The End of the World

The End of the World

An Annotated Bibliography

by
TOM MCIVER

McFarland & Company, Inc., Publishers
Jefferson, North Carolina, and London

5755

Library of Congress Cataloguing-in-Publication Data

McIver, Tom, 1951–
    The end of the world : an annotated bibliography / by Tom
McIver.
        p.   cm.
    Includes index.
    ISBN 0-7864-0708-5 (library binding : 50 # alkaline paper) ∞
    1. End of the world — Bibliography.   I. Title.
Z7786.M35   1999
[BL503]
016.2912'3 — dc21   99-15154
                                                                          CIP

British Library Cataloguing-in-Publication data are available

Manufactured in the United States of America

McFarland & Company, Inc., Publishers
  Box 611, Jefferson, North Carolina 28640
    www.mcfarlandpub.com

To Katie, Kerry, and Eileen

*May they live in a world which cherishes
freedom of thought and expression,
a society tolerant of diverse ideas and beliefs,
while never forgetting the importance of critical
evaluation and healthy skepticism.*

Acknowledgments

I would like to thank the following libraries: Cleveland Public Library (and the West Park branch); Kent State University; Case Western Reserve University; the academic libraries accessed through OhioLINK, especially Cedarville College, Ashland University and Theological Seminary, and Oberlin College; the Popular Culture collection at Bowling Green State University; Aurora University (which houses the most comprehensive Advent Christian collection and archives); Andrews University (home of the premier Seventh-day Adventist collection and archives); Cincinnati Bible College and Seminary; Fuller Theological Seminary; and the Library of Congress.

This book is dedicated to my daughters, who wondered why I spend so much time looking at all these odd books and running off to libraries both near and far. My preoccupation with the End of the World meant I was usually busy when they wanted my time and attention. I hope they will realize the importance of trying to understand such beliefs as are included here, and why it took me away from them so often.

Table of Contents

Preface

I became interested in beliefs about the end of the world as a consequence of studying creationism — research which resulted in a similar annotated bibliography (*Anti-Evolution*, 1988, McFarland). There is of course an obvious symmetry and complementarity between beliefs about the beginning and the end of the world — one need not be a bibliophile to think of them as "book-ends" — but the relation is even deeper than that of mere formal chronological relationship. For religious beliefs about Creation and the End, it turns out, are directly and intimately related. This is so precisely because they *are* religious, and thus seek to impose ultimate meaning upon history and upon the universe — even more than that, to discern meaning *behind* and *beyond* history, meaning behind and beyond the universe. Creation is the foundation of all that exists, including all meaning, and the End is its culmination, in which everything comes out the way it is supposed to — the way God intended it from the beginning.

The works here are by believers; all are religiously based or inspired. Though in a few cases this religious motivation is not openly displayed, in the vast majority it is quite explicit. Most are openly Bible-based. The great majority are Christian, but I have also included some Jewish and Islamic works and a few items from other religions. Works based on psychic and occult beliefs are also represented, including Pyramidology, Lost Tribes of Israel, astrology, and UFOlogy. Some fictional works are included: Novels allow believers to show events turning out just as they expect them to.

What the works in this collection have in common is that all are convinced the world is coming to an end, one way or another, and that this End constitutes a divine judgment or is somehow preordained.

The works listed cite their original publication date (first or earliest known edition). Multiple works by the same author are listed in order of publication. Posthumously published works are listed as if published in the author's lifetime (for instance, an author who died in 1960 but whose book was published in 1975 is listed in the *pre*-1970 section).

The Pre-1800 section is conceived and arranged differently from the sections for later works. It is intended to be as much a survey of historical sources

1

as a listing of available works, and is arranged chronologically, while later sections are arranged alphabetically by author. Some of the pre–1800 works are still available in many editions, while others are rare, existing only in manuscript (sometimes several variant forms).

Most of the works in the next section, titles from 1800 to 1910, are available in libraries, though some in microform only.

The third section comprises works from 1910 to 1970. The year 1910 is a somewhat arbitrary dividing point, but does lie in the period between the predominantly post-millennial nineteenth century and the emergence of the fundamentalist movement in the twentieth, when pre-millennialism became the dominant view.

The final section consists of works written in 1970 and later. The year 1970 is used as a boundary not because of any major doctrinal shift, but as a convenient dividing point. It was the year Hal Lindsey published his enormously popular *Late Great Planet Earth*. The post–1970 section includes Internet websites that contain substantial material in themselves rather than primarily links to other sites.

This is by no means a comprehensive listing. Hundreds of titles not included here can be found, for instance, in Jon Stone's bibliography *Guide to the End of the World: Popular Eschatology in America* (1993, Garland) which focuses on dispensational pre-millennialism, the predominant fundamentalist view. LeRoy Froom discusses (from a decidedly Adventist perspective) many more of the earlier sources in his *Prophetic Faith of Our Fathers* (1946-54, Review and Herald). Ted Daniels' *Millennialism: An International Bibliography* (1992, Garland) lists sources on millennialism, eschatology, and related topics concerning the End mostly by scholars studying these beliefs rather than by believers themselves. Another good source is the Center for Millennial Studies (available on the Internet at <http://www.mille.org/>), run by scholarly authorities such as Richard Landes, Stephen O'Leary, and Michael Barkun.

There is an index of authors, titles and subjects, keyed to entry numbers, at the back.

Introduction

Different Meanings of the End

"The end of the world" can mean quite different things, from complete destruction of the entire universe and extinction of all life, to the close of the present age — the end of the world "as we know it" — and beginning of a new age, or the end of history, or of time.

The End, in mythology and in religious accounts, has a close and direct logical relationship to the Beginning — to Creation. Religions in general have the concept of a return (via myth and ritual) to the original mythic state, of contrast between the present, mundane existence and the original timeless, unchanging past. In most religions, history and change are viewed as degenerative and generally evil.

Christianity and Judaism differ from most other religions in their avowedly *historicist* emphasis, viewing time and history as *progressing* from a definite moment of Creation through to the End. Unlike religions in which the aim of existence is to return to an original mythic state, this monotheistic grand narrative or drama of divine history, as a unique sequence of nonrepeatable, dateable events, moves forward in historical time rather than simply returning to the beginning or cycling endlessly. However, despite this novel historicist emphasis, the cyclical element common to all religions is nonetheless quite evident in Judeo-Christianity, and even the End is in many respects a return to the Beginning.

Indeed, the Judeo-Christian tradition includes a prior End of the World: the Flood of Noah, which destroyed all life except that aboard the Ark; Earth was in effect re-created afterwards. The notion of the End varies, but even within the Judeo-Christian tradition it generally involves a return to originally created perfection before the Fall; a return to Eden or Paradise; to timelessness, Eternity; an abolition of history, decay, and change. Many "old-earth" creationists maintain that the Flood was not even the first End of the World, pointing to a previous destruction of the world before the Six Day creation of Genesis, which was really a *re*-creation some six thousand years ago. The original creation, they believe, was ages prior to this; but Satan — the fallen angel Lucifer — corrupted

3

the Earth following his rebellion against God, and God destroyed it utterly, re-creating it in the familiar Six Day account.

The idea of the Millennium has its own peculiarities. It is generally taken as implying the End, but strictly speaking is more of an interregnum — a thou-sand-year *interlude* of reign either by Christ in person or by his saintly follow-ers — before the absolute end of time and commencement of Eternity.

What is meant by the End of the World, then, varies substantially, and believers may be highly ambivalent towards it, both fearing it as a final terror-filled Doom and yearning for it with expectant, even ecstatic, joy — a curious mixture of hope and anticipation, anxiety and fear. This ambivalent attitude varies according to doctrine: whether it is believed one can know for sure who will be saved, and whether believers think they must undergo terrible tribula-tions. Much also depends on strength of religious conviction: believers' certainty or uncertainty regarding whether or not *they* belong to the Saved Elect.

A common theme of the works included in this collection is that all sup-pose some existence *after* the End — some if not all souls survive beyond the "End" into Eternity or Paradise. Because these are all more or less religiously-inspired, all assume that the End is the culmination of a divine Plan, that it embodies ultimate Meaning and is not merely a matter of chance — of purely naturalistic forces and happenings. It must be somehow foreordained; it must be an ultimate making-right of all things by a personal, eternal Mind or Soul, the deliberate result of personal, supernatural will. It has meaning and moral dimension: It is the necessary justifiable conclusion of the Divine Plan, the ulti-mate settling of accounts of good and evil.

Eschatological Terms

In presenting works devoted to the End of the World certain terms and concepts need explanation. There is a bewildering profusion of eschatological terms, many with synonymous, overlapping, or variant meanings, different meanings for different religious groups, or theological meanings different from ordinary usage.

Eschatology itself is Greek for study of "last" (or "farthest") things and events. It is thus largely resonant with terms such as "End Times," "Final Things," or "Last Days." Eschatology is that branch of religion which deals with "final things" or End Times — the final destiny of mankind and the end of the world; and, in Christianity, with the Battle of Armageddon, Rapture of the Faithful, Great Tribulation, Second Coming of Christ, the Millennium, Resurrection of the Dead, and Last Judgment. (Some theologians speak of "personal eschatol-ogy" — the destiny of the *individual* after death — but that is another topic.)

The *Millennium* is Latin for "thousand year" period (*mille* + *annus*), and refers to the era prophesied in the Bible's Book of Revelation when righteous-ness prevails after Armageddon and before the Final Judgment at the End of Time. Though generally "*the* Millennium" is held to be future, "a-millennialists" may interpret it symbolically or historically as having begun in the past (and not necessarily as literally a thousand years). ***Millennialism*** means belief in the coming Millennium, in biblical eschatological prophecies in general; and is sometimes also used as more or less synonymous with "eschatology." "Millennialism" can also be extended even wider to refer to belief in a future period of perfection on earth (generally accomplished by violent destruction of evil) in *any* religious or cultural tradition. ***Chiliasm*** is the Greek equivalent to "millennialism" (it too is derived from "thousand") and refers to the doctrine that Jesus will reign for a thousand years; it is often equated more with "millenarianism."

Millenarianism, is often used, especially by social scientists, in a broad sense to encompass beliefs in a coming period of prosperity, justice, goodness and perfection in any religion or culture, often following a violent overthrow of the present evil order.

Messianism is the belief that an end-time king or savior will lead the suffering oppressed into this just rule.

Apocalypticism is used in a similar sense to refer to belief in the violent and usually imminent End of the World, and "The Apocalypse" is often taken to mean the final violent destruction — God's sudden, cataclysmic intervention. However, its literal meaning is simply "uncovering": it is Greek for *revelation*— the "revealing" of the hitherto hidden future. The New Testament Book of Revelation, along with the Old Testament Book of Daniel, is the chief apocalyptic book of the Bible, and it and Daniel contain the major eschatological prophecies. "Revelation" likewise implies a dramatic and violent scenario, and indeed that is what is described in the Book of Revelation.

Terms such as "End Times," "Final Things," "Last Days," "Judgment Day," "Doomsday," "Day of the Lord" and "Day of Wrath" are even more general but many biblical interpreters assign them specialized and distinctive (often conflicting) meanings. "Armageddon" refers to the final battle or apocalyptic confrontation. "Tribulation" or "Great Tribulation," "the Seven Years," "Rapture," "Parousia," and "Second Coming" are terms referring to penultimate events whose chronological relationships, are, however, much disputed by interpreters.

The ***Second Coming*** (or "Second Advent"), or ***Parousia*** (Greek for "presence"), refers to Christ's return to earth in the Last Days. Depending on interpretation, this may occur simultaneously with, or just prior to, End Time events such as Armageddon and the Final Judgment, or it may precede them by some time; and it may occur either before or after the Millennium. In some interpretations the Second Coming is in two (or more) stages; the first being the ***Rapture*** (see below).

The Resurrection of the Dead and the Final Judgment may likewise be subdivided into several stages, depending on interpretation.

"The Church" (in Christian tradition) may mean either the True Church — the body of righteous, faithful believers — the Elect; or the evil, apostate institution of false religion which persecutes true believers and serves as Satan's tool. To Augustine, and his Catholic followers, it constituted the Millennium itself.

The English term "Doomsday" is obviously apocalyptic. (The famous *Domesday Book* compiled by the Norman conquerors of England, however, was not apocalyptic — at least not directly so. An official assessment of population, land, and other property undertaken in 1086 primarily for tax purposes, it received its popular name because its judgments were considered final and unappealable — taxation being dreaded as much as that other inevitability, death itself.)

Apocalyptic Literature

"Apocalyptic" is also used as the name for a *literary genre* closely related to prophetic literature. While much prophecy is concerned with the present and immediate future, apocalyptic literature refers to the ultimate future — the End Times. When the northern kingdom of Israel was destroyed in the eighth century B.C. and the southern kingdom of Judah in the sixth century, Jewish prophets urged faith by prophesying that the oppressing forces would be overcome, the evil order violently destroyed, and after this destruction, a Golden Age lay ahead for righteous believers, an age outside of history. Apocalyptic literature stresses dualist themes of good versus evil — the notion that this present age is dominated by evil, but that the future age will be one of purity and goodness. The genre is characterized by fantastic imagery and warnings of doom and the end of the world. The apocalyptic genre was the chief form that prophecy took in the Greco-Roman era, when Israel was dominated and threatened by these imperialist powers. Afterwards it became a popular genre for Christians during Roman persecutions.

Though Daniel in the Old Testament and Revelation in the New Testament are the only fully apocalyptic books in the Bible, many others contain apocalyptic sections. Noncanonical apocalypses include the Books of Enoch, the Apocalypse of Peter, and other apocryphal works (works not considered officially part of the sacred scripture). *Apocryphal* is not a term of opprobrium: it means "hidden away" (i.e., books not displayed as part of the officially authorized canon); or of doubtful authorship or authenticity. According to denominational tastes apocryphal works may be included or consulted as worthwhile supplements to the biblical canon, or considered suspect and inferior.

Among other books of the Bible containing apocalyptic passages often cited in End of the World interpretations is the Book of Amos (written about 760 B.C.), which speaks of the "Day of the Lord" in eschatological terms as a terrible time of darkness and wrath. Isaiah (700s B.C.) prophesies retribution and judgment but also ultimate salvation for Israel, portraying the Assyrians, soon to conquer the Northern Kingdom of Israel, as instruments of God's punishment of Israel. Part of the Book of Isaiah is acknowledged by experts to have been written considerably later, however, during the Babylonian Captivity (500s B.C.). This later author, referred to by many biblical scholars as Deutero-Isaiah, predicts a coming Messiah, wholesale devastation at the Day of Lord, then a new creation.

Jeremiah, written around 600 B.C., grimly and persistently preaches Israel's impending submergence by Babylonia — the Day of the Lord, when God makes the world waste and void. This was considered fulfilled in 587 B.C. by the Babylonian conquest. Ezekiel, written in exile following this conquest, is replete with strange images and visions such as fiery wheels and dry bones coming to life (a metaphor for renewal of the Jewish nation). Prophecies found in Ezekiel include the rebuilding of the Temple and the End Time invasion of Gog and Magog from the North (likely referring to Scythians).

Prophecies and visions from many other Old Testament books, such as Zechariah (200s B.C.), which includes a vision of horses of four colors, and Joel (300s B.C., around the time of Alexander the Great's conquests), which includes a prophecy of demonic locusts, are incorporated into or referred to by the author of Revelation.

The Book of Daniel

One of characteristics of apocalyptic literary genre is that authorship is usually attributed to ancient prophets and revered wise men. An advantage of this is that "prophecies" can be attributed to these ancient worthies which were seemingly later "fulfilled" but which actually came to pass in the real author's past or present — and were therefore not genuine prophecies at all, but instead post-dated history. Such seems to be the case with the Book of Daniel, though biblical literalists stoutly deny this. Daniel was ostensibly written during the Babylonian Exile, like Ezekiel, but much internal textual evidence indicates it was composed much later — the 160s B.C., when the Jews were being persecuted by the Seleucid Greeks. Another advantage of attributing authorship to earlier prophets is that criticism of the current regime can be somewhat disguised, making it less overtly seditious. While Daniel ostensibly protests "Babylonian" oppression, his Jewish audience easily recognized it as referring to contemporary Seleucid tyranny.

The first six chapters of Daniel encourage Jews to resist the Seleucid ruler Antiochus IV Epiphanes by praising past Jews who remained true to the faith while exiled in Babylon under Nebuchadnezzar, especially urging resistance to forced worship of the king and the pagan gods. It contains such stories as the three companions of Daniel thrown into the furnace, Daniel himself cast into the lion's den, Nebuchadnezzar's going mad for seven years, and the divine handwriting on the wall foretelling the fall of Babylon during Belshazzar's feast on the eve of Babylon's capture by the Persians.

Of particular importance to End Time belief is the statue or "image" dreamed of by Nebuchadnezzar, which Daniel interpreted as a succession of world empires lasting until the Last Days. The statue was in four parts, each composed of a different metal. The first part, the head, was of gold, and represented Nebuchadnezzar's own Babylonian (Chaldean or "Neo-Babylonian")

Empire. The second, the chest and arms, was of silver, and represented the empire which was to succeed Babylonia. This is presumably the Median Empire, based in what is now northern Iran and later absorbed into the Persian Empire. The third part of the statue, the belly and thighs, are of brass, presumably representing the Persian Empire. The fourth, of the legs, is of iron, but the feet are of iron and clay mixed (the "feet of clay" symbolizing instability or weakness). Presumably this is the Macedonian Greek empire founded by Alexander the Great, which split into unstable successor kingdoms after his death, with two, the Ptolemaic and Seleucid dynasties, struggling for domination in the Near East. A stone "cut out without hands" smites the feet of this mighty image, shattering it to pieces, and itself becomes an even more powerful kingdom. This "stone kingdom" is the Kingdom of Heaven or millennial reign which the Book of Daniel assures its readers is imminent. (The Jewish revolt of the Maccabees had in fact broken out at about this time, and resulted in a century of Jewish independence, until the Roman conquest.)

In Christian times, these Four Kingdoms were generally assumed to be Babylonia, Medo-Persia *combined*, Greece, and *Rome*. The second-century author of Daniel would have been familiar with Media, Persia, and Greece (though presenting these as much earlier prophecies yet to be fulfilled); he would not, however, have known of Rome's expansion into a world empire, which was genuinely future. In Christian interpretations, the ten toes of the statue represent either ten stages of the Roman Empire, barbarian kingdoms or successor states to Rome, or ten nations which will comprise the "revived Roman Empire" in the End Times.

The second half of Daniel (chapters 7–12) is overtly apocalyptic. Chapter 7 is Daniel's own dream of Four Beasts, who correspond to the four metals of the statue. The first is like a lion with eagle wings and human legs. The second is like a bear (raised "on one side," taken to mean lopsided) chewing three ribs. The third is like a leopard with four heads and wings. The fourth is a strange composite creature, the most horrible of all, with iron teeth and ten horns, from which a "Little Horn" emerges, uprooting three of the other horns. This fourth beast represents an empire which will "devour the whole earth." The horns are ten kings which will arise out of it; and the "Little Horn" is presumably the Seleucid ruler Antiochus IV Epiphanes, who subdues three rivals. The final beastly manifestation is opposed by the "Ancient of Days" and "Son of Man," with the prophecy that after 2,300 days the sanctuary would be cleansed (the Temple in Jerusalem, the center of Jewish worship, which Antiochus had deliberately and ostentatiously defiled). In the next chapter, Daniel sees a ram with two horns, one higher than the other (presumably Media and Persia). A goat with one horn comes from the west (Greece), and triumphs over the ram. Four horns grow out of the goat's great horn (the four successor kingdoms to Alexander's empire), then one Little Horn "waxes great," establishing dominance.

Daniel 9 contains the prophecy of the 70 Weeks, which has assumed tremendous importance in much eschatological theorizing. Jeremiah had prophesied "seventy years" captivity in Babylon while the land of Israel lay desolate; Daniel cites this, then modifies it to "seventy *weeks* (or *heptads*—'sevens')," which fundamentalists assume means "weeks of *years.*" These are divided into three parts: seven from the commandment to restore and rebuild Jerusalem to the arrival of a messiah, 62 more till the city is rebuilt (for a total of 69), after which (another?) messiah is "cut off"; then, a covenant is confirmed for one week, and in the middle of this last week an abomination desolates the land.

Daniel 11 begins with mention of kings of Persia, then a veiled reference to Alexander the Great, followed by kings of the South and North who battle each other, with the King of the South retiring to Egypt after defeating the North, but then warring again. The King of the North then invades (there are references to a "raiser of taxes" and a "vile person") but is prevented from overwhelming the South by the "ships of Chittim." The King of the North then defiles the Sanctuary with the "abomination of desolation" and "exalts himself above God." War recommences against the King of the South, with the King of the North re-entering the "glorious land." The Kings of the North and South are presumably the Ptolemaic and Seleucid successor states, based respectively in Egypt and Antioch (north of Israel, in what is now southern Turkey). Daniel continues with a reference to "turning towards the isles," the ships of Chittim come against the King, and troubling news from the east and north results in further fighting. "Chittim" is Cyprus, probably referring to Rome (which lies past Cyprus, beyond the western horizon).

In Daniel 12, Daniel is told to seal the book to the "time of the end" when "many shall run to and fro, and knowledge shall be increased." The time till "the end" is then declared to be "time, times, and a half," and also as 1,290 days till the defilement caused by the Abomination of Desolation is cleansed and purified.

Such prophetic numbers seem to be not only symbolic representations but also attempts to guess how long foreign oppression would last. For instance, counting from 586 B.C., the full 70 Weeks of years (490 years) would end about 96 B.C., some years into the future from the presumed time Daniel was writing. About seven "weeks" of years later — 538 B.C. — the Persian emperor Cyrus, after defeating Babylonia, issued his decree for the Jews to rebuild the Temple. Cyrus ("Koresh" in Hebrew) may in fact be the "messiah" referred to following the first seven weeks; the messiah who is "cut off" after the next 62 weeks is apparently a later, different figure. Most fundamentalists, however, assume the "Messiah" in all cases refers to Christ, and many begin the 70 Weeks count somewhat later, with Artaxerxes' subsequent decree to Nehemiah in 445 B.C.

New Testament

How apocalyptic Jesus himself was continues to be a matter of intense debate, and is outside the scope of this work. Words attributed to him in the

Bible certainly speak of promises of an imminent end, in the lifetime of his listeners ("Verily I say unto you, This generation shall not pass, till all these things be fulfilled"), but elsewhere he counsels patience and insists that the end is "not yet," that "no man knows the day or hour," and that many signs and events remain to be fulfilled. John the Baptist was definitely apocalyptic, proclaiming "Repent, the Kingdom of Heaven is at hand!" In Matthew 24, the "Olivet Discourse," Christ's disciples inquire when the end will come. He replies that signs of the end include "false Christs" displaying signs and wonders, "wars and rumors of wars," famines, pestilences, earthquakes, and accelerating evil, as in the days of Noah prior to the worldwide destruction by Flood. Also, the Gospel will have been preached in all nations before the End. As the sprouting of leaves on a fig tree heralds the soon approach of summer, so too these signs of the times will indicate the Last Days. Christ emphasizes to his disciples the necessity of eternal watchfulness, as some will be taken while others will be left behind when the End comes. Following the "Abomination of Desolation," the faithful will flee to the mountains to escape the great "Tribulation," whose days God shortens for the sake of the elect. Immediately after the Tribulation, the sun darkens, stars fall, then Christ returns at his Second Coming.

Matthew, Mark, and Luke are called the "Synoptic Gospels" because much of their content overlaps, providing three versions of the same events and stories. Passages corresponding to Matthew's Olivet Discourse appear in Mark 13 (the so-called Little Apocalypse) and in Luke 21.

Revelation

The Book of Revelation was written by someone named John, who said its revelatory visions came to him while in exile on the Isle of Patmos. Some have tried to identify this John with the Apostle who wrote the fourth (and nonsynoptic) Gospel, but most consider him a different (and otherwise unknown) seer. Revelation was probably written in the A.D. 90s, during Emperor Domitian's reign, which followed Nero's cruel scapegoating of Christians and Titus' bloody suppression of the Jewish revolt and destruction of Jerusalem. "Antichrist," the "Beast," and "666" likely refer to Domitian or Nero. Particularly repugnant to Christians was required worship of pagan imperial gods as a mark of loyalty to Roman overlordship, with refusal considered traitorous. Like Daniel, Revelation was written to encourage resistance to pagan worship and foreign domination, and to reassure the faithful (this time Christians) facing persecution and martyrdom that their religion would triumph in the end over the present evil regime, and that all martyrs would be rewarded, resurrected to rule with the Messiah in the millennial kingdom. Old Testament visions and prophecies are cited and incorporated into Revelation, which reinterprets them as referring to Jesus as the prophesied Messiah.

The first part of Revelation is a set of epistolary admonitions addressed to the "seven churches of Asia" (Asia Minor; i.e., Anatolia). Seven is a highly significant theme throughout Revelation, with most events occurring as seven-fold series. Next, God appears at His throne, with the "lamb" (Christ), who opens the seven seals of the book that seal it until the End Times. The first four seals are the famous Four Horsemen of the Apocalypse. The first, on a white horse, carries a bow, and probably represents foreign invasion. (In Roman times, Parthian horsemen epitomized external military threat, having annihilated an entire Roman army in the first century B.C. and hovering menacingly on the horizon ever since. The signature tactic of these skilled mounted archers was the "Parthian shot" fired at pursuers while feigning retreat by turning around in the saddle at a gallop.) The second horseman, riding a red horse, wields a sword, probably symbolizing internal warfare: civil war and revolution. The third, riding a black horse, holds scales for weighing grain, and represents famine. The fourth, on a pale horse, is called Death, probably referring to death from pestilence and disease.

At the Fifth Seal, martyred believers cry out for vengeance. At the Sixth Seal, earth is devastated by earthquake, the sun is blackened, stars fall, the sky rolls up, mountains shake, and people hide in caves and mountains. At the Sixth, God seals 144,000 faithful, 12,000 from each of the twelve tribes of Israel. This is followed by cryptic references to an unnumbered "multitude" who come out of the great tribulation.

Prior to the Seventh Seal there is an ominous half hour of silence, then seven angels sound Seven Trumpets announcing a series of calamities. The First Trumpet brings hail and fire which destroy a third of all vegetation. At the Second Trumpet a mountain is hurled into the sea, turning a third of the sea to blood. At the Third a star falling from heaven — Wormwood — ruins a third of all rivers. At the Fourth a third of the day is darkened.

The last three trumpets are sometimes called the "Woe Trumpets" after the angel's cry which announces them. The Fifth summons forth locusts from the Bottomless Pit with human faces and scorpion tails, who savagely torment all those not sealed by God for five months. At the Sixth, 200 million horsemen kill a third of mankind. Then comes a vision of Two Witnesses who prophesy for 42 months under divine protection, and prevent all rain from falling. After the 42 months, they are killed by the Beast. They lie dead in the street for 3½ days, then are revived and ascend to heaven, seen by all.

The Seventh Trumpet brings a vision seen in the sky, of a child born to a woman "clothed with the sun." A great Dragon tries to devour the child, and Michael and his angels battle the Dragon and his evil angels. Following this, a terrible Beast emerges from the Sea, with seven heads and ten horns — a sort of composite of Daniel's four beasts. Then a second Beast emerges from the Earth, with two horns "like a lamb" but speaking "as a dragon." This second Beast causes the world to worship the first Beast by performing miraculous signs and wonders; and he fashions an image (statue) of the first Beast, causing it to talk and come alive. The second Beast demands that everyone receive a "mark" on his hand or forehead of the name or number — 666 — of the Beast, without which no one is allowed to buy or sell. Three angels fly by: the first preaching the Gospel to the world, the second announcing that Babylon is fallen, and the third explaining that all who accept the Mark of the Beast are doomed, but that all who resist and are martyred will be blessed and rewarded by God. Then comes a vision of the "Son of man" reaping the Earth, casting grapes into the winepress of God's wrath. Blood from the winepress runs as high as a horse's bridle for 1,600 furlongs.

Next (though always bearing in mind that the chronological relationships of Revelation are very confused and ambiguous), the Seven Vials (Bowls) are poured out — seven horrible plagues. First are loathsome sores afflicting all who have the Mark of the Beast. The second vial turns the sea to blood. The third turns rivers to blood. The fourth brings scorching heat. The fifth plunges the world into darkness. The sixth dries up the Euphrates, enabling the kings of the East to advance, and includes a vision in which three unclean spirits "like frogs" come out of the mouth of the Dragon (Satan), the Beast, and the False Prophet (the second Beast). These demonic spirits cause all the kings of the world to gather at Armageddon (about which location nothing further is said explicitly). The Seventh Vial produces a tremendous earthquake that dissolves islands and crumbles mountains, and a storm of hailstones weighing a talent each. Then comes a vision of woman wearing gaudy scarlet and purple raiments, called Mystery Babylon, Mother of Harlots and Abominations, riding a beast "that was, and is not, and yet is," with seven heads (described as standing for seven mountains) and ten horns. The horns are said to be "five kings who are fallen, one is, and another to come." The beast itself is "*of*" the seventh and "*is*" the eighth (future) king. The woman, Mystery Babylon, rules the world, but the ten horns are to destroy her, leaving her utterly desolate.

Finally, a rider on a white horse — Christ — throws the False Prophet and Dragon in the lake of fire. Satan (the Dragon) is cast into the bottomless pit for a thousand years. Those martyrs killed for resisting the Beast and remaining faithful to Christ are resurrected, to rule with Christ for a thousand years. The rest of the dead are resurrected at the end of the thousand years. Also at the end of the thousand years, Satan is "loosed a little season" to deceive the nations one last time, and Gog and Magog assemble a vast force for battle. God destroys this last rebellion. There follows the judgment of all the dead, then the New Jerusalem descends, the first heaven and earth pass away, and God creates the new heaven and earth.

Apocalyptic Symbols of the Bible

It must be kept in mind that the Bible is a collection of disparate sources presenting varying and often conflicting points of view (edited and carefully reworked, to be sure). The apocalyptic sections are composed in ambiguous, mystical language, and are filled with horrific, nightmarish, almost hallucinatory visions, characterized by vague and confusing chronological relationships and interrupted by bizarre allegorical interludes, all of which later exegetes can easily enough manipulate to advocate radically different and totally new interpretations, especially by treating some passages as flashbacks or jumps further into the future, or even as both at once. Many interpreters maintain that events of near and distant future may be telescoped together in prophecy. Another principle frequently invoked is "double fulfillment": prophecies are fulfilled both in the biblical writer's immediate future (our past) and in the End Times. Related to this principle, many figures and events are said to be "types" (prototypes; forerunners or precursors) of their primary or final fulfillment; for instance Antiochus or Nero as "type" of (the future) Antichrist.

The seven-fold series of seals, trumpets, and bowls of Revelation may be interpreted either as consecutive, subsets, or concurrent. The War in Heaven of Revelation 12:7 is assumed by many to occur midway through the final seven-year Tribulation, but others see it as a pre–Adamic flashback. The fatal wound of the beast that then wondrously heals is associated with the legend of "Nero redivivus"— the belief that Nero would return to life to subject Christians to further tribulation. The seventh and eighth horn (king) of the beast ridden by Mystery Babylon may be another reference to Nero come back to life.

2 Thessalonians 2 speaks of a "restrainer" (or "hinderer") who when removed allows the "mystery of iniquity" to be fully revealed or operational. This Restrainer has variously been interpreted as the Church, Rome, Holy Spirit, Antichrist, and others. The omission of Dan from the naming of the Twelve Tribes in Revelation has led to the assertion by some that Antichrist will arise from that tribe. The Beast from the Sea (the First Beast) is commonly held to be Antichrist (the term "antichrist" does not appear in Revelation), who becomes empowered or possessed by Satan, and the Beast from the Earth (the Second Beast), the False Prophet. But every permutation possible has been advanced as to their identities and relationships to the other End Time beasts and entities. The Mark and Number of the Beast has been taken as literal tattoo, an electronic implant or biochip, or some other distinctive device. The 666 has, notoriously, been applied to the most diverse candidates.

Most interpreters acknowledge that the author of Revelation equated "Babylon" with Rome, but many claim it refers to present or future *literal* Babylon. Many make a distinction between Mystery Babylon, which they assert refers to some present or future city, system, or nation, and the literal Babylon. The Ten Kingdom confederacy, inferred from Revelation as well as Daniel, has likewise been interpreted as either past, present, or future. It is generally assumed to be a direct descendant or revival of the Roman Empire (with the European Common Market a favorite choice), but others insist it will be (or already is) some other league of states.

Among other points of contention are whether additional souls will be saved during the Tribulation, if true Christians are raptured before it begins, how many (if any) survive into the Millennium, and who remains on earth during the Millennium. (While considered a Utopian return to Eden by most fundamentalists, Seventh-day Adventists conspicuously hold that no one will be left alive on earth during the Thousand Years, as the wicked are all killed and the righteous translated to heaven.) Some make a distinction between the seven-year period of tribulation (the Seventieth Week) and the Great Tribulation, which they limit to the second 3½ years of the seven; or between the "wrath of God" or final plagues and the earlier series of punishments and horrors, which they attribute to Antichrist and Satan. The Woman clothed in the sun is variously interpreted as Mary, Jerusalem, Israel, or the Church; and the "man-child" she bears as Christ, the Church, or the 144,000.

Armageddon is popularly taken to be the final, climactic battle, but fundamentalist interpreters differ on whether it is the last, decisive clash or an extended campaign or war. Some insist Armageddon is simply the field of assembly for the armies, with the actual fighting in other places culminating in the siege of Jerusalem, or with no actual fighting at all, God simply obliterating the armies by supernatural means. "*Har-Megiddo*," the term used in Revelation, means "Mount of Megiddo." Megiddo is an ancient fortified site bordering a broad plain extending to the Mediterranean coast. (Sometimes the fighting is described as occurring in the Plain of Jezreel or Esdraelon, also referring to the area around Megiddo.) This is a geographically and militarily critical location on the coastal route between Egypt and Mesopotamia. The earliest well-documented battle in history was fought at Megiddo between Thutmose III and a Canaanite-Syrian coalition in the fifteenth century B.C. In the seventh century B.C. the Egyptians, while attacking Assyria, crushed the Israelite army here. In the First World War, British General Allenby, following his entry into Jerusalem, decisively defeated the Turks at Megiddo on his way to Damascus. (It is also possible that "Har-*Megiddo*" in Revelation is a mistranslation, and really means "Mount of Assembly" or Mt. Zion. There is no real mountain at Megiddo.)

The whole End Time war sequence is open to a broad range of interpretation. Most fundamentalists posit an invasion of Israel by Russia, allied with Middle Eastern and African nations, at or near the beginning of the Seven Years, followed by war between Antichrist and his European forces and Israel or the Russians and the 200-million man army of the Far East. Many interpreters foresee all the world's armies attacking Israel, or battling each other in Israel, then uniting in desperation to resist the heavenly forces of Christ when he returns at his Second Coming. Especially in the last century, Gog and Magog have confidently been equated with Russia or the Soviet Union, though even more recently with a resurgent Islam or some Russian-Islamic combination. (Prior to the twentieth century, interpreters had often equated the Moslems with Antichrist, frequently calling the Papacy the Western manifestation of Antichrist and Islam the Eastern.)

The invasion of Israel prophesied in Ezekiel is by Gog and Magog. Five-sixths of the invaders are slaughtered, and it takes seven months to bury the dead, the Jews burning the weapons of the defeated enemy for seven years. Revelation also refers to Gog and Magog as assembling vast forces for the final rebellion against God led by Satan at the *end* of the Millennium. Some interpreters maintain that here Gog and Magog represent *all* the nations and are different from the specifically "northern" Gog and Magog of the pre–millennial invasion. Many exegetes also maintain that Gog is a *person* while Magog is his *kingdom*.

The World Week

The World Week concept, or 6,000 Year Theory, exerted tremendous influence on early Christian thought, and still resonates powerfully. Associated with the Judaic idea of cosmic history as composed of three two-thousand year ages, it is the belief that as creation took six days, followed by a day of rest, so too all world history will last six periods of a thousand years each, followed by a seventh, final thousand years or Millennium. Claimed scriptural support is the verse in 2 Peter 3 which says that "one day is with the Lord as a thousand years" and a similar phrase in Psalm 90:4. The 6,000 Year scheme was initially endorsed by early church authorities in part as a way to control dangerously destabilizing popular millennialist expectations — the conviction that the world would end any moment, and resultant temptation to hasten and usher in Christ's Return by force. Now that the church was an established institution, its leaders desired stability rather than agitation and revolution. Relying on the Septuagint (Alexandrian Greek) translation, the date of Creation was calculated (notably by Hippolytus in A.D. 203) as about 5500 B.C., thus making the End still several hundred years in the future. As A.D. 500 approached, Church authorities again sought to dampen incendiary millennialist expectations by switching to a creation date of 5200 B.C., moving the End back a few hundred years, again safely in the future (A.D. 800, the projected date of the End, was notable for Charlemagne's crowning as Emperor in Rome by the Pope). The degree of millennialist excitement as A.D. 1000 approached has been much debated. The year 1000 was not linked to a standard creation date, but it certainly carried the appeal and dread of an even millennial number, at least for those who were aware of exactly how many years had elapsed since Christ (standardized A.D. calendars not being in common household use then).

The year 1000 also became associated with Augustine's teachings of the Church as the Millennium, though in a literalist way that violated the intent of his a-millennial theory and symbolic approach. If taken literally as a thousand years after the First Coming of Christ, then the Millennium would end A.D. 1000 (or so). Or, if ending a thousand years after his death or resurrection, or the establishment of the Church at Pentecost, then it would end around 1033, or possibly later with different start dates for the Church.

With widespread adoption of the Masoretic (Hebrew) text, the End was again shifted into the future. Calculations based on the Masoretic text generally date creation to around 4000 B.C., which, in the 6,000 Year scheme, put the

Millennium about 2000. This had the additional attraction of nice, round, undeniably millennial dates. Archbishop Ussher's famous date of 4004 B.C. for Creation was but one of many such biblical chronologies which set creation around four thousand years before Christ. His became the best known because of his scholarly reputation and especially because it was enshrined in marginal notes of the King James Bible from 1701 onwards. Ussher believed his meticulous calculations (based on far more than simply adding up biblical "begats," by the way) indicated there were exactly 4,000 years from creation to Christ's Incarnation at His First Coming (allowing for a calendrical discrepancy which put his birth at 4 B.C.), which in turn supported the notion that there would be an even two thousand years *after* Christ, followed by the final Millennium.

This World Week scheme profoundly affected date-setting for the End, and remains a powerful influence even today. It is still openly appealed to by many who preach an imminent End. The 6,000 Year concept satisfies the irresistible urge to prefer a neatly symmetrical chronological pattern for a supernaturally ordained Plan encompassing all past and future. Assumption of an overarching 6,000 Year Plan helps provide meaning to the flux and babble of history by subsuming human events to an overall divine Planner, and guarantees a tidy wrapping-up, with everything concluding how and when it is supposed to, all within an easily comprehensible framework.

Date-Setting by Prophetic Numbers

Besides dates for the End based on Creation and the World Week, the prophetic numbers of Daniel and Revelation could be used to determine when the End would arrive, independently or in conjunction with the 6,000 Year theory. Such thinking derives from biblical literalism. During the nineteenth century, when the doctrine of biblical literalism was formally developed, literalists sought to study the hard, literal *facts* provided by Scripture to arrive at "scientific" conclusions. These methods were used to calculate many nineteenth and twentieth century dates for the End, notably 1843-44, the 1860s, 1914 or 1917, and 1988, to name only the most common. In "historicist" interpretations that relied on the Year-Day principle (which assumes that "day" in the Bible really means "year"), the number 1,260 was especially significant. Revelation 13:5 speaks of 42 months as the reign of the Beast; assuming 30-day months, this works out to 1,260 days. Daniel 7 and 12 refer to "time, times, and a half," which many fundamentalists interpret as 1,260 by assuming "time" to refer to a 360-day year (thus 360, plus 2 x 360, plus half of 360). Taken literally, the 1,290 "days" of Daniel and Revelation 12:6 equal 3½ years and are applied as such to the Tribulation, but if interpreted as years are also often used to calculate the date of the End. The 1,335 "days" mentioned in Daniel 12:12 are also used this way to measure years till the End, as are the 2,300 "days" till the defiled sanctuary (Temple) is cleansed.

One might object at this point that interpreting "day" as "year" is not as literal as simply assuming it means *day*. Despite the appeal to literalism, an even more important principle for fundamentalists is biblical *inerrancy*: the assumption that the Bible contains no error whatsoever. Even the most dedicated literalists concede that not everything in the Bible can be interpreted literally — the Book of Revelation especially is filled with obviously symbolic passages — and the trick then becomes which to interpret as strictly literal and which to treat as symbolic. Believers then manipulate both the "literal" facts and figures and their reinterpretations of the "symbolic" words or passages to make them fit the theory being argued.

Such numerical calculations and interpretive manipulations may be combined with the 6,000 Year scheme by, for instance, pointing to the Bible verse which states that the Tribulation is "shortened for the sake of the Elect" since otherwise all would die, and reasoning that therefore the 2,000 year period after Christ will be shortened a certain number of years. But now, as earlier predicted dates have passed, and A.D. 2000 is here, the even 2,000 years since Christ's birth tends to assume overwhelming importance, and may be appealed to even if disconnected from any creation date. The 2,000 Year Christ-to-End assumption, previously a component or corollary of the 6,000 Year theory, now exists independently, though a surprisingly large number of fundamentalists still prefer to retain the more comprehensive (and seductively symmetrical) 6,000 Year theory in its full, original form.*

Early History

The early Christians assumed the Second Coming was imminent. The Book of Revelation was intended to reassure believers then undergoing persecution that the prophesied scenario would unfold as promised despite the delay of several decades since the death of Jesus; that Christ would definitely return, and that the faithful would be rewarded. In the second century A.D., Montanus declared a Third Age of the Holy Spirit with an imminent Second Coming. This belief was declared heretical, and millenarianism was discredited by ecclesiastical authorities, but millennialist expectations for the imminent return of Christ remained strong for several hundred years. Eventually, as Christianity became accepted rather than persecuted, there was a corresponding shift from expectation of an *imminent* Second Coming to more symbolic allegorical interpretations by religious authorities. In the 200s, Origen suggested a more allegorical, symbolic interpretation, and in the 400s the enormously influential Augustine taught that the Millennium had been realized with the establishment of the Church, and that the spiritual City of God coexisted with the evil of this world.

The predicted Y2k computer glitch, by definition striking on the year 2000, serves simply to compound belief in the significance of the 2,000 Years.

But millennialism remained a readily-tapped undercurrent, especially in times of deprivation and oppression, erupting with occasional spectacular outbursts during the Middle Ages and Reformation among radicals, rebels, and the downtrodden. Bohemian Hussites (especially the most radical Taborites) tried to establish a millennial kingdom militarily. Prophets and millennialist reformers such as Thomas Müntzer and John of Leiden arose in the German Peasant's War (1524–25) and the violent Anabaptist takeover of Münster (1534–35). In the following century, independents from the Church of England such as the Fifth Monarchy Men (so called from the millennial kingdom which is to follow the four world empires prophesied by Daniel) also sought to usher in the Millennium.

The most significant medieval interpretative development was Joachim of Fiore's theory of history as divided into an age of the Father (God), an age of the Son (Christ), and the imminent age of the Holy Spirit. This notion of Three Ages retained its mystical appeal through the centuries. Hitler echoed it, declaring his Third Reich (which he maintained would last a "thousand years") the fulfillment of history. (Hitler's ideology drew heavily on millennialist tradition and concepts — and became increasingly apocalyptic when the Reich was faced with defeat. Similarly, Marxist ideology assumed a three-stage progression, culminating in a millennialist Paradise. That these were modern reflections of medieval millenarianism was proposed by Norman Cohn in his classic 1957 study *Pursuit of the Millennium*, especially the 1970 edition.)

Historicist, Preterist, and Futurist Interpretations

As the Reformation eventually led to abandonment of Augustine's assumption that nature and society were beyond man's control, the allegorical interpretation lost its attraction. During the Reformation, Protestant leaders retained Augustine's a-mill view but frequently interpreted Rome and Babylon as the Catholic Church. Protestants developed the *historicist* interpretation, in which the prophecies regarding the End are gradually fulfilled from the time of Christ up to the present, with only the very last events still to come. ("Historicist" in this sense should not be confused with the "historicism" of Judeo-Christian tradition spoken of earlier.) The historicist approach relies on the Year-Day principle of supposing "days" to mean years, and typically views the Catholic Church as apostate and evil, the counterfeit Rome-based Papacy simply replacing *pagan* Rome as the enemy and oppressor of true Christian faith.

Preterism is a belief that the events prophesied in the New Testament have *already* been fulfilled, except for the very last events and final judgment. The Great Tribulation and Armageddon occurred in the first century A.D. when the Temple in Jerusalem was destroyed and the Jews dispersed. The preterist interpretation was developed by Catholics (who interpret the Millennium as establishment of the Church), initially by Alcazar in the early seventeenth century, largely to counter the often stridently anti–Catholic historicist schemes being promoted by Protestants.

The *futurist* interpretation holds that most prophecy remains unfulfilled and will be fulfilled only in the Last Days. Proposed by Catholics, in particular by Ribera in the late sixteenth century, it was later adopted by Protestant fundamentalists. In the futurist scenario, all the seals, trumpets, bowls, and so forth occur during the coming End Times.

A-mill, Pre-mill, and Post-mill

As already noted, the millennialism of the early Christians was largely replaced by Augustine's a-millennialism, which became the "official" Church position through the Middle Ages, and remains Catholic orthodoxy. (It is also the position of most Lutherans, Churches of Christ, and others.) *A-millennial* means "*no* Millennium": a-millennialists deny a future, literal thousand-year Millennium, instead interpreting it symbolically or allegorically. (This term can be somewhat misleading, as most a-millennialists believe in a Millennium of *some* sort, though non-literal.) While Augustine taught that it was the establishment of the Church, some later a-mill believers interpreted it as being fulfilled in Heaven on a spiritual level.

In the seventeenth century Joseph Mede promoted a new, more literal interpretation of Revelation, proposing that the prophetic timetable could be calculated from the text. He advocated a *progressive* rather than apocalyptic millennialism — the result of true religion gaining over evil and Satan rather than God's abrupt supernatural intervention. Around 1700 Daniel Whitby taught what became known as the "*post- millennial*" interpretation. **Post-millennial** means that Christ's Second Coming occurs *after* the Millennium, which is an earthly period of peace, prosperity, and justice brought about by the eventual triumph of Christianity in this world.

Jonathan Edwards popularized the post-millennial view in America in the eighteenth century, and it flourished in the nineteenth, with many seeing America as God's favored land being transformed into the Millennial Kingdom. But there was still Tribulation to be endured before triumph, and evil to be overcome before the establishment of the Christian paradise. The Kingdom had to be fought for: God's truth was marching on, and the whole world would eventually see the glory of the Coming of the Lord, but not before He trampled the bloody winepress of the grapes of wrath.

Post-millennialism remained the dominant view through the nineteenth century, linked with concepts such as Manifest Destiny and the Social Gospel, but its optimistic assumptions that the world was progressively becoming better and more Godly were severely shaken — almost extinguished — by the carnage of the First World War. For most fundamentalists, the Second World War served merely to confirm the inadequacy of post-mill belief.

By the time of the First World War, a new, rival interpretation called ***pre-millennialism*** was already gaining popularity, and has remained the most popular since then amongst fundamentalists. It began around the 1830s with doctrinal innovations of John Nelson Darby and was developed and promoted at late nineteenth-century Bible conferences. The earlier millennialism of the first centuries of Christianity is sometimes labeled "pre-mill" but this tends to be misleading, especially as there was not really a distinct post-mill alternative then. It is worth keeping in mind that though pre-mill fundamentalists claim the early Christians as pre-mill predecessors, the pre-millennialism developed in the nineteenth century and preached today is substantially different from the millennialism of the early church. Some refer to the earlier pre-millennialism as "historic" or "classic" pre-millennialism to distinguish it from modern "dispensational" pre-millennialism.

Additionally, a new form of post-millennialism has emerged in the last few decades. This new post-millennialism differs significantly from the earlier nineteenth century post-millennialism. It is being actively promoted today by the Christian Reconstruction movement, whose highly contentious members insist on literal application of all Old Testament laws and a strict theocracy, and by groups promoting "Kingdom Now" or "Dominion Theology." A variety of other groups have adopted post-millennialism (and preterism) recently, but unlike other post-mills they are convinced that rather than becoming more Godly, society is increasingly controlled by evil conspiracies, and that believers will endure bloody tribulation and must battle to survive, following which the righteous survivors will impose righteousness and exterminate evil by force; these include Christian Identity sects and certain Christian Patriot, survivalist, and militia groups. (This, incidentally, demonstrates that it is merely a shift in emphasis from viewing history as Divine Plan to seeing it as dominated by *conspiracies against* this divine purpose and intention.)

The Rapture

In the second quarter of the 1800s, Darby introduced the notion of a "two-stage Second Coming," making a distinction between Christ coming secretly *for* his saints prior to the Tribulation — the Rapture — and coming publicly *with* his saints at the (final, public) Second Coming at the end of the Tribulation and Armageddon. At the Rapture, Christ comes secretly, "like a thief in the night" (1 Thessalonians 4) to "rapture" the faithful up to meet him in the air. Instantly, all who have truly accepted Christ disappear from the earth. The new pre-trib Rapture doctrine got an enormous boost when incorporated by Scofield into his Reference Bible in 1909 and 1917.

The word "rapture" itself is not in the Bible; 1 Thessalonians 4, the passage claimed to refer to the Rapture, says that at the coming of the Lord "the Lord himself shall descend from heaven with a shout," with the dead believers rising up to join Christ, then living believers "caught up" in the clouds to meet Christ in the air. The Greek word used in verse 4:17 for "caught up" is *harpazo*, meaning "to seize." The English word *rapture* comes from the Latin for "to seize." In its nonbiblical sense it means the state one is in after being transported or gripped by excitement or enthusiasm ("enthusiasm" itself means god-possessed), and the biblical doctrine is referred to popularly by many fundamentalists as the "Great Snatch." It is cognate with "raptor" (an animal which seizes its prey); also with "rape" (in its earlier sense of seizing by force — abducting; the current meaning of forced sex originally being a secondary meaning).

Pre-trib, Mid-trib, and Post-trib

Fundamentalists differ in views on the timing of the Rapture. The view that the Rapture will precede (and may in fact trigger) the Seven Year Tribulation is known as **pre-tribulationism**. By contrast, **post-tribulationists** believe that all Christians, even the most faithful true believers, must undergo the Tribulation, with survivors raptured only at its conclusion, rising up to meet Christ just as he begins his descent for the Second Coming. **Mid-tribulationists** hold that the Rapture occurs halfway through the Seven Year Tribulation, the halfway point being marked by even greater persecutions and disasters. (A confusing point is that since many mid-tribbers believe that the Great Tribulation is limited to the second half of the Seven Years, the Rapture is really *pre*-trib even though midway through the Seven Years.) Others argue for "*pre-wrath* Rapture" in which believers must endure Antichrist's Tribulation horrors but are raptured before God's Tribulation judgments ("wrath") which they maintain are unleashed only after Antichrist's, towards the end of the seven years. Another interpretation is the "*partial* Rapture" theory, which holds that only *some* Christians are raptured at the beginning of the Tribulation (the most faithful believers), while the remainder are raptured later.

Pre-trib pre-mills generally remain friendly with post-trib pre-mills, though post-tribbers may object that pre-tribulationism fosters the dangerous delusion that those who miss the Rapture still get a second chance of salvation if they become Christians during the Tribulation. The pre- versus post-trib distinction within pre-millennialism is not nearly as divisive as the debate between pre- and post-millennialists, which remains hotly contested and causes great dissension. Pre-mills accuse post-mills of endorsing humanist, evolutionist notions because of their belief in progress and eventual earthly triumph of Christianity, and of seeking worldly success at the expense of spiritual purity by embracing materialist heresies such as the "Prosperity Gospel." Post-mills in turn accuse pre-mills of succumbing to defeatist pessimism by passively waiting for the Rapture instead of energetically working to transform society into a totally Bible-based theocracy.

Dispensationalism

Along with the Rapture, nineteenth-century pre-millennialists developed the doctrine of ***dispensationalism***: the view that God established distinctly different covenantal relationships with mankind during the different "dispensations" of history, and that a proper understanding of Scripture requires a determination of which dispensation each biblical passage is referring to. There are a number of dispensationalist schemes, but the most common posit seven periods (dispensations). These seven are usually defined as Creation to the Fall, to the Flood, to Abraham (or, alternatively, the Tower of Babel), to Christ, to the Tribulation, and the Millennium. This seven-fold division echoes the World Week, though except for the last, the Millennium itself, the dispensations are not even thousand-year periods. (Nevertheless, the urge to symmetricalize induces many theorists to try to fit at least some of the dispensations into thousand-year blocks.)

Besides these successive dispensations, dispensational pre-mills also argue that the Bible makes a crucial distinction between Jews and the Church (Christians), and that it is necessary to know which passages and prophecies in both the Old and New Testaments refer to Jews and which to the Church, as well as to what dispensation is involved. This picking and choosing which passages refer to which group (Jew, Church, or heathen gentile) and to which dispensation is what dispensationalists call "rightly dividing the word of truth."

The most dramatic chronological innovation in dispensational pre-mill interpretation concerns Daniel's prophecy of the 70 Weeks. The final, Seventieth Week follows the "cutting off" of the Messiah during the Sixty-ninth (the Crucifixion, according to Christian interpreters). Dispensationalists argue that because the Jews rejected their Messiah, the 70 Weeks were interrupted, and there followed a centuries-long Gap or *Parenthesis* between the Sixty-ninty and the Seventieth Week, which is yet to come. This Parenthesis is the entire Church Age, during which prophetic time is put on hold. The prophetic clock begins ticking again when the Seventieth Week resumes in our near future (the End Times), beginning with the Rapture (for pre-tribs) or the Seven-Year Covenant (equated with the Tribulation). The supposed dividing line occurs between Daniel 9:26 and 27, when "he" (the pronoun is ambiguous) makes a covenant for one week. Previous exegetes had considered that "he" refers to the messiah, but dispensationalists assume it refers to Antichrist, the coming False Messiah.

From its nineteenth-century doctrinal roots, Protestant fundamentalism coalesced into a powerful movement by the end of the First World War. Dispensational pre-millennialism remains the majority eschatological view, though strongly contested by rival interpretations. Many pre-mills who assert that the Rapture may occur at any moment but that it cannot be predicted, nonetheless insist that once this precipitating event *does* occur (or Antichrist's seven-year treaty with Israel, which the Rapture makes possible), the events of the final Seven Years culminating in the Second Coming and Millennium will unfold with clock-like precision according to the prophetic schedule, just like the successful resumption of a postponed rocket-launching countdown. Many fundamentalists assert that the Rapture and the seven-year period of the End must occur soon after re-established Israel returns (1948); often claiming within a generation of this return (or within a generation of the 1967 recapture of Jerusalem, or some related event). Earlier dates previously seen as the start of the Return include 1917, when the British expressed support for a Israeli state in the Balfour Declaration and when the Ottomans surrendered Jerusalem to Allenby; and 1890, when the Zionist movement was born.

In the most popular pre-trib pre-mill dispensationalist End Times scenario, Antichrist comes to dominate the Ten-Nation revived Roman Empire, especially after all true Christians are removed by the Rapture. He signs a seven-year treaty with Israel; and is hailed as Messiah by presenting himself as a wonder-worker who brings peace to Israel. During the first half of the Tribulation he rebuilds the Temple, but halfway through the Tribulation (3½ years) he breaks the treaty and commits the Abomination of Desolation, ordering Jews to worship him as God and persecuting them dreadfully. The Two Witnesses preach in Jerusalem against Antichrist and the False Prophet. Armies of the South, North, and West battle each other and the Jews in Israel (in many versions the Seven Years is preceded by, or begins with, a Russian invasion of Israel). The 200-million man army of the East invades across the dried Euphrates. All converge at Armageddon, which is interrupted by the Second Coming followed by the Millennium. Christ binds Satan for a thousand years, till the end of the Millennium, then Satan leads a final rebellion against God, the Gog-Magog war.

If there is anything scary in all this, it is the almost gleeful anticipation of the expected Tribulation horrors and exterminations exhibited by some fundamentalists who believe that they, as true believers, will escape via the Rapture. The most radical may even seek to hasten or trigger these expected events. Post-tribbers and post-mills can be frightening too: they may try to make their scenarios of Tribulation and Armageddon self-fulfilling prophecies by preparing to resist by force the evil forces they believe surround them.

Dispensational pre-mills exhibit a marked ambivalence toward the Jews. Because of the prophetic significance of Israel and the Jews in their interpretation, they are strident supporters of the modern state of Israel. But they assume that Jews will suffer most terribly under Antichrist during Tribulation, more so even than during the Nazi Holocaust, and that all surviving Jews will convert to Christianity at or before the Second Coming. Pre-mills accuse post-mills of engendering anti–Semitism due to post-mill belief that the Church has entirely replaced Israel as God's favored, with the Jews no longer heir to any of the prophecies or promises; while post-mills reply that pre-mills happily consign Jews to a Tribulation fate worse than Nazism.

The dispensational pre-trib pre-mill interpretation which began largely with Darby was popularized in the early twentieth century by Scofield, and has been championed at many fundamentalist institutions such as Dallas Theological Seminary (in 1999 presided over by John Walvoord), where Hal Lindsey picked it up. Best-selling authors promoting this interpretation include Tim LaHaye (who collaborated with Henry Morris to set up the most influential creationist institution), Dave Hunt, Grant Jeffrey, Salem Kirban, and Charles Ryrie, and by televangelists Jerry Falwell, Jimmy Swaggart, and Jack Van Impe (vigorous promoter of the 6,000 Year theory).

Another line of interpretation derives from William Miller, who predicted the End for 1843 (then for 1844). After the Great Disappointment which followed, some Millerites reorganized into the Advent Christian denomination, retaining their belief in an imminent Coming. Ellen G. White, who founded the Seventh-day Adventist denomination (which in turn began offshoots, and offshoots of offshoots such as Branch Davidians), took a somewhat different approach, reinterpreting 1844 as Christ's *secret* coming. (1844 is also a key date for Baha'is: their founder proclaimed himself the return of the Shia Moslem's Hidden Imam, who went into occultation a thousand years earlier.)

Pentecostals believe their often flamboyant manifestations of the Holy Spirit such as speaking in tongues are Last Days gifts and signs, but these very manifestations may be denounced as demonic End Time deceptions by unsympathetic "Bible-only" fundamentalists.

Mormons (Church of Jesus Christ of *Latter-day* Saints) hold to a literal premillennial Second Coming, with Christ ruling from both Old and New Jerusalems (the latter in Missouri).

Worldwide Church of God founder H.W. Armstrong was clearly apocalyptic. Since his death church doctrine has been much altered, but some splinter groups retain his apocalyptic teachings.

The resolutely apocalyptic Jehovah's Witnesses set a number of dates for the End, notably 1914, which they later reinterpreted as Christ's *invisible* return before assuming heavenly rule, leaving earth to Satan.

Jews have generally abandoned apocalyptic expectations since ancient Roman times, but self-proclaimed Jewish Messiahs have appeared through the centuries, and many orthodox Jews are strongly messianic.

Despite Roman Catholicism's traditional a-millennial stance, a number of fringe and extremist Catholic groups now entertain apocalyptic expectations, stressing the imminent End-time "Chastisement" (Tribulation). A number have adopted the Rapture doctrine as well, and see abortion and apocalyptic Marian apparitions as End Time signs.

This bibliography comes out as the Millennium is but months away. One of the major lessons to be appreciated from a large compilation such as this is how long, and how often, the End has been predicted, and how certain those who proclaim it are of their beliefs; how wrong many of these beliefs have already turned out to be; how violently these beliefs often contradict each other; and how certain it is that failed predictions do not deter similar predictions, when these too are based on deeply held religious convictions.

Pre-1800 Works
(Chronological)

1. Enoch (Books of). 2nd-1st cent. B.C., with substantial later additions and revisions. 1 Enoch ("Ethiopic") is an apocalyptic collection which includes the legend of the Watchers — fallen angels who mate with human women and corrupt humanity — and God's imminent judgment, with doom for the unjust, and divine rewards for the righteous Elect. 2 Enoch ("Slavonic") is a Christian (7th cent.?) reworking of a first(?) century Jewish version.

2. *War of the Sons of Light Against the Sons of Darkness* (the "*War Scroll*"). 1st cent. B.C.? One of the Dead Sea Scrolls of the Qumran community (presumably Essenes). Describes the final apocalyptic war between evil army (troops of Belial, and "Kittim" of Assyria and Egypt) and divinely-aided Sons of Light (members of the Qumran sect themselves). 1962 ed. by Oxford Univ. (Yigael Yadin, ed.).

3. *Apocalypse of Baruch.* Late first cent. A.D. Ostensibly written by Jeremiah's scribe after Babylonian conquest, but actually written after Roman destruction of Jerusalem in A.D. 70. Promises restoration and a glorious Messianic age before final consummation of the world.

4. Esdras (Book of). Ca. A.D. 100 (preface and appendix later — ca. 150 and 250). One of the apocryphal books of the Bible (accepted as "deuterocanonical" in the Catholic Bible), ostensibly written by Ezra after return from Babylonian exile. Series of visions of "Signs of the End" and

coming disasters, with Israel's oppressors violently terminated by the Messiah. The preface refers to the Church superseding Israel. 14:10-11—"For the world hath lost his youth, and the times begin to wax old." 10½ out of 12 parts gone already. God promises terrible judgments to unbelievers: plagues, famine, war, destruction.

5. *The Shepherd of Hermas.* Early 100s A.D.? Complex Christian apocalypse written in stages (perhaps from A.D. 90-150, probably composite authorship). In his fourth vision, Hermas comes across a 100-foot Beast; an angel (representing the Church) explains to him it signifies the Great Tribulation about to transpire. Considered canonical in some early churches.

6. *Didache* (Early 100s?) (*Teaching* ["Didache"] *of the Twelve Apostles*). Chapter 16 warns of sudden, imminent, and apocalyptic Second Coming (following or during the Tribulation). False prophets and corrupters in Last Days. World Deceiver (Antichrist) subjects mankind to "fiery trial." Three Signs: opening of heaven; sound of trumpet; then resurrection of dead; then, Second Coming with saints.

7. *Epistle of St. Barnabas.* Ca. 120. Accepted in the Alexandrian (Orthodox) Church as canonical. Stated that 6 Days = 6,000 years (Cosmic Week) and that "in 6000 years, the universe will be brought to its end." Antichrist = Roman Empire. Highly esteemed in Alexandrian Church for its symbolic approach but not included in Bible canon. Chapter 15 refers to Cosmic Week, Millennium, judgment of wicked, new order and renewal of all things. "Of the Sabbath He speaketh in the beginning of the creation; And God made the works of His hands in six days, and He ended on the seventh day, and rested on it, and He hallowed it. Give heed, children, what this meaneth; He ended in six days. He meaneth this, that in six thousand years the Lord shall bring all things to an end; for the day with Him signifyeth a thousand years. and this He himself beareth me witness, saying: Behold, the day of the Lord shall be as a thousand years. Therefore, children, in six days, that is in six thousand years, everything shall come to an end." Christ comes soon to abolish Satan, judge ungodly, and usher in "day" of rest.

8. *Sibylline Oracles.* Orig. written 1st cent. B.C. to 2nd cent. A.D. Widely disparate writings, supposedly written by Roman prophetesses of doom and woe and much imitated. Adopted by Christians to proselytize pagan Romans. VII:148 predicted the End in A.D. 195. Influenced *Dies Irae* ("Day of Wrath") of Requiem Mass.

9. *Apocalypse of Peter.* Early 100s. Apocryphal work.

10. Polycarp. *To the Philippians.* Early 100s. Believed he was living in Last Times. Warns (7:1) of false leader, the "first-born of Satan."

11. Akiba ben Joseph. *Sepher Yezirah* Ca. 130. Early systematizer of rabbinical Judaism; associate of messianic aspirant Bar Kochba who led revolt against Romans. End = 6,093rd year after Creation.

12. Justin Martyr. *Apology.* Ca. 150. Syrian Greek; first prominent Christian apologist. Emphasized the Second Coming. Resurrection of the saints prior to the Millennium, during which "Christ will dwell a thousand years in Jerusalem," followed by eternal resurrection and judgment of all men. Second Coming delayed to allow more sinners to repent (maybe even some who are not even born yet).

13. _____. *Dialogue with Trypho.* 150s. Affirmed literal Millennium.

14. Montanus. Ca. 156. Original writings lost; known mostly through refutations by opponents who condemned him as heretical. Declared himself prophet of new Third Age of Holy Spirit. Based in Phrygia (in Anatolia), stressed imminent Second Coming, with New Jerusalem to descend in local town. (Tertullian was, for a while, a Montanist.)

15. Irenaeus. *Against Heresies.* Ca. 130-200. Pupil of Polycarp. Concludes with survey of biblical apocalypses; taught Antichrist would reign for 3½ years. After condemnation of millennialism (Augustine, Council of Ephesus 431 A.D.) church expurgated Irenaeus's works. 38:3: "For in as many days as this world was made, in the same number of thousands of years will it be concluded": i.e., the 6,000 year theory — as God rested on the 7th Day, so the 7,000th year (the Millennium) will be the final age. Christ to come with His saints. Discusses unfilled prophecies in Revelation, Daniel. Antichrist = a Jew.

16. Theophilus of Antioch. *To Autolycus.* 180. 6,000 years nearly up. Relies on Sibylline Oracles; knowledgeable about Greek philosophy, demonstrates historical priority of Moses and Old Testament over other civilizations

17. Rashi. *Commentary on the Talmud (Sanhedrin* 97d). Ca. 200? 2,000 years of desolation, 2,000 years under the Torah, then 2,000 years intended for messianic age — but this timetable ruined by iniquity (Messiah delayed).

18. Tertullian. *Against Marcion.* Ca. 200. 4:31: Insisted on literal interpretation of Revelation. Jews to be restored to Palestine, Jerusalem to descend from heaven, 1,000 year reign of faithful. Jerusalem seen hovering for 40 days over Asia Minor. Millennialist sections in *Apologetics* and *Resurrection of the Dead.* Already in "last days." Decline of Rome, rise of Antichrist, Christ to re-appear suddenly. Breakup of Roman Empire among 10 kings leads to Antichrist.

19. Hippolytus. *On Daniel.* 204. II:4: Predicted End for A.D. 500 by arguing for World Week of 6,000 years (with creation 5500 B.C.). Hippolytus hoped to dampen apocalyptic expectations and millenarian fever of his own day by deferring the End hundreds of years.

20. _____. *On Christ and Antichrist.*

Jewish Antichrist regarded by Jews as Messiah, leads Jewish army against Christians led by Christ. "Woman with child" of Revelation = the Church.

21. Julius Africanus. *Chronicles.* Ca. 220. XVIII: "5531 years can be counted from Adam and the Creation to the coming of Christ and his resurrection." The world's 6,000 years coming to a close.

22. Origen. Various works. Early 200s. Allegorized the Bible, including the Book of Revelation. Neoplatonist; rejected apocalyptic literalism, hostile to chiliasm.

23. St. Cyprian. *Exhortation to Martyrdom Addressed to Fortunatum.* Ca. 250. Bishop of Carthage, martyred in Roman persecution. "The Day of Judgment is at hand" — the "end of the world and the time of Antichrist."

24. Victorinus (of Pettau). *Commentary on the Apocalypse.* Ca. 300. First systematic commentary on Revelation. Proposed successive or repeating fulfillments. Antichrist is Roman.

25. Lactantius. *Divine Institutes.* Ca. 308. Theologian admired by Constantine; expressed strong apocalyptic strain. Draws on Sibylline Oracles. 7:14-26: The 6,000 Year theory — world to last from 5500 B.C. to A.D. 500. 7:25.5: Affirms "not more than 200 years to go" til End. Antichrist revealed when Roman Empire finished, just prior to End. "Let the philosophers who would compute the age of the world, know that the sixth millennium of years has not yet reached its close, and that on the completion of that number the consummation is to take place. That the close of the six thousand years is now approaching, may be discerned from the predictions of the prophets, for they foretold signs from which the consummation may be expected daily. [Experts agree that] by computing from the Scriptures the ages that have elapsed since the creation of the world, who although they vary somewhat, yet unite in the expectation that not more than two hundred years remain. As God labored during those six days in creating such good works, so His religion and truth must labor during these six thousand years, while wickedness prevails and bears rule. And again, since God, having finished

His works, rested on the seventh day and blessed it, at the end of six thousand years all the wickedness must be abolished from the earth, and righteousness reign for a thousand years...." Won't be the End until Rome falls, but when it does, "who will doubt that the end of human affairs and the world itself has arrived."

26. *Tiburtine Sibyl.* Ca. 350. Especially popular set of Sibylline prophecies. Constans (son of Constantine) is Great Emperor of the Last Days, unites divided and defeated Roman Empire, established millennial reign, defeats Gog and Magog, then hands over rule to God.

27. St. Cyril. *Catechetical Lectures.* Ca. 360. Bishop of Jerusalem. Rome: Daniel's Fourth Kingdom. Antichrist appears after Rome divided, takes over ten member nations and rules 3½ years. Then, when Gospel preached to all, Second Coming and end of the world.

28. Ephraem Syrus [Ephrem the Syrian]. *Antichrist & the End of the World.* 373? 1988 edition: Willits, CA: Eastern Orthodox Books. Saints and Elect "gathered together before the tribulation which is about to come and are taken to the Lord." During tribulation, some new believers are able to resist Antichrist become saved. This is taken by Grant Jeffrey as proving early origin of pre–trib position, but the "tribulation" here probably refers to the "Day of the Lord" (the Second Coming, Armageddon, and Judgment combined), and occurs after what is now called "the Tribulation." Other scholars attribute this work to a later "Pseudo-Ephraem."

29. Tichonius. *Commentary on the Apocalypse.* Ca. 380. Expected Second Coming soon, but this involves the world gradually converting to the true Church, a symbolic interpretation further developed by Augustine. Two Witnesses = Old and New Testaments. Antichrist = totality of forces opposing Christianity. Number of the Beast is 616 (not 666).

30. Martin of Tours. Late 300s. Apocalyptic millennialist who evangelized much of France; work known mostly through biography by contemporary Sulpicius Severus. Believed Antichrist already born.

31. Sulpicius Severus. *Sacred History*. Ca. 400. Daniel's Fourth Empire — Rome — now separating into iron and clay components: final stage before Christ's Kingdom.

32. Jerome. *Commentary on Daniel*. Ca. 400. Translator of Bible into Latin (the Vulgate). Expressed doubt whether to retain Revelation in canon. Historical interpretation; rejects millenarianism. Beast of Revelation is Nero, who will come again as the Antichrist. Two Witnesses = Elijah and Jeremiah. Incorporated Victorinus' commentary in his work.

33. Augustine. *City of God*. 413–426. Augustine's theology was shaped by eschatology but he resisted End Time speculation, arguing for an allegorical, spiritual Kingdom of God. John's Apocalypse is being fulfilled in the present; only Last Judgment really in future. Expressed an a-millennial view, which (due to his enormous influence) became the dominant official interpretation during the Middle Ages. Interpreting Revelation allegorically, he held that the Millennium referred to the Church Age (the church since its establishment). Evil is already conquered in spiritual level, through Christ; Satan rules only the world, which coexists with City of God. The "Millennium" is not a literal thousand years. However, if taken literally (and contrary to Augustine's intentions), then the Millennium started with Christ and ends ca. A.D. 1000 when Judgment is expected. Such notions may have influenced the Crusades. 12:10: World not more than 6,000 years old.

34. Commodian. *Instructions* and *Apology*. 400s? End comes 6,000 years after creation. End Times Tribulation starts with Seventh Persecution, begun by Nero with Jewish instigation. Two successive Antichrists, then Second Coming. Heavens and Earth burn; Heavenly City descends.

35. Andreas of Cesarea. 400s. 7 Kings = 7 historical Roman emperors. Constantine to be succeeded by Antichrist. Millennium began with founding of Christian Church; ends ca. A.D. 1000.

36. *Christian Legend Concerning Alexander*. 400s? Legend that Alexander the Great built gate in northeastern mountains to keep Huns confined and enclosed. Alexander said after 826 years Huns would burst forth from gate; after 940 years another horde would follow, and world would end. Appeals to authority of Jeremiah. (See A.R. Anderson's *Alexander's Gate, Gog and Magog* [1932] and Budge's *History of Alexander the Great* [1889].)

37. Jacob of Sarug (Mar Jacob). *Syrian Discourse* [or *Homily*]. Early 500s. Similar to earlier *Christian Legend Concerning Alexander*, but peoples confined by Alexander's Gate are Gog and Magog. They burst forth in the seventh thousand year as Antichrist's army. Related to Sura XVIII of Qu'ran: Dhu'l-Qarneyn ("the Two-Horned") = Alexander the Great (but also associated with Moses), shuts up Gog and Magog. (This sura opens with story to sleepers in the cave, related to Hidden Iman of Shi'ite belief, and German legend of return of Barbarossa.)

38. Gregory of Tours. *History of the Franks*. Late 500s. 6,000 years with Creation 5200 B.C., thus the End not till A.D. 800. Describes — critically — a self-proclaimed Christ who preached imminent End of World in 591.

39. Gregory, Pope, "The Great" (590–604). Various homilies and epistles. Convinced the End was near. Christ "predicted the evils that are to attend [the world's] old age, and the calamities that are immediately to precede its termination … some of which events we know have already taken place, and others we fear as nigh: for we see that our times are marked more than all former periods" by these signs (earthquakes, wars, famines, pestilences). Earth now "depressed by its old age, and driven on as it were to the verge of death by increasing troubles." "Antichrist the enemy of the Almighty is nigh." "… the end of the present world is nigh, and the kingdom of the saints about to come, which is never to end." Saw Lombard invasions as presaging End.

40. Pseudo-Methodius. *Epistle on Antichrist* and the *Apocalypse*. Late 600s. Moslems to bring about Tribulation (this is phrased as prediction, as if written before rise of Islam). Emperor of the Last Days defeats Gog and Magog when they burst forth from Alexander's Gate, then establishes millennial rule, finally yielding his crown to Christ in Jerusalem. History of mankind from creation to end of world covers 6,000 years plus Millennium.

41. St. Odile (Odilia) Late 600s. Patron saint of Alsace. A prophecy attributed to her received attention in 1916 for predicting German invasion of France but eventual triumph of France. Also said to have predicted Hitler ("conqueror from the banks of the Danube").

42. The Venerable Bede. *De Temporibus.* 703. Bede: English historian, theologian; promoted A.D. system of dating. Advocated Hebrew Masoretic text of Bible, from which he figured creation at 3952 B.C. Though he believed in Six Ages, he denied that date of end could be known (but would be 2048 if each age a thousand years). Expanded arguments in *De Temporum Ratione* (725) and *Explanation of the Apocalypse.*

43. Beatus of Liébana. *Commentary on Revelation.* 786. 14 years till the End, which is A.D. 800—6,000 years after Creation. Richly illustrated.

44. John of Modena. 800. Preached the End would come within a year, relying on the 6,000 year scheme.

45. Cynewulf. *Christ.* Early 800s. Anglo-Saxon poem in three parts; third is "Last Judgment" or Day of Doom.

46. Adso, Abbott of Montier-en-Der. *De Ortu et Tempore Antichristi.* 950? Following world apostasy, the appearance of Antichrist, and Final Judgment, the world will end. Antichrist, a demon-inspired magician, will be a Jew born in Babylon, revealed when coming reunited Roman Empire falls; reigns 3½ years till Second Coming. 1976 edition (Belgium: Brepols).

47. Bernard of Thuringia. *Apocalypse* and *Antichrist.* 960. Declared his calculations proved the End would come in 32 years.

48. Völuspá (Seeress' Prophecy). Late 900s? First section of *Poetic* (or *Elder*) *Edda*—a collection of Norse skaldic poems. Icelandic manuscript. Ca. 1270, but much of material predates introduction of Christianity to Scandinavia (ca.

1000). After describing the creation, the seeress relates the end of the world: *Ragnarök* ("doom of the powers" [gods]); *Götterdämmerung* ("twilight of the gods" in German). The story of *Ragnarök* is also featured in Snorri Sturluson's *Prose Edda* (1220s).

49. Wulfstan of York. *Sermo Lupi ad Anglos.* 1014. "Sermon of the Wolf" (his pseudonym) to the English. Wulfstan: Bishop of London, and Worcester; Archbishop of York. Advisor to kings; wrote their law codes. Pessimistic, impassioned call for repentance and reform during traumatic period of Danish raids and occupation of much of England. Wulfstan was concerned with assimilation of occupying Danes, and tried to enforce Christian standards. He was "preoccupied with nearness of the end of the world" and saw the invasions as God's wrath against evil of society. "This world is in haste and is drawing ever closer to its end ... the coming of the Anti-Christ grows ever more evil because of the sins of the people and then truly it will be grim and terrible widely in the world." 1976 edition (England: Univ. Exeter).

50. Glaber, Radulfus. *Historiarum Libri Quinque* ("Five Books of the Histories") ca. 1040. 1989 ed. Oxford Univ. Press. Burgundian monk; described millennial portents and beliefs on eve of A.D. 1000, and in the years 1030–33 (a thousand years after the death and resurrection of Christ). "It was believed that the order of the seasons and the elements ... had fallen into perpetual chaos, and with it had come the end of mankind.... It could portend nothing other than the advent of the accursed Anti-Christ who, according to divine testimony, is expected to appear at the end of the world." In a separate account, Abbo of Fleury described a preacher in Paris who predicted imminent End of the World.

51. Bruno of Segni. *Exposition of the Apocalypse.* Ca. 1100. Influenced by Carolingian bishop Haymo's exposition. Two Witnesses = Old and New Testaments.

52. Hildegard of Bingen. *Scivias.* 1100s. Hildegard: German abbess, mystic, and composer. Account of her prophetic visions. Many visions of Antichrist.

53. Bernard of Cluny. *De Contemptu Mundi* (Contempt of the World). Early 1100s. The Pope is "King of this odious Babylon." (About the same time, the Cistercian Bernard of Clairvaux held that Antichrist would come in the future.)

54. Otto, Bishop of Friesing. *The Two Cities* [*Historia de Daubus Civitatibus — Chronicles, or the History of the Two Cities*]. 1928 [1143-47]. Cistercian abbot, uncle of Frederick Barbarossa, participated in 2nd Crusade; called the "greatest medieval historical thinker." *Two Cities* derives from Augustine and other chronicles (especially Eusebius); used Augustine to construct complete history of world. Endorsed Augustine's view of City of God as the Church: all saints dead and alive; City of Earth is "Babylon." City of God to continue til End (thus later followers of Otto saw 16th cent. decline of Holy Roman Empire and Roman Church as signs of End). Church claimed succession to Rome: e.g. Charlemagne's authority from Church — but still competition between Church and state. Four World Empires; Rome was "translated" to Constantinople, then to Franks. Pagan empires where two cities overlapped. Roman Empire to prepare mankind for City of God. Heavenly Jerusalem only realized at End. 4th Empire must last til End. Confident of nearness of End; living in "closing days." Church grows in power as Empire declines. "Mixed city" phase near end (because of competition between Pope and Emperor). Other worldly phase about to start: Last Judgment, End of World. End also near because geographic limit reached of westward movement of civilization. Linear concept of predetermined time. Satan bound during Constantine's reign, but not for a literal thousand years. Resurrection *after* destruction of world, new heavens and earth. Speculates on resurrection of monsters — whether they will remain deformed. Antichrist from tribe of Dan.

55. St. Malachy. *Prophecies.* 1148? Archbishop of Armagh. List of 112 future Popes up to the End, each identified with distinctive epitaph. These prophecies discovered in 1590s in Rome (and suspected by many to be forgeries). Last three popes: "From the Labor (or Eclipse) of the Sun," "Glory of the Olives," and "Peter the Roman." (John Paul II is 110th Pope.)

56. *Letter of Toledo.* 1186. Prophesied imminent doom.

57. Joachim of Fiore. *Liber Concordie Novi ac Veteris Testamenti* (Harmony of Old and New Testaments). Late 1100s.

58. ____. *Expositio in Apocalypsim* (Exposition of the Apocalypse). Cistercian abbot. Proposed and popularized scheme of Three Ages of the world: Age of the Father, under Old Testament law; Age of the Son, under New Testament grace; and coming Age of the Spirit, to be ushered in by monastics. Calculated 1200-1260 as End (Millennium), claiming the 1,260 Days of Revelation 12:6 are really the number of years before the true Church is revealed openly in the New Age. After A.D. 1260, his followers calculated 1290, then 1335, etc., for End. Joachim's Seal; Trumpet, Vial series concurrent from Christ to 1260 A.D. Seven-headed Beast = Herod, Nero, Mohammed, Saladin, and Antichrist. Locusts: Cathar heretics. Richard the Lionheart reportedly met with Joachim on his way to the Crusades. (Richard assumed Antichrist would be a Jew from Babylon or Antioch; Joachim said he was already born, in Rome, and would become universal Pope.) Many later works by various writers were attributed to Joachim.

59. *De Semine Scripturarum* (Seed of the Scriptures). Ca. 1200. Joachite author. Mystical gematria. 2,300 Years: 700 from founding of Rome to Christ, then to 1600. A new era to begin 1215.

60. "Pseudo-Joachim." *De Oneribus Prophetarum.* 1240s. Joachimist prophecies against the reigning Hohenstaufens. 1260 is critical year.

61. Bacon, Roger. *Opus Maius.* 1267. Bacon: philosopher and scientist; attempted to forecast, from astronomical calculation of configuration of planets from creation to the future, the coming of the Antichrist, heralding the imminent end of the world.

62. Arnold of Vilanova. *De Tempore*

Adventu Antichristi.(Time of the Coming of the Antichrist). 1288-90. Joachite alchemist and physician. 1,290 years ends ca. 1378: coming of Antichrist. 2,300 years from Belshazzar (Arnold erroneously guessed he lived in 800s B.C.) to the End (late 1400s).

63. ____. *Expositio Super Apocalypsi.*

64. Olivi, Petrus Johannis (Pierre Jean). *Postilla Super Apocalypsim* (Commentary on the Apocalypse) and *Lectura in Apocalypsim.* 1290s. Franciscan Spiritualist: Joachite. Babylon = corrupt Church of Rome. 1,260 Years from Peter's establishment of the Church (ca. A.D. 40) to 1300. 2,300 Years from Antiochus to A.D. 2100.

65. Ibn Kathir, Isma'il Abul-Fadl Umar. *The Signs Before the Day of Judgment.* 1300s. Islamic eschatology. 1992 edition (London: Dar Al Taqwa; 96 p. bibl. refs.) From hadith (traditional sayings of Prophet Mohammed) concerning *Akhir al-Zaman* (end times). The Mahdi (Savior) rules until the False Messiah (*al-Masikhal-Dajjal*) takes power (this Mahdi is not the Hidden Iman of the Shi'ite Moslems). *Ya'juj wa-Ma'juj* = Gog and Magog. *Fitan* = the Tribulations. Antichrist (*Dajjal*) marks all non-Moslems on forehead with letters KFR (*Kafir*: unbeliever). Beast from Earth emerges. Messiah Jesus descends, kills Dajjal at gate of Ludd (now Lod, the Airport site). Jesus refutes Christian claim that he (Jesus) is divine; explains he was not crucified, but taken to heaven by God. Signs of End included prevalence of high buildings.

66. Rolle de Hampole, Richard [attributed to]. *The Pricke of Conscience.* 1300s. Signs of Doomsday and Second Coming; much on Heaven and Hell. First sign: Rome destroyed. Then Antichrist, a Jew from the tribe of Dan, establishes himself in Jerusalem and proclaims himself Christ. He performs miracles, re-animating the dead with demons, who are loosed upon the world, and reigns for 3½ years. Gog and Magog, confined beyond the Caspian, will break loose to persecute Christians (Gog secretly, and Magog openly). Enoch and Elijah prophesy against Antichrist for 1,260 days. Antichrist kills these Two Witnesses, but reigns only 15 days more, then is killed by God. "What tyme the day of dome shall be" is not revealed by God; we should not seek to learn when, "but we suld mak us redy alle, as the day of dome to morn suld falle"—i.e., be ready always. Rolle lists various signs of Doomsday such as commotions in the heavens, and the "15 Tokens" attributed to Jerome (great disturbances in the seas, in the earth, and in the heavens; rising of the dead, burning of the earth). All the resurrected dead will be given bodies of 32-year-olds. The righteous dead are "ravyste" (ravished; raptured), rising to meet Christ in the air. Christ then pronounces Judgment on all at the Valley of Jehoshaphat.

67. Militz (Milíč) of Kromeriz. *On the Antichrist.* 1368. Militz: Archdeacon at Prague; affiliated with Franciscan Spirituals; forerunner of Hus. Antichrist already active, but fully revealed only when, 1335 years ends 1363-67. End 1365-67.

68. Wycliffe, John. *De Papa.* 1379. Wycliffe: first complete English translation of Bible. This is one of three tracts definitely by Wycliffe, of many attributed to him. The Pope is the Antichrist. Time, times, and a half = early Papacy, Islam, and current years.

69. ____. *The Last Age of the Church* (1840; 1536). Also attributed to Wycliffe.

70. *Summula seu Breviloquium Super Concordia Novi et Veteris Testamenti.* 1300s. A restatement of Joachimism, probably written in Catalonia.

71. Huska, Martin, of Bohemia. Taborite (radical Hussite). In 1420 announced End would come February 10-14.

72. d'Ailly, Pierre. *De Legibus et Sectis* 1480 (written ca. 1400) D'Ailly: French theologian and cardinal. Astronomical conjunctions portend successive dominance of religions; Saracans (Islam) to be overthrown soon by Tatars or Christians, and followed by Antichrist. Tatars have already burst from Caspian gates, and will embrace Antichrist. Uprising of Ishmael's line against Romans in 7th millennium, Saracens overrun Holy Land, great desolation and persecution. Then Emperor-

Messiah arises, takes fiery revenge, then new millennial peace until End of Time. Earlier(?), another disruption as Gog and Magog forces unleashed from Asia for a "week of years"; Emperor-Messiah lives in Jerusalem 10 years, during which Antichrist appears. World to last 7,000 years (cites Augustine); 6,845 years already elapsed. Columbus took d'Ailly's *Imago Mundi* with him on his voyages.

73. Nicholas of Cusa. *Conjecture Concerning the Last Days.* 1452. Nicholas: Cardinal and noted scholar. 559 B.C. + 2,300 years. End perhaps 1700–1734.

74. Hilten, John. *Commentary on Daniel and the Apocalypse.* Late 1400s. Franciscan monk. Predicted that a religious reformer would overthrow Papacy in 1516. Turks = Gog.

75. Savonarola, Girolamo. *Compendio delle Revelationi.* 1495. Florentine religious reformer and theocratic leader. Preached doom and destruction, and necessity of repentance.

76. Stoeffler, Johannes. *Ephemerides.* 1499. Astrologer, predicted End for 1524 by universal flood, triggering ark-building panic in Germany. Over a hundred pamphlets based in his prediction were published. After 1524, he recalculated date for 1528. Also wrote *Almanach Nova in Annos 1499-1531; Tabulae Astronomicae; Coelestium Rerum Disciplinae.* Similar predictions in 1503, from similar astrological conjunctions. (Astrologer Nicolaus Peranzonus de Monte Sancte Marie also predicted End by Flood for 1524.)

77. Columbus, Christopher. *The Book of Prophecies.* Ca. 1501-02.

After his 3rd voyage in 1500, Columbus attempted to justify importance of his discovery of the Indies by compiling biblical texts and patristic and medieval commentaries, relating these to the End. Columbus "came to believe that he was predestined to fulfill a number of prophecies in preparation for the coming of the Antichrist and the end of the world." His apocalyptic vision and conviction of his special role in these events presaging the End of Time was a major stimulus for his voyages. Came to see himself as "divinely inspired fulfiller of prophecy." According

to contemporary sources, Eden lay eastward in Asia; Gog and Magog were imprisoned in the walls built by Alexander. World to last 7,000 years (citing d'Ailly and Augustine); it began 5343 B.C., thus ends by mid-1600s. People in all islands converted before End; Columbus believed that his discoveries of Indies would aid this: pictured himself as a divinely inspired fulfiller of prophecy, discoverer of "the new heaven and new earth," and "bearer of Christ" (*Christo-ferens*) to these new lands. 1996 edition (Univ. Calif.; ed. by Roberto Rusconi; xiv, 419 p.).

78. *Book of a Hundred Chapters.* Ca. 1510. Author known only as "Revolutionary of the Upper Rhine." Prophesies the return of Frederick Barbarossa for millennial reign, preceded by bloody elimination of all sinners and unbelievers. Four Empires are France, England, Spain, and Italy; Germany, the Fifth, will be restored to its original supremacy. Earth to be destroyed if program not followed.

79. Müntzer, Thomas. *Die Fürstenpredigt.* ["Prince's Sermon"] 1520s.

Sermon preached to Duke of Saxony. World is now entirely Satan's; the Elect should kill all non-believers. Müntzer was radical Protestant reformer who split from Luther, and became leader of the 1524-25 Peasant's Revolt.

80. _____. *Ausgedrückte Entblössung* ... 1520s. "Explicit Unmasking of the False Belief of the Faithless World."

81. Gaurico, Luca. *Sigismondo Tizio Historiae Seneses.* 1522. Predicted End in 1524 by Flood, from astrological conjunction.

82. _____. *Prognosticum Astrologicum, ad Annum Christi MDXLIIII.* 1543 [1535]. ([32] p. illus. [listed under Achils Gasser, author]).

83. Virdung, Johann. *Practica von dem Entcrist vn[d] dem jüngsten Tag auch was geschehen sal vor dem Ende der Welt.* 1523? ([Speyer: Jakob Schmidt.) [8] p.

Occult prophecies about Antichrist in the Last Days.

84. Paracelsus. *The Prophecies of Paracelsus.* 1992 [originally early 1500s]. Edmonds, WA: Alchemical Press. 54 p. illus.

85. Luther, Martin. *Ein Sermon von des judische Reichs und der Welt Ende: Math. 24.* 1525 [Wittemberg] [20] p.

Called Pope the Antichrist in his 1530 Bible and earlier, and said the Turks were Gog. "I am persuaded that verily the day of judgment is not far off; yea, will not be absent three hundred years longer." But Luther generally accepted Augustinian view, not apocalyptic. Initially skeptical of Millennial prophecies (he stridently condemned the millennialist Peasant War), he later assumed the Millennium lasts from the writing of Revelation to Pope Gregory VII, followed by 666 years of anti-Christian Papacy (historicist interpretation). Gog and Magog = Turks and the "red Jews; then the Last Judgment."

86. _____. *Sermon on Matt. 24:8-13.* 1539. No literal Millennium on earth. Luther rejected Book of Revelation in 1522, but significantly changed his opinion by 1530. In 1529 (*Revelation of Antichrist*) said Turk = Gog; Pope = Magog. In 1517 said: "I believe that all the signs which are to precede the last day have already happened. The gospel is preached throughout the world: the Son of perdition is revealed."

87. _____. *Supputatio Annorum Mundi.* 1541. 6,000 years for world, followed by the End.

88. Stifel, Michael. *Apocalypsis in Apocalypsim.* 1532. Wittenburg. [104] leaves.

Stifel: German. Numerology. Calculated Second Coming, from Daniel and Revelation, for 1533, Oct 19, 8 A.M.

89. Hoffmann, Melchior. *Prophetische Gesicht vn Offenbarung, der gotliche Wurckung zu diser letste Zeit, die vom .xxiiij. Jar biss in dz .xxx. einer gottes Liebhaberin durch den heilige Geist geoffenbart seind, welcher hie in disem Buchlin .lxxvij. verzeichnet seindt.* 1530. [Strassburg: Balthasar Beck]. 39 p.

German Anabaptist Reformer. Second Coming = 1553. Gog and Magog = the Turks.

90. Carion, John. 1550 [1532]. *The Thre Bokes of Cronicles ... London.*

Called *Carion's Chronicle.* Revised by Melancthon, who may have inserted the Prophecy of Elias, and of Daniel. Three

Books = 3 two-thousand year ages: Adam to Abraham, to Christ, to End. Four Monarchies (empires): end to come when Christ's stone breaks feet of 4th Monarchy (Rome). Ends with exhortation to fight against "malaciouse kyng of Egypt or blasphemouse Byshop of Rome and all his trayterouse trayne...." Pref.: "The Sayenge of Helias House. The worlde shall stande syxe thousand yeares and after shall it falle. Two thousande yeares wythout the Law. Two thousande yeares in the lawe. Two thousande yeares the tyme of Christ. And if these yeares be not accomplyshed, oure synnes shall be the cause, whyche are greate and many." "The last age from the nativitie of Christ untyil the worldes ende, doth likewise contayne two Th. yeres, although we have said before, that the yeres of this age wulde not be whole, that the two thousand yeres may be complete." Turks = Gog- Magog, Little Horn.

91. Rothmann, Bernhard. *Eyne Restitution edder Eine wedderstellinge rechter vnde gesunder christlicher leer, gelouens vnde leuens vth Gades genaden durch de gemeynte Christi tho Munster an den dach gegeuenn.* 1534. Münster : [s.n.], [114] p.

92. _____. *Eyn ganz troeslick Bericht van der Wrake unde Straffe des Babilonischen Gruwels.* 1534. Münster.

Anabaptist disciple of Jan Bockelson (John of Leiden: the "New David") during his millenarian theocratic (and despotic) reign in Münster. The 3rd Age first lasted till Flood, second included Christianity (corrupted by Catholic Babylon). "The glory of all the Saints is to wreak vengeance.... Revenge without mercy must be taken upon all who are not marked with the Sign [all except the Elect Anabaptists]." All who oppose the Elect must be exterminated. Whole world would be destroyed except purified community of the Elect in Münster. Jan Matthys, the "Prophet" of the Münster rebellion, declared himself Enoch who was to prepare for the Second Coming.

93. _____. *Van verborgenheit der schrifft des Rykes Christi, vnde van dem daghe des Heren, durch de gemeinte Christi tho Münster.* 1535 [Münster, s.n.] [87] p.

94. Calvin, John. *Commentaries on*

the Book of the Prophet Daniel. 2 vols. 1948 [1540s?] Grand Rapids, MI: Eerdmans.

Translation of *Praelectiones in Librum Danielis*. Antichrist = the Papacy.

95. Melancthon, Phillip. *Commentary on the Prophet Daniel*. 1557.

Melancthon: German Reformation leader, along with Luther. Mahometan Empire and Papacy to be destroyed about the same time, then the Millennium, when Earth is 6,000 years old. End possibly in 1588, probably before 1600. "This aged world is not far from its end." 1557 = 5,519th year of world.

96. Osiander, Andreas. *Vermutung von der letzten Zeiten und dem Ende der Welt, aus der Heiligen Schriften gezogen*. 1545 [1544]. Nurnberg. [110] p. Pub. 1548 as *The Conjectures of the Ende of the Worlde* (Antwerp; 61p. illus).

German protestant astronomer, wrote preface to Copernicus' 1542 *De Revolutionibus*. 6,000 Year prophecy of Elias. 1,656 years from Christ to End, because of 1,656-year Creation to Flood span. Christ's 33 years as types too. Little Horn = Julius Caesar; his assassination and emergence of Augustus was healing of the fatal wound. A.D. 412 + 1,260 (Papacy dominant) = 1672 — End soon after. Ten Horns = Spain, Portugal, France, England, Scotland, Denmark, Poland, Bohemia, Hungary, Holy Roman Empire.

97. Ambach, Melchior. *Vom Ende der Welt, und Zukunfft des Endtchrists: Wie es vorm jungsten Tag in der Welt, ergehn werde*. 1545. Frankfurt.

"Alte und newe Propheceyen, auff diese letzste böse Zeit...."

98. Bale, John. 1550 [1545?] *The Image of Bothe Churches: After the Most Wonderfull and Heavenly Revelation of Sainct John ...* London. 872 p. illus.

Verse-by-verse commentary on Revelation. Bales: British Protestant, playwright, later a bishop. The "first systematic chronological interpretation of Revelation." True and False Church. Pope (general, not individual) = Antichrist. Revelation as Christ vs. Antichrist (the Pope — the Ten Horn Beast). Millennium began 606; Papal power has lasted less than 1,000 years, but God will shorten time for the sake of the Elect. Whore of Babylon = Catholic Church. Islam also = Antichrist. 1st-3rd Seals: occurred 1st-6th centuries. First Seal, White Horse rider = Christ. Third (black) horse = Satan. 4th = Mohammed and Pope Boniface III. 6th = Wycliffe. Trumpets synchronous with seals, and refer to church history. 6th Vial = Henry VIII's defiance of Rome. 7th Seal imminent. Locusts = papal agents. Two Witnesses = Moses and Christ (Old and New Testaments). First Beast (from the sea) = Antichrist (wounded by Reformation). Satan released from bondage ca. A.D. 1000 by Pope; Antichrist gains power through control of Papacy and Islam ca. 600 (Gog and Magog).

99. Grünpeck, Joseph. *Propheceien und Weissagungen: Vergangne, Gegenwartige, unnd Kunfftige Sachen, Gesicht und Zufall, hoher und niderer Stande ...* 1549. Frankfurt / Augsburg. 128 p.

Astrology and occult prophecies. Also wrote about the "French evil" (syphilis).

100. Turrel, Pierre. *Le Periode, Cest a Dire, La Fin du Monde: Contenant la Disposition des Chouses Terrestres, par la Vertu & Influence des Corps Celestes*. 1550. [Lyon?]: s.n.

French astrologer. Claiming religious orthodoxy, predicted End for 1537 (and later for 1544, 1801, 1814) by various computations.

101. Mandel, Christof. *Rechnung der lxx. Wochen Danielis: Sampt Zwayen Vermuetungen von dem Ende der Welt auf der ailigen Geschrifft vnd warhafftigen Historien gezogen*. 1552. Dillingen: Sebaldus Mayer. [58] p.

102. Latimer, Hugh. 1500s. "Antichrist is known throughout all the world. Wherefore the day is not far off.... The world was ordained to endure, as all learned men affirm, ... six thousand years." 5,552 already past, so 448 left. But these *"shall be shortened* for the elect's sake." Thus Second Coming very near: "it may come in my days ... or in my children's days"; "the last day cannot be far off."

103. Ridley, Nicholas. 1566. *Piteous Lamentation of the Miserable Estate of the Churche of Christ in England, in the Time of Queen Mary, wherin is Conteyned a*

Learned Comparison Betwene the Comfortable Doctryne of the Gospell, and the Traditions of the Popyshe Religion ... [57 p]

Ridley: English bishop and martyr (d. 1555). Antichrist and Babylonish Beast = Papacy.

104. Nostradamus. *The True Centuries.* 1555. Many subsequent editions; various translations.

French astrologer-physician of Jewish descent. Rhymed quatrains written in mixture of languages; with highly ambiguous meanings that have provided later interpreters with an almost unlimited and highly adaptable source of predictions. Mentions year 1999 and Antichrist, also various wars and disasters.

105. Leowitz, Cyprian. *Eclipsium Omnium ab Anno Domini 1554 Usque in Annum domini 1606 Accurata Descriptio Et Pictura.* 1556. Augsburg: P. Ulhard.

Astrologer; predicted End for 1584.

106. Bullinger, Heinrich. *A Hundred Sermons upon the Apocalyps of Jesu Christe.* 1573 [1557]. [55], 699 p.

Translated from Latin. Seals of Revelation run concurrently until the End. 5th-6th Trumpets = Mohammedans and Turks. Antichrist = Pope. Millennium began 1st cent. A.D.

107. ____. *Of the End of the World and Judgement of Our Lord Jesus Christe to Come: And of the Most Perillous Dangers of This Our Moste Corrupt Age.* 1580. London.

108. Musculus, Andreas. *On the Last Days.* 1557?

Frankfurt theology professor.

109. *Geneva Bible.* 1560. Prepared for English Protestants in Calvin's Geneva. Heavily annotated, especially Revelation. Depicted Pope as Antichrist. Babylon = Catholic Church. Magog = Turks, Saracens. Locusts = monks, friars, other papal agents. Interpretation of Millennium largely follows Bales; also influenced by Bullinger. 666 = "Lateinos" (Roman Church). Geneva Bible became "vehicle for the widespread dissemination of the apocalyptic tradition."

110. Foxe, John. *Acts and Monuments of These Latter and Perilous Days ... (Book of Martyrs.)* 1563.

Based on Revelation. Theme: the oppressed and persecuted Elect. 1563 edition has millennial binding of Satan from the Ascension (loosed around A.D. 1000); in 1576 edition Satan's binding starts with Constantine and ends ca. 1300.

111. ____. *Eicasmi seu Meditationes in Sacram Apocalypsin* (Conjectures on the Apocalypse). (1587, London?)

First British author to present Protestant apocalyptic history as unfolding pattern of events. Foxe writing commentary on Revelation when he died. 5th seal = birth of Christ. World-Week starting 4000 B.C., but 6th (present) millennium shortened by God, so End is near. Locusts = barbarians; scorpions = Moslems. 666 = Year Islam started. Second Beast (land) = Papacy. First Beast = Pagan Rome. Two Witnesses = Hus and Jerome of Prague. But prophecies not numerically exact, only fully understood when fulfilled.

112. Funck, Johann. *Chronologia; Hoc Est, Omnivm Temporvm et Annorvm ab Initio Mvndi vsqve ad Resvrrectionem Domini Nostri Iesv Christi, Computatio.* 1545. Nuremburg [18], 123 p.

113. ____. *Guide to the Understanding of the Apocalypse.* 1564.

A.D. 216 + 1,260 = 1521 (Diet of Worms); + 1,335 = 1595. 457 B.C. + 490 (70 Weeks) = A.D. 34. (457 B.C. = 3,506th year since Creation.)

114. Faber, Basilius. *Christliche, notige und nutzliche Unterrichtungen, von den letzten Hendeln der Welt.* 1569. Leipzig: Vogelin. [183] p. Also 1594.

115. Wigand, Johann. 1571. *Von den Letzten Tagen vnd verenderung der Welt. Eine Predigt Aus der Epistel 2. Pet. 3. Dominica 26. gethan zu Speier.* Jena. [22] p.

116. Krenzheim, Leonhard. *Coniecturae Piae et Eruditae de Impendentibvs in Ecclesia et Imperiis, Horum Temporum Mutationibus, & Calamitatibus: Sumptae ex Collatione Annorum atq[ue] Euentuum Veteris & Noui Testamenti, Prima & Ultimae Monarchiae, Numerorum in Daniele & Apocalypsi* ... 1580. Gorlicii: Ambrosius Fritsch. [72] p.

117. Ribera, Francisco. Ca. 1580 1603. *In Sacram Beati Joannis Apostoli & Evangelistae Apocalypsin Commentarii.* Antwerp.

Jesuit; originated futurist interpretation as refutation of Protestant claims that the Pope was Antichrist. Seals: five for early church, two for End (none for present or medieval period). Antichrist still in future (thus not the Pope); conditions for Antichrist's coming not yet met. Antichrist will rule for 3½ years. Millennium is heavenly, after First Coming. First part of Revelation refers to pagan Rome, the rest to future.

118. Batman, Stephen. *The Doome Warning all Men to the Judgment.* 1984 [1581]. Delmar, NY: Scholars' Facsimiles & Reprints. xii, 437 p. illus.

"Wherein are contayned for the most parte all the straunge prodigies hapned in the worlde, with divers secrete figures of Revelations tending to mannes stayed conversion towardes God."

119. Winckler, Nicolaus. *Bedencken von kunfftiger Verenderung weltlicher Policey, vnd Ende der Welt, auss heyliger gottlicher Schrifft vnnd Patribus, auch auss dem Lauff der Natur des 83. biss auff das 88. vnd 89 Jars.* 1582. Augsburg: Michael Manger. [68] p.

120. Geveren, Sheltco a. *Of the End of this World, and Second Comming of Christ a Comfortable and Most Necessarie Discourse, for these Miserable and Dangerous Dayes.* 1583 [1577]. London: Andrew Maunsell. [2], 88 p. bibl refs. Transl. by Thomas Rogers.

Destruction of world, judgment of mankind at Second Coming. Prophecy of Elias: "the world shall not endure six thousand yeres"—the 6,000 Years are "shortened" for the Elect. "Among all sinners, none is more odious before God, than is Incredulitie, doubting both of divine promises & threatnings." Daniel's final kingdom = Turkish Empire. "Now what is more evident in these our daies?" than that Pope is False Prophet. Locusts = friars. Contemporary flood, earthquakes, comets and meteors, new star 1572-3. Astronomers predict great world change for 1583. 73 years from Christ to destruction of Jerusalem; likewise 73 from Luther (1517) to 1583. 1,500 years from apostolic era to End. 1058: start of papal tyranny. A.D. 97 (Revelation written) + 666 = 763

(Merovingians grant Papal authority). Quotes Sybils; much Platonic numerology.

121. James VI of Scotland (James I of England). *A Paraphrase Upon the Revelation of the Apostle St. John.* 1588.

Babylon = Papacy. Beast of Revelation and Antichrist = Pope. Plague of deadly locusts = monks. When he became King of England, James authorized the Bible translation that bears his name; its dedication alludes to this work. James also wrote book on demonology.

122. _____. *A Fruitfull Meditation Containing a Plaine and Easie Exposition, or Laying Open of the VII, VIII, IX, X Verses of the 20th Chapter of the REVELATION* ... 1616. London.

Turk and Pope both Antichrist.

123. Barrow, Henry. 1590. *A Briefe Discoverie of the False Churches* ... sl: sn.

Imminent End, with warfare of Christ vs. Antichrist. Separatist: attacked established church for tolerating ungodly.

124. Napier, John. 1593. *A Plaine Discoverie of the Whole Revelation of St. John.* Edinburgh [6], 269, [11] p. 1611 ed. (London).

Napier: inventor of logarithms. Calculated current age would end 1688-1700. Many editions, especially popular during English Civil War. Abridged, reissued as *The Bloody Almanack* (1643). Seven Seals: in 7- year intervals from A.D. 29 to 71. Trumpets same as vials (concurrent, same events), both occurring at 245 year intervals. 2nd = A.D. 316 (Eastern Empire established). 3rd = 561 (Rome burned). 4th = 806 (Charlemagne emperor). 5th = 1051 (Turks under Zadok). 6th = 1296 (Osman, Ottoman founder). 7th = 1541 Reformation, ends 1786. Napier first to propose that 666 = "Lateinos" (not number of years). Antichrist = Pope. Urges "utter extirpation" of "devilish seat" (Rome). Last Day between 1688 and 1700. Satan bound A.D. 300: start of Millennium. Gog-Magog = Papacy, Islam (and Mongols). Two Beasts = Latin Empire and Pope. Denied millenarian notion of perfect life during earthly thousand year reign. Last trumpet and vial begins 1541. 1260 year rule of Antichrist ends ca. 1560. A.D. 1699 = 1,600 (furlongs of blood from winepress — Rev. 14:20) + A.D. 99 (the year Rev. was written).

125. Poyssel, Eustachius. *Etliche Tratetlein jetziger Zeit nutzlich und notig zu lesen.* 1595 Rupertum Fluuium. 82 p. illus. End of world 1623. Numerology. Includes poems.

126. Pont, Robert. 1599. *A Newe Treatise on the Right Reckoning of the Yeares and Ages of the World, and Mens Lives, and of the Estate of the Last Decaying Age Thereof, this 1600 Yeare ... Which is from the Creation, 5548 Yeare....* Edinburgh: 105 p.

Son-in-law of John Knox. Comets and eclipses signs of impending End. Creation 3947 B.C. (agreeing with Scaliger). 6,000 Year theory — Prophecy of Elias. Six ages: Adam to Noah, to Abraham, to Solomon's Temple, to Christ, to 1056 A.D. (when Antichrist achieves supremacy), to End (very soon). 1600 as critical date.

127. *Books of Chilam Balam* ("Jaguar Prophet") 1600s. "Quasi-historical and prophetic" texts from Yucatan, Mexico. Written in Colonial period, like Popol Vuh (sacred book of highland Quiché Maya). "The Maya wise men all across the Yucatán predict that the world will end in the year 2000 y pico — 'and a little'... The Great Cycle of the Maya calendar which began in darkness on 13 August 3114 B.C. will come to an end after almost five millennia on 23 December A.D. 2012...." (Michael Coe, 1992). Book of Chilam Balam of Tizimín prophesies "great flooding of the Earth."

128. Willet, Andrew. *Synopsis Papismi, that is, A Generall View of Papistrie: Wherein the Whole Mysterie of Iniquitie, and Summe of Antichristian Doctrine is Set Downe, which is Maintained This Day by the Synagogue of Rome, Against the Church of Christ.* 1600. London. [20], 1114, [28] p. Editions through the 17th century. "Together with an antithesis of the true Christian faith, and an antidotum or counter-poyson out of Scripture, against the whore of Babylons filthie cuppe of abominations: confuted by Scriptures, Fathers, councels, imperiall constitutions, pontificall decrees, their owne writers, and our martyrs." Argues against Catholic attempts at futurist

interpretation (in order to avoid Antichrist label). Willet affirms that Pope is indeed Antichrist and Mystery of Iniquity. A.D. 666 Pope makes Latin service compulsory. Paul V (Pope til 1621) = 666. Willet refutes Catholic claim that Antichrist will be a Jew. Gospel already preached to whole world (contra Catholic denials). Denies that greatest persecutions of believers will be in future, under Antichrist; says they are "overpast," and have since subsided. Condemns Papist "boldness" in declaring that Antichrist will rule for 3½ years in future, and in precisely dating Second Coming for end of 1,290 plus 45 "days." Instead argues these already fulfilled (preterist interpretation). Exact date of End can't be determined.

129. Abbott, Robert. *Antichrist Demonstratio.* 1603.

Refutation of Cardinal Bellarmine (who refuted Protestant claim that Pope was Antichrist)

130. Downame, George. *A Treatise Concerning Antichrist ... Proving that the Pope is Antichrist ...* 1603.

Refutation of Bellarmine's denial that the Pope was Antichrist.

131. Dent, Arthur. *The Ruine of Rome, or, An Exposition Upon the Whole Revelation.* 1633. London. 406 p.

"Wherein is plainely shewed and proved, that the Popish religion, together with all the power and authority of Rome shall ebbe and decay more and more throughout all the churches of Europe, and come to an utter ouerthrow even in this life, before the end of the world: written especially for the comfort of Protestants, and the daunting of papists, seminary priests, Jesuites, and all that cursed rabble."

132. Brightman, Thomas. 1615 [1609, 1611]. *A Revelation of the Revelation.* Amsterdam. 921 p. 1609 edition (Heidelberg) titled *Apocalypsis Apocalypseos.*

Many editions Puritan. Seven Churches of Revelations = seven church ages. Ephesus = up to Constantine. Smyrna = to Gratian (382). Pergamon = to 1300. Thyatira = to 1520. Sardis = German Reformation. Philadelphia = Genevan Reformation. Laodicea = Church of England.

Complex interpretation of prophecies: double fulfillments, repetitions: e.g. 5th Trumpet is both Mohammed and the Pope; locusts both Saracens and papal agents (monks and friars). Thousand Year binding of Satan = A.D. 300 to 1300 (Church age); Satan now loose, working with Pope and Turks. Fall of Papacy and defeat of the Turks by 1650, conversion of Jews and Armageddon by 1695. Gave nationalist interpretation to Foxe; later interpreters saw England as Elect nation. Three Angels of Rev. 14 = Wycliff, Hus, Luther. *Revelation of the Revelation* was response to Jesuit refutations (especially Bellarmine's) of Protestant interpretations of Pope as Antichrist. Brightman saw England as elect nation and church. Seven Seals: up to Constantine. Trumpets started in 4th cent. Antichrist in control of church by A.D. 607. Two Beasts = spiritual and temporal power of Papacy. 7th trumpet = 1558. Seven Vials start 1563 with Queen Elizabeth; Vials 5-7 still in future. Armageddon = defeat and annihilation of the Turks in the East by the Jews, and defeat of the Catholics in the West by Protestants. Then the New Jerusalem descends; literal Millennial reign.

133. Broughton, Hugh. 1610. *A Revelation of the Holy Apocalypse.* Amsterdam. 339, [9] p.

3926 B.C. Creation + 6,000 = A.D. 2072 (Second Coming). Broughton's chronology was not popular because it put the End too far in the future for popular taste. Also wrote 1599 *Commentary on Daniel.* Third Beast is Alexander's empire; 4th its divided successor states (Seleucid).

134. _____. 1590. *A Concent of Scripture.* London. [76 p] [5] leaves plates, illus.

Tried to reconcile Hebrew and Christian interpretations. Assumed that chronology, with actual dates, was obtainable from the Bible. Uses prophecies of Elias, Daniel, John. Concerned with conversion of Jews. Daniel's 4th Beast = Antiochus (not Rome or Papacy). 6,000 years til Babylon/Pope fully overthrown.

135. Roeslin, Helisaeus. *Ein Tabella des Welt Spiegels: Darinnen geistliche goetlliche und politische weltliche Sachen in einer*

Harmonia und Vergelichung gegen einander gestellt werden, nahe den sieben Revolutionen der Planeten und zehen altern von Anfang der Welt bis zu Ende.... 1612. Frankfurt am Main. [6], 30 p.

Alsatian astrologer, in 1578 predicted End in 76 years, by study of 1572 nova.

136. Alexander, William. *Doomes-Day, or the Great Day of the Lords Judgement.* 1614 [s.l.]: Unpaged.

Alexander: Earl of Stirling. Also 1720 London edition titled *Doom's Day, or, The Last Judgment: A Poem.*

137. Andreä, Johann Valentin. 1620. *Christianopolis.*

Utopia based on description of the New Jerusalem and prophecies of Revelation. Valentin: Lutheran pastor. Also wrote the Rosicrucian manifesto *The Chemical Wedding of Christian Rosenkreuz* (1616).

138. Alsted, Johann Heinrich [John Henry]. *Treatise on the Thousand Years.* 1618.

139. _____. *Theologia Prophetica Exhibens....* 1622 Hanover: C. Eifridi. 1019 p.

140. _____. *The Worlds Proceeding Woes and Succeeding Joyes, 1. In Cruell Warres and Vehement Plagues, 2. In Happy Peace and Unity Amongst All Living Creatures, or, The Triple Presage of Henry Alsted ... Depending As Well on the Oracles of Heaven as On the Opinions of the Greatest Astrologers with an Addition of the Fiery Conjunction of Saturn and Jupeter, This Instant February, Denouncing Many Calamities to the World, Or Certaine Regions Thereof: In Which Discourse is Discovered the Opinions of Many Learned Men Concerning Christs Personall Reign Upon Earth and Confirmed by the Most Comfortable Prophecie of Tycho Brahe, Touching the Most Blessed Age Even Now at Hand.* 1642 London. 16 p.

Reformed theologian, devised more scholarly form of (pre-)millennialism as against official a-mill tradition. Inspired Puritan belief in establishment of literal earthly millennial kingdom in England.

141. _____. 1643. *The Beloved City, or, the Saints Reign on Earth a Thousand Years ...* London. viii, 84 p.

Binding of Satan in future, when

saints rule for thousand years. Millennium = 1694 (but disavows "chiliasm"— notion of a perfect age with no evil). Transl. of *Diatribe De Milleannis Apocalypticis no illis Chiliastarum & Phantastarum sed BB. Danielis & Johannis* (1627, Frankfort).

142. Alcazar, Luis de. *Vestigatio Arcani Sensus in Apocalypsi* (Investigation of the Hidden Sense of the Apocalypse). 1618 [1614] xxi, 778, [72], 74 p. illus. map indexes. Orig. pub. Antwerp?

Alcazar has been called the first systematic preterist. Developed preterist interpretation as means of countering Protestant assumptions that Pope was Antichrist. Rev. 1-11: up to A.D. 70 destruction of Jerusalem; Rev. 12-19: the triumph of the Church over pagan Rome.

143. Raleigh, Walter. *History of the World.* 1614. London.

The English soldier-explorer and courtier. Creation 4031 B.C. Literal interpretation of Daniel and Revelation. False Prophet = Mohammed. Insisted on relating all history to First Causes; non-biblical sources not as trustworthy as Bible. Magog = both Turks and Spaniards.

144. Lapide, Cornelius A. 1861 [1620?]. *Commentaria in Scripturam Sacram.* Vol 21: *Apocalypsis Sancti Joannis.* Paris: Vives.

Duration of the world is six millennia, corresponding to the Six Days of Creation. Creation=3950 B.C.; thus A.D. 1620=5,570th year of the world, or 430 years til the End.

145. Lichtenberger, Johann, Johann Carion, Joseph Grumpeck, "der Sibyllen," and others. *Propheceyen und Weissagungen jetzt gegenwertig und künfftige sachen, Geschicht und Zufäll, biss zum Ende der Welt ankündend.* 1620 s.l.

146. Meyfart, Johannes Matthaeus. *Tuba novissima, das ist, Von den vier letzen Dingen des Menschen.* 1626. Tubingen: M. Niemeyer. 119, 108 p.

Much here also included in Meyfart's 1642 book on the Prophet Jeremiah (Nuremburg).

147. Mede, Joseph. *The Key of the Revelation* (*Clavis Apocalyptica*). 1627, Cambridge). 2nd ed.: "whereunto is added a conjecture concerning Gog and Magog." London.

Very influential. Similar to Alsted, and largely based on Bale's work. "Synchronist" interpretation: all leading events of Revelation are contemporareous (not successive). Advanced Year-Day theory: 3½ Times = 42 Months = 1,260 Days (years). Ignored allegorical views, interpreting Revelation as describing literal Kingdom of God. In contrast to apocalyptic millennialism, Mede largely invented "progressive millennialist" view of unfolding of Millennium in future according to prophetic timetable. Influenced Milton, Newton, Ussher; and claimed as predecessor by both post-mills and dispensational pre-mills. Antichrist appeared A.D. 456; End in 1660. The Ten Nations (Ten-Horn Beast) = Britons, Saxons, Franks, Burgundians, Visigoths, Sueres and Alans, Vandals, Alemanes, Ostrogoths, and Greeks.

148. _____. *The Apostasy of the Latter Times.* 1641. London: Samuel Man. [16], 152 p. "In Which (According to Divine Prediction) the World Should Wonder After the Beast, the Mystery of Iniquity Should so Farre Prevaile Over the Mystery of Godlinesse, Whorish Babylon Over the Virgin-Church of Christ, as that the Visible Glory of the True Church Should be Much Clouded, the True Unstained Christian Faith Corrupted, the Purity of True Worship Polluted...."

149. _____. *A Paraphrase and Exposition of the Prophesie of Saint Peter, Concerning the Day of Christs Second Coming* ... 1642. London. 25 p.

"As also how the conflagration, or destruction of the world by fire, (whereof Saint Peter speaks) and especially of the heavens, is to be understood." Bible passage that "this generation should not perish till all these things were fulfilled" refers to "nation of the Jews." 1,260 Years = A.D. 395 to 1655 (age of apostasy). Beast = Roman Church, to fall in 1655. Seals 1-6: Rome from Christ to Constantine. Trumpets start with barbarian invasions of Rome. 7th trumpet during Millennial reign, which is future. 1,260 Years of Antichrist's great apostasy begins with 1st trumpet, thus less than 25 years til Millennium and End. 10 Horns = successor kingdoms to Rome.

150. Leighton, Alexander. 1628. *Speculum Belli Sacri: or the Looking-Glasse of the Holy War.* Amsterdam.

Very militant; calls for holy war against Spain and Catholics. End is near, but doesn't set dates. British must lead apocalyptic mission, purge popish elements.

151. Burton, Henry. 1628. *The Seven Vials or a Briefe and Plaine Exposition Upon the 15: and 16: Chapters of the Revelation.* London. [12], 144 p.

152. _____. 1641. *The Sounding of the Two Last Trumpets* ... London. [6], 93 p.

Armageddon to be fought mainly in England; English Civil War is start of Armageddon. Condemned Arminianism in English church, Jesuits. Thirty Years War as 6th Vial.

153. Grotius, Hugo. *Von der Wahrheit der Christlichen Religion.* 1631. [Breslau]: D. Muller. [18], 159, [1] p.

154. _____. *Commentatio ad Loca Quaedam N. Testamenti Quae de Antichristo Agunt, aut Agere Putantur Expendenda Eruditis.* 1641. Amsterdam: Joh. & Cornelium Blaeu. 93 p.

Preterist; influenced by Alcazar. Millennium began A.D. 311 (Constantine's Edict); ends with Ottoman Islamic expansion (= Gog and Magog) of 14th century into Europe. 666 = Trajan. Millennium = A.D. 311 (Constantine) to 1311 (Turkish Empire).

155. Sheldon, Richard. 1635 [1634]. *Man's Last End: The Glorious Vision and Fruition of God.* London. [6], 109 p.

156. *A Briefe Explanation of the XX Chapter of the Revelation of Saint John.* 1641. London.

"Wherein is contained the binding of the Dragon for a thousand yeares: the thrones, and who were to sit upon them, while the Dragon lay bound, and the Judgment that was given unto them: the Saints, (whose bodies they that sate on the thrones should kill, because they would not worship the Beast, nor his image, nor receive his marke) which is called the First Resurrection: the losing of the Dragon after the thousand yeares of his binding: the coming downe of Gog and Magog, and their destruction; the Great Day of the Lords

Coming in glory: the general Resurrection of the bodies of all, good and bad, and the generall Judgement: written for the edification, and confirmation of the faithfull, in their comportable expectation of the Day of the Lord, now neare approaching."

157. Burroughs, Jeremiah, and Thomas Goodwin. 1641. *A Glimpse of Sions Glory.* London.

Based on Revelation 19:6: Prophecies unfolding in England, as Long Parliament to result in collapse of Babylon, rise of Zion. Earthly reign (not in heaven) since afterwards enemies arise (Gog and Magog). Co-author Goodwin? Radical Puritan view. Considered themselves the Two Witnesses of Revelation. Antichrist's activity to climax in 1666. Papacy and Turks collapse by 1700.

158. Archer, Henry. 1642. *The Personall Reign of Christ Upon Earth.* London: Benjamin Allen. 59 p.

Proves that "Christ, together with the saints, shall visibly possesse a monarchicall state and kingdom in this world": the "Fifth Monarchy" (Daniel's godly kingdom following the four earthly empires) — an imperial political reign of the Elect. Christ organizes government for 40 days, then returns to heaven, leaves Elect to rule earth. Rome = 4th empire; 5th is coming. A.D. 406 (eclipse of Rome) + 1,260 = 1666. 365 A.D. (Julian the Apostate) + 1,290 + 45 = 1700 (Second Coming).

159. Shipton, Mother [Ursula]. *The Prophesie of Mother Shipton in the Raigne of King Henry the Eighth: Fortelling the Death of Cardinal Wolsey, the Lord Percy and Others, as Also What Should Happen in Insuing Times; Strange and Wonderful Prophesies.* 1641. London. 6 p.

Popular prophecies issued in many publications and editions since the 1640s, including many attributed to Shipton but written much later. Not clear whether Shipton actually existed. Widely regarded as having predicted 1666 London fire.

160. _____. *Six Strange Prophecies Predicting Wonderfull Events, to Betide These Yeares of Danger, in This Climate Whereof Some have Already Come to Passe Well Worthy of Note* ... [also includes]

"Sybilla's prophecies, Merlins prophecies, Otwel Bins prophecies, Mr. Brightmans prophecies." [London]

Also twentieth-century versions: e.g. *Mother Shipton's Prophecy* (1960s?; Shoals, IN: Old Paths Tract Society).

161. Sedgwick, William "Doomsday". 1642. *Zions Deliverance and Her Friends Duty.*

Proclaimed the Millennium. Devil tries to prevent Long Parliament from reforming church. Antichrist about to be defeated. Christ about to return to usher in Millennium. An "exceptionally powerful apocalyptic interpretation of the [English] Civil War."

162. Cotton, John. *The End of the World.* 1982 [1642] New York: AMS. 292 p. vol 14: Library Amer Puritan writings. Two works: *The Churches Resurrection* [1642; London; 30 p]; *An Exposition upon the Thirteenth Chapter of the Revelation* [1655, London; iv, 268 p].

Churches Resurrection: Resurrection of Martyrs and Saints after Antichrist and destruction of Rome (Armageddon): change from *spiritual* death to spiritual life — a *reformation* of churches. Episcopacy almost as bad as the Papacy. *Expos. of the 13th Chap. Rev.*: Beast from the Sea, the Antichrist, is not Pagan Rome, but Roman Catholic Church. Seven Heads = types of Roman government prior to Papacy. Fatal wounding which heals = Rome overrun by barbarians. Healing was "by degrees," starting with retaking by Belisarius under Justinian. Ten Kingdoms include England, France, Spain, Navarre, Sweden, Denmark. Predicts giant blow to Beast in 1655 (A.D. 395 + 1,260). Beast warring with the saints = persecution of Waldenses, Albigensians. Second Beast = Pope personally. Mark of Beast = swearing of loyalty to Papacy. Christ uses number 12; Popish laws and decrees use number six, multiplied (tithing) = 666.

163. *A Brief Discovery of the Estate of the Church of Christ in the Apostles Times and of Her Great Persecution by the Dragon* ... 1644. [London.] [6]. 97 p.

"A brief explanation of the eleventh, twelfth and thirteenth chapters of Revellation." "What the two Witnesses are and how they are said to finish their testimony and to prophesie: the rising of Antichrist and his killing the two witnesses...: of the second beast ... and what Service he hath done ... against Christ and his church ... and what estate the church of Christ is to be in from the end of the beast to the end of the world.

164. Huit, Ephraim. *The Whole Prophecie of Daniel Explained.* 1644.

Huit: Connecticut pastor; first complete commentary by American. 3 times = 1,300 + 350. Antichrist = Pope and Turk, from ca. A.D. 600. King of North = Turkey. A.D. 360 + 1,290 = 1650; + 1,335 = 1695.

165. Petrie, Alexander. *Chiliasto-Mastix.* 1644 Rotterdam. [8], 70 p.

"The prophecies in the Old and New Testament concerning the Kingdom of our Saviour Juesus Christ: vindicated from the misinterpretations of the millenaries and specially of Mr. Maton...."

166. Lady Eleanor. *A Prophesie of the Last Day to Be Revealed in the Last Times and Then the Cutting Off the Church, and of the Redemption Out of Hell: The Word of God.* 1645 London: s.n. 8 p.

Eleanor excommunicated 1649.

167. Parker, Thomas. *The Visions and Prophecies of Daniel Expounded:* 1646. London: Edmund Paxton 160 p.

"Wherein the mistakes of former interpreters are modestly discovered, and the true meaning of the text made plain ..., here is propounded a new way for the finding out of the determinate time signified by Daniel in his Seventy Weeks, when it did begin, and when we are to expect the end thereof, in respect of the great stirs and tumults of this present age wherein we live." Parker: Massachusetts minister. Antichrist, Millennium = ca. 1650. Or, ca. 1860. 70 Weeks: 7 years (1160 to 1209) + 62 years (to 1642) + year (ends 1649). Or, 1370 (Wycliffe) + 490 (70 Weeks) = 1860.

168. Royle, Thomas. *A Glimpse of Some Truths to be Made Known in these Last Times.* 1648. London. 12 p.

Includes "The Day of Judgment, What it is, and When it is."

169. Coppe, Abiezer. *A Fiery Flying Roule: A Word from the Lord to All the*

Great Ones of the Earth, Whom This May Concerne: Being the Last Warning Piece at the Dreadful Day of Judgement. 1649. [12,] 15 [1,] 22 p.

Coppe: prominent Ranter (antinomian sect with reputation for cursing and shouting).

170. Owen, John. *Predicted Events Coming Upon the Nations of the Earth: A Sermon Preached Above Two Hundred Years Since, before Oliver Cromwell and the Houses of Parliament, on a Special and National Fast Day.* 1854. 2nd ed. London: Houlston & Stoneman, G., J. & R. Banks. 40 p.

Original sermon preached to Cromwell's Parliament (ca. 1650) on Hebrews XII:27 under title "The Shaking and Translating of Heaven and Earth."

171. Hartlib, Samuel. *Clavis Apocalyptica, or, A Prophetical Key by which the Great Mysteries in the Revelation of St. John and the Prophet Daniel are Opened: It beeing Made Apparent that the Prophetical Numbers Come to an End with the Year of Our Lord, 1655.* 1651 London. 85, 168 p.

Based on Mede's *Clavis Apocalyptica.*

172. Weldon, Robert. *Of Antichrist, and the End of the World.* 1651. London. 147 p.

The Day of the Lord is "at hand."

173. Maton, Robert. *A Treatise of the Fifth Monarchy, or, Christs Personall Reigne on Earth One Thousand Yeares with His Saints ...* 1655 [1652]. London. 329 p.

174. Aspinwall, William. *A Brief Description of the Fifth Monarchy or Kingdome that Shortly Is to Come into the World.* 1653. [2], 16 p.

Describes the coming new order. Conclusion includes "a prognostick of the time when the Fifth Kingdome shall begin." To start by 1673.

175. Canne, John. *A Voice from the Temple to the Higher Powers: Wherein is Shewed, that It is the Work and Duty of Saints, to Search the Prophecies and Visions of Holy Scripture, Which Concern the Later Times: and that Jesus Christ Will Reveal the Understanding of Them, Near the End of Their Accomplishment ...* 1653. London. 39 p.

176. _____. *Truth with Time, or,*

Certain Reasons Proving that None of the Seven Last Plagues or Vials are Yet Poured Out. 1656. London: J.C. [15], 101 p.

177. _____. *The Time of the End.* 1657. London: L. Chapman. [32], 275 p.

"Shewing, first, until the three years and an half are come ... the prophecies of the Scripture will not be understood, concerning the duration of the period of the Fourth Monarchy and the Kingdom of the Beast. Then secondly, when that time shall come, before the expiration the knowledge of the end will be revealed, by the rise of a little horn, the last apostacy, and Beast slaying the witnesses...."

178. Tillinghast, John. *Generation-Work.* 1653 London.

Subtitled in part "Being an Exposition of the Seven Vials Rev. 16, and Other Apocalyptical Mysteries." 1,290 Days of Daniel = A.D. 366 to 1656, when Jews convert and return to Palestine.

179. _____. *Knowledge of the Times; or, the Resolution of the Question, How Long It Shall Be Unto the End of Wonders.* 1654. London. 346 p.

Jews return, become Kings of the South; opposed by Kings of the North — Turks and Papal forces combined. 1,260 and 1,290 years end in 1656 (fall of Antichrist). 1,335 and 2,300 years end 1701 (Second Coming and Millennium).

180. Burden, William. *Christs Personal Reign on Earth One Thousand Yeers ...* 1654 London. [4], 10 p.

181. Homes, Nathanael. *The Resurrection Revealed; or, The Dawning of the Day-Star, About to Rise, and Radiate a Visible Incomparable Glory, Far Beyond Any, Since the Creation, Upon the Universal Church on Earth, for a Thousand Yeers Yet to Come, Before the Ultimate Day, of the General Judgement ...* 1654 London.

182. Manasseh ben Israel. *The Glorious Stone; or, On the Statue of Nebuchadnezzar.* 1654. Two legs of Daniel's statue: Papal Romanism and Mohammedanism. Stone = coming of the Messiah. Believed American Indians were Ten Lost Tribes of Israel. Rembrandt provided etchings.

183. Rogers, John. *Sagrir, or, Doomes-Day Drawing Nigh, with Thunder and Lightening to Lawyers in an Alarum for*

the *New Laws, and the Peoples Liberties
from the Norman and Babylonian Yokes.*
1654. London. [24], 150 p.

"Making discoverie of the present
ungodly laws and lawyers of the Fourth
Monarchy, and of the approach of the
Fifth, with those godly laws, officers and
ordinances that belong to the legislative
power of the Lord Iesus : shewing the glorious work incumbent to civil-discipline,
(once more) set before the Parliament,
Lord Generall, army and people of England, in their distinct capasities, upon the
account of Christ and his Monarchy."

184. Moore, Thomas. *An Antidote
Against the Spreading Infections of the Spirit
of Antichrist, Abounding in These Last Days
Under Many Vizors: Being a Discovery of a
Lying and Antichristian Spirit in Some of
those Called Quakers* ... 1655. London:
Livewell Chapman [17], 199, [8] p.

Rebuttal of James Naylor's *Satan's
Designs Discovered.*

185. Muggleton, Lodowick. *A
Stream from the Tree of Life Wrote by the
Two Last Witnesses of Jesus Christ Wherein
Truth Rides Triumphant* ... 1758 [1650s?]
88 p.

Founder of Muggletonians (antinomian sect); one of Two Witnesses of the
Last Days (with John Reeve).

186. Reeve, John. *A Divine Look-
ing-Glass, or, The Third and Last Testament of Our Lord Jesus Christ, Whose Personal Residence is Seated on His Throne of
Eternal Glory in Another World.* 1656. 5th
ed. London. 1846: xv, [1], 184 p.

Reeve: "Prophet of God." Imminent
doom of mankind and Millennial rule of
the Saints. He and his cousin Lodowick
Muggleton taught that they were the Two
Witnesses of the Last Days.

187. Durham, James. *A Commen-
tarie Upon the Book of Revelation.* 1658.
Edinburgh. [16], 787, [17] p.

"Wherein the text is explained, the
series of the several prophecies contained
in that book, deduced according to their
order and dependance upon each other;
the periods and succession of times, at, or
about, which, these prophecies, that are
already fulfilled, began to be, and were
more fully accomplished, fixed and ap-

plied according to history; and those that
are yet to be fulfilled...."

188. Smith, Humphrey. *An Alarm
Sounding Forth unto All the Inhabitants of
the Earth: As a Warning Before the Vials of
Everlasting Wrath be Poured Forth Upon
Them.* 1658. London. 8 p.

189. *A True Narration of the Two
Wonderful Prophets at Rome Presaging the
End of the World to Be in the Year 1670.*
1660 London. 8 p.

190. Biddle, Ester. *The Trumpet of
the Lord Sounded Forth Unto These Three
Nations as a Warning from the Spirit of
Truth, Especially Unto Thee, Oh England*
... 1662. London. 24 p.

Quaker. "Likewise, unto thee, thou
great and famous city of London, doth the
Lord God of vengeance found one warning more into thine ear ... with a word of
wholsome counsel and advice unto thy
kings, rulers, judges, bishops, and priests
... together with a few words unto the
royal seed." Wickedness of London sur-
passes even that of Sodom and Gomorrah.
God to rain fiery judgment down soon.

191. Serrurier, Petrus. *An Awakening Warning to the Wofull World, by a Voyce
in Three Nations....In Which It Is Clearly
Evinced ... that the Glorious Coming of
Jesus Christ Is at Hand* ... 1662 Amsterdam. 42 p.

192. Wigglesworth, Michael. *The
Day of Doom: or, A Poetical Description of
the Great and Last Judgment.* 1662.

Very widely read in New England.
Sinners dragged down to pit of woe, saints
ascend to glory. 1867 ed: NY: America
News, from 6th [1715] ed. 119 p.

193. Coale, Josiah. *A Salutation to
the Suffering-Seed of God: Wherein the
Things are Declared and Signified Before-
Hand that Must Shortly Come to Pass.* 1663
London. 9 p.

194. Eccles, Solomon. *Signes are
from the Lord to a People or Nation to Forewarn Them of Some Eminent Judgment
Near at Hand.* 1663. London: s.n. Broadside.

Prophetic omens. Eccles: London
Quaker, declared Black Death prelude to
the End. During the Plague, often walked
semi-naked with pan of burning brim-

stone on his head announcing coming End. Often disrupted church and cathedral services to denounce the ministers, priests, and con-gregation. Before (and possibly after) his prophetic career he was a successful composer and music teacher.

195. Bayly, William. *The Great & Dreadful Day of the Lord God Almighty (Which is Hastening as a Flood Upon the Whole World of the Ungodly Once More Proclaimed): That All People May Again Be Warned to Repent with Speed and to Be Left Without Excuse.* [1664?] [London?] : s.n. [8] p.

196. E[llington], F[rancis]. *Christian Information Concerning These Last Times.* 1664. London. 16 p.

Quaker. Daniel's prophecy coming to pass, "how very near Antichrist, or the great Whore of Babylon, is to Her End...."

197. Sherwin, William. *Eiphnikon, or, A Peacable Consideration of Christ's Peaceful Kingdom on Earth to Come: Rev. 20.4, Rev. 5.10.* 1665. [London.] [16], 110 p.

"Peaceable Kingdom" on earth: the Millennium. Historicist. First resurrection of the just "to begin not long after the glorious appearance of Christ, and his said Kingdom." False, apostate church established A.D. 406: 406 + 1,260 = 1666. 6,000 Years; Solomon's Temple built 3,000 years after Creation. The "End" is not absolute annihilation, but rather wiping clean and re-constituting, as with the Flood. Appeals to Lord's Prayer regarding earthly millennial reign of Christ ("Thy Kingdom come on earth as it is in heaven"). Moses, Daniel, and John (Revelation author) are "God's three great chronologers." Three Babylons: Tower of Babel (described by Moses), Kingdom of Babylon (by Daniel), and Mystical Babylon (Revelation).

198. _____. *Prodromos: The Fore-Runner of Christ's Peaceable Kingdom Upon Earth.* 1665. London. 48 p.

Historicist. Fourth and Fifth Kingdoms of Daniel and Revelation: Rome and Christ's. A.D. 366 (Emperor Julian the Apostate) + 1,290 = 1656. Gog and Magog: Turks and the Pope. But also a second Gog-Magog at end of Millennium.

Rapture. Armageddon = Pope and Turks both destroyed simultaneously. Jews: Kings of the East.

199. _____. *Eiro-Metropolis, or, The Holy, the Great, the Beloved New Jerusalem: Shortly to Come Down from God Out of Heaven: Being the Work of God's Own Hands ...* [1670?]. London. [6], 26 p.

The New Jerusalem is cubical.

200. _____. *A Plain and Evident Discovery of the Two Personal Comings of Christ.* [1670?]. [London.] 51 p.

"One at the beginning of His Thousand Years Reign, Rev. 20,4, with his holy and blessed raised Saints in the Now [sic] Jerusalem, come down from God out of Heaven, Rev. 21, the other after the Little Space when the Thousand Years are ended...."

201. _____. *Oikoumeme Mellousa: The World to Come, Heb. 2,5: or, The Doctrine of the Kingdom of God and His Christ to Come on Earth ...* 1671. London. [2], 38 p.

202. _____. *A Scheme of the Whole Book of the Revelation of Jesus Christ: Of Very Great Use: With the Following Summarie of Daniels Visions &c.* 1671. [London.] 8 p.

"For the right understanding of the parallel of that book and the Revelation...." 2,300 (and 1,335) years end ca. 1700 (Papal armies gathered for final battle).

203. _____. *Exanastasis, or, The Saints Rising Up Out of the Heap or Mass of Dead Bodies Contained in the Globe of the Earth and Sea ... Rev. 20.5.* 1674. London. [2], 83.

The first bodily resurrection. Then, at end of the Millennium, rest of dead resurrected. Even though the world's 6,000 years won't be over until A.D. 2000, the Millennium will probably begin before then. The "little space" of Satan's loosing after the Millennium "may be allowed to make up some part of the sixth [millennium] before it." "Creature-Redemption-Infidels" (those who deny restitution of all things and raising of the dead) are as obviously and dangerously wrong as "Creation Atheists" (advocates of chance origin and development). These truths will inspire believers to steadfastly oppose Babylon and hasten its final defeat.

204. _____. *Chronoi Apykatastaseoz Panton, or, The Times of Restitution of All Things: With Their Neer Approach Upon the Ruine of the Beast.* 1675. London. [2], 81 p.

"Manifest by two tracts on Rev. 20.5 & Rev. 21.5 containing the main scope of all Revelation prophecie ... which said two last tracts may fitly be entituled An Alarm to This Present World...." Still over 200 years to go until completion of world's 6,000 years. But Millennium may be very soon, because post-Mill years of Satan's loosing (unspecified duration) must be subtracted from the 6,000 to remain at 7,000 at final End. Or, 6,000 may be shortened by God for the sake of the Elect. Also, must subtract time spent getting Adam and Eve evicted from Eden.

205. _____. *The True News of the Good New World Shortly to Come (Heb. 2. 5.) for All Such as Then Shall Be Found Real Saints: With the Sudden End of All the Enjoyments of this Present World....* 1675. [London?]: s.n. [2], 12 p., plates; chart.

206. D. R. [Daniel Roe]. *God's Judgments Still Threatened Against Thee, O England for the Great Abominations that Have Been, and Are Committed in Thee.* 1666. [London] 19 p.

"London's dissolution a figure of the downfall of Babylon : with a call unto all people to come out of Babylon which stands in confusion, and to repent and seek the Lord while he many be found: also a manifestation of love of the seed of God, and a warning to the inhabitants of the earth of the great and notable, terrible and dreadfull day of the Lord near at hand." London = Babylon. London unrepentant even after great Plague. Written while imprisoned.

207. Sabbetai Tzevi (Shabbetai Tsevi). Jewish cabalist; in 1665 declared he was the Messiah, and that 1666 was the apocalyptic year and start of Messianic Kingdom. When detained by Ottoman sultan, he converted to Islam.

208. Comenius, Johann Amos. 1667. *The Way of Light.*

Czech author. Inspired by Thirty Years War to predict imminent Second Coming. Messianic Age preceded by return of the Jews

209. "S.H. of Boston." 1667. *A Declaration of a Future Glorious Estate of a Church to be Here Upon Earth at Christ's Personal Appearance for the Restitution of All Things, a Thousand Years Before the Ultimate Day of the General Judgment ...* London : [s.n.] 36 p.

210. Mather, Increase. *The Mystery of Israel's Salvation.* 1669. London. 181 p. Boston ed 1686. [2], 6, 212, [2] p. 1983 reprint ed. New York: AMS Press.

"A Discourse concerning the general conversion of the Israelitish Nation, wherein is shewed (1) That the Twelve Tribes shall be saved, (2) When this is to be expected, (3) Why this must be, (4) What kind of salvation the Tribes shall partake of, a glorious, wonderful, spiritual, temporal salvation...." Jews return, convert; but great wars and commotions before conversion.

211. _____. *Heavens Alarm to the World, or A Sermon Wherein is Shewed, that Fearful Sights and Signs in Heaven are the Presages of Great Calamities at Hand.* 1681. Boston: printed by John Foster. [6], 17 p.

"Wherein the nature of blazing stars [comets] is enquired into...." The End: "You must not only look for, not only believe that such a day will come, but you must hasten to it — that is, by earnest desire and longing wishes." Second Coming and Millennium are near. King of North = Ottoman Empire. A.D. 1050 + 666 = 1716. Significance of comet of 1680.

212. Vincent, Thomas. *Christ's Certain and Sudden Appearance to Judgment.* 1817 [1808]. New Brunswick [NJ]: 388 p.

Vincent: d. 1678.

213. Franklin, Richard. *A Discourse on the Antichrist, and the Apocalypse: Shewing that the Number of the Beast Ought Not to be Translated 666 but 42 Only: That Christians have Reigned a 1000 Years, and that Mohamet is the Grand Antichrist.* 1675. London: author. 32 p.

214. Jones, Andrew. *Dooms-Day, or, The Great Day of the Lord Drawing Nigh, by Certain Signs and Tokens Thereof, Foretold by Our Lord Jesus Christ: Wherein*

is Declared that there Shall Be an End of the World.... 1678. 25th ed. London: W. Thackeray, etc.

Half-title: "Dooms-Day at Hand."

215. *An Alarm to Judgement, or, An Assay to Rouse Up All of All Sorts (Before it is Too Late) to Prepare to Meet the Bridegroom.* 1679 s.l.: s.n. 234 p.

216. Burnet, Thomas *The Sacred Theory of the Earth.* 1681. First published in Latin (*Telluris Theoria Sacra*) 1681- 9. bibl refs. 1965 ed.: Carbondale: Southern Illinois Univ. Press, 412 p, illus, maps.

Purifying conflagration burns entire Earth, then the Millennium or End, with Earth returned to its original created state of perfect smoothness. Burnet approvingly cites authorities who accept the 6,000 year scheme of Earth's duration.

217. *Two Remarkable Paradoxes: I. That the World was Created in an Instant, and Not in Six Days. II. That the World at the Last Day Shall Not Intirely be Consumed by Fire.* 1681. London: R. Baldwin. 1 p. l., 17 p.

218. Bernoulli, Jakob. *Conamen Novi Systematis Cometarum: Pro Motu Eorum Sub Calculum Revocando & Apparitionibus Praedicendis.* 1682. Amsterdam: Henr. Wetstenium. [8], 95 p., plates, illus.

Swiss mathematician (dicovered the "Bernoulli Numbers"); predicted disastrous return of comet of 1680 for 1719.

219. *A Calendar of Prophetick Time, Drawn by an Express Scripture-line, from the Creation to the New Jerusalem.* 1684.

Numbers of Daniel. Two Witnesses: Luther (1517) to 1697. Beast destroyed completely in 1727: A.D. 437 + 1,290 = 1727. End in 1772: 1727 + 45 "Days" (end of 1,335 days). A.D. 33 (Crucifixion) + 666 = A.D. 700 (almost): apostasy established. Turks: King of North and Second Woe.

220. Baier, Johann Wilhelm. 1686. *De Termino Vitae.* Jena. [40] p. (Andreas Cöler, respondent.)

221. Jurieu, Pierre. *The Accomplishment of the Scripture Prophecies, or, the Approaching Deliverance of the Church.* 1687 London: s.n. 2 vols. Translation of *L'Accomplissement des prophéties, ou la délivrance prochaine de l'église* (1686).

"Proving that the Papacy is the Antichristian Kingdom ... that the present persecution may end in three years and-half, after which the destruction of Antichrist shall begin, which shall be finisht in the beginning of the next age, and then the Kingdom of Christ shall come upon earth." Huguenot. Predicted downfall of Antichrist Roman Church for 1689. The 3½ Years the Two Witnesses lie dead might date from 1684 Revocation of the Edict of Nantes (renewing French persecution of Huguenots). France = the "tenth part" of the city which is destroyed — coming fall of France.

222. Cressener, Drue. *The Judgments of God Upon the Roman-Catholick Church from its First Rigid Laws for Universal Conformity to It Unto its Last End.* 1689. London. 315 p.

"With a prospect of these near approaching revolutions, viz. the revival of the Protestant profession in an eminent kingdom where it was totally suppressed, the last end of all Turkish hostilities, the general mortification of the power of the Roman Church in all parts of its dominions; in explication of the trumpets and vials of the Apocalypse upon principles generally acknowledged by Protestant interpreters." 1,260 years from Justinian to the 1800s, when Beast's rule ends.

223. Keach, Benjamin. *Antichrist Stormed, or, Mystery Babylon the Great Whore, and Great City, Proved to be the Present Chruch of Rome Wherein All Objections are Fully Answered: To Which is Added, the Time of the End....* 1689 London. 243 p., plates.

Includes confutation of P. Jurieu and review of Thomas Goodwin.

224. Beverley, Thomas. *The Prophetical History of the Reformation; or, The Reformation to Be Reform'd; in That Great Reformation; That Is To Be 1697.* 1689 London. 7, 84, [6], 10 p.

"The 1260 Years Allowed to the Beastian Kingdom, or to the Roman Apostasie (Which Because It Is to End 1697, Must Therefore have Begun 437")."

225. _____. *A Scheme of Prophecy Now to Be Fulfilled Beginning This Present Year 1691, and So To Be Carried on to the*

Succession of the Kingdom of Christ, 1697.
1691. London: s.n.

226. _____. *The Grand Apocalyptic
Question; When the Reign of Antichristian-
ism, or the Papacy Began? and Consequently,
When It Shall End? in the Assertion of the
Epoch, or Beginning at* A.D. *437, and the
Period of End, at 1697.* 1701. London: W.
Marshall. 46 p.

"Humbly debated with Mr. [Robert]
Fleming, in answer to his fixation of the
epoch at 606, and the period at 1800 or
after."

227. Bossuet, J. B. *L'Apocalypse avec
une Explication.* 1690.

Catholic. Two Witnesses are past
Christian martyrs, followed by persecution from Diocletian, who is 666. Locusts
= ancient heretics. End of Millennium =
expansion of Turks into Europe, and the
heretics of the Protestant Reformation.

228. Baxter, Richard. *The Glorious
Kingdom of Christ: Described and Clearly
Vindicated Against the Bold Asserters of a
Future Calling and Reign of the Jews, and
100 Years Before the Conflagration.* 1691.
London. 73 p.

Refutation of Thomas Beverley.

229. Lee, Samuel. *A Summons or
Warning to the Day of Judgment.* 1692.
Boston: B. Green.

Rhode Island minister. Millennium
starts 1811-12.

230. Ray, John. *Miscellaneous Dis-
courses Concerning the Dissolution and
Changes of the World.* 1692. London:
Smith. 259 p.

From Earth's "primitive chaos and
creation" through the Flood and the "universal conflagration and future state."

231. _____. *Three Physico-Theolog-
ical Discourses.* 1721. 4th ed. London: William and John Innys. xxxi, 456 p. plates.

"Concerning I. The primitive chaos,
and creation of the world. II. The general
Deluge, its causes and effects. III. The dissolution of the world and future conflagration."

232. *Millennianism: Or Christ's
Thousand Years Reign Upon Earth, Considered* 1693. London. [3], 76 p.

Refutation of millennialism as igno-
rant and fanciful wish. Even the earliest

disciples "hanker'd after, what they most
desired, a pompous temporal Kingdom,"
and chiliasts ever since vainly imagine a
sensual earthly millennial kingdom, and
often seek to impose or hasten it by violence. But Christ's Kingdom is in heaven,
and the Millennium refers to the Church.

233. van Helmont, Franciscus Mer-
curius. *Seder Olam, or The Order, Series or
Succession of All the Ages, Periods, and
Times of the Whole World, is Theologically,
Philosophically and Chronologically Expli-
cated and Stated.* 1694. London 236 p.
illus.

"Also the Hypothesis of the Pre-Ex-
istencey and Revolution of Human Souls;
Together with the Thousand Years Reign
of Christ on Earth."

234. Philo Chronographus. *Perspec-
ulatus, oder Die Beschauung der letzten Zeit:
so da ist, das Vale Mundi, oder der Welt
Kehrab.* 1690s? [Augsburg?: J. Ender-
lin?[4+], 26+ p. Tentative title from prefa-
tory matter.

235. Keith, George. 1694. *A
Chronological Account of the Several Ages of
the World from Adam to Christ and from
Thence Continued to the End of the World.*
[New York]: 32 p.

Keith: Quaker. "Showing, by scripture account: I. The time of the churches
going into the wilderness, her continuance
there, and time of return and full restoration; II. The intervals of time belonging to
the seven seals, seven trumpets, and seven
vials, called, the seven last plagues, and
the various dreadful effects that are like to
ensue at the pouring forth of each of the
vials, which is near at hand; III. Concerning the personal anti-Christ yet to come,
and the time and manner of his appearance, and continuance of his reign; IV.
The time of the prophecying, killing and
rising again of the two witnesses, Rev. 9;
V. The time of the appearance of the Virgin Company, of 144,000, Rev. 14; VI.
The time of the angels flying through the
midst of heaven, having the everlasting
gospel to preach; VII. And lastly, concerning the thousand years reign of the
saints with Christ, yet to come, and the
time of beginning thereof, by way of essay
and hypothesis."

236. Whiston, William. *A New Theory of the Earth, From its Original, to the Consummation of All Things.* 1696 London: Benjamin Tooke. [1978. Arno Press reprint ed.]

"Wherein the CREATION of the World in Six Days, the Universal DELUGE, and the General CONFLAGRATION, as laid down in the Holy Scriptures, are shewn to be perfectly agreeable to REASON and PHILOSOPHY." Whiston: mathematician; Newton's successor at Cambridge. Hypothesized Earth was originally a comet; that another comet caused the Flood; and that a future comet will precipitate Earth's final destruction by fire.

237. _____. *An Essay on the Revelation of St. John.* 1706. Cambridge.

A.D. 606 + 1,260 = 1866. 552 B.C. + 2,300 (of 360-day years) = 1716. Predicted 1716, then 1734, then 1766 as start of Millennium.

238. _____. *A Supplement to The Literal Accomplishment of Scripture Prophecies.* 1725. London. [4], 136 p.

239. Theobald, Francis. *Eclectical Chiliasm; or, a Discourse Concerning the State of Things from the Beginning of the Millennium to the End of the World.* 1700. London. 62 p.

240. Fleming, Robert. *Apocalyptical Key, a Discourse on the Rise and Fall of Anti-Christ.* 1849 [1701]. Cincinnati: John D. Thorpe. Many editions up to 1860, variously titled.

Pastor of Scottish church in Rotterdam. Also wrote *Rise and Fall of Antichrist* and *Rise and Fall of Rome Papal* (both 1701). French king overthrown (1793), Papacy weakened 1794, further wounded in 1848; then Ottoman Empire will fall, then the End (Millennium perhaps 2000). France exhausted by end of century. 5th Vial: weakening of Papacy 1794-1848, but not destroyed. 6th Vial: against Islam. 4th Vial 1717-1794. 5th Vial: to 1848. A.D. 606 + 1260 = 1848.

241. _____. *The Fulfilling of Scripture.* 1806 [1743]. Charlestown, MA: 394 p.

Earth to be destroyed as in Noah's day — Ark was precursor of Christ. Pope = Antichrist. Turkish empire as Satanic chastizer. Future fulfillments: Fall and ruin of "Babylon" (Papacy) — already underway; conversion and "incalling" of Jews; expansion of both Jewish and Gentile churches (already underway); fall of Turkish Empire (already in decline); Gog and Magog battle; Second Coming. Satan bound after Antichrist's reign.

242. Mather, Cotton. *Magnalia Christi Americana.* 1702. London: T. Parkhurst. In 7 books. 1st American ed 1820, Hartford: S. Andrus [from 1702 ed.]. 1967 ed 2 vols.; New York: Russell & Russell.

In 1691 suggested end of world for 1697. Saw New England as capital of Millennial Kingdom, and Indians as demonic Antichrist forces following the Millennium. All prophecies for the End fulfilled. Ca. 456 + 1,260 = ca. 1716 — fall of Papacy, Second Coming, and Millennium (the "Happy Estate"). Also wrote *Fall of Babylon* (Antichrist = Pope).

243. Whitby, Daniel. *A Paraphrase and Commentary on the New Testament: With a Treatise on the True Millennium, and the Examen Millii.* London: Thomas Tegg. 1842 [1703] 1238 p. bibl notes, indexes.

Whitby: Anglican. Post-millennialist: first formulation or popularization of hopeful, reformist interpretation of Bible prophecy. Kingdom of God will arrive with more of present effort: "progressive millennialism." First resurrection = revival of martyr's spirit by church, nation, people. Millennium is yet to come, preceded by triumph over papacy and heathenism, conversion of world. Satan will be bound (rendered inactive). Church to triumph completely, despite short rebellion at close of Millennium. Then final Judgment and eternal Kingdom. Includes "A Treatise on the Millennium: Shewing that It Is Not a Reign of Person Raised from the Dead, But of the Church Flourishing Gloriously for a Thousand Years Afer the Conversion of the Jews, and the Flowing In of All Nations to Them thus Converted to the Christian Faith."

244. Bull, Digby. *A Farther Warning of Popery and of the Second Dreadful Wo that are Now Certainly at Hand, and of the Third Dreadful Wo which Cometh*

Soon After Them ... 1710. 2d ed. London. 47 p.

245. Vitringa, Campegius. *Hypotyposis Historiae et Chronologiae Sacrae, a M.C., Usque ad Finem Sace I. AE. V. Accedit Typus Doctrinae Propheticae.* 1708. Franequerae: Halman.

246. _____. *Anakrisis: Apocalypsios Joannis Apostoli: Qua in Vera Interpretandae Ejus Hypotheses Diligenter Inquiritur* ... 1719 [1705] Amsterdam: Franeker?. [34], 918, [63] p.

A response to Mede, arguing for Whitbyan post-mill interpretation. Revelation is progressive (successive), not contemporaneous. Influenced German Pietists. Used historical, archeological, and other extra-biblical sources. Seven Churches = seven periods till End.

247. Wadsworth, Benjamin. *The Great and Last Day of Judgment.* 1709. Boston: Nicholas Buttolph. [10], 132 p.

"The Last Trumpet sounding, the graves opening, all the dead arising, to receive their last sentence from the Lord Jesus Christ, who will descend from heaven in matchless glory, to reward the godly, and punish the wicked to all eternity."

248. Allen, James. 1855 [orig. early 1700s?]. *Old Testament Prophecies, Relative to the Return and Restoration of the Twelve Tribes to the Land of Palestine: Together with the Setting Up of Messiah's Kingdom on Mount Zion, During a Period of 1000 Prophetic Years.* London: Wertheim and Macintosh. xvi, 420 p.

249. Hildrop, John. *A Treatise of the Three Evils of the Last Times.* 1826 [1711]. London: Hatchard. li, 211 p.

"I. The Sword, II. The Pestilence, III. The Famine; and of their natural and moral causes. As also of the ensuing coming of Antichrist...."

250. Flint, Henry. *The Doctrine of the Last Judgment.* 1714. B. Green, for Benj. Eliot.

Preface by Increase Mather. When wickedness reaches its maximum, then Judgment and Second Coming (any day now).

251. Sewall, Joseph. *The Certainty and Suddenness of Christ's Coming.* 1716.

Pre-mill view of Doomsday.

252. Daubuz, Charles. *A Perpetual Commentary on the Revelation of St. John.* 1730 [1720] London. 631 p.

"New modell'd, abridg'd, and render'd plain to the meanest capacity by Peter Lancaster." (1720 ed. much longer.) Daubuz: Huguenot exiled to England. Fifth Trumpet = Islam A.D. 612-762. Two Beasts: civil and ecclesiastical Rome.

253. Burnet, William. *An Essay on Scripture-Prophecy, Wherein it is Endeavoured to Explain the Three Periods Contain'd in the XII Chapter of the Prophet Daniel: With Some Argument to Make it Probable that the First of the Periods Did Expire in the Year 1715, etc.* 1724. [New York?] 167 p.

254. Newton, Isaac. *Observations Upon the Prophecies of Daniel and the Apocalypse.* 1831 [1733]. London: James Nisbet. xvi, 250 p. Also 20th century eds.

Posthumous pub. (Newton: d. 1727.) Influenced by pre-mill implications of Alsted and Mede. Opines End is near but doesn't give date. Historicist. Revelation sealed only until End Times, then widely interpreted and understood. Babylonian, Persian, Greek, Roman empires. Clay-iron mix feet of image = barbarian kingdoms incorporated into Roman Empire. Ten Horns of 4th Beast: Vandals, Suevians, Visigoths, Alans, Burgundians, Franks, Britons, Huns, Lombards, Ravenna. Little Horn that prevails = Papacy, which achieves temporal dominion. 70 Weeks = 490 years, from return from Captivity to the death of Christ (457 B.C. to A.D. 34). 70th Week, Abomination of Desolation = Jewish War and Roman destruction of Jerusalem A.D. 70. Kings of North and South = various historical elements: Seleucid, Ptolemaic Egypt, Roman conquest of Macedon; also relates to division of Empire into East and West, where Saracens = South, and Turks = North. Newton on Daniel: "There is scarcely a prophecy in the Old Testament concerning Christ that does not in some way or other relate to this second coming." Implies that Millennium could be A.D. 2132, 2370, or 2436 (2,300 "days" from 168 B.C., A.D. 70, or 135).

255. Sewall, Samuel. *Phaenomena Quaedam Apocalyptica ad Aspectum Novi Orbis Configurata. Or, Some Few Lines Towards a Description of the New Heaven as* *it Makes to Those Who Stand Upon the New Earth* ... 1727. 2d ed. Boston, MA: 4 p. l., 64, 24 p.

"The fountain opened: or, the admirable blessings plentifully to be dispensed at the national conversion of the Jews."

256. Ambrose, Isaac. *Christ in the Clouds Coming to Judgment: or The Dissolution of All Things.* 1729. Boston: Benjamin Gray. [4], 20 p.

A "substance of sermons preached by ... Dr. [William?] Bates." Some editions listed under "Bates." Extracted from chapter on "Dooms-Day" in Ambrose's *Prima, Media, et Ultima.*

257. Abauzit, M. [Firmin] *Discour Historique sur l'Apocalipse.* 1770 [1730?]. London. 104 p. bibl refs.

258. Knight, James. *A Discourse on the Conflagration and Renovation of the World.* 1736. London: C. Corbet. 31 p.

259. Bengel, Johann Albrecht. *Erklärte Offenbarung Johannis* (Interpretation of the Revelation of John). 1740. Stuttgart; English transl. 1757. (London).

Distinguished exegete, foremost post-Reformation theologian in Württemberg; pietist. Influential in England as well as in Germany. Historic pre-mill. 42 Months each 15½ years; prophetic "day" = one-half year. Grand crisis in 1836, precipitates Millennium and End. Preliminary Millennium begins 1836, followed by Millennium proper and End. Antichrist = Pope. A.D. 1143 + 666 = 1809. Various mystical calculations: all end on 1836.

260. _____. *Gnomon Novi Testamenti.* 1773.

Mathematical calculations to fix future dates.

261. Watts, Isaac. *The End of Time.* 1825 [1740]. Boston. 45, [3] p.

The famous hymn-writer. Pre-mill. (Watt's carol "Joy to the World" really concerned the Second Coming, not Christmas, the First.)

262. Schubert, Johann Ernst. *Johan Ernst Schuberts derer hochlobl. philosophischen Facultaten zu Witttemberg [sic] und Jena adjuncti Vernunftige und schriftmasige Gedanken von dem Ende der Welt.* 1742. Frankfurt: J.A. Melchior. 94, [2] p.

263. Edwards, Jonathan. *Some Thoughts Concerning the Present Revival of Religion in New-England.* 1803 [1742]. Lexington, KY: Joseph Charles. [Orig. pub. Boston] 390 p.

Prime mover of the Great Awakening. Post-mill, but believed Millennium was near. Earth destroyed after the Millennium and transfer of Saints to heaven. Expected Islam to be overthrown, Jews converted. Influenced by post-mill implications of Whitby.

264. _____. *Apocalyptic Writings.* 1977. Yale Univ. Press. x, 501. bibl. refs, indexes. Vol 5 *The Works of Jonathan Edwards.*

265. _____. *History of the Work of Redemption.*

Uncompleted. Significance of the New World. Anticipated Kingdom near end of 20th century Ends with Millennium, apostasy, Last Judgment, End of world. Disputed Lowman's date of 1,260 + A.D. 765 (the Merovingians) = 2016. Rather, A.D. 456 + 1,260 (= 1716). Then, when this date passed, suggested A.D. 606 + 1,260 (= 1866).

266. Amory, Thomas. *Eight Sermons on a Future General Judgment.* 1748. London: J. Waugh. 218 p.

267. Gill, John. *An Exposition of the New Testament.* 1954 [1744].

Grant Jeffery (in Ice and Demy) claims Gill taught pre-trib Rapture in the air, preserving saints and elect from conflagration of earth. Believers stay with Christ in heaven, then descend to earth with Him to reign at Millennium.

268. Newton, Thomas. *Dissertations on the Prophecies, Which Have Remarkably Been Fulfilled and at This Time Are Fulfilling in the World.* 1833 [1754]. 17th ed. London: T.T.& J. Tegg. xxiv, 730 p.

Lord Bishop of Bristol. Figures 6,000 years of earthly history, then the Millennium. "Popery the great corruption of Christianity"—Antichrist and Babylon. 1850 edition "revised by the Rev. W[illiam] S. Dobson." Islam prevails for 1,260 years, then restoration of Jews, destruction of Antichrist, then Millennium = 1868. Four Kingdoms: Babylonia, Medo-Persia, Macedonia, Rome. Rome and Ottoman

Empire fall, then Jews restored. Millennium = 1966 or 1987 (2,300 days from 334 B.C. and 1,260 days from A.D. 727).

269. Wesley, John. *Explanatory Notes Upon the New Testament.* 1754. New York: Eaton and Mains. 734 p. Many later eds.

Welsey: founder of Methodism. Follows Bengel; tentatively accepts his date of 1836 for fall of Turkish and Papal Beasts, and the Millennium. "Perhaps the times mentioned might be fixed thus— ...[A.D.] 1077. The beast ascends out of the sea ... 1836. The beast finally overthrown." Two distinct, non-overlapping thousand-year periods in Revelation: the binding of Satan, and the millennial rule of the saints.

270. Imrie, David. *Speedy Accomplishment of the Great, Awful and Glorious Events which the Scriptures Say are to be Brought to Pass in the Latter Times.* 1755. Edinburgh. Reprinted Boston, 1756.

538 B.C. + 2,300; End ca. 1794.

271. Alcock, Thomas. *A Sermon on the Late Earthquakes, More Particularly That at Lisbon.* 1756.

The devastating 1755 earthquake in Portugal as a warning and judgment from God.

272. Prentice, Thomas. *Observations ... on the Late Terrible Night of the Earthquake.* 1756. Boston: D. Henchman.

New England Congregational minister. Lisbon earthquake harbinger the End.

273. Burr, Aaron. *The Watchman's Answer to the Question, What of the Night.* 1757. Boston: S. Kneeland.

Burr: president of Princeton; father of Aaron Burr the statesman. Pope and Islam as Antichrist; Protestants as the Two Witnesses. 6th Trumpet not yet ended.

274. Cheever, Ezekiel. *Scripture Prophecies Explained.* 1757. Boston: Green and Russell.

Cheever: teacher. Pre-mill.

275. Torrey, William. *A Brief Discourse Concerning Futurities of Things to Come, viz.: The Next, or Second Coming of Christ; of the Thousand Years of Christ's Kingdom; of the First Resurrection; of the New Heavens and New Earth; and of the Burning of the Old....* 1757. Boston. [2],iv,iii, [1], 76 p.

276. Bellamy, Joseph. *The Millennium: or, The Thousand Years of Prosperity, Promised to the Church of God.* 1794 [1758]. Elizabethtown: S. Kollock. 49 p.

Bellamy: Connecticut minister, disciple of Jonathan Edwards. Millennium to begin when Papal period ends (1,260 years after Papacy achieved dominance: A.D. 606-765).

277. Swedenborg, Emanuel. *A Treatise Concerning the Last Judgment and the Destruction of Babylon: Shewing that all the Predictions Contained in the Revelation, are at This Day Fulfilled.* 1788 [1758]. London. xvi, 154 p. Originally published in Latin.

Swedenborg: Swedish scientist, philosopher, theologian. In 1757 Swedenborg saw vision of Last Judgment, and descent of literal New Jerusalem from Heaven. Spiritual fulfillment of End, though external world continues.

278. _____. *De Miraculis, et Quod Hodie Circa Finem Saeculi Mulla Exspectanda.* 1947 [1943]. London: Swedenborg Soc. 27 p.

"Miracles, they are not to be expected at this time when the end of the age is near"

279. Clarke, Richard. *The Prophetic Numbers of Daniel and John Calculated.* 1759. Boston. 24 p.

Popular work; predicted End by 1766. Subtitle: "in order to shew the time, when the Day of Judgment for this first age of the Gospel, is to be expected: and the setting up the millennial Kingdom of Jehovah and his Christ."

280. *Some Thoughts on the Duration of the Torments of the Wicked, and the Time When the Day of Judgment May Be Expected.* 1759. Charlestown. 37 p.

Response to Clarke's *Prophetic Numbers of Daniel and John Calculated.*

281. *The Strange and Wonderful Predictions of Mr. Christopher Love.* 1759 [Boston]; Newport. Broadside.

Purported to be written by minister executed by Cromwell. Predicts Antichrist in 1761, End in 1763. 1760 London edition subtitled "Giving an account of the time of Babylon's fall, or the destruction of Popery...."

282. March, Edmund. *Divine Providence (to Appearance) Visibly Engaged in Fulfilling Scripture-Prophecies, Which Relate to the Purity, Peace and Glory of the Church of God in the Latter Days.* 1762, Boston. 40 p.

283. Eyre, Joseph. *Observations upon the Prophecies Relating to the Restoration of the Jews.* 1771. London. xvi, 166 p.

284. Killingsworth, Grantham. *Paradise Regained: Or, the Scripture Account of the Glorious Millennium.* 1772. London: printed for J. Buckland and W. Davenhill. ii, 44 p.

"When it will start, the Anti-Christ, Satan bound 1,000 years, Gog and Magog, Second Resurrection, Final Judgement, eternal kingdom."

285. Cooper, Samuel. *A Discourse on the Man of Sin.* 1774. Boston: Greenleaf.

Part of Harvard lecture series on prophetic significance of the Papacy, established by Paul Dudley (who wrote 1731 pamphlet on subject).

286. Walmesley, C[harles]. 1807 [ca. 1776?]. *The General History of the Christian Church from her Birth to Her Final Triumphant State in Heaven: Chiefly Deduced from the Apocalypse of St. John, the Apostle and Evangelist.* 4th ed. New York: xxiv, 456, vii p.

Pseud. "Signor Pastorini." British Catholic. Locusts = Protestant Reformers. 666 and Little Horn = Mohamedanism. Antichrist (future Mohammedan prince) overthrown about 1825.

287. Dwight, Timothy. *The Conquest of Canaan: A Poem in Eleven Books.* 1785. Hartford [1970 reprint of 1788 ed. by Greenwood Press, Westport]

Grandson of Jonathan Edwards; later became president of Yale. Eschatological interpretation of American Revolution; thought Millennium would begin "near the year 2000." Vigorously opposed French atheism. SEE ALSO 1800-1910.

288. Apthorp, East. *Discourses in Prophecy.* 1786. London: Rivington. viii, 392, [8] p.

Daniel's 70 Weeks = 490 years, from Artaxerxes's 457 B.C. edict. No gap between 69th and 70th Weeks. Stresses "Perspicuity of Prophecy." Creation 4004 B.C.

289. Remusat, Jacinto Maria [Hyacinthe Marie]. *Carta de un Canonigo a un Amigo Suyo Sobre la Proximidad del Fin del Mundo.* 1841 [1786] Mexico: Cumplido. 27 p.

290. _____. *El Fin del Mundo, Para el Ano de 1860, a Sea Carta de un Canonigo a un Amigo Suyo.* Mexico. 1852. 29 p.

291. Foster, Benjamin. *Dissertation on the Seventy Weeks of Daniel.* 1787. Newport: 40 p.

Daniel as chronological guide to End Time events.

292. Edwards, Morgan. *Two Academical Exercises on Subjects Bearing the Following Titles; Millennium, Last-Novelties.* 1788. Philadelphia: Dobson and Lang. 56 p.

Historicist: Tribulation lasts 1,260 years; Rapture 3½ years before end of Tribulation.

293. Gale, Benjamin. *A Brief Essay, or, An Attempt to Prove, From the Prophetick Writings of the Old and New Testament: What Period of Prophecy the Church of God is Now Under; and from Them to Shew What Events Revelationists May Expect Will Take Place During the Present Period.* 1788. New Haven, CT. 63 p.

Gale: Connecticut physician. Premill. Seals began in early centuries; Seventh Seal, Trumpet, and Vial all to occur soon at fall of mystical Babylon; then Second Coming and Millennial rule of saints.

294. Crawford, Charles. *Observations Upon the Downfall of the Papal Power, and Consequent Events.* 1788 "new ed." Philadelphia. 44 p.

295. Jones, William. *Popular Commotions Considered as Signs of the Approaching End of the World.* 1789. London: Robinson. 15 p.

296. Lacunza y Diaz, Manual de [pseud. "Ben Ezra"]. *The Coming of the Messiah in Glory and Majesty.* 1827 [1790]. London: L.B. Seeley. 2 vols. Orig 1790, Spanish. 1833 ed. (abridged) Dublin/London: William Curry; xiv, 575 p.

Lacunza: Spanish-Chilean Jesuit. This work written under the name "Juan Josafat Ben Ezra, a converted Jew." Considered originator or precursor of modern pre-mill interpretation (Second Coming *before* the Millennium). Describes a "great space of time between the glorious coming of the Lord ... and the general judgment and resurrection..." Rapture of believers at time of Second Coming; most others killed; "these few who shall remain alive" survive into the Millennium. Edward Irving wrote 1827 *Preliminary Discourse* to "Ben Ezra's" book.

297. Waring, George. *The End of Time.* 1790. London 44 p.

Judgment Day sermon.

298. Bicheno, James. *Signs of the Times; or, The Overthrow of the Papal Tyranny in France, the Prelude of Destruction to Popery and Despotism; but of Peace to Mankind.* 1793. London. 67 p.

Restoration of Jews a necessary condition. 481 B.C. + 2,300 = 1819. A.D. 529 + 1,260 = 1789; + 1,290 = 1819; + 1,335 = 1864 (End).

299. Murray, John. *The Last Solemn Scene!* 1793. Newburyport, MA: 69, [3] p.

Sermon preached in Boston, 1768.

300. *Prophetical Extracts: Particularly Such as Relate to the Revolution in France and the Decline of the Papal Power in the World: Selected from Fleming, Usher, Jerieu, Goodwin, Gill, Love, Brown, Knox, Willison, More, and Dr. John Owen, in an Extraordinary Sermon, he Preached Before the Honourable House of Commons, April the 19th, 1649. Intitled the Shaking and Translating of Heaven and Earth.* 1793. London: 8, [2], ii, 5-56 p.

Added to title page: "Ouraneon Ourania, the shaking and translating of heaven and earth."

301. Brothers, Richard. *A Revealed Knowledge of the Prophecies and Times, Wrote Under the Direction of God By the Man Who Will Be Revealed to the Hebrews as Their Prince.* 1794. London. Various pagings.

Brothers: retired sailor. Early promoter of British-Israelism; preached that ancestors of Ten Tribes merged among English (other two in Europe). End is near; he would lead Jews to Promised Land as rightful king and leader of Jews. Told George III to yield crown to him.

Predicted war between France and Austria-Prussia to usher in Millennium. Called himself God's Almighty Nephew. Expected millennial rebuilding of Jerusalem by 1798. Book enormously popular, several editions. Millennium = 1793-95. The mortally wounded head that revives = Charles I (executed) and Charles II (reinstated as King). Daniel's Lion = George III. Leopard = Louis XIV.

302. *A Dissertation on the Existence, Nature, & Extent of the Prophetic Powers in the Human Mind: with Unquestionable Examples of Several Eminent Prophecies, of What in Now Acting, and Soon to Be Fulfilled, Upon the Great Theatre of Europe* ... 1794. London: B. Crosby. 40 p.

"Particularly those of Dr. John Harvey, Michael Nostradamus, William Lilly, Anna Trapnel, Mr. Love, John Tillinghast, Peter Jurieu, Seth Darwin, Robert Nixon, Robert Flemming, John Lacy, John Maximilian Daut, Rev. Mr. John Wilson, Bishop Newton, Baron Swedenbourg, Daniel Defoe, Dr. Pricotley, Dr. Goldsmith, James Lambert, Dr. Smollet, Martha Ery, Hannah Green, St. Thomas of Becket, Dr. Sibley."

303. Hopkins, Samuel. *A Treatise on the Millennium: Shewing from Scripture Prophecy, That It Is Yet to Come, When It Will Come, In What It Will Consist, and the Events Which Are First to Take Place, Introductory to It.* 1794. Edinburgh: John Ogle. 200 p.

Hopkins: New England theologian, Congregationalist, associated with Jonathan Edwards. Post-mill: Millennium to begin in about two years after gradual decline of Papacy and growing dominance of true Christianity.

304. Jung-Stillung, Johann Heinrich. *Das Heimweh.* 1994 [1794]. Verlag am Goetheanum.

Novel; includes author's "Schlüssel [Key] zum Heimweh." Influenced by Bengel (1740) and John Bunyan. French Revolution: chaos and impending doom; Prussia-Austria-Russia alliance. Introduction discusses Masonic and alchemic links. Euro-Asian empire threatened by secret conspiracy from France. Emperor's followers form counter-organization. Hero and others seek to establish final kingdom of peace among Tartar tribes around Samarkand and Bokhara in Turkestan (north of Afghanistan)—the only region inaccessible to Antichrist.

305. Priestly, Joseph. *Present State of Europe Compared with Ancient Prophecies.* 1794. Philadelphia: Dobson. 106 p.

Priestly: Unitarian-Universalist Church. Restoration of Jews must occur before End.

306. Austin, David. *The Millennium Promised to the Church of God, in the Old Testament and in the New, Shortly to Commence* ... 1794. Elizabeth Town: Shepard Kollock. 426 p.

Williston (1854) says Austin predicted "very day" of start of Millennium. New Jersey Presbyterian.

307. _____. *A Prophetic Leaf.* 1798 New Haven: author. 64 p.

Addressed to newspapers titled *The Stone Against the Image*, for serialization. "Containing an illustration of the signs of the times, as now displaying themselves to the eye of a spiritual observer, in the natural, in the moral, and in the invisible heavens: collected from the fountain of truth, from the events of Providence, and from the inditings of the spirit of grace; designed to unfold an astonished world, the purpose of God in the convulsions which now shake the thrones of the earth and threaten the demolition of the prophetic heavens: preparatory to the introduction, irresistible progress, and final consummation of the glory of the latter day, absorbed in the princely reign of the mighty Redeemer."

308. _____. *The First Vibration of the Jubilee Trump!* 1799. Elizabeth-Town: S. Kollock. 16 p.

309. Halhed, Nathaniel Brassey. *A Calculation on the Commencement of the Millennium* ... 1795. London.

310. _____. *Testimony of the Authenticity of the Prophecies of Richard Brothers* ... 1795. London. iv, [5]-45 p.

Orientalist scholar. Gave speeches in Parliament supporting Brothers and urging his release. Nov. 19, 1795 = the 6,000 years of world history will end.

311. Watkins, John. *An Essay on the End of the World.* 1795. Worcester [MA]: Isaiah Thomas. 36 p.

312. Winchester, Elhanan. *Lectures on the Prophecies That Remain to Be Fulfilled.* 1795.

Evil winning in the world

313. Belcher, William. *A Guide, Spiritual and Temporal. Comprising Twelve Prognostics of the End of the World* ... 1796. London: Original Asylum of Genius. xv, 48 p.

314. Spalding, Joshua. *Sentiments Concerning the Coming and Kingdom of Christ Collected from the Bible and from the Writings of Many Ancient and Some Modern Believers.* 1841 [1796]. 2nd ed. Boston: J.V. Himes. 258 p.

315. Cummings, Abraham. *A Dissertation on the Introduction and Glory of the Millennium.* 1797. Boston: Manning & Loring. 118? p.

316. Gleason, James. *An Exposition of the Three First Chapters of Genesis Explained and Improved; Wherein the Four Dispensations Contained in the Scriptures from Age to Age are Revealed* ... *Until the Opening of the Last Great and Seventh Seal, When the Mystery of God is Finished* ... 1797. Norwich 190 p.

317. King, Edward. *Remarks on the Signs of the Times.* 1798. London 40 p.

Capture and deportation of Pope by Napoleon in 1798 as fulfillment of 1,260 years (from 538).

318. Wrangham, Francis. *Rome is Fallen!* 1798. York, England. 38 p.

Capture and deportation of Pope by Napoleon in 1798 as fulfillment of 1,260 years (from 538).

319. Abbott, Abiel. *Traits of Resemblance in the People of the United States of America to Ancient Israel.* 1799. Haverhill, MA: Moore & Stebbins. reprinted in *The American Republic and Ancient Israel,* 1977, NY: Arno Press

320. Kett, Henry. *History the Interpreter of Prophecy.* 1799. 2nd ed. 2 vols. Oxford: University Press. Bibl. refs.

"A view of Scriptural prophecies and their accomplishment in the past and present occurrences of the world: with conjectures respecting their future completion." Preterist.

Works from 1800 to 1910 (Alphabetical)

321. A.D.D. *Approach of the Apocalyptic Troubles: The World's Crisis; Antichrist, or, "The Coming Man."* 1853. 2nd ed. London: Ward & Co., J. Lund. 31 p.

"With a Refutation of the Sentiments Referring to Great Britain, Put Forth in a Work Entitled 'The Coming Struggle Among the Nations of the Earth'" (David Pae's 1853 work).

322. *Advent Tracts.* 1845–1849. Boston: J.V. Himes. 2 vols. 246 p.

Vol. 2 includes William Miller; Mourant Brock, James Haldane Stewart.

323. Aldersmith, Herbert. *The Fulness of the Nations; or the ABC of the Promises Given to the House of Israel Considered in Relation to the Second Advent.* 1889. London: Hodder and Stoughton. xix, 350 p. foldout chart index.

These are "last days"—"very near" the End. Personal pre-mill reign. Denies gap before 70th Week. Rather, promises and prophecies of latter days apply to Israel (the Ten Tribes). Distinction between Israel and Judah: "Israel" must be mighty, multitudinous company of nations prior to Millennium. Gog= Russia. 2,520 Years: from Captivity 721 B.C. to 1800, when England became supreme. Age ends 1844–48, and finally (fully) in 1919–23. Denies partial or "first fruits" secret rapture of 144,000: Rapture will be public and visible, just prior to Millennium but *after* Tribulation.

324. Alger, William Rounseville. *The End of the World, and the Day of Judgment.* 1870. Boston: Roberts Bros. 75 p.

"Two discourses preached to the Music-Hall Society."

325. Allwood, Philip. *A Key to the Revelation of St. John, the Divine: Being an Analysis of Those Parts of That Wonderful Book, Which Relate to the General State of the Christian Church, Through All the Times Since It Was Written, and to the Peculiar Signs of Those Times.* 1829. London: C.J.G.& F. Rivington.

326. An American Layman. *The Second Advent; or Coming of the Messiah in Glory, Shown to be a Scripture Doctrine, and Taught by Divine Revelation, from the Beginning of the World.* 1815. Trenton, NJ: Fenton & Hutchinson.

327. Anderson, Robert. *The Coming Prince.* 1984 [1884]. Kregel. lviii, 320 p. bibl refs, index.

10th edition 1915; 12th edition 1940; 19th edition 1975.

Subtitles vary: *Daniel's Seventy Weeks / Prophecy Concerning the Antichrist / Answer to the Higher Criticism.* Anderson: chief criminal investigator of Scotland Yard; Plymouth Brethren. Updated edition notes increased interest in prophecy after World War. This book still much and respectfully cited. Anyone who doubts Second Coming has "no claim whatever to the name of Christian." Intricate computation of biblical dates. Daniel's 69 Weeks: 7 x 360 days (prophetic years) x 69 = 483 years to the exact day from Artaxerxes' decree (445 B.C.) to Jesus's entry into Jerusalem as Messiah (A.D. 32). 70th Week begins when treaty signed with Israel by coming King who controls Ten Nations. Postulated series of Comings: pre-trib Rapture; at End of Tribulation for Jewish converts; for destruction of Antichrist; End of Millennium; maybe others too.

328. ____. *Daniel in the Critic's Den.* 1990 Kregel (reprint of 3rd ed. 1909, J. Nisbet). xvi, 186 p. 4th ed. 1910/1919 [1895] Subtitles vary: "A Reply to Dean [F.W.] Farrar's Book of Daniel" e.g.

Denies late authorship of Daniel (i.e. after-the-fact prophecies). SEE ALSO 1900–1970.

329. Andrews, John Nevins. *The Three Messages of Revelation XIV, 6–12: Particularly the Third Angel's Message and Two-Horned Beast.* 1872. 3rd ed. Battle Creek, MI: Steam Press of the Seventh-Day Adventist Pub. Assoc. viii, 126 p. bibl. refs.

330. ____. *The Judgment: Its Events and their Order.* 1890. Oakland, CA: Pacific Press. Bible Students Library No. 5. 133 p. Reprinted 1992 Leaves-Of-Autumn Books.

3rd President of General Confederation of Seventh-day Adventists. U.S. = Two-Horn beast. "Investigative Judgment" at end of period of human probation. Jesus comes to God before Second Coming.

331. Andrews, Samuel James. *Christianity and Anti-Christianity in Their Final Conflict.* [1898]. Chicago: Bible Institute Colportage Assoc. xxviii, 358 p.

Foreword by James M. Gray. Socialism, pantheism, evolution weakening church, leading to apostasy. Antichrist, probably head of Ten Nation league, will take over apostate world church, assisted by False Prophet.

332. Andros, Thomas. *The Place of the Church, on the Grand Chart of Scripture Prophecy, or The Great Battle of Armageddon.* 1814. Boston. 48 p.

Re: Napoleon.

333. *The Apocalypse Popularly Explained.* 1853. London: Wertheim & MacIntosh. 80 p.

1,260 years: Papal "horn" arises 533, ends 1793. Follows 10-Horn beast, which ends A.D. 476 (Britain, Spain, France, Portugal, Austria, Naples, Piedmont, Lombardy, Ravenna, Rome). Trumpets: against ancient Rome; Seals: Western Roman Empire. White Horse Rider = Constantine. Red Horse = Theodosius. Black = Alaric the Goth. Pale = Justinian. 5th Woe = Saracens; 6th = Turks. Awaiting 7th now. Four Vials: revolutionary France. 5th = invasion of France. Great Britain escaped wrath (successfully resisted Napoleon). Great Earthquake = 1848 revolutions. The Papacy is "Satan's deepest and mightiest achievement..." Final battle and Day of God not the end of world, but the Millennium. Urges British to remain faithful to be saved, though England will eventually rejoin 10-Horn confederation.

334. *Armageddon, or, A Warning Voice from the Last Battle-Field of Nations.* 1858. London: Wertheim, MacIntosh, and Hunt. 3 vols., (approx. 1,800 p.), illus. Charts.

By "A Master of Arts of the Univ. of Cambridge." (M. Baxter 1863 attributes authorship to "Mr. Beale.") "Proclaiming by the mouths of prophets and apostles, that the close of the times of the Gentiles, the second personal Advent, and Millennial Reign of our Lord and Saviour Jesus Christ, are nigh at hand..." Vol. 1: Personal Second Coming, Millennium. Vials 1–5 = 1789 to 1848. Vol 2: Restoration of Israel. End 1865–6, shown by various cycles, calculations. Millennium starts 1869. Vol 3: Appendix with foldout charts, indexes, maps, tables. Lost Ten Tribes in Central Asia. (Appendix also pub. as separate suppl. vol.) A.D. 530–3 + 1,335 = 1865–9. 70th Week is "insulated portion" deferred until End. Antichrist = Louis Napoleon; will probably sign 7-year treaty 1862; revealed as persecuting tyrant midway through.

335. *Armageddon: or, the Battle-Field on Which Antichrist and His Armies Are to Be Overthrown, as Seen Through the Telescope of Divine Prediction.* 1853. London: Houston & Stoneman. 32 p. Catholic Apostolic Church.

336. Armstrong, Amzi. *A Syllabus of Lectures on the Visions of the Revelation.* 1815. Morris-town, NJ: P.A. Johnson, H.P. Russell. 238 p.

1,260 years ends 1826.

337. _____. *The Last Trumpet.* 1824. New York: G.F. Hopkins. 18 p.

Pre-mill.

338. Auberlen, Karl A. *The Prophecies of Daniel and the Revelations of St John: Viewed in Their Mutual Relation, with an Exposition of the Principal Passages.* 1857 [1856]. Andover: W.F. Draper. xx, 458 p.

Originally in German.

339. Bacon, John. *Conjectures on the Prophecies.* 1805. Boston: D. Carlisle. 31 p.

Bacon: Congregational minister, judge. A.D. 606 (Bishop of Rome claims universal authority) + 1,260 = 1866; + 1,335 = 1941 (start of Millennium). (Written in 1799.)

340. Baines, Thomas Blackburn. *The Lord's Coming, Israel, and the Church.* 1900 [1875]. London: Rouse. xii, 451 p. index.

341. Baker, W[illiam] A[dolphus]. *The Day and the Hour, or Notes on Prophecy: a Sketch of the Future, Extracted from the Bible.* 1865. London: for author [by] William MacIntosh. xii, 270 p.

1,290 Years ends in 1878: the Second Coming.

342. Baldwin, Samuel Davies. *Armageddon: or, The Overthrow of Romanism and Monarchy; the Existence of the United States Foretold in the Bible, Its Future Greatness, Invasion by Allied Powers; Annihilation of Monarchy; Expansion into the Millennial Republic, and Its Dominion over the Whole World.* 1878 [1854]. Rev. ed. Nashville: Southern Methodist Pub. 480 p. Orig 1854; Cincinnati: Applegate. Also subtitled *The U.S. in Prophecy.*

"Dedicated to the friends of Bible Democracy and the foes of monarchy and Romanism." Baldwin: Methodist; Murfreesboro, TN; pres. of Soule Female College. Says his book is of "incalculable importance" to U.S., as warning of Armageddon. U.S. is "Israel restored"; heir to prophecies regarding Israel. The Return is immigration to America, not restoration of Israel state. Theory that Jewish state to be restored to rule as world capital "absurd, fanatical, and repugnant to scripture, as well as to common sense." Gog = Russia and confederated Europe, also much of Africa and Asia. Invasion of America, not Palestine: "Now in the name of all that is rational, is it probable or possible to excite and muster such a force, to put down a few feeble Jews restored to Palestine? ...common sense and revelation both coincide in determining the United States as the Israel to be invaded by confederate Europe." Daniel's prophecies run from A.D. 68 (cessation of Temple sacrifice) to July 4, 1776. Russian-led alliance attacks U.S., is annihilated; U.S. then dominates world. Shem, Japhet: race of true religion; Ham, Canaan: race of "serpent and his seed." Semitic (yellow) race "vastly inferior to the white race": Hamitic (black) "early sunk into great inferiority." Japhethites emigrated to America; will hold sway during Millennium. "Equality of political rights will not be held in common by the three races during the Millennium." Israelite dispensation "typical," not "realizing"; it foreshadows what Christian fulfills: carnal vs. spiritual Israel, respectively. Bible and U.S. Constitution both recognize Hamitic slavery. Cites Maury on central geographical position of America. Christ won't come *during* Armageddon but later. Ten Lost Tribes amalgamated, gone. Russia and European confederacy, with Africa, Asia, invade U.S. U.S. is 5th Kingdom. Ten Horns of Beast: Huns, Goths, Vandals, Franks, Germanic tribes; also first 4 Trumpets. Little Horn is Papacy. 3½ times = 529,984 days of overthrow of church/state union, beginning with Council of Nice A.D. 325, ending July 4, 1776. Millennium to begin 1878; U.S. to destroy Europe within 26 years. Four Horsemen: Christ, Papacy, Islam/Saracens, French atheism. Persecution of Christians to cease 1865; monarchy destroyed worldwide 1878 by U.S. Seven-headed Beast = Rome, with Western, Charlemagne, Papal, Spanish, British, French, Russia offspring. Beast from Sea:

Imperial Church. Beast's wounded head: Pope Gregory VII humbled by Henry IV, survived. Two-Horn Beast from Earth and False Prophet = England ("infallibly predicted"). 666 = *Lateinos*, also *H. Latinh Basileia*. 5th Trumpet = Saracens. 6th = Turks (to fall in 1861). Makes much of 13 Colonies as direct reflection of Israelite tribes, and many convergences to July 4, 1776. 144,000: number of true Christians in U.S. in 1776. 1st Vial: wrath against England; 2nd: Revolutionary France; 3rd: Germany, 4th: Napoleonic France, 5th: French invasion of Russia, 6th: Waterloo, 7th: Western Church. Trumpets: 1st: Germanic invasions of Roman Europe, 2nd: Atilla and Huns, 3rd: Vandals, 4th: fall of Western Empire, 5th: Saracen invasions, 6th: Turkish, 7th: rise of U.S. and fall of monarchies. Site of "Armageddon" metaphorical; this battle of the End actually to be fought at Mississippi or Ohio valley. Millennium to establish pure Christian religion in America, Europe, and adjoining Mediterranean regions; false religion remains in rest of Africa and Asia. End of Millennium: America remains true Christian, but Europe, others, apostasize and degenerate. Second Coming in U.S., either at start, during, or end of Millennium. "Is it not plain that any theory of exposition is in error, if proposed prior to the "time of the end?" (i.e. all earlier theories are wrong). 70 Weeks begins with Cyrus, ends A.D. 68 (desolation). 70 Weeks count "labor time" only (abbrev. years), to which "sacred time" must be added.

343. Ballou, Hosea. *Brief Reply to a Pamphlet Entitled A Vindication of the Common Opinion Relative to the Last Judgment and End of the World.* Boston: Henry Bower. 40 p.

Reply to Timothy Merritt's refutation of earlier work by Ballou. Denies accusation that he denies future judgment and punishment, Last Day, End of World. Does deny "unmerciful eternal punishment," however; argues for continuing chances for salvation.

344. Barbour, Nelson H. 1877. *Three Worlds, and the Harvest of This World.* Rochester: C.T. Russell. 194 p. illus

Independent Adventist, editor of *Herald of the Morning.* 1873 = 6,000 years since Adam created. When End didn't come, decided 1873 was Coming of invisible presence of Christ. Chronological interpretation was later adopted by Russell and Jehovah's Witnesses. A 1,845-year dispensation up to Christ, and 1,845-year dispensation after Christ (1,845 + 33 = 1878).

345. Barnes, C.E. *The Second Personal Coming of Christ.* [1874]. Boston: Advent Christian Publication Soc. 12 p.

Advent Christian.

346. Barrett, B.F. [Benjamin Fiske] *The End of the World, or, Consummation of the Age.* 1848 [1843]. Boston: Otis Clapp. 54 p. Tract #6 for the New Church in the U.S.

Literal interpretation is wrong (e.g. Millerites), follows Swedenborg's spiritual interpretation. Earth = Church. "End" is end of old Christian Church, beginning of Swedenborg's New Church.

347. Bates, Joseph. *A Seal of the Living God; And Hundred Forty-Four Thousand, of the Servants of God Being Sealed, in 1849.* 1849. New Bedford [MA]. 72 p.

Four Angel Messengers of Revelation 7: Britain, France, Russia, America. Bates first declared 1845 the Day of Atonement, then 1851 (realized he had to add seven years).

348. Baxter, Michael Paget. *The Coming Battle and the Appalling National Convulsions Foreshown in Prophecy Immediately to Occur During the Period 1861–67.* 1860. Philadelphia: W. Harbert. 32 p. map bibl. refs.

Indefatigable date-setter: here predicts End for 1861–67, but in later works confidently predicted later dates for End — always within a few years. Historicist but also advocates secret Rapture.

349. _____. *Louis Napoleon the Infidel Antichrist Predicted in Prophecy to Confirm of Seven Years Covenant with the Jews, About the Year 1861 and Nearly to Succeed in Gaining a Universal Empire...After Which Napoleon, Their Destroyer Together with the Pope, Will Be Cast Alive Into the Lake of Fire at the Descent of Christ at Armageddon About the Year 1868.* 1860. London: Wertheim & MacIntosh. 40 p.

350. ____. *End of the World About 1864–69: As Held and Clearly Demonstrated by More than Fifty Expositors … Whose Predictions of Coming Calamities are Verified by the Present American Commotion Which is Only a Prelude to the Dreadful Wars, Famines, Pestilences, and Earthquakes, That Will Prevail Until the End in 1869.* 1861 Boston: E. Dutton. 16 p. maps.

England subjugated by Napoleon the Antichrist "about 1864–5."

351. ____. *Louis Napoleon the Destined Monarch of the World, and Personal Antichrist, Foreshown in Prophecy to Confirm a Seven Year's Covenant with the Jews About, Or Soon After 1864–5, and (After the Resurrection and the Translation of the Wise Virgins has Taken Place Two Years and from Four to Six Weeks After the Covenant,) Subsequently to Become Completely Supreme Over England and Most of America, and All Christendom, and Fiercely to Persecute Christians During the Latter Half of the Seven Years, Until He Finally Perishes at the Descent of Christ at the Battle of Armageddon, About Or Soon After 1871–2* 1863. Philadelphia: Wm. S.& A. Martien. 355 p.

Cites over 70 other works predicting End for 1866–68, including Frederick Sargent's *Essay on Personal and Pre-Millenial Advent of Messiah* (1833); James Verner's *Battle of the Nations as Revealed in Daniel's Vision* (1853, London/Dublin) W. Goble's *The Beast* (1861 [same as 1862 *The Beast* by "X, Y, Z"?]); and in E. Davis's *Seven Thunders; or the Mighty Crash of Europe's Royal and Papal Thrones, About to be Cast Down by the Awful Judgments of God* (1855, New York/Louisville, KY). Seals — 1st: A.D. 33–323; 2nd: to 534; 3rd: to 1073; 4th: to 1438; 6th: to French Revolution; 7th: 1863–68 to 1871–73. Vials: from French Revolution and Napoleonic Wars to the Armageddon. Wicked resurrected one thousand years later. Antichrist to make 7-year covenant with Jews soon, then engages in "exterminating persecution" against Christians, slaughtering most who oppose him, branding others with his name or 666. Also "unparalleled wars, earthquakes, pestilences, and famines"

during this Tribulation. Armageddon and Second Coming to follow soon after. As End will be 1871–3, Antichrist must reveal himself now. As prophesied, Louis Napoleon is 7th-restored (i.e. 8th) head of Beast — the "deadly wound which healed," is of Grecian ancestry, has taken over Roman Empire, controls the Pope, is "addicted to spiritualism, has a "Sphinx-like impenetrability," is eager to seize Palestine, and his name = 666. Ten-Horn confederacy = England, France, Spain, Italy, Austria, Tripoli, Greece, Egypt, Syria, Turkey. "ABSOLUTELY CERTAIN" Napoleon III will conquer England. He will ally with Confederacy against North (he has already landed forces in Mexico), then conquer the continent. Both yearday and literal-day fulfillment of 2,520: from 724 B.C. (+ 75) to 1872, and 648 B.C. to 1871; also the future Tribulation (seven years, plus 75 days). 2,300 = 456–7 B.C. and 428 B.C. to 1843–4 and 1871. 1,335, 1,290, 1,260 = 534–7 A.D. to 1794–7, 1844–7, 1872. Rapture two years after treaty; five years from End. Great Tribulation 3½ years, begins when Satan cast down with demons after war in heaven. Saints flee to remote region of U.S. Millennium population to increase to 200 billion, ruled over by raptured (and returned) saints. New Jerusalem suspended over Earth.

352. ____. *Forty Prophetic Wonders from Daniel to Revelation: Some Already Fulfilled, Some in Process of Fulfillment, and Others Yet Unfilled.* 1918 [1866]. Cleveland: Union Gospel.

11th ed. 1903; lxii, 531 p. illus.

353. ____. *Future Wonders of Prophecy.* 1894 [1866]. lxiii, 543 p. Appendix VII added 1895. 1894 ed. subtitled *Between 1896 and April 23, 1908: As Foreshown in the Prophecies of Daniel and Revelation.*

The end of the Age is set for April 23, 1908. Forty wonders included the defeat of Germany by France ten years before End. The ten-Horn Beast is equated with England, France, Italy, Austria, Greece, Egypt, Turkey, Bulgaria. A Napoleon will arise, become King of Syria

(=North), make 7-year treaty with Jews. Translation of believers to heaven (Second Advent of the Air: dead saints plus 144,000 living)= 2:30-3:00 PM March 12, 1903. Napoleon vs. Egypt in three wars; then becomes Antichrist (1902-3). White Horse rider represents Gospel. Trumpets are interpreted literally, begin in 1903. Michael vs. Satan war in heavens: late 1903-04. Christians increasingly persecuted, flee to wilderness. Baxter assigns dates to all woes, plagues, disasters, seals, trumpets. 666=Mark. Armageddon: 1908, at End. Many engravings illustrating all episodes of Tribulation and End. 200,000,000 lion-headed demon horses, ridden by demons, kill a third of mankind in 1906.

354. _____. *Coming Wonders Expected Between 1867 and 1875: Explaining the Future Literal Fulfilment of the Seals, Trumpets, Vials, and other Prophecies of Revelation and Daniel, within the Final Seven Years....* 1867 [1866]. Philadelphia: J.B. Lippincott. xv, 447 p. plates, illus.

355. _____. *Forty Coming Wonders: During the Final 10 or 12 Years Preceding the End of this Age, in Fulfilment of the Prophecies of Daniel and Revelation.* 5th ed. enl. London: Christian Herald Office. By the "Editor of the Christian Herald." lxiv, 527 p. illus.

356. _____. *Forty Future Wonders of Scripture Prophecy.* 1930 [1923]. 16th ed. (Christian Herald: London).

357. Baxter, Robert. *Narrative of Facts, Characterizing the Supernatural Manifestations in Members of Mr. Irving's Congregation...* 1833. London: J Nisbet. ix, 155 p.

Baxter was follower of Irving, then returned to post-trib belief.

358. Beet, Joseph Agar. *The Last Things.* 1905 [1897] London: Hodder and Stoughton. xxii, 326 p. bibl. refs, index.

Also 1913 abridged ed.

Methodist. Removed from post in England for these views, but claims they are orthodox Wesleyan. Bodily Coming, preceded by new and terrible form of evil. Post-mill: coming years will see "still further progress" of Gospel's victorious war, and advance of its Kingdom. But evil will still be in power at Second Coming. Immediate Final Judgment; wicked not eternally punished(?). End not real soon, as Gospel is progressing now, and prophesied "new" evil hasn't arisen. Heavenly Kingdom set up "suddenly" on ruins of sinful earthly life. Parousia = Day of Lord = Revelation (appearing) = Second Coming. Continued and continuing progress of Gospel until future unleashing of great Evil —"terrible revolt." Millennium *precedes* this Evil (a prior, divine intervention). Denies pre-mill Coming because of its "insuperable difficulties." Second Coming thus not soon, as all this must be precede it. Book also has much on "Doom of the Wicked": whether soul is immortal and wicked are eternally punished (says no proof in Bible).

359. Begg, J[ames] A. *A Connected View of Some of the Scriptural Evidence of the Redeemer's Speedy Personal Return, and Reign on Earth with His Glorified Saints, During the Millennium: Israel's Restoration to Palestine, and the Destruction of Anti-Christian Nations.* 1830. 2nd ed., enl. London: J. Nisbet. 254 p.

360. Berg, Joseph F[rederick]. *Prophecy and the Times; or, England and Armageddon.* 1856 Philadelphia: Higgins & Perkinpine. 200 p. [also discussed in following work].

Lives in Philadelphia. Nations now "mustering for the fierce conflict at Armageddon." Christ to remain in Heaven, with *spiritual* reign (denies pre-mill). Gog and Magog again after Millennium for final rebellion. Beast = Papal Rome. 1866-70: 1,260 Years expire, destruction of Papacy, "arch-enemy of Christ"; start of Christian Age. Drying up of Euphrates = decline of Islam. Horns = 10-Kingdoms, now including Britain, France, Sardinia, Spain; opposed by Russia. Crimean War is preliminary to Armageddon (same forces involved). Austria, Prussia, Holland, Belgium, Naples, Portugal will join later. Siege of Sebastopol in Crimea is start of Armageddon. 6th Seal = occurring now. Two Witnesses will lie unburied in England. France = Scarlet Beast ridden by Woman.

361. ____. *The Stone and the Image, or, The American Republic, the Bane and Ruin of Despotism; An Exposition of the Fifth Kingdom of Daniel's Prophecy, and of the Great Wonder in Heaven of the Apocalypse.* 1856. Philadelphia: Higgins & Perkinpine.

Berg: Pastor of 2nd Reformed Protestant Dutch Church, Philadelphia. Rejects pre-mill. Biblical prophecies not intended to be understood till fulfillment at hand. U.S. is "hope of the world," land of true religion founded by believers fleeing false religion. U.S. is the "stone" which breaks the "image" (statue) of Daniel 11:44–5. Four Empires: Babylonia; Medo-Persia; Graeco-Macedonia; Roman. Clay: maybe the suspicious Roman/Papal matrimonial political alliances, or barbarian admixture into Rome. Slavery: Japhetic race must govern over nations, but abuses of slavery must be answered. Popery is antichristian (Beast = Rome), Mormonism a "foul excrescence," spiritualism demonic. Armageddon: 6th and 7th Vials, just prior to Millennium. English-French alliance fatal; England to undergo Tribulation, where greatest persecution will occur. 1,260 days = domination of Rome — ends 1870, when Papal apostasy will be destroyed. France = Scarlet Beast of Rev. 16. French-English alliance will lead to 10-Nation confederacy. Signs in Heaven not literal; refer to the "political firmament." Child born to woman = U.S. republic (Rev. 12:1–6) = A.D. 1620. "War in Heaven" is final pre-mill conflict, fought in U.S. These events "cannot…be very far distant." Papal Antichrist to perform "hellish miracles" to deceive world. Gathering of Armageddon distinct from actual last pre-mill battle. Current French mobilization may be first stages of Armageddon. Millennium may begin A.D. 2000 (World Week scheme): a "providential and gracious administration in contradistinction to the miraculous manifestation" of pre-mill belief. U.S. will progress toward and inaugurate Millennium. Includes Appendix with excerpts of Ethan Smith (1814).

362. Berick, Francis H. *The Fulfilment of Prophecy: or, a Prophetic History of the World; Including a Few Suggestions on the Probable Termini of the Chronological Periods.* 1852. Lowell [MA]: S.J. Varney. 137 p.

363. ____ [supposed author]. *Gog and Magog: or, An Exposition of Ezekiel 38 and 39.* 1854. Lowell [MA]: S.J. Varney. 28 p.

364. ____. *The Grand Crisis in Human Affairs: The Lord Soon to Come.* 1854. Lowell, MA: Stereotyped by J.E. Farwell. 383 p.

365. ____. *An Investigation of the 1,260, 1290 and 1335 Days: as Given by Daniel and John.* N.d. [s.l. : s.n.]

366. *The Biblical History of the World, During the Period of the Time of the End of Gentile Rule Over All the Earth, as Foretold by Daniel, by Christ and by John the Revelator …* [ca. 1870s] Weldon, NC: Harrell. 21 p.

367. Bickersteth, Edward. *The Restoration of the Jews to Their Own Land, in Connection with Their Future Conversion and the Final Blessedness of Our Earth.* 1862. 3rd ed., enl. London: L. Seeley. vi, 415 p. 2nd ed. 1841.

368. ____. *A Practical Guide to the Prophecies.* 1884 [1839]. 7th ed. London: Seeley, Burnside, and Seeley.

Also included in *The Literalist* (1840 1842; Philadelphia: Orrin Rogers), along with other authors on Second Advent and Millennium. Part of this work co-written by T. Birks. Double fulfilment (day-year but also literal-day). 458 B.C. + 490 = A.D. 33. 451 B.C. + 483 = A.D. 33. 70th Week in future. A.D. 533 + 1,260 years = 1793 (beginning of fall of Papacy); A.D. 608 + 1,260 = 1868. 1,335 years to 1868. 420 B.C. + 2,300 years = 1880. Antichrist's 7-year covenant (70th Week) ca. 1862–3; Rapture ca. 1864. End 1869–70.

369. ____. *The Divine Warning to the Church: At This Time, of Our Enemies, Dangers and Duties, and as to Our Future Prospects; with Information Respecting the Diffusion of Infidelity, Lawlessness, and Popery.* London: W. H. Dalton. xxv, [332] p. bibl. refs.

370. Birchmore, John W. *Prophecy Interpreted by History; Including Present*

Events. 1871. New York: E.P. Dutton. 279 p.

Birchmore: At Christ Church, Hyde Park, MA. Historicist interpretation of Daniel and Revelation.

371. Birks, Thomas Rawson. *First Elements of Sacred Prophecy.* 1843. London: W.E Painter. xi, 438p.

Birks: theologian and professor of moral philosophy at Cambridge Univ.; Bickerteth's son-in-law. "Including an examination of several recent expositions and of the year-day theory." 6,000 years for world. End = 1880. Also wrote *The Scripture Document of Creation,* 1887. Historic pre-mill.

372. _____. *The Four Prophetic Empires and the Kingdom of Messiah.* 1845 [1844]. London: Seeley, Burnside and Seeley. viii, 446 p.

373. _____. *The Two Later Visions of Daniel: Historically Explained.* 1846. London: Seeley, Burnside and Seeley. xii, 390 p.

374. _____. *The Mystery of Providence: or The Prophetic History of the Decline and Fall of the Roman Empire.* 1848. London: Nisbet. xvi, 452 p.

Rev. VIII–IX

375. _____. *Outlines of Unfulfilled Prophecy, Being an Inquiry into the Scripture Testimony Respecting the "Good Things to Come."* 1854. London: Seeleys. viii, 378 p.

376. _____. *Thoughts on the Time and Seasons of Sacred Chronology.* 1880. London: Hodder & Stoughton. xii, 130 p.

Early Christians weren't allowed to know the time of End, but *we* can. "'Such knowledge,' our Lord implies, 'may hereafter be given to others, but it is not for you.'" For us, clear signs that Second Coming is at hand.

377. Bishop, S. W. *The Time Appointed.* 1860. [United States: s.n.] 24 p.

1,290 Years ends in 1815. 45 more (1,335 Years) ends in 1860, "which year will bring the awful day of doom..."

378. Blackstone, William Eugene. *Jesus Is Coming.* c. 1932 [1878] (3rd rev. ed.) New York: Fleming H. Revell. 252 p. illus bibl refs, Scripture index. 1989 up-

dated ed. Kregel. 1908 ed. reprint by Garland in *The Premillennial Second Coming.*

Widely read. Reissue sent to hundreds of thousands of religious leaders. Blackstone: Methodist Episcopal; strong Zionist supporter. Dispensationalist pre-trib. Heavily footnoted with scriptural citations and explanations. Literal fulfillment of prophecy. Seven arguments for pre-mill Second Coming; distinction between Rapture and Revelation (at Second Coming), Church and Kingdom. Time of Gentiles: 2,520 "days" (years) = 606 B.C. to 1915, or 595 B.C. to 1927, or 587 B.C. to 1935. If 1915 or '16, then years til 1934 or '35 will include Ten-King confederation, Antichrist, Restoration of Israel. Six thousand years, then the Millennium — 7,000-year "Plan of the Aions." Rapture: principal event, "great hope" of believers. Can't predict date, but must be expectant, vigilant, as it is "any moment" and "imminent." World getting worse, won't be converted. Tribulation includes 70th Week, but probably will last *more* than seven years. Unparalleled wickedness, sorrow. Some (especially from remnant Israel) saved during Tribulation. 12 Tribes all return. Antichrist = 666 Beast, arises during Tribulation. Covenant with returned Israel. Assisted by False Prophet. Antichrist destroyed by Christ before Millennium. Believers resurrected first; Tribulation Saints at start of Millennium; others after Millennium. "Last Days" = Millennium = "Kingdom." Personal reign. End of Millennium — Gog and Magog revolt.

379. _____. *The Millennium: A Discussion of the Question, "Do the Scriptures Teach That There Is to Be a Millennium?" Affirmative.* 1918 [1904]. Chicago: Fleming H. Revell. 64 p . SEE ALSO 1910–1970.

380. Bliss, Sylvester. *An Exposition of the Twenty-Fourth of Matthew: in Which It Is Shown to be an Historical Prophecy, Extending to the End of Time and Literally Fulfilled.* [ca. 1860?]. Boston: Joshua V. Himes. 69 p.

381. _____. *Sacred Chronology.* 1887 [ca 1860?]. Oakland, CA: Pacific Press. 40 p. index.

In same vol: *The Peopling of the*

Earth, by Alonzo T. Jones (pp 245–299). Reprinted 1995 by Leaves-Of-Autumn. Earth's 6,000 years up ca. 1873.

382. Bogie, Brackenbury Dickson. *The Crisis Is Come.* 1843 [1839]. Edinburgh. vi, 258 p.

"The crisis of the Church of Scotland; the apostasy in the Church of England; and the fall of the Church of Rome." Great changes of the last thirty and especially the last six years: "The next generation will behold more wonderful things, and may see the commencement of the thousand years."

383. Bonar, Horatius. *The Coming and Kingdom of the Lord Jesus Christ: Being an Examination of the Work of the Rev. D. Brown on the Second Coming of the Lord.* 1849. Kelso: J. Rutherford. xviii, 462 p. index.

Historic pre-mill (post-trib). Response to David Brown's *Christ's Second Coming* (post-mill).

384. Booth, A.E. *Chart of the Ages.* 1896. New York: Loizeaux Bros.—Bible Truth Depot. 8 p. illus.

See also Daniel, Roger P. (1980s?), which is based on Booth.

385. Boudinot, Elias. *The Second Advent, or Coming of the Messiah in Glory: Shown to Be a Scripture Doctrine, and Taught by Divine Revelation from the Beginning of the World.* 1815. Trenton, NJ: Fenton & Hutchinson. xix, 578 p.

Also wrote *The Age of Revelation: or, The Age of Reason Shewn to Be an Age of Infidelity* (against Thomas Paine).

386. Bradshaw, Wesley. *Washington's Vision.* 1864 [1859]. Philadelphia: C.W. Alexander. 11–26 p. ill.

387. Brewer, S[idney]. S. *The Last Day Tokens.* 21st ed. 1840s. Yarmouth, ME: Scriptural Publication Society. 32, 96, 88 p. illus.

388. _____. *The Laodicean Church: Or, the Judgment Age.* 1854. Concord, NH. 48 P.

389. _____. *The Wine Cup of God's Wrath.* 1854. Concord, NH: Printed by O. Hart. 24 p.

The world now feverishly preparing for war.

390. _____. *The Time at Hand: or, Evidences that the Coming of Our Lord Jesus Christ Will Occur the Present Year, 1867.* 1867. Newark, NJ: Herald of Bridegroom. 72 p.

391. _____. *Evangels of the Coming One; or, Divine Utterances and Their Accomplishment, Showing Conclusively that the End of This World Is Specially Nigh.* 1870. Concord, NH: C. W. Sargent. 40 p.

392. _____. *Ancient and Modern Gog and Magog.* 1884. Boston: Advent Christian Publication Soc. 84 p.

Advent Christian Church

393. Brewster, James Colin. *An Address to the Church of Christ and Latter Day Saints.* 1848. Springfield, IL. 24 p.

Mormon prophecies on End of World

394. Brighouse, James. *The Voice of the Seventh Angel!: The Unfolding of the Mystery of God!: The End of Time!: Described in a Series of Several Hundred Questions and Answers....* 1892 [1887]. Salt Lake City: s.n. 267 p.

"Unorthodox" Mormon. 5 parts: parts 2–5 signed (written) by Brighouse and Henry I. Doremus.

395. Brookes, James H[all]. *Maranatha: or, The Lord Cometh.* 1870. (10th ed. 1889 Revell) 3rd ed. 1874; St. Louis: E. Bredell; 545 p.

Brookes: Presbyterian pastor, St. Louis; prominent in Niagara conferences. Strong pre-mill, promoted futurist interpretation and "any moment" Rapture (prophetic clock stopped till 70th Week begins); two-stage Second Coming. 70 Weeks really "heptads." 69 Weeks = 453 B.C. (Artaxerxes' decree to rebuild Jerusalem) to A.D. 29, then "cut off" and interrupted by great "Parenthesis." In periodical *The Truth* said that Christians should "keep aloof from the whole defiling scene" of reform. No Bible passages support pre-mill Coming; all early Christians were millenarians. Great Tribulation ahead, not worldly triumph of Christianity. Even "important discoveries and wonderful inventions" of science can't halt humanity's downfall. True Christianity beleaguered, on the retreat. Post-mill belief makes Coming less urgent, imminent. Vigorous defense of personal pre-mill Second Coming. Christ comes *for* saints (secret Rapture), then *with* saints (Second Coming). Shout and Last Trumpet heard only by believers. 1 Corinthians: "Anathema maranatha" — if not saved by Second Coming, then cursed. Bible's meaning must be accessible, not hidden. "This generation" = Jewish/Hebrew race; or, when prophecies *begin* to be fulfilled. Resolute insistence on literal interpretation (including Six Day creation). Israel must return. But Jews will return only after treaty with Antichrist, Prince of revived 10-Nation Roman Empire. Antichrist demands he be worshipped as divine: mid-70th Week. "Cruel persecution of the godly remnant of the Jews by the Antichrist." Separate resurrections of just and unjust, at Coming, and end of Millennium.

396. Brooks, Cyrus E. *The End Near; and On the Brink.* 1897. Malvern Link, England: "The Faith" Press. 29 p.

Pre-mill. Only 2% of world population Christian believers. End of Gospel Age probably 1896–97; certainly by 1923. Earth's allotted 6,000 years either already expired or just about up: now Year 6027 by Clinton's chronology (6,000 years ends 1872), and six years to go by Ussher's (adjusted by 93 years). Antichrist regimes of Catholic Papacy and Islamic Ottomans in decay.

397. Brooks, Joshua William ("Abdiel" pseudonym) *Essays on the Advent and Kingdom of Christ and the Events Connected Therewith.* 1843 [1840]. 4th enl. ed. London: Simpkin, Marshall. 356 p.

398. "Brother Sailor." *Breakers Ahead! A Warning from the Faithful Pilot to Keep a Good Look-Out for Danger at the Close of the Voyage.* 1843. Boston: J.V. Himes. 18 p. illus.

The 1,260 Years now completed. Nautical conceit. Millerite Adventist.

399. Brown, A. *London, the Babylon of the Apocalypse.* 1849. Fitchburg, MA: Printed by W.J. Merriam. 36 p.

The Papacy is the "Abomination," but London is "Babylon": the great city and commercial capital described in Revelation.

400. Brown, Alexander. *The Great Day of the Lord: A Survey of New Testament Teaching on Christ's Coming in His Kingdom, the Resurrection, and the Judgement of the Living and the Dead.* 1894 [1890]. London: Elliot Stock. xiv, 403 p. bibl. indexes.

Says that the Second Coming, "whatever it may mean," is "invariably" stated to be near. Spiritual coming. No catastrophe to physical world. No Rapture.

401. Brown, David. *Christ's Second Coming: Will It Be Pre-Millennial?* 1846. Edinburgh: John Johnstone. vi, 368 p. indexes. 1990 reprint ed. of 1882 ed. (Edmonton, Canada: Still Waters Revival Books; ed. by K. Gentry).

Brown: Scottish Presbyterian; president Free Church College. Post-mill.

402. _____. *The Apocalypse.* 1891.

403. Brown, John A. *The Even-Tide; or, Last Triumph of the Blessed and Only Potentate... Being a Development of the Mysteries of Daniel and St. John, and of the Renovated Kingdom of Israel.* 1823. 2 vols. London: Offer [Offord?].

2,520 Years from 604 B.C. (fall of Judah, start of Gentile rule) to A.D. 1917. Nebuchadnezzar's madness as prophetic key. Brown's arguments were employed by Russell and the Jehovah's Witnesses.

404. Brown, M[arvin] H. *The Sure Word of Prophecy: A Study of the Book of Daniel.* 1979 [1895]. Payson, AZ: Leaves-of-Autumn. 96 p. illus.

405. Browne, J.H. *The Age in Which We Are Living and the Time of the End.* 1905. Bardstown, KY: Kentucky Standard Printing. unpaged pamphl.

406. Bryant, Alfred. *Millennarian Views; With Reasons for Receiving Them, to Which is Added a Discourse on the Fact and Nature of the Resurrection.* 1852 New York: M.W. Dodd. 252 p.

Pastor of Presbyterian Church, Niles, MI. 1,260 years + 606 A.D. = 1866. Gog = Russia.

407. Buck, Charles. *A Theological Dictionary.* 1800. [Philadelphia?] 631 p.

Many subsequent editions; used by most Protestants throughout first half of 19th century. Millennium is near.

408. Buck, Daniel Dana. *Our Lord's Great Prophecy and Its Parallels Throughout the Bible, Harmonized and Expounded ... with a Particular Examination of the Principal Passages Relating to the Second Coming of Christ, the End of the World, the New Creation, the Millennium, the Resurrection, the Judgment, the Conversion and Restoration of the Jews.* 1857 [1856]. Nashville: Graves, Marks. xvi, 472 p.

409. Buck, James A. *The Saviour's Second Coming. A Great Mystery of Babylon Unravelled. The Great Judgment Day at Hand...* 1884. Belleville, Ontario: 27 p.

Poetry and prose.

410. Bullinger, Ethelbert. *The Lord's Day: (Rev. I 10): Is It a Day of the Week? Or, the Day of the Lord?* 1907. London: Spottiswoode. iv, 35 p. bibl. refs.

Historicist; pre-trib. Interprets "firstfruits" (1 Cor. 15:23) as pre-trib Rapture prior to general post-trib "harvest." SEE ALSO 1910–1970.

411. Burdick, Elias. *An Essay on the Millennium: In Which the Theory is Built Upon Plain Revelation — a Long Millennium Before the Second Advent.* 1852. Norwich, NY: J. D. Lawyer. [6]-36 p.

Post-mill. Seventh Day Baptist. Millennium will last 365,000 years.

412. Burgh, William. *The Apocalypse Unfilled, or, An Exposition of Revelation...* 1833. 2nd ed. Dublin: Richard M. Tims. iv, 265 p. 5th ed. 1839; 432 p; titled *An Exposition of the Book of Revelation.*

Antichrist will make 7-year covenant with Jews, rebuild the Temple, then set up Abomination of Desolation and kill all who resist his worship.

413. _____. *Lectures on the Second Advent of Our Lord Jesus Christ...* 1841. 3rd ed. Dublin: R.M. Tims. vii, 314 p.

414. Burridge, J.H. *God's Prophetic Plan: A Comprehensive View of God's Dealing with Man from Creation to the New Heavens and New Earth.* 1909. St. Louis: Fred. Hammond. xxix, 311 p. illus.

415. _____. *The Best Reform: The Perfect Law of Liberty for One Thousand Years.* 1831. [London?]: Causton. 8 p.

416. _____. *The Coming of Christ: What Is It? Will All or Only Part Be Caught Up? Will or Will Not the Church Pass Through the Great Tribulation??* n.d. Glasgow: Pickering & Inglis. 136 p. illus.

417. Burton, Alfred H. *The Future of Europe: Politically and Religiously, in the Light of Holy Scripture; and, Russia's Destiny in the Light of Prophecy.* 1967 [1915]. 7th ed. Oak Park, IL: Bible Truth. 106 p. [orig 1896?].

418. Burwell, Adam Hood. *A Voice of Warning and Instruction Concerning the Signs of the Time, and the Coming of the Son of Man, to Judge the Nations, and Restore All Things.* 1835. Kingston, Canada. Irvingite. 453 B.C. + 2,300 = 1847.

419. Bush, George. *A Treatise on the Millennium in Which the Prevailing Theories on that Subject are Carefully Examined, and the True Scriptural Doctrine Attempted to be Elicited and Established.* 1832. New York: J.&J. Harper. xv, 277 p. 2nd edition titled *The Millennium and the Apocalypse.*

Bush: professor of Hebrew at NYU. Post-mill. Critical of dispensationalism and Jewish 6,000 year scheme. Prophetic fulfillment of "this generation" began with destruction of Jerusalem A.D. 70; Millennium is already past. Gog-Magog = Turks.

420. _____. *The Millennium of the Apocalypse.* 1842. Salem: Jewett. 2nd edition of earlier work with different title.

"The Millennium, strictly so called, is PAST..."

421. _____. *Valley of Vision: or The Dry Bones of Israel Revived.* 1844. New York: Saxton & Miles. vii, 60 p. Plate, map. "An attempted proof, from Ezekiel, chap. xxxvii, 1-14, of the restoration and conversion of the Jews."

Jews to abandon Talmud and convert. King of North: originally Babylon, then Medes, then (in future) Russia.

422. Cachemaille, E[rnest] P. *Daniel's Prophecies Now Being Fulfilled.* 1888. London: Hodder and Stoughton. vi, 133 p. SEE ALSO 1910–1970.

423. Cairns, Adam. *The Second Woe.* 1854 [1852]. Glasgow: J. Keith.

Refutes Elliott. Bound with Alexander MacLeod's *Principle Prophecies of the Revelation.*

424. Caldwell, John R. *Things to Come: Being a Short Outline of the Great Events of the Events of Prophecy.* N.d. [ca. 1900?]. 10th ed. Glasgow: Pickering & Inglis. 112 p.

425. Campbell, Alexander. *Millennial Harbinger* vol. 1. 1830. Bethany, VA, index.

Campbell: revivalist; founded Disciples of Christ (Campbellite) Church. Dedicated to propagating Millennium; also urges emancipation of slaves. Imminent pre-millennial Second Coming and literal earthly Millennium. Mostly written by Campbell but contributions by Walter Scott and others.

426. _____. *Popular Lectures and Addresses.* 1863. Philadelphia: James Challen. 647 p.

427. Carter, R[ussell] Kelso. *Alpha and Omega: or the Birth and Death of the World: The Science of the Creation, the Coming Crisis, and the Golden Age.* 1894. San Francisco: O.H. Elliott. 613 p. illus.

Carter: military school teacher, hymn-writer; Methodist Holiness member. Advocates Isaac Newton Vail's Water Canopy Theory as literal interpretation of Genesis — Flood waters came from immense ring of water formerly suspended above Earth's atmosphere — and similarly attempts "literal" interpretation of Revelation and the End. Earth will undergo catastrophic cosmic collisions and geophysical convulsions at Second Coming. The Canopy will be restored at the Millennium, though at a lower altitude than before, since it need last only a thousand years (not the 1,656 years from Creation to the Flood of the previous Canopy). The Canopy will make Earth an Edenic paradise once again during the Millennium.

428. Cary, Clement C. *The Second Coming of Christ: Showing Pre-Millenarianism to be Unscriptural and Unreasonable.* 1902. Atlanta: Doctor Blosser. 138 p.

Cary: Methodist Episcopal Church, Southern; supporter of Holiness doctrine (second sanctification), but opposes premillennialism, which many Holiness Wesleyans advocate. Claims Methodist doctrine and tradition is contrary to pre-mill

(though interpretations vary). Notes that Calvinists are especially susceptible to pre-millennialism because of doctrine of Elect. Insists Christ comes only at End, with single resurrection of all. Agrees with Adam Clarke on danger of basing literalist doctrines on figurative passages. Reign of saints: living Christians, spiritual reign of Christ. World to be destroyed by fire at Second Coming = Day of Judgment = Last Day. Millennium inaugurated gradually, by Gospel advances, not personal reign of Christ. Points to improvements wrought by Christianity in world. Silly to suppose resurrected saints in immortal bodies to live amongst others during Millennium.

429. Cassels, Samuel J. *Christ and Antichrist, or, Jesus of Nazareth Proved to be the Messiah and the Papacy Proved to be the Antichrist Predicted in the Holy Scriptures.* 1846. Philadelphia: Presbyterian Board of Publication. 348 p.

Antichrist = Catholic Church

430. Chamberlain, Walter. *The National Restoration and Conversion of the Twelve Tribes of Israel; or, Notes on Some Prophecies Believed to Relate to Those Two Great Events; and Intended to Show that the Conversion will Take Place After the Restoration; and that the Occasion of It has Been Uniformly Predicted.* 1854. London: Wertheim and Macintosh. xx, 578 p.

Tarshish = England. Also wrote *The Time of the End.* [1880s] and *Isaiah's Call to England.*

431. Charles, Benjamin H. *Lectures on Prophecy: An Exposition of Certain Scriptures with Reference to the History and End of the Papacy; the Restoration of the Jews to Palestine, Their Repentance and Enlargement Under the Reign of the Son of David; and the New State in the Millennium.* 1897. New York: Fleming H. Revell 320 p.

Pre-mill. Tribulation, then Second Coming, then Millennium, then Third calamity (Flood was first, Tribulation second). 6,000 years creation to end. Papacy = Little Horn (Beast). Mystical Babylon (Harlot) = Rome 1848–1870 (when temporal power lost). Vials 1–6 = French Revolution, Napoleonic Wars, 1848 revolutions. Unclean frogs of Revelation 16:13 = spiritualism, Communistic anarchism, Mormonism. Great increase in armed forces as sign of imminent Tribulation. Two Witnesses = Christian ministry and Gospel (1,260 "days" really years). Jews to be restored to Israel, will repent and convert after Tribulation. Gog, Rosh = Russia; will invade Israel, last battle near Jerusalem at Jehoshaphat Valley. Now in Last Days: Gospel already preached to almost all nations; Pope humiliated. 1,260 years from 533 and 610 to 1793 (First Vial) and 1870 (Last). Jewish Captivity: 2,520 Years from 606 B.C. to 1914 (with calendar correction) = Second Coming, or thereabouts. "Millennium" will actually last 360,000 years.

432. Chater, E[dward] H. *The Coming and Reign of Our Lord Jesus Christ.* 1963 [1880]. Orange, CA: Ralph E. Welch Foundation. 127 p.

433. Clarke, Adam. *The Duration of the Earth.* 1859 [1820]. New York: H.L. Hastings.

6,000 years for the world — less than 150 to go. End Times for 20th century; Islam to wither, Millennium to start before 1950. Suggested Millennium to last 365,000 years. A.D. 612 + 1,335 = 1947. Alexander's invasion of Holy Land (332 B.C.?) + 2,300 = 1966–7 (cleansing of the Sanctuary).

434. Clarke, J[ohn] A[lgernon]. *What the Prophets Foretold: A Compendium of Scripture Prediction, with Special Reference to the Duration and Doom of the Papal Antichrist, the Judgments of the Great Day of God Almighty, and the Dawn of Millennial Glory.* 1862. London: Nisbet. viii, 304 p. scripture index, foldout chart.

Jews falsified Creation to 3760 B.C. to keep Jews "in expectation of the Messiah at least for 240 years after that date" (of First Coming). 70 Weeks from 7th year of Artaxerxes to A.D. 33. Historicist, but literal interpretation of remaining (future) events. Papal Rome: 1,260 year reign (but gradual beginning and end). 1,260 year periods end 1793, 1848, 1867, 1869 — all blows to Papacy. 10-Horns: Huns, Ostrogoths, Visigoths, Franks, Vandals,

Sueves and Alans, Burgundians, Heruli and Turingi, Saxons and Angles, Lombards. Later other combinations of 10 nations also. Little Horn = Papal Rome. Four Horsemen refers to Jews vs. Romans. Revelation not in chronological order. Seals, trumpets, etc.= fall of ancient Rome, Catholic atrocities. Currently awaiting 7th vial (or undergoing 5th), so End is imminent. Rome probably will be destroyed by violent earthquakes, volcanoes. Catholic nations = Beast; Papacy = False Prophet. Restoration of Jews, Armageddon to occur, final slaughter in Valley of Jehoshaphat. Gog = Russia. Millennium: literal, or nearly so. "Gog and Magog" of final post-mill war symbolic of all anti-Christians. Second Coming may be pre- or post-mill. New Heaven and Earth follows "day of doom" (Judgment).

435. Clarke, John Edward. *Dissertation on the Dragon, Beast, and False Prophet, of the Apocalypse: In Which the Number 666 is Satisfactorily Explained.* 1814. London: author. viii, 400 p.

436. Cleveland, J.J. *The Prophetic Dates: Or the Days, Years, Times, and other Epochs Spoken of by the Prophets, Which Point Out the Rise and Fall of Kingdoms and Churches, the Coming of Christ, the End of the World, and the Resurrection.* 1883. San Franciso: J.B. Hill. 83 p.

437. *The Close of the Millennium: The Present War Clearly Explained as Being the Battle of "That Great Day of God Almighty" and the Coming of Our Lord and Saviour Jesus Christ at Armageddon.* 1855. London: Houlston and Stoneman, Coultas. 35 p.

The Crimean War.

438. Cochran, Mary. *The Signs of the Times!* 1838. Rochester, NY: Hackstaff, Printer. Broadside.

Poem describing portents in sky of imminent end of world.

439. Coffin, William H. *The Millennium of the Church, to Come Before the End of Time: Being an Examination of such Prophecies as are Supposed to Related to the End of Time.* 1843. Baltimore: Parsons and Preston. 85 p. refutation of Millerism.

440. Cogswell, William. *The*

Harbinger of the Millenium. 1833. Boston: Pierce and Parker. 362 p.

441. Cohn, Joseph Hoffman. *Will the Church Escape the Tribulation?* 1900. Englewood Cliffs, NJ: American Board of Missions to the Jews. 31 p.

Also wrote *The Man from Petra* (1961; Charlotte: Chosen People Ministries).

442. Coleridge, Henry James. 1894. *The Return of the King: Discourses on the Latter Days*. New ed. London: Burns and Oates. xvi, 420 p. bibl. refs.

443. Collin de Plancy, Jacques Albin Simon. 1871. *La Fin des Temps confirmer par des Prophéties authentiques nouvelle recuilles*. Paris: H. Plon. 211 p. illus.

444. Collom, John. *The Prophetic Numbers of Daniel and the Revelation: An Identification of the Times and Events Referred to in Prophecy; Together with Coincident Facts Respecting the Great Pyramid of Egypt and the Approaching Planetary Perihelia*. 1880. Chicago: Wilson & Jones. 467 p. Chronological index.

Includes advertisement for *Star Prophecies Concerning Coming Disasters on the Earth from 1881 to 1885* (Knapp).

445. *The Coming Crisis: How to Meet It*. 1968 [1853]. 3rd ed. rev. Salt Lake City: Truth Publishing. 24 p.

Reprinted from 1853 *Millennial Star*.

446. *The Coming Struggle Among the Nations of the Earth: or The Political Events of the Next Fifteen Years Described in Accordance with Prophecies in Ezekiel, Daniel and the Apocalypse*. 1853. New York: John Moffet. 32 p.

Anglo-Saxon race exempted from coming doom of other nations. England not a member of 10-Horn confederacy. 9th and 10th horns added only in 1820 and 1830. Two Witnesses = civil and religious democracy. 1,260 Years ends 1848 and 1791. 6th and 7th Vials occur first half 19th century. Austria, Turkey, Rome all doomed to fall. Russia conquers Turkey, France defeats Austria. Magog and Gomer = Germany and France. Britain not involved in these wars; later leads world into Millennium with U.S. and Australia. Tarshish = British East India Co. Final

Battle = Armageddon: in Israel, Russians and continental Europe armies vs. England and U.S. But God Himself destroys Russian forces. Anglo-Saxons destined to remain "leading people...unrivalled in intellectual greatness." Jews will be "*officially* greater" but intellectually inferior.

447. *The Coming Whirlwind Among the Nations of the Earth: Daniel's Iron Kingdom, and "Time of the End."* 1868. London: Houlston & Wright. 52 p.

448. *The Computation of 666*. 1891 London: James Nisbet. xiv, 398 p. illus.

The coming Antichrist and his overthrow by God, written by "Two Servants of God"

449. *Conditions of Society and Its Only Hope, in Obeying the Everlasting Gospel, as Now Developing Among Believers in Christ's Second Appearing*. 1847. Union Village, OH: Day-Star. 120 p.

Shaker.

450. Congleton, Lord. *The Rapture of the Church: or, Are Any Events To Be Expected Before the Rapture of the Church?* 1853 London: Campbell, Holborn. 24 p.

Bound with *The Apocalypse Popularly Explained*. Church to be "caught up." "*Now* is the time for the rapture of the Church." Any-moment Rapture: no events still left unfulfilled. Rapture includes both dead and living. Later, Millennium, then New Heaven and Earth.

451. Connelly, William Montague. *The Four Beasts: An Identification of Antichrist, that Fixes the Time of the End*. 1875. Baltimore: s.n. vi, 178 p.

452. Cook, J. B. (John B.). *A Solemn Appeal to Ministers and Churches, Especially to Those of the Baptist Denomination, Relative to the Speedy Coming of Christ*. 1843. Boston: Joshua V. Himes. 62 p.

Millerite Adventist. A.D. 508 + 1,335 Years = 1843.

453. Cotton, John Frederick. *The Light-Ship*. 1860. Boston: [s.n.]. 59 p. "Published for the benefit of seamen."

454. Couch, J[ohn]. *A Prophetic Echo*. 1874. Boston: Advent Christian Publishing Society 18 p.

Advent Christian. King of South =

Egypt. King of North = Syria. Turks loom large in biblical End Times prophecy.

455. _____. *The End at Hand.* 1898. Boston: Advent Christian Publication Society. 23 p.

456. _____. *The Two-Horned Beast.* Boston: Advent Christian Pub. 11 p.

Two horns: Roman Catholic Church and Eastern Orthodox Church (dominated by Russia).

457. Cowles, Henry. *Ezekiel and Daniel with Notes, Critical, Explanatory, and Practical.* 1875. New York: D. Appleton.

Oberlin College minister. Russia = Gog.

458. Crandall, A. L. *A Brief Explanation of the Book of Revelations: In Chronological Order.* 1841. Troy, NY: James M. Stevenson. 106 p.

A.D. 563 + 1,260 = 1793. Antichrist = Papacy. Two Witnesses = Bible and true Christianity ("killed" 1793–97, but revived). 1,335 and 2,300 years both end 1868: the Millennium

459. Croly, George. *Apocalypse of St. John, or, Prophecy of the Rise, Progress, and Fall of the Church of Rome, the Inquisition, the Revolution of France, the Universal War, and the Final Triumph of Christianity.* 1838 [1827]. Philadelphia: E. Littell. xvi, 319 p.

A.D. 533 + 1,260 = 1793. Seals, Trumpets and Vials contemporaneous — Church Age. Two Beasts: Papacy and Dominican Order. "Tenth part" of city destroyed: France.

460. Crosby, Alpheus. *The Second Advent: or, What Do the Scriptures Teach Respecting the Second Coming of Christ, the End of the World, the Resurrection of the Dead, and the General Judgment?* 1850. Boston: Phillips, Sampson. 173 p.

No Third Coming. Second Coming is single event, associated with End, Resurrection, and Judgment. Jesus said Second Coming within lifetime of listeners. Second Coming figurative not literal: already happened. Denies "double sense" theory (both historical and future fulfillments).

461. Cross, Joseph. *Pizgah-Views of the Promised Inheritance.* 1856. New York:

Carlton & Phillips; Nashville: Stephenson & Owen. vii, 293 p.

462. *A Cry from the Desert.* 1841. Philadelphia: Orrin Rogers. 54 p. Also included in *The Literalist.*

Debate between "Aquila" and "Philater," who warns of imminent Second Coming and End.

463. Cumming, John. *Signs of the Times.* [Orig 1853, London, 43 p].

1854 enlarged ed. London: Arthur Hall, Virtue. 1859 ed. Philadelphia: Lindsay & Blackiston, 288 p.

Cumming: Scottish minister, popular in U.S. Pre-mill. Said that all prophetic dates "meet and mingle about the year 1864." Two Witnesses = Luther in 1517. Locusts = Moslems.

464. _____. *The End; or, The Proximate Signs of the Close of this Dispensation.* 1855. Boston: J.P. Jewett / Cleveland: O. Jewett, Proctor and Worthington. viii, 356 p.

Popularized idea that Gog = Russia. In Last Days, Russia will "burst forth, overcome all resistance … march to Palestine…perish ultimately … amid tremendous scenes." Proves Magog settled on north coast of Black Sea — Scythians; "Caucasus" = "Gog's fortified place"; then moved north to Russia proper. Meschech, Tubal = Moscow, Tobolsk. Gomer = Cimmeria = Germany. Tarshish = England. Russia and Germany form giant conspiracy (Northern Confederacy) and attack Israel, which is defended by England. Prophecies fulfilled by 1864.

465. _____. *Apocalyptic Sketches: Lectures on the Book of Revelation: Second Series.* 1856. Philadelphia: Lindsay and Blakiston. 532 p. 12th ed. 1852.

Apocalyptic prophecies "about to emerge far sooner than many believe."

466. _____. *The Great Preparation: or, Redemption Draweth Nigh.* 1872 [1860]. New York: G.W. Carleton. 2 vols.

Some editions titled *Redemption Draweth Nigh: or the Great Preparation.*

467. _____. *The Destiny of Nations as Indicated in Prophecy.* 1864. London: Hurst & Blackett. x, 334 p.

Israel to return to Palestine.

468. _____. *The Last Warning Cry: With Reasons for the Hope That Is In Me.* 1867. New York: G.W. Carlton. 327 p.

469. _____. *Soundings of the Last Trumpet.* 1867.

470. _____. *When Shall These Things Be?, or, Signs of the Last Times.* 1868. London: J. Nisbet & Co. 414 p.

471. _____. *The Seventh Vial: or, The Time of Trouble Begun, as Shown in the Great War, the Dethronement of the Pope, and Other Collateral Events.* 1871. New York: G.W. Carleton. 418 p.

All Europe now massing for war. 1870 Franco-Prussian War was preliminary to Armageddon. Papacy nearing its end. Rosh and Gog = Russia. Russia, Germany and Italy emerging as dominant End Time powers.

472. _____. *The Great Consummation: The Millennial Rest; or, The World As It Will Be.* 1872 New York: G.W. Carleton. 307, 295 p.

Pre-mill. Seven dispensations in history: Adamic, Antediluvian, Noachian, Abrahamic, Mosaic, Gospel (present), Millennium (future). Seven dispensations totally 6,000 years correspond to the six days of creation plus the 7th (Sabbath). Accepts vast pre-Adamic ages. 1,260 Years from A.D. 532 to 1792; adding other periods of Daniel gives 1867. Denies he predicted 1867 as definite End; but maybe real End will come when Mahometanism and Papacy both fade away. Discusses whether will be births and deaths in Millennium. Righteous resurrected at Second Coming, unbelievers and wicked at end of Millennium. Earth purified by fire, not destroyed. 1,335 Days ended in 1865; 6,000 years ended in 1862. End signs include decline of Islam and settlement of Jews in Jerusalem. By 1861 Cumming included France as well as Germany with "Gomer." Guessed Jewish persecution would cease by 1867, and Jews would return (American and British Jews already buying up land in Palestine).

473. Cuninghame), William. *A Dissertation on the Seals and Trumpets of the Apocalypse, and the Prophetical Period of 1260 Years.* 1843 [1813]. London: Thomas Cadell. 4th ed. 1843; lxvi, 550 p. bibl refs. Orig. 1813 London: Hatchard; xxiv, 372 p.

474. _____. *A Synopsis of Chronology from the Era of Creation; According to the Septuagint, to the Year 1837.* 1837. London: James Nisbet, Hatchard, L.&.G. Seeley. xxxi, 149 p.

475. _____. *The Septuagint and Hebrew Chronologies: Tried by the Test of their Internal Scientific Evidence....* 1838. London: J. Nisbet. xvii, 122 p.

"Also, on the great periods which terminate in, and mark the year 1838, as the point of time, that sums up and concentrates as in a focus, the chronology of all past ages, and appear likewise to show, the approach of the end." All of prophecy, "every sign, every promise, every testimony,— unite in announcing his [Christ's] approach." Pre-mill. Creation 5478 B.C. (Septuagint). "Chronological forgers" corrupted text of Daniel with 70-week prophecy. Various math cycles (Jubilees, Metonic, etc.) produce dates 1789, 1813, 1846. Chronology of all past ages concentrated and summed up in 7,316th year of world (A.D. 1838), and shows approach of the End. Calculates 58 series from various events which all end in 1838. "Unequivocal chronological indication of the nearness of the end." 1,260 Years: ended 1792; 1,290 Years ended 1822; 1,335 ended 1867. By then, destruction of Fourth Kingdom (Christian Europe), restoration of Jews, invasion and overthrow of God, Second Coming, Rapture. These events must begin immediately in order to finish within the 28 years allowed. Interprets Revelation symbols historically: French Revolution, Napoleon, etc. Pope = apostate Man of Sin.

476. _____. *The Season of the End; Being a View of the Scientific Times of the Year 1840.* 1841 London: Nisbet, Hatchard, Seeley, and Cochran. xvi, 90 p.

Includes refutation of Buckland's Flood-denying geology. Timespans from 62 events and dates which all end at 1840. 457 B.C. + 2,300 = 1843.

477. Cunningham, L[uther] T. *The End of "the King of the North," and the Impending Time of Trouble, and the Near*

Coming of Christ. 1877 [1864]. Boston: Advent Christian Publishing Society 45 p.

478. _____. *Saints Lift Up Your Heads! Sinners Flee from Coming Wrath!* 1880. [England: s.n.] 4 p.

A.D. 533 + 1,260 Years = A.D. 1793. Sun and moon darkened in 1780; stars fell (meteorites) in 1833. The Papacy — the "desolating abomination" — will be overthrown in 1889.

479. _____. *Chronological Dates Adjusted: St. Luke Against Josephus on the Date of the Birth of Christ: The End of the Six Thousand Years Determinable, Consequently the End of This Age*. [1890s] s.l.: s.n. 26 p.

480. Curtis, Chandler. *The Mystery of Iniquity Unveiled: or, Popery Unfolded and Refuted, and Its Destination Shown in the Light of Prophetic Scripture*. 1866. Boston: Crocker & Brewster.

481. Dallas, Alexander R.C. *The Prophecy Upon the Mount: A Practical Consideration of Our Lord's Statement Respecting the Destruction of Jerusalem, His Own Appearing and the End of the Age*. 1843. London : James Nisbet. xiv, 158 p.

482. _____. *Look to Jerusalem: A Scriptural View of the Position of the Jews in the Great Crisis of the World's History*. 1847. 4th ed. London: J. Nisbet. iv, 139 p.

483. Darby, John Nelson. *The Hopes of the Church of God in Connexion with the Destiny of the Jews and the Nations as Revealed in Prophecy*. 1841, London: F. Baisler, 187 p.

Joined new Brethren sect, became leader of stricter faction (Plymouth Brethren) when it fissioned in 1840s and popularized Brethren doctrines in U.S. Darby developed the idea of the secret Rapture and the dispensational interpretation. Prophesied events stopped with the Crucifixion, will restart with Rapture as prophetic clock begins ticking again. There is a great "Parenthesis" or gap between the 69th and 70th of Daniel's 70 Weeks; prophecy is silent on the entire intervening Church Age. Daniel's 1,260 days are literal days: second half of Tribulation. Rejected historicist interpretation of U.S. as "Israel," etc.; assigned prophetic role to Jews — their

return to Israel, rebuilding of Temple, Jewish remnant to embrace Messiah.

484. _____. *What is the World and What is Its End? A Serious Question for Those Who Are Of It*. [1880s]. London: W. Gibling. 15 p.

485. _____. *Lectures on the Second Coming*. 1909. London: G. Morrish. 188 p.

Taught two stage Second Coming: first a secret "catching away" (Rapture) of saints, removing church before Tribulation; then Christ appears visibly with saints to earth to rule thousand years (Millennium).

486. Davidson, James. *Lectures on the Second Coming*. 1909 reprint (London: Marshall, Morgan and Scott). 1913 ed. London: Nisbet, Ballantyne, Hanson, vii, 133 p.

Edinburgh minister.

487. Davis, Timothy. *Anti-Christian Religion Delineated, in a Treatise on the Millennium, or, the Fulfillment of Old Testament Prophecies Completed*. 1807. Leominster, MA: author. 36 p.

Davis: claims to be illiterate and blind. Argues that prophecies have already been fulfilled — otherwise Jesus would be a liar. Symbolic (a-mill) interpretation. New Heaven and Earth are new covenant: Grace replacing Law. Elements melting at End = end of Temple authority. Christ already came: to say he didn't is to heretically downgrade the importance of his First Coming.

488. Davis, William Cummins. *The Millennium; or A Short Sketch on the Rise and Fall of Antichrist, etc*. 1817 [1811]. Frankfort, KY: Beard & Berry.

489. _____. *A Treatise on the Millennium, Shewing...When It Will Commence...How It Will End*. 1827. Yorkville, SC: Advocate Office. 136 p.

Millennium will commence 1847 (or 1843). 453 B.C. + 2,300 = 1847; A.D. 587 + 1,260 = 1847.

490. Dennett, Edward. *The Blessed Hope: Being Papers on the Lord's Coming and Connected Events*. 1879. London: G. Morrish. ii, 130 p. 1987(?) reprint ed.: Orange, CA: Ralph E. Welch Foundation.

Pre-trib, any-moment Rapture. "The

difference between the Lord's coming and His appearing is, that in the former case He comes *for* His saints [the Rapture], and in the latter *with* His saints [the Second Coming]." Saints reside in heaven during the Tribulation, then return with Christ at Second Coming. "There is nothing more certain from the word of God than that the Jews, who are now dispersed throughout the world, will be restored to their own land…"

491. Denny, Edward. *A Prophetical Stream of Time; or, An Outline of God's Dealings with Man, From the Creation to the End of All Things.* 1849. London: J. Nisbet; W.H. Broom. viii, 45, with folded chart.

"Companion to a Chart, Illustrated Throughout with Pictorial Designs." 457 B.C. + 69 Weeks (483 yrs) = A.D. 26. Seven years to A.D. 33, but this last week disallowed because Israel rejected Messiah — deferred to future: "*cancelled and blotted out.*" Forfeited 70th week only resumed after end of "whole period of Israel's dispersion." Ten-Kingdom leader Antichrist received as Messiah by Jews, mighty deceiver, revealed as terrible deceiver and tyrant; destroyed at Armageddon end of 70th Week. Chart orig. ca. 1845.

492. _____. *The Strong Delusion and Lie on the Last Days.* N.d. London: W. H. Broom. 29 p. Reprinted from "The Great Epistle General of John, to the Seven Churches in Asia…".

493. Desprez, Philip S[oulbien] *The Apocalypse Fulfilled: in the Consummation of the Mosaic Economy and the Coming of the Son of Man.* 1861. London: Longman, Green, Longman, and Roberts. 3rd ed. xvi, 511 p.

"An Answer to the *Apocalyptic Sketches* and *The End* by Dr. [John] Cumming."

494. Dimbleby, J[abez] B. *The New Era at Hand: or The Approaching Close of the Great Prophetic Periods…* 1893. 3rd ed. London: Book Society. 24 p. charts.

495. _____. *The Appointed Time: Being Scriptural, Historical, and Astronomical Proofs of the End of the Gentile Times in 1898¼ and the Coming of the Lord.* 1896. 2nd ed. London: E. Nister. viii, 295 p.

1898¼ = 5896½ Anno Mundi (years since Creation), the end of the 2,520 years. Rapture. Tribulation 3½ years, Second Coming, Return of Jews (who then evangelize world), Millennium. Millennium 1928¼ (5926 AM) to 2928¼, then 75 lunar years to end of 7,000 Years. 1898 ends 1,260 of Muslim rule of Jerusalem. Rome lasted 666 years. 30 years from end of Gentile age to Millennium (1898–1928). Tribulation first 3½ years following 1898¼, to 5900 AM. On 6,000 Years: Millennium starts 5926½ so 74 years short of 6,000, but Satan loosed for a "little season" at end of Millennium-probably for that long, thus completing the 7,000 Year total.

496. _____. *Why and When We Expect the Fulfilment of Daniel's Prophecies, and the Coming of the Lord.* 1897 London: E. Nister. 30 p.

497. _____. *The Climax of the Ages; or, The Coming of the End. Shown to be Near at Hand from Recent Wonderful Astronomic Discoveries.* [1899?] San Francisco: J.D. Hammond. 24 p. tables.

498. Dixon, John. *A Treatise on the Fate of the Ottoman Empire in 1844: The Great Popish Revolution in 1866, with the Fall of the Pope and the Utter Extinction of Many Catholic Nations; the Commencement and Duration of the Millenium, and the Last Apostasy at the Extreme End of Time.* 1843. Worcester: National Aegis Office. 22 p.

499. _____. *A Key to the Prophecies: Containing an Explanation of the Symbols Used for Prophetic Declarations in the Bible…* 1844. Boston: author. 342 p. illus.

More about the Ottoman Empire.

500. Dobbs, Francis. *A Concise View from History and Prophecy, of the Great Predictions in the Sacred Writings, that Have Been Fulfilled; Also of Those That Are Now Fulfilling, and That Remain to Be Accomplished.* 1800. Dublin: author. vi, 289 p.

Letters to son. Creation 4004 B.C. Follows Isaac Newton: 10 Kingdoms = Vandals, Suevians, Visigoths, Alans, Burgundians, Franks, Britons, Huns, Lombards, Ravenna. Little Horn = Papacy. A.D. 455 + 1,260 = 1715. Papacy thwarted in attempt to claim British throne. English and

Irish union bill indicates Second Coming within the year: Messiah will come to prevent it. Millennium won't result from Christianization of world, but only by Second Coming. Personal Antichrist. Two Beasts (including Antichrist) destroy residue of Papacy. Antichrist = Caesar Augustus, to return (the "healed head") as leader of revived Rome. Antichrist battles Christ on earth at End; Christ appears in Ireland, Antichrist in France. Armageddon = Ardmaceaddon (in Britain). The 144,000 (Christ's army) gather from around world. The worst people also reborn for battle of final conflict. All alive today have lived before: reincarnation is the "great key to the Scriptures." Thus "same generation" alive with Christ will see the Second Advent. Two races of man: evil from Eve and Satan, the other from Adam and Eve. Secret "society of Avignon" (headed by Polish nobleman) vs. evil spirits of Illuminati (spiritism).

501. Douglas, J[ames] S. *The Reign of Peace Commonly Called the Millenium...* 1867. Toronto: W.C. Chewett. 319 p.

"In which it is shown that the Millenium there spoken of is to be a reign of peace on earth: not the end, but the summer time of the world, before the coming of Christ to judgment, and the final restitution of all things."

502. Dow, Lorenzo. *A Hint to the Public, or Thoughts on the Fulfilment of Prophecy.* 1811. 3rd ed. Salisbury, NC. 24 p.

Babylon = London. Two-Horn Beast = Napoleon. Magog = Russia, Popish nations, and England. America = God's instrument for the Millennium.

503. Dowling, John. *An Exposition of the Prophecies: Supposed by William Miller to Predict the Second Coming of Christ, in 1843.* 1840. Providence, RI: G.P. Daniel. 1842; New York: J.R. Bigelow. Answered by Josiah Litch: Refutation of "Dowling's Reply to Miller (1842, Boston: Himes, 90 p) with Preface by Joshau V. Himes.

504. Drummond, Henry. *A Defence of the Students of Prophecy.* 1828. London: James Nisbet. 127 p.

Also edited 3 vol *Dialogues on Prophecy* (1827–29).

505. Duffield, George. *Dissertations on the Prophecies Relative to the Second Coming of Christ.* 1842. New York: Dayton & Newman. xv, [9]-434 p.

Presbyterian minister, Detroit. Historic pre-mill.

506. _____. *Millenarianism Defended.* 1843. New York: Mark H. Newman. 183 p.

Refutation of Moses Stuart's refutation of former work. Ten Kingdoms from Rome = Vandals, Suevi, Alans, Burgundians, Franks, Visigoths, Ostrogoths, Anglo-Saxons, Heruli-Turingi, Lombards; Pope absorbs three of them. 1,260 years ends 1792, 1798, 1866, or 1910. 2,250 years ends 1780–1844. "Time of the end": 1843–47.

507. Dwight, Timothy. SEE ALSO PRE-1800. *A Discourse on Some Events of the Last Century.* 1801. New Haven: Ezra Read.

Sermon delivered as president of Yale. Prophesied overthrow of Antichrist under way. "The reign of the spirits of deceit is exhibited in prophecy as short, and the coming of Christ to destroy them, as sudden, unexpected, and dreadful." Terrible convulsion of nations as Papal power declines — Armageddon. But Millennium inaugurated gradually, underway around 2000.

508. Edson, Hiram. *The Time of the End: Its Beginning, Progressive Events, and Final Termination.* 1849. Auburn, NY. 31, 16 p.

Inc. *Review and Herald* "Extra": "Dream of William Miller," with remarks by David Arnold

509. Elliot, Edward Bishop. *Horae Apocalypticae: Commentary on the Apocalypse, Including also an Examination of the Chief Prophecies of Daniel.* 1862 [1844]. London: Seeley, Burnside, & Seeley. 5th ed. rev. 4 vol. xxv plates map, foldout diagr.

Pre-mill; historical school. Summarizes and criticizes many interpretations, especially Whitby's post-mill view, and discusses many works not listed here, e.g. W.G. Barker's "modified futurist scheme

(1850). Objects to futurist's "supposed instant plunge of the Apocalyptic prophecy into the distant future of the Consummation." "It is my settled conviction...that each and either of these prophetic counter-theories, the prœteristic and that of the futurists, in any of the multitudinous and mutually contradictory forms of either, may be shown to be self-refuting." A.D. 530 (Justinian's Pope-recognizing decree) + 1,260 = 1790 (French Revolution). A.D. 606 + 1,260 = 1866. Accepts Fynes Clinton's creation date of 4138 B.C., so 6,000 Years ends ca. 1862, which is also end of 1,260 years. Papacy "singularly answering to the characteristics of the little horn," thus Antichrist. Millennium preceded by triumph over Papal Antichrist and conversion of Moslems. Trumpets: A.D. 395–1453 (1st: Alaric; 2nd: Genseric; 3rd: Attila; 4th: Odoacer; 5th: Moslem hordes (= locusts); 6th: Turkish spread [Euphrates]). Revelation 8:7 "hail and fire from north": Goths.

510. _____. *Reply* [to Rev T.K. Arnold's futurist argument against *Horae*] 1845 London: Seeley, Burnside, and Seely. 78 p.

Four Horsemen: ancient Roman Praetorians and administrators. First Woe: Saracens. Second Woe: Turks. Two Witnesses: Paulikien sectaries ca. A.D. 1500. Beast, Antichrist = Pope.

511. _____. *The Last Prophecy.* 1884 London: Nisbet. 375 p. illus.

Abridgment of *Horae*.

512. Emeric de St.Dalmas, H.G. *Harmony of the Time Prophecies in Daniel and Revelation.* 1906. London: R.F. Hunger. 45 p. Paper read before Prophecy Investigation Society. SEE ALSO 1910–1970.

513. Emerson, Joseph. *Lectures on the Millennium.* 1818. Boston: S.T. Armstrong. 288 p.

A.D. 606 + 1,260 = 1866; + 1,335 = 1941–the Millennium.

514. *The End of the World in 1867: A Condensed Report, with Observations, of Dr. Cumming's Lecture, in the Town Hall, Leeds, on "The Last Prophecy of Daniel."* London: Thomas William Grattan. 16 p.

515. "Enquirer." *An Attempt to Prove the Calculations of the Rev. Robert Fleming Incorrect, and the Shew the Termination of the "Two Thousand Three Hundred Days,"—Dan. VIII, in Combination with the other Prophetic Numbers: At the Time Appointed the End Shall Be."* 1849. London: Simpkin and Marshall, Keble. 100 p. bibl refs.

516. Epp, Claas. *Die entsiegelte Weissagung des Propheten Daniel und die Deutung der Offenbarung Jesu Christi.* 1878. Alt-Schau bei Neusalz: F.A. Ruhmer.

"The Unsealed Prophecy of the Prophet Daniel and the Interpretation of Revelation." In 1880, Epp, inspired by Jung-Stilling's 1794 novel *Das Heimweh*, seeking to avoid State interference, and believing the Antichrist was about to appear in Europe, led 600 German-Swiss Mennonites to Turkestan (recently acquired by Russia; now Uzbekistan), following stays in Poland and the Ukraine. Believing he was Elijah and Melchizedek, Epp taught that the Tribulation was underway, that the Second Coming would occur at Shar-i-Sabs south of Samarkand, and that the End was March 8, 1889 (advanced to 1891 when that date passed). Pre-mill (but other Mennonites have been a-mill and post-mill).

517. Erdman, William J. *The Parousia of Christ: A Period of Time; or When Will the Church Be Translated?* [1880.] Chicago: Gospel Pub. 146 p.

Historic pre-mill. How long between Rapture and Second Coming with its outpouring of wrath upon the wicked? Are these events near-simultaneous, or in two stages? Examines and distinguishes various terms e.g. Day of Lord, of Christ. Toes, Horns, Beast, Stone, yet to appear. Argues for the "Exemption of the Church from the Tribulation" (pre-trib).

518. Evill, Thomas. *The Apocalypse of Jesus Christ, Commonly Called the Revelation of St. John the Divine.* 1829. London: Andrew Paton. xii, 110 p.

"Briefly, yet minutely, explained and interpreted, to the XIXth chapter inclusive: being the history of the Christian Church, until the destruction of the Roman empire at the coming of Our Lord with all his saints ... Consisting of a select compilation from the most approved and learned commentators both ancient and modern."

519. *Extracts on Prophecy.* 1835. Glasgow: James A. Begg. viii, 360 p.

Contributors: W. Burgh, W. Anderson, G.T. Noel, Irving, S. Maitland, Cuninghame, J.A. Begg, S. Madden, B.A. Simon, J. Mede, J.M. Campbell, J. Hooper, J.E. Sabin, W.W. Pym, Bishop Newton, J. Fletcher, W. Dodsworth, T. Goodwin, Bickersteth, T,. Erksine, W. Marsh, C.S. Hawtrey, J. Fry, and Toplady.

520. Faber, George Stanley. *A Dissertation on the Prophecies that have been Fulfilled, Are Now Fulfilling, or will Hereafter be Fulfilled, Relative to the Great Period of 1260 Years; the Papal and Mohammedan Apostacies; the Tyrannical Reign of Anti-Christ; and the Restoration of the Jews.* 2 vols. 1811 [1807]. 2nd Amer. ed. New York: Duyckinck. Orig 1807; London: Rivington.

Faber: English vicar. Napoleon = Antichrist; destroyed in Palestine. Kings of East = restored Ten Lost Tribes. A.D. 606 (Pope acquires universal powers, start of Mohammedan heresy) + 1,260 years = 1866.

521. _____. *A General and Connected View of the Prophecies, Relative to the Conversion, Restoration, Union, and Future Glory of the Houses of Judah and Israel; the Progress, and Final Overthrow, of the Antichristian Confederacy...* 1809 [1808]. Boston: William Andrews. xvi, 384 p.

Napoleon head of revived Roman Empire. Tarshish = England (maritime power). Russia is *good* King of North. Antichrist (Papal Roman Empire) attacks Israel, then is itself attacked.

522. _____. *The Sacred Calendar of Prophecy; or A Dissertation on the Prophecies which Treat of the Grand Period of Seven Times, and Especially of its Second Moiety, or the Latter Three Times and a Half.* 1853 [1828]. London: C.&J. Rivington. 3 vols bibl refs. (1828 ed.)

1864: probably End of Gentile apostasy, Time of End begins. 1865: Son of Man (Second Coming); then Millennium

(1866). Satanic degeneration for 335 years after Millennium — Gog and Magog confederacy. Papacy, Islam, French infidelity. "This generation" (shall not pass): refers to race or nation.

523. _____. *Napoleon III, the Man of Prophecy; or The Revival of the French Emperorship Anticipated from the Necessity of Prophecy.* 1865 [1859]. New York: D. Appleton. 102 p.

524. Falconer, Hugh. *The Unfinished Symphony the Eternal Life Begun.* 1909. London: Duckworth. xii, 304 p.

525. Farnham, Benjamin. *Dissertations on the Prophecies.* 1800. East-Windsor [CT]: Luther Pratt. 155 p.

"On the Jews. On the fifth and sixth trumpets. On Antichrist. On the sixth and seventh vials. On the seventh trumpet. Observations concerning the signs of the times. On the millennium. On the general resurrection and judgment. On the new heavens and new earth." 2,300 and 1,290 years may end 1819.

526. Farnham, C[harles] O[rland]. *What About Gog and Magog?* 1952 [1903]. Boston: Advent Christian Society 12 p.

527. Farquharson, James. *Daniel's Last Vision.* 1838. Aberdeen, Scotland.

"Prophecy, Respecting which Commentators have greatly differed from each other, showing its Fulfilment in events recorded in Authentic History." Preterist.

528. Fausset, A[ndrew] R. *The Second Advent of Christ: The Millennium; Enlarged from "The Englishman's Critical & Expository Bible Cyclopedia".* 1880. London: Hamilton and Adams. 16 p.

529. Fereday, W[illiam] W[ooldreidge]. *Coming Events, on Earth and in Heaven.* [ca 1900?] London / Boston: Pickering & Inglis / Scripture Truth Depot. 48 p.

Wrote for pre-mill journal *Our Hope.*

530. *Fifteen Solemn Facts Taken from Holy Scripture.* 1859. 5th ed. enl. London: G. Morrish. 4 p. With *What is the Difference Between the Coming of Christ...and His Appearing in Glory...?*

531. *The First Fruits: A Scriptural Inquiry Into the Time and Season of the First Resurrection, and the Change of Those*

Who are Alive and Remain. 1856. Philadelphia 48 p.

"The author of this is John Cox of England" handwritten on page 1. M. Baxter 1863 attributes authorship to Alexander Porter. Antichrist = Louis Napoleon. End is seven years after he signs covenant with Jews.

532. Fitch, Charles. *A Wonderful and Horrible Thing*. 1842. Boston: Joshua V. Himes. 24 p.

Millerite Adventist.

533. Fleming, L.D. *First Principles of the Second Advent Faith*. 1844. 2nd ed. Boston: Joshua V. Himes.

Pre-mill, Millerite Adventist. Jews won't return to Israel; Christian believers are the true Jews now. Wicked will be destroyed.

534. Folsom, Nathaniel S., and John Truair. *A Dissertation on the Second Coming and Kingdom of Our Blessed Lord and Savior, Jesus Christ, Upon the Earth*. 1840. Cazenobia, NY: printed at Union Herald Office. 92 p.

535. Frere, James Hatley. *A Combined View of the Prophecies of Daniel, Esdras, and St. John: Shewing That All the Prophetic Writings are Formed Upon One Plan*. 1817 [1811]. London: J. Hatchard. xxxviii, 491 p., plate.

"Accompanied by an explanatory chart." Armageddon and Second Coming = 1867. Napoleon was 7th head of Rome; Armageddon fought against 7th-revived (8th) head. "Ships of Chittim" refers to English naval victory over Napoleon in Aboukir Bay, Egypt.

536. _____. *Three Letters on the Prophecies*. 1859 [1833]. London: Hatchard. xix, 89 p.

Bound with *Apocalypse Popularly Explained*. Rev.: Three separate parallel histories, but strictly chronological within each. Follows Mede; criticizes Faber's historicist identifications. Many prophecies fulfilled 1814–48. France to destroy Austria. 1848 = Time of Gentiles ends. Different manifestations of Antichrist include Papal, Mahometan, Infidel (many of these fulfilled by Napoleon). Napoleon III fulfills rest of prophecies.

537. Furlong, Charles Joseph. *The Times of the End: Five Sermons on the Apocalypse*. 1849. Boulogne-sur-Mer: 62 p.

538. Fysh, Frederic. *The Time of the End, or, The Sultan of Turkey the Wilful King, and Mehemet Ali the King of the South Pushing at Him, as Foretold by Daniel*. 1839. Bath: Binns and Goodwin; London: Simpkin, Marshall. 20 p.

539. Gaebelein, Arno C. *The Harmony of the Prophetic Word; A Key to Old Testament Prophecy Concerning Things to Come*. [c1907]. New York: Our Hope Publication Office. 211 p. Foreword by Scofield. Also pub. F.H. Revell.

Gaebelein: Methodist minister, editor of *Our Hope*, director of Hope of Israel Mission. In 1894 Gaebelein said soon the "world shall behold the Jewish state." Pre-mill; futurist. SEE ALSO 1910–1970.

540. Galloway, Joseph. *Brief Commentaries Upon Such Parts of the Revelation and Other Prophecies as Immediately Refer to the Present Time: With the Prophetic, or Anticipated History of Rome*. 1809 [1802]. Trenton [NJ]: 2 vols.

Dragon = Pagan Rome. First Beast (from sea) = Papal Rome. Second Beast (from land) = atheist France. Two Witnesses = Old and New Testaments—lying "dead" in atheist France 3½ years 1792–96.

541. _____. *The Gate of Prophecy*. 1846. London: Rivington. 2 vols.

542. Galusha, Elon. *Address of Elder Elon Galusha: With Reasons for Believing Christ's Second Coming at Hand*. 1844. Rochester [NY]: E. Shepard.

543. Garnier, John. *The Great Pyramid, Its Builder and Its Prophecy with a Review of the Corresponding Prophecies of Scripture Relating to Coming Events and the Approaching End of the Age*. 1912 [1905]. rev. ed. London: R. Banks. xvi, 385 p. illus. bibl refs.

544. Garratt, Samuel. *Signs of the Times Showing that the Coming of the Lord Draweth Near ... : With the Added Signs of the Last Few Months*. 1869. 2nd ed. London: William Hunt. xv, 121 p.

545. Gascoyne, Richard. *The Ten-Horned Beast of Daniel and St. John: Showing that the Present Kingdoms of Europe*

Will Destroy the Popedom Before the Coming of the Son of Man, or the Millennium. 1853. London: Wertheim and Macintosh. 36 p.

546. Gauntlett, Henry. *An Exposition of the Book of Revelation.* 1821. London: L. B. Seeley. xlvii, 480 p.

Armageddon = 1866. 7th Head of Beast killed at Waterloo, but will be revived.

547. *Geometrical Digest of the Sacred and Prophetic Numbers.* 1859. [Montreal?: Salter and Ross]. 31 p.

"Showing that the world has entered upon the seventh millenary, that the time of the end has commenced, that the great Anti-Christ has come and entered upon his fearful mission, and that the end of this dispensation and Second Advent of Christ are near at hand."

548. Gesenius, Wilhelm. *A Hebrew and English Lexicon of the Old Testament.* Boston. Transl. of *Hebräisches und chaldäisches Handwörterbuch über das Alte Testament.* 1836 [1828]. Leipzig.

Influenced Darby and the dispensationalists. German Hebraicist, Univ. Halle, said "Rosh" (Ezek. 38) was proper name, "undoubtedly the Russians." Also, Meshech and Tubal = Moscow and Tobolsk. Gomer = Germany.

549. Gillings, G.W. *Our Lord's Return: What Is "Maranatha"?—A Dialogue.* 1901 [1880s?] Chicago: Bible Institute Colportage Association (Revell). 126 p.

550. Gillson, Edward. *The Coming of the Lord to Judge the Earth.* 1846 [1845]. London: James Nisbet. 127 p.

Also wrote *Table-talking: Disclosures of Satanic Wonders & Prophetic Signs.*

551. Girdlestone, Henry. *Notes on the Apocalypse.* 1847. London: William Edward Painter. 89 p.

"Enquiry into the Mystery of the Seven Stars and Seven Lamp Branches of the Apocalypse... Illustrative, the One of the Chronology, the Other of the Geography of the Apocalypse."

552. _____. 1901. *The Grammar of Prophecy: An Attempt to Discover the Method Underlying the Prophetic Scriptures.* London: Eyre & Spottiswoode. xiii, 192

p. Also 1955 Kregel reprint ed. [subtitled "A Systematic Guide to Biblical Prophecy"]

Also wrote *The Divine Programme* (1915; London: C. J. Thynne, 104 p.).

553. Gloag, Paton J. *The Messianic Prophecies.* 1879. Edinburgh: T. & T. Clark. xv, 368 p.

The Baird Lectures.

554. Godbey, W[illiam] B[axter] *Second Coming.* [ca. 1900?] Cincinnati: God's Revivalist Press. 29 p.

Second Coming in 36 years. "Divine intimation that *Paul will be President* of the United States."

555. _____. *An Appeal to Postmillennialists.* 1900s? Nashville, TN: Pentecostal Mission.

556. _____. *Millennial Restoration of Israel's Lost Tribes.* [1900s?] Louisville, KY: Pentecostal Publishing Co.

557. _____. *Armageddon.* [1910s?] Greensboro, NC: Apostolic Messenger. 30 p.

558. _____. *Tribulation Revivals.* [1910s?] Apostolic Messenger Office. 32 p.

559. _____, B[axter], and Seth Cook Rees. *The Return of Jesus.* [1900s?] Cincinnati: M.W. Knapp. 105 p.

560. Gordon, A[doniram] J. *Behold He Cometh. = Ecce Venit.* 1889. New York: Fleming H. Revell. vii, 311 p.

Reprinted in *The Premillennial Second Coming* (1988, Garland)

Gordon: Baptist minister, Boston. Both the "certainty" of the Second Coming and the "uncertainty" of when it will occur are necessary in order to maintain any-moment expectancy, otherwise the "wing of hope is paralyzed." Seven Churches = ages of Christendom. Antichrist = Pope (anti = "in place of," not "against"). Catholic Church = Harlot. Beast = Papal Empire. Millennium: populated by hierarchy of resurrected saints, highest suffered the most. Stresses failure of all "human rule" in history up to End. Apostasy and Tribulation "preempt" present dispensation, preventing Millennium for Church or for Israel, til Second Coming and destruction of Antichrist.

561. Gorton, Benjamin. *A Scriptural Account of the Millennium: Being a*

Selection from the Prophecies Concerning Christ's Second Coming and Personal Glorious Reign on Earth a Thousand Years... 1802. Troy NY: 216 p.

Includes "observations calculated to stimulate man to an enquiry into the matter, and to make the necessary preparation for that all-important event."

562. _____. *A View of the Spiritual or Anti-Typical Babylon, with Its Downfall Exhibited, By a Vision of Elisha Peck: as Well as Sundry Scripture Prophecies and Revelations...: A Warning to Making, the Certainty of the Near Approach of the Great and Terrible Day of the Lord.* 1808. Troy [NY]: author. 179 p.

563. Govett, Robert. *Entrance Into the Kingdom: or, Reward According to Works.* 1922 [1853]. 2. ed. London: C.J. Thynne. *Reward According to Works* (4th ed.) also published in 1989 by Schoettle (Miami Springs, FL).

Partial Rapture. Only faithful, deserving believers raptured initially (beginning of Tribulation); other believers raptured mid- or post-Trib.

564. _____. *The Apocalypse Expounded by Scripture.* 1951. Washington DC: Voice of Deeper Truth. 395 p.

Orig. 1861. 1865 London: James Nisbet. 4 vol illus.

Govett used pseudonym. "Matheetees."

565. _____. *How to Interpret the Apocalypse: As Naturalists? Or, as Supernaturalists?.* 1985 Miami Springs, FL: Conley & Schoettle. 60 p.

"A Refutation of the Historic Interpretation, with Especial Reference to the Rev. G. Guinness' "Approaching End of the Age.""

566. _____. *The Future Apostasy.* 1989. Miami Springs, FL: Schoettle. 42 p. Orig pub s.l.: Josiah Fletcher, 18 —?

567. _____. *Leading Thoughts on the Apocalypse.* 1989 [1885]. Miami Springs, FL: Schoettle. 73 p. bibl refs.

568. "Graduate of the University of Cambridge." *The Rule, Based on the World of God, for the Calculation of the Time in the Prophecies of the Old and New Testament: With an Application of Same, as a First Example, to the Three Times and a Half of the Apocalypse....* 1843. London. Simpkin, Marshal. 73 p.

569. Grant, Frederick W. *Ought We to be Watching? A Reply to Mr. Laing's Tract on the "Second Coming of the Lord."* 1877. [Toronto?]. 30 p.

Grant: Plymouth Brethren; later worked with Loizeaux brothers. Pre-trib; Second Coming in a few years. Also wrote *Creation in Genesis and Geology.*

570. _____. *The Numerical Structure of Scripture.* 1887. New York: Loizeaux Bros. 143 p.

571. _____. *The Prophetic History of the Church: Or Some Evils Which Afflict Christendom and their Remedy.* 1955 [1902]. New York: Loizeaux Brothers. 183 p.

Revelation 2–3: the Seven Churches.

572. _____. *The Numerical Bible.* 7 vols. 1903. New York: Loizeaux Bros., Bible Truth Depot.

573. _____. *Present Things, as Foreshown in the Book of Revelation.* N.d. New York: Loizeaux Brothers, Bible Truth Depot. 237 p.

574. Grant, James. *The End of Things.* 1867. London: James Nisbet. xviii, 434 p. 1866. London: Darton & Co.

Jews return to Israel, and are attacked by armies from all over the world. Second Coming and Millennium follow.

575. Grant, Miles. *Divine Chronology: An Examination of the Seven Prophetic Periods in the Prophecy of Daniel, Showing that the Second Coming of Christ is in the Near Future.* 1910. Oakland, CA: Messiah's Advocate. 22 p.

576. Gray, James M. *Satan and the Saint; or, The Present Darkness and the Coming Light; Popular Bible Studies on the Personality of Satan, the Evil of Christian Science, the Power Behind the Medium, the Heresies of the "Millennial Dawn," the Characteristics of the Age End, and the Second Coming of Christ.* 1909. Chicago: Bible Institute Colportage Assoc. 124 p.

Gray: head of Moody Bible Institute. Refutes occultism, Jehovah's Witnesses, Christian Science. Advocates pre-mill Second Coming, Millennium, but cautions it is "foolish and sinful" to set dates. Rapture,

10-Nation Roman Empire under Antichrist, Israel returns, Temple rebuilt, Second Coming. Remnant survives into Millennium. SEE ALSO 1910–1970.

577. *The Great Battle: Remarks on "The Battle of that Great Day of God Almighty."* 1845. New York: J.S. Redfield. 65 p.

"Rev. 16:14, taken from a series of unpublished letters on various subjects, for the use of his children."

578. *The Great Harvest, or, the End of the World Sermon.* [1800s]. London: W. Clowes and Sons [for the Religious Tract Society]. 12 p. Matthew XIII:39.

579. *The Great Roman Eclipse, With the Visions of Locusts and Horsemen.* 1882. London: E. Stock. viii, 412 p. Bibl. refs. Index.

"An exposition of the eight and ninth chapters of the Apocalypse."

580. Gregg, Tresham Dames. *On the Sacred Law of 1866, Conferring Perpetual Life with Immunity from Decay and Disease.* 1875. London: Simpkin, Marshall. 112 p.

"A cento of decisive scriptural oracles strangely discovered showing whence, from the Old Testament, the mystical number 666 is drawn into the Apocalypse, and that it constitutes the key to the gate of immortality." Gregg believed that he was immortal, and that the Millennium had started in 1865. "It is my position that it is demonstrable that 1866, and no other year, was the Year of Doom!" Insisted people could now be "translated" (raptured) to heaven without dying. Also wrote *Leviathan, the Ironclads of the Sea Revealed in the Bible* (1864); *The Steam Locomotive Revealed in the Bible* (Ezekiel is "otherwise absolutely unintelligible"); and *The Abomination of Desolation Spoken of by David the Prophet* (the abomination is "the most holy and adorable sacrifice of the [Catholic] Mass").

581. Griffin, Edward D. *The Kingdom of Christ.* 1805. Philadelphia: Jane Aitken.

Great crisis in 1847–48 (end of 1,260 years), and Millennium around 1922 (end of 1,335 years).

582. Guers, Emile. *Israel in the Last Days of the Present Economy: or, An Essay on the Coming Restoration of This People. Also, a Fragment on Millenarianism.* 1862 [1856]. London: Wertheim, Macintosh, and Hunt. viii, 382 p.

Translation of *Israel aux derniers jours de l'economie actuelle; ou, Essai sur la restauration prochaine de ce peuple, suivi d'un fragment sur le millenarisme...* Future 70th Week: Antichrist makes 7-year covenant with Jews, Great Tribulation in second half, ending with Armageddon and Second Coming.

583. Guinness, H. Grattan. *The Approaching End of the Age Viewed in the Light of History, Prophecy and Science.* 1881 [1878]. New York: A.C. Armstrong. 706 p. illus.

1887 ed. 10th xxxvi, 776 p.

Guinness: English. Pre-mill; historicist (also futurist?). End not later than 1923. New ed: 1918. New York: George H. Doran. xii, 372 p. index. 13 editions up to 1897.

584. _____. *Divine Programme of the World's History.* 1888?

585. _____. *On This Rock.* 1909.

End ("fulfillment of the prophetic times") = 1945.

586. _____, and Mrs. [Fanny Emmy] Grattan. *Light for the Last Days: A Study in Chronological Prophecy.* 1917 [1886]. "New ed., edited & rev. by E.P. Chachemaille." London: Morgan & Scott. xxiv, 333 p. Many reprint editions. 1886 ed. xxxi, 673 p., foldout charts.

1923 as maximum for prophecies of Daniel; Armageddon soon; Israel to be restored. Biblical "time" = 360 years. "Day" = year. "Babylon" = Catholic church. The two Little Horns = Papacy and Islam. 1699 as beginning of decline of both Turkish and Papal powers — "obvious" drastic decline of both in last two centuries. Three kinds of years — solar, lunar, calendar — so several different end points for each prophetic span. 2,520 Years from 747–587 B.C. to 1699–1934 (fall of Papal and Mohammedan power to re-birth of Israel). 2,520 lunar years from 587 B.C. to 1860 (Garibaldi establishes Italian Kingdom, demoting Pope), calendar years to 1898, solar to 1934. From 598 B.C., extends to 1848, 1887, and 1923. From 606 B.C. to 1840, 1878, and 1915. 2,300 Years from 480–395 B.C. to 1821–1903. 1,260 Days (42 Months) from 533–637 to 1793–1933. 476–637 rise of Papal power; 610 rise of Mohammedan. 1,260 (lunar) = 747 B.C. to 476 (last Western Roman emperor). 1917 as "final crisis date" of "these terminal years of crisis": 662 (Mohammed) + 1,335 (lunar) = 1917; also 604 B.C. + 2,520 (solar) = 1917. Jews now attaining disproportionate power and influence after centuries of unspeakable degradation and persecution. 1917, 1923, or 1934 as maximum for Daniel. Jewish Age: 2000 to 740 B.C.; Gentile Age to A.D. 1930; then Millennium.

587. Guiteau, Charles Julius. *A Lecture on Christ's Second Coming, A.D. 70.* 1877. Albany: Weed, Parson. 24 p. 2nd ed. pub. Washington, DC and Hartford, CT.

Guiteau: sometime lawyer; assassinated President Garfield in 1881. Former member of Noyes' Oneida Community; like Noyes, Guiteau believed Second Coming was A.D. 70: the Roman destruction of Jerusalem "in the clouds directly over Jerusalem." "I hold that for all these eighteen centuries the churches have all been in error in supposing the second coming of Christ to be in the future."

588. _____. *A Reply to Recent Attacks on the Bible, Together with Some Valuable Ideas on Christ's Second Coming, and on Hades...* 1878. Syracuse: Masters & Stone.

589. _____. *The Truth: A Companion to the Bible.* 1879. Chicago: Donnelley, Gassette & Loyd. 98 p.

590. Gunn, Lewis Carstairs. *The Age to Come! The Present Organization of Matter Called Earth, to be Destroyed by Fire at the End of This Age or Dispensation: Also, Before the Event Christians May Know about the Time When It Shall Occur.* N.d [1844] Rev. ed. Devonport [England]: 64 p. bibl. refs.

1844 ed. Boston: J.V. Himes; with appended paraphrase of Daniel 10–11 by Sylvester Bliss.

591. H.W.H. *The Church and the Great Tribulation.* 1906. Dublin: R. Stewart. 46 p.

592. Habershon, M. 1834. *A Dissertation on the Prophetic Scriptures, Chiefly Those of a Chronological Character; Shewing Their Aspect on the Present Times, and on the Destinies of the Jewish Nation.* 1834. London: James Nisbet.

Second Coming "undoubtedly now near at hand." Russia (not Turks) is Gog, the "King of the North."

593. _____. *A Guide to the Study of Chronological Prophecy.* 1841 Philadelphia: Orrin Rogers. 54 p.

Also included in *The Literalist*, v. 5; abridged from larger work. Dedicated to E. Bickersteth. 2,300 Years ends 1843–44. 1,260 Years covers rise and fall of Papacy, ending 1793 and 1843–44 (double start and stop dates). "Drying up" of Euphrates = decay of Ottoman Empire. Sudden universal destruction to come. England one of Ten Papal Kingdoms of Western Roman Empire.

594. Haldeman, Isaac M[assey]. *The Coming of Christ: Both Pre-Millennial and Imminent.* 1906. Los Angeles: Bible House of Los Angeles. 325 p.

Haldeman: minister First Baptist Church, Manhattan. Pre-mill. Coming must be imminent in order to maintain hope and preparation. Professing Church — Rome — corrupted by Satan. Post-mill thoroughly refuted by condition of world today. Second Coming notable for Christ vengefully trampling out evil, which is impossible if Millennium first.

595. _____. *The Signs of the Times.* 1910. New York: C.C. Cook, 455 p. 1929 8th ed. New York: F.E. Fitch, ix, 366 p. also published 1919 Philadelphia School of the Bible.

New York as Babylon. Even marvels of modern science can't stop world from plummeting into destruction .

596. Hale, Apollos. 1843. *Herald of the Bridegroom: In Which the Plagues that Await the Enemies of the King Eternal are Considered: and the Appearing of Our Lord to Gather His Saints is Shown to Be the Next Event Before Us ...* 1843. Boston: Joshua V. Himes. 36 p.

Millerite Adventist. Papacy fell from power in 1793, so Second Coming is next event.

597. Hales, William. *A New Analysis of Chronology.* 1830 [1809]. London.

Rev. Hales: University of Dublin professor Creation = 5411 B.C. 420 B.C.: start of 70 Weeks and 2,300 days. End = 1880. First Horse = Christ A.D. 31. Other 3 = early Christian era. Barbarian, Islamic, Saracenic and Turkish invasions. 70 A.D. = 70 Weeks end, 1,290 and 1,335 days begin. A.D. 620 = 1,260 days begin (Islam and Popery both rose then, both had zenith ca. 1300, and declined since). A.D. 622 = locusts. 1281 = 6th trumpet / 2nd woe. 3rd Angel of Revelation = Luther, 1517. 1793 = 7th trumpet, 3rd woe, 1st vial. 1810 = 2nd vial. 1880 = 7th vial, last woe. Then Millennium. First Beast, from Sea = Roman empire, then Papal; deadly wound is Papacy (little horn). Second Beast, from Earth = Turkish Empire; False Prince = Mahomet = 666 (in Greek). 7 heads = types of Roman leaders. Says 1880 date "analytically" determined from prophetic numbers, not mere historical resemblances. Two Witnesses will preach in London.

598. Hampden-Cook, Ernest. *The Christ Has Come: The Second Advent an Event of the Past.* 1905 [1894]. 3rd ed. rev. London: Simpkin, Marshall, Hamilton, Kent. xxviii, 195 p.

Preterist. Second Coming occurred shortly after First, during Apostle's lifetime.

599. Hanes, Elias. *The Three Unclean Spirits Which are to Go Forth to the Kings of the Earth and to the Whole World to Gather Them Together to the Battle of the Great Day.* 1862. [United States]: Published for the benefit of blind E. Hanes. 46 p.

600. Harbert, W.Z. *Our Country: What Is to Become of It?* 1863. Philadelphia: W.Z. Harbert. 24 p.

601. _____. *The Coming Battle.*

Cited in Sears 1961:24. 1453 (fall of Constantinople) plus 390 years of Revelation 9:15 = 1843. Clear proof that this date foretold Christ's Second Coming.

602. Harris, J.L., and B[enjamin]

W. Newton. *Lectures on Prophecy.* 1842. London: s.n. [90] p.

Series of lectures, several dated 1842.

603. Hastings, H[orace] L[orenzo]. *The Last Days.* 1859. New York: H.L. Hastings. [23 p.]

Part of compilation by Hastings which includes Adam Clarke 1820.

604. _____. *The Signs of the Times; or a Glance at Christendom As It Is.* 1863. Boston: H.L. Hastings. 415 p. index.

Worldwide corruption today as in Noah's day. Second Coming results in horrible destruction: "earth's final scene of conflict and of carnage" which is imminent.

605. Hawley, S[ilas]. 1843. *The Second Advent Doctrine Vindicated.* Boston: Joshua V. Himes. 107 p.

Millerite Adventist.

606. [Hawtrey, C.D.] "Spiritual Watchman." *The Nature of the First Resurrection, and the Character and Privileges of Those That Shall Partake of It.* 1828. 2nd ed. corrected. 48 p.

607. Hemenway, James. *Signs in the Heavens of the Second Advent Near.* 1894 [1874]. Boston: Advent Christian Publication Society. 12 p.

Hemenway: Advent Christian editor.

608. _____. *The End At Hand.* Boston: Advent Christian Publication Society. 24 p.

609. Henshaw, J[ohn] P[rentiss] K[ewley]. 1842. *An Inquiry into the Meaning of the Prophecies Relating to the Second Advent of Our Lord Jesus Christ.* Baltimore: Daniel Brunner. 228 p.

Pre-mill.

610. Herschell, Ridley Haim. *The Mystery of the Gentile Dispensation, and the Work of the Messiah.* 1848. London: Aylott & Jones. iv, 319 p.

Also wrote *Jewish Witnesses that Jesus is the Christ.*

611. Hewitt, H.W. *Cumulative Signs of Our Lord's Return.* 1910. Foldout tract. [Aurora, IL]

612. Higgins, Elon G. *The Closing Events of This Dispensation.* 1896. Boston: Advent Christian Publication Society. 32 p.

613. Highton, Henry. *Essays Towards a Right Interpretation of the Last Prophecy of Our Lord Concerning the Destruction of Jerusalem and the End of the Present World.* 1841. Oxford: Joseph Vincent; London: Hatchard. 50 p.

614. Himes, Joshua V. *Address of Adventist Believers: Being a Re-Examination of Their Faith, and a Warning Against Certain Defections From It.* [1850?] 34 p.

Delivered at Adventist General Conference, New York, 1850. Himes: Pastor of Chardon St. Baptist Chapel, Boston; primary publisher and publicist of William Miller's works.

615. Hindley, Charles, ed. 1862. Reprinted "garbled" edition of Richard Head's 1687 edition of *The Life and Death of Mother Shipton* [1667], inserting prediction of End for 1881. Later admitted making up that rhyme, plus Shipton's foretelling of telegraph and steam-engine. Widely quoted, though.

616. Hinton, Isaac Taylor. *The Prophecies of Daniel and John: Illustrated by the Events of History.* 1843. St. Louis: Turnbull & Pray. 375 p.

617. Hitchcock, *The Future Condition and Destiny of the Earth.*

"In a very short time—far shorter than we imagine—all the scenes of futurity will be to us a thrilling reality!"

618. Hitzig, Ferdinand. *Das Buch Daniel.* 1850. Leipzig: Weidmann. xiv, 228 p.

619. Hoare, Edward. *Palestine and Russia.* 1877. London: Hatchards.

See also 1918 "update" by Langston titled *Great Britain, Palestine, Russian, and the Jews.*

620. Hofer, Mrs. Angeline. *The Conspiracy of the Kings; or, Prophecy Fulfilled.* 1872. Cleveland, OH: M.W. Viets. 40 p.

Historicist. Eternal heavenly (not earthly) rule of Christ—no millennium. Wicked destroyed at End.

621. Holbert, Charles. *X Rays on the Future: A Study of Ten Prophecies Which Must be Fulfilled Before Christ Comes: Undenominational and Independant.* 1898. Minneapolis: Berger-Kohlstedt Printing Company. 47 p.

"A study of the religious and military future of our country."

622. Holcombe, William Henry. *The End of the World, With New Interpretations of History.* 1881. Philadelphia: Lippincott. 395 p. Holcombe: MD.

623. Holmes, James Ivory. *The Fulfilment of the Revelation of St. John Displayed, from the Commencement of the Prophecy, A.D. 96, to the Battle of Waterloo, A.D. 1815.* 1819. London: Ogle, Duncan. xv, 508 p.

Refutation of interpretations of G.S. Faber, Cuningham, and "Catholic author Pastorini."

624. Holzhauser, Bartholomaus, and Ignace N. Wuilleret. *Interpretation de l'Apocalypse, Renfermant l'Histoire des Sept Ages de l'Eglise Catholique.* 1856. Paris: L. Vives.

625. Hooper, John. *The Present Crisis: or, A Correspondence Between the Signs of the Times in which We Live and the Prophetic Declarations of Holy Scripture.* 1842. Boston: J.V. Himes. 54 p.

"Considered in Relation to the Blessed Hope and the Glorious Appearing of the Great God and Our Saviour Jesus Christ."

626. Horne, E.H. *Divine Clues to Sacred Prophecy.* 1901. London: S.W. Partridge. tables diagrams 79 p.

Horne: English vicar. Prophecy must be understood "progressively"—applicable to (all) contemporary times—"keeping pace with the progress of history." Deliberate intent to make us *always* expect Second Coming as imminent. The "worldwide influence of Christianity today amply fulfills" prophecy of Stone Kingdom, but will additionally be fulfilled at Second Coming. 70 Weeks fulfilled both as 490 years to A.D. 32, and also as 476 lunar ("sacred") years to A.D. 32. Messiah "cut off" middle of 70th Week. Horne denies "double fulfillment"—rather, prophecy may have two senses, or two parts, but no part is fulfilled twice over. Gentiles "made equal" end of 70th. 1,260 years ended 1870. Beast is Italy (not Papacy). Trumpets 1–6: Goths, Vandals, Huns, mixed barbarians, Saracens, Turks.

7th: Revolution era (France, Europe) political decadent Church. Vials end with Papal and Turkish decline, and Second Advent. Then Millennium. 10-Horn empire: division of ancient Roman Empire.

627. Hough, Sabin. *The Judgement Day: Showing Where, How, and When the Last Judgement Takes Place.* 1849. Columbus, OH: Siebert & Lilly. 214 p.

General Convention of the New Jerusalem in the United States of America.

628. Houghton, G. Warrand. *The Expected Rapture of the Church, or, The Analogy of Prophecy & Established Fact.* 1884. London: Elliot Stock. xxx, 350 p.

629. Houliston, William. *The Coming of the Great King.* 1897. Minneapolis: Great Western. 184 p.

"An examination and discussion of the Second Coming of Christ, with a concluding chapter on the Millennium and the future life."

630. Howard, Harry F. *The End of the World: And the Opening of the Book of Life.* 1908. Rochester, NH: priv. pub.

631. Howard, J. *Sign of His Coming: What Shall Be the Sign of Thy Coming, and of the End of the World?* 1874. Boston: Advent Christian Publication Society. 4 p.

Advent Christian.

632. Huchede, P. *History of Anti-Christ.* 1968 [1884] Rockford, IL: Tan Books. 59 p [1884; New York: Bray; 134 p.] Transl from French *Histoire de l'Antechrist.*

633. Hughes, Nimrod. *A Solemn Warning to All the Dwellers Upon Earth.* 1811. Trenton. 34 p.

"Given forth in obedience to the express command of the Lord God, as communicated by him, in several extraordinary visions and miraculous revelations, confirmed by ... signs, unto N. Hughes, upon whom the awful duty of making this publication has been laid ... wherein he was shewn that the certain destruction of one third of mankind, as foretold in the Scriptures, must take place on the fourth day of June, 1812."

634. Hunter, James. *The Personal Coming and Reign of the Lord Jesus Christ Over the Earth.* 1854.

Revived Roman Empire under Antichrist; 7-year covenant with Jews; Antichrist worshipped last 3½ years, then Armageddon and Second Coming.

635. Huntingford, Edward. *A Harmony of the Chronological Prophecies of Daniel, on a New Principle; Answering the Requirements of Scripture and History.* 1854. 23 p.

Bound with *Apocalypse Popularly Explained.* Historicist. Personal Antichrist. 10-Horns = Christian kingdom. Two Beasts = Holy Roman Empire and Papacy.

636. Huntington, William. *The Time of the Fall of the Papacy, the Previous Declension, and the Means of its Overthrow, Calculated from the Dates of the Prophets: With a Scriptural Discovery of the True Millennium, and the Year of its Commencement.* 1851. London: W.H. Collingridge. 12 p.

Huntington: d. 1813.

637. Hyren, Frederic. *Principles and Rules for the Establishment of the Millennial Church of the Lord Jesus Christ, Called the Church of the Holy Spirit.* 1858. [Cleveland, OH]. iv, 16 p.

638. *The Identity of Napoleon and Antichrist Completely Demonstrated.* 1809. New York Erza Sargeant. 47 p.

Scriptural references to Antichrist "apply to Napoleon in the most striking manner": "the prophetic number 666 is found in his name, with perfect exactness."

639. "Incognito, E." *The End of the World: Being an Exposition of the Prophecies of Our Lord and Saviour, Jesus Christ, and His Apostles Concerning that Important Event.* [1811] [Philadelphia: author] 48 p.

Debate between "Christus" (a believer) and "Theorus" (a theist). Christus argues for figurative, spiritual accomplishment following end of evil reign, not literal Coming.

640. Inglis, James. *The Destiny of the Earth Under Its Coming King.* 1854. 2nd ed. New York: J. Moffet. 48 p.

American promoter of Darby.

641. Irving, Edward. *For the Oracles of God: Four Orations; For Judgement to Come.* 1825. New York: S. Marks. xii, 427 p.

Irving: London-based Church of Scotland minister. Encouraged glossolalia (speaking in tongues) as sign of Last Days. Followers founded Catholic Apostolic Church; expected some leaders to be alive for Second Coming. Apocalyptic expectations and dispensationalism. Irving was first to popularize two-stage Coming with secret Rapture prior to Tribulation.

642. ____. *Babylon and Infidelity Foredoomed of God: A Discourse on the Prophecies of Daniel and the Apocalypse, Which Relate to These Latter Times*. 1826 Glasgow: Chambers and Collins. 2 vols. 1828 ed 588 p.

Book led to yearly conferences at home of Henry Drummond. Predicted Second Coming for 1864.

643. ____. *Preliminary Discourse to Ben-Ezra's Work on the Second Advent*. 1859 [1827]. London: Bosworth & Harrison. Vi, 222 p.

Translation, analysis, and discussion of Lacunza's ("Ben Ezra's") 1790 *Coming of the Messiah*. Argues that the concept of the "millennium" (post-mill Utopian age on earth) derives from dangerous "optimism of the German and French infidels!" Criticizes post-mill postponement of Christ's Second Coming as being "discouraging." Suggests pre-mill interpretation, inspired by Lacunza.

644. ____. *The Last Days: A Discourse on the Evil Character of These Our Times: Proving Them to be the "Perilous Times" of the "Last Days"*. 1850 [1828]. London: James Nisbet. xl, 531 p.

Pref. by Bonar. Dedicated to leaders of National Scottish Church. Last Days of Christian, not Jewish, dispensation. Irving is extremely stern about wickedness of the times. God's vengeance on "backsliding and incorrigible Church." 1,260 Days of Daniel (= Years of Papal Usurpation) end in A.D. 1792 (and 1832); the Last Days begin 1823. "Therefore give heed to these things, seeing that now, by more than the space of two years, I have given you warning of them." Most of book proof that world now fulfilling II Tim. 3:1–5 that in the Last Days men shall be blasphemers, lovers of self, proud, disobedient to par-

ents, wicked. Denounces Papacy, Unitarians, Arianism as "blasphemous." Sunday Schools are proof of degeneracy (because parents not educating kids themselves). Travel books no longer focus on religious and moral climate of foreign lands, but on scenery and Papal abominations such as statues and paintings. Complains that kids now given children's books instead of just reading Bible and adult religious commentaries. Modern authors "silly, saucy, pert, forward, and hasty," compared to ancient intellects. Bewails post-mills as arrogantly expecting betterment; world is actually getting worse. Counsels followers to quote Bible to skeptics and doubters, steel themselves to withstand scoffers, and to trust faith over reason.

645. ____. *Daniel's Vision of the Four Beasts and of the Son of Man Opened, and Applied to Our Present Crisis in Church and State*. 1829. London: J. Nisbet. 307 p.

646. ____. *Exposition of the Book of Revelation*. 1831 London: Baldwin and Cradock. 4 vol in 2 (x, 1428 p).

The Ten Kings from A.D. 476: France, Britain, Spain, Portugal, Naples, Tuscany, Austria, Rome, Lombardy, Ravenna (last two absorbed into Rome). 1,335 to 1867–8 = Second Coming. 6th head of Beast is German; 7th = Napoleon. 8th may be Napoleon's son.

647. ____, and John Hampden. *Foredoomed and Forewarned, Both by Daniel and St. John: Written for Our Admonition, Upon Whom the Ends of the World are Come*. 1867. Bristol, England: W. Mack; London: J. Stevenson. 36 p.

648. *Isaiah's Message to the American Nation: A New Translation of Isaiah, Chapter XVIII, with Notes Critical and Explanatory: A Remarkable Prophecy, Respecting the Restoration of the Jews, Aided by the American Nation, with a Universal Summons to the Battle of Armageddon, and a Description of that Solemn Scene*. 1814. Albany, NY: 50 p.

649. Jacobs, E. *The Doctrine of a Thousand Years Millennium, and the Return of the Jews to Palestine, Before the Second Advent of Our Saviour, Without*

Foundation in the Bible. 1844. Cincinnati. 76 p.

Pre-mill.

650. Jezreel, James Jershon [White]). *Flying Roll* (1). 1879. "Jerusalem" [i.e., New York].

Jezreel (James White; probably an American), a British army private, joined New House of Israel in 1875, then took over. His "New and Latter House of Israel" members were known as Jezreelites. Addressed to "Lost Tribes of the House of Israel" scattered among the Gentiles (i.e. British-Israelism). Introduction by Elizabeth Easton (a New York City convert). 12 vols. planned. 4004 B.C. + 6,000 years = almost A.D. 2000. Jezreelites are nucleus of the 144,000 elect; survive until Millennium; will gather together in New Jerusalem and "break covenant with death." "Utterings of the seven thunders" kept secret until End Times. "We are now living in the third and last watch of the eleventh hour;— the end of the sixth thousandth year"— last watch of last dispensation. 1875 = end of second watch. 20 years 10 months = "watch" of one hour. 666 years = "watch" of 2,000 years. Non-stop jumble of biblical references and disjointed commentary strung together. Female spirit of God seeking new vessel after Eve sinned. Jezreel is the Sixth Trumpeter; previous five sounding the alarm were Richard Brothers, Joanna Southcott, George Turner, William Shaw, John Wroe.

651. Johnson, Ashley. *Opening the Book of the Seven Seals.* 1902 [1896]. Knoxville, TN: Ogden Bros. 269 p.

Disciples of Christ. Roman Catholicism as Beast.

652. Jones, Henry. *The Scriptures Searched or, Christ's Second Coming and Kingdom at Hand ...* 1839. New York: Gould, Newman & Saxton.

653. _____. *Compend of Parallel and Explanatory References on Christ's Second Advent at Hand.* New York: Piercey and Reed. 16, [8] p.

654. _____. *Modern Phenomena of the Heavens, or Prophetic "Great Signs" of the Special Near Approach of "the End of All*

Things." 1843. New York: Piercy & Reed. 48 p.

Blood, smoke, and fire in the skies. Stars falling from sky prophesied in Revelation: the 1833 meteorite shower.

655. Junkin, George. *The Little Stone and the Great Image: or, Lectures on the Prophecies Symbolized in Nebuchadnezzar's Vision of the Golden Headed Monster.* 1844. Philadelphia: James M. Campbell. viii, 318 p. index.

656. Keil, C.F., and F. Delitzsch. *Biblical Commentary on the Old Testament.* 1866 Edinburgh: T.& T. Clark. viii, 512 p. Also Eerdmans; many editions 1950 to 1971.

657. Keith, Alexander. *The Signs of the Times, as Denoted by the Fulfillment of Historical Predictions, from the Babylonish Captivity to the Present Time.* 1847 [1832]. 2 vols. Edinburgh: William Whyte. 450 p.

Historicist; Rome, Europe, Ottoman, Papacy. Examines Elliott's theory.

658. _____. *The History and Destiny of the World and of the Church, According to Scripture.* 1861. London: T. Nelson & Sons. xxxiii, 479 p. illus.

659. Kelber, Leonhard Heinrich. *Das Ende kommt: Aus dem Worte Gottes und den neuesten Zeitereignissen grundlich und uberzeugend bewiesen, nebst...* 1842. Stuttgart: Verlag der Blauen Bibliothek. 126 p.

660. Kelly, James. *The Apocalypse Interpreted in the Light of "the Day of the Lord."* 1851 [1849]. London: J. Nisbet. 2 vols.

Futurist literal-day interpretation of numbers but also historicist year-day interpretation (double fulfillment).

661. Kelly, William. *Lectures on the Book of Daniel.* 1972 [1881]. Charlotte, NC: Books for Christians. 270 p.

Kelly publicized and promoted Darby, and was a major pre-trib proponent.

662. _____. *Lectures on the Book of Revelation.* 1861. London: Williams and Norgate. xv, 416 p.

663. _____. *Lectures on the Second Coming and Kingdom of the Lord and Saviour Jesus Christ.* 1970 [1865]. Sunbury, PA:

Believers Bookshelf. 395 p. Orig 1865, London.

664. _____. *The Second Advent of Christ Premillennial.* 1868. viii, 130 p.

A reply to Rev. D. Brown.

665. _____. *Elements of Prophecy.* 1876. London: G. Morrish. xxxv, 263 p.

666. _____. *The Coming, and the Day of the Lord.* 1903. London: T. Weston. 135 p.

Also wrote *Babylon and the Beast.* SEE ALSO 1910–1970.

667. Kelsall, Henry. *Antichrist.* 1846.

Futurist, literal-day. Antichrist's reign in 70th Week; Abomination of Desolation is image animated by Satan. Ten-Nation Empire includes England.

668. Ker, John. *The Day Dawn and the Rain.* 1875 [1869?] New York: Robert Carter. 450 p.

669. King, John. *Observations on the Prophecies which Relate to the Rise and Fall of Antichrist and Such as Appear to Point to the Events of Our Times.* 1809. Chambersburg [PA]. 32 p.

"With some calculations on prophetical members to show that his fall may not now be far off." 1,260 years ends 1860; 2,300 ends 1867. Napoleon may be Two-Horn Beast (horns = "liberty and equality").

670. King, W. *Tract: For the Times.* 1847. Utica, NY.

Great increase of knowledge as sign of the End, which immediately follows Second Coming

671. *The Kings of the East: An Exposition of the Prophecies, Determining, from Scripture and from History, the Power for Whome the Mystical Euphrates is Being "Dried Up;" with an Explanation of Certain Other Prophecies Concerning the Restoration of Israel.* [1842]. London: R.B. Seeley and W. Burnside. xvi, 355 p. illus.

Historicist. Britain = Tarshish. English in India and East India Company fulfill prophecies of ruling over kings; "righteousnes" of England foretold. Britain to restore the Jews, will be opposed by Russia, Persia, Egypt, France. Britain: "deliverer of the Jews and the Light of the Gentiles."

672. Kingsford, Anna Bonus, and Edward Maitland. *How the World Came to an End in 1881.* 1884. London: Field & Tuer [etc.]. 83 p. Based on ideas expressed in *The Perfect Way; or, The Finding of Christ,* published anonymously by Kingsford and Maitland in London, 1882.

673. Kinnear, Beverley O. *Impending Judgments on the Earth; or, "Who May Abide the Day of His Coming".* 1892. New York: James Huggins. xxviii, 265 p., plate.

Russia's "armed interference and aggression" in East Europe and Afghanistan signs of imminent End Times invasion.

674. Knapp, M.L., and others. *Astronomical Etiology; Or, Star Prophecies Concerning Coming Disasters on the Earth from 1881 to 1885.* Chicago: Thomas Wilson.

Perihelia (closest approach to sun) of the four largest planets coincide, producing catastrophic effects on Earth.

675. "Knoxite." *Tekel: The Coming Struggle and Its Reviewers Weighed and Found Wanting.* 1853 [1849?]. 2nd ed. Edinburgh/London: Jameswood; J. Nesbit: 30 p.

676. Koresh [Cyrus Teed Reed]. *The Great Red Dragon: The Flaming Devil of the Orient.* 1908. Esotero, FL: Guiding Star. 149 p.

Novel. Set in future. Japan and China (the "Yellow peril") overrun the West; Islam does also. Christians flee to U.S. Planet Earth shifts with catastrophic consequences.

677. _____. *Interpretation of the Book of Revelation.* 1925. Estero, FL: Guiding Star. 121 p.

Koreshan series. Koresh (d. 1908) taught that the Earth is hollow, and that we live on the *inside* surface. Also preached British-Israelism and Pyramidology, and denounced evolution. Koresh called his theory "Cellular Cosmogony," and his religious beliefs "Koreshanity."

678. Kramer, George A. *The Second Coming of Christ.* N.d. Boston: Advent Christian Publication Society 24 p.

Advent Christian.

679. Kurtz, Johann Heinrich. *Manual of Sacred History.* 1883.

"Coming of the last times" dependent on "missionary zeal" in preaching to all men. Then, Millennial period. Powers of Darkness at their strongest then, church greatly afflicted — exceeding in severity all that preceded it." But then reign of Christ, not visible and earthly (contra chiliasm) but invisible and celestial (though it will influence terrestrial life, and Christianity will triumph). End of Millennium: great Tribulation as Satan loosened, evil has final convulsive fury, Antichrist is ruler.

680. Labagh, Isaac P. *Twelve Lectures on the Great Events of Unfilled Prophecy, which Still Await their Accomplishment, and are Approaching their Fulfillment.* 1859. New York: author. 288 p.

Rev. Labagh: Calvary Church, Brooklyn; ed. of *American Millenarian and Prophetic Review.* Dispensational pre-mill. Restoration and conversion of Jews. Recovery of Ten Lost Tribes, reunion with other tribe. Rise and fall of Antichrist. Two Witnesses. Fall of Papacy and Islam. Great calamities of Last Days. Antichrist, Armageddon, Second Coming, Millennium ("Paradise regained"). Lost Tribes probably hidden in Central Asia. Papacy and Islam = two Little Horns; both show "utter hostility" to Bible. "When the Son of Man cometh, he will scarce find faith on the earth." Battle of Armageddon in Israel: incalculable slaughter, but God intervenes. Islam = False Prophet. Satan cast into "Bottomless Pit" at center of earth.

681. Lannin, W[illiam] H. *Earth's Harvest Time as Revealed in the Bible.* 1890. Boston: Advent Christian Publication Society. 26 p.

Advent Christian. Signs show "divinely fixed harvest, or judgment, ... imminent now." Also wrote *Ishmael: Mohammed and the Turk in History and Prophecy* (1896).

682. *The Last Battle After "The Coming Struggle;" a Study for Christians, Infidels, & the Man of Sin.* 1905. London: B. Green; Glasgow: Oliphant & White. 32 p.

Possible that "Coming Struggle" refers to David Pae's 1853 book.

683. *The Last Judgment and Second Coming of the Lord.* 1899. 7th ed. Philadelphia: Swedenborg Pub. Assoc. 55 p.

684. Lathrop, Joseph. *The Prophecy of Daniel, Relating to the Time of the End Opened.* 1811. Springfield, MA. 32 p.

1,260 years of Papal domination ends 1842 or 1866. Now living amid "gloomy signs of the last days."

685. *The Latter Days: Railways, Steam, and Emigration with its Consequent Rapid Peopling of the Deserts: Also the Present Going To and Fro, and Increase of Knowledge, Fortold by Isaiah, Daniel, and Joel, and Indicating the Rapid Approach of the End of the Latter Days.* 1854. Dublin: London: Samuel B. Oldham; Seeleys, (W. Porteous). 24 p.

686. Launder, Charles Henry. *The Word of God; Prophecy Unfolded; the End of the Age Is At Hand ...* 1900. Chicago: The Messengers of God. 487 p. illus.

687. Lee, Charles [and Julia Lee?]. *History of the Human World: As to Its Rise, Progress and Final End, and the Great Labor Movement of Our Time, Viewed in the Light of Prophecy.* 1891. S.l.: s.n. 247 p.

688. Lillingston, I. W. *An Exposition of Part of the 24th and 25th Chapters of St. Matthew Together with the Signs of Christ's Coming with the Clouds of Heaven, That is, the Glorious Appearing of the Great God and Our Saviour Jesus Christ.* 1838. Edinburgh: John Lindsay & Co. 38 p.

689. Lincoln, L.E. *Disquisitions on the Prophecies of Daniel.* 1843. [Lowell, MA.] 168 p.

2,300 Year/Days to 1843 — but God may postpone End a bit.

690. Lincoln, William. [d.1888] *The Church of God and the Apostasy.* Kilmarnock: John Ritchie. 102 p.

691. _____. *Lectures on the Book of Revelation.* [1875]. Chicago: Revell. 450 p. [London: Yapp & Hawkins] Reprinted from *The Latter Rain.*

"As in Genesis is seen the germ, so in Revelation is found the ending or summing up of all things. Pre-eminently a book of judgment, showing us things that must shortly come to pass...."

692. _____. *Typical Foreshadowings in Genesis: or, The World to Come and the*

Divine Preparation for It. [1880s?] Glasgow. viii, 214 p.

693. _____. *The Epistles of John: Revealing the Family of God; With Their Father in the World, in the Last Days.* [1890?] Glasgow/ London: Pickering & Inglis : A. Holness. 192 p.

694. Litch, J[osiah]. *An Address to the Clergy, on the New Approach of the Everlasting Kingdom of God on Earth; ...* 1840. Boston: Dow & Jackson [publisher of William Miller's books].

Also wrote *Christ's Second Coming about A.D. 1843.* Millennium: eternal not temporal; "unending duration" (calls belief in literal thousand year Millennium "dangerous error"). Second Coming by 1843. Ottoman Empire falls 1840. Anti-post-mill position: equates literal Millennium belief with false expectation of conversion of world to Christianity. Resurrection of the just at end of world. Satan and wicked set free after thousand year rule of Christ over godly, but God destroys them. Then Judgment. Restoration of Jews: "Spiritual" Jews, not literal descendants; restoration fulfilled at Resurrection. Antichrist = Pope. 1,260 years: A.D. 538 to 1798. Ten Kingdoms: Huns, Ostrogoths, Visigoths, Franks, Vandals, Sueves/Alans, Burgundians, Heruli, Angles/Saxons, Lombards. Time of End started with "demoniac equality" and "frantic atheism" of French Revolution (= Beast). King of North = Syria, who stopped Napoleon, made him retreat to South (Egypt). Locusts = Moslems. Two Witnesses = Old and New Testaments.

695. _____. *The Doctrine of the Millennium.* 1840. S.l.: s.n. 14 p.

696. _____. *The Probability of the Second Coming of Christ About A.D. 1843.* Boston : David H. Ela. 204 p.

697. _____. *Prophetic Significance of Eastern and European Movements; Being a Plain, Literal, and Grammatical Construction of the Last Five Chapters of Daniel, Applied to Passing Events; Showing Conclusively that a Syrian Prince, Not Napoleon III, Is the Antichrist of the Last Days.* 1867. Boston: J. Litch. 35 p.

698. _____. *A Complete Harmony of Daniel and the Apocalypse.* 1873. Philadelphia: Claxton, Remson and Haffelfinger. 300 p.

699. Livermore, Harriet. *The Glory of the Lord: In the Land of the Living by Redemption of the Purchased Possession, to the Praise of His Glory.* 1848. 2nd ed. Philadelphia. 48 p.

Second Coming 1843 or 1847. 677 B.C. + 2,520 = 1843; 457 B.C. + 2,300 = 1843. Includes epistle by Joseph Wolff (both believed Indians were Lost Tribes of Israel).

700. Looker On. *A View of the Late Momentous Events: as Connected with the Latter Days.* 1830. London. 116 p

"Wherein the Shaking of the Nations, the Fall of the Power of the Romish Church, and of the Turkish Empire, the Past and Present State and Appearance of the Speedy Restoration of the Jewish nation, the Approach of the Spiritual Reign of Christ, and the Glorious Millennium, are Considered."

701. Lord, David Nevins. *An Exposition of the Apocalypse.* 1847 [1846]. New York: Harper & Bros. 542 p. bibl. refs. Orig. Franklin Knight.

Lord: editor of *Theological and Literary Review* (1848–61). Promoted non-dispensational pre-millennialism: historical rather than futurist interpretation of Revelation. Rev. not poetry because not "personification" of things but rather "thingification" of people, nations, etc. Introduction explains "laws of symbolization" and analogy. Rest of book verse-by-verse exegesis. In each section discusses (generally erroneous) interpretations of the symbols of other commentators: Whiston, Grotius, Rosenmüller, Mede, Jurieu, Bishop Newton, Vitringa, Faber, Woodhouse, Stuart, etc. Useful descriptions of their (generally historicist) interpretations. Four Horsemen: Church/Roman Empire history up to Antichrist. 12 Tribes (144,000) — church denominations. 7 Trumpets: Roman Empire history. Wormwood = Huns. Locusts: Saracens. 6th trumpet: Cyrus conquering Babylon, also Mongols, Tartars, Turks. Rainbow angel is Reformation leaders, as are Two Witnesses. 10-

Horn Beast: Rulers from fall of Rome to present. 2-Horn Beast: Papacy. Vials 1–4: French Revolution and Napoleonic Wars. 5th vial: 1815–48. 6th Vial now in process: withdrawal of believers from state churches. 7th Vial and Armageddon still to come; Second Coming immediately followed by literal war with combined Anti–Christian forces. Satan = dragon; literally imprisoned in Abyss. Restoration of Israel immediately after Second Coming. First resurrection beginning of Millennium, Second at Judgment and End. Millennium = 360,000 years [sic]. New Jerusalem symbolic.

702. _____. *The Coming and Reign of Christ.* 1858. New York: Franklin Knight. 430 p.

Strict young-earth creationist. Emphasizes *un*filled prophecies. Their fulfillment "may probably burst on the world ere the present generation passes from the scene." Strong refutation of post-mills and "Anti-millenarians." The "present dispensation is drawing to its close, and … is in its last stages to be marked by avenging judgments on the nations, instead of their conversion, and by great apostasies" and persecutions. Presents "established laws" by which to interpret prophecy. Special laws for each type of figurative speech. (Presented these fully in his magazine, and his book *The Characteristics and Laws of Figurative Language*). Christ didn't establish his Kingdom immediately after his own resurrection in order to allow men's belief and resolve to be tested — "act out their hearts." 2 Peter: teaches that planetary collisions wouldn't be heard on Earth. Earth itself won't be burned up, just stuff on it. Earth and mankind will be eternal. New regimes (Beasts) to arise before Second Coming; collapse of Turkish domination, slaughter of Witnesses. Pre-mill, with personal earthly reign of Christ. Millennium soon, perhaps a few years, maybe somewhat longer. Expounds Laws of Figurative Language and of Prophetic Symbols with great confidence. Historicist interpretation, but some events still future. Earth not annihilated by fire, because occupied by humans eternally. Wicked probably destroyed by volcanoes, earth-

quakes, and flammable ejected gases. Resurrection of holy dead at Second Coming, to reign with Christ. Literal Armageddon battle in Palestine, armies of all nations destroyed, thus ridding world of corrupters of Christianity. Literal invasion of Israel by Gog; bows and arrows then used for fuel by Israelites. Four vials: French Revolution and Napoleonic Wars; Fifth: 1848; Sixth: continuing at present. 330: Drying of Euphrates: withdrawal of people and nations from control of established churches and Vatican rule. Wild Beast of Revelation: Roman rulers through ages. Ten horn beast: Gothic rulers of Roman lands, to be overwhelmed by great political convulsions in future, with even worse governments, then coming again under Catholic control (all of Europe). Two Witnesses: really large number of people, to occur in a European capital. 144,000 symbolic of Christian denominations. Cautions against late 19th-century date-setting of Elliott, Faber, e.g., for Millennium; precise date is unpredictable.

703. Lord, Nathan. *The Millennium: An Essay Read to the General Convention of New Hampshire.* 1854. Hanover: Dartmouth Press. 56 p.

President of Dartmouth; father of David Lord above.

704. Lord, Willis. *The Blessed Hope, or, The Glorious Coming of the Lord.* 1877. Chicago: W.G. Holmes. 176 p.

Revell ed. 250 p. [1888].

705. Loughborough, John Norton. *Last-Day Tokens.* 1904. 4th ed. Mountain View, CA: Pacific Press. 206 p. illus.

1995 ed.: St. Maries, ID: LMN Pub. International. 158 p. illus. bibl. refs.

706. Lyon, R.V. 1861. *The Suffering and Restoration of Israel.* Seneca Falls, NY? 51 p.

Published at the offices of *Millennial Harbinger.*

707. "M.D." *A Warning and an Encouragement to England.*

Popularization of Fleming's *Apocalyptic Key.*

708. Macartan, Michael. *The Michael Foretold by Daniel: The Time of his Standing Up and the Duties of his Mission.* 1865–

1866. Buenos Ayres: Printed at the "Buenos Ayres" Printing-Office. 2 vols.

709. M'Causland, Dominick. *The Times of the Gentiles as Revealed in the Apocalypse.* 1857. Dublin; London: McGlashan & Gill ; J. Nisbet. xi, 247 p.

Abomination of Desolation: statue of Antichrist "endowed with life" by "miraculous and diabolical agencies" in rebuilt Temple midway through 70th Week (Tribulation). 455 B.C. + 69 Weeks = A.D. 29.

710. _____. *The Latter Days of Jerusalem and Rome, as Revealed in the Apocalypse.* 1859. London: R. Bentley.

711. McCartney, Richard Hayes. *The Coming of the King.* 1897. Chicago: Revell. 224p. Poem.

712. _____. *The Secret Rapture Delusion and Snare.* 1926. Chicago: J. Watson. 103 p.

713. McConkey, James H. [James Henry?] *The End of the Age: A Series of Prophetic Bible Studies Upon the End of this Present Age.* 7th ed. 1921 [1897]. Pittsburgh: Silver Publishing. 15th ed. 1924; Pittsburgh: Silver; 129 p. 15th ed. 1964.

Book sent free, not sold. Glorification (Rapture) for Church, Restoration for Jews, Judgment for unbelievers. Today world is "red with blood. Kingdoms rising and falling in a night. Thrones are tottering. Armies are battling in earth, sea and sky. The sons of men are being slaughtered by the millions. Civilization is shot through with the barbarism and savagery of by-gone ages. The foundations of human government and society are reeling under earthquake blows." Special signs of End: 3½ year Tribulation, rule of Antichrist, then Second Coming. World won't be converted; increasingly wicked. Communing with demon spirits sign of End. "The Anti–Christ is as surely a human being as Christ was the God-man." Satan's counterfeit of Christ, the World Emperor, a blasphemous boaster, to control all business, finance, and plunge world into last war. 10-nation confederacy will be destroyed suddenly, violently, supernaturally at Second Coming. Then Millennium: personal earthly reign of

Christ with saints. Iron-clay mix: future states descended from Roman Empire.

714. M'Corkle, Samuel M. *Thoughts on the Millennium: with a Comment on the Revelations.* 1831. New York. iv, 76 p.

Pre-mill. First Beast is Catholic Church; Second Beast is Protestantism. 453 B.C. + 2,300 = 1847. A.D. 587 + 1,260 + 1847. Millennium to last 360,000 or 365,000 years.

715. M'Donald, Donald. *The Subjects of the Millennium Traced in their Downward Progress from their Ancestry through the Three Pre-Millennial Dispensations: Together with a Scriptural View of the New Jerusalem, Coming of Messiah, Sacred Numbers, and Signs of the Times, the End of the World, and Last Judgment …* 1849. Charlottetown [P.E.I.], Canada: J.D. Haszard. v, 417 p.

716. MacDonald, James M. *The Coming of the Lord: A Key to the Book of Revelation.* 1846. New York: Baker and Scribner. viii, 210 p.

717. M'Farland, Asa. *Signs of the Last Times.* 1808. Concord [NH]. 32 p.

Papacy and Islam to dominate 1,260 years; both begin about A.D. 600.

718. McFeeters, J[ames] C[alvin]. *America in the Coming Crisis: An Appeal to Christian Patriots to Align Our Country with Jesus for Her Safety in the Next War.* 1923. 2nd ed. Boston: Christopher Publishing House. viii, 122 p.

719. McLeod, Alexander. *The Character, History, Death, and Resurrection of "The Two Witnesses."* 1843 [1814]. 3rd ed. Edinburgh: W.P. Kennedy. 24 p.

Revelation 11:3.

720. _____. *Lectures Upon the Principal Prophecies of the Revelation.* 1844 [1814]. New York: Whiting and Watson. xii, 480 p. bibl. refs. 1844 ed. pub. in Glasgow.

Bound with Cairns' *Second Woe.* Author: Reformed Presbyterian Church, New York. Historicist. Revived fatal wound = Charles Martel and Merovingian-Carolingian successors.

721. _____. *A Scriptural View of the Character, Causes, and Ends of the Present War.* 1815. New York: Eastburn, Kirk and

Co.; Whiting and Watson; Smith and Forman, Paul & Thomas. 224 p.

War of 1812.

722. _____. *The Cherubim and the Apocalypse.* 1853. Edinburgh: William Whyte. viii, 464 p.

723. Maitland, Charles. *A Brief and Connected View of Prophecy: Being an Exposition of the Second, Seventh, and Eighth Chapters of the Prophecy of Daniel Together with the Sixteenth Chapter of Revelation.* 1814. London: Printed for J. Hatchard. 95 p.

"To which are added, some observations respecting the period and manner of the restoration of the Jews." Future 70th Week: Antichrist rebuilds Temple, then Armageddon and Second Coming.

724. Maitland, Samuel R. *An Enquiry Into the Grounds on Which the Prophetic Period of Daniel and St. John, Has Been Supposed to Consist of 1260 Years.* 1826. London: Hatchard and Son. 175 p. bibl. refs.

Maitland: Anglican. Historic premill; first Protestant futurist. Antichrist is yet to come.

725. _____. *A Second Enquiry Into the Grounds on Which the Prophetic Period of Daniel and St. John, Has Been Supposed to Consist of 1,260 Years.* 1829. London : C. and J. Rivington. vi, 175 p. bibl.

"Containing an examination of the arguments of Mede — remarks on a passage in the dialogues on prophecy,— on various reviews of the first inquiry,— and on the common interpretation of the seven heads of the Beast.

726. _____. *An Attempt to Elucidate the Prophecies Concerning Antichrist.* 1853 [1830]. 2nd ed. London: Rivington. 77 p.

727. Martin, James. *The End of the World: Coming Struggle Among the Nations.* n.d. London: Martin, Boundy. 15 p.

Includes "correct copy of the will of Peter the Great" and "opinion of Napoleon on the Turkish crisis."

728. Mason, Archibald. *The Fall of Babylon the Great, by the Agency of Christ, and Through the Instrumentality of His Witnesses in Four Discourses.* 1821. Glasgow: Printed by Young and Gallie. 112 p.

729. Matteson, J. G. *Prophecies of Jesus: or, the Fulfillment of the Predictions of Our Saviour and His Prophets.* 1895. Battle Creek, MI: International Tract Soc. 566 p. illus. index.

Jesus is source of all prophecies, including Dan. and Rev. Wars increasing, also famine, pestilence, earthquakes, false prophets. Christianity preached to whole world: sign of End (but world doesn't convert). Tribulation = 1,260 years of Papacy from 538 (after Bishop of Rome made head of all churches and Goths depart) to 1798 (Papal power broken by France). "Dark Day": 1780; falling stars 1833. Quotes many Danish sources. "All Protestant expositors agree" that First Beast = Papacy. 666 = "vicarious filii dei." 10 toes = 4th-5th century barbarian successor states, which will "never reunite." Little Horn = Papacy (uproots Heruli, Vandals, Ostrogoths to establish Papal State). Healing of deadly wound: Papal power will be restored. 2,300 days = 457 B.C. to A.D. 1844. 70 weeks = 457 B.C. to A.D. 34. In 1844 Jesus began but the "sanctuary cleansing"; (see below) "not revealed" how long to last. King of North and South = Napoleon sails to Egypt; Turkey vs. France in Syria; part still to be fulfilled. Euphrates dries up = Turkey withers. Woman = Church. Man-Child = Christ. Dragon = Pagan Rome. 10-Horn Beast of Sea = Papal Rome = 10 Kingdoms in Roman areas (including France, Germany, England). Michael = Christ. Stresses crucial importance of Sabbath; continuing gifts of prophecy, praising E.G. White. 2nd Beast = U.S., arose as 1st mortally wounded. False Prophet (corrupted Protestantism) induces worship of 1st Beast for 2nd Beast (Papacy will take over U.S. government). Mark of Beast = changing and violating Sabbath laws. Warns of pending Sunday laws, state takeover of religion in U.S. 144,000 = true Sabbath keepers; divinely protected during plagues, raptured up end of Tribulation. 7 last plagues, Armageddon, then Second Coming. Earth burns; New Heaven and Earth. New Jerusalem descends from Heaven, 119,025 sq. miles. Discusses Scandinavian 1840s millenarian "Crying Voices" revival.

730. Maurice, Frederick Denison. *Lectures on the Apocalypse, or, Book of the Revelation of St. John the Divine.* 1893 [1885]. London: Macmillan. xi, 368 p. 2nd ed.

Preterist. Most events of Revelation already fulfilled in Christ's time and ancient Rome. Earthquakes = effect of Gospel. Locusts = superstitions. Two Witnesses = city of Jerusalem. 1st Beast = Roman emperorship. 2nd Beast = ancient Roman religion. Babylon = Ancient Rome. Millennium = Christ's death, resurrection and ascension.

731. Mauro, Philip. *The Number of Man: The Climax of Civilization.* 1909. Boston, MA: Hamilton Bros. ; Scripture Truth Depot. 384 p. SEE ALSO 1910–1970

732. Mayer, Lewis. *Bonaparte the Emperor of the French, Considered as Lucifer and Gog of Isaiah and Ezekiel.* 1806. 3rd ed. London: priv. pub. ii, 70 p. illus.

Includes "an hieroglyphic ... of the destiny of Europe, the fate of the German Empire, and the fall of Russia. And a new explanation of Daniel's Seventy Weeks." Bound with author's *The Prophetic Mirror; or, A Hint to England* (1806, 3rd ed., iv, 56 p.), which also proves Napoleon is the Beast of Revelation.

733. Mead, Willis W. 1909 [1908]. *The Apocalypse of Jesus Christ.* New York: author. iii, 354 p. Index.

Parallels between first chapters of Genesis (1–4) and last chapters of Revelation (14–22).

734. Medill, William. *Key to a Part of the Book of Revelation.* 1855. Cleveland, OH: printed by Cowles, Pinkerton.

735. Merrill, Stephen Mason. *The Second Coming of Christ: Considered in its Relation to the Millennium, the Resurrection, and the Judgment.* 1879. Cincinnati: Hitchcock and Walder. 282 p.

Methodist Episcopal Church.

736. *The Millennial Kingdom.* 1852 London: J.F. Shaw. xii, 365 p.

Lectures by Church of England clergymen.

737. *Millennial Tidings.* 1831. Describes work of Joseph Wolff, a converted Jew who predicted Second Coming for 1847.

738. Miller, William. *Evidence from Scripture and History of the Second Coming of Christ, About the Year 1843, and of His Personal Reign of 1000 Years.* 1842 [1835]. Boston: Joshua V. Himes. Reprinted 1994 by Leaves-of-Autumn Books. 304 p. With "Chronological Chart of the World." 1835 ed. pub. Syracuse, NY; 64 p. Also pub. 1833 as pamphlet.

First Coming happened according to prophecy, so the Second must also. "If I have erred in my exposition of the prophecies, the time, being so near at hand, will soon expose my folly; but if I have the truth on the subjects treated on in these pages, how important the era in which we live! What vast and important events must soon be realized!" At Second Coming, wicked will be destroyed, death will be abolished, all earth's interior fires will be spent (after burning the earth). 6,000 Years from Creation of Adam 4157 B.C. to A.D. 1843. Then the Millennium. 457 B.C. + 2,300 (days/years till the Sanctuary is cleansed) = 1843. Crucifixion was end of 70 Weeks. 457 B.C. (Ezra's decree) + 490 (70 Weeks) = A.D. 33. A.D. 538 (rise of Papacy) + 1,260 (reign of Beast: "time, times and a half") = 1798. 1299 + 150 years = 5th Trumpet — the Ottoman Empire. Locusts: turbaned Turkish cavalry. 1449 + 391 years = start of 7th Trumpet. 1798 = end of Papal power over kings. 45 years from 1798 to End = 1843 (45 is difference between 1335 and 1290). Pagan Rome 158 B.C. + 666 =A.D. 508 (last of ten successor states becomes Christianized). 508 + 1,290 = 1798. 538 (when Papacy declared to be infallible) + 1,260 = 1798. Kings of South (Sardinia, Italy, Spain), plus North (England, under Nelson) vs. Napoleon in Egypt and Italy. Disturbing tidings from North and East were Holy Alliance and Russian campaign. Great Tribulation will start "on or before A.D. 1839." Seven Churches: historical periods; the seventh beginning 1798. Seven Seals refers to Church history. Seven Trumpets judgments against pagan Rome. Seven Vials against papal Rome. Two Witnesses: the

Old and New Testaments. Dragon vs. Woman in Revelation = Luther, Calvin, etc. Sea turned to blood = Huguenot massacres. Rivers turned to blood = religious wars. Euphrates dried up: decline of Ottoman Empire. Seventh Vial about 1840; Armageddon.

739. _____. *Views of the Prophecies and Prophetic Chronology, Selected from Manuscripts of William Miller, with a Memoir of his Life.* 1842. Boston: Joshua V. Himes. Edited by Himes. 252 p. illus, chart. 1980 reprint edition Yountville, CA: Carl E. Prosser.

Authorship sometimes credited to Himes, the editor. Includes biographical material by Himes and accounts of lectures and sermons. The End = ca. 1843 (from Daniel 8:14-"2,300 days" = years from 457 B.C. decree to Ezra to rebuild Temple. 2,520 - 677 (Babylonian Captivity) = 1843. 2,300 - 490 (7 x 70) + 33 (Christ's age) = 1843. Himes also published *Synopsis of Miller's Views* (1843, Boston; 32 p.). The *1843 Prophetic Chart* (1842) used at Millerite meetings was designed by Charles Fitch and Apollos Hale; then revised for 1844. The broadside *End of the World, October 22, 1844!!* attributed to Miller was really a parody. The chief Millerite serials were *Signs of the Times* (Boston; Himes, ed.); *Midnight Cry* (New York); and *Second Advent of Christ* (1843; Cleveland; Fitch, ed.).

740. Milligan, William. *The Revelation of St. John.* 1886.

Milligan: professor at University of Aberdeen. A-mill; non-literal interpretation. Critically discusses historical ("Joachist"), preterist, and futurist interpretations. Apocalypse refers to whole Christian age from First to Second Coming.

741. Minton, Samuel. *Our Present Position: The 1260 Years of Papal Domination Just Expiring, and "the Time of the End" Commencing.* 1867. London: Seeley, Jackson & Halliday. 63 p.

The world's 6,000 years just about over. Popery as false religion: the False Prophet and the Beast. Decisive crisis expected 1866-67: A.D. 607 plus 1,260. [1869 annotation by "R. Robertson" in

Aurora Univ. copy adds 75 years (1,335 total) for "many Antichrists," with End thus extended to 1942.]

742. Mitchell, W[illiam] H[obbs]. *A Striking Resemblance: or, A Contrast Between the Days of Noah and the Days of the Coming of the Son of Man.* 1894. Boston: Advent Christian Publication Society. 25 p.

Advent Christian. Prevalence of unbelief, violence, materialism, and corruption.

743. Molyneux, Capel. *The World to Come.* 1853. London: Partridge and Oakey. xv, 295 p.

744. _____. *Israel's Future.* 1860. 6th ed. London: James Nisbet. xvi, 269 p.

70th Week future; at end of age, when Israel restored. Antichrist makes 7-year covenant with Israel; breaks it midway, persecutes Jews horribly. Two Witnesses oppose him, but Antichrist gathers world armies to crush Israel. Defeated at Armageddon by Second Coming.

745. Moody, Dwight L. *The Second Coming of Christ.* 1877. Rev. ed. Chicago: Revell. 27 p. Also 32 p. ed. Also pub. 1898, 1913 Boston: Advent Christian; 1899 Oakland, CA: T. Wilson; inc. in Bible Inst. Colportage Assoc. series.

Moody: Congregationalist; famed evangelist. Preached imminent Second Coming. [Moody Bible Institute in Chicago has been a major dispensational pre-mill fundamentalist center.]

746. Moore, Irvin. *The Final Destiny of Man.* 1869. Ann Arbor, MI: author [printed by Detroit Daily Post]. 80 p.

"Giving a most interesting exposition of all the different times spoken of in prophecy: being the only true theory ever offered to the public on latter day matters and the only one calculated to clear away the most of the mysteries that has been thrown over the important subject of the End of the World, the Second Coming of Christ, and the ushering in of the Millennium, etc. The Year 1870 is the correct date of the End of the World, and that is but the beginning of greater events, as proven within." The Seven Times of Lev. XXVI:18 = 2,520 years of Jewish captivity (Time of Gentiles), from 677 B.C. to

1843. 1,260 days = A.D. 538 (Papacy established control over 3 of the 10 Horns) to 1798. 2,300 Days = Sanctuary cleansed = 1843: when Turkish Empire dries up. Dan. XII: 1,290 and 1,335 days = start A.D. 538, to 1828 and 1873. 1870: Gospel preached worldwide, France will fall, Jerusalem becomes world capital; then Millennium, with Christ ruling. Moore denies Trinity; just single God instead. No Hell, no devil. Two Witnesses = "waldences and albigences" and other anti-papal true Christians. 3½ years = 1866 to June 28, 1870. David, not Christ, is commander on white horse at Gog battle in Revelation between "true church and the antichristian Romans."

747. Morrison, H.C. *Will God Set Up a Visible Kingdom on Earth?* 1934. Louisville, KY: Pentecostal Publishing Co.

748. Morse, Jedediah. *Signs of the Times.* 1810. Charlestown [MA].

Congregational minister; father of telegraph inventor. Mohammedan Antichrist will be overthrown by Russia, and Papal Antichrist will fall about the same time, probably around 1866. Then, the Millennium.

749. Munhall, Leander W. *The Lord's Return and Kindred Truths.* 4th ed. 1888. New York: Fleming H. Revell. 192 p. Also 1962 reprint of 8th [1898?] ed. (Grand Rapids, MI: Kregel).

Munhall: itinerant Methodist evangelist who reached perhaps 17 million listeners; preached imminent Second Coming and wrote books against Higher Criticism. Pre-trib. Satan used Millerite disappointment to discourage pre-millennialism. Early church was strongly pre-mill until Origen's allegorizing. Praises great pre-millers: Ussher, Milton, Bunyan, Newton, the Wesleys (Charles was the "Millennial Poet"), Delitzsch, Kurtz, Faussett, Spurgeon, Melancthons' Augsburg Confession, Nicene Creed, Book of Common Prayer. Post-mill theory "entirely indefensible." Bible teaches "most explicitly" that world will not be converted. At end of this dispensation "... Christ comes to catch his bride away to save her from the fires of the great tribu-

lation, and the end of which time he returns with his bride to judge the world in righteousness and destroy the antichrist and his armies...." Bible assures us "that more fearful atrocities, by far, than the Neronian, will befall God's people in the last days." "Real, literal, personal" Coming in very near future. "He will not tarry.... The King, in regal beauty — our Beloved — riding majestically upon the clouds of heaven, with all the royalty of the skies, will soon appear." End occurring during "this generation" probably refers to Israel as a people. Resurrection of saints at start of Tribulation, of the unjust only after Millennium; God comes *for* the saints, then *with* the saints. Jews not to possess land of Israel until end of Tribulation and Advent. Summary: God now gathering church; will hurl Satan to earth to wreak havoc (Tribulation); God raises saints to heaven; Tribulation; Jews convert during Tribulation; Second Coming; Millennium; many others convert; Satan loosed at end of Millennium; leads unsaved nations (Gog, Magog) to defeat; Judgment and Resurrection of wicked. All dispensations ended in man's failure: Fall; Flood; Babel; Babylonian Captivity; rejection of Christ; and soon, reign of Antichrist. Miller was a "fanatic" — his failure caused swing to post-millennialism (which Satan capitalized on). Accuses post-mills of non-literal interpretation; says pre-mills make better evangelists and missionaries. Decries Sunday business, theater-going. "Coming of the Lord"= start of Millennium; "Day of the Lord" = judgment at end of Millennium. Rejects as "Miltonic" the idea that Satan is a fallen angel; says he was evil from beginning.

750. Nagnatus. *The Connection Between Famine and Pestilence and the Great Apostasy.* 1847. Dublin: Philip Dixon Hardy. 51 p.

751. Needham, Elizabeth Annable [Mrs. George C.] *The Antichrist.* 1901 [1881]. Philadelphia: A.W. Needham. 103 p.

752. Needham, George C. (ed?). *Prophetic Studies of the International Prophetic Conference.* 1886 Chicago: F.H. Revell. 214 p. [8] leaves. illus.

2nd International Prophetic Conference, 1886, Chicago. Also called American Bible and Prophetic Conference. Title page: "Critical and scholarly essays ... upon the near Coming of the Lord, its literal and personal character, the development of the Antichrist, the First Resurrection, the Jews and their future predicted judgments, the Millennium, and kindred topics and events..." The "restrainer" of Satan is Satan himself.

753. Newbrough, John Ballou. *A Hand Book of the Millennium According to Oahspe, the Cosmic Bible.* 1911. Los Angeles: Brewer. 63 p.

Extracts from last four books of *Oahspe*, an occult American "Cosmic Bible" written by Newbrough (d. 1891) in King James style. Published (and edited?) by Charles L. Brewer, who is sometimes listed as the author.

754. Newton, Benjamin Wills. *Thoughts on the Apocalypse.* 1844. London: Hamilton, Adams. 377 p. 3rd ed 1904; London: Houlston & Sons; xii, 515; index.

Plymouth Brethren, but opposed Darby's Rapture doctrine and pre-trib theory. Verse-by-verse commentary; premill. All dispensations of history have been "disastrous failure." Revelation says path of humanity is toward evil. Sometimes results are announced first in Revelation; not their order of fulfillment. Israel to regather in unbelief; undergo Tribulation. Antichrist servant of Harlot; then False Prophet teams up with Antichrist after Antichrist and 10-King future Roman league destroy Harlot. First Horseman of Four = Christ. Woes all in future: Tribulation. Seven Trumpet woes punish Israel; Vials punish Antichrist and Gentiles. Literal Witnesses, demonic locusts. "Day" never means year! Antichrist/10-Horn Beast supported by Mystical Babylon but later destroys it (= wounding of head). 10-Horn system carrying Harlot not yet manifest. Popery is "chief channel towards Antichrist" but not the focus of Revelation. Second Coming: nations will have rejected Christianity. Armageddon: Roman world gathers there, immediately followed by barbarous Eastern nations attacking literal Babylon. Armies annihilated by God. Millennium itself described in Old Testament, not Revelation. Gog and Magog = Central Asia (not Russia); their second appearance, at end of Millennium, is to the nations generally.

755. _____. *Prospects of the Ten Kingdoms of the Roman Empire Considered: Being the Third Series of Aids to Prophetic Inquiry.* 1863 [1849]. London: Houlston & Wright. 275 p. index. Rev. abridged ed. 1955. Wembley: G.L. Silverwood Browne; vi, 271 p.

Christ will govern through Israel in Jerusalem. Recommends Tregelles. Insists on coming Ten Monarch confederation, a revived Roman Empire, which must include eastern (Greek) half. Iron-clay mix = popular/monarchic governments — constitutional monarchy. Insists revived Empire will have same boundaries; thus Ireland to break away from England, some German states to be annexed by "Roman" states. Austro–Prussian War confirmation that Austria will rejoin Roman but most of Germany to remain outside. Little Horn = Antichrist; from Greek part; arises only after Ten Kingdoms. 70 hebdomads from 454 B.C. (Artaxerxes) to A.D. 29–30. 70th Week when full national regathering of Israel. Luke 21 predicted that persecution of Jews would cease, as Newton says it has. But after Return will again have to be chastised. Jews return, rebuild Temple; Antichrist then directs fury against them. Antichrist will move base to Babylon and Jerusalem. Second half of 70th Week: Antichrist as Desolator in Jerusalem, makes image speak, requires he be worshipped. Attacked by Kings of North and South (Syria, Egypt), defeats them. Brings Ten Kingdom army to Armageddon when Babylon attacked by East and North; moves to attack Jerusalem but destroyed by Lord at Jehoshaphat. Those who aid or follow Antichrist will be resurrected with "revived bodies" to be tormented during Millennium; rest of wicked only resurrected at end of Millennium. Rapture at beginning of Second Coming (end of Tribulation) so that saints can accompany

Christ's descent to earth a few minutes later. Millennium begins later. Gog-Magog invasion while whole of Israel gradually regathered at beginning of Millennium. New Jerusalem descends to earth during Millennium but doesn't land until after Millennium. Some people saved during Millennium, others regenerate; newly saved resurrected with wicked at end of Millennium. Final Gog-Magog revolt at end of Millennium. This edition includes Appendix on Franco-Prussian War: concedes results opposite to predicted revival of Roman imperial boundaries, but claims war was prophetically necessary because it foiled "atrocious plot" by wicked France to form coalition with Papacy. England is headed toward Babylonish system, forsaking true religion.

756. _____. *Aids to Prophetic Inquiry*. 1853. 2nd ed. enl. London: Sovereign Grace Advent Testimony. 220 p.

757. _____. *Europe and the East: Final Predominance of Russia Inconsistent with the Declarations of Scripture*. 1878 [1855]. London: Houlston. 2nd ed. 176 p.

Ten Toes: reconstituted "Roman" federation prophesied; will include Egypt, Greece, Syria, Turkey, England, Spain, France. 1st ed. during Crimean War. Author erroneously predicted England would take over much of Islamic dominions. England so far privileged, but will be tempted into apostasy by Eastern and German infidelity. Antichrist reigns after this dispensation ends. Discusses dire effects of atheistic socialism, sacerdotalism, anti–Christianism.

758. _____. *Antichrist Future*. 1859. 2nd ed. 1900.

759. _____. *Events that are to Precede the Return of Our Lord*. 1972 [1861]. 4th ed. London: Sovereign Grace Advent Testimony. 23 p.

760. _____. *Babylon, its Future History and Doom*. 1890. London: Houlston. 3rd ed. xvi, 642 p. map plate. Orig. ed. "more than 40 years ago."

The "awful end of *unbelieving* Israel's history when gathered (as they soon will be) back to Jerusalem, there to be 'trodden down' [and] the scarcely less awful history

of the end of Christendom." Rage and fury of Satan at end of dispensation, great destruction, First Resurrection of dead and Reign of Saints.

761. _____. *The New World Order or Premillennial Truth Demonstrated: An Answer to the Post–Millennial, A-Millennial and Anti-Millennial Theories*. 1900. London: Sovereign Grace Advent Testimony. 19 p.

Also wrote *Facts of Prophetic Scripture: Studies in Daniel & Revelation* (date?) reprinted *from Watching & Waiting*.

762. _____. *Expository Teaching on the Millennium and Israel's Future*. 1913 London: Sovereign Grace Advent Testimony. v, 192 p. index.

"Abomination of desolation" was Antiochus; preceded by invasions by Syria (North) and Egypt (South).

763. Newton, William. *Lectures on the First Two Visions of the Book of Daniel*. 1859. Philadelphia: Martien. 250 p.

1866 as End/Millennium.

764. Nichols, J. H. *The Approaching Crisis and End of the World*. 1890. Stanberry, MO: Advent and Sabbath Advocate Press. 48 p.

765. Nichols, L.T. *Bible Chronology*. 1899. West Concord, MN: Enterprise Print. 106 p.

766. _____. *The Coming of Jesus and Elijah and the Great Battle of Armageddon*. 1968 [1905]. Rochester, NY: Megiddo Mission church. 64 p.

Nichols: former Christadelphian; proselytized at turn of century on custom-built riverboat *Megiddo* (from Hebrew for "gathering of God's army") on Ohio River. Followers founded Megiddo Mission Church in Rochester.

767. Norton, Robert. *The Restoration of Apostles and Prophets: in the Catholic Apostolic Church*. 1861. London: Bosworth & Harrison. 191 p.

768. *Notes on the Apocalypse*. Anon. [From 1842 lectures]. London: G. Morrish. 165 p.

Symbolic interpretation of seals, trumpets, vials, as representing apostasy. 70th week not yet fulfilled. Can't interpret 666 yet. 10 Horns = future confederation of kings. Christ's Millennial Reign is "spiritual as well as personal" but real thousand years. Two resurrections, of just and unjust; second after Second Advent. Calls on Jesus to come quickly.

769. Nott, Eliphalet. *A Sermon Preached Before the General Assembly of the Presbyterian Church in the United States of America.* 1806. Philadelphia. 39 p.

World is advancing "towards that dreadful catastrophe, of which revelation pre-admonishes the saint. The six thousand years of Satan's triumph is almost over." But Millennium will be ushered in by "human exertions": i.e. post-millennialism.

770. Noyes, John Humphrey. *A Treatise on the Second Coming of Christ.* 1840. Putney, VT. 32 p.

Second Coming occurred immediately after Jewish Revolt A.D. 70—a spiritual rather than physical event. Noyes: founded perfectionist commune ("Bible communism") in Oneida, NY, 1848.

771. "Omicron." *The Millennium, or the Doctrines of the Second Advent.* 1844. London: Nisbets.

Coming revival of Roman Empire, led by the Beast, for 70th Week.

772. Osler, Lemuel. *The Historical Prefigurations of the Kingdom of God.* 1861. Boston: American Millennial Assoc. [35]–89 p. Address to Evangelical Advent Church, Providence, RI.

773. Ottman, Ford C. *The Unfolding of the Ages in the Revelation of John.* 1967 [1905]. Fincastle, VA: Scripture Truth. xxx, 510 p. indexes.

"One of the earlier premillennial commentaries." Pre-trib pre-mill. Chapter-by-chapter exposition of Revelation. Gap Theory creationism (cites Pusey's *Daniel*): Satan and his rebel angels occupied pre–Adamic earth. Last Days characterized by demon worship. Tribulation after Satan defeated and expelled from heaven. Church "summoned out of the world to meet her Lord" (Rapture). Then 70th week. 200 million horsemen demon possessed. Gog-Magog = Russia. Mystery Babylon = Roman Catholic Church.

774. Pae, David. *The Coming Struggle Among the Nations of the Earth, or, the Political Events of the Next Fifteen Years: Described in Accordance with Prophecies in Ezekiel, Daniel and the Apocalypse, Showing Also the Important Position Britain and American Will Occupy During and at the End of the Awful Conflict.* New York: G. Taylor. 1853. 48 p.

Credits Dr. Thomas (American) as first to find key. Babylonian, Persian, Greek, Roman empires. Restoration of Jews is key to "awful events of the coming years." Refutes theory that Armageddon is moral triumph over Popery. Ten Kingdoms: Bavaria, Lombardy, Hungary, Greece, Sardinia, Naples, Portugal, Spain, France, Belgium. They will be destroyed within 15 years (by 1868) at end of 1,260 days. A.D. 531 + 1,260 = 1791: end of Beast's reign. Two Witnesses were slain by Louis XIV in 1789. England and America to conduct moral progress of world and prepare it for Millennium, while others nations destroy each other. 6th Vial began 1820, still in progress (Turkey withers). 7th Vial began 1830. "Frog-power" is France. Russia to take over Austria and conquer Germany, France. Britain aloof, then expands East, restores Jews. Then Russian invades Israel, army destroyed at Armageddon by Britain, U.S., and Jews (Americans sail over to help).

775. Pagani, Giovanni Battista. *The End of the World, or, The Second Coming of Our Lord and Saviour Jesus Christ.* 1855. London: Charles Dolman. viii, 367 p.

776. Parker, William. *The Bible Unveiled.* 1851. London: Sampson Low.

"The Anglo-Saxon Bible — The Papacy — The Millennium," etc.

777. Paton, John H. *The Day Dawn.* 1890 [1880]. Almont, MI: J.H. Paton. 399 p.

778. Peabody, Andrew P. *Sermon on the End of the World.* 1843. Portsmouth, NH: 15 p.

779. Pearson, Abel. *An Analysis of the Principles of the Divine Government... and a Dissertation on the Prophecies, in Reference to the Rise and Fall of the Beast.... Together with a Calculation Showing the Exact Time of the Death of Christ ... and* *the Beginning of the Millennium, Etc.* 1833, 1823. Athens, TN: T.A. Anderson. 419 p.

780. Pember, G[eorge] H[awkins]. *The Great Prophecies Concerning the Gentiles, the Jews and the Church of God.* 1984 [1881]. Miami Springs: Conley & Schoettle. xvi, 458 p. bibl. refs.

"*Our age has entered upon its last days....*"

781. _____. *The Antichrist, Babylon, and the Coming of the Kingdom.* 1988 [1886]. 3rd ed. Miami Springs: Schoettle Publishing Co. xiv, 171 p.

Parallels between Christ and Antichrist. Dispensationalist. Applauds return to literal, futurist interpretation of prophecy (Trumpets, Vials, 70th Week all in future). Papal power is increasing and still a menace — the Harlot Church of Satan. World now "in an advanced state of preparation for the Antichrist." Spiritualism = Satanism. Antichrist = Beast; becomes leader of 10 Kingdom Empire of Rome, overthrows Harlot Church (Mystery Babylon) in first half of Tribulation. False Prophet = 2nd Beast; organizes worship of Antichrist. Mark of Beast, ghastly persecutions. Antichrist's armies destroyed at Armageddon by Second Coming. Babylon was the original center of Satan's evil conspiracy; Satan then transferred his headquarters to Rome. Literal Babylon to be rebuilt, as Antichrist's capital; world center of commerce and wickedness. Pretrib, but partial (selective) Rapture. Vulture carcass parable: corpse = the spiritually dead.

782. _____. *Mystery Babylon the Great and The Mysteries and Catholicism: An Exposition of Revelation 17 and 18 and An Account of the Rise of the Roman Catholic Church Under Pagan Influence.* 1998 [sic]. Miami Springs, FL: Schoettle. x, 147 p.

783. Pettingill, William. *History Foretold: Simple Studies in Daniel.* 1941 [1901]. 8th ed. Findlay, OH: Fundamental Truth. 117 p.

"The Time of the End is here." Dispensational pre-trib pre-mill. Rapture, then 7-year Tribulation. Unlike Revelation, Daniel was "sealed book" until Time of the End. Jewish remnant to suffer awful horrors of Great Tribulation. Antichrist = "last Gentile World-Monarch"; King of Syria, then dominates world; destroyed at Second Coming. Denies literal Babylon; "contrary to Scripture" that it will be rebuilt. Little Horn = Antichrist, from final tenfold form of Roman Empire; from eastern (Greek) part of Empire. 70 "sevens" of 360-day years. 69th = 445 B.C. to Christ's entry into Jerusalem. Then long Gap. 70th Week = Tribulation. Pettingill: Baptist; co-founder Philadelphia School of Bible. SEE ALSO 1910–1970

784. Phelps, Enoch. *Gog in the Land of Magog.* 1897. Boston: Advent Christian Society. 87 p.

785. Phillips, J[oseph] Scott. *Interpretations.* 1860. London.

Antichrist = 1,260 years of Papal dominance; but also literal 1,260-day future Antichrist: Louis Napoleon. Will make 7-year covenant with Israel. At Second Coming, great earthquake will open channel connecting Mediterranean to Dead Sea, then to Red Sea, making Jerusalem trade center of the world.

786. _____. *Original Discoveries Concerning the Resettlement of the Seed of Abraham in Syria and Arabia. With Mathematical and Geographical Scripture Proofs.* 1860. Geneva, IL: "Gospel Banner" Office, by the Christian Publication Co.

Restoration of the Jews.

787. "Philo-Basilicus." *Essays on the Coming of the Kingdom of God.* 1842. Philadelphia: Orrin Rogers. 92 p. Also included in *The Literalist.*

Jews restored prior to Second Coming and End, but this Return may occur suddenly.

788. Philpott, J.P. *The Kingdom of Israel.* 1883. Southern Methodist Publishing House, 533 p. Orig 1864. (Fairfield, TX: Pioneer Office, 50 p.).

"From its inception under Joshua, its first president, in the year of the world 2553, to the second advent of Christ...." Dedicated to S.D. Baldwin (author of *Armageddon*). Three Israelitish kingdoms, successively headed by Ephraim, Judah (David), and Manasseh. Just as Judah seceded from the Israelite confederacy, modern Judah has seceded from Manasseh. And just as Manasseh and Ephraim rejoined Judah in the past, so must they now. U.S. is now Manasseh, and Confederate States are Judah. Manasseh had 13 children (13 colonies in America), five of them female (five of the colonies had female names). Washington, D.C. = Sodom (Ezek. 16:49–50). CSA is Zion; also the Stone Mountain which succeeds the Four Kingdoms, born without labor in a day. Jefferson Davis = David (almost). Confederacy also Two Witnesses who prophecy in Sodom/Washington, and are killed and resurrected. "Fiery serpents" are abolitionists. The ten Western states — Ephraim — will soon secede also from Manasseh. Then all three Israelite nations (Confederate states, Union states, and Western states) will join together under Judah's leadership. This unification will definitely be accomplished between Nov. 1865 and Jan. 1867. Then, Israel , under Confederate rule, will fight the world's monarchies in the battle of Armageddon. Noah's sons Japheth, Shem, and Ham: "Perpetual rule to Japheth" which 'must become Israel" in the last days. Ham (Egypt) formerly enslaved Israelites; so now Japheth (Israel) enslaves Ham.

789. "Phylos the Tibetan." *A Dweller on Two Planets.* 1952 [1886]. Los Angeles: Borden [distr. by DeVorss]. 432 p. Illus.

Wisdom from Atlantis includes coming "end of the Age ... awful woe ... terminal horror" before New Heaven and New Earth. War involving many million soldiers, then catastrophic natural disasters. The Great Master says these things shall be "when you see surrounded by encampments the Jerusalem, then you may know that has come near the desolation.... For days of vengeance these are, to be fulfilled of all the judgments."

790. Pickett, L[eander] L. *The Blessed Hope of His Glorious Appearing.* 1901. Louisville, KY: Pentecostal Publishing Co. vii, 370 p. illus.

Pre-mill; Methodist. The Millennium — "Imagine Paul under Immanuel as President of the United States, Peter King of England, James superceding the Czar of Russia, John as Emperor of China, Bartholomew succeeding to the throne of Kaiser William of Germany"; Nathaniel the president of France, John Wesley mayor of London, John Bunyan as mayor of Paris, Moody mayor of Chicago, Jonathan Edwards mayor of New York. SEE ALSO 1910–1970.

791. Pile, William N. *The Coming Reign of Terror: or, The Commune.* [1890s]. 2nd ed., rev. and enl. [Springfield, MA: author?] 28 p.

792. _____. *Perils of the Last Days.* 1905. Boston: Advent Christian Publication Soc. 41 p.

Advent Christian. We are now "in the 'last days,' and the predicted perils of these days are all about us."

793. Pitts, Fountain E. *A Defence of Armageddon; or, Our Great Country Foretold in the Holy Scriptures.* 1859 [1857]. Baltimore: John W. Bull. 116 p.

Orig. day-long sermon "delivered in the Capitol of the United States, at the request of several members of Congress" in 1857, about America's prophetic destiny. Elaborates on Baldwin's scenario; Armageddon fought in Mississippi Valley.

794. [Plinth, Octavius]. *A Crude Picture of Latter Ages, or an Undisguised Scrutiny of the Modern Predominant Knowledge, Social Order and Happiness.* 1817. [n.p.] vi, [7]–185 p.

"To which is prefixed the living Hebrews' illustration, and the plain investigation of the profuse bliss that the rambling Jews have successfully dispensed in the northern hemisphere.... Also terminated by a series of quotations of the obvious fulfillment of the Holy Scripture, giving explicit warning to the inadvertent human species of this desolated and devastated planet that they are fast approaching the time of the disastrous catastrophe generally predicted by the godly inspired prophets, the grievous observations are dedicated to the serious cogitation of the afflicted, having no delight in the afflictions of others, and the sincere believers in the Sacred book of Divine Revelation."

795. Pollok, Robert. [d. 1827]. *The Course of Time.* 1833 New York: Charles Wells. 338 p. index Many eds. 1850s etc. (e.g. National School Series).

Poem in ten books. Bard sings of the "Millannium" and 1000-year "millannial rest" of Messiah's reign and destruction of the world and Final Judgment in last several books.

796. Post, Truman. *Outlook of the Times.* 1881.

797. Potts, James Henry. *The Golden Dawn: or, Light on the Great Future.* 1882 [c1880]. Philadelphia/Chicago: P.W. Ziegler. 608 p. illus. index.

"The best thoughts of over 300 authors and scholars." Potts: editor of *Christian Advocate* (Detroit). Many short entries, on death, afterlife, immortality, Millennium and Second Coming, resurrection of dead and final judgment, Heaven and Hell. Including dying words of infidels and atheists, and Christian believers. W.X. Ninde presents overview of Millennium and Second Coming: favors post-mill but presents pre-mill as also possible. Other entries examine e.g. how both cannibals and their human meals can both be resurrected physically. Generally nonsectarian and inspirational, but stresses certainty of coming End and of everlasting Judgment, punishment and reward.

798. Pratt, Parley J. *A Voice of Warning and Instruction to All People: or an Introduction to the Faith and Doctrine of the Church of Jesus Christ of Latter Day Saints.* 1950 [1837]. Lamoni, IA: Reorganized Church of Latter Day Saints. Also pub. 1950 Salt Lake City: Church of Jesus Christ of Latter-day Saints. "Also an Analysis of Isaiah" (subtitle of some editions.). Many editions.

Fulfilled prophecy. These are the "last days." Future: Return of Jews, God's Army (the Nations) attacks, is destroyed. Messiah Comes, resurrects dead, Millennium. The Lamanites are "dark and benighted." Decries "slander" against Mormons.

799. *The Premillennial Advent.* 2nd ed. 1851 London: J.K. Campbell. Various pagings. "Tracts on Prophecy" (orig 1840–1860).

800. Priest, Josiah. *A View of the Expected Christian Millennium: Which is Promised in the Holy Scriptures, and is Believed to be Nigh its Commencement, and Must Transpire Before the Conflagration of the Heavens and the Earth.* 1828. Albany NY: Loomis Press. 5th ed. 408 p. illus.

"Embellished with a chart, of the dispensations from Abraham to the End of Time."

801. *Prophetic Light: The Date Marking the End of the Two Thousand and Three Hundred Day Period, a God Appointed Epoch, From Which Radiates Prophetic Light Indicating the Limitation of the Measuring Periods Which Point to the End of the Gentile Times.* 1870. [U.S.: s.n.] 30 p.

2,300 "Days" ended 1814. End was expected in 1844, but 45 years have to be added.

802. Purdon, Robert A. *The Last Vials.* 1852. London: Seeley. [172] p.

From Purdon's journal of the same name. Antichrist = Louis Napoleon. Jews return under Antichrist. "Translation" of 144,000 prior to 3½ years but after Antichrist's 7-year treaty (70th Week).

803. Pym, William Wollaston. *Word of Warning in the Last Days.* 1839. 2nd ed. Philadelphia: Dobson and Whetham. 129 p.

Later (1836) wrote *A Defense of A Word of Warning in the Last Days* (London: James Nisbet; 107 p.). Also wrote *Thoughts on Millenarianism.*

804. Ramsey, William. *The Second Coming of Our Lord and Saviour Jesus Christ in Power and Great Glory Before the Millennium.* 1841. Philadelphia: O. Rogers. 144 p.

Pre-mill.

805. Read, Hollis. *The Hand of God in History: or, Divine Providence Historically Illustrated in the Extension and Establishment of Christianity.* 1860 [1849]. Hartford: Robins. 432 p. illus.

Millennialism being fulfilled in America (Manifest Destiny) in 19th century Encouraged imperialism to spread Gospel and hasten Millennium.

806. _____. *The Coming Crisis of the*

World, or, The Great Battle and the Golden Age: The Signs of the Times Indicating the Approach of the Great Crisis and the Duty of the Church. 1861. Columbus: Follett, Foster. xv, 345 p.

Congregational minister, Boston. "There is a feeling in the human breast that despotism, bloodshed, fraud, oppression, and unbridled lust, have, in defiance of Heaven, rioted long enough, and that a righteous God will soon rise in his wrath and make a short work."

807. Redding, William A. *Our Near Future: A Message to All the Governments and People of the Earth.* 1896. Peekskill-on-Hudson, NY: Loomis. 216 p. illus. Also pub. 1900; Chicago: Loomis.

Bible prophecies.

808. Rees, Arthur Augustus. *The Death of Wellington and the Resurrection of Napoleon.* 1853. London: J. Nisbet.

Napoleon III as Antichrist; he will restore Jews to fulfill prophecy.

809. Rees, Seth Cook. *Fire from Heaven.* 1899. Cincinnati: Office of God's Revivalist. 329 p.

Holiness church. Pre-mill. The Bride (Church) will know when Christ is coming, though world won't. *Burning Coals* is vol. of excerpts from this work.

810. Reid, Robert. *The Seven Last Plagues: or, The Vials of the Wrath of God.* 1828. Pittsburgh: D. & M. Maclean. 305 p.

Dan. 7–9, 12; Rev. 11–16. Heavenly Sanctuary is cleansed around 1850; Millennium 45 years later.

811. Rice, N. L. (Nathan Lewis) 1855. *The Signs of the Times in a Series of Eight Lectures.* St. Louis, MO: Keith & Woods. 220 p.

Rice: Presbyterian pastor, St. Louis. Post-mill. Soon overthrow of Romanism, Mahometanism; Jews to return, Christianity to triumph (U.S. having leading role), then the Millennium in 1866 (or so). 1866 = A.D. 606 (start of Papal supremacy) + 1,260.

812. Riddall, Walter. *The End of the World.* 1890s. Booklet.

Similar to Dimbleby but prefers 5926 over 5826 Anno Mundi terminus.

(Anno Mundi: years since Creation.) Papal domination extends to 5926, so Second Coming must be later than this.

813. Roberts, Robert. *Thirteen Lectures on the Things Revealed in the Last Book of the New Testament Commonly Known as "Revelation" But More Appropriately Distinguished as the Apocalypse.* 1880. Birmingham Eng.: R. Roberts. viii, 220 p.

"Shewing their bearing on the events of history, and on those mightier events of the near future to which they have all been leading." Christadelphian.

814. Rohling, August. *Der Antichrist und das Ende der Welt: Zur Erwägung für alle Christen dargestellt.* 1875. St. Louis MO: B. Herder. 77 p. bibl. refs.

Rohling: Catholic priest, professor at theological Academy, Munich, and Salesianium of Milwaukee; author of notoriously anti–Semitic work *Der Talmudjude,* also wrote *Meine Antworten an die Rabbiner, oder Fünf Briefe über den Talmudismus und das Blut-Ritual der Juden* (1883).

815. _____. *Das Buch des Propheten Daniel.* 1876. Mainz: Franz Kirchheim. vi, 374 p. bibl. refs.

816. _____. *Erklarung der Apokalypse des h. Johannes des grossen Propheten von Patmos.* 1895. Munich: Liebfraumen-Druckerei. 315 p.

817. _____. *Die Zukunft der Menschheit als Gattung: Nach der Lehre der h. Kirchenvater.* 1907. Leipzig: Carl Beck. 369 p.

818. Ross, Albion. *Great Events Showing Our Nearness to the End.* [1885]. Boston: Advent Christian Publication Soc. 20 p.

Advent Christian. "Soon shall time no longer be." Six Trumpets: judgments against pagan Rome. Six Vials: against Papal Rome and Mohammedans.

819. _____. *Tokens of the Hour: The Last Phases of the Papacy Marked in Prophecy.* 1885. Boston: J.E. Ballou. 47 p. Daniel VIII.

820. Rosselet, G.A. *The Apocalypse and History.* 1878.

Euphrates dries up: Turkish Empire fades. 10-horn Beast: Catholic nations.

821. [Rossi, Gaudentius] "Pellegrino." *The Christian Trumpet: or, Previsions and Predictions about General Calamities, the Universal Triumph of the Church, the Coming of Antichrist, the Last Judgment, and the End of the World.* Compiled by "Pellegrino" (Rossi). 1873. Boston: Donahoe. xvi, 272 p.

Rossi: concerned with converting English to Catholicism. Compilation of over forty selections, transl. from French, Italian, other languages. Prophecies and predictions from early medieval to modern times. 1st part: warnings to mankind regarding impending serious calamities. 2nd part: eventual triumph of true Catholic religion. 3rd part: Last Judgment. Predictions of Charlemagne, Napoleon, Franco-Prussian War (1870), future wars, Antichrist. 1839 D'Orval predictions: End in about a hundred years. St. Bridget (Sweden): world religion in 1890, 1980 triumph of wicked (Tribulation), sun and stars cease to shine in 1999. 1830 prophecies: Babylon = Paris. La Sallette prophecies (1846, but written later?): Lucifer unchained 1864; Abomination of Desolation and Ten Kings in 1865; Antichrist at turn of century. Many prophets denounce republicanism, say communism will spread in America. Future Pope "Angelicus" from Dalmatia. (Rossi:) 6,000 year theory endorsed by many Catholic authorities, especially Cornelius Lapide. Creation ca. 4025 B.C.; less than hundred years left because Tribulation will be "shortened." "Hence, this world is doomed to utter destruction in much less than a century from the present date of 1873." Antichrist born 1860. Says infidelity is a greater sin than immorality.

822. Royse, P[leasant] E. *The Voice of the Prophets; and the Oracles of Omega: Proclaiming Wonderful Tidings About the Time of the End of this Dispensation and the Commencement of the Millennium.* 1866 [1860]. Cincinnati: Royse. 753 p.

823. Rozas, José Maria de. *Consulta a los Sabios, Sobre la Aprocsimación de la Segunda Venida de Nuestro Señor Jesucristo.* 1835. Toluca: Estado de Mexico, a Cargo de J. Matute. 239 p.

De Rozas: Catholic; Mexican judge. Supporter of Lacunza. 2,300 years ends ca. 1847. 6,000 Year theory.

824. Rupert, G[reenberry] G. *The Gathering of the Nations to Armageddon.* 1903. Oklahoma City: Union Pub. Co. viii, 266–543 p. illus., charts. SEE ALSO 1910–1970.

825. Rupley, H. *The Prophetic History of Time: With the Outlines of the Four Great Empires, Including the Tribulation and the Antichrist.* 1903. Huntington IN: U.B. Pub. 260 p.

826. _____. *The World's Great Crisis: or, The Signs of the Second Coming of Christ.* 1910 Huntington, IN: U.B. Pub. 230 p.

827. Russell, Charles Taze. *The Object and Manner of the Lord's Return.* 1877. Rochester, NY: Office of Herald of the Morning. 64 p.

1874 = invisible presence + 40 years = 1914 (Second Coming).

828. _____. *The Plan of the Ages.* 1914 [1886]. Brooklyn: Watch Tower Bible & Tract Soc. 316, [48] p. Foldout chart.

Russell: Jehovah's Witnesses founder. Vol. I of *Studies in the Scriptures* (many eds.; series titled *Millennial Dawn* in earlier editions.; orig pub. Pittsburgh: Zion's Watch Tower). Pre-mill. 4th Beast = Roman, with Papal horn. Papal power wanes 1798, 1870. 70 Weeks was continuous, ended in past. Predicted End for 1914; credibility boosted by outbreak of World War. 606 B.C. + 2,520 = 1914.

829. _____. *The Time is at Hand.* 1915 [1889]. *Studies in the Scriptures* vol. 2. Brooklyn: International Bible Students Association. 371, [47] p.

6,000 years from creation of Adam to 1872. Millennium started 1874, saints resurrected 1878, Age ends 1914. Now in 7th Millennium, gradual reduction of evil, perfection. Gentile Age 606 B.C. to A.D. 1914 (2,520 years). Declares it "established truth that the final end" will occur 1915. Second Coming in spiritual body, Christ reveals himself gradually. 40 years of "harvest" from 1874 to 1914. Jubilee period = thousand year Millennium, began 1875. After 1915 Jews return to favor, not persecuted. Antichrist = Papacy; False Millennium lasted A.D. 800 to 1800.

830. _____. *Thy Kingdom Come.* 1915 [1891]. *Studies in the Scriptures* vol. 3. Brooklyn: International Bible Students Association. 384, [44] p. index.

Includes historical and prophetic chronology from the Great Pyramid.

831. _____. *The Battle of Armageddon.* 1915 [1897]. Brooklyn: International Bible Students Association. xvi, 11–660, [39] p. indexes. *Studies in the Scriptures* vol. 4.

Gog-Magog attack on Israel from Europe. Stars fell in 1833 (great meteor shower), heavens darkened in 1780. God will "establish righteousness by force" at his Day of Vengeance, and will inaugurate Messianic Kingdom after 1914.

832. _____. *The New Creation.* 1915 [1904]. *Studies in the Scriptures* vol. 6. Brooklyn: International Bible Students Association. 738, [71] p. indexes.

833. Russell, James Stuart. *The Parousia: A Critical Inquiry into the New Testament Doctrine of Our Lord's Second Coming.* 1996 [1887]. Bradford, PA: Kingdom Publications. xvi, 561 p.

Preterist. Originally published anonymously. (1878). Nero = Beast, Man of Sin. Saints (the 144,000) raptured in earliest church years, during Apostolic age. Claims historical records show sudden absence of believers at that time. Scripture references all assert Last Days are come, End of Age imminent (then), Day of Lord at hand. Rejects "double fulfillment" interpretation — that End was partially fulfilled then but will only be fully fulfilled in future. Christianity is now stronger than ever. "This world belongs no more to the devil, but to God." Jerusalem obliterated, nation destroyed, because Jews rejected Messiah. End of Jewish dispensation, Mosaic economy. Asserts this is simplest, plainest, most literal interpretation. End Times requirement that Gospel must be preached to "all nations" referred to Palestine only.

834. Ryle, J[ohn] C[harles] *When Will He Come?* [1850s]. Providence, RI: H.L. Hastings. 4 p.

Second Advent will be soon and sudden.

835. _____. *Prophecy.* Fearn: Christian Focus. 254 p. Orig 1867 under title *Coming Events and Present Duties.*

"The last days of the earth shall be its worst days. The last war shall be the most fearful and terrible war that ever desolated the earth."

836. _____. *Perilous Times! A Forecast.* 1911. Taunton: E. Goodman. 12 p.

837. _____. *The Second Advent.* 1985. Chelmsford, England: Sovereign Grace Advent Testimony. 12 p. illus.

838. Sargent, C. W. *The Gathering of the Nations to the Battle of that Great Day!* 1854. Concord, NH: O. Hart. 12 p.

839. Savage, Mrs. *Watch, the Prophecy [of the] Scripture and Truth which Came to Pass in the Year 1851 that Thing is Proved Herein [and] Published Among All Nations, Observe It, Be Watchful.* 1856. Toronto: author. 19, [1] p.

840. Schmucker, John George. *The Prophetic History of the Christian Religion Explained, or, A Brief Exposition of the Revelation of St. John According to a New Discovery of Prophetic Time: By Which the Whole Chain of Prophecies is Arranged, and Their Certain Completion Proved from History Down to the Present Period: With Summary Views of those Not Accomplished Yet.* 1821 [1817]. Baltimore: Schaeffer and Maund. 2 vols.

Originally German. Pastor of Evangelical Lutheran Church, Yorktown, PA. Fold-out chart. Intricate date calculations. Promotes Bengel's system, with his own modifications. Beast's 42 months = 666 lunar years. Translates "prophetic time" to much longer "common time." First horse of 4 = Christ. Red horse = Bar Kochba revolt A.D. 133. Black horse = famine in Roman empire. Pale horse= A.D. 250–56 plague. Other seals: conversion of Constantine, barbarian invasions. Woes: Muslim conquests. Woman with Child = Church. Moon= Islam. Escape to wilderness: in Europe during the Reformation. Angel saying "Babylon is fallen" is Bengel (and others who discovered prophetic key). Vial poured into air = Revolutions of 1829. Seven heads of Beast: mountains the Popes sat on. Second Beast = Jesuits. Satan loosed "a little while" = 950 years. Vials begin at end of 666 year Beast reign. 5th: 1798. Second Beast to help revive papacy; terrible persecution of Protestants. Future Antichrist will be even worse. End is very near. 42 months = 666 lunar years; thus "year" = 196 years, "hour" = 8 days, "month" ca. 16 years. 70 weeks ended A.D. 72. 7 Churches: periods, to A.D. 104, 324, 700, plus Roman, Greek, Jewish/infidel, and Russian systems. 4 Beasts = Patriarchal, Mosaic, Christian, and Millennial ages. Seven Seals = A.D. 72–122 to 172, 222, 272, 322, and 372. Seven trumpets: first four to A.D. 572; 5th-6th to 1063 (Islam, Arabs, Turks, Tartars). Two Witnesses after 1845. Woman, child, dragon = Charlemagne's Empire (= sun; Saracens = moon); conquers paganism (dragon), establishes Church in realm. A.D. 832 + 1,260 =1509. Woman's Flight = 1509 to 1859 (Reformation, missionary activity). 777 years of Land Beast; 666 years of Sea Beast (from Pope Gregory VII to 1798, with pause). Wounded head = papal schism 1378–1428. War against saints: crusades against Waldenses, Albigensian anti-papal sects. 144,000: Bohemian Church (true Christians). Earthquakes = political convulsions. 7 Vials = started in 1789 (French revolution and wars; 6th is breakup of Ottoman Empire). Ten-King alliance to emerge, led by Antichrist; will destroy Rome and papacy. Tremendous war in Israel just before Millennium: Ten-King and Eastern armies gather at Armageddon. Then Second Coming; Millennium = 1850. Gog and Magog after Millennium; Satan loosed 950 years; then 200 years Judgment: up to 4000 A.D. Earth burns; new Heaven and Earth. Literal New Jerusalem descends. One-twelfth cubic stadia for each resident. Calculation of dates may be off a few years due to uncertainty of Christ's birthdate.

841. Scofield, Cyrus. 1909. *Reference Bible*. 1917 [1909]. Oxford: Oxford Univ. Press. Also 1967 rev. ed.

Between 5 and 10+ million copies (2.5 million copies by 1990 for 1967 ed.). Scofield: studied under J.H. Brookes; Congregational minister in Dallas, then at Moody's Northfield Bible School (MA), then an independent promoter. Polished Darby's dispensational scheme, made it enormously popular. 1967 edition still identifies Gog with Russia. Israel subject to Gentile rule until Second Coming; chastised by other nations, though those in turn afflicted.

842. _____. *Addresses on Prophecy*. 1914 [c1910]. A.D. 104. Swengel, PA: Bible Truth Depot. 134 p. 1955 ed. Findlay, OH: Dunham; 159 p.

Must understand dispensational divisions to clarify Bible. 800,000,000 haven't yet heard Gospel. Rapture: "I believe that the day is drawing very near." To ignore Tribulation is "shallow and senseless." Jews as great miracle of history and proof of prophecy. Israel restored, then Rapture and seven year Tribulation, then literal Millennium — a Jesus-run theocracy. Then world ends. Beast from the Earth = Antichrist — the False Prophet; Beast from Sea is emperor of Ten-Nation Roman Empire.

843. _____. *Prophecy Made Plain: Addresses on Prophecy*. 1967 [1910]. Grand Rapids, MI: Grand Rapids Book Manufacturers. 171 p. SEE ALSO 1910–1970.

844. Scott, James. *The Coming King; or, A Simple Introduction to the Subject of the Second Coming of Christ*. 1891. London: Nisbet. 104 p.

845. _____. *After These Things — What?* [ca 1945?]. Glasgow: Pickering & Inglis. 165 p.

Original articles. Blames German rationalism, Higher Criticism. Pre-trib Rapture. "That the Roman Empire will re-appear is so fully attested in the prophetic Scriptures that it is not even open to debate." "That the Jews will go back to Palestine is a divine certainty"; they make covenant with Beast (European ruler); build Temple. Jewish leader is Antichrist. King of North = Assyrian leader. Immense army includes hordes from East, invades. Roman Prince, the Beast, sends armies to defend Israel. God makes Northern army crush Roman Prince : Armageddon (end of 70th Week); uses Assyrian as His instrument. Tarshish = Rome. Assyrian continues to Egypt, then returns (hears threats from East and North) to exterminate Jews. False Prophet = Antichrist. 144,000 mostly Jews, to witness in Tribulation. Jehoshaphat battle *after* Armageddon battle. Nations allied with North = Day of Jehovah, Day of Wrath. Finally, Russia (= Gog) participates, but only after Second Coming, and after new revolution overthrows communism. Dispensationalism essential for proper interpretation. Zionist movement won't bring blessing but rather wrath of God.

846. Scott, Thomas. *Commentary on Revelation.* [1800s].

Millennium either 1866 or 2016, from either A.D. 606 or 756, + 1,260 years.

847. Scott, Walter. *At Hand; or, Things Which Must Shortly Come to Pass.* 1920s [1908]. 4th ed. London: Pickering & Inglis. 213 p.

Plymouth Brethren; helped with Scofield Reference Bible. Futurist. Roman Empire resurrected "in a ten-kingdomed form." Antichrist will be a Jew.

848. _____. *Future Events, with Numerous Prophetic Details.* 1910 [1881]. Glasgow: R.L. Allan. 97 p. Also pub. 1985? (Los Angeles: Berean Bookshelf).

Includes relation of Jews to prophecy, the Millennium, etc. Predicted Russia as End Time power.

849. _____. *Exposition of the Revelation of Jesus Christ.* 1968. 4th ed. Westwood, NJ: Revell; 1979 Grand Rapids, MI: Kregel. 2nd ed. 1900? [d. 1933]. 456 p. bibl., index.

Detailed, careful study. Pre-trib; futurist. Clear which verses refer to future, which don't. Assumes 6,000 year scheme. 70th Week: prophetic timetable resumes after Rapture. Seal, Trumpets, Vials: possibly Roman Empire emerging again near end. 70th week: concerns Jews, Israel — treaty, abominations. 70 weeks = 455 B.C. (Artaxerxes allows return of Jews) to messianic entry of Jesus in Jerusalem. Locusts = literal insects. 2-part Second Coming (Rapture, then Millennial appearance). Gog = Czar of Russia. Papal Church is "Satan's masterpiece.... Popery blights everything it touches." Constantine led church to "fatal union" and down path to ruin. Most of book verse-by-verse exegesis. Modern Judaism condemned by God. Islam is "greatest curse on the face of the earth," Mohammed "devil-inspired." Rapture not mentioned in Revelation, but Scott assumes it occurs before Rev. 4. White Horse rider of Revelation 4 is *not* Christ. 200 million cavalry not literal; hail, fire, blood devastations symbolic, also Two Witnesses. Ten Kingdom division yet to arise, but imminent. 1,260 Days: literal. Beast who "was, and is not," and emerges yet again (in 3 phases) is Roman Empire of past and future (revived): slain in A.D. 476; revived in future ("assassination" of Beast). Satan wars with Michael in heaven, cast down to earth, turns full fury against Israel in last half of Tribulation. Beast of Sea: revived Roman Empire. Beast of Earth = Antichrist = False Prophet. Antichrist of Jewish descent, performs supernatural miracles, pretends to be Messiah, leads "most awful system of corrupt and damnable evil ever known." Arises at end of Ten Kingdom period as Jewish lieutenant of first Beast, religious leader based in Palestine, but taken over by first Beast. Second Beast sets himself up as divine. 666 = symbolic of human limitations. Babylon: two senses — literal and historical; also mystical (includes the future) — the false religious system of the world, the Harlot. Mystical Babylon destroyed by Beast, who then rules by force. Attacked by North and South in Palestine, after destruction of West and East. Armageddon not merely the literal valley. Vial plagues, blood sea, etc., probably symbolic, but Euphrates will literally dry up. Second Coming: Christ arrives with armies of believers (not angels); his garment covered with blood of enemies (not of Cross). Destroys armies of world. Millennium literal. Literal resurrection of unjust after Millennium. "Gog" after Millennium: metaphorical for whole earth.

850. *The Second Advent Introductory to the World's Jubilee.* 1845. London: Ward. By "A Protestant Non-conformist Layman." 32 p. (Bound with *Apocalypse Popularly Explained.*)

Letter to Rev. Raffles refuting post-millennialism. World conditions not improving but instead like in Noah's day. Messiah to come "not when that [millennial] glory is over and gone, but to create it — to be the seal and centre of it." Urges dispensational interpretation.

851. *The Second Coming, the Judgment, and the Kingdom of Christ.* 1844. London: J. Nisbet. viii, 375 p.

Contributors: H.M. Villiers, Edward Auriol, William Pym, C.J. Goodhart, W. Dalton, J.W. Brooks, T.R. Birks, Alexander Dallas, W.R. Fremantle, Thomas Hill, E. Bickersteth, J.H. Stewart.

852. Seiss, Joseph Augustus. *The Last Times and the Great Consummation: An Earnest Discussion of Momentous Themes.* 1864 [1856]. 6th ed. Philadelphia: Smith, English. 438 p. bibl., index. 1902 abridged ed. (Cincinnati: Office of God's Revivalist); also 1901 excerpt *Be Ye Also Ready.* 1878 (7th) ed. titled *Last Times or Thoughts on Momentous Themes.*

Seiss: Lutheran minister, Philadelphia, editor of *Prophetic Times.* End = 1870. Christ resurrected in spirit, not flesh. Like Cumming, vividly portrayed pre-mill message. "This world is a disjointed and dilapidated fabric.... Cold, storms, earthquakes, volcanoes, barren fields, pestilential airs, smiting sunshine, tearing briars, and noxious things, combine in the terrific accusation against man, and utter the bitter manifesto of protestation against his unholy deeds." "All society, everywhere, with its politics, its philosophy, and its religion, is in a perturbed condition.... Old systems and modes of thought and belief, which have stood for ages, are everywhere tottering upon their thrones, and many of them reeling as for their final fall." Second Coming is central doctrine of Christianity. Vigorously refutes post-mill. "Natural justice seems to demand that he should come again" to right wrongs and confound his detractors. Denies as "falsehood forged by Satan" view that world is converted to Christianity before End. Prophecies refer both to end of Israel and of World; Israel foreshadows World; thus both about past destruction of Jerusalem and coming destruction of world. Insists on simple interpretation; symbolic interpretations are absurd, bunk. Advent "not a *post*-millennial, but a *pre*-millennial coming.... *It is Christ's coming that is to make the millennium,* not the millennium which is to prepare the world for Christ's coming." "Criminally indifferent, arrogant, and unbelieving" not to believe in imminent End. Bible declares world gets worse, then Tribulation, then Millennium. Satan is master of world now. But world won't be destroyed: "I do not, I *cannot* believe it." "World" not meant literally; rather present arrangement. Fires of the End are erupting subterranean fires. Resurrection: "God knows each atom, and where it rests" (can reunite them again). Literal resurrection of righteous dead before Millennium, then another after of wicked dead. Millennium will be "Christocracy": personal earthly reign. "Day of Judgment" is progressive: "day" not literal; mostly concerns Millennial period. Dispensations overlap: Millennium commences with world as is, not sudden change, but sneaks in as thief in night. We may not notice when Millennium, Judgment start. Papal Antichrist. "Babylon" = nationalized (political) religion, both Papal and Protestant. Israel restored to Palestine, most Jews embrace Messiah. Then, World Confederacy vs. Israel. Jerusalem to be world capital (since center of Old World). Glorified saints may be invisible. Appeals to Barnabas: Six Days Creation = 6,000 years. Until Origen's "fanciful" interpretation, everybody agreed with this World Week. Millennium to be 6,000 years after Creation. Millenarianism "fell only as Popery rose." Many wanted to believe Millennium began with Constantine: i.e. that Antichrist = Pagan Rome, but really Antichrist = Papal Rome. Millennium to start within 7 years. Tribulation: probably 1865–70. Creation 4131 B.C. Many say A.D. 606 (first supremacy of Pope) + 1,260 = 1866. Vials: French Revolution, 1848 revolutions, denationalization of the church. Last Day apostasy: almost half of "Christians" now in the "foul embrace of Popery"; many Protestant branches "fearfully corrupt." Quotes many authors on imminent Coming, End. "This generation" means race, nation (Israelites). Insists that Luther, Lutherans, Augburg Confession condemn only *Anabaptist* chiliasm. Antichrist = Napoleon III, probably. Probably 2-stage translation: of faithful believers first, before Tribulation, then others after (Partial Rapture theory).

853. _____. *The Apocalypse.* 1988 [c1865]. Kregel [1962 Zondervan] 1901 ed. with 1880 pref. vii, 503 p. index. Many 2- and 3-vol eds.

Insisted that Civil War deepened his pre-mill convictions. Carcass and vulture parable: Carcass is Christ. Also wrote *A Miracle in Stone: or, The Great Pyramid of Egypt* (1877).

854. Shaw, John Gilder. *Britain (or Israel) the Fifth and Last and the Unconquerable Empire as Depicted in Nebuchadnezzar's Dream and its Interpretation, Viewed in Connection with the History of the Nations Represented by the Image...: To Which is Added Britain (or Israel) the "Ancient of Days".* 1878 London: S.W. Partridge; Montreal: W. Drysdale. viii, 60 p.

Anglo-Israel.

855. Shedd, William Greenough Thayer. *The Doctrine of Endless Punishment.* 1886, 1885. New York: Charles Scribner. vii, 163 p.

1986 reprint of 1885 edition Edinburgh: Banner of Truth Trust; vii, 201 p. 1980 reprint of 1886 edition by Minneapolis: Klock & Klock Christian Pub.

856. Sheldon, William. *The Millennium: The Good Time Coming. With a History of Experiments on the Odic Force.* 1862. Springfield, MA: S. Bowles. 196 p.

Also wrote *The 7th Vial* (1849).

857. _____. *The King of Glory Soon to Be Revealed from Heaven to Destroy All Earthly Kingdoms and Set Up the Kingdom of God on Earth.* 1866. Buchanan, MI: WACP Assoc. 48 p. illus.

858. _____. *The "End of the World" At Hand.* N.d. [1856]. 15 p.

Adventist. A.D. 533 + 1,335 Years = 1868. Papal power in decline.

859. Shepheard, H. *The Tree of Life; or, Redemption and Its Fruits in Grace*

and Glory. 1864. London: J. Nisbet. viii, 344 p.

Pre-mill.

860. Shimeall, R.C. *Age of the World as Founded on the Sacred Records, Historic and Prophetic; and the "Signs of the Times," Viewed in the Aspect of Premonitions of the Speedy Establishment on the Earth, of the Millennial State, by the Second, Personal, Pre-Millennial Advent of Christ.* 1842. New York: Swords, Stanford. xxvii, 364 p.

Episcopal Church in New York. Pre-mill. Assuming 6,000 year duration for world, by various calculations the Millennium starts 1868. But great crisis in 1847. "Look to 1847! May Heaven prepare us all to meet undismayed the *terrors*, and to share triumphantly in the *glories*, of 'THAT DAY!'"

861. _____. *Prophecy, Now in the Course of Fulfillment, As Connected with the 2,300 days of Daniel VIII, 14.* 1844. New York: Stanford and Sword's. 51 p.

"Delivered at NYU chapel, 1884 [sic; 1844?]." Predicts subversion of Millerism to take effect in 1844. Appended to work is prospectus for forthcoming *Systema Theologiae Propheticae, or, the General Scope of Prophecy Unveiled.*

862. _____. *Our Bible Chronology, Historic and Prophetic, Critically Examined and Demonstrated, and Harmonized with the Chronology of Profane Writers....* 1867. New York: A.S. Barnes. 234 p. illus.

Refutes Egyptologists' chronology.

863. _____. *The Second Coming of Christ: or, The Impending Approach of the Restitution of All Things by the Power and Coming of the God-Man, the Lord Jesus Christ: Scripturally, Philosophically, and Historically Demonstrated.* 1873. New York: Henry S. Goodspeed. xxxi, 320 p. 15 leaves illus.

Pre-mill but distances himself from Millerism; says it is not equivalent to "millenarianism." Asserts "predestined six thousand years from the creation and fall to the close of 'the times of the Gentiles'" Bound with *Reply* to an article on eschatology, which has index to both Shimeall works.

864. Sibley, A. W. (Abiel Willard).

Signs of the Present Time: Their Relation to the Immediate Personal Coming of Our Lord Jesus Christ. 1889 [1886]. New edition with supplement. Boston: Advent Christian Publication Soc. 44 p.
Advent Christian. Physical, moral, political, and financial signs of imminent End.

865. _____. *Omens of the Coming One.* Boston: Advent Christian Publication Soc. 15 p.
Papacy and Islam as antichristian powers; accelerating evangelism as sign of imminent End.

866. *Signs of the End.* 1890. Mountain View, CA: Pacific Press. 16 p.

867. Silliman, Anna. *The World's Jubilee.* 1856 [1855]. New York: M.W. Dodd. 343 p.

868. Skinner, H. B. *A Synopsis of the Views of Those Who Look for the Coming of the Lord Jesus Christ in 1843.* 1842. Ashburnham [MA]: A. Ward. 108 p.

869. Smith, Elias. *The Day of Judgment.* 1805. Exeter [NH]. 35 p.

870. _____. *Sermons Containing an Illustration of the Prophecies to be Accomplished from the Present Time Until the New Heavens and Earth are Created, When All the Prophecies Will be Fulfilled.* 1808. Exeter [NH]. 300 p.

871. _____. *The History of Anti-Christ: In Three Books, Written in Scripture Stile, in Chapters and Verses, for the Use of Schools.* 1811. Portland, ME: Herald Printing. 120 p.
Critical of state-supported religion, but expects "kingly government of Christ" to be fulfilled by U.S.

872. Smith, Ethan. *A Dissertation on the Prophecies Relative to Antichrist and the Last Times.* 1814. 2nd ed. Boston. 588 p. folded charts bibl. refs.
A.D. 606 + 1,260 = 1866. Rise of Antichrist in French Revolution

873. _____. *Key to the Revelation.* 1833. New York: J.& J. Harper.
Trumpets 1–4: barbarian invasions of Rome; 5–6: Arabs and Turks; 7th will destroy Antichrist just prior to Millennium. 481 B.C. + 2,300 = 1819 (end of Turkish period). "Millennium" is indefinite period starting at end of 1,335 years

874. Smith, John. *A Summary View and Explanation of the Writings of the Prophets.* 1804. 2nd ed. Cambridge: Longman, Hurst, Rees, and Orme. [8], 192 p.
Preterist. Second Coming followed destruction of Jerusalem A.D. 70.

875. Smith, Uriah. *The United States in the Light of Prophecy, or, An Exposition of Rev. 13:11–17.* 1980 [1872]. Payson AZ: Leaves-of-Autumn. 160 p. Orig. pub. Battle Creek, MI: Steam Press of the Seventh-day Adventist Pub. Assoc.

876. _____. *Man's Nature and Destiny: or, The State of the Dead, the Reward of the Righteous, and the End of the World.* c1884. 3rd ed. rev. enl. Battle Creek, MI: Review and Herald. 443 p.

877. _____. *The Prophecies of Daniel and the Revelation.* 1951 [1897]. Mountain View, CA: Pacific Press. 830 p. illus., bibl. refs. indexes.
Many eds. Revelation section also pub. 1904 [1897] by Review and Herald. 1907 edition subtitled *The Response of History to the Voice of Prophecy.* Verse-by-verse study. Historicist. Armageddon = Islam (Ottoman Empire) vs. Christianity.

878. Snell, H.H. *Prophetical Outlines. Seven Lectures on the Second Coming and Kingdom of the Lord Jesus Christ.* 1868. London: W.H. Broom. 227 p.
Rapture, personal Second Coming, dispensational pre-mill (70th week in future). Beast (who is not the Pope) and False Prophet will hold sway until Second Coming. Millennium is the Day of the Lord.

879. Snow, Samuel Sheffield. *The Voice of Elias; or, Prophecy Restored.* 1863. New York: Baker & Godwin. 395 p.
"Being a complete and truthful exposition of the visions of the prophet Daniel and the Book of the Revelation."

880. Southcott, Joanna. *The Strange Effects of Faith: With Remarkable Prophecies (Made in 1792, &c.) of Things Which Are to Come.* 1801. 3rd ed. Exeter: T. Brice.
After publication Southcott began certificating and "sealing" the faithful (10,000 of the 144,000 by 1805). In *Third Book of Wonders* (1813) announced she was pregnant with the second Christ.

881. _____. *Prophecies. A Warning to the Whole World, from the Unsealed Prophecies of Joanna Southcott.* 1803. London: E. Spragg. ii, 123 p.

882. _____. *The Full Assurance that the Kingdom of Christ is at Hand from the Signs of the Times.* 1806. London. 64 p. World to last 6,000 years after Six Days of creation (4000 B.C.), but last thousand years will be cut short by God.

883. _____. *Scriptures of the Revelation of the Most High.* 1843. [London.] 32 p.

"Being the three-fold cord, which cannot be broken; whereby the whole human family who now exist, have, or shall exist, are comforted, in the sure interpretation of dark sayings, traced from the 22nd chapter of the Revelation of Jesus Christ to John of Patmos, back to the chaotic — 'In the beginning God created the heavens and the earth': Making thereby the divine trinitarian scriptures interwoven into unity, for Jew and Gentile."

884. Speer, Robert E. *The Second Coming of Christ.* 1903. Chicago: Winona. 46 p.

885. Sprunger, John Abraham. *Outline on Prophecy: Israel in the Past and in the Future. The Kingdom of Antichrist. The Coming of the Lord. The Millennium. The New Heaven and New Earth.* [1903]. Cleveland, OH: Light and Hope. 287 p. plates.

886. Spurgeon, C[harles] H. *Twelve Sermons on the Second Coming of Christ.* n.d. New York: F.H. Revell.

Late 19th cent. sermons at Metropolitan Tabernacle, London.

887. Stanley, Charles. *What God hath Said on the Second Coming of Christ and the End of the Present Age.* 1877 [1857?]. London: G. Morrish. 32 p.

888. _____. *The Second Coming of Christ and the End of the Present Age.* [1859?] Oak Park, IL: Bible Truth. 31 p.

889. Steen, J. Charleton. *God's Prophetic Program: As Revealed in the Book of Daniel; Indicating the Consummation of "the Times of the Gentiles".* 1900. Kilmarnock, Scotland: John Ritchie. 128 p. index charts.

Future 10-nation league. 69 Weeks; Gap; 70th Week. Rapture, Millennium, Judgment.

890. Steward, T[heophilus] G[ould]. *The End of the World, or, Clearing the Way for the Fullness of the Gentiles.* 1888. Philadelphia: A.M.E. Church Book Rooms. iv, 182 p.

"End of the world" really consummation of this age. "Roman" (Gentile) age is ending. Historicist interpretation of 10 Nations as successor kingdoms to ancient Rome; i.e. mix of peoples. Largely eloquent criticism of white racial arrogance (Steward is black) and appeal for racial equality as true Christianity. Anglo-Saxons seek to dominate world, assuming their superiority, but in fact are corrupting it. They spread Christianity and developed concept of justice but have yet to extend it to other races. Predicts "great crash of the Christian nations, and a liberation of the Christian idea from the dominance of the principle of clan [i.e. insiders vs. outsiders], and a consequent purification of the Christian Church." Then, true Christian brotherhood extended to non-white races, who will convert from heathenism.

891. Stockman, E[dward] A[insley]. *The Moral Signs of Christ's Coming.* 1894 [1874?] Advent Christian Publication Society. 16 p.

892. _____. *Our Last Work.* 1923 [1903?]. Boston : Advent Christian Publication Society. 7 p. Reprinted from the *World's Crisis.*

893. _____. *The Amazing Changes Connected with the Second Advent: or, What Events will Occur when the Savior Comes?* N.d. [ca 1890?]. Minneapolis: Interstate Evangelistic Association. 32 p

By the "editor of *The World's Crisis.*"

894. Stowe, H[arriet] B[eecher] et al. *He's Coming Tomorrow: and Other Papers.* 1896. New York: Fleming H. Revell. 127 p.

Also includes *The Second Coming* (D.L. Moody), *Occupy Till I Come* (J.C. Ryle), *The Second Coming of Christ* (G. Muller), *The Second Coming of Our Lord* (D.W. Whittle), *The Blessed Hope* (G.C. Needham), *The Second Coming of Christ* (C.H. Spurgeon), *The Missing Ones* (J.W.).

895. Strange, Thomas Lumisden. *The Light of Prophecy: Being an Attempt to Trace Out the Coming Judgments and the Promised Glory.* 1852. London: J.K. Campbell. xxiii, 406 p. illus.

69 Weeks = 450 B.C. to A.D. 33. 70th Week future, ends with Second Coming. Also wrote *Scripture and Science* (1876), and *Development of Creation on the Earth* (1874).

896. Streator, Martin Lyman. 1900. *The Anglo-American Alliance in Prophecy, or the Promises to the Fathers.* New Haven: Our Race. 565 p. Map.

Prophets foresaw America as God's Elect, the favored race, the true descendants of Israel. Russia (= Rosh, Magog) will lead anti-American forces at End (cites Louis Tracy's novel *Final War*). 1898 (notably Spanish-American War) as beginning of Last Years. "The crisis is at hand. The conflict is impending. The war of races for the supreme dominion of the world in inevitable, and let it come."

897. Stuart, Moses. *A Commentary on the Apocalypse.* 1845. Andover; Allen, Morrill and Wardwell; New York: Newman. 2 vols. 1864. Andover: Warren Draper. xii, 504 p. (vol 1).

Stuart: Andover Theological Seminary. Introduced preterism to U.S. Scholarly work. Refers to apocryphal apocalypses for comparative interpretation; summarizes these and other works; also various interpretations of Rev. "Historico-critical" interpretation; emphasize literary structure, poetic framework, figurative language. Revelation mostly about *moral* future. Gog and Magog symbolic for end of Millennium. Locusts and 200 million cavalry symbolic. 3 part division of Revelation: first catastrophe: persecution by Jews, devastation of Jews in 70 A.D.; second catastrophe (partially fulfilled): persecuted by Rome, Babylon and Rome, finally (future) destroyed, Millennium; third catastrophe: defeat of Satan after Millennium.

898. _____. *A Commentary on the Book of Daniel.* 1850. Boston: Crocker & Brewster. viii, 496 p.

899. Sturdevant, Hervey S. *Signs of His Coming: or Prophecy Fulfilled: The Rea-* sons for Christ's Coming: Wonders of the Last Days Historic and Prophetic. 1912 [1907?]. 2nd ed. Oakland, CA : Messiah's Advocate. 16 p.

900. Sulley, Henry. *Is It Armageddon?.* 1915 [1904]. London: Simpkin, Marshall. 107 p. illus. maps.

Reprint of *Britain in Prophecy.*

901. Swartz, D.W. 1841. *The World's Ruins, or A Sermon on the General Judgment.* Frankfort, KY: A.G. Hodges. 13 p.

Whole world destroyed at End.

902. Swete, H.B. [Henry Barclay]. *The Life of the World to Come.* 1917. London: Soc. for the Promoting of Christian Knowledge. xi, 114 p. Pub. posthumously.

903. _____. *The Apocalypse of St. John.* 1922 [1906]. London: Macmillan. 3rd ed. 1909. 1906. ed. ccxv, [1], 335 p. illus. maps.

A-mill (preterist): Millennium is Christianity's accomplished triumph over paganism.

904. Swormstedt, James M. *The End of the World Near: Or, Antichrist, the Beast of Rev. XIII.* 1877. Cincinnati: E.W. Swormstedt. 338 p.

"Containing a prophetic history from the Bible of the wonderful events which are to happen during the next fifty years, including the first resurrection and translation in November, 1878; the forty years of retribution on all nations; the universal reign of Antichrist; the visible Coming of Christ; the Judgment; the world melted by fire and made into a beautiful Eden; and the Millennial Reign of Christ and His glorified Saints." World was 6,000 years old in 1871. "Translation" (Rapture) of church in Nov. 1878, then 40 years of God's Wrath. Overturning world kingdoms 1878 in "sea of blood." Sultan of Turkish Empire (= King of the South; Two-Horned Beast) allies with Antichrist, Sultan becomes miracle-worker aided by Satan. Vials of Wrath after "translation" of church is horrific civil war in Antichrist's huge empire. Antichrist's vast armies invade U.S. via Atlantic and Mexico, but God causes earth to swallow them up. War in Heaven fought on Moon; Satan still hurls meteorites at Earth from

Moon, which is location of Hell. Victor Emanuel of Italy is "King of the North"; he will defeat Turkish invaders and enter Jerusalem. Antichrist succeeds him as King of Italy. Antichrist fights Turkey, then Sultan becomes his ally. Reign of Antichrist as world controller starts in 1911. Russia invades Europe, then all nations invade Palestine: Armageddon, from 1914 to 1918. Total destruction of all life on earth before Millennium; earth itself breaks up. "Victor Emanuel" = 664th ruler of Italy; the Beast will be 666th. Rome = Mystery Babylon, the Abomination, the Harlot.

905. T., E.J. *The Time of the End But the End Not Yet: Some Explanation of the Prophecy of Matthew XXIV.* 1910. London: T. Weston. xii, 164 p.

906. Tait, Asa Oscar. *Heralds of the Morning: The Meaning of the Social and Political Problems of To-Day and the Significance of the Great Phenomena in Nature.* c1906 [c1899]. Mountain View, CA: Pacific Press. Rev and enlarged ed. 380 p. illus. drawings photos. Also 1916, 1915. Nashville: Southern Publishing Assoc.

Much on the 1906 San Francisco earthquake and fire.

907. Talmage, T[homas] De Witt. *Dr. Talmage's View of the Dawn of the Millennium.* 1890. Allegheny City, PA: Tower Tract Soc. 32 p.

Cited as authority on Last Days cyclone activity by D.T. Taylor.

908. Tanner, Joseph. *Daniel and the Revelation: The Chart of Prophecy and Our Place In It, a Study of the Historical and Futurist Interpretation.* 1898. London: Hodder and Stoughton. xx, 539 p. index

Tanner: Oxford Univ. "A study of the historical and futurist interpretations"—argues for historicist (and against symbolic interpretation). Present time: end of dispensation, near close of 6th Vial, just prior to Second Coming and 1st Resurrection. Then Millennium, Second Resurrection, Final Judgment, Eternity. Decline of Pope and Islam signal end; also Zionism, evangelism. "The Second Advent is at hand." Denies Gap for 70th week. Papacy the Beast) will embroil world in final war: Ar-

mageddon. King of North= Russia. King of South= England and dependencies. Israel not regathered until Second Advent.

909. Taylor, D[aniel] T[hompson]. *The Voice of the Church, on the Coming and Kingdom of the Redeemer, A History of the Doctrine of the Reign of Christ on Earth.* 1855. Peace Dale, RI: H.L. Hastings. xii, 406 p. index, bibl. refs.

Massive compendium of pre-mill statements by authorities through the ages.

910. _____. *It Hasteth Greatly* [1850s]. Rochester, NY: Advent Harbinger. 16 p.

911. _____. *The Coming Earthquake, and the Signs That Betoken Its Approach.* 1870. Boston: Scriptural Tract Repository.

Science teaches that Earth "is an enormous 'terrestrial bombshell'..., its hidden interior ... an intensely heated mass in a condition of molten fluidity, agitated, restless, and rolling its fiery waves hither and thither age after age, incessantly seeking with a terrible expressive power an outlet to diffuse its igneous elements.... On this thin, rocky film, or outer surface, dwells a fallen, sinful, and dying race of mortals.... Is it any wonder that thinking, sober people have from the earliest ages looked for a final, awful convulsion and burning day?"

912. _____. *The Great Consummation and the Signs that Herald Its Approach.* 1891. Boston: Advent Christian Publication Soc. 454 p.

Also wrote *The Coming Glory; The Chariots of Fire and Steel* [modern transportation as sign of inaminent End]; *Voice of Warning from the Four Winds* (1859). "Not to know these tremendous truths pertaining to the last things when we can know them is a sin. To know them and not speak them out loud is a crime." Calls his conclusions "impregnable and irrefutable." "History teems with its evidence on every page." Eagerly awaits Advent in the "glory-clouds." Abomination of Desolation is Papacy, not Roman Empire; Pagan Rome destroyed Israel but Papal Rome destroyed Christian Church. Rejects both ancient and futurist interpretations. Demands "literal" interpretation. All signs show "the last great catastrophe is near." Rome is "the beast dreadful and terrible," "Satan's masterpiece": Pagan Rome crushed Israel, Papal Rome crushed Christian Church. Tribulation not the "time of trouble" immediately before End, but the 1,260 year-long afflictions through Church history up to present (beginning to wane during Reformation). "No one prophecy has ever been so accurately, so conspicuously, so terribly fulfilled" as the persecutions and massacres of the Tribulation. Aurora Borealis among signs in heavens of End; hardly noticeable before 1700s. Long description of 1755 Lisbon Earthquake as greatest in world, and "signalized the near ending of the dark and bloody days for the elect of God." Great darkness of 1780; great star (meteor) showers 1799, 1832–3, 1866–8. Earth to be burned, either by nature or miracle: maybe atmosphere or ocean oxygen will separate, sunspots may trigger electrical catastrophes, etc. Solar eruptions and storms, coronas, celestial signs, began in 1780s right after Tribulation ended. 1870 solar commotion precipitated 1871 Chicago and Western fires. 1880s: Krakatoa; electrical disturbances from sun. "A merciful God means that all shall behold his wonders and be without excuse, because duly warned." God can easily end all life with solar catastrophe in single day. "On the wings of steam and electricity the *last message* is flying..."; Gospel brought to whole world, though world will reject it.

913. Terry, Milton S. *Biblical Apocalyptics.* 1898. New York: Eaton & Mains; Cincinnati: Curts & Jennings. 513 p. index.

Preterist and historical, but attempts to conserve substance of fundamental Gospel doctrines. Symbolic interpretation of Millennium: Church Age may last 1,000 x 1,000 years. Apocalypses of Creation, of Flood, Babel, etc., of other Old Testament books, John.

914. Thom, Adam. *Chronology of Prophecy: Tracing the Various Courses of Divine Providence, from the Flood to the End of Time, in the Light as Well of National*

Annals as of Scriptural Predictions. 1848. London: Longman, Brown, Green, & Longmans. xxxii, 300 p.

915. Thomas, John. *Elpis Israel: Being an Exposition of the Kingdom of God, with Reference to the Time of the End, and the Age to Come.* 1897 [1849]. 7th ed, rev. Birmingham: Robert Roberts. vi, 410 p. illus.

"Millenary Week of Seven Thousand Years" from Creation 4089 B.C. to End exactly 7,000 years later (6,000 years plus the Millennium). 1864–68 as the End, plus 40 years to restore Israel. Millennium starts 1912. Vials = Napeolonic Wars; Turkey. Beast and Little Horn: Turkey and Austro-Papal power. False Prophet = Pope. Papacy probably ends 1865. 2,300 years ends 1846. Two Witnesses = Calvinism and democracy (revived 1798 in France). 1,260 years = 529 to 1789. Unclean Spirits from Three Frogs = the French. "Gogue" = "Emperor of Germany and Autocrat of All the Russias." Tarshish = England; Merchants of Tarshish = British East India Co. Tarshish Lion helps restore Israel (*Elpis* = "hope").

916. _____. *The Coming Struggle Among the Nations of the Earth; or, The Political Events of the Next Thirteen Years: Described in Accordance with Prophecies in Ezekiel, Daniel, and the Apocalypse: Shewing also the Important Position Britain will Occupy During, and at the End of, the Awful Conflict.* 1853. Toronto: T. MacLear. iv, 36 p. Revised and corrected version of the Edinburgh ed.

917. _____. *Anatolia: Or Russia Triumphant and Europe Chained.* 1854. Mott Haven, NY: priv. pub. 102 p.

"Being an exposition of prophecy: showing the inevitable fall of the French and Ottoman Empires: the occupation of Egypt and the Holy Land by the British...: and consequent establishment of the kingdom of Israel."

918. _____. *Chronikon Hebraikon; or, The Chronology of the Scriptures: As Contained in their Historic and Prophetic Numbers and Dates* (New York, 1865 ["A.M. 5974"]; 43 p.). 11th ed. 1924.

919. _____. *Eureka; an Exposition of*

the Apocalypse. 3 vols. 1895. Birmingham. Previously published 1866 West Hoboken, NJ, by author.

920. Thompson, H.E. *Destiny of the Earth as Revealed by Science and the Scriptures.* 1898. Boston: Advent Christian Publication Soc. 26 p.

End will be a terrific fiery catastrophe, but the saints will be raptured just before this.

921. Thomson, George. *Trumpet for the Watchman on the Walls of Zion.* 1874 [1870?]. Boston: Advent Christian Publication Soc. 124 p.

922. Thurman, William C. *Our Bible Chronology Established: The Sealed Book of Daniel Opened: or, A Book of Reference for Those Who Wish to Examine the "Sure Word of Prophecy."* 5th ed., rev. 1867 [1864]. Boston: Office of the World's Crisis. 350 p. illus. index.

The 6,000 Years since Creation ends 1875.

923. *The Time of the End.* By "a Congregationalist." 1856 [1855]. Boston: New York: J.P. Jewett ; Shelton, Lamport & Blackman. 408 p. illus.

Subtitled "a prophetic period, developing, as predicted, an increase of knowledge respecting the prophecies and periods that foretell the end: illustrated by the history of prophetic interpretation, the expectation of the church, and the various computations of the times of Daniel and John, by commentators, who generally terminate them between A.D. 1830 and 1880; also, our present position in the prophetic calendar, with his Apocalypic seven-sealed scroll, by the Rev. E.B. Elliot, A.M. lectures on the nearness of the advent, by the Rev. John Cumming, D.D.; lectures on the new heavens and new earth, by Dr. Chalmers, Dr. Hitchcock, and John Wesley; and the testimony of more than one hundred witnesses against the modern Whitbyan theory of a millennium before the Advent." Cites plethora of writers who predict Millennium or End around mid-nineteenth century. Opposes Whitby's post-mill. Includes long extract from Elliott, also quotes many others.

924. Totten, Charles A.L. *The Hope of History. The Millennium.* 1892. New Haven, CT: Our Race Publishing Co. xvi, 289 p. illus. *Our Race* series.

"Possible reading" of Daniel: 5,897th year of world = A.D. 1899. End of the Age and the restoration of Judea (Zionism) to occur soon after close of 19th century.

Totten: promoter of British-Israelism (Ten Lost Tribes = British and Americans).

925. Townley, Robert. *The Second Advent of the Lord Jesus Christ: A Past Event.* 1845. London: Simpkin, Marshall. ix, 172 p.

926. Townsend, Edward Erwin. *The Time of the End; or, The Slaveholders' Rebellion Predicted More than Two Thousand Years Ago by the Prophet Daniel: The Government Vindicated in Suppressing the Rebellion....* 1865 Emira, NY: Fairman & Caldwell. 20 p.

God foresaw slavery and its overthrow by Union. Daniel 12: Lincoln = Michael; Holy Mountain = U.S. Daniel 11: King of South and of North = Confederacy and Union: "full and complete history of the Slaveholder's Rebellion" (Civil War). When war is finally over, then the End. Chariots = horse-drawn field artillery. 1,260 days = A.D. 606 (Papacy begins) to A.D. 1866. Though Lincoln assassinated, unfilled term would fulfill time prophesied. "Christ comes *prior* to the Millennium ... rather than after." That day is "without doubt" very near.

927. Tregelles, Samuel P. *The Man of Sin.* 1850. London: Sovereign Grace Advent Testimony. 31 p.

Babylon = New York; to be annihilated near End.

928. _____. *Remarks on the Prophetic Visions in the Book of Daniel: With Notes on Prophetic Interpretation in Connection with Popery, and a Defence of the Authenticity of the Book of Daniel.* 6th ed. 1883 [1845–47]. London: Sovereign Grace Advent Testimony. xvi, 308 p.

Plymouth Brethren, but rejected pretrib Rapture. Also wrote *The Man of Sin* [Antichrist]. Future ten-part division of renewed Roman empire (not past kingdoms arising from Empire); Stone which destroys is Christ. Little Horn in future.

"Time, times, and a half" = period the little horn acts in defiance of God, blaspheming. Little horn not Papacy. Arises from Eastern (Grecian) part of Empire. The 70 Weeks = 69 from 455 B.C. to A.D. 29 (Crucifixion). Then, later, the 70th or "reserved week." Seven year treaty, broken half way through, desecrates the rebuilt Temple (abomination of desolation). "Weeks" really "heptads" (seven part divisions). Israel established as nation; wars between Egypt (King of South) and Syria (King of North). North and South war against Israel-based Antichrist, after he persecutes faithful of Israel. North ravages Israel, but checked by Western (European) power. North invades Egypt, but maritime European power ("Chittim") aids Egypt; North returns to Israel. Remnant of Jews who fled are saved. Papal claims and doctrines are indeed "fearful falsehoods ... Satanic delusions" but Papacy is not prophesied Antichrist.

929. _____. *The Hope of Christ's Second Coming: How Is It Taught in Scripture? And Why?* 1964. 5th ed. 11 p.

930. Trench, George F. *After the Thousand Years: The Glorious Reign of Christ as Son of Man in the Dispensation of the Fullness of Times.* 1908 [1899?]. London: Morgan and Scott. viii, 120 p.

At end of Millennium, world belongs to Christ but most conversions not genuine. Outward peace and calm, but souls still possessed by Satan. Satan finally destroyed at end of Millennium. (Not the same as contemporary "Archbishop [Richard] Trench," philologist and any-moment Second Coming advocate.)

931. Trenwith, William H. *The Time of the End, or, Remarks on the Book of Revelation ... and Shewing Also, the Near Approach of the Second Advent of Messiah.* 1845. Cork, Ireland: G. Purcell. ix, 55 p.

932. _____. *God and His Wisdom, Satan and His Sin, Man and His Filth—Results.* 1877. New York: Polhemus. 44 p.

933. _____. *Antichrist.* 1885. New York: s.n. 8 p.

Anti-Catholic. Reprint from *Protestant Times* (London).

934. Trotter, William. *Plain Papers on Prophetic Subjects.* 1985 [1853]. Glenside, CA: Church Press; Denver: Wilson Foundation. 572 p. [568 p.] index. New ed., rev. 1863?; Chicago: Fleming H. Revell. 582 p.; also Loizeaux Bros., etc.

Strong pre-mill argument; pre-trib. "Any day, any hour." Increasing number of conversions proof of imminent Judgment. Christianity hasn't converted world, but has itself become corrupted. Judgment lies ahead, not conversion of World. Grand Prophetic Question: which is first, Millennium or Second Coming? After "translation" (Rapture) of true church, wickedness comes to full head. Gog and Magog active both before and after Millennium. Jews must return, Tribulation. 10-Horn Beast exists now. "Blasphemous" claims of Rome; Popery is corrupt; apostasy, ecclesiastical corruption, "absurd superstitions and immoral practices." Mystic Babylon mostly but not entirely Rome. Remnant of Jews to be preserved through Tribulation. The Coming and Day of the Lord not the same (former is pre-mill Second Coming, latter is post-mill Final Judgment). Literal Millennium, but battle against and subduing of Antichrist occupies some time after Second Coming. "The Church": all Saved people up to Second Coming (there will be others later). "Mystery of iniquity": vast amount of evil, apostasy in nominal church. Gentile power will be energized by Satan, will take over worldly government of the ten kings, work miracles, require Mark and worship of Beast, Jews return in unbelief (except for remnant) in league with Antichrist, who deceives them, undergo Tribulation ("Wrath ... to the uttermost" upon Israel), many martyred. War of Beast confederacy against Christ. After Antichrist overthrown and Millennium begins all 10 Lost Tribes also restored. Iron/clay: monarchical and constitutional governments in states of former Roman Empire. Satan will produce real miracles, give life to Beast image. Literal Two Witnesses. Literal Beasts, False Prophet, lake of fire. Two Gog-Magog battles, at start and end of Millennium.

935. Turner, Joseph. *A Scriptural View of the Close of the Present Dispensa-*

tion.... *To Be Succeeded by the Restitution or Everlasting Kingdom of God.* 1849. Hartford, CT. 72 p.

936. T[ustin], E.W.P. *The Days in Which We Live.* 1857. [Philadelphia:] Merrihew & Thompson. 21 p.

M. Baxter 1863 attributes authorship to "E.W.P. Taunton." Soon Second Coming. Jews starting to return. Ten Nations: Turkey, Greece, Austria, Sardinia, Naples, Spain, France, Belgium, England, Portugal. Napoleon, 7th Head, extinguished 6th — Holy Roman Empire. Napoleon III is Antichrist and 8th Head: ruler of Ten-Nation Roman Empire. Second Beast = Papal Kingdom. Pope will become False Prophet 3½ years prior to Second Coming. 666 = Lvdovicus (Louis [Napoleon]). Rapture ("translation" of the expectant) before 3½-year Great Tribulation (second half of 70th Week), following which a "flood of demons will be cast down from the heavenlies into the earth." After meeting Christ in the air, believers return with him at Second Coming for Armageddon.

937. *Twenty Reasons for Believing that the Second Coming of the Lord Is Near.* 1878. Chicago: F.H. Revell. 34 p.

Evidence that "we are living in the latter days" includes Zionism, the Great Pyramid (which indicates 1881 as the End), Russian role in Crimean War. 6,000 Year theory.

938. Two Servants of Christ. *The Computation of 666 and Its Relations to Antichristian Systems, But Having Reference to a Person, the Coming Antichrist, Who Is to Be Overthrown by the Sun of Righteousness.* 1891. London: James Nisbet. xiv, 398 p. illus.

Futurist. 2,520 Years = 2,516½ years from Creation to Exodus, plus 3½ years during Antichrist's manifestation. Catholicism is really pagan.

939. Tyng, Stephen H. *He Will Come; or Meditations Upon the Return of the Lord Jesus Christ.* 1877. New York: Mucklow & Simon. 212 p.

Second Coming 1868: "all the lines of prophecy meet in this designated year 1868, as the time of the glorious coming of the Son of Man...."

940. Urquhart, John. *The Wonders of Prophecy: Or, What Are We to Believe?* 1981. 9th ed., rev. Harrisburg, PA: Christian Publications. x, 241 p. 3rd ed 1906.

Already fulfilled prophecies are proof. Decline, degradation of Egypt foretold. Roman Empire (4th Empire) would become twofold (East and West), with fragments enduring until (still future) End. Nations already in prophesied tenfold division: five in the West (England, France, Spain, Germany, Italy , with Belgium, Switzerland, and Portugal to be absorbed); and in the East (Austria, Greece, Turk, Egypt, Danubian states). 70 weeks. 360 day prophetic year. 483 = 446 B.C. (decree to restore Jerusalem) to 30 A.D.

941. "Veritas." *An Answer to "The Mission and Destiny of Russia": the Last Published Work of the Author of "The Coming Struggle of the Nations."* 1853. London: Wertheim and Macintosh. 16 p.

942. *The Voice of God: or An Account of the Unparalleled Fires, Hurricanes, Floods and Earthquakes Commencing with 1845: Also, Some Account of Pestilence, Famine, and Increase of Crime.* 1847. Albany NY: Printed by Joel Munsell. 84 p.

"Collected ... from the various journals of the day" [Thomas Preble, comp.].

943. Waggoner, E[llet] J. *Prophetic Lights: Some of the Prominent Prophecies of the Old and New Testaments, Interpreted by the Bible and History.* 1888. Oakland, CA: Pacific Press. Reprinted 1982 by Leaves-of-Autumn. 180 p. illus.

944. Waite, John. 1896. *The Coming of Christ and Signs Preceding His Coming.* London: Stoneman. 77 p.

945. Wale, Burlington B. *The Closing Days of Christendom as Foreshadowed in Parable & Prophecy.* 1883 [1879]. 2nd ed. enlarged London: S.W. Partridge. xi, 548 p.

Author: minister Trinity Church, Plymouth. "The Author has long been impressed with the conviction that the present dispensation has nearly run its course, and that the 'time of the end' is near." This book presents "proofs" that this conviction is founded on the Bible and that signs of the End "are in manifest operation around us." Presently world in greatest crisis since the Reformation. Cites many writers who all predict End ca. 1840–1880; since everybody expects End in same period, this proves it. Drying up of Euphrates: fall of Turkish Empire. All writers focus on France, Turkey, and the Papacy. Not exact dates but "characteristics" of the period are important. Signs: increase of knowledge, commercial dishonesty, development of democracy, fall of Papacy, Turkey, rise of spiritualism. 6,000 year lifespan of earth reaching completion (endorses chronology of Hales, Shimeall, Fynes (Clinton — not Ussher's). Concludes that "year-day" theory is valid; prophetic numbers *can't* be literal. "This generation shall not pass away" refers to (future) Tribulation.

946. _____. *The Day of Preparation, or, the Gathering of the Hosts to Armageddon: A Book for the Times.* 1893. London: Eliot Stock. 358 p. illus.

947. Waller, Charles B. *The Apocalypse Viewed Under the Light of the Doctrines of the Unfolding Ages and the Restitution of All Things.* 1878. London: C. Kegan Paul. xii, 403 p.

948. Wardell-Potts, E. *The Time Is At Hand: Or, Things Which Must Shortly Come to Pass.* ? N.d. London: W.B. Horner. 158 p. Scripture index.

Pre-mill, pre-trib. 70th week, Tribulation, Gog invades, etc.— standard scenario, end of world prophecies

949. *The Warning of the Lord.* N.d. Plymouth [England:] J. Clulow & H. Soltau. 12 p.

950. Warren, Israel P. *The Parousia: A Critical Study of the Scripture Doctrines of Christ's Second Coming, His Reign as King, the Resurrection of the Dead, and the General Judgment.* 1884. 2nd ed. Portland ME: Hoyt, Fogg, & Dohnham. 394 p.

Parousia began when Christ ascended to heaven(?)

951. _____. *The Book of Revelation.* 1886. New York: Funk & Wagnalls. 300 p.

"An exposition, based on the principles of Prof. Stuart's Commentary and designed to familiarize those principles to the minds of non-professional readers." Also wrote refutation of "saduceeism": doctrine of the final annihilation of the wicked.

952. Weethee, J[onathan] P[erkins]. *The Coming Age: Its Nature and Proximity.* 1884. Chicago: C. H. Jones. ix, 506 p.

953. Wellcome, I[saac] C[ummings]. *A Treatise on the 24th and 25th Chapters of Matthew: Showing the Fulfillment of Most of the Predictions of Christ, by Copious Extracts from History; Consequently, that the Gentile Times are Nearly Ended, and the Kingdom of God Soon to Come.* 1872 [1856]. 6th ed. Boston: Advent Christian Publication Soc. 150 p.

954. Wemyss, Thomas. *A Key to the Symbolical Language of Scripture: by Which Numerous Passages are Explained and Illustrated: Founded on the Symbolical Dictionary of Daubuz, with Additions from Vitringa, Ewaldus, and Others.* 1840 [1835]. Edinburgh: Thomas Clark. viii, 512 p.

Also titled *The Symbol Dictionary.*

955. Wendell, Jonas. *The Present Truth, or, Meat in Due Season.* 1870. Edenboro, PA: author. 48 p.

Taught Russell. 1874 = Second Coming. Then advanced date to 1914 when 1874 passed. The Witnesses got "Seven times" doctrine from Nebudchadnezzar's madness.

956. West, Nathaniel. *The Thousand Years in Both Testaments.* 1880. Chicago: Fleming H. Revell. xxii, 493 p.

"With supplementary discussions upon symbolical numbers, the development of prophecy, and its interpretation concerning Israel, the nations, the church, and the kingdom, as seen in the apocalypses of Isaiah, Ezekiel, Daniel, Christ, and John." West: Presbyterian; Cincinnati. Post-trib pre-mill. Asserted that pre-mill belief was great incentive to missionary efforts to preach to all before Christ returns: "not to make the world better [but] to save the people out of [the world]." "Christian State" = Beast, 10-Horns, 10-Toes. 1993 reprint of 1899 ed. published as *The Thousand Year Reign of Christ: The Classic Work on the Millennium* (Grand Rapids, MI: Kregel). Also published by Scripture Truth (Fincastle, VA) titled *The Thousand Years: Studies in Eschatology in Both Testaments.*

957. _____. *Daniel's Great Prophecy. The Eastern Question. The Kingdom.* 1898. New York: Hope of Israel Movement. 307 p. index.

958. _____, ed. *Pre-Millennial Essays of the Prophetic Conference.* 1879 Chicago: Revell. 528 p. bibl. refs. index.

Second Coming of Christ, with appendix of critical testimonies. 1878 Conf. Contributors include Stephen H. Tyng. West also edited the proceedings of the 1875 Niagara Bible Conference (including "Pre-Millennian Creed" of John Charles Ryle).

959. *What is the Difference Between the Coming (Parousia) of Christ to Receive His Saints and His Appearing (Epiphaneia) in Glory With Them.* 1859. London: G. Morrish, G. Littlewood. 36 p.

Rapture, 3½ year Great Tribulation in second half of 70th Week, then Second Coming. The *Parousia* is the Rapture; the *Epiphaeia* the Second Coming.

960. White, Ellen G. *The Great Controversy Between Christ and Satan: From the Destruction of Jerusalem to the End of Time.* 1887. 6th ed. Oakland, CA: Pacific Press. 506 p. illus. Also 1986 ed. pub. 1870–78 under title *The Spirit of Prophecy.* Pub. 1988 under title *America in Prophecy* (Jemison, AL: Inspiration Books East).

"The great controversy between Christ and Satan, that has been carried forward for nearly six thousand years, is soon to close...." Before the creation of Adam, Lucifer (Satan) rebelled in heaven. Later, Satan deceived Christians into false Sunday worship. The 1,260 years began with 6th-century. Papacy: the abomination of Babylon and "apostasy of the latter times." U.S. is Beast from the Earth, with "lamb- like horns." Mark of the Beast is enforced Sunday worship. Deadly wound was 1798 abolition of Papacy. Revealing identity of Mark is message of 3rd angel of Revelation; 1st and 2nd were Millerite Adventists and their 1844 prediction. As end approaches, miracle-work-

ing demons produce fearful signs in heavens; Antichrist will impersonate Christ. Coming plagues "the most awful scourges that have ever been known to mortals." Believers will be hunted down for extermination. Then, Second Coming, Earth rent by mighty convulsions. All righteous dead resurrected, wicked all annihilated. "At the coming of Christ the wicked are blotted from the face of the whole earth...." Earth utterly desolate, devoid of life for Millennium, except for Satan and wicked angels. "For a thousand years Satan will wander." Judgment of wicked during Millennium. Second resurrection, of wicked, at end of Millennium. Satan mobilizes all resurrected wicked for last assault, but he is blasted into oblivion by God.

961. _____. *Almost Armageddon.* 1973. Jemison, AL: Audio Visual Production. 218 p.

962. _____. *Final War.* 1980, 1979. Phoenix, AZ: Inspiration Books. 218 p. "Parts taken from *The Great Controversy.*"

963. _____. *What's Behind the New World Order?* (1991, Jemison, AL: IBE; 80 p. illus.) "contains excerpts from *America in Prophecy* ... originally published under the title *The Great Controversy*"

964. _____. *Last Day Events: Facing Earth's Final Crisis.* 1992. Boise, ID: Pacific Press. 330 p. indexes.

965. _____. *World Peace!— Or Final War?* 1992 Graham, WA: Cornerstone. 1992. iv, 106 p. Selections from *The Great Controversy.*

966. _____. *Daniel and the Revelation.* Compiled by Walter T. Rhea. Reprinted 1994, Leaves-Of-Autumn Books. 200 p.

967. _____. *An Adventist Apocalypse: Last-Day Events.* 1994. s.l. LMN Pub. Intl. 144 p.

968. _____. *Promises for the Last Days.* 1994. Hagerstown, MD: Review and Herald. 155 p.

969. White, James. *A Word to the "Little Flock."* 1847. [Maine:] priv. pub. 24 p.

Husband of Ellen G. White. Includes E.G. White's vision "To the Remnant Scattered Abroad" and "Remarks" by Joseph Bates. Declares that Sunday worship is the prophesied Mark of the Beast.

970. _____. *Bible Adventism: or, Sermons on the Coming and Kingdom of Our Lord Jesus Christ.* 1877. Battle Creek, MI: Seventh-day Adventist Pub. Assoc. 198 p.

971. _____. *The Second Advent? Manner, Object, and Nearness of the Event.* n.d. Battle Creek, MI: Review and Herald. 31 p.

972. Whitman, A. *Prophecy Opened: Illustrating the Character of God, as Shown in His Providential and Gracious Administration on Earth.* 1874. Carthage, MO: Advance Book and Job Printing House.

973. Wickes, Thomas. *An Exposition of the Apocalypse.* 1851. New York: M.W. Dodd. viii, 437 p. Foldout chart.

Wickes: First Congregational Church (Marietta, OH). Four Horsemen: clergy from A.D. 100 to 400. 144,000: the true Church Militant of medieval times. Trumpets = Huns, Vandals, Saracens, Turks. Vials = French Revolution and Napoleonic Wars. Armageddon and Millennium will be in 1800s. Illuminati Conspiracy is part of First Vial: infection of unbelief.

974. _____. *The Economy of the Ages.* Long ages required to prepare Earth for mankind (pre–Adamic creation). Then 6,000 years of human history. Numbers of Revelation are symbolic. Second Coming and First Resurrection (of the good), then the "Millennium," which will last 365,000 years (Wickes assumes it has to be longer than the 6,000 years of mundane history). "Satan loosed" at end of Millennium also to last thousands of years.

975. Wilcox, Charles F. *The World's Rebellion, or, The Great Drama of Sin in Seven Acts.* 1901. MS [6], 140 leaves

976. Wilcox, Milton Charles. *The Heralds of His Coming: Is the End Near? May We Know the Time?* 1898. Oakland, CA: Pacific Press. 23 p.

977. _____. *The Great Day of the Lord.* N.d.: 40 p.

978. Wild, Joseph. *How and Why the World Will End.* 1879. New York: James Huggins. 422 p. 4th ed. 1886.

Congregational church sermons. 1880 excerpt titled *The Future of Israel: Being the Discourses on the Lost Tribulationes from How and Why [...]* Also wrote *The Lost Ten Tribes and 1882* and *Manasseh and the United States.* Pastor Union Congregational Church, Brooklyn. Pre-Adamic races; Flood destroyed all of Adamic race and all Nephilim, but not all Rephaim. Cites pre–Adamic Ohio Valley mound-builders. Translation (Rapture) only at very End (not before Tribulation). Before the Millennium, the Lost Tribes will "perish by the million in heroically struggling for God."

979. Wilkinson, Benjamin. *The Seven Last Plagues.* 1901. Battle Creek, MI: Review and Herald. 47 p.

980. Williston, Seth. *Christ's Millennial Reign; or, A Scriptural View of the Coming Thousand Years of Holiness, and Especially of Our Duty in Regard to It.* 1854 [1849]. Hudson, OH: Sawyer, Ingersoll. Revised and enlarged ed. 489 p.

Set of "discourses" (lectures). Urges missionary proselytizing. "Great Commission" to save as many as possible. Protestant truth; Catholic is "Abomination," Greek and Russian Orthodox also apostate. First Resurrection is spiritual: conversion of apostate prior to Millennium. Second Coming is after Millennium; with literal resurrection of dead; then End of World. Argues contra "millenarians" (pre-mills). Millennium *may* come in lifetime of "the present generation." All will be Christ's Disciples during Millennium. Christ reigns but does not dwell on Earth during Millennium. Orig. ed. 1849 titled *Millennial Discourses* ("and to Suggest Means for Hastening Its Introduction").

981. Williston, T[imothy]. *Christ's Millennial Reign and Second Appearing.* 1885. New York: Microcosm Pub. 130 p.

982. Wilson, Thomas. *The Terrible Day of the Lord; the Darkening of the Sun and Moon, and the Falling of the Stars.* [1901]. San Francisco: Last Days. 22 p.

Wilson: editor of *Last Days.* 1780 as Dark Day; star fell 1833.

983. _____. *The Drying Up of the Great River Euphrates.*

1822 as start of End Times — Ottoman Empire in death throes.

984. Winthrop, Edward. 1843. *Lectures on the Second Advent of Messiah.* Cincinnati: J. B. Wilson. iv, [5], 281 p.

Pre-mill. Two manifestations of Second Coming; Rapture is the first.

985. _____. *The Premium Essay on the Characteristics and Laws of Prophetic Symbols.* 1854. New York: F. Knight. xiii, 191 p.

Prize essay in competition conducted by the *Theological and Literary Journal.*

986. [Wolcott, Eseck] "A Servant of Christ." *Last Things: A Warning to All.* 1885. Eatontown, NJ: ["by Brethren"]. 12 p.

Especially concerned about activity of Communist Anarchists.

987. _____. *No Millenium Future.* [ca. 1900]. Eatontown, NJ. 24 p.

Also wrote *A Judgment Message* (1912; 15 p.).

988. Woodard, D.H. *World Politics at the Close of the Nineteenth Century in the Light of Prophecy.* 1899. Boston: Advent Christian Publication Soc. 23 p.

Russia to lead End Time alliance in a "deluge of war." The Beast that was, is not, and shall come: Russia, which will rule Greek Orthodox nations and take over Constantinople.

989. Woodward, E[dward] P[ayson]. *Christ's Last Prophecy: Concerning the Destruction of Jerusalem, and His Own Second Advent.* 1898. Portland, ME: Safeguard. 134 p.

990. _____. *The Two-Horned Beast: Its Image, Its Mark, Its Number, Its Name (Revelation XIII, 11–18).* 1904. Portland, ME: Safeguard. 90 p. illus. SEE ALSO 1910–1970.

991. Wordsworth, Christopher. *Lectures on the Apocalypse.* 1852 [1849]. Philadelphia: H. Hooker. xxiv, 535 p. 2nd ed. 1849. bibl. refs.

Excerpted in *The Church of Rome, or, the Babylon of the Apocalypse* (1853, 122 p.). Also wrote *On the Millennium* (1848). Hulsean Lectures to Cambridge students "for their guidance, warning, and encouragement, in the trials of the latter days." Author: Canon of Westminster, Public Orator — Univ. of Cambridge. Much discussion of history of exegesis. Literal Millennium and millenarianism rejected by Church of England, Luther, Calvin. Millennium is "repugnant to Scripture." Apocalypse (i.e. Revelation) a "synoptical system of co-ordinate Prophecies," with anticipations and recaps, not consecutive prophecies. Resurrection of saints and Universal Judgment same event: Last Day; no Millennial interval. "[V]ery little of the Apocalypse *remains to be fulfilled,* and that, therefore, the time to the end is probably very short...." Severe trials in time remaining: great earthquake, physical calamities. All men and nations combine vs. Christ in last age, last conflict of Armageddon, with Beast, False Prophet, Satan.

992. *The World to Come!: The Present Earth to be Destroyed by Fire at the End of the Gospel Age.* 1849. Boston: Joshua V. Himes.

Excerpted from *The Age to Come.*

993. Wright, Charles H. H. *Biblical Essays, or, Exegetical Studies on the Books of Job and Jonah, Ezekiel's Prophecy of Gog and Magog, St. Peter's "Spirits in Prison," and the Key to the Apocalypse.* 1886. Edinburgh: T. & T. Clark. xxxii, 261 p.

994. Wroe, John. *Communications for the Members of the Israelite Church.* 2nd ed. 1862. Gravesend: Printed for the Society, Surnamed Israelites.

In 1823 became leader of "Christian Israelite" faction of Southcottians after Turner's failed prophecy. Prophesied 1863 for beginning of Millennium. Predicted End for 1977. Also *Abridgement of John Wroe's Revelations,* 3rd ed. Boston 1849; etc.

995. Wylie, James Aitken. *The Great Exodus, or "The Time of the End": How Near Are We To It?* 1892. London: James Nesbet; Edinburgh: Andrew Elliot. iv, 408 p.

Includes The Four Monarchies; The Four Beasts; The Dragon; The Seven Times; The Three Times and a Half;

Length of the Judgment Day; The Apocalypse, or Unveiling; The Vials; etc.

996. Youngs, Benjamin Seth. 1856. *Testimony of Christ's Second Appearing, Exemplified by the Principles and Practice of the True Church of Christ: History of the Progressive Work of God, Extending from the Creation of Man to the "Harvest" Comprising the Four Great Dispensations Now Consummating in the Millennial Church....* 1856. 4th ed. Albany: United Society of Shakers. xxiv, 631 p.

997. Zezschwitz, Gerhard von, ed. *Das Drama vom Ende des romischen Kaisertums und von der Erscheinung des Antichrists.* 1878. Leipzig: C. Hinrich. 75 p.

From medieval manuscript from Tegernsee, Germany.

998. Zook, J.R. *The Bible Its Own Commentary on the Second Coming of*

Christ. 1903. Des Moines: Iowa Printing Co. 199 p. [Cover title *He Is Coming: Who Is Ready?*]

Creation ca. 4000 B.C. "It is quite evident that this age will close at the consummation of the 6,000 years, which time no man is able to give accurately." Papacy = Beast, Little Horn. Deadly wound = separation of Roman Empire into East and West (A.D. 476); revival is re-established power under Charlemagne. Islam is other Little Horn and False Prophet. Jews punished for rejecting Christ, but will regain Palestine. Christ will "utterly destroy" the nations and all the wicked at Second Coming (Armageddon). First Resurrection (at Second Coming), then Millennium, then Second Resurrection (when resurrected wicked and fallen angels battle Millennial forces.

Works from 1910 to 1970 (Alphabetical)

999. "Abu-ru-shin." *In the Light of Truth: The Grail Message.* 3 vols. 1996 [1933]. 10th ed. Gambier, OH: Grail Foundation Press. 1061 p. Index. Orig. German (*Im Lichte der Wahrheit*).

Metaphysical, occult. Antichrist is already on earth, but not publicly apparent yet. Humans incapable of managing this Creation, so God must "*forcibly* intervene. *Hence the Millennium!*" Cause of this will be monstrous comet now headed towards Earth. Stresses importance and reality of Holy Grail.

1000. Adams, Jay Edward. *The Time Is At Hand.* 1970 [1966]. Nutley, NJ: Presbyterian and Reformed. ix, 123 p. illus. Rev. ed. of *I Will Tell You the Mystery.*

A-mill; preterist. Argues that pre-mill interpretation ignores simpler and more logical interpretation, and was advanced largely because the 19th century post-mill view sounded too similar to the liberal notion of continued progress and triumph. Wants to construct a positive a-mill eschatology. Says "a-mill" is misleading term: prefers "realized" millennialism. Christ will come again. "Diplopia" of premill view: Millennium duplicates events of Second Coming, scenario repeated. Preterist interpretation of Apocalypse, like Calvin's; refers to literal, historical Rome. Revelation largely fulfilled soon after writing. Ten Horns probably provincial governors of Roman Empire. 144,000 sealed witnesses: Christian Jews who escaped to Pella from Romans. Beast = Nero = 666. Fifth Kingdom — stone that broke Roman Empire — is Kingdom of God: the Church. "Mystery": after A.D. 70 destruction of Temple, Gentile converts in church become equal to Jewish Christians. Satan cast to earth at Crucifixion. Millennium: ideal time, not literal thousand years — Church Age, not utopian paradise.

1001. Adams, John Quincy. *Babylon and the Present Apostasy: A Study of the Babylonian Apostasy that Now Grips the World.* 1924. 2nd ed. Dallas: Prophetical Society of Dallas. 78 p. illus.

1002. _____. *His Apocalypse.* 1924. Dallas: Prophetical Society of Dallas. 485 p. index.

Parousia probably Apr. 11, 1925; Tribulation 1925–28; Advent probably Oct. 11, 1931. "Futurist" interpretation.

1003. Alderman, Paul R. *The Unfolding of the Ages: Prophecy Fulfilled, Prophecy Being Fulfilled, Prophecy to Be Fulfilled.* 1965 [1954]. Neptune, NJ: Loizeaux Bros. 148 p.

Introduction by E. Schuyler English. Antichrist: Jew from revived Roman Empire with Satanic powers. "As the horrible Tribulation roars towards its awful climax, with Satan personally on earth, his Antichrist on the world throne, and the False Prophet (the religious counterpart of Antichrist) holding sway in Jerusalem, all the nations of the earth join in sending their mighty armies into Palestine...." "The spotlight of prophecy" is shining "its all-revealing rays upon *Russia*, that sinister nation...."

1004. _____. *God's Spotlight on Tomorrow: Seven Sevens Concerning the Return of Christ.* 1960. New York: Loizeaux Bros. 32 p.

1005. Allen, A.A. *Seven Women Shall Take Hold of One Man!* 1954. Dallas: A.A. Allen. 69 p. illus.

1006. Allis, Oswald Thompson. *Prophecy and the Church* . 1978 [1945]. Phillipsburg, NJ: Presbyterian and Reformed. x, 339 p. bibl. refs, indexes.

"An examination of the claim of dispensationalists that the Christian church is a mystery of parenthesis which interrupts the fulfillment to Israel of the kingdom prophecies of the Old Testament." A-mill; refutes dispensationalist eschatology. Allis: Presbyterian, prof. and co-founder of Westminster Seminary.

1007. Anderson, A.W. *The World's Finale, a Brief Exposition of the Prophecies of the Seven Churches, the Seven Seals, and the Seven Trumpets of Revelation.* 1932 [1912]. Warburton, Victoria, Australia: Signs Publishing Co. 95 p. illus.

1008. Anderson, H. S. (Hans Steele). *The Spirit of Elijah in the Closing Work.* N.d. Fort Meade, FL: s.n. 16 p.

Seventh-day Adventist.

1009. Anderson, Robert. SEE ALSO 1800–1910. *Unfilled Prophecy and "The Hope of the Church."* 1918 [1917]. London: Charles J. Thynne / James Nisbet. xii, 105 p.

Justifiable increase in interest in prophecy due to the War. Restoration precedes 70th week, though; Tribulation not yet. Second Coming = Judgment at End of World. Bible nowhere speaks of "secret" coming (Rapture). 445 B.C. to A.D. 32 = 69 weeks of years to the day. "No Christian doubts the Messianic fulfillment of the 69 weeks of this prophecy. And ... no less certain is it that the 70th week awaits fulfillment." Coming of Christ not the same as Coming of Son of Man, which follows Anti–Christ and the Tribulation. But Coming of Christ could be any mo-

ment. 70th Week announced by clear change of Dispensation, then saintly believers called up to heaven. Antichrist will be "energized" by Satan — "false Messiah and mighty Kaiser." Three future Comings: end of Dispensation, with elect to heaven; Son of Man; Judgment in "far-distant future" after Millennium.

1010. Anderson, Roy Allan. *Unfolding the Revelation.* 1974 [1953]. revised edition Mountain View, CA: Pacific Press. vii, 223 p.

1011. _____. *Unfolding Daniel's Prophecies.* 1975. Mountain View, CA: Pacific Press. 192 p. index bibl.

1012. Anderson, Wing. *Seven Years that Change the World: 1941–1948.* 1940. New York: Kosmon Press [The Book of Gold]. xviii, 266 p. bibl.

Anderson: Custodian of Archives, American Essences of Kosmon. Based on *Oahspe*, the 1881 occultic "American Cosmic Bible" by John Ballou Newbrough (the "greatest prophet of them all"), but quotes many other prophecies as well. "We are living in 'The Time of the End'" — but a utopian new age lies ahead. 1914–1948 is the rebel generation of Kosmon (*Oahspe*), or biblical Time of Trouble, including Armageddon (the World Wars). The building generation of Kosmon starts in 1948. Hitler is the Vile Person predicted in Daniel; Mussolini the King of the South. Hitler will conquer Europe and head new confederation of nations. A Catholic-Capitalist coalition will briefly subject U.S. to fascist rule. Mankind 72,000 years old, with 1848 the halfway point of mankind's 144,000 years total existence. A Sixth Race will arise in 1948. Many other races, angels, monstrosities (hybrids), planes of existence and stages of materialization too. Includes psychic phone messages from dead leaders. Anderson also wrote *The Next Nine Years: An Analysis and a Prophecy* (1938, 1939; Los Angeles: Kosmon Press), and *The Year of Crisis* (1952; Los Angeles: Kosmon Industries).

1013. _____. *Prophetic Years, 1947–1953.* 1946; Los Angeles: Kosmon. Cosmic cycles of *Oahspe*. Kosmon era began 1848. 1941–48 = Time of Trouble. 1947–53 = end of cycle of destruction. Millennium starts 1980. Quotes many recent prophecies, about Germany, U.S.S.R., Britain, U.S. , China; also Mormon prophecies. 4046 B.C. + 6,000 years = 1954. Nazis and the Vatican are "blood brothers."

1014. Angley, Ernest. *Raptured: A Novel on the Second Coming of the Lord.* 1950. Akron, OH: distr. by Winston Press. 218 p.

Novel. Angley: Akron, OH, televangelist. Rapture results in utter chaos. Antichrist rushes in when Church removed. Antichrist — the Beast — will please Jews, until he desecrates Temple mid–Tribulation. Newspaper headlines scream: "*Thousands of People have Mysteriously Disappeared!*" All babies vanish. Mark of Beast required to buy or sell. Typical dialogue: "The demons of hell are here to usher my soul into that terrible place called Hell! I feel the flames of Hell!" Persecutors drink blood of martyred Christians, much description of burnings at stake, torturing to death. Jews (the Woman) flee to wilderness; Man-Child = 144,000. Literal demonic locusts; other woes, plagues. 200 million horsemen. "Antispirit" = False Prince = Antichrist's colleague. Ends with Second Coming.

1015. Anscombe, Francis C. (Francis Charles). *The Day of the Lord: What the Bible Says: a Modern Interpretation.* 1962. Winston-Salem, N.C.: F.C. Anscombe. 134 p.

1016. Anstey, Martin. *Romance of Bible Chronology.* 1913. London: Marshall Bros. 2 vols.

Adam created 5,955 years ago (4042 B.C.); 1913 is 45 years til End.

1017. *The Antichrist and the Armageddon: A Prophetic Forecast of the Joys and Sorrows that Are to Come Upon this Sin-Sick and War Stricken Planet.* 1944. Los Angeles: The Gleaners. 64 p. illus. "Jewish Hope Pub. Co." stamped on title page.

1018. Appelman, Hyman Jedidiah. *The Battle of Armageddon.* 1944 [1942]. Fairfield, AL: Faith of Our Fathers Broadcast. 62 p. (Also published by Zondervan.)

Appelman: Converted Jew from Ukraine; lawyer and Southern Baptist evangelist.

1019. _____. *Antichrist and the Jew; and, The Valley of Dry Bones.* 1950. Grand Rapids, MI: Zondervan. 25 p.

1020. _____. *The Atomic Bomb and the End of the World.* 1954. Grand Rapids, MI: Zondervan. 28 p.

1021. Armerding, Carl Edwin. *Signs of Christ's Coming—as Son of Man.* 1971 [1965] Rev. ed. Chicago: Moody Press. 126 p.

Book adapted from articles in *Moody Monthly.* Pre-trib. The 70th Week and Second Coming. SEE ALSO 1970+.

1022. Armstrong, Garner Ted. *When God Shakes the Earth.* 1969. Tyler, TX: Worldwide Church of God. 26 p.

"Bible Prophecy Says Massive Earthquakes, Tidal Waves, Huge Storms and Catastrophes in Unimaginable Intensity Are to Shake this Earth Just Prior to Christ's Return: Are We Now Entering a Time of Increasingly Devastating Natural Calamities?: Is the Eruption of Mount St. Helens Only Another in a Long History of Natural Disasters, Or a Harbinger of Something Much Worse to Come?" Armstrong: son of Herbert W. Armstrong; Worldwide Church of God. SEE ALSO 1970+.

1023. Armstrong, Hart. *Even So Come.* 1950 Springfield, MO: Gospel Publishing House. 128 p.

Second Coming.

1024. _____. *To Those Who Are Left.* [ca 1960]. Kansas City, MO: Defenders of the Christian Faith. 64 p.

The Rapture and Tribulation

1025. _____. *The Beast.* 1967. Kansas City, MO: Defenders of the Christian Faith. 64 p.

A Defender Mity Mite book (another is on the Devil). Armstrong: editor of Defender since 1968; Defenders of the Christian Faith.

1026. _____. *Primer of Prophecy.* 1970. Kansas City, MO: Defenders. 3 vol. illus. SEE ALSO 1970+.

1027. Armstrong, Herbert W. *Who or What is the Prophetic Beast?* 1960 [1952].

Pasadena, CA: Worldwide Church of God. 45 p. illus. chart

"Deals with governments and wars that will bring this world to its final end." Armstrong: founder of Worldwide Church of God, Ambassador College, *Plain Truth* magazine. In earlier (unpub.) work, *Third Angel*, Armstrong said Armageddon would be in 1936.

1028. ____. *The Book of Revelation Unveiled at Last!* 1972 [1959]. 44 p.

Now in the "Time of the End," "the very END TIME ... just prior to the Second Coming of Jesus Christ."

1029. ____; *The United States and Britain in Prophecy.* 1980 [1967]. xii, 192 p. Indexes. illus.

British-Israelism: Joseph's sons Ephraim and Manasseh inherited promises of Israel; Ephraim's descendants are the British; Manasseh's are the Americans. SEE ALSO 1970+.

1030. Arnot, A.B. *The World's Midnight Hour (Armageddon Foretold).* 1957 London/Edinburgh: Oliphant's. 128 p. index bibl.

Gog = Northern Confederacy — Russia vs. Tarshish = British Commonwealth, which comes to defense of Israel at Armageddon. Based largely on 1936 sermon "Armageddon" — in which he predicted Russia (not Germany) as Gog.

1031. Atkinson, Tacy W. *A Guide to the Study of Revelation.* 1937. Burlington, IA: Lutheran Literary Board. 86 p. chart.

1032. Axelson, A.E. *Last Day Events.* 1957. Berrien Springs, MI: Emmanuel Missionary College. 2 vols.

1033. Ayer, William Ward. *God's World of Tomorrow.* 1939. Grand Rapids, MI: Zondervan. 59 p.

"Meditations on God's world to come, in the light of man's present World's Fair."

1034. ____. *What Goes On Here!* 1947. Grand Rapids, MI: Zondervan.

Ayer: pastor N.Y. Calvary Baptist Church; radio preacher. "The Jew is going back to his land in unbelief" (assumes that restoration of Israel will follow Second Coming). A jeremiad about world conditions. Civilization is "dust," will be de-

stroyed at Second Coming. Warns that world is still evil even though Nazis defeated. Seduced by hope of peace, prosperity; rotten with rampant materialism, blasphemy, selfishness, lawlessness. Russian atheism a huge menace. Iron and clay = fascism and communism, now mixing in Europe headed for totalitarianism. "Divine dictatorship" under Christ the ultimate solution. Noted he predicted in earlier work that Russia would triumph over Germany. "Evolution is manifestly not true because obviously it is not working." Section on "Evolution Creates Fatalism"; is "refuge of lies"; "the most deadly and destructive force" in the world. Also rails against communism and liquor. Einstein was an "ingrate" who preached atheism. Future "Translation" of church, 7-year Tribulation, Coming. Mystery of Iniquity, Babylon, Harlot, rules during Tribulation: false religion, led by Antichrist, the False Prophet. True church is raptured pre-trib. Jews "spiritually blind," deluded by Satan. God now focusing on Gentiles, though later will again bless Israel, purifying and restoring it. Bible shows Arabs are inherently aggressive, and are not to own Palestine, but "not the divine will" that Jews return to homeland unconverted either. "Obviously, modern Zionism is not a truly Biblical movement." Too many are communist. "I say authoritatively, supported by God's Word, that the Jew cannot have his land permanently until he has his Messiah" i.e. accepts Christ. Repentance and restoration for Jews. Second Coming will be unexpected and sudden because it is "not evolutionary but cataclysmic."

1035. Baker, Alonzo L. *Is Our World Facing Twilight Or Dawn?* [ca. 1930]. Arlington, CA: Home Bible Study League. [8] p.

Seventh-day Adventist.

1036. ____. *Christ or Chaos! A War-Wracked World Cries for the Coming of the Prince of Peace.* 1943. Nashville: Southern Publishing Assoc.

1037. Baker, C.J. *An Examination of the Scriptures on the Length of the "Times of the Gentiles."* 1917 [1914]. 7th ed. Kansas City, MO: C.J. Baker. 64 p.

"The Coming of the Lord Draweth Nigh." Pre-mill; pre-trib Rapture. Criticizes historicist interpretations; 70th Week still to come; 1,260 Days are literal (second half of 70th Week: the Tribulation). Antichrist won't be revealed until after Rapture. 2,520 "Days" (Time of Gentiles) are years, though. Year of 70th Week and End events not known for certain, but will start on Jewish New Year, and the World War is a prelude to Armageddon.

1038. Baker, Nelson B. *What Is This World Coming To?: A Study for Laymen of the Last Things.* 1965 Philadelphia: Westminster Press. 157 p. bibl. refs.

Baker: prof. E. Baptist Theol. Sem. A-mill. Millennium was resurrection of souls at First Coming. Second Coming, with Final Judgment but no Millennium. Antichrist — ruler of satanic lawlessness — at end of history.

1039. Baldwin, H[armon] A. *The Coming Judgment, General and At the End of Time.* 1927 Chicago: Free Methodist Pub. House. 184 p. bibl.

1040. Ballard, J. Hudson. *Delusions of the Last Days.* [1920s?] Toronto: A. Sims. 16 p.

1041. Ballenger, A[lbion] F. *Before Armageddon.* 1918. Riverside, CA: author 180 p.

Seventh-day Adventist

1042. _____. *Bible Predictions of World Events Before Armageddon: A Study of the Prophetic Symbols of Daniel and Revelation in the Light of World Conditions.* 1953. 2nd ed. rev. Riverside, CA: The Gathering Call. 157 p.

1043. Barbarin, Georges. *Le Secret de la Grand Pyramide: ou, La Fin du Monde Adamique.* 1966? [1936]. Paris: Editions Adyar. viii, 119 p. illus. maps diagrams bibl. refs.

Also wrote book on Sphinx. "Prophetic geometry" of Pyramid. Adam 4000 B.C., Flood 1,656 years later, First Tribulation 1914–18, Second Tribulation to 1936. Anglo-Saxons as Israel.

1044. Baron, David. *Israel in the Plan of God.* 1983 [1925]. Kregel. Orig. pub. London: Morgan & Scott. Orig. title *The History of Israel.*

Baron: Converted Jew, born in Poland; leader of Hebrew Christian Testimony to Israel. Historic pre-mill.

1045. Barton, Harold Edwin. *It's Here: The Time of the End.* c1963. New York: Exposition Press. 221 p.

Barton: Baptist minister. Second half of book chapter-by-chapter exegesis of Revelation. Rejects futurist interpretation; advocates historicist — Guinness, Cachemaille, Elliott — [and?] "presentist" or "historical Protestant" (Waldenses, Wycliffites, and Hussites, then the Reformers). "Supreme desire" of author is to "*prove* that the 'time of the end' is here." Crucifixion in middle of 70th week. 10-Horn nations: Lombards, Franks, Burgundians, Ostrogoths, Visigoths, Vandals, Heruli, Sueves, Huns, Saxons. Papacy = Antichrist. Little Horn: Islam. "The power of the Moslems for evil is only exceeded by that of the Papacy." Much discussion of evils and horrors of Papacy. 666= Lateinos, Romiti, Vicarivs filii dei. Time of Gentiles ends 1699–1934: decline of Papacy and Islam. 1,260 and 2,520 Years, solar and lunar, to and from various dates; Captivity of Israel, and establishment of Islam and Papacy. The Four Horsemen: White = A.D. 96–180, Red = Roman Civil War 192–284. Black = decline of Rome. Pale = 250–265 Plague years. 6th seal earthquake= fall of Roman paganism. 12 tribes symbolic of Christians. Trumpets = Alaric the Goth, Vandals, Huns, Odoacer and Theodoric, Saracens (5th), Turks (6th). French revolution = 3rd Woe. 7-headed Beast of Sea = Roman rulers: Kings, consuls, dictators, decemvirs, military tribunes, emperors, absolute monarchs, last rulers (to be revived). Vials = wars of Catholics, up to Napoleon; 6th is Turkey. Russia and Arabs soon will try to crush Israel. Armageddon: Antichrist and all forces of evil vs. Christ at Second Coming, followed by Millennium.

1046. Barton, Michael X. *Time No More.* 1965. Los Angeles: Futura Press. 37 leaves illus.

Flying saucers.

1047. _____. *Amazing Visions of the Endtime.* 1967. Los Angeles: Futura Press; Clarksburg, WV: Saucerian Books. 37 p.

New Age prophecy connected with UFOs.

1048. Bate, L.F. *Happening Unaware.* 1963. Dallas: L. Bate. 96 p. illus. maps bibl. refs.

End of world conspiracies.

1049. Battenfield, J.A., and Philip Y. Pendleton. *The Great Demonstration: A Harmony of All the Prophetic Visions of the Holy Bible. I: Daniel and Revelation.* 1914. Cincinnati: Standard. 462 p.

Battenfield: Disciples of Christ; also edited *Primary Lessons in Science of Prophecy* (1921 [1918]; Olney, IL: The Incoming Kingdom Missionary Unity; 3 vols.). Jews return to Palestine in 1897. 1972: the Millennium begins. A.D. 637 + 1,335 years = 1972. 328 B.C. + 2,300 years = 1972. 1960: fall of paganism. Creation: 4028 B.C. A.D. 666 + 1,260 years (of Dark Ages) = 1927.

1050. *The Battle of Armageddon : Where Will It Begin?* 1939. Boulder, CO: Enterprise Mission. [8] p.

1051. Bauman, Louis S[ylvester]. *God and Gog: or The Coming Meet Between Judah's Lion and Russia's Bear.* 1934. Priv. pub.

Bauman: Grace Brethren. Pre-mill. Stalin = "steel" of Jer. 15:12.

1052. _____. *Shirts and Sheets; or, Anti–Semitism, a Present-Day Sign of the First Magnitude!* c1934. Long Beach, CA: A.S. Pearce. 52 p. illus.

Typical pre-mill ambiguity of attitude towards Jews. Persecution of Jews bad, but necessary because they killed Christ, and ordained by God. Jews responsible for most revolutions and for Depression. Anti–Semitism leads to Armageddon.

1053. _____. *Light from Bible Prophecy: As Related to the Present Crisis.* 1940. New York: Fleming H. Revell. 169 p.

Turks chanted "*Allah-Bey!*" (= "Allenby"); didn't oppose British General Allenby's entrance into Jerusalem, because prophesied that Jerusalem to be returned to Jews when "Prophet of God" arrives.

1054. _____. *Russian Events in the Light of Bible Prophecy.* 1952 [1942]. Phil-adelphia: The Balkiston Co. [1942 ed NY: F.H. Revell; 191 p.]

Russia as Gog. Gomer is Germany; will ally with Russia.

1055. _____. *The Approaching End of This Age.* 1952. Grand Rapids, MI: Zondervan. 64 p.

Bauman: evangelist, Brethren Church minister; this book originally articles from *King's Business.* Months, not years, til armies march to Armageddon. King of South = Britain, allied with Italy in new Roman Empire. A-bombs and H-bombs won't destroy world, but world is sinking into apostasy. Bauman rails against world government and is horrified by ecumenicism. Notes he declared Russia was Gog in 1939, and that Scofield did so in 1909. Red Horse of Apocalypse is Soviets. Man created 6,000 years ago. "Keep your eye on the Jew" for prophetic insight. New Roman Empire, an alliance of ten European nations, will defeat Gog and his allies. Rapture, then 7-year Tribulation, then Armageddon. Antichrist demands worship of Beast in Jerusalem; his earthly armies then defeated by Christ at Armageddon. In his previous book, Bauman predicted Stalin would defeat Hitler, and that Gomer of Ezekiel was Germany.

1056. Bauman, Paul, et al. *The Prophetic Word in Crisis Days.* 1961. Findlay, OH: Dunham. 215 p. Also pub. 1964.

Prophetic Messages Delivered at the West Coast Prophetic Congress (Los Angeles) in 1961. Contributors: Bauman, Simon Forsberg, H. Hoyt, J.V. McGee, J.D. Pentecost, J. Walvoord, Charles Woodbridge. Bauman: son of L.S. Bauman. Pre-trib Rapture, Tribulation, Second Coming, Millennium. 10-nation confederacy: revived Roman Empire of southern Europe, also North Africa and West Asia. Roman ruler makes covenant with Israel. World War of all nations foretold: Armageddon. Gog = Russia. Catholic Church = "Harlot." Awakening of China = Eastern forces. Atomic bombs = melting of earth. World Church movement as End sign. Communism destroyed mid-trib. U.S. may be part of 10-nation confederacy. Burning weapons for 7 years may indicate disarmament. European Confederation destroys Roman Church, the "Harlot" political-religious system, mid-trib.

1057. Beach, Raymond. *Crepusculo ou Aurora?: Una Respuesta a la Pergunta: Qual Sera Destino do Mundo?* 1946. Lisbon: Publicadora Atlantico. 190 p. illus. Portug.; orig French. 3rd ed. 1944.

"Dusk or Dawn?"

1058. Becker, Klaus. *Die Nacht ist vorgerucht. Eine Analyse unserer Zeit im Licht der Bibel.* 1967. Bad Liebenzell/ Wurttemburg [Germany]: Verlag der Liebenzeller Mission. 63 p.

1059. Beirnes, William F. *The Tribulation.* 1948 [1930]. 3rd ed. Denver, CO: William Beirnes. 60 p. illus. foldout chart.

1060. _____. *Questions and Answers on the Second Coming.* [1969?]. 3rd ed. Tequesta, FL: Midnight Cry. 128 p. indexes.

1061. _____. *Revelation.* 1969. Summerfield, FL: Midnight Cry. 4 vol.

1062. _____. *The Sealed Book Revealed: A Commentary on the Book of Daniel.* [1969?]. Tequesta, FL: Midnight Cry. 101 p.

1063. _____. *That Man of Sin.* [1969?]. Tequesta, FL: Midnight Cry. 45 p. Antichrist.

1064. _____. *Wrath Outpoured: A Study of the Great Tribulation.* [1969?]. Tequesta, FL: Midnight Cry. 88 p.

SEE ALSO 1970+.

1065. Bell, Clinton C. *Ten Lessons on Our Lord's Return: As Taught by the Old Testament and New Testament Scriptures Relating to Church History and World-Wide Conditions.* 1919 [1918]. New York: Revell. 148 p.

1066. Benavides, Rodolfo. *Dramatic Prophecies of the Great Pyramid.* 1969 [1968]. Mexico: D.F. Editores Mexicanos Unidos. 479 p., illus. Orig. Spanish. Many editions.

Dire predictions for remaining years of this millennium, which confirm Bible, including pole shift 1977–1982, Jews to disappear, Messiah by 2001.

1067. Bendle, Arthur J. M. *The End Time.* Geistown, PA: A. Bendle. 30 p.

"Daniel 12:9: a brief treatise on chronology and eschatology, the Jewish question, denominational heresies, Catholicism and Modernism."

1068. Benham, Charles O. *101 Signs of Christ's Coming, X-Raying Today's Crisis.* 1940 [1935]. Joliet, IL: National X-Ray Publications. 140 p.

1069. _____. *The New Order Is at Hand: God's Greatest Program for the World.* 1941 Joliet, IL: National X-Ray Pub. 62 p. illus.

1070. _____. *Great Britain and the United States in Prophecy.* 1942. Joliet, IL: National X-Ray Publications/ Dr. C.O. Benham. 63 p.

1071. _____. *101 Roadsigns to Our Next Pearl Harbor and to Armageddon.* 1945 [1939]. Washington, D.C.: National Forecast. 156 p. 1939 ed. priv. pub. (Joliet IL), titled *101 Roadsigns to the Soon Coming Armageddon: "The Battle of that Great Day of God Almighty."*

1072. Benjamin, Ethel. *A Message.* 1922. [Dayton, OH: s.n.]. 39 p. illus.

1073. Benson, Carmen. *This Earth's End.* 1971 [1970]. Watchung, NJ: Charisma Books. 152 p. Contains the text of the last three chapters of her *Supernatural Dreams and Visions* (1970; Logos).

1074. Berke-Muller, Paul. *Unser Jahrtausend geht seinem Ende entgegen.* 1965. Stuttgart-Hohenheim: Hänssler-Verlag. 42 p., [16] p. of plates. illus., charts; bibl.

1075. Berry, George Benton. *The End of All Things: Studies in the Revelation of Jesus Christ, as Written Down by St. John the Divine.* 1912. Plymouth. 150 p. illus.

1076. Beskin, Nathan Cohen. *The Mark of the Beast: Some Startling Signs of the End.* 1935 [1931]. [Chicago:] Evangel. 14 p.

Dispensationalist.

1077. _____. *Return of the Jews and the End of the World.* 1931. Chicago: Peacock Press, for author. xvi, 156. p.

Beskin: "The Converted Jew"; rabbinical training in Russia. With British General Allenby in Palestine in WWI, including fighting at Megiddo ("Armageddon") and entrance into Jerusalem. Jews to return in unbelief, then convert. 360-day prophetic years. 69 Weeks = 457 B.C. to A.D. 30. 606 B.C. + 2520 = 1917 (surrender of Jerusalem to Allenby; Balfour Declaration). Future Armageddon prompted by Dead Sea riches, oil. Gentile era coming to an end. Rapture soon. *When Will It End?* (1931; Los Angeles: Free Tract Soc.) includes sermon by Beskin. End begins 1934.

1078. _____. *Signs of the Antichrist: "The Fasces": Is It "the Mark of the Beast"?* 1932. Evangel. 43 p.

1079. _____. *The Chart of the Eternities.* [1930s?]. Fort Wayne, IN: Old Time Religion Tabernacle. 22 p., plates, illus., fold-out chart.

1080. Biederwolf, William E. *The Second Coming Bible Commentary.* 1985 [1924]. Grand Rapids, MI: Baker 728 p. Orig. 1924; prev. titled *The Millennium Bible* and *The Second Coming Bible.* Reprint ed. of 1924 ed. titled *The Amazing Prophecy Second Coming Bible* (1974; Orange, CA: Amazing Prophecy).

Biederwolf: evangelist; worked with Billy Sunday; later president of School of Theology. All scripture verses pertaining to Second Coming, with commentary; citing many experts. "Impartial," but Biederwolf himself is pre-mill, post-trib.

1081. _____. *The Great Tribulation and the Second Coming of Christ: A Study of Matthew 24.* 1929. Boston: Hamilton Bros. 32 p.

1082. Bietz, Arthur L. *Last Day Events.* 1957. [S.l. : s.n.] 95 p. bibl. refs.

Seventh-Day Adventist

1083. Bjaanaes, Erling. *Stormvarsler.* 1951. Oslo: Nosk Bokverlag. 160 p. illus.

Biblical prophecies; Second Coming; End.

1084. Black, Harry. *What About Between Now and 1936–1937?* [1930s?]. Los Angeles: author. 32 p.

"When will the Gentile Age end?"

1085. _____. *Is the End of the Age At Hand.* ? [1940s]. Los Angeles: author. 31 p.

Free Methodist Church. Luke XXI: 24–28

1086. Blackstone, William Eugene. SEE ALSO 1800–1910. *The Times of the*

Gentiles, and, The Time of the End. [1920s] New York: Fleming H. Revell. 28 p.

1087. Blanchard, Charles A[lbert]. *Light on the Last Days; Being Familiar Talks on the Book of Revelation.* 1913. Chicago: Bible Institute Colportage Assoc. 149 p.

Blanchard: Congregationalist; president Wheaton College.

1088. _____. *The World War and the Bible.* 1918. Chicago: Bible Institute Colportage Assoc. 22 p.

1089. Bloomfield, Arthur E. *What Daniel Knew About Hitler.* 1936. Rochester, NY: Interstate Evangelistic Assoc. 72 p.

Hitler is Little Horn arising out of modern Ten-Nation Roman Empire (Germany as eleventh nation: not actually part of Roman Empire but extending from inside it). Hitler = Antichrist and Seventh Head of Revelation. Rapture; then Satan comes to earth personally (becoming the Eighth Head).

1090. _____. *All Things New: A Study of Revelation.* 1959. Minneapolis Bethany Fellowship. xi, 335 p. index.

1091. _____. *The End of the Days: A Study of Daniel's Visions.* 1961. Minneapolis: Bethany Fellowship. 279 p. illus.

1092. _____. *Signs of His Coming: A Study of the Olivet Discourse.* 1962. Minneapolis: Bethany Fellowship. 160 p. charts.

1093. _____. *The Ark of the Covenant.* 1965. Minneapolis: Bethany Fellowship. 76 p. bibl.

The Ark in prophecy. SEE ALSO 1970+.

1094. Boettner, Loraine. *The Millennium.* 1986 [1957]. Grand Rapids, MI: Baker Book House. 325 p. 1984 rev. ed. Phillipsburg, NJ: Presbyterian and Reformed; 411 p. bibl. index.

Study of various views; defends postmill; Millennium to come gradually as world is Christianized.

1095. Bolton, Thomas. *Where We Stand To-Day: Being an Application of Biblical Chronology (After Anstey) to the Study of Unfilled Prophecy.* [1928?]. London: Charles J. Thynne & Jarvis. 95 p. foldout charts.

Chronology points to 1930. 70 Weeks

consecutive, ended A.D. 32. 6,000 years ("Anno Homini") ends A.D. 1954.

1096. Borden, E[li] M. *The Millennium, or, The Plan of the Ages: Eleven Sermons.* 1941. Austin, TX: Firm Foundation. 64 p.

1097. Borduin, M[enno]. *The Great Battle and Our Glorious Victory.* N.d. Grand Rapids, MI: Zondervan. 23 p.

Pre-mill.

1098. Bosworth, William A. *Prophecies Relating to the Time of the End.* 1918. Boston: Gorham Press. 165 p.

The First World War.

1099. Boyd, Frank Matthews. *Prophetic Light.* 1984 [1948]. Springfield, MO: Berean School of the Bible. 148 p.

22 lessons from the Correspondence School of Assemblies of God.

1100. Bradbury, John, ed. *Light for the World's Darkness.* 1944. New York: Loizeaux Bros. 254 p. 2nd New York Congress on Prophecy, Calvary Baptist Church, 1943. Held under auspices of American Board of Missions to the Jews. Also pub. 1944 (Fleming H. Revell).

Bradbury: ed. *Baptist Watchman-Examiner.* "We all know that the day is coming when Israel is to be restored to the Land of Promise to enjoy what God has covenanted she should have." Second Coming is personal, pre-mill, pre-trib. W.W. Ayer: war, apostasy, decay and darkness. "The nations are working their way to Armageddon, to antichrist, to judgment." Walvoord: Nazi persecution of Jews, God's chosen people, will continue to play special role in Tribulation. Speculates on Japan and China in biblical prophecy: Kings of the East of Rev. 17:16. R.L Powell: Armageddon imminent, but present war hasn't triggered it; must directly involve Jerusalem, literal fulfillment, including armies of Heaven and Hell. Chafer: Israel's "final regathering" only at Second Coming. H.J. Hager: Armageddon must be fulfilled literally, not WWII. D.C. Bedford: "Jews = communists" is Satanic propaganda. Albert Lindsey: urges homeland for Jews and afterwards missionary efforts to them. C.D. Brownville urges homeland for Jews. Other contrib-

utors: Zwemer, L.E. McNair, J.P. Muntz, Ironside.

1101. _____, ed. *Hastening the Day of God.* 1953. Wheaton, IL: Van Kampen Press. 262 p. "Prophetic Messages from the International Congress on Prophecy" (Calvary Baptist Church, New York, 1952).

Conference "Manifesto" affirming Rapture, Tribulation, Second Coming (in that order). Rapture is any moment, but can't set date. Insists on pre-mill. Spread of communism and 1948 Israel show approaching consummation of history. Alva McClain: Four Endtime powers: North — Soviet Russia, West — incipient European Federation, East — Communist China, South — U.S.-England. Russia will invade Israel. J.P. Muntz: denounces Ecumenical Movement. Talbot: Tribulation will include great plagues, earthquakes, burning heat, famine.

1102. Branham, William. *Will the Church Go Through the Tribulations.* [1950s?]. Los Angeles: Sacred Records; Jeffersonville, IN: Mercier [distr]. Cassettes.

Branham: Pentecostal faith-healer. Presented himself as Herald of the Second Coming.

1103. _____. *The Laodicean Church Age.* [1965?]. s.l.: s.n. 48 p.

Revelation III:14–22.

1104. _____. *The Revelation of the Seven Seals: As Given to Our Precious Brother William Marion Branham.* 1967. Jeffersonville, IN: Voice of God Recordings. 523 p.

1993 reprint ed. 1963 messages delivered at Branham Tabernacle. Excruciatingly verbatim. Rambling, anti-intellectual; talks interrupted by miraculous healings, speaking in tongues, personal revelations from God. Photos of author with supernatural manifestations. Secret Rapture, Tribulation. Catholic = Harlot, killed 68 million Protestants. Catholics and Jews hold world's wealth. Satan cast out of heaven, incarnated as Antichrist. Satan is Trinity: manifests as Antichrist, then False Prophet, then Beast. Four Horsemen also stages of Antichrist. After Rapture, Rome and Jews make covenant, Antichrist breaks it halfway through. Two Witnesses call out the 144,000 redeemed Jews, then Mark of Beast. Armageddon: End of Tribulation. Second Gog-Magog battle at end of Millennium. Mentions Cain as "serpent seed" (Eve mated with Satan).

1105. ____. *The Seventy Weeks of Daniel.* 1970 Jeffersonville, IN: Spoken Word. 142 p.

1106. ____. *Exposition of the Seven Church Ages.* N.d. Jeffersonville, IN: Spoken Word.

Millennium begins 1977.

1107. Brasington, Virginia F. *Flying Saucers in the Bible.* 1963. Clarksburg, WV: Saucerian Books. 78 p. illus.

1108. Breyer, Jacques. *Arcanes Solaire; ou, Les Secrets du Temple Solaire.* 1959. Paris: "Histoire et tradition," Société d'études philosophiques solaires, La Colombe. 268 p. diagrams

Various predictions calculated for the End from astrological and occult charts, from 1995–96 to 1999. This book later consulted by Order of the Solar Temple.

1109. Brinsmead, Robert D. *Kings of the East.* [1960s]. Springfield, MO: Prophetic Research International. 48 p.

1110. ____. *Revelation.* 1963. Bryn Mawr, CA: Prophetic Research International. 110 p. illus.

1111. ____. *The Battle for the Mind, as Portrayed in Daniel and the Revelation.* 1971. Denver: International Health Inst. 101 p.

1112. Britt, George L. *When Dust Shall Sing: The World Crisis in the Light of the Bible.* 1958 Cleveland, TN: Pathway Press. 203 p.

1113. ____. *The Hour Has Come.* 1966. Cleveland, TN: Pathway. 96 p.

1114. Brooks, Keith L. *Prophecies of Daniel and Revelation.* 1927 [1925]. Los Angeles: Biola Book Room.

Verse-by-verse Bible studies, with cross-references, originally presented to Men's Bible Class of the Glendale (CA) Presbyterian Church. Brooks: Baptist; professor at Biola. "Present order" to be destroyed, but not world itself. Revelation

4 makes switch from Church Age to the future.

1115. ____. *Prophecy and the Tottering Nations.* 1938 [1935]. Grand Rapids, MI: Zondervan. Orig 1935, Los Angeles: author. 100 p.

We are now "unmistakably" in the "consummation of the age." Mussolini is not the Antichrist, but he will rebuild the Roman Empire according to prophecy. Illuminati was a Satanic conspiracy to undermine the Bible. Evolution is part of the "stupendously wicked modern program" to discredit Christianity.

1116. ____. *The Certain End as Seen by the Prophet Daniel: A Fresh Examination of these Prophecies by the Cross-Reference Method of Interpretation.* 1942. Los Angeles: American Prophetic League. 61 p.

1117. ____. *Biblical Prophecy: Fulfilling and Unfilled.* 1944. Glendale, CA: American Prophetic League. 93 p.

Prophecy, Israel, Second Coming, End of the World.

1118. ____. *Coming Events: Prophecy Answered.* 1960. Westchester, IL: Good News Publishers. 64 p. illus.

1119. ____, ed. *Prophetic Questions Answered.* 1954. Wheaton, IL: Van Kampen. 165 p. topical index.

By editors of *Prophecy Monthly* (Brooks: editor-in-chief). Condensed version *Prophecy Answered* (1960, Good News, Westchester IL; 63 p.).

1120. Broomall, Wick. *The Antichrist: A Brief Scriptural Study of the Coming Satan-Inspired World Dictator.* N.d. [1940s]. Columbia, SC: W. Broomall. 15 p.

1121. ____. *The Apostasy: A Study of the Scripture Doctrine of Apostasy and the Apostasy of the Last Days.* N.d. [1940s]. Columbia, SC: W. Broomall. 16 p.

1122. Brown, Arthur I. *What of the Night?* 1931. Toronto: Christian Outlook. 63 p.

1123. ____. *Light on the Hills.* 1934. Hoytville, OH: Fundamental Truth. 87 p.

1124. ____. *Into the Clouds.* 1938. Findlay, OH: Fundamental Truth. 220 p.

Includes Times of the Gentiles; Matt 24; Next war, Armageddon; Communism,

Fascism, Nazism; Palestine and the Jew; Rise of Dictators; The Antichrist; Mussolini; The Days of Noah; The Great Tribulation.

1125. _____. *The Eleventh "Hour."* 1940. Findlay, OH: Fundamental Truth Publishers. 159 p.

Pre-trib. World has reverted to "antediluvian wickedness." "Civilization drifts rapidly towards the precipice — men sense impending dissolution and stand helpless and impotent, overcome by the dread of threatening calamity. Governments and legislatures, science and philosophy, confess failure." Hitler, Mussolini and Stalin as Satanic triumvirate. Emphasizes Hitler-Stalin non-aggression pact as prophetic fulfillment of Russo-German alliance. Russia (not Germany) will emerge as dominant nation. Mussolini reviving Roman Empire. Antichrist will be successor to Mussolini (if not Mussolini himself), and become World Dictator. One half of world will be killed by Tribulation judgments and woes. King of the South (England, operating through Egypt) will attack Antichrist's Roman Empire. Then Russia (King of the North), with German and African allies, also attacks Israel. Later, all nations attack Israel and Christ's forces: Armageddon. Palestine given to Jews by God. Chastizes Anglican Church for accepting evolution.

1126. _____. *I Will Come Again.* 1947. Findlay, OH: Fundamental Truth 115 p.

Seven Ages, all end in chaos, including this. Secret Rapture, pre-trib. 70 Weeks = 490 years; 69 Weeks 445 B.C. to A.D. 32, final week to come. Second Coming this generation, within 70–80 years. Matt. 24: World War as sign of Coming — WWI, II and III as this single prophesied war. "Without doubt Russia is one of the outstanding 'signs' of the times — pointing directly to the 'time of the end.'" Russia (= Rosh) will attack Palestine with airborne army (Ezek. 38); also attacks U.S. ("unwalled villages") via Canada. "Gomer, undoubtedly, is Germany." Roman Catholicism now evidencing its predicted role as Mystery Babylon, Harlot, Abomi-

nations. Antichrist from Roman Empire (maybe resurrected Emperor), with armies of U.S., Britain, Europe attack Jerusalem, but are destroyed by Christ, who rules at Millennium.

1127. Brubaker, Ray. *Signs of Christ's Soon Return.* N.d. St. Petersburg, FL: God's News ... Behind the News. 32 p. illus.

"These are the latter days." Rapture any-moment, but partial (testing of Christians — only firmest believers raptured initially). 6,000 Year lifespan for world. Creation 4026 B.C.; End in 1974–75. UFOs, earthquakes, rebuilding of Temple. SEE ALSO 1970+.

1128. Brumbaugh, Roy Talmage. *Nations in Commotion; Rome Revived.* 1934. Findlay, OH: Fundamental Truth Publishers. 79 p.

1129. Bullinger, Ethelbert. SEE ALSO 1800–1910. *Four Prophetic Periods: A Key to the "Things Which Must Shortly Come to Pass."* 1922. London: Eyre & Spottiswoode. 16 p.

1130. _____. *Commentary on Revelation.* 1984 [1935]. Grand Rapids, MI: Kregel Orig titled *The Apocalypse.*

1131. Buroker, L. Peres. *Today in Bible Prophecy.* 1937. Lapeer, MI: W.E. Cole. 63 p.

1132. _____. *The Five Horses and Horsemen of Revelation.* 1940. Almont, MI: author. 62 p.

Buroker: Michigan evangelist. White = democracy; Red communism; Black fascism; pale (actually green) maybe Balkan Iron Guards. Pre-mill.

1133. Cachemaille, E[rnest] P. SEE ALSO 1800–1910. *XXVI Present Day Papers on Prophecy: An Explanation of the Visions of Daniel and of the Revelation, or the Continuous-Historic System.* 1911. London: Seely, Service. xii, 694 p. indexes maps diagrams.

1134. _____. *The Seventy Weeks and the Messiah.* 1918. London: C.J. Thynne.

1135. _____. *The Warfare of the End.* 1920. London: Charles J. Thynne. 79 p.

Addresses to Prophecy Investigation Soc., 1920. Other contributors include

W.E. Vine, E. Bendor Samuel ("Russia in Prophecy"), Alfred H. Burton ("The Assyrian").

1136. _____. *The Prophetic Outlook Today: Where Are We Now in Prophecy?* 1918. London: Morgan & Scott. viii, 164 p. plates illus., maps, index.

"Essays on Second Advent Subjects."

1137. _____. *The Three Angels of Rev. XIV. 6-11, and their Parallels: Final Events.* N.d. London: Chas. J. Thynne.

1138. Caldwell, William. *When the World Goes Boom.* 1962. Tulsa, OK: Front Line Evangelism. 64 p. Also pub. 1970. Kisumu, Kenya.

1139. Cale, John, and George B. Rickard. *The End Time and God's Gospel.* 1915. Paris, Canada: John H. Cale. 100 p.

1140. Cameron, Robert. *Scriptural Truth about the Lord's Return.* 1922. New York, Chicago: Fleming H. Revell. 176 p.

Post-trib pre-mill (argues against imminency of Rapture).

1141. Cardey, Elmer L. *Countdown of History.* 1962. Grand Rapids, MI: Baker Book. 198 p.

Also wrote books on Daniel and on Revelation. "The onrush of history seems to be bringing the world as we have known it to its end, to be followed by a rebirth of history of history in an eternal, better world." Evolution e.g. as sign of world's decline, sinfulness. Book of Isaiah says that atomic and H-bombs will kill most people. Second Coming any moment; all prophecies either fulfilled or in process of fulfillment.

1142. _____. *Feet of Clay : Who is Holding the World Together?* N.d. Atlanta, GA: School of Bible Prophecy. 56 p.

1143. Carpenter, Ellsworth. *Coming to Earth! (Very, Very Soon) "The Mighty God, the Everlasting Father, the Prince of Peace."* 1940. Prohibition Park, NY: Newer-Knowledge. 212 p. illus.

Seventh-day Adventist.

1144. Carter, Mary Ellen. *Edgar Cayce on Prophecy.* 1968. Warner Books. 205 p. "Under the editorship of Hugh Lynn Cayce."

1145. Cayce, Edgar in *Earth Changes* extracts from Edgar Cayce Readings,

Edgar Cayce Foundation. 1959 [1934]. Virginia Beach, VA: A.R.E. Press. 80 p. illus.

Cayce: the American trance healer known as the "sleeping prophet." Ca. A.D. 2000: "There will be a shifting of the poles. There will be upheavals in the Arctic and the Antarctic that will make for the eruption of volcanoes in the Torrid areas.... The upper portion of Europe will be changed in the twinkling of an eye. The earth will be broken up in the western portion of America. The greater portion of Japan must go into the sea."

1146. Chafer, Lewis Sperry. *The Kingdom in History and Prophecy.* 1944 [1915]. Chicago: Moody Press 167 p. bibl. refs. indexes. Also pub. 1943 Dunham (Findlay, OH); orig 1915 (Revell; Bible Inst. Colportage Association).

Chafer: Presbyterian; follower of Moody and Scofield; founded Dallas Theological Seminary.

1147. _____. *Seven Biblical Signs of the Times.* 1919. Philadelphia: Sunday Times. 30 p.

1148. _____. *Dispensationalism.* 1951 [1936]. 108 p. Dallas: Dallas Seminary Press. Orig. 1936, reprinted from *Bibliotheca Sacra.*

1149. Chaij, Fernando. 1966. *Preparation for the Final Crisis.* SEE ALSO 1970+.

1150. Chestnut, Lawrence J. *The Battle of Armageddon: What, Where, and When.* 1949. Oklahoma City, OK: L.J. Chester. 61 p.

1151. Chick, Jack T. *The Beast.* 1985 [1966]. Chino, CA: Chick Pub. 20 p. illus.

Pre-trib. One-world dictator, along with False Prophet. Tribulation: 10 leaders rebel against Beast. 666 tattoos on forehead. Temple rebuilt, desecrated. Satan leads world armies at Armageddon; then Second Coming, Millennium. Revised edition changes instigator from godless communism to Vatican. SEE ALSO 1970+.

1152. Christian, Lewis Harrison. *Facing the Crisis in the Light of Bible Prophecy.* [1937]. Takoma Park, DC: Review and Herald. 320 p. illus

Describes worsening conditions of world. Evolution is mental aberration that has done the worst harm. Rampant materialism and militarism; whole world now gearing for war. 69 Weeks: 457 B.C. + 483 = A.D. 27, with 70th Week continuing to A.D. 34 (no gap). A.D. 1844 = end of 2,300 and 1810-year prophecies (end of Papal power; cleaning of Sanctuary). Denies secret Rapture. Seven Last Plagues just before Second Coming. Mid-trib: Northern (Russian) and Southern (Arab) confederacies both attack Israel, but are destroyed by God. Then the West (United States of Europe) moves in under the Beast's leadership. At close of Tribulation, the East (200 million soldiers) invades.

1153. Clark, A.H. *The Prophecy of Revelation.* [1950s?]. sl: sn. 87 p.

1154. Clark, Doug. *The Kingdom of the Antichrist.* [1960s]. Placentia, CA: Amazing Prophecy Ministry. LP disk. SEE ALSO 1970+.

1155. Clarke, James W. *Is Armageddon at Hand?* 1965. 2 cassettes.

Second Presbyterian Church, Richmond, VA.

1156. Close, Albert. *Babylon, or, The Divine Foreview of the Rise, Reign and Destiny of the Church of Rome: A Study Historic and Prophetic of Revelation XVII.* 1910. London: Marshall Brothers. xi, 144 p. 2nd ed. titled *Babylon: The Scarlet Woman....*

1157. _____. *Antichrist and His Ten Kingdoms.* 1944 [1917]. 4th ed. London: Thynne and Co. viii, 208 p. illus. Orig. pub. Protestant Truth Soc.

Also wrote *The Great Harlot on the Seven Hills, the Enemy of Britain* (Ilford, [England]: Thynne; 96 p. illus.), and *Jesuit Plots against Britain from Queen Elizabeth to George V* (1936; Protestant Truth Soc.).

1158. Cohen, Gary G. *The Chronology of the Book of Revelation.* 1966. x, 345 p. Grace Theological Seminary Th.D. thesis.

1159. _____. *Understanding Revelation: An Investigation of the Key Interpretational and Chronological Questions which Surround the Book of Revelation.* Chicago: Moody 1978 [1968]. 187 p. Revision of thesis. SEE ALSO 1970+.

1160. Cole, E.L. *Chronology and Destruction.* 1969. New York: Carlton. 51 p.

1161. Collier, Gordon W. *Closing Events.* 1963. [San Diego].

Seventh-day Adventist.

1162. Collins, Nina L. MacFadyen. *What Shall be the Sign of Christ's Coming and the End of the World?* 1920. Los Angeles: W.H. & F.M. Society of the Advent Christian Church, Pacific Tract Office. [4] p.

Advent Christian. 70 million people martyred by Catholic Church 6th through 18th centuries.

1163. *The Coming Great War: The Greatest Ever Known in Human History.* [1920s?]. Toronto : A. Sims. 50 p.

1164. Cook, Charles C. *End of the Age Themes.* 1917. New York: author. 116 p.

1165. Cooper, David L. *Future Events Revealed.* 1983 [c1935]. rev. ed. Los Angeles: Biblical Research Soc. xviii, 249 p. illus. Orig. 1935, author.

Matthew 24–25. Cooper: founder and dir. of Biblical Research Society. Time of Gentiles ends when Jews recover land of Israel. The World War, with attendant famines, pestilences, earthquakes, was sign that End is within a generation. Trumpet judgments all part of 7th Seal; Bowl judgments all part of 7th Trumpet. Unparalleled calamities during Tribulation, but also mighty revival led by Jewish evangelists.

1166. _____. *When Gog's Armies Meet the Almighty in the Land of Israel.* 1970 [1940]. 4th ed. Los Angeles: Biblical Research Society. 116 p. plates, foldout plan.

Prior to the Tribulation, when Jews return to Palestine, a North-East Confederacy, led by Russia allied with Persia, Ethiopia, Germany, and Turkey, will invade Israel. This invasion is opposed by Western Confederacy. King of South then attacks "world dictator." Church raptured, then 144,000 Jews evangelize the world during Tribulation. Another invasion at end of Tribulation. All armies destroyed by the Almighty. Jews returning now to Palestine, so these events imminent. 1939 non-aggression treaty between Germany and Russia may indicate this North-East Confederacy prophesied by

Ezekiel is already in existence. Mechanized armies foretold in Bible.

1167. _____. *The 70 Weeks of Daniel*. 1941. Los Angeles: Biblical Research Society. 71 p.

1168. _____. *Messiah: His Glorious Appearance Imminent*. 1961. Los Angeles: Biblical Research Society. xii, 202 p. indexes.

Dispensational pre-trib. Denies year-day theory. 144,000 Jews witness during Tribulation; those they convert suffer persecution and martyrdom. Great Northeastern confederacy will invade Israel. "Chariots" = tanks.

1169. Corbin, Bruce. *This Fateful Generation: Light for these Last Days*. 1941. Guthrie, OK: Truth Publishing.

1170. _____. *Will This Age End with This Fateful Generation: and, What Will Happen in the Days Ahead?* 1944. 3rd large ed. Enid, OK: Truth Pub. 127 p.

1171. _____. *The Third World War and the Battle of Armageddon*. 1945. Enid. OK: Truth Publishing. 140 p.

1172. _____. *Great Prophecies: Relating to this Fateful Generation and the End of this Age*. 1953. Enid, OK: Bruce Corbin Ministries / Marrs. 80 p.

1173. _____. *What Lies Ahead?* Enid, OK: Truth Publishing. 159 p.

1174. Corfield, Virginia. *Sow the Wind*. 1979. Covina, CA: Provident Press. 144 p.

About Amos (Old Testament).

1175. Corliss, Benjamin W. *The Physical Signs: Past or Future*. 1956 [1938]. Rev. Milltown, ME: B.W. Corliss. 12 p. "A brief exposition of the Seven Seals."

1176. Cornelison, I.B. *Grat* [sic] *Events of the Last Days*. [1910s?]. Dallas: Holiness Messenger Publishing Co. 42 p.

1177. Cottrell, Raymond F. *The Coming Crisis: A Composite Paraphrase from the Bible and the Spirit of Prophecy*. 1947. Angwin, CA: Bible Research Fellowship. 3rd ed. 1948. 22 p. 1952 ed. titled *Crisis and Victory* (Mountain View, CA: Pacific Press).

1178. _____. *Beyond Tomorrow*. 1963. Nashville: Southern Publishing Assoc. 380 p.

Many paintings. Easy-to-read ac-count giving Seventh-day Adventist scenario and interpretation. Bible foretold history with "incredible accuracy" up to modern times, warning of "great global holocaust soon to burst upon the world." Lord's Kingdom to come "cataclysmically." Harlot of Revelation (apostate religion) fornicates with Kings (the result of not keeping church and state separate). Satan's pre-Adamic rebellion. Ten Horns may be barbarian successor states. Northern Kingdom = Seleucid Syria; Southern = Ptolemaic Egypt. Little Horn = End Time Tyrant who destroys and desecrates Temple. Rejects Antiochus as prophesied desecrator, and "Gap [i.e. Parenthesis] Theory." Great Apostasy, Tribulation, Second Coming, End. 1780 = Dark Day; 1833 = falling stars: Signs of Coming. A.D. 538 + 1,260 = 1798 — reign of Beast (Papal Rome, great deceiver and clever counterfeiter of Christ); mortal wound was when deported by Napoleon. "Vicarius Filii Dei" = 666. Sabbath switch to Sunday was tampering with Holy Commandments. Second Beast = U.S. "Babylon" = Rome, false religion. Warns of impending Sunday laws engineered by Catholics. 490 years (70 Weeks) = 457 B.C. to A.D. 27 (Messiah revealed) plus 3½ years (Crucifixion). 2,300 Years = 457 B.C. to A.D. 1844: Sanctuary cleansed (Miller) in heaven (as later understood, after 1844). Examination of eligible subjects for heaven began in 1844. A Remnant keeps Sabbath, entrusted with prophetic gifts. "Armageddon" not actual geographic location. Horrible plagues prove wicked still unrepentant after deadline for "sealing" heaven-bound. Cottrell rejects secret Rapture; it will be spectacular, public Coming, with righteous all swept up to heaven. Righteous dead resurrected; souls are "sleeping" until then (not in heaven now). During Millennium, the righteous review all unredeemed dead. Wicked alive at Second Coming are slain. Wicked are resurrected at end of Millennium; they then attack Christ and saints. Earth burns, wicked sent to eternal death (not eternal torment).

1179. Cottrell, Roy Franklin. *The Challenge of the Twentieth Century*. 1932.

Mountain View, CA: Pacific Pres. 96 p. illus.

Seventh-day Adventist. 1844 = the Sanctuary in Heaven cleansed.

1180. ____. *After Tomorrow—What?* 1942. Nashville: Southern Pub Assoc. 96 p. illus.

1181. ____. *Tomorrow in Prophecy: God's Preview of the World's Climax.* 1942 Nashville: Southern Pub. Assoc. 96 p. illus. 1959 ed. (Manila: Philippine Pub. House).

1182. ____. *The Jews and Palestine.* 1947 Mountain View, CA: Pacific Press. 96 p. illus.

1183. Court, Norman. *The Red Beast and His Ten Horn Satellites; Some Thoughts on Last Day Events as Recorded in Revelation 17, Ezekiel 38 and 39, and Daniel 2 and 7, Together with Evidence Supplied by History and Ethnology.* 1956. Woodford Green, Essex, English Society for Proclaiming Britain is Israel. 27 p. illus.

1184. Cox, Clyde C. *Apocalyptic Commentary: An Exposition of the Book of Revelation.* 1959. Cleveland, TN: Pathway. 351 p. illus.

1185. Cox, William E. *The Millennium, with an Exposition of Revelation Twenty.* 1964. Philadelphia: Presbyterian and Reformed. 67 p. bibl.

A-mill.

1186. ____. *In These Last Days: New Testament Eschatology.* 1964. Philadelphia: Presbyterian and Reformed. 109 p. bibl.

1187. ____. *Biblical Studies in Final Things.* 1974. [NJ:] Presbyterian and Reformed. xiv, 226 p. bibl. refs.

1188. Criswell, Jeron. 1968. *Criswell Predicts from Now to the Year 2000!* Anderson, SC: Droke House (distr. Grosset & Dunlap). 141 p. illus.

1189. Crow, R. *Storm Over Israel: A Look at Israel, the Nations and the Church as They Will Appear at the End of the Age According to the Bible.* 1968. Bombay: Gospel Literature Service. viii, 155 p.

1190. Crowley, Dale. *The Soon Coming of Our Lord.* 1961 [1958]. New York: Loizeaux Bros. Orig. pub. Washington, D.C.: Capitol Voice Press.

Material from radio sermons on general theme "Bible Prophecy and the End of the Age."

1191. Culbertson, William, and Herman B. Centz, eds. *Understanding the Times.* 1956. Grand Rapids, MI: Zondervan. 290 p.

2nd Intl. Conf. on Prophecy, New York, 1955. Produced for Amer. Assoc. for Jewish Evangelism, Winona Lake, IN. Pre-trib pre-mill. Gog and Magog rebellion at end of Millennium not worldwide. Contributors include McClain, John G. Mitchell, Wilbur Smith, William F. Kerr, Richard A. Elvee, Walvoord, Roy L. Laurin, Hoyt, Claude Ries, Code, Robert T. Ketcham, W.R. Wallace, Harry Hager, Peter Hoogendam, Gaebelein, DeHaan.

1192. Culleton, Richard Gerald. *The Prophets and Our Times.* 1974 [1941] Rockford, IL: Tan Books. 251 p.

Catholic. Prophets from early church and Talmud to modern times. Attempts to generalize End chronology from these many sources. False doctrine and evil spread after birth of Antichrist. Two Witnesses; Jews convert, general apostasy. Prophecies of German Anti–Pope who takes over Italy; Russia, Japan, Turkey, and Arabs attack Europe. England defeated. Russia overruns Germany. Japan conquers western U.S. Last Battle of Christian vs. Anti–Christian forces to be fought near Essen, Germany. Afterward, a Great Monarch and Angelic Pastor spread Catholicism across world. "It would seem that there is nothing we can do to avert these various catastrophies [sic]." Prophets quoted include St. Columbkille (d. 597), Merlin, St. Odile, the Monk Hilarion (d. 1476), Hildegard of Bingen, various English, Scottish, German, and Italian folk prophecies, Brother John of the Cleft Rock (1340), Bridgit of Sweden (d. 1373), St. Francis de Paul (1470), Mother Shipton, Nostradamus, Holzhauser (d. 1658), Father Nectou (d. 1772), Mothia Maria Rafols (1815), Maria Taigi (d. 1837), Catherine Emmerich (d. 1824), St. John Bosco (d. 1888), the Fatima visions, Berry (pub. 1920), and many others.

1193. Culligan, Emmett J. *The Last*

World War and the Battle of Armageddon. 1970 [1950]. xvi, 210 p. plates. illus.

Catholic. Marian apparitions and miracles. Also wrote on secret of Fatima vision.

1194. _____. *The Last World War and the End of Time.* 1966 [1950]. Oceanside, CA: St. Charles Priory. xvi, 210 p. plates. Also pub. 1975 (Rockford, IL: Tan Books).

1195. _____. *The 1960 Fatima Secret and the Secret of La Salette.* 1967. San Bernardino: Culligan Book Co. 37 p. Bibl. refs, plates, illus.

1196. Culver, Robert Duncan. *Daniel and the Latter Days.* 1964 [1954]. 2nd ed. Chicago: Moody. 224 p. index bibl.

Well argued defense of pre-mill position. Ten-Nation Roman Empire; Antichrist rules during Tribulation (70th Week), literal Millennium after Second Coming.

1197. _____. *The Histories and Prophecies of Daniel.* 1980. Winona Lake, IN: BMH Books. 191 p.

1198. Cummins, Alvin Pender. *This Generation Shall Not Pass Till All These Things be Fulfilled.* 1939. Grand Rapids, MI: William B. Eerdmans. 182 p.

Fiction.

1199. Dabold, Frederick W. *The Mystery of Iniquity: or, The Final Phase of the Apostasy.* 1966. Fort Pierce, FL: author. 125 p.

1200. Dahl, Mikkel. *The Book of Revelation Unveiled.* 1989 [1950]. Fulton, MO: Shepherdsfield. 160 p.

Pyramidology. Great Pyramid dates start at 4000 B.C., with 1844, 1914, 1918, and 1929 as key years. 1844 significant as meeting of Marx and Engels. 1936–53 is epochal time. Ending date of Pyramid seems to be 1984.

1201. _____. *The Pyramid Speaks Prophetically & Symbolically.* 1975 [1950]. Windsor, Ont., Canada: M. Dahl. 239 p. illus. Folded leaf of charts. Index. Orig 2 vols.

1202. _____. *Tomorrow's Empire of the Beast.* 1965.

1203. _____. *The Day After: Portraying in Narrative Form Startling Events on the Near Horizon.* N.d. Windsor, Ontario: Dawn of Truth. SEE ALSO 1970+.

1204. Dake, Finis Jennings. *Revelation Expounded: or, Eternal Mysteries Simplified.* 1950 [1931]. Lawrenceville, GA: Dake Bible Sales. 320 p. Also many other editions, including 1948, 1977, 1991.

Pre-trib. 70th Week will start when Israel recovers Jerusalem. Antichrist rules over Ten Kingdom European realm. Tribulation primarily against Jews. Sun-clothed Woman = Israel; man-child = 144,000 Jewish witnesses. Seal, Trumpet and Vial judgments all literal. Whore of Babylon = Roman Catholic Church. Three more European wars before Second Coming: first to form Ten Kingdom realm, second when Antichrist overthrows three of the ten; third the great war between Antichrist and the Northern league (led by Russia and Germany) and the East. Then, one-day battle of Armageddon: Antichrist vs. the armies of Christ.

1205. _____. *God's Plan for Man.* 1977 renewed ed. Lawrenceville, GA: Dake Bible Sales. 1081 p.

52 lessons, with questions. Part 1: origins; 2: God in history; 3: God's present dealings with man; 4: God's future dealings with man. Also published by Bible Research Foundation (Atlanta, 1949). Widely used by Pentecostalists.

1206. _____. *The Two Future World Empires: World Wars, World Rulers, World Changes.* 1955. Atlanta: Bible Research Foundation. 32 p. SEE ALSO 1970+.

1207. Dalrymple, Gwynne. *Feet of Clay.* 1938. Mountain View, CA: Pacific Press. 96 p. illus.

1208. _____. *The New Caesars.* 1938. Mountain View, CA: Pacific Press. 96 p. illus.

1209. Daniells, Arthur Grosvenor. *The World War, its Relation to the Eastern Question and Armageddon.* c1917. Washington, D.C.: Review and Herald. 128 p. maps, illus.

Constantinople to revert to another power. Time of End dates from 1798 (limit of Papacy). 1,260 Years: from A.D. 533–38 (Papacy under Belisarius's protection) to 1798. WWI, greatest war in history, is prelude to Armageddon. Kings of North and South again active. A.D. 538 to 1798 = 1,260 "days." Turkish victories over Napoleon foretold (Daniel's King of North), also subsequent decline of Turkish power. The war will probably drag in whole world, culminating in Armageddon itself. Armageddon "ends with the extermination of the human race, except those who have before found refuge in God, and it leaves the world in utter ruin."

1210. *The Darkening of the Sun, Moon and Stars.* [1946]. Oregon, IL: Restitution Herald [6] p.

This will be "very literal," occurring end of Tribulation just prior to Second Coming.

1211. Darter, Francis M. *The Gathering of Israel from a Scriptural Standpoint: The Coming of John the Revelator, the Elias, and Forerunner of the Second Coming of Jesus Christ....* 1915. Long Beach, CA. 123 p.

1212. _____. *The Lord's Strange Work; The Return of John, the Revelator; A Voice of Warning; The Approaching End.* 1917. Long Beach, CA: 186 p.

Mormon. *Zion's Redemption* (1933) apparently expanded version. Literal interpretation. Adam created 4000 B.C. Second Coming ca. April 1953. Millennium began 1843: complete restoration of Gospel (sealed by Smith's martyrdom in 1844). 1,260 Years of Catholic domination: from A.D. 538 to 1798 (the deadly wound that healed). 1843 = end of 1,335 and 2,300 Years. A.D. 1928: "The Approaching End." Gog and Magog led by Russia allied with Turkey, Germany, etc. Accept "restored Gospel" (Mormonism) to avoid fate; gather and seek refuge. Gog has openly boasted to defeat God in heaven. Russia now collecting horses in South, "whence Gog's armies will start on their long march." Not farm horses, but bred for mountain passage. Endorses Pyramidology. 1928–36 in Pyramid: predicted Depression and religious strife. 200,000,000 soldiers; half will be slain. 666 = "Vicarivs Filii Dei." Setting of Center Stake of Zion in Missouri — Kingdom of God. Tribulation= began 1928. Quotes 1877 revelatory

dream of fourth President of the Church, Wilford Woodruff, of an American apocalypse and resulting desolation.

1213. _____. *"The Time of the End."* 1928. Los Angeles: Wetzel. 295 p.

"Daniel identifies latter day temples and Jesus as the Christ, the voice of God, the mysteries of Daniel unveiled, God sets a date for the restoration of the Gospel of Jesus Christ including his Holy Latter Day Sanctuary — the Temple".

1214. _____. *Our Bible in Stone: Its Divine Purpose and Present Day Message: the Mystery of the Ages Unveiled.* 1931. Salt Lake City: Deseret News. 179 p. illus.

Great Pyramid shows 6,000 years since Adam (when humanity entered mortality state.) Final Trouble from 1928 to 1936; "colossal calamities and appalling slaughter" by 1934; Sept. 1936 is closing of this generation; Armageddon is 1940. Lucifer's final reign — the "little season" he is loosed — lasts to A.D. 2000, when Gog/Magog battle occurs. Pyramid reveals 28,826-year cycle of solar system orbiting star Alcyone, which is Kolob of Mormon doctrine, God's home. Evolution is "insult to human intelligence." Relates Joseph Smith's "White Horse Prophecy" (1843), recorded by Edwin Rushton and Theodore Turley, of great revolution in U.S., with populace fleeing to West, and worldwide war.

1215. _____. *Zion's Redemption: The Return of John the Revelator, the Elias, the Restorer, the Gatherer of All Israel and Forerunner of Christ's Second Coming.* 1933. Salt Lake City: *Deseret News.* 224 p.

Apparently expanded edition of his 1915 *Gathering of Israel.*

1216. _____. *Oh America, Stop and Think, Christ Or Chaos; the God, Whom You have Forsaken, is About to Withdraw His Spirit from You, Hence Disaster and Dissolution.* 1935. Salt Lake City: Deseret News Press. 77 p.

Last Days.

1217. _____. *End of Our Generation; or, Christ's Second Coming.* 1940. [Salt Lake City]. 16 p.

1218. _____. *The Mystery of John the Revelator and the Seven Last Plagues; the*

Seventh Seal; Who Will Win the War, the "One Mighty" Indian Prophet; the Prophecy of Enoch Confirming "Mormonism." 1942. Salt Lake City. 31 p.

Also 1965 version.

1219. _____. *Armageddon ... Christ's Second Coming.* 1943. Salt Lake City: author. 39 p.

Includes excerpts from R.H. Charles' book on Book of Enoch. Also wrote *Jesus Christ versus Lucifer* (1957) sanctioning race segregation as "divine," and book on the "racially 'marred' Indian" (1949?) concerning the Last Days.

1220. _____. *"God Will Send a Man": The "One Mighty"—"Choice Seer" of Yucatan—The Foretold "Branch" Who Will Soon Complete Joseph Smith's Mission—Behold: "That Day" Is Here.* 1956. 2nd ed. Salt Lake City: author. 4 p.

1221. _____. *Amazing L.D.S. Prophetic Dates.* 1959. [Salt Lake City?] author. 5 p.

1222. Daugherty, Kathryn. *The Time of the End: The Story of Mankind and His Destiny.* 1962. New York: Exposition Press.

1223. Davis, George T.B. *Israel Returns Home, According to Prophecy.* 1950. Philadelphia: Million Testaments Campaign. 114 p. illus.

Also wrote other books on fulfillment of biblical prophecy, especially in Palestine.

1224. Davis, W[illiam] M[orton]. *The End of the World.* 1944. Austin: Firm Foundation. 59 p.

1225. Dawson, W[illiam] B[ell]. *The Time Is At Hand: As Indicated by the Periods in Prophecy Already Fulfilled.* 1926. London: Thynne & Jarvis. 141 p.

Historicist. 70 Weeks finishes A.D. 33 (Crucifixion "cuts off" Messiah A.D. 30 midway through 70th Week). Antichrist = Papacy, and Islam. Intricate chronological calculations: "Closing eras" measured by various types of years and start dates, all end 1932–34.

1226. Dayhoff, Irvin E. *The Majestic Hand in Bible Prophecy.* 1968. University Park, IA: I.E. Dayhoff. 111 p. illus.

1227. Dean, I[bzan] R. *The Time of the End.* 1918. Toronto: Evangelical Publishers. 166 p.

Rosh (= Russia), Gomer (= Germany), and others = King of North, who battle King of South (Jews allied with Egypt, Anglo-Americans). 70th Week = 7 year Tribulation after Rapture. 7 Churches: ages of Church. Davidic king crowned in 1922. 1928: End of Tribulation, Second Coming. 1933: Israel finally cleansed, and restored. Arrives at these dates (and 1914) by adding 2,520 Years to B.C. dates. Dates not "dogmatic," but "they must be nearly correct." Papacy = Babylon the Great, commits "spiritual fornication." Armageddon: decisive battle. Jews vs. Beast and Prophet (10-nation confederacy) and North. First Beast = Antichrist as Emperor. Millennium; then New Heavens and Earth. Rejects any-moment Rapture, because 70th Week hasn't started yet.

1228. _____. *The Coming Kingdom the Goal of Prophecy.* 1928. Philadelphia: Phil. School of the Bible. 245 p.

Said he made the mistake of suggesting dates in his 1918 book, and doesn't do so here. Admits he doesn't know, or know when Israel will be re-established.

1229. DeForest, Eleanor. *Armageddon, a Tale of the Antichrist.* 1938. Grand Rapids, MI: William B. Eerdmans. 219 p.

1230. DeHaan, M[artin] R[alph]. *The Second Coming of Jesus.* 1944. 4th ed. Grand Rapids, MI: Zondervan. 178 p.

1231. _____. *Coming Events in Prophecy.* 1962. Grand Rapids, MI: Zondervan 151 p.

"The only way out is up"—only the Second Coming will end the nuclear threat.

1232. _____. *The Atomic Bomb in Prophecy: An Examination of Scripture Passages Dealing with the Devastation of the Earth in the Day of the Lord: Will It Be by Atomic Explosions?* N.d. Grand Rapids, MI: [Radio Bible Class]. 27 p.

1233. _____. *The Return of the King: Revelation 22:20: A Bible Study Concerning the Certainty, Imminency, and Results of that Blessed Hope of Christ's Return.* [1940s]. [Grand Rapids, MI: Radio Bible Class. 30 p.

1234. _____. *Russia and the United Nations in Prophecy.* [1940s]. Grand Rapids, MI: Zondervan. 27 p.

Also wrote *Russia and the Final War.*

1235. _____. *The Days of Noah and Their Prophetic Message for Today.* 1973? [1963]. Grand Rapids, MI: Zondervan [orig 1963, Radio Bible Class]. 184 p.

DeHaan: MD. Orig. booklets from broadcasts. Second Coming is "the most certain future event"; world's only hope; any moment Rapture. Abandoning fundamentalism means going the way of Cain: to pre-Flood wickedness. World today like Noah's time: great technical advances, knowledge, decadence, violence, deception. Ark is symbol of death and resurrection; safety during Tribulation. Pre-trib Rapture. Man would destroy himself but God will intervene to prevent this. Enoch raptured before Flood, like believers before Tribulation. Raptured saints = "Bible astronauts." "Remember the Flood!" Church is like Methuselah, Enoch's son: extended life till Second Coming. Flood caused by demons (fallen angels) mating with women, just as today's greatest sin is "going after strange flesh": sexual perversions. Elaborates on Christ as Ark metaphor.

1236. _____. *Israel and the Nations in Prophecy.* 1971 [1968]. Grand Rapids, MI: Zondervan. 120 p. [1968 ed. 146 p].

Russian invasion half way through Tribulation. Since it will take seven months to bury all the Russian dead, there must be hundreds of millions. Armageddon at *end* of Tribulation, though.

1237. _____. *Christ and Antichrist in Revelation: An Exposition of Revelation Eleven, Twelve, Thirteen and Fourteen.* N.d.? : Grand Rapids, MI: [Radio Bible Class]. 38 p.

Antichrist = Judas returned.

1238. Denman, Francis L. *The Day of the Lord.* [ca 1914].

1239. Denton, J[oshua] William. *The Consummation of the Ages.* 1945. Boston: Advent Christian Publication Soc. 22 p.

Advent Christian. All earthly governments coming to an end.

1240. Dickens, J.L. *The Second Com-*ing of Christ and Last Things. 1921. Houston: Houston Bible Inst. 168 p.

Dickens: ex-president of Bethel Coll. (TN) and Trinity Univ. (TX). Pre-trib pre-mill.

1241. Dodson, Charles A. *At the Time of the End.* 1960. Greenville SC: House of David. xiv, 247 p. bibl.

1242. Donahue, C.B. *Last Day Tongue Speaking in the Light of Prophecy.* 1965. Hixon, TN: C.B. Donahue. 24 p.

Glossolalia.

1243. Downing, Barry H. *The Bible and Flying Saucers.* 1970 [1968]. New York: Avon Books [orig. Lippincott]. 191 p. bibl. refs.

Includes chapter "Flying Saucers and the Future."

1244. Drake, B.G. *Tomorrow Unveiled.* 1960. 2nd ed. Peoria, IL: Bible Prophecy Books. 24 p.

1245. Drake, H.M. *The Plan of God for the Ages; a Book on Revelation.* 1966. Cleveland, TN: Pathway. 121 p.

1246. Drake, Katherine. *In the Last Days.* 1932 London: Advent Testimony and Preparation; Pickering & Inglis. 158 p.

Omens and natural signs in sky of End. "The signs are all around us now that this Great Tribulation is getting rapidly nearer." A third of world to be killed in Tribulation and Armageddon. Papacy will dominate, then Beast (= Mussolini) will take over. Says "chronology puts the last date on which anything whatever is foretold to happen as between 1935 and 1936." Translation of believers may have been delayed, since nothing prophesied left to occur before it. Spiritualism, counterfeit Christianity, Communism, Zionism, resurrection of Papacy discussed.

1247. Drinhaus, Paul. *Weltkrisis und ihr Ausgang.* 1925. Hamburg: Advent-Verlag. 78 p. illus. Also 1932 Dutch ed. *(Wereldnood, Wereldredding*; Dem Haag: Advent-Zendingsgenootschap).

1248. _____. *In der Entscheidungs-Stunde.* 1930. Hamburg: Advent-Verlag. 201, [3] p. illus. maps. bibl. refs.

1249. Duff-Forbes, Lawrence. *Peril from the North.* 1958. Whittier, CA: Review Publishing Co. iii, 990 p.

Jewish; has radio program "Treasures from Temach." Gog = Russia. "Double Sense" canon: prophetic fulfillment both historical (near future of prophet) and future. Cites contemporary use of armor now, and wooden weapons (including planes). "Invasion of Israel by Gog and his hordes in the latter days." Seven months to bury all corpses. Ezekiel: relates to Second Coming of Messiah. Caucasus = Gog's Fort. Gomer = Germany. Soviet Russia with satellite Germany and Pan-Islamic Arab confederacy (including Turkey).

1250. Dugger, Andrew N., and Clarence Orvil Dodd. *A History of the True Church, Traced from 33 A.D. to Date.* 1936. Salem, WV: A.N. Dugger and C.O. Dodd for the Bible Advocate. 318 p.

Church of God (Adventist). Editor of *Bible Advocate.* In 1927 said Tribulation = May 29, 1928. 2,520 Years = 7 x 360 = 606 B.C. to 1914.

1251. Duncan, Everett E. *Christ Is Coming.* 1949. Los Angeles: Voice of Prophecy. 95 p.

1252. Duncan, Homer. *The Millennial Reign of Christ.* [1960s?]. Lubbock, TX: World-Wide Missionary Crusader. 112 p.

1253. _____. *The King Is Coming: Ninety-Seven Scriptural Signs that Indicate the Imminent Return of the Lord Jesus Christ.* 1977 [1960]. Lubbock, TX: Missionary Crusader. 122 p. 4th enl. ed.

1254. _____. *Seventy-One Scriptural Signs that Indicate Jesus Is Coming Soon.* 1960. Lubbock, TX: Missionary Crusader. 100 p. Graphs. SEE ALSO 1970+.

1255. Duncan, Mildred H. *A Revelation of End-Time Babylon.* 1968. Second edition revised. Dallas, TX.: Voice of Healing. 325 p.

1256. Dunham, Truman Richard, ed. & comp. *Unveiling the Future: Twelve Prophetic Messages.* 1934. 4th ed. Findlay, OH: Fundamental Truth. 165 p.

Also wrote *The Great Tribulation.* Contributors include Harry Rimmer, Arno Gaebelein, W.B. Riley, Charles G. Trumbull, James Gray, Keith Brooks, Sale-Harrison, A.I. Brown, Donald Grey Barnhouse, Roy Brumbaugh, Pettingill, Dunham. Rimmer: discusses Satan's pre-Adamic revolt — Satan victor over earth. Second Coming soon, literal. Gaebelein: Rapture must precede Tribulation. Morning Star (= Rapture) prior to Sun (= Second Coming). Riley: Turks surrendered Jerusalem in 1917 because planes were prophesied. "Intellectualism … has run its course." Trumbull: Evangelizing rather than converting world is true mission of church, because end is soon. Greatest war (WWI), famine (Russia 1920s), pestilence (1918 influenza), earthquake (China), all occurred 1912–22. Sale-Harrison: God allowed WWI to free promised land from Turks. Return of Jews promised by God. Barnhouse (editor of *Revelation*): Christ to be world's "benevolent Dictator." Brumbaugh: Antichrist, from Roman Empire, makes covenant with Israel. Invades South (Egypt). Naval campaign thwarted by British ships. Then 200 million-man army from Far East attacks, followed by Second Coming. Brown: Vast army at Armageddon to fight Jews and God. Led by Russia, with Germany (Gomer), Turkey (Togarmah). Germany will fall to communists. Setup for Armageddon complete now: all nations in place. World War — Armageddon — inevitable and imminent. Dunham refutes the "General Judgment" theory (single resurrection at End).

1257. Dupont, Yves. *Catholic Prophecy: The Coming Chastisement.* 1970. Rockford, IL: Tan Books. 125 p. Index. bibl. refs. 1973 edition lists author as Dupont-Fournieux. Condemns critical analysis of Revelation as "Satanic" effort.

1258. Eade, Alfred Thompson. *The Plan of the Ages.* 1947. Westwood, NJ: Revell. 26 p. illus.

1259. _____. *The Expanded Panorama Bible Study Course.* 1961. Westwood, NJ: Fleming H. Revell. 192 p.

Compilation of Eade's other entries (all part of Panorama study series).

1260. _____. *The Second Coming of Christ.* 1966. Westwood, NJ: Revell. 34 p. illus.

1261. _____. *A Visual Study of the Book of Revelation.* 1970. Westwood, NJ: Revell. 32 p. illus.

1262. Eagon, I.G. *A New World Order and Lasting Peace.* 1944. Delaware, OH: priv. pub. 66 p.

"The End of the Age is imminent." 7th Vial: WWII aerial bombardment. Also wrote *Antichrist: His History and His Final End*; and *After the War; or the Consummation of God's Purpose.*

1263. Eames, Roger B. *The End Times and Related Subjects.* 1944. New York: Loizeaux Bros. 63 p.

1264. Eddleman, H. Leo, ed. *Last Things: A Symposium of Prophetic Messages.* 1969. Grand Rapids, MI: Zondervan. 160 p. bibl. refs.

Eddleman: president New Orleans Baptist Theological Seminary. Contributors include C.H. Dodd: "realized eschatology" (no further fulfillments; *now* and continuing time is end of age); B. Graham; B. Ramm ("inaugurated eschatology"— realized in present but also End Time to come); R.L. Lindsey; J.G. Dukes; W.R. White; Peter Stoner; D.A. Warriner (at End, God will cease to hold the atoms together); H. Hartzler; W.O. Vaught; Grady Cothen; W.K. Harrison, E.A. McDowell.

1265. Edgar, John, and Morton Edgar. *The Great Pyramid Passages and Chambers.* 1976 [1912–1913]. Glasgow: Bone & Hulley. illus, maps.

"In which is shown how the Great Pyramid of Gizeh, symbolically and by measurement, corroborates the philosophy and prophetic times and seasons of the divine plan of the ages, as contained in the Holy Scriptures."

1266. Edwards, Wesley G. *The End Draweth Nigh.* 1941. 4th rev. ed. [s.l. Fargo, ND]: [distr. by Prophetic Book Concern] 58 p.

1267. _____. *The Rapture of the Church: Pre or Post Tribulation?* 7th ed. 1941. [Los Angeles]: Distr. by Prophetic Book & Film Service. 46 p.

1268. _____. *The Day of Vengeance.* [1970s?]. Los Angeles: Prophetic Book and Film Service. 84 p. illus. foldout chart. Post-trib.

1269. Ehlert, Arnold D. *A Bibliographic History of Dispensationalism.* 1965. Grand Rapids, MI: Baker Book House. 110 p. bibl. refs., index.

Books promoting 6,000 year theory and dispensationalism. Ehlert: librarian of Bible Institute, Los Angeles, later of Institute of Creation Research.

1270. Elderdice, J.L. *How Near Is the End of the Age?* 1916. Buffalo, NY: Sword and Shield Tract Soc. 20 p.

1271. Ely, James E. *Glimpses of Bible Climaxes: From "The Beginning" to "The End."* 1927. Garden City, KS: Businessman's Gospel Assoc. vi, 302 p.

Pre-mill. Largely a denunciation of evolution as opposed to the Bible and Christianity and therefore opposed to law and government. We are headed towards "GRAND IMPOSING CLIMAX." Symmetry of beginning (Creation and Eden) and the end (Kingdom of God, New Earth). Satan in rebellion before Adam; thus Firmament of Day 2 not declared "good." Evolution = "revamped paganism" reactionary and obstructionist since interferes with Christian progress. Christ's comment that "this generation" would witness the End referred to the Jews. Earth is wallowing in suffering and sin. Wars, earthquakes, false teachings (especially evolution) abound. "A 'league of nations' is in the air," and Jews are starting to return to Palestine. 6,000 Year theory: creation was about 4000 B.C. "WE KNOW WE ARE GOING TO HAVE WAR." "Scripture reveals that the world will be devil-looted, not evoluted": Russia-Gog, Rosh, King of the North will attack Israel and try to eliminate all Jews. Numeric design of Bible; cites Panin.

1272. Emeric de St. Dalmas, H.G. SEE ALSO 1800–1910. *The Time of the End and the "Weeks" of Daniel: A Discovery and Restatement.* 1917. London: Charles J. Thynne. ix, 166 p. index.

1273. Emmerson, George J. *The End in View.* 1920. London; New York: Marshall Bros. 120 p. bibl. refs. Index.

1274. English, E. Schuyler. *The Shifting of the Scenes: A Survey of the Signs of the Times.* 1945. New York: Our Hope.

48 p. Also published by E. Stroudsburg, PA: Pinebrook Book Club.

English: 1967 Scofield Reference Bible editorial review committee.

1275. _____. *The Rapture.* 1981 [1954]. 2nd ed. Neptune, NJ: Loizeaux Bros. 123 p. Prev. pub. 1954, 1970 as *Re-Thinking the Rapture: An Examination of What the Scriptures Teach as to the Time of the Translation of the Church in Relation to the Tribulation.*

Pre-trib pre-mill. Material first published in *Our Hope* 1949–51. Daniel's 70 Weeks: 69 "weeks" from 445 B.C. (decree of Artaxerxes to rebuild Jerusalem) to A.D. 31. "Parenthetic age" since then; 70th week will be the Tribulation, immediately following the any-moment Rapture. Antichrist only revealed after the "departure" of the Church (i.e. the Rapture), not "departure from faith" (i.e. apostasy). Holy Spirit is the "Restrainer" preventing emergence of Antichrist, who is free to emerge after Church is raptured away.

1276. *Entering the Shadow of the "Last Days"; or, The Signs of the Times in the Light of Prophecy.* 1921. Kingston [Jamaica] : Printed by the Gleaner Co. 145 p.

1277. Epp, Theodore H. *Russians Doom Prophesied: In Ezekiel 38 and 39.* 1953. Lincoln, NE: Back to the Bible. 64 p. 2 leaves plates folded map. Also 1961 "correspondence school compact course" edition.

Mennonite. Also wrote *God's Program for Israel* (1952, 1957).

1278. _____. *Things That Will Survive.* 1954 Lincoln, NE: Back to the Bible. 61 p.

Former title *Things That Cannot Be Shaken.*

1279. _____. *The Rise and Fall of Gentile Nations.* 1956. Lincoln, NE: Back to the Bible. 80 p.

Regarding Daniel and Revelation.

1280. _____. *Why Must Jesus Come Again?* 1960 Lincoln, NE: Back to the Bible. 79 p.

1281. _____. *Practical Studies in Revelation.* 1969. Lincoln, NE: Back to the Bible.

1282. _____, comp. *A Brief Outline of Things to Come.* 1950. Chicago: Moody Press. 128 p.

1283. Erdman, Charles R. *Return of Christ.* 1922. New York: George H. Doran. 108 p.

Erdman: Presbyterian; professor at Princeton Theological Seminary, a founder of Moody Bible Inst. Post-trib pre-mill; argues against pre-trib Rapture. Second Coming may be soon, or may be long delayed. In "The Coming of Christ" (ca. 1913, in *The Fundamentals* vol. XI), Erdman argued for personal, imminent Second Coming. "'The end of the world' does not mean, in prophecy, the end of the earth and the destruction of its inhabitants; but the end of 'the present age,' which is to be followed by *an age of glory.* The 'present evil age' is predicted to close amid scenes of fiery judgment upon the enemies of God, and with portents and convulsions which will affect the very earth itself...."

1284. Estep, Howard C. *He's Coming Again!* 1964. Colton, CA: World Prophetic Ministries. 24 p.

1285. _____. *Armageddon.* 1965. Colton, CA: World Prophetic Ministry. 32 p.

Final War "fast approaching": follows Tribulation, just prior to Millennium. Antichrist, False Prophet, and Gentile armies versus Christ, His heavenly armies, and the Israelites.

1286. _____. *God's Pay Day.* 1973. Colton, CA: World Prophetic Ministry. 24 p.

Judgment Day.

1287. _____. *Daniel's Seventy Weeks.* 1975. Colton, CA: World Prophetic Ministry. 28 p.

1288. Evans, William. *The Coming King; the World's Next Great Crisis.* 1923. New York; Chicago: Fleming H. Revell. 244 p.

Presbyterian.

1289. Everest, Quinton J. *Perilous Times.* 1943. South Bend, IN: Your Worship Hour. 59 p.

1290. _____. *Awake or Perish.* South Bend, IN: Your Worship Hour, E.V. Publishing House. 40 p.

1291. ____. *Then Shall the End Come.* 1966. South Bend, IN: Your Worship Hour. 76 p.

1292. Everson, Charles T. *The Last Warning Message to This World.* 1927. College Place, WA: Walla Walla College Press. 36 p. Also published 1945 by Elmshaven Press; Review and Herald. Later incorporated into *The Last Warning Message and Other Bible Lectures,* Pacific Press, 1929.

Seventh-day Adventist.

1293. ____. *The Mysterious Number of Prophecy 666.* 1927. College Place, WA: Walla Walla College Press. 30 p.

1294. ____. *The Mark of the Beast in the Forehead.* 1928. Angwin, CA: Pacific Union College Press, 48 p.

1295. Ewing, Albert M. *The Antichrist: Who Is He? Is He Here Now? If Not, When Will He Come? 666 His Number.* 1950. Frankfort, IN: s.n. 48 p.

1296. F., C. H. *Concerning the Nations: World Anxiety! What of Tomorrow? What of You?* 1960. Epping [Australia]: Gospel Publicity League. 18 p.

1297. Fehr, Edward. *Prophetic Bible Course.* 1942. Inman, KS: Salem; Topeka, KS: Prophetic Conference Bureau [distr.] 110 p. charts

Dispensationalist.

1298. Feinberg, Charles, ed. *Focus on Prophecy.* 1964. Fleming H. Revell.

Includes V. Raymond Edman, Pres. Wheaton Coll. "Habakkuk in the Nuclear Age" (Hab. describes "the horrendous cancer of communism"). Coder: Dan. 11 "King of the South"= African confederacy led by Egypt.

1299. ____, ed. *Prophetic Truth Unfolding Today.* 1968. Westwood, NJ: F.H. Revell. 160 p.

Talks presented at Congress on Prophecy (5th, 1967, New York) of American Board of Missions to the Jews. Feinberg also wrote *Premillennialism or Amillennialism*)1954; Wheaton, IL: Van Kampen; 354 p.), arguing for pre-mill.

1300. Ferris, Alexander James. *Armageddon is at the Doors.* 1934. Keston, England: 2nd ed. 88 p. illus

Anglo-Israel advocate.

1301. Fineren, W[illiam] W. *The Times of the Gentiles and the Time of the End.* 1944. Gainesville, FL: W. Fineren. 132 p. illus. map.

Daniel and Revelation.

1302. Finlay, William Golden. *Nations in Confusion.* 1968. Johannesburg: Federation of the Covenant People. [viii], 146 p. illus.

Anti-communist. Condemns racial miscegenation. UN is modern Tower of Babel. Communists infiltrating and brainwashing using beat music with hypnotic rhythms. Anti-evolution. True Israel = Anglo-Celto-Saxon peoples; British folk rightful world leaders. Revelation judgments started with WWI brought on by communist-led conspiracy and racial strife. "Slowly but surely the life blood of the nation is being drained away in this time of the end — the closing stages of this era when the mystery of iniquity is rampant." God will supernaturally destroy Russian-African invasion of Israel. This invasion possibly opposed by UN forces. Papacy may try to take over after invaders destroyed.

1303. Finney, John E. *Events of the Last Days.* 1939. Grand Rapids, MI: Zondervan. 161 p.

Pre-mill. Jews don't accept Christ but resist Antichrist, suffer Tribulation; Antichrist violates treaty, stops Temple worship, Antichrist persecutes Jews so awfully that by comparison the modern German pogroms "will pale into utter insignificance." Iron/clay mix in Daniel = political and ecclesiastical Rome.

1304. Finney, Rodney Earnest. *The End of the World.* 1959. Los Angeles: Voice of Prophecy. 72 p. illus.

Seventh-day Adventist. From radio program.

1305. Fischer, Saxon. *Christ Has Come the Second Time.* 1916. Richmond, VA: Fischer, Virginia Stationery Co. 31 p.

Shaker. Christ reborn as Ann Lee. God lives in the Pleiades. Good angels are "Electrians"; Lucifer uses bad electricity.

1306. Fisher, H.A. *Soviet Russia and Palestine.* 1946. Los Angeles: author.

1307. Fletcher, George B. *The*

Millennium: What It Is Not and What It Is. 1972 [1944]. Swengel, PA: Reiner [Bible Truth Depot]. 64 p.

A-mill. Argues against pre-mill interpretation. Satan is bound during the Christian era.

1308. Francis, Gwilym I. *The World's Next Great Event—And After.* 1950 [1938]. Marshall, Morgan & Scott.

1309. Fraser, Alexander. *The Return of Christ in Glory.* 1943. Scottdale, PA: Evangelical Fellowship. 158 p.

"Consolidating *Is There But One Return of Christ?* and *The Any Moment Return of Christ—A Critique.*" Reprinted 1947 with "a few additions."

Historic pre-mill. Rapture not until the Second Coming; Christians must undergo the Tribulation. Nazi Holocaust was prelude to the Tribulation.

1310. Frazee, Willmonte Doniphan. *Coming Events and Crisis at the Close.* 1978 [1950s?]. Payson, AZ: Leaves-of-Autumn. xiii, 160 p. Orig. pub. Wildwood, GA: Wildwood Medical Missionary Institute.

Seventh-day Adventist.

1311. French, W.R. *Armageddon.* 1942. Angwin, CA: priv. pub. 72 p.

Seventh-day Adventist.

1312. Frodsham, Stanley H. *Things Which Must Shortly Come to Pass.* 1928. Springfield, MO: Gospel Publishing House. 117 p.

Pentecostal

1313. _____. *The Coming Crises and the Coming Christ.* N.d [1930s?] Springfield, MO: Gospel Publishing House. 64 p.

1314. Fromow, George H. *The Italo-Abyssinian Crisis and the Revival of the Roman Empire: The End Not Yet.* 1935. London: Sovereign Grace Advent Testimony. 39 p.

1315. _____. *Will the Church Pass Through the Tribulation?: An Affirmative Reply.* 1937. London: Sovereign Grace Advent Testimony. 23 p.

Paper presented to Prophecy Investigation Soc., 1937, London. J. Sidney St. Clair argued for negative versus Fromow. Post-trib: Tribulation began with Adam.

1316. _____. *Christ and Antichrist Contrasted: An Analysis of Prophecy.* 1967. London: Sovereign Grace Advent Testimony. 24 p.

1317. _____, ed. *Watching and Waiting.* London: Sovereign Grace Advent Testimony (serial only?).

1318. Froom, LeRoy Edwin. *Civilization's Last Stand and Other Studies on the Fundamental Issues of the Hour.* 1928. Mountain View, CA: Pacific Press. 126 p.

Seventh-day Adventist. Sinful conditions worldwide. Tribulation = Papal supremacy. "*This generation is the last.*"

1319. _____. *Meteoric Showers Seen as Heralds of Advent.* 1951. Priv. pub. 33 p.

In Advent Source Collection at Andrews University, which also includes Froom's *Number of the Beast, 666.*

1320. _____. *The Prophetic Faith of Our Fathers.* 1946–1954. Washington, D.C.: Review and Herald. 4 vols. illus., charts, tables, bibl.

Exhaustive, scholarly study of prophetic and End Time views and sources from the earliest Church Fathers to Seventh-Day Adventists. Thousands of works discussed.

1321. Frost, F[rank] D[utton]. *The Appointed Time, or, The Present World Crisis, the Disease and the Cure.* 1932. 4th ed. rev. London: Pickering & Inglis. ix, 106 p.

1322. Frost, Henry Westo. *The Second Coming of Christ.* 1934. Grand Rapids, MI: William B. Eerdmans. 251 p.

Frost: Presbyterian. Historic pre-mill.

1323. Gaebelein, Arno C. SEE ALSO 1800–1910. *The Revelation: An Analysis and Exposition of the Last Book of the Bible.* 1915. New York: Our Hope. 225 p.

Gog invasion at beginning of Millennium.

1324. _____. *The League of Nations in the Light of the Bible.* 1920. New York: Our Hope. 50 p.

1325. _____. *The Thousand Years in Both Testaments.* 1933. New York: Our Hope. 31 p.

1326. _____. *World Prospects; How Is It All Going to End? A Study in Sacred Prophecy and Present Day World Conditions.* [1934]. New York: Our Hope. 190

p. Also pub. London: Pickering & Inglis; 1935.

After the Rapture.

1327. _____. *As It Was— So Shall It Be: Sunset and Sunrise: A Study of the First Age and Our Present Age.* 1937. New York: Our Hope. 190 p. bibl.

Litany of End Time signs. "The sun of our age is setting, the evening is here. The prophecies relating to our age-ending are rapidly approaching their fulfillment." After Rapture, evil breaks forth unrestrained; Antichrist becomes world dictator; earth overrun with demons. First Beast possible Mussolini. Second Beast a Jew: the Antichrist.

1328. _____. *Will There Be a Millennium ? When and How?* 1943. New York: Our Hope. 82 p.

"The coming reign of Christ in the light of the Old and New Testaments."

1329. _____. *Our Age and Its End.* [1940s?] New York: Our Hope. xv, 134 p.

With Scofield's Lectures on Prophecy.

1330. _____. *Hopeless, Yet There Is Hope: A Study in World Conditions and their Solution.* New York: Loizeaux Bros. 193 p.

The world is rushing to war. Russia will ally with Gomer (probably Germany), after Hitler.

1331. _____. *Daniel: A Key to the Visions and Prophecies of the Book of Daniel.* 1985 [1955]. Grand Rapids, MI: Kregel. 212 p. 1955 ed. titled *The Prophet Daniel.*

1332. Garrison, George C. *The End of the Age.* 1913. Los Angeles: author. 45 p.

Besides long-known signs, author describes others: Balkan War (Ottoman Empire). "The Automobile Sign": Nahum 2:3-4 "chariots raging in the streets" and "broad ways," like "torches," running like "lightning," in the Last Days. Satan's deception of spiritualism another sign. Stages of the End: like 3-part stages of Israel's destruction. 457 B.C. + 69 Weeks = A.D. 27. Then 2,300 year Desolation, to 1844. 1844 beginning (not end) of "cleansing of the sanctuary": preparation of Holy Land for restoration by Jews. 1923 and

1934 also probably significant End Time mileposts. Scoffers will rationalize Rapture as due to "electricity." Tribulation, then Second Coming with Saints. Christ's Second Coming would lose its "charm" if not prior to Tribulation: it wouldn't be fair to believers. Tribulation to fall mainly on Jews, thus on Christendom (where most Jews live). All signs now fulfilled for Coming, including preaching to entire world. Pyramidology indicates 1914–16 End for Church. "Never in all the past has there been such a host of warnings!"— even more than for First Coming and Flood.

1333. Gerber, Charles. *Le Christ Revient.* 1949. Dammarie-les-Lys: Editions "Les Signes des Temps." 286 p. illus. bibl. refs.

1334. Gerbrant, John J. *Things That Must Shortly Come to Pass.* 1943. San Jose, CA: author. 16 p. illus.

1335. Gerling, Reinhold. *Der Weltkrieg 1914/15 im Lichte der Prophezieung.* 1916. Oranienburg: Orania-Verlag. 62 p.

Gog = England, because it is allied with Russia in the World War.

1336. Gilbert, Dan. *The Red Terror and Bible Prophecy.* 1944. Grand Rapids, MI: Zondervan. 40 p.

1337. _____. *What Will Become of Germany in the Light of Bible Prophecy?* 1945. Washington: Christian Press Bureau. 34 p.

Russia will be chief jailor of Germany; Germany to remain anti-God; to invade Palestine; Ezekiel prophesies new military empire in Europe.

1338. _____. *Who Will Be the Antichrist?* 1945. Washington: Christian Press Bureau. 36 p.

Antichrist will be Judas returned.

1339. _____. *What Will Happen Next in America?:* 1946. Los Angeles: Jewish Hope Publishing House. 24 p.

Also wrote *Russia's Next Move in the Light of Bible Prophecy* (1945; Russia allies with Iran, occupies Turkey, Ethiopia, Libya); *The End of Stalin in the Light of Bible Prophecy* (1943); *The United Nations and the Coming Antichrist; Mark of the*

Beast (1951); *Will Russia Invade Palestine?*; *Will Russia Fight America?* (yes).

1340. Gilbert, Fred Carnes. *Time for the Messiah.* 1946. Mountain View, CA: Pacific Press. 96 p.

Seventh-day Adventist. Gilbert: "Hebrew-Christian minister."

1341. Gill, A. R. *Daniel's Remarkable Vision of Hitler; or, Hitler's End Foretold.* 1944. Ilfracombe [England]: A.H. Stockwell. 64 p.

1342. Gillatt, J.J. *Prophetic Light for the Last Days.* 1925. Garston, England: author. 372 p. illus., charts.

Denies evolution. "We are living in momentous times." Lord "even now at the door." Infidelity is rampant. Papacy vs. Protestants (especially in Britain). Signs of times: WWI, religious apostasy, social decay, political turmoil. 1844 was "investigative Judgment of the Righteous." Standard scenario: Tribulation disasters, Armageddon, Second Coming, Millennium. 70 Weeks ended A.D. 34. Crucifixion was middle of 70th. "Indefinite time of the End": 1844 to Second Coming. Chapter "The Divine Mathematician": computes dates, from Revelation and Daniel.

1343. Gordin, Morris. *Culmination of Evil: Satan Behind Bolshevism and Nazism.* 1939. Los Angeles: American Prophetic League. 22 p.

1344. Gordon, S[amuel] D. *Quiet Talks About Our Lord's Return.* 1912. New York: Fleming H. Revell. 266 p.

War, famine, earthquakes, persecution intensify during Tribulation, which may start any moment; then Second Coming. Surest sign will be return of Israel, though growth of evil in the world is general sign. Also wrote *Quiet Talks on the Deeper Meaning of the War and Its Relation to Our Lord's Return* (1919; Revell).

1345. _____. *Quiet Talks on the Crisis and After.* [1926]. New York: Fleming H. Revell. 224 p.

Plan of history ever since Adam: age-old "racial" struggle between evil descendants of Cain and godly descendants of Seth, and various mixed stocks. World War (I) was this "racial crisis" coming to a head. (By "race" seems to mean all of humanity.) Africans and Asians corrupted by European materialism, and Europeans in turn corrupted by African savagery. Germany now building up for new war, with Italy and Japan seeking to join her, expecting Germany to win. Jews will "re-nationalize" as result of persecution. Coming "racial" crisis will be centered in eastern Mediterranean, with prophesied Northern and Southern confederations being drawn in; then Second Coming. Rejects evolution as unscientific speculation.

1346. Gortner, J. Narver. *Studies in Daniel.* 1948. Springfield, MO: Gospel Publishing House. 204 p.

Pentecostal (Assemblies of God), Calvary Tabernacle, Queens, NY; grandfather of Marjoe Narver. Germany allied with Russia vs. Israel.

1347. _____. *Studies in Revelation.* 1948. Springfield, MO: Gospel Pub. House. 276 p.

1348. _____. *Are the Saints Scheduled to Go Through the Tribulation?* N.d. Springfield, MO: Gospel Pub. House. 45 p.

1349. Graebner, Theodore. *War in the Light of Prophecy: "Was It Foretold?" A Reply to Modern Chiliasm.* 1942 [1918]. St. Louis MO: Concordia. vii, 143 p. bibl.

Updated version of *Prophecy and the War* (1918, Concordia). Strong refutation of pre-mill and chiliasm ("religious disease") as illogical, fanciful, unjustified imaginings and inventions. Urges literal interpretation where possible but figurative and symbolic if text itself suggests it. Most Lutherans "believe in no millennium at all" though do have "joyous expectancy of the Second Advent." "From prophecy we know that we are now living in the last era of the world's history." WWII indeed heralds End but Graebner deplores date-setting and Millennialist mania. Refutes huge mass of literature claiming WWI = Armageddon. Ridicules idea of converted Jewish peerage in Israel; national return of Jews is "pure fiction" and general conversion "impossible" as Jews still "irreconcilable enemies of Christ." Rise of Papacy from Rome genuinely prophesied.

1350. Graham, Billy. *World Aflame.*

1965. Garden City, NY: Doubleday. xvii, 267 p. bibl. refs.

Also 1967 ed. Penguin Books. "We seem to be plunging madly toward Armageddon." "Jesus said there would be a future generation with certain characteristics to indicate the end is near.... Today it would seem that those signs are indeed converging for the first time since Christ ascended into heaven." SEE ALSO 1970+.

1351. Grant, W[alter] V. *The Great Dictator: The Man Whose Number is 666.* Dallas: Grant's Faith Clinic, n.d. 31 p. illus.

1352. _____. *Men in the Flying Saucers Identified: Not a Mystery!* [1950s].

1353. Gray, James M. SEE ALSO 1800–1910. *A Text-Book on Prophecy.* 1918. New York: Fleming H. Revell. 215 p.

1354. _____. *The Second Coming of Christ: The Meaning, Period and Order of Events and How I Came to Believe in Our Lord's Return.* [1950s]. Chicago, IL: Moody Bible Institute. 14 p.

1355. _____. *Studying the Second Coming for Yourself.* 1914. Chicago: Bible Institute Colportage Assoc. 14 p.

1356. Greene, Oliver B. *The Revelation: Verse by Verse Study.* 1976, 1963. Greenville, SC: The Gospel Hour. 543 p.

Greene: Baptist.

1357. _____. 1963 [1958]. *Russia, Israel and the End.* Greenville, SC: Gospel Hour. 50 p.

1358. _____. *Bible Prophecy.* 1970. Greenville, SC: Gospel Hour. 578 p.

Pre-trib. SEE ALSO 1970+.

1359. Greenway, W. Norman. *When the Vultures Eat the Dictators: A Clear Analysis of the End-Times in the Light of God's Word.* 1941. Grand Rapids, MI: Zondervan. 112 p.

1360. Gregory, Benjamin F. *Schedule of Events in the Time of Trouble.* 1963. Bakersfield, CA: [s.n.]. 29 p.

1361. Grier, William James. *The Momentous Event: A Discussion of Scripture Teaching of the Second Advent.* 1945. Belfast [N. Ireland]: Evangelical Book Shop. 98 p. 1970 ed. London: Banner of Trust.

Orig. 1944–45 articles. Calvinist; a-mill: Millennium is spiritually fulfilled. "Our Lord plainly teaches a general and universal judgment at His second coming. That coming will be visible and glorious, For the wicked it will mean final and irrevocable judgment. For the saints it will mean, not millennial bliss, but the very heaven of heaven itself as the seat of their abode...." Jews not returned to Palestine — the New Testament gives an "enlarged meaning and spiritual significance to Old Testament promises" which now refer to all believers in Christ.

1362. Haberman, Frederick. *Armageddon has Come: The Climax of the Ages is Near.* 1940. 2nd. ed. St. Petersburg, FL: Kingdom Press: 116 p, plates illus. bibl. refs. 3rd ed. 1941.

1363. Haddon, L. *The End of the World: The World That Was — The Present Evil World — The World to Come* [ca. 1915?]. Haddonfield, VA. 40 p.

1364. Haines, Perry F. *The End from the Beginning.* 1942. Grand Rapids, MI: Zondervan. 97 p.

"The significance of Jewish Persecution and Looking into the Future through God's Ancient Newspaper." Haines: Methodist pastor (PA). First half of book written before WWII; Haines claims he predicted Hitler's attack on Poland and anti-Jewish persecutions. "God has permitted these persecutions and in some case may have used them for a scourge" to punish Jews for not recognizing Christ as Messiah and to force them to return to Israel. Italy will not fight with Germany in present war (WWII), and U.S. won't be involved until after Ten Nation revived Roman Empire arises. This Ten Nation federation will be formed to oppose Germany, Russia, or both together. Then Ten Nation ruler will sign seven-year treaty with Israel. The present World War "will not be decided in Europe, nor Germany,... but will be brought to an abrupt close by the appearing of the Lord Jesus Christ" in Israel.

1365. Haldeman, Isaac M[assey]. SEE ALSO 1800–1910. *Why I Preach the Second Coming.* [1919]. New York: Fleming H. Revell. 160 p.

Christ's coming for His church (the Rapture) is the "most important event on the horizon of time" and central concept of Bible. Bible also full of warnings about Armageddon. Antichrist revealed after Rapture. Describes horrors of WWI. League of Nations now restoring the old Roman empire (to become Ten-Nation confederation under Antichrist). Jews, guilty of killing Christ, will return only at Second Coming.

1366. ____. *The Falling Stone, or the Overthrow of the Last Kaiser.* 1917. New York: C.C. Cook. 73 p.

Rome revived; the Ten Kings invite Antichrist (military leader from Babylon) to rule from Rome; he sets up Zionist state to prevent Russo-Germany alliance, breaks seven-year treaty, precipitating Tribulation. Confronts rebellion in Egypt, returns to face North and East armies at Armageddon.

1367. Halff, Charles. *Palestine, the Land of Fulfilled Prophecy.* 1955. San Antonio, TX: Christian Jew Hour. 45 p.

1368. ____. *Will There Be a War Between Russia and America?* 1961.

Also wrote *Israel — Nation of Destiny.* Futurist. Halff: converted Jew. SEE ALSO 1970+.

1369. Hall, John G. *Prophecy Marches On.* 1994 [1963]. Newcastle, OK: author. 246 p.

1370. ____. *God's Dispensational and Prophetic Plan.* 1994 [1966]. [Newcastle, OK]: J.G. Hall. 202 p.

1371. Halsey, W[allace] C. *Cosmic End-Time Secrets.* 1965. Los Angeles: Futura Press. 102 p. illus.

Author: founder of Christ Brotherhood; cousin of Admiral "Bull" Halsey. Channeled End-Time message; much on UFOs, vibrations, densities. Earth is hollow, with opening at North Pole; some flee to interior during Tribulation; some evacuated by flying saucers. Halsey's wife is reincarnated Venusian. English peoples are true Israelites. Flood caused when Earth flipped over, collapsing the Water Canopy. Earth will flip again. Crust of Earth, formed of fallout from breakup of evil planet Marduk-Lucifer, will be discarded, leaving 800-mile translucent shell, transmitting light into hollow interior.

1372. Hamilton, Floyd Eugene. *The Basis of Millennial Faith.* 1955 [1942]. Grand Rapids, MI: William B. Eerdmans. 162 p. bibl. refs.

A mill.

1373. Hamilton, Frank. *The Bible and the Millennium, Being a Compilation of the Two Books, the Old Testament & Messiah's Reign on Earth and the New Testament and the Millennium.* [1940s?]. Ventnor, NJ: Hamilton. 66, 82 p.

1374. Hamilton, Gavin. *Quiz, Queer & Co.* [1940?]. Oak Park, IL: Gavin Hamilton; Good News Pub. 64 p.

1375. ____. *Will the Church Escape the Great Tribulation?* 1944 [1941]. 3rd ed. New York: Loizeaux Bros., Bible Truth Depot. 79 p.

1376. ____. *Is This the End Time?* [ca 1970?]. Westchester, IL: Good News Publishers. 22 p.

1377. Hamon, L. *Cheiro's World Predictions ...* 1927. London: The London Pub. Co. xvi, 240 p. plates, tables.

Political prophecies, astrology, earthquakes. Jews return to Israel, this triggers WWIII, then Armageddon.

1378. Hare, R[obert]. *Earth's Last Generation: What Will It See?* 1923. Warburton, Australia: Signs. 143 p. illus.

1379. Hargis, Billy James. *Today in Bible Prophecy.* 1967. Tulsa OK: Christian Crusade. 36 p.

Director of Christian Crusade. World being sucked into "convulsive lawlessness" is proof of end of the age. Increasing apostasy (including voting against school prayer) and emerging world government and world church. 70th Week begins as Israel re-established as nation. Armageddon — Christ and His heavenly army vs. Antichrist and earthly armies — at end of Tribulation.

1380. Harrington, Wilfrid J. *Understanding the Apocalypse.* 1969. Cleveland: Corpus Books. ix, 278 p. bibl.

1381. Harrison, Norman B. *His Sure Return.* 1926. Chicago: Bible Institute Colportage Assoc. 84 p.

1382. ____. *The Partial Rapture Theory.* 1940 Dallas Theological Seminary thesis. bibl. refs.

1383. _____. *The End: Rethinking the Revelation.* 1948 [1941]. Minneapolis: The Harrison Service. 244 p. illus. charts.

"The End of all things is at hand." Revelation "purposely" written to baffle unprepared reader. Daniel was "sealed" (not understandable) until End Time. Half-hour silence in Revelation = period between World Wars I, II — "day" = thousand years, so half hour = 20 years, 10 months. "Beasts!" — Daniel saw terrifying sights of future: our world today. Church Age overlapped Jewish Age A.D. 30-70, and will overlap first half of 70 Weeks. Seven Churches: "typical" (representative) of historical periods; seven successive spiritual states. First-Love, Persecuted, Married, Papal, Reformation, Missionary, and Rejected Church. Emphasizes structural patterns, repeated themes, of Revelation and rest of Bible. Rapture mid-trib (though Harrison calls it "pre-trib" because the "Great" Tribulation is the second half of 70th Week). Rapture occurs at Revelation 4:1 (start of Great Tribulation, just before first appearance of the Beast). Tribulation can also be applied to the World Wars: the Seals to WWI, the half hour of silence before the Trumpets to the 20-year interval between wars. Second Trumpet = Germany; destruction of the ships = wartime losses. First Horse: Anti–Christian Ideology. The Seals are man's doings; the Trumpets are Satan's; the Bowls are by God Himself (Wrath of God). Woman = Israel; Dragon = Satan; Child = Christ; Remnant = Jews. First Beast = Antichrist. Second Beast = False Prophet. Jews flee to Petra. "Beast" is both man and empire. Antichrist Beast: most terrible dictator in world; may be Germany. Mark is "like the swastika"; denotes allegiance and ownership. Armageddon = all armies of Antichrist's world empire converge at Armageddon. Papal Church = Mystery Babylon. Harlot = Romanism and apostate Protestantism. Millennium "typified" by Adam's lifetime (nearly thousand years). Gog Magog attackers from North, pre-mill; Gog and Magog rebellion at end of Millennium so named because it resembles earlier attack.

1384. _____. *This War? If We Win, If We Lose.* 1942. Minneapolis: Harrison Service. 48 p.

1385. _____. *His Coming: Seven Significant Signs of the Times; Seven Reasons Why Christ Must Come Again.* 1946. Minneapolis: The Harrison Service. 72 p.

1386. Haskell, Joe S. *The Seven Seals.* 1951. Angwin, CA: Bible Research Fellowship. 35 p.

1387. Havner, Vance. *Repent or Else!* 1958. [Westwood, NJ:] Revell. 121 p.

1388. Haynes, Carlyle B. *Our Lord's Return.* 1964 [1918]. rev. ed. Nashville: Southern Publishing Assoc. 125 p. illus.

1918 ed. titled *The Return of Jesus.*

1389. _____. *What Is Coming?* 1920. Southern Pub. Assoc.: Nashville. 128 p. illus. Former title *Bible Prophecies Unfolding.*

1390. _____. *On the Eve of Armageddon.* 1946 [1924]. Rev. ed. Washington, D.C.: Review and Herald. 96 p. illus.

"An account of the Scriptural teaching relating to the war among the nations which will engulf civilization, and will immediately precede the universal and eternal kingdom of peace." After Armageddon, "utter depopulation and ruin of the earth — such is the terrible destiny" — earth remains completely lifeless all through the Millennium. Wicked resurrected at end of Millennium to be destroyed forever. Seventh-day Adventist.

1391. _____. *Our Times and Their Meaning.* 1929. Nashville: Southern Pub. Assoc. 416 p. illus.

1392. _____. *Earth's Last Hour; An Analysis of the Evidences Now Manifesting Themselves Everywhere of the Nearness of the Long-Foretold Return of Jesus and the Establishment of an Enduring World Government.* 1937. Takoma Park, Washington, D.C.: Review and Herald. 96 p. illus.

Second Coming in "very near future ... in our time." World is now frantically preparing for war.

1393. _____. *The Blackout of Civilization and Beyond.* 1941. Nashville: Southern Pub. Association. 96 p. illus.

"A searching Scriptural analysis of the cosmic catastrophe into which the world is plunging, the essential causes which have produced it, the world government which will follow, and the program of the coming world ruler." WWII as sure sign of the End. "Six thousand years of criminality is approaching its termination." Satan to be "securely shut up in a concentration camp" during Millennium. Wicked all killed at start of Millennium — nobody left alive on earth. Wicked are resurrected end of Millennium for Judgment.

1394. _____. *When God Splits the Atom: An Explanation of the Meaning of the Discovery and the Principles of Nuclear Fission in the Light of the Ancient Prophecies of the Bible.* 1946. Nashville: Southern Publishing Assoc. 94 p. illus.

Also 1951 ed. Also wrote *America in Bible Prophecy* (1947).

1395. Haynie, Burl. *Time of Jacob's Trouble Approaching: Israel, God's Timepiece.* 1965. Los Angeles: Biblical Research Society. 174 p. "Prepared especially for the New York World's Fair 1964–1965 ministry of the American Board of Missions to the Jews, Inc. cooperating agency Biblical Research Society."

1396. Hayward, James L. *The Time of the End: Chronological Study of Last Day Events.* [1960s?]. Fort Worth, TX: s. n. 173 p. illus. Chart.

1397. Heer, Johannes de. *De komende Rechter en de Eindcrisis der Volken in Armageddon.* [1930s?]. Zeist: Zoeklicht-Boekhandel. 237 p. map.

1398. Hegy, Reginald. *The Hour Approaches.* 1941. [Johannesburg:] Central News Agency. xvi, 253 p.

1399. Heim, Karl. *The World: Its Creation and Consummation: The End of the Present Age and the Future of the World in the Light of the Resurrection.* 1962. London: Oliver and Boyd. xi, 159 p. Transl. from German; orig. 1958 (*Weltschöpfung und Weltende*).

1400. Heindel, Max. *How Shall We Know Christ at His Coming?* 1914. Oceanside, CA: Rosicrucian Fellowship. 29 p.

Rosicrucian interpretation.

1401. Heinecken, Martin J. *Beginning and End of the World.* 1960. Philadelphia: Muhlenberg Press. 62 p. illus.

1402. Hendley, Jesse M. *Satanic Trinity of the End Time.* 1968. Cassette. [Atlanta, GA: Radio Evangelistic Publications.]

Broadcast of the Radio Evangelistic Hour. Also many similar tapes.

1403. Hendriksen, William. *Lectures on the Last Things.* 1951. Grand Rapids, MI: Baker Book House. 65 p. bibl. refs.

Return of Israel in unbelief and lists of earthquakes (e.g.) are "mistaken signs," not proof of imminent End. World evangelism, and Great Tribulation after Antichrist are still required before End. Unclear how much of Bible prophecy is literal, how much figurative. Real signs of End: increasing wickedness and materialism. Second Coming will be public, Antichrist defeated, then immediate Judgment. Denies separate resurrection of good and wicked.

1404. _____. *More Than Conquerors: An Interpretation of the Book of Revelation.* 1990 [1939]. Grand Rapids, MI: Baker. 216 p. index bibl. refs. Commemorative ed.

A-mill. Binding of Satan follows *first* Coming of Christ; no triumphant Millennium.

1405. Herrstrom, W.D. *The Atomic Bomb and the End of the World.* 1945. Faribault, MN: Bible News Flashes. 48 p.

1406. Hicks, W. Percy. *The Second Coming of Our Lord Jesus Christ in Relation to the Present World Crisis.* 1925. London: Charles J. Thynne & Jarvis, for The Advent Testimony and Preparation Movement. 77 p.

1407. _____. *Dictatorship, Fascism and Communism.* N.d. Foldout tract. [National Bible Inst.: Oregon, IL]

"All things indicate that we are in the preparatory stages for the appearing of the Antichrist," followed by Armageddon and Second Coming. Reprinted from *Prophetic News* and *Jewish Hope.*

1408. Higdon, David Andrew. *The End of the World and the World to Come.* 1936. Louisville, KY: Standard. 221 p.

Minister: Oxford, MS. Asserts "the end is not far off, even at the doors." Most or all prophecies already fulfilled. America is "Raiser of Taxes" of Dan. 11:20; PWA and other government projects are "lying wonders." Denounces evolution as "devil's doctrine"; insists Hell is located inside Earth.

1409. [Hill, Ethel P.] "Ashtar" (pseud.). *In Days to Come.* 1965 [1957?]. Los Angeles: New Age. 1957; Clarksburg, WV: Saucerian Publications. 90 p.

Channeled by "E.P.H." from Ashtar of the planet Venus. Ashtar first contacted by flying saucer contactee George Van Tassel in early 1950s.

1410. Hogg, C.F., and Thomas Stockdale. *The Progress of Revelation Concerning the Coming of Messiah.* 1923. London: Thynne & Jarvis.

1411. Hogg, C[harles] F., and W[illiam] E[dwy] Vine. *Touching the Coming of the Lord.* 1932 [1919]. Edinburgh: Oliphants. 173 p. indexes.

Brethren. "Last Day" includes Rapture before Millennium and resurrection of non-believers at end of Millennium. "Parousia" really means (silent, secret) "presence."

1412. Holden, J. Stuart. *"Behold He Cometh!"* 1918. London: Morgan and Scott. 77 p.

Rapture, Tribulation (probably seven years) under Antichrist, then Second Coming.

1413. Holland, Herbert H. *The Time is at Hand.* [1940]. 8 p.

Advent Christian. Three Frogs (Unclean Spirits) of Revelation: Communist, Fascist, and Catholic propaganda. Last Day at hand.

1414. Hollenbeck, James Carlton. *The Coming World Climax: Inspirational, Prophetic, Educational, Illustrated.* 1943. [Chicago]: J. Hollenbeck. 64 p. plates illus.

1415. Honert, Wilhelm Hermann. *Prophetenstimmen; die zukunftigen Schicksale der Kirche Christi im Lichte der weissagungen des Herrn und seiner Heiligen.* 1919. Regensburg: G.J. Manz. iv, 270 p. 4th ed.

Honert: Regensburg priest.

1416. Hopkin, Mary Elizabeth Philpott. *Israel and the End of Time.* 1969. [Llanelli, Wales: M.E.P. Hopkin]. 75 p.

Only remnant of Jews saved, and larger remnant of Christians. Israel is the True Church (not Jews). Denies Rapture and dispensationalism (two covenants only: Old and New Testaments). Second Coming = Resurrection of all; no literal Millennium. Return of Jews not relevant. All promises to Israel already fulfilled. Earth destroyed, then remade at End.

1417. Hörbiger, Hanns, and Phillip Fauth. *Glazial-Kosmogonie.* 1913. Leipzig: Voigtlanders. xxxii, 790 p. illus, charts, bibl.

Hörbiger: Viennese mining engineer. Our Moon is latest of series of ice-covered moons, each of which spirals into Earth causing global destruction. Atlantis and Flood are racial memories of collision of past moon. Hörbiger's *Welt-Eis-Lehre* ("cosmic-ice theory") inspired dozens of books (including novels) and journals, and had many Nazi supporters (some who wrote explicitly Nazified versions describing the rise and destruction of a series of fabulous races and a primeval Aryan homeland).

1418. Horsefield, F.J. *Return of the King: Its Certainty; Its Meaning; Its Nearness.* N.d. [ca. 1917]. London: Marshall Bros. 125 p.

Horsefield: Bristol, England, minister. Pre-trib Rapture. The World War is "undoubtedly preparing the way" for Armageddon. Russia will be leader of Northern Confederation.

1419. Hoste, William, and Charles Askwith. *The Seven Vials of God's Wrath.* 1920. London: C.J. Thynne. 40 p.

Addresses delivered at meetings of the Prophecy Investigation Society Vol. also includes F.J. Horsefield's and Earle L. Langston's *Judgment of the Nations.*

1420. Houghton, Henry. *New World Coming!* 1941[1930]. Haverhill, MA: Destiny Publishing vi, 208. Orig. pub. London: Covenant [also published in Canada].)

"Anglo-Saxondom" (British-Israelism).

1421. [Houteff, Florence]. *Christianity, from Retreat to Triumph.* 1961 Waco, TX: Universal. 51 p. Also abridged ed.

Wife of Victor Houteff; became

leader of Davidian Seventh-Day Adventists after his death. Predicted End for April 22, 1959.

1422. Houteff, Victor T. *The Shepherd's Rod, the 144,000 of Revelation 7 — Call for Reformation.* 1980 [1932]. Salem, SC: General Assoc. of Davidian Seventh-Day Adventists. 2 vol. illus. Orig pub. 1932. Waco, TX.

Houteff: founder of Davidian Seventh-Day Adventists (later renamed Branch Davidians). Expected to establish Davidic Kingdom with 144,000 believers.

1423. _____. *Behold, I Make All Things New.* 1940. Waco, TX: Universal. 112 p. illus.

Millennium and Second Coming.

1424. _____. *The Great Paradox of the Ages: A Timely Revelation.* 1948 [1941]. Waco, TX: Universal. 72 p. index.

Bible prophecies.

1425. _____. *At the Eleventh Hour: Judgment of the Living.* 1983 Exeter, MO: Universal. 67 p. illus.

1426. _____. *America: King of the North, Sixth Regime, 666: Assyria Phase, Babylon Phase.* 1994. Tamassee, SC: D. Adair. 324 p. illus.

1427. Howden, J. Russell. *The Wars of the Lord.* London: Marshall Bros. 160 p.

Based on 1926 Keswick Convention.

1428. Howe, H.G.J. *The Dawning of that Day.* 1930. London: Advent Testimony and Preparation Movement. 108 p. foldout chart.

1429. Hoyt, Herman A. *The End Times.* 1973 [1969]. Chicago: Moody Press / B M H Books. 256 p. bibl., index.

Imminent, pre-mill pre-trib. "Clear chronology of end-time events" possible. Explanation of terms, doctrines, refutation of false interpretations of Second Coming: crisis that terminates End Times. Hell is inside Earth. New Jerusalem descends end of Millennium — enough room for it because sea is gone. Antichrist = Beast from Sea; amazing intelligence, "evil genius," physically attractive, forges 10-King confederacy of revived Roman Empire. First Horse rider probably a Jew. Antichrist revealed right after Rapture. Destroys apostate Church mid-tribula-

tion. Destroyed at Armageddon by Second Coming. Tribulation = 70th Week = Day of Lord. Antichrist establishes world super-church (= Harlot), gains world domination, moves capital to Jerusalem. Most of world killed. Armies of all world gather at Armageddon, "doubtless approaching 400 million." Northern Confederacy (Russia and allies), Southern Confederacy (Egypt and allies), Eastern Confederacy (China, Japan), and Western Confederacy (Antichrist's Roman Empire) converge. Demons from Hell, then "supernatural invasion from outer space": Second Coming. Sealed 144,000 witness to Gentiles, save multitudes. Southern Confederacy falls to Antichrist's armies. Northern Confederacy invades Israel, fails, annihilated. Jews flee to wilderness, pursuing Antichrist armies swallowed by earthquake. Armageddon is the siege of Jerusalem by all armies. Just as finally being defeated, Jews are saved by Second Coming. Literal 200 mile blood to bridles. Millennium = "mediatorial Kingdom of God." Insists on everlasting punishment of wicked. SEE ALSO 1970+.

1430. Hubbard, Joseph. *The Times of the Gentiles.* 1919. Tisdale, CA: s.n. 301 p.

1431. Hughes, Archibald. *A New Heaven and a New Earth: An Introductory Study of the Coming of the Lord Jesus Christ and the Eternal Inheritance.* 1958. Philadelphia: Presbyterian & Reformed. 233 p.

1432. Hull, William L. *Israel — Key to Prophecy: The Story of Israel from the Regathering to the Millennium, as Told by the Prophets.* 1957. Grand Rapids, MI: Zondervan. 104 p. illus. map.

Novel. "We live in the last days." Most of book is fictional account of End Time events. Following Rapture, Russia (Gog) attacks Israel, aided by Iran, Iraq, Arab nations, but God destroys invading armies. Catholics gain control of U.S., which becomes new religious-political "Roman empire" overseeing ten dictatorships. Supreme leader, Antichrist, is Satan incarnated. Antichrist signs 7-year pact to rebuild Israel after devastation of Russian attack, and to rebuild Temple. Then unveils huge talking statue of himself that demands he be worshipped as God. Most Jews refuse and are massacred. Survivors flee to Petra, and discover Bibles hidden there by Blackstone and by Charles S. Price. Arab armies try to eliminate remaining Jews but are supernaturally destroyed. Christ makes his Second Coming at Petra; all Jews tearfully convert, then follow Christ and his returning raptured saints to Armageddon where they annihilate assembled world armies of Antichrist.

1433. Humberd, Russel I. *The Book of Revelation.* 1944. Flora, IN: Christian Book Depot. 279 p. 6th ed. (orig. same year).

Beast = Antichrist; King of revived Roman Empire. He is healed from deadly wound, performs miracles and thrills crowds to delirious acceptance. Literal judgments and plagues. Babylon rebuilt. Japanese, Chinese, Indian armies cross Euphrates to Armageddon. War rationing as prelude to Mark of Beast. Humberd denounces ecumenicism (and coming World Church): "God's command is absolute separation." Church returns at Second Coming with Christ to Armageddon, then rules in Millennium. Mentions story that Edison believed all words ever spoken still exists as vibrations, and sought to recover Christ's actual speech. At Final Judgment, God similarly examines speech record. Humberd hopes that "new heavens" is remaking of atmosphere only, as he enjoys looking at the old stars.

1434. Hurst, William D. *Hooks in Their Jaws: A Premillennial Study of Bible Prophecy.* 1969 [1968]. New York: Exposition Press. 95 p.

Pre-mill. Seven dispensations, each ends with catastrophe (Fall, Flood, Babel, Crucifixion, Rapture, Second Coming, Judgment). Now at end of 5th; Tribulation and Millennium to follow soon. Imminence of Rapture. Denounces deadly infiltration by atheistic communism. Cites friend W.H. Rogers (*End from the Beginning*). Great Northern Confederacy during Tribulation, also 10-Nation revived Roman Empire led by Antichrist (both anti-Jewish). Gog = Russia. Tarshish probably

Britain. Literal Armageddon, then Second Coming, Millennium, Gog-Magog rebellion.

1435. Ironside, H.A. [Henry Allan] *The Midnight Cry.* 1928 [1915]. 4th ed., rev. and enl. New York: Loizeaux Brothers. 63 p.

1436. _____. *Lectures on the Book of Revelation.* 1919. Oakland, CA: Western Book & Tract. 366 p. 1920. Neptune, NJ: Loizeaux Bros. ("First ed."). 367 p., fold-out chart. 1981: 35th printing.

Dispensationalist, futurist. Popular lecture style. Antichrist = Second Beast.

1437. _____. *The Lamp of Prophecy; or, Signs of the Times.* c1940. Grand Rapids, MI: Zondervan. 159 p.

"Armageddon is really the clashing of vast Eastern and Western armies contending for the possession of Palestine."

1438. _____. *The Great Parenthesis: Timely Messages on the Interval Between the 69th and 70th Weeks of Daniel's Prophecy.* 1943. Grand Rapids, MI: Zondervan. 131 p.

Reprinted as *Studies in Biblical Eschatology* (1983, Minneapolis: Klock & Klock) along with Ottman's *God's Oath.* Parenthesis or gap between 69 prophetic weeks and 70th Week, which is still in future. Gap covers entire Church Age; End Time events unfold in final, 70th week.

1439. _____. *Expository Notes on Ezekiel, the Prophet.* 1949. New York: Loizeaux Bros. xiii, 336 p.

Russia covetous of Holy Land resources.

1440. _____. *Not Wrath ... But Rapture: or, Will the Church Participate in the Great Tribulation?* n.d. Neptune, NJ: Loizeaux Bros. 48 p.

Tribulation in future. Any moment Rapture: "blessed hope" must be imminent. Comparison of various verses, looks at various books of Bible for references to Tribulation, destruction of our civilization. "Time of Jacob's Trouble" means Jews suffer primarily, but apostate nations too (but not the Church). Tremendous supernatural afflictions and cataclysmic disasters. Day of Christ = Final Judgment; of the Lord = Tribulation (70th Week) and

Second Coming. Satan's "hinderer" is Holy Spirit, which departs with Church at Rapture. Beast = Roman Prince, makes league with Antichrist, received by Jews as Messiah. Tribulation saints: individual believers but not part of "Body of Christ." Denies that futurist view was merely Ribera's attempt to divert opprobrium from Rome.

1441. *Jacob's Trouble: Gog and Magog at the End of the Age: An Exposition of Ezekiel 38/39.* 1968 [1942]. Bible Fellowship Union. 2nd ed. 31 p. illus.
Reprinted from *Bible Study Monthly.*

1442. Jaggers, O.L. *Flying Saucers.* 1952. Los Angeles: B.N. Robertson. 47 p.
California televangelist.

1443. Jarnes, Peter C. *The Battle of Armageddon.* 1960. rev. ed. [58] p.

1444. Jehle, Friedrich. *Weltschöpfung und Weltvollendung.* 1922. Hamburg: Agentur des Rauhen Hauses. 79 p.
Pre-mill.

1445. Jenkins, Ethel Stout. *The Time of the End.... A Verse by Verse Study of Daniel and the Revelation....* 1944 [1939]. Murfreesboro, TN. 355 p. [244 p] foldout diagr.

1446. Jennett, E. W. *Eschatology: The Doctrine of the Last Things.* 1922. Detroit: Detroit Bible & Tract Depot. 78 p.

1447. Jennings, Frederick, Charles. *The World Conflict in the Light of the Prophetic Word.* 1917 [1915 pref.]. 3rd ed. New York: Our Hope. 173 p.
"Futurist": most of Revelation to occur after Rapture. But the World War suggests some "historicist" interpretation too: "in the present war, *that very end has been reached, and now absolutely nothing remains unfulfilled....*" Revived Roman Empire to arise. Restoration of Jews is aided by War. 6 Seals: A.D. 1-400. 1st-4th Trumpets: end of 5th century. 5th Trumpet: end of 10th century. 6th: 18th century. 1st-5th Vials: early 19th. 6th Vial: present. Iron/clay of Daniel's statue: hybrid democracy and absolutism. Thus probably the war will end in compromise. Rapture: might cause war to end, then provoke nations to form confederation. "Armageddon" means "gathering" of

armies, like WWI. Also wrote *The End of the European War in the Light of Scripture* (1915) and *Satan: His Person, Work, Place and Destiny.*

1448. _____. *The Time of the End: A Criticism.* N.d. New York: C. Gaebelein. 14 p.

1449. Jessop, Harry E. *The Final Counterfeit: Antichrist, Superman, Incarnate Devil.* 1940. Kansas City, MO: Nazarene. 61 p.

1450. _____. *The Day of Wrath, a Study of Prophecy's Light on Today.* 1943. New York: Fleming H. Revell. 119 p. Rev. & enl. ed. of *Final Counterfeit.*
Jessop: dean of Chicago Evangelistic Inst. "Surely hell has opened her mouth and spewed out her most vicious demons." War is "link in a chain of events which only satanic sources could inspire and explain." End of the age — termination of the present world order ending in "fearful disasters," followed by personal reign of Christ. Any-moment Rapture. Then Antichrist as world emperor in Rome. Russia, with Germany and others, will invade Palestine. Then 200-million man Eastern army (China, maybe India too). "Without a doubt, Antichrist is coming...." Coming Roman leader (not Mussolini, but a successor) — Antichrist, the counterfeit Messiah — will offer pact to Jews, leading to Tribulation. Last battle in and around Armageddon (Megiddo). Bible describes aerial bombardments, paratroopers, etc.

1451. Johns, Varner J. *The Secret Rapture and the Antichrist.* 1942. Mountain View, CA: Pacific Press. 95 p. illus.
Seventh-day Adventist. Antichrist = the Pope.

1452. Johnson, Ashley S. *The Resurrection and the Future Life.* 1913. Knoxville: Press of Knoxville Lithographing. 531 p.
Johnson: Tennessee evangelist.

1453. Jones, Russell Bradley. *The Things Which Shall Be Hereafter.* 1947. Nashville: Broadman Press. ix, 186 p.
New Testament always interprets Old — inseparably linked. Strict literalism wrong; predictions can't all be literally interpreted; much is figurative, symbolic.

No gap between 69th and 70th Week. Jews are no longer Chosen People; now under a curse for rejecting Messiah. New Testament does not promise restoration of Israel (adds paragraph in later ed. denying new State of Israel refutes this). God's Chosen are believers in Christ. Promises realized in spiritual realm and in Christ and born-again state. Kingdom began with First Advent. "Binding" of Satan during Millennium is figurative (triumph over Death). Tribulation is past, Millennium is present. *When* of Second Coming is incidental; Armageddon symbolizes active rebellion against Christ. Single bodily resurrection of dead. "All date-setters are wrong."

1454. _____. *The Latter Days.* 1961. Grand Rapids, MI: Baker. ix, 196 p. indexes bibl. refs. (New ed. of 1947 book above.) SEE ALSO 1970+.

1455. Jordan, Willis F. *The Present Great World Crisis.* 1917. Zion City, IL. 102 p. A revision of *The European War from a Bible Standpoint.* 3rd ed. 1918.

1456. Kac, Arthur W. *The Rebirth of the State of Israel: Is It of God Or of Men?* 1976 [1958]. Grand Rapids, MI: Baker Book House. 384 p. Rev. ed.

Kac: physician.

1457. "Kalamos" [pseud. of M.M Wilson]. *Prophetical Suggestions: Being Expository of the Books of Revelation and Daniel.* 1909 [1906]. London: Digby, Long. xvi, 760 p. index, foldout charts.

Historicist interpretation of Revelation (partly figurative, partly literal; refers to ancient Rome and barbarians), but last part is futurist. Denies eternal retribution, Hell. Wicked not resurrected but remain dead. 666 = King Antiochus Epiphanes. Millennium: A.D. 2000. 1920s–50s: Tribulation, 70th Week. Britain = King of South, with Egypt. Russia = King of North; vs. Antichrist (from Rome, ruling over ten feudatory kings). Antichrist defeats both, invades Israel. Satanic false prophet aids Antichrist, works miracles. Jewish-Christians flee, Great Tribulation begins. Antichrist requires subjects receive Mark of Beast and worship him. Rapture, then 7th vial, Second Coming, Armaged-

don (Christ's armies vs. Antichrist's). Denies that Pope is Antichrist.

1458. Kastberger, Francisco. *El Juicio Universal y el Fin del Mundo.* 1968. [Buenos Aires]: Manas. 174 p. bibl.

1459. Kaye, James R. *The Coming Crisis: Are We Approaching the End of the Age?* 1927. Chicago: Buxton-Westerman. 128 p.

1460. Kee, Jack H. *The End of the World.* [1960s?]. Powderly, TX: priv. pub. 48 p.

1461. Keefer, Glen Elgin. *Definite Signs of This Age Closing.* 1925. Westport, CT/Antwerp, OH: G. E. Keefer. 68 p.

1462. Kellogg, Howard W. *The Coming Kingdom and the Re-Canopied Earth.* 1936. Los Angeles: American Prophetic League. 87 p.

Pre-Flood Water Canopy above Earth re-established during Millennium.

1463. Kellogg, Jay C. *The United States in Prophecy and Other Messages.* 1931. Rev. 2nd ed. Chicago: Chicago Gospel Tabernacle. 54 p.

1464. _____. *The Midnight Cry: Do We Face the Golden Age, or the World's Darkest Midnight?* 1932. Tacoma, WA: Whole Gospel Crusaders of America. 54 p.

1465. _____. *A-Millennialism: How Does it Differ from the Pre-Millennial Views?* 1939. Los Angeles: American Prophetic League. 22 p.

1466. Kelly, William. SEE ALSO 1800–1910. *The Prospects of the World.* 1945. London: C.A. Hammond. 39 p.

1467. Keyes, Henry S. 1940 [1937]. *World Peace Through Satan.* 4th ed., rev. Los Angeles: Henry S. Keyes. 65 p.

1468. Kies, Reinhold Friedrich. *Wonders of the Approaching End: Indications and Proofs of the Near Return of the Lord.* 1939. Adelaide: [priv. pub.?]

Each of seven chapters also published as separate booklet.

1469. Kinley, Henry. *Elohim the Archetype Pattern of the Universe* c1961. Los Angeles: Institute of Divine Metaphysical Research. Recently, IDMR members believed End would occur 1996, but no literal Millennium.

1470. Kirban, Salem. *Guide to Survival.* [1968]. Huntingdon Valley, PA: 278 p. illus. bibl.

"How the World Will End." Russia needs to invade for food as prophesied famines cause starvation.

1471. _____. *666.* 1970. Wheaton, IL: Tyndale House. 285 p. photos, charts.

Novel of the Tribulation. Sequel is *1000* (1973). Nuclear-tipped arrows and spears thus preserving biblical literalism. Unspeakable agonies of dying hordes of Russian invaders. Antichrist blasts Mosque of Omar on Jerusalem Temple site with laser. SEE ALSO 1970+.

1472. Knechtle, Emilio B., and Charles J. Sohlmann. *Christ's Message to the Last Generation.* 1971 [1967]. Mountain View, CA: Pacific Press. 160 p.

1473. Knoch, Adolf E. *The Unveiling of Jesus Christ: Commonly Called the Revelation of St. John; With a Revised Concordat Version, Including the Mystery of the Seven Stars, the Mystery of God Finished, the Mystery of Babylon.* 1935. Los Angeles: Concordant Publishing Concern. 591 p.

1474. Knopf, Eugene. *When God Comes Down.* 1959. New York: Pageant Press. 64 p.

1475. Koch, Kurt E. *Day X: The World Situation in the Light of the Second Coming of Christ.* 1969. Berghausen: Evangelisation Publishers. 128 p. Transl. of *Tag X: Die Weltlage im Blick ouf die Widerkunft Jesu* (1968; Berghausen: Evangelisation.)

Includes "Christus Ante Portas; Time is Short; Characteristic Signs of the Present Age: The Dethronement of the White Man; The Decreasing Impulse of Missionary Work; Racial Hatred; The Advance of the Colored Peoples: Ascendancy in the Birth Rate; Ascendancy in Missionary Advance; The Flood of Occultism; The Hunger Catastrophe of the Last Days; Radioactivity and the Fear of the Atom; The Breakdown of Mental Health in the White Race; Natural Disasters; The Breaking Down of Standards: The Break-up of Family Life...." Nearness of Day of the Lord. White race is breaking down, whites declining in influence because Satan wants to destroy Christianity.

"White races are the object of Satan's greatest interest" because they are bearers of Christianity. Flood of occultism, communism, sex, drugs. Nuclear weapons are of "eschatological character." Conditions ripe for coming Antichrist. Israel to be attacked from North (Gog-Magog) but God intervenes. Israel still "smitten with blindness" but Jews will convert.

1476. _____. *World Without Chance?* 1974 [1968] Grand Rapids, MI: Kregel. 96 p. Transl. of *Welt ohne Chance?*

1477. _____. *The Coming One: Israel in the Last Days.* 1972. Grand Rapids, MI: Kregel, 94 p. illus. orig. German.

Stories of divine intervention in the 1967 six-day war, and of Arab-Russian hatred of Israel. Antichrist then the Second Coming: "we are nearer to the time than the world suspects, and nearer even than many Christians care to know." The Return to Israel was the "greatest event in mankind's salvation" since Jesus was on earth. But Israel will suffer fearful woes, then the Gog-Magog invasion from the North. All Israel will convert at the Second Coming. Antichrist is probably a Jewish convert to Bahaism.

1478. Koehler, Anna Lewis. *The Drama of the Ages.* 1941. [Chadron, NB]: priv. pub. 87 p. foldout chart.

1479. Kraemer, Augustus. *Coming, the World's Greatest Crisis.* 1947. Angwin, CA. 163 p. illus.

1480. Kratzer, G[lenn] A. *The End of the Age: A Study of Present World Conditions and a Revelation of Mysteries.* 1917. Chicago: Central Christian Science Inst. 112 p. Rev. ed. pub. Rochester, NY: Liberator (no date).

1481. Kromminga, Diedrich Hinrich. *The Millennium in the Church; Studies in the History of Christian Chiliasm.* Grand Rapids, MI: Eerdmans. 1945. 360 p.

Leans towards premill; covenant theology.

1482. _____. *The Millennium: Its Nature, Function, and Relation to the Consummation of the World.* 1948. Grand Rapids, MI: Eerdmans 121 p.

Second Coming must be emphasized "especially against a false Christianity that thinks its task is to bring about a millennium without Christ" (i.e. post-mill). Historic (non-dispensational) pre-millennialism: appeals to "continuous historical trail which the Apocalypse maps out for us through Christian history...." The Millennium will involve Christianization of the rest of the world. Millennium "is to serve the purpose of *undoing* the amalgamation of the nations": good and evil are now mixed, but humanity will be separated into Gog- Magog peoples and nations of the saints, the former to be wiped out at Armageddon.

1483. "Kueshana, Eklal" [Richard Kieninger]. *The Ultimate Frontier.* 1992 [1962]. Quinlan, TX: Adelphi Org. 285 p.

Written as novel; brotherhood of scientist-philosophers dedicated to preserving civilization. Inspiration for Stelle Group community, Stelle, IL. Universal Wisdom of the ancient Brotherhoods. Lemuria. 1980s: economic and political strife, natural and ecological disasters. Armageddon: a series which began in 1914, ends in 1999. May 5, 2000: cataclysmic reapportionment of earth's land masses. Oct. 2001: a new nation emerges; the Golden Age. Denies chance evolution. Life, mankind created by angels. Kieninger founded Stelle community, but was expelled; he now heads "Builders of the Nation" near Dallas.

1484. Kuyper, Abraham. *The Revelation of St. John.* 1964 [1935]. Eerdmans. 360 p.

Transl. from Dutch; orig. larger part of 4th (last) vol. of Kuyper's *The Consummation of the World.*

1485. Lacy, S.L. *The End of the World: A Comprehensive View of the Meaning and Purpose of Life, Death, the Closing of This Age and Eternity.* 1941. West Point, VA: author. 210 p. illus. bibl.

1486. Ladd, George. *The Blessed Hope.* 1956. Grand Rapids, MI: Eerdmans. 167 p. bibl. refs.

Ladd: Baptist; prof. at Fuller Theological Seminary Second Advent. Historic pre-mill: post-trib. Irenic approach, charitable to both views (pre- and post-trib). Good historical summary of positions; re-

liable source. The "Blessed Hope" is Christ's personal Second Coming, not the Rapture. Pre-trib Rapture *may* be true, but (unlike Second Coming) it is only an inference, and may not occur. Jews will refuse to worship Antichrist, and suffer fearful martyrdom.

1487. Lamb, W[illiam]. *Dark Days and the Signs of the Times.* 1918. Sydney: Australian Baptist Pub. 3rd ed. rev. 283 p.

Also wrote *Great Future Events.*

1488. _____. *The Great Pyramid Witness and Near Eastern Nations: in the Light of Christ's Second Coming.* 1923. [Sydney, Australia: Worker Trustees]. 232 p. illus.

"The time is now right at hand. Nothing else matters." Coming Great War: Gog (= Russia) invades Israel (literal Armageddon), then invades again after Millennium. Job built the Great Pyramid.

1489. _____. *Signs Showing the Return of the Lord to be Near at Hand.* 1929. Sydney: Worker Trustees. 405 p.

1490. _____. *The Wise Shall Understand.* 1932. Sidney, Australia: Worker Trustees. 415 p.

Lamb: editor of *Advent Herald.* Second Coming "very near." End of the Age will come suddenly; End of the World comes later. World tragedy, rise of Antichrist (more terrible than anything the world has ever known), Rapture, Tribulation, Second Coming. 69 weeks, then long gap, then 70th Week (the present).

1491. Lancaster, G.H. *Prophecy, the War and the Near East.* 1919 [1916]. London, New York: Marshall Bros. 272 p. indexes map, foldout chart, bibl.

Lancaster: vicar of St. Stephen's, London; also wrote *The British Empire, the War, and the Jews.* 1934 is Final End of Time of the Gentiles. Historicist: some prophecies fulfilled, some still future. British occupation of Jerusalem discussed in later editions. British Empire: "Davidic Throne." World War *must* have prophetic significance. "Latter Days": all A.D. years. Prophets didn't always understand their own prophecies. Two Little Horns: Islam and Papacy (7th century plus 1,260 years). 2,520 years: four great empires chastising

Israel; Time of Gentiles. "Black indeed is the story of the Papal influence...." Prophecies fulfilled according to solar, lunar, and "calendar" reckonings. Jews persecuted viciously. "Promised Land" = Palestine plus much of East Africa and Near East. "That we are now living in 'the Time of the End' there is no doubt whatever...." Parallel decline of Islam, Papacy. 70 Weeks = 490 years; continuous (no gap). Assyrian = Gog = King of North. Kills ⅔ of Israel, God's People, at Armageddon in final battle. WWI proves British is the true "Christian Empire," greatest ever in the world.

1492. Lang, G[eorge] H[enry]. *Coming Events: An Outline of Bible Prophecy.* 2nd ed. 1988. Miami: Schoettle. 31 p.

Lang: d. 1958. Also wrote *Histories and Prophecies of Daniel.* Partial rapture theory.

1493. ____. *The Revelation of Jesus Christ.* 1945. London: G.H. Lang. 420 p. foldout charts. 1985 reprint ed. Miami Springs: Conley & Schoettle.

Partial Rapture: only faithful, deserving believers raptured initially; other believers raptured later.

1494. Langelett, D.W., and Andreas Bard. *The World-War in the Light of Prophecy.* 1915. Burlington, IA: German Literary Board. Orig. title *Was sagt die Bibel vom Weltkrieg?*

1495. Langston, E.L. *Great Britain, Palestine, Russia, and the Jews.* 1918. London: Charles J. Thynne.

Update of Hoare 1877.

Hails 1917 Balfour Declaration as "beginning of a series of events that are destined to establish God's kingdom here upon earth."

1496. ____. *Ominous Days! or, The Signs of the Times.* 1925 [1914]. London: Thynne & Jarvis. xvi, 213 p. illus.

1497. ____. *The Last Hour.* 1951. London & Worthing: Henry E. Walter. viii, 102 p.

1498. Larkin, Clarence. *Dispensational Truth: or God's Plan and Purpose in the Ages.* 1920 [c1918]. Philadephia: Rev. Clarence Larkin Est. iii, 176 p. plus many charts (unpaged).

Larkin: Baptist. This book, and his others, filled with intricate hand-drawn charts showing order of dispensations, historical and prophesied events.

1499. ____. *The Book of Revelation; a Study of the Last Prophetic Book of Holy Scripture.* 1919. Fox Chase [Philadelphia] PA: C. Larkin. x, [2] 210 p. illus., plates, map.

1500. ____. *The Second Coming of Christ.* 1922. 6th ed. Philadelphia: Rev. Clarence Larkin Estate. 71 p many charts.

Larkin popularized multiple Raptures.

1501. Latimer, David A. *Opening of the Seven Seals and the Half Hour of Silence.* Salt Lake City: Pyramid Press.

Second Coming = 1956 or '58. Latimer earlier prophesied 1936 as End date, but the "Half Hour of Silence" needs to be added. Because biblical "day" = thousand years, this "half-hour" is nearly 20 years. Pyramidology. Armageddon just prior to the Second Coming.

1502. Laughlin, Elsie M. *The Last Frontier; Reflections on a World at the Crossroads of Time.* 1965. New York: Exposition Press. 141 p.

1503. Lawrence, J[ohn] B[enjamin]. *A New Heaven and a New Earth: A Contemporary Interpretation of the Book of Revelation.* 1977 [1960]. Orlando, FL: Christ for the World. 165 p.

1504. Lea, Charles. *World Events in the Light of God's Word.* 1959. New York: Comet Press. 47 p.

1505. Lee, Frederick. *Our Amazing Times: The Challenge and the Meaning of the World-Shaking Happenings of Our Day.* 1947. Nashville: Southern Pub. 96 p. illus.

1506. Lenfest, Edna T. *Revelation for the End of the Gospel Age.* 1965. Sanford, ME: s.n. 132 p.

1507. Leonard, R. Cedric. *Flying Saucers, Ancient Writings and the Bible.* 1969. New York: Exposition Press. 282 p. bibl.

1508. Lewis, C.S. *The World's Last Night.* 1959 [1952]. New York: Harcourt, Brace. 93–113 p.

In title essay, Lewis emphasizes importance of expectation of any-moment Second Coming and Judgment (he does not refer at all to any separate or prior Rapture) as encouraging moral behavior. Argues that denial of this belief is derived from popular belief in evolution as continued progress.

1509. Lewis, Oscar. *The March of the Dictators.* 1933. Long Beach [CA]: Lewis. 46 p.

1510. Lewis, W. Myrddin. *God's Ultimate.* 1969. Eastbourne, England: Prophetic Witness Pub. House. 164 p.

Welsh, Pentecostal, supports divine healing. Many now alive will witness Rapture. Mankind today "more evil and diabolical" than ever. Lewis bewails modern Britain as "Godless and Churchless," and decries appalling collapse of morals. World won't convert. Babylon = modern Rome. Gog = Russia (Rosh). First Beast = leader of communist Russia. 10 Horns = satellite nations of Russia. Antichrist = Man of Sin in Jerusalem, worshipped as God; first of Four Horsemen. Antichrist = False Prophet (head of Rome's false religious system) = Second Beast. 7-year Tribulation (70th Week) will be by far "greatest horror and murderous persecution" of Jews. Literal Tribulation judgments, woes. Will be great revival during Tribulation led by 144,000 converted Jews aided by Two Witnesses (Enoch and Elijah). Antichrist and Jews oppose two Beasts, but Jews revolt against Antichrist. One, not two, invasions. Armageddon at end of Tribulation: all Israel overrun by 200-million-man army led by Russia, includes China (the East); saved by Second Coming, Christ devastates armies, creates giant new valley of Jehoshaphat. Antichrist destroys Rome ("Babylon"). After Armageddon whole earth devastated. Christ rules from Jerusalem. Gog again attacks with world's armies. Earth "completely and utterly destroyed" (not mere purification). Then Last Judgment, Second Resurrection. New Jerusalem will be suspended above Earth. Ridicules "obsolete" theory of evolution.

1511. Lindberg, C.E. *Beacon Lights of Prophecy in the Latter Days.* 1930. Rock Island, IL: Augustan Book Concern. xiv, 256 p.

Lutheran, pre-mill.

1512. Lindberg, Milton. *The Jew and Modern Israel in the Light of Prophecy.* 1930. Chicago: Moody Press. 1969 revision by Archie A. MacKinney.

Lindberg: American Messianic Fellowship; Chicago Hebrew Mission; father of David Lindberg. Russia strengthened hold on Turkey and Persia in WWII.

1513. ____. *Is Ours the Closing Generation of the Age?: An Exposition of Matthew 24.* 1938. Findlay, OH: Fundamental Truth Pub. 39 p.

Orig. a stereopticon lecture. 2nd ed. pub. 1940. Chicago: Chicago Hebrew Mission.

1514. ____. *Gog All Agog: "In the Latter Days": Russia and Palestine in the Light of Ezekiel 38 and 39.* 1953 [1938]. 7th ed. Chicago: Chicago Hebrew Mission. 40 p. [orig. Findlay, OH: Fundamental Truth].

1515. ____. *Jonah: Amazing Parallelisms Between the Story of Jonah and the Prophetic Picture of End-Time Events.* [1960s]. Chicago: American Messianic Fellowship. 32 p.

1516. ____. *The Jews and Armageddon: The Relation of Current News to Coming Events in the Light of Bible Prophecy.* 1968 [1940]. 11th ed. rev. Chicago: American Messianic Fellowship. 40 p.

Exposition of Psalm 2.

1517. Lindsay, Gordon. *The Mystery of the Flying Saucers in the Light of the Bible.* [1950s]. Dallas: Voice of Healing. 88 p.

Lindsay: Pentecostal faith healer, took over Branham's *Voice of Healing* (now *Christ for the Nations*).

1518. ____. *The Antichrists Have Come!* 1965. Dallas: Voice of Healing. 79 p.

Prepared for World Correspondence Course. Includes UFOs as false Messiahs.

1519. ____. *It's Sooner Than You Think!* 1967. Dallas: Christ for the Nations. 32 p. SEE ALSO 1970+.

1520. Lindstrom, Paul D. *Armaged-*

don: The Middle East Muddle. 1967. Mt. Prospect, IL: Christian Liberty Forum. 112 p.

1521. Linton, John. *How Near Is Christ's Coming?* 1946. Philadelphia: Westbrook. 132 p.

1522. _____. *The Battle of the Ages.* [1940s]. Toronto: Livingstone. 16 p.

1523. _____. *Is Modernism the Forerunner of Antichrist?* [1940s]. Philadelphia: J. Linton. 13 p.

1524. _____. *Will Christ Come in the Lifetime of This Generation?* [1940s]. sl: sn. 24 p.

1525. _____. *Will the Church Escape the Great Tribulation?* [1940s]. Riverside, Ontario: John Linton. 96 p.

1526. Loasby, Roland E. *Har-Magedon.* 1950. [S.l. : s.n.]. 26p.

Seventh-day Adventist.

1527. Lockyer, Herbert. *Russians and Romans: or Will the European Crisis Result in the End of the Age?* 1940. Grand Rapids, MI: Zondervan. 28 p. illus. Reprint from *Grace and Truth* (Denver Bible Inst.).

1528. _____. *Cameos of Prophecy: Are These the Last Days!* 1942. Grand Rapids, MI: Zondervan. 128 p.

Lockyer: editor of *Christian Digest.* Pre-trib. "We live in a world of collapse....The floodgates of Hell are open. Iniquity abounds." World needs "revival of first-century Christianity." 6,000 Year theory: Creation 4004 B.C., Seven-Year Tribulation starts 1989. Satan now very active knowing little time is left; dictators are "demon-possessed." Russia will defeat Germany in this war (WWII) even though on the verge of collapse. Jews will survive Hitler and return to Israel. Post-war planning futile because Russia will lead Northern Federation, and Great Britain (maybe with U.S.) will join revived Roman Empire. Antichrist will then foment further war. Armageddon even worse than WWII. Condemns increasing freedom of women (wartime work), comparing it to women living with evil angels in Genesis 6.

1529. _____. *The H-Bomb and the End of the Age.* 1950. Grand Rapids, MI: Zondervan. 32 p.

1530. _____. *The Thousand Year Reign of Christ.* 1958. Grand Rapids, MI: Zondervan. 30 p. SEE ALSO 1970+.

1531. Logsdon, S. Franklin. *Profiles of Prophecy.* 1970 [1964]. Grand Rapids, MI: Zondervan [orig. pub. Bowdon].

"One bright, golden, fast-approaching daybreak, all divine plans will be fulfilled, all things will be made right."

1532. _____. *Is the U.S.A. in Prophecy?* 1974 [1968]. rev. ed. Grand Rapids, MI : Zondervan. 98 p.

Dispensational pre-trib. Antichrist = Beast = World Dictator. Two Prophetic Babylons: political (national) and ecclesiastical. Harlot: organized world religion, ecclesiastical Babylon. Antichrist kills Harlot. U.S. = prophetic Babylon. Babylon destroyed first half of Tribulation. Then Russia "supernaturally disposed of" when it invades Israel and Egypt, opposed by 10-Nation confederacy. Antichrist is wounded this conflict, then resurrected. SEE ALSO 1970+.

1533. Longley, Arthur. *The International Situation in Prophecy.* 1941. London: Victory Press. 58, [2] p.

1534. _____. *Christ's Return to the World.* 1965. Yorkshire, England: Hamilton, OH: Expositor Publications. Inspired word. 114 p. bibl. refs.

Also wrote *Heaven on Earth* (the Second Coming).

1535. *The Loud Cry of the Gospel of the Kingdom: The Last Warning Before the End of this World.* 1930. Montreal: The Loud Cry. various pagings.

1536. Lovett, C[ummings] S[amuel]. *Jesus Is Coming: Get Ready Christian!* 1981 [1969]. Baldwin Park, CA: Personal Christianity. 127 p. illus.

Retired Air Force chaplain; president of Personal Christianity. The Rapture, a worldwide "trumpet blast," will be "some day soon...." SEE ALSO 1970+.

1537. Lowry, Oscar, Rev. *The Second Coming of Christ.* 1940 [1936]. Chicago, IL: Bible Institute Colportage Association 36 p.

Pentecostal; also wrote sex books, book on Hell and who's going there.

1538. MacArthur, Harry H., et al.

The Rapture: Our Lord's Coming for His Church. 1940. American Prophetic League.

1539. McBirnie, William Steuart. *50 Progressive Messages on the Second Coming of Christ.* 1940. Norfolk, VA: McBirnie Publications. xv, 474 p.

McBirnie: Southern Baptist minister.

1540. _____. *Mussolini is the Anti-Christ.* 1940. Fremont, NE: McBirnie Publications Association. 65 p. illus.

1541. _____. *50 Progressive Messages from Armageddon to New Earth.* 1944. 2nd ed. Norfolk, VA: McBirnie Publications.

1542. _____. *What the Bible Says About Mussolini.* 1944. Norfolk, VA: McBirnie Publications Assoc. 122 p.

1543. _____. *World War III and the United States.* [1965]. Glendale, CA: Community Churches of America. 48 p. illus. 1979 ed. Dallas: Chaplain Ray.

1544. _____. *What the Soviets Will Do Next in the Middle East.* n.d. Community Churches of America. 54 p. SEE ALSO 1970+.

1545. McClain, Alva J. *The Four Great Powers of the End Time and Their Final Conflicts.* 1938. Los Angeles: American Prophetic League. 24 p.

McClain: Brethren minister; founder and president of Grace Theological Seminary. (Winona Lake, IN). King of South = Britain, which is allied with Russia; vs. Italy

1546. _____. *Daniel's Prophecy of the Seventy Weeks.* 1970 [1940]. 6th ed. Grand Rapids, MI: Zondervan. 62 p. [1969 Winona Lake, IN: B M H Books. 73 p. chart.]

Popularization of Anderson's *Coming Prince* exposition. Dedicated to L. Bauman. "Indispensable chronological key to all New Testament prophecy." 70 Weeks of years, beginning March 14, 445 B.C. (rebuilding of Jerusalem). 69th Week ends April 6, A.D. 32 (Jesus revealed as Prince of Israel). Great Parenthesis before 70th Week; Messiah "cut off," Church Age intervenes. Makes exact date-setting of End impossible, but provides "exact chronological framework" for events of Revelation 6–19, the 7 year Tribulation. Antichrist to arise from Ten Horn Roman Empire of End-Time, rules world, makes 7 year covenant with Israel to protect from Russia. Two Witnesses killed midpoint of Tribulation; Antichrist then begins terrible persecution of Israel, and demands he be worshipped (the Abomination of Desolation).

1547. McCrossan, T[homas] J. *The World's Crisis and the Coming Christ.* 1934. Seattle: author. viii, 245 p.

Pre-trib. Failure of U.N. prophesied in Luke. Second Coming this generation. Holy Spirit protecting the Church. When Church is raptured away, the Holy Spirit will attend to believers converted during the Tribulation.

1548. McDougall, Duncan. *The Rapture of the Saints.* 1970 [1962]. Blackwood, NJ: O.F.P.M. 63 p. bibl. refs. Orig. pub. Vancouver: British Israel Assoc.

McDougall: Free Church minister. "A Documented Exposé of the Future Antichrist Story," from lectures in Vancouver.

1549. McFeeters, J[ames] C[alvin]. SEE ALSO 1800–1910. *The New Heaven and the New Earth.* 1926. Boston: Christopher Publishing House. 67 p.

Reformed Presbyterian Church of North America.

1550. McGee, J. Vernon. *Reveling Through Revelation.* 1962. Pasadena: Thru the Bible Books. 2 vols. bibl.

McGee: Presbyterian minister. Orig. notes for Bible Study group at McGee's Church of the Open Door, Los Angeles.

1551. _____. *He is Coming Again.* 1963. S.l.: s.n. 23 p.

1552. _____. *Thru the Bible* (5 vols). 1981–1983 [1975]. Nashville: Thomas Nelson.

Based on McGee's radio program. SEE ALSO 1970+.

1553. MacGregor, Daniel, and Margaret MacGregor. *The Time of the End.* [1920s?] S.l.: s.n. 25 p. illus.

Mormon.

1554. McKay, Edward James. *Prophecies, Warnings and Instructions in View of End-Time Events and New-Age Conditions.* 1938. Dunn, NC: s.n. 40 p.

Apocalyptic poetry

1555. _____. *The Final Antichrist*

and World Government: His Words, Actions, Reign and End. 1952. Dunn, NC: [Pope Printing Co.?]. 7 p.

1556. McKee, Gus. *Time Cycles in the Bible.* Los Angeles: Free Tract Soc.

End 1931–38. 6,000 years allotted for world.

1557. McPherson, Aimee Semple. *The Second Coming of Christ: Is He Coming? How Is He Coming? When Is He Coming? For Whom Is He Coming?* 1921. Los Angeles: A. McPherson. 120 p. 1 plate.

McPherson: Pentecostal evangelist, Los Angeles; founded Foursquare Gospel Church. (In 1926 claimed she was abducted by evil conspiracy.)

1558. _____. *Behold! Thy King Cometh.* 1925. n.p. 64 p.

1559. _____. *The Last Days.* 1945 [1935]. Los Angeles: Bridal Call. 2 p.

1560. _____. *The Zero Hour.* 1984. Los Angeles: Foursquare Publications. Cassette.

Recorded sermons (McPherson d. 1944). Impending World War heralds Second Advent and Judgment Day.

1561. McPherson, Norman. *Triumph Through Tribulation.* 1944. Otego, NY: author. 77 p.

1562. MacTyre, Paul. *Doomsday 1999.* 1962. New York: Ace Books. 158 p.

1563. Mancuso, Peter. *The Outcome of This Conflict and Russia's Destiny.* 1943. Valley Park, Sherman Oaks, CA : Peter Mancuso. 77 p.

1564. Mankamyer, Orlin Leroy. *The Signs of the Times, the Return of the Jews, the Restoration of Palestine, and the Battle of Armageddon.* 1947. [Sandpoint, Idaho: priv. pub.] 63 p.

"World War One and World War Two were just child's play" compared to imminent Armageddon. Atomic weapons, radiation sickness, bacteriological warfare. "Fatal wound that healed" is totalitarian dictatorship. Hitler and Mussolini are gone, but totalitarianism is stronger than ever under Stalin. Harlot Church = papacy.

1565. Manker, Dayton A. *They That Remain: A Story of the End Times.* 1941. Grand Rapids, MI: Zondervan. 229 p.

Fiction. SEE ALSO 1970+.

1566. Marsh, F[rederick] E[dward]. *Why Will Christ Come Back?* [ca. 1918]. London: Advent Testimony Movement 152 p.

1567. _____. *What Will Take Place When Christ Returns?* 1919. 2d ed. London: Charles J. Thynne. 221 p. 3rd ed. 1931.

"The prophetic word will be verified.... The sleeping and living saints will be unified.... Believers will be glorified.... The saints will be classified.... Israel will be vivified.... Hell will be stultified.... Mankind will be pacified.... Creation will be gratified.... The earth will be beautified.... The Holy Spirit will be justified.... Christ will be satisfied.... The Father will be magnified."

1568. Marsh, Joseph. *The Bible Doctrine: or True Gospel Faith Concerning the Gathering of Israel, the Personal Coming of Christ, Resurrection, Renovation of the Earth, Kingdom of God, and Time of the Second Advent of Christ.* 1849. Rochester, NY: Advent Harbinger and Bible Advocate Office. 64 p.

1569. Marshall, James, and Margaret Scott Marshall. *1960: (A Retrospect).* 1919. Los Angeles: J.F. Rowny. 96 p.

WWI was a "mere drop" compared to "coming annihilation," but this terrible holocaust will be followed by wonderful new era for survivors.

1570. Martin, Cora. *The World's Last Dictator.* 1943. Sl.:s.n. x, 343 p. plates, illus.

1571. Martin, James. *The End of the World: Coming Struggle Among the Nations.* N.d. London: Martin, Boundy. 15 p.

Includes a "correct copy of the will of Peter the Great" and "opinion of Napoleon on the Turkish crisis."

1572. Marystone, Cyril [pseud.?]. *The Coming Type of the End of the World and the Universal Conversion of the Nations.* 1963. Beirut. viii, 370 p. bibl.

1573. _____. *Grave and Urgent Warnings from Heaven: The Communist World Revolution and the Intermediate Coming of the Messiah.* No copyright [1970s] s.l.: s.n.

1574. Mason, W.A. *Signs of the*

Times. 1911. Snellman, GA: priv. pub. 52 p.

6,000 years for world. Apostasy, corruption, and evangelism indicate End is near. Also wrote *The Great Tribulation.*

1575. Masselink, William. *Why Thousand Years?: Or, Will the Second Coming Be Pre-Millennial?* 1953. Grand Rapids, MI: Eerdmans. 4th ed. 222 p.

Also wrote *Chiliasm* (1923 Th.D. thesis, Southern Baptist Theological Seminary).

1576. Mattison, James. *Prophecies of the End of the World.* 1962. Oregon, IL: Restitution Herald.

From radio broadcasts. Egypt, Libya, Iran ally with Russia against Israel. Russia invades but disastrously defeated. Armageddon is later rebellion of China against Russia.

1577. _____. *Signs of Jesus' Coming and of the End of the World.* 1967. Oregon, IL: Restitution Herald. [6] p.

"Watch the Common Market!" Ethiopia, Libya, and China as End Time invaders.

1578. Mauro, Philip. *God's Present Kingdom.* 1919. Boston / New York / Chicago: Hamilton Bros. / Revell. 270 p. scripture index. Appendix "The World War: How It is Fulfilling Prophecy" also pub. separately.

Mauro: lawyer; initially dispensationalist; later rejected dispensationalism.

1579. _____. *The Seventy Weeks and the Great Tribulation: A Study of the Last Two Visions of Daniel, and of the Olivet Discourse of the Lord Jesus Christ.* 1988 [1923]. Reprint of 1944 rev. ed. Sterling, VA: Grace Abounding Ministries. 279 p.

70 Weeks consecutive from Cyrus's decree to end of Christ's ministry on earth. Jesus crucified middle of 70th Week; covenant is Christ's. Then 40 years probation for Israel til its destruction A.D. 70: the Great Tribulation. "He" of Dan. 9:27 = Christ, not Antichrist. Latter Days = final years of Jewish history; End Times = last years, extinction of Jewish national existence. Abomination of Desolation = Roman armies besieging Jerusalem. Impossible to date Second Coming. Future

Tribulation and End too, but different than above.

1580. _____. *How Long to the End?* 1927. Boston: Hamilton Bros. 64 p.

League of Nations being made into Superstate because of Red and Yellow menaces (Communist and Oriental).

1581. _____. *Of Things Which Soon Must Come to Pass.* 1972 [1933]. Swengel, PA: Reiner. xxviii, 623. Orig. 1933, Eerdmans. Expanded version of 1925 work *The Patmos Visions.* Also 1990 reprint: Sterling, VA: GAM.

"General abandonment of futurist position, with spiritualized Millennium." Millennium = spiritual triumph of martyrs now reigning with Christ.

1582. _____. *The Last Call to the Godly Remnant: A Study of the Five Messages of Haggai.* 1976. Swengel, PA: Reiner Publications. 64 p.

1583. Mawson, J. T. *Jerusalem: The Coming Metropolis of the Earth; Her Sins, Sorrows and Saviour.* 2nd ed. [1905?] Newcastle-on- Tyne : Northern Counties Bible and Tract Depot. 120 p.

Pre-trib. Imperial Beast (leader of Ten-Nation confederacy based in Rome) and Antichrist persecute Jews. Jerusalem invaded from North and South, then armies of East and West collide there.

1584. Maxwell, Arthur. *History's Crowded Climax.* 1940. Mountain View, CA: Pacific Press. 160 p. illus.

Editor of Seventh-day Adventist *Signs of the Times.* "Suddenly, in the midst of the brilliant civilization of the twentieth century, all the worst attributes of humanity have come to the front; all the most evil passions have been unleashed; all the evil spirits some thought were exorcised centuries ago have returned sevenfold, more loathsome and diabolical than of old." Previously wrote *Looking Beyond World Problems* (1923), *Great Issues of the Age* (1927), *This Mighty Hour* (1933), *These Tremendous Times* (1938).

1585. _____. *So Little Time: The Atom and the End.* 1949 [1946]. Singapore: Malayan Signs Press. [156] p. illus. 5th ed.

Published in other East Asian languages too, as are many of Maxwell's works.

1586. _____. *Time's Last Hour.*
1948. Mountain View, CA: Pacific Press.
96 p. illus.

1587. _____. *Time Running Out:
New Evidence of Approaching Climax.*
1963. Mountain View, CA: Pacific Press
116 p. illus.

Catholic Church mortally wounded
in 1798, but then healed, starting with
Mussolini, and now undergoing amazing
revival. Catholics are behind Common
Market and will try to reunify Europe.
But "Great Second Advent Movement"
will spread like lightning during Last
Days, dedicated to keeping proper Seventh-Day Sabbath, and publishing a lot.
Second Coming: a "vast, spectacular
pageant," cities collapse, most people destroyed, faithful dead resurrected from
sleep of death, living saints "translated."
Followed by a glorious life free from all
ills. Also wrote *Great Prophecies for Our
Time* (1943), *The Coming King* (1953).

1588. _____. *This Is the End.* 1967
Mountain View, CA: Pacific Press. 96 p.
illus.

1589. Messenger, F[rank] M. *The
Time of the End: or Book of Revelation.* 1925.
Kansas City, MO: Nazarene. 192 p. illus.

Nazarene. Dispensational pre-mill,
imminent Rapture. Now "very near to the
midnight hour of the six thousandth year
period of the world's existence" so Millennium must be close. Six Day creation
"leads us to the general belief that the duration of the earth in its present form will
last seven of God's thousand year days, the
first six thousand to represent the six
working days of God's creation, and the
seventh thousand year day represents
earth's sabbath of rest on the glorious millennium...." Christ predicted global war
like WWI would mark start of End. Antichrist system being set up by atheist
communists. Book of Revelation in two
parts: "things to come shortly" (already
fulfilled), and those still in future. Recent
earthquakes in Japan killed half million,
but because of God no missionaries among
the dead. Ten Tribes incorporated into
north and west Europeans and Americans.
Half hour pause before Trumpet judg-

ments of Revelation = 21+ years according
to year-day theory, thus renewed horrors
to begin 1939. Antichrist will beguile
world into accepting him as leader. False
Prophet's animated statue of the Beast will
be as yet unknown combination of radio
and cinema technology (i.e. television):
"Who can say that the time is not near
when we may sit and not only listen, but
see the actor as he delivers his speech although thousands of miles distant?"

1590. Meyers, Cecil K. *The World
in Preparation.* 1927. Mountain View, CA:
Pacific Press. 128 p. illus.

Seventh-day Adventist. New weapons
(airplanes, etc.) and increased missionary
activity as signs of End. 69 Weeks from
457 B.C. to A.D. 27; 70th Week to A.D. 34.
2,300 "Days" from 457 B.C. to 1844.

1591. Michael, Cecil. *Round Trip to
Hell in a Flying Saucer.* 1955. New York:
Vantage Press. 61 p. illus. Also pub 1971 in
New Zealand.

1592. Middleton, R. *Not Far Off:
The Gathering Signs of Christ's Speedy Re-
turn.* [1919?]. 3rd ed. London: Jarrold &
Sons. 101 p.

1593. Miles, F[rederic] J. *Even at
the Doors: The Coming King and the Coming Kingdom.* 1936. London: Marshall,
Morgan & Scott. vi, 144 p. index.

1594. _____. *Russia and Palestine in
Prophecy.* 1942. 4th enlarged ed. Chicago:
Russian Missionary Soc. 28 p. bibl. refs.

1595. _____. *Prophecy, Past, Present
and Prospective.* 1943. Grand Rapids, MI:
Zondervan 143 p.

Pre-trib pre-mill. Jews returning to
Palestine. Gog-Magog and Rosh = Rus-
sia; to ally with Germany (Gomer) and
Turkey (Togormah) and invade Palestine.
Russian hosts slaughtered, then Second
Coming, Millennium. Russian invasion
may be a counterattack triggered by an at-
tempt by Mussolini to seize Palestine.
Signs of End include massive famines in
China and Russia, 1920 Chinese and 1923
Japanese earthquakes, and Communist
and Nazi religious persecution.

1596. _____. *The Horsemen Are
Riding.* 1947. London: Marshall, Morgan
& Scott. 96 p.

1597. Milholland, John H.E. *Two Signs of the End Time: Daniel's Prediction of the Scientific Age and Rapid Transit Development....* 1918. New York: Our Hope. 33 p.

Delivered at Prophetic Conf., Carnegie Hall, 1918.

1598. *The Millennium Manifested.* N.d. London: Sovereign Grace Advent Testimony. Various pagings. bibl. refs.

"An answer to the post-millennial, a-millennial and anti-millennial theories." E. Kirk, B.W. Newton, R.L. Wheeler, Percy W. Heward, G.H. Fromow, Frank H. Kingsbury, H.G. Harvey, James Payne, Frank H. White, Herman Newmark, Jack Barkey, B.G. Wheatley, W.J. Rowlands, A.I. Burch. Sovereign Grace Advent Testimony published journal *Watching and Waiting* ("Perilous Times").

1599. Miller, Samuel Martin, and Halvar G. Randolph. *The Word of Prophecy.* 1937. Minneapolis: Lutheran Bible Inst. iv, 172 p.

Presents four main interpretations: idealist, preterist, historical, futurist. Unclear whether Millennium is Church, or will follow Second Advent; Lutherans have espoused both views. Author favors premill. Quotes other pre-mill Lutherans. Rapture, then public personal Coming. Antichrist appears earlier, Tribulation. End is near: increasing signs, especially feverish war preparations.

1600. Milligan, E[zra] M. *Is the Kingdom Age at Hand?.* 1924. New York: George H. Doran. xii, 354 p.

1601. Moeller van den Bruck, Arthur. *Das Dritte Reich.* 1922. Authorized English ed. titled *Germany's Third Empire* (1971 [1934]; New York: H. Fertig).

Prophesies a great imperial future for Germany, which will arise from the cataclysmic defeat of the Great War (WWI). Draws on tradition of Joachim's Third Age; popularized term Third Reich prior to Hitler's rise. Dismisses materialist science (including evolution) as inadequate.

1602. Moffett, J.W. *The Second Coming of Christ: The Great Tribulation, Battle of Armageddon, and Signs of His Coming, from a Lawyer's Standpoint.* 1925. Abilene, TX. 75 p.

1603. Mohr, Viktor. *Katastrophen und Menschheitsschicksal.* 1962. [Bietigheim, Germany]: Lorber. 14 p.

Pseud. "M. Kahir." Biblical prophecies. Also wrote *Nahe an Zweitausend Jahre.*

1604. Montgomery, G[ranville] H. 1963. *I Predict: Things Which Must Shortly Come to Pass.* 5th ed. Wichita, KS: Mertmont. 63 p.

1605. Morris, A[lvin] M[arion]. *The Prophecies Unveiled: or, Prophecy a Divine System.* 1952 [1914]. Rosemead, CA: Old Paths Book Club. xvi, 496 p. diagr. Reprint ed. [orig. 1914; Winfield, KS: Courier Press].

Largely a refutation of Battenfield 1914.

1606. Morrison, H[enry] C[lay]. *The World War in Prophecy: The Downfall of the Kaiser and the End of the Dispensation.* 1917. Louisville, KY: Pentecostal Publishing Co. 5th ed. [orig. ed. same year]. 128 p. [2nd ed. 95 p.].

Morrison: evangelical/pentecostal minister. Dispensational. The World War (One) is Satan's last effort to gain world control, using the Kaiser, the immediate forerunner of Antichrist. Rapture and Great Tribulation about to occur.

1607. Mountain, James. *British-Israel Truth Defended, a Reply to the Rev. Samuel Hinds Wilkinson.* 1926. London: Covenant Pub. viii, 225 p.

Prophecies historically fulfilled, still being fulfilled (now by Great Britain).

1608. Munro, Clayton A. *The Kingdom and Coming of Christ: A Study of Millennialism.* 1919. Boston: Richard G. Badger. vi, 316 p.

1609. Murray, George Lewis. *Millennial Studies: A Search for Truth.* 1972 [1948]. Grand Rapids, MI: Baker 207 p. bibl. refs.

A-mill; argues against pre-millennialism.

1610. Nagel, Sherman A. *John the Baptist, a Type: A Message to All Who Proclaim the Second Advent of Christ and Profess to Belong to the Remnant.* 1935. [Beaverton, OR: author]. 141 p.

1611. _____. *The Little Time of*

Trouble: A Word Picture of What is Soon Coming. [Loma Linda, CA :] author. 84 p.

1612. Naish, Reginald T. *The Midnight Hour and After!* 1928 [1920]. 7th ed. London: Charles J. Thynne & Jarvis. ix, 244 p.

World War (One) ended on eleventh hour (Armistice signed 11 PM 11/11/18), eleven days after Turks driven out of Syria, a prophesied sign of the End. Prophetic "day" is a thousand years, so "hour" is 15 years; Armistice is start of "Last Hour" before Second Coming and Millennium, ending Nov. 11, 1933. Rev. 8:1 "half hour of silence" before 7th Seal = 7½ years from 1919. Anti-evolution. 6,000 Year theory. Creation 4000 B.C.; God promised Palestine to Abraham in 1917 B.C. 747 B.C. + 2,520 = 1774 (Islam receives first great blow); 606 B.C. + 2,520 = 1914 (start of World War); 587 B.C. + 2,520 = 1934: the end of the Time of the Gentiles, so Rapture "very imminent." Also natural disasters and heavenly signs since 1917. Postwar Council of Ten of monarchical and republican nations (iron and clay mix). 1934 also start of 70th Jubilee period. 1943 is 57 years short of 6,000 years since Creation, but God shortened the days "for the sake of the elect." World War prophesied in Jer., Hag., and Zech., but Armageddon yet to come: Russian attack on British-sponsored Jewish state of Israel. Then the Millennium. Tarshish: England and colonies, including U.S.

1613. _____. *The Last Call: or, The Trumpet Shall Sound.* 1935. London: Thynne. 240 p.

Sequel to above book: beginning of the predestined "hour." The World War was the "last great Trumpet Blast to the world announcing the approach Return of the King of Kings to this earth!" 2,520 Years after Jeremiah's prophecy. 6,000-year history of world indicates time remaining before the Second Coming. Jews now returning; strange signs in the skies; economic depression. Gog = Russia. Believers raptured prior to "that ghastly struggle." "First-fruits" raptured first, then other Christians. Also wrote *Spiritual Arithmetic.*

1614. Nee, Watchman. *Aids to "Revelation."* 1983. New York: Christian Fellowship Publishers. 122 p.

1615. Neff, Merlin L. *Our Exploding Age.* 1959. Mountain View, CA: Pacific Press. 45 p. illus.

1616. Neighbour, Ralph E. *The Out-Resurrection and the Prize of the Up-Calling.* 1930. Elyria, OH: McMillen-Neighbour. 37 p.

1617. Nelson, Nels L[ars]. *The Second War in Heaven as Now being Waged by Lucifer Through Hitler as a Dummy.* 1941. Independence, MO: Press of Zion's Printing and Pub. 296 p.

Also wrote *Scientific Aspects of Mormonism.* Stresses pre-existence of souls. Lucifer's Revolt was first cosmic war; World War II is second. Nazis are "sub-human" agents of Satan; Hitler is literally possessed by demons who "antedate the solar system." Millennium will follow this war.

1618. Newell, William R. *The Church and the Great Tribulation.* 1933. Chicago: Scripture Press. 31 p.

1619. _____. *The Book of the Revelation.* 1994 [1935]. Kregel. ix, 404 p. Orig. 1935, Chicago: Scripture Press; also pub. Chicago: Grace; Chicago: Moody.

Verse-by-verse commentary; strongly futurist, pre-mill. Church judged unworthy by Christ; seals trumpets, vials follow; Second Coming, Great Day of Wrath, Millennial reign; Satan loosed, defeated, heavens and earth destroyed; Great White Throne Judgment of non-saints; New Creation. "Whatever judgments fall, they do *not* fall on the saints, the Body of Christ!"— believers are raptured prior to Tribulation. Rejects "historical" interpretation of Rev.; judgment is "imminent" "'The time is at hand' should be in the heart of every believer, every day!" Seven churches represent historical periods and spiritual states up to the End. Parousia, then 3½ years of Great Tribulation, then "public" Second Coming. Christ "must have come *for* His saints in order to come *with* them." Bible says "at least seven years between His coming *for* His Church and His coming *with* them." Denounces "Romanism." Third of Earth burning up "will occur literally!" Fire and brimstone plagues "*must* be literal — there is no possible escape *if we believe the Bible true at all!*" Sorcery prophesied for Last Days refers to drug abuse. First and Second Beast: Antichrist and his prophet. That many names fit 666 shows Satan ceaselessly trying to put plan in action. 666 deliberately used for "advertising commercial products!" Tribulation judgments occur before Day of Wrath (Second Coming), though some verses describing them occur afterwards. 10 Horns = ten (historical) kings (not present/future kingdoms). Armageddon: "direct warfare of hell against heaven"; forces led by Antichrist; just before Second Coming. Millennium: personal reign of Christ. Literal New Jerusalem, parked above Old. Revelation is "unsealed book" — symbolic only where so stated. Church will escape Tribulation.

1620. Nicklin, J. Bernard. *The Great Tribulation.* 1941. London: Covenant. 167 p. index.

Based on 1936 British-Israel World Federation Conference. Hitler = Beast; Second Beast = Mussolini. Tanks, planes, torpedo boats, paratroops in Bible. "Nazi-Rosh league" = King of North. Israel = England (inc. Commonwealth and U.S.) = merchants of Tarshish. Great Tribulation directed against Jews in Palestine. Present war (WWII) "exactly fits in with Daniel's prophecy."

1621. Norris, Harold. *When Will Our Lord Return? Prophetic Times and Warning Events.* 1915 [1914]. London: Charles J. Thynne. 125 p.

Also wrote: *The Millennium: When?*

1622. _____. *The End of the Age, How and When?* 1932. Bath, England: Advent Herald Pub. House. 80 p.

Seven Dispensations. All believers raptured. Euphrates dried up: Ottoman Empire abolished (1923). The World War is either Armageddon or first stage of it. King of North: Japan; also coming "Yellow Plague" — Mongol confederation. 568 B.C. + 2,520 Years = 1953. 1915, 1934, 1953, 1972 as decisive years. 1972 proba-

bly End (A.D. 647 + 1,335 Years; also other calculations from Daniel's dream).

1623. Ober, Douglas. *The Great World Crisis.* 1950. Wheaton, IL: Van Kampen. 141 p.

Rosh = Russia, citing 5th cent. Proclus. Two invasions by Gog, neither one is Armageddon.

1624. Ockenga, Harold John. *Bible Prophecy and the End Times.* 1967. s.l.: s.n. 28 p.

Sermons preached in Boston; Congregational. Post-trib pre-mill.

1625. Oilar, Forrest Loman. *Be Thou Prepared, for Jesus Is Coming.* 1937. Boston: Meador. 356 p.

Prophecy novel, based largely on Blackstone. The Kolzon family: converted Jews in the U.S.; son and daughter go to Israel. The Rapture causes worldwide chaos: cars and planes crash as occupants disappear; headlines scream: "EXTRA! THE CHURCH OF LIVING GOD RAPTURED FROM THE EARTH TO GLORY." Revived Roman Empire led by Antichrist. Jews return to Palestine in unbelief. Two Witnesses — Elijah and Enoch — perform miracles in Jerusalem, preach against Antichrist. 144,000 Jewish witnesses horribly persecuted. Satan expelled from heaven, savagely attacks Jews. False Prophet, a Jew, uses TV and radio to promote Antichrist. Daughter taken on tour of Hell, then accepts martyrdom. Mark of Beast required. Horrible Tribulation plague transmitted by cigarettes. King of South (Egypt) rebels, crushed by Antichrist. Then Northern Kingdom (Russia) attacks, then East with 200-million man airborne army. All forces collide at Armageddon; immense slaughter of all armies as Christ returns. Many long descriptions of tortures undergone by courageous believers who secretly maintain faith, memorized forbidden Bible, resist Mark and Antichrist. Also dwells on certainty of eternal punishment for non-believers.

1626. Oliver, French E. *Signs of the Times.* [1914]. Los Angeles: Biola Book Room. 15 p.

Pre-trib secret Rapture.

1627. Olson, Arnold T. *Inside Jerusalem: City of Destiny.* 1968. Glendale, CA: Regal Books (G/L). 241 p. illus. map.

President of Evangelical Free Church. 1967 War as Sign of End. "The Temple will be rebuilt. Israel has the will, access to the means, and now the site."

1628. Orr, William W. *A Simple Picture of the Future: A Dispensationalist View.* [1957?]. Wheaton, IL: Scripture Press. 32 p. bibl. refs.

1629. _____. *Antichrist, Armageddon and the End of the World.* 1960. Temple City, CA: William W. Orr. 32 p.

1630. Osgood, Dewitt S. *The Midnight Cry: Radio Sermons Featuring Prophecy in the News and Vital Bible Truth.* [ca. 1950]. 12 vols. Priv. pub.

Indianapolis, Chicago, Seattle, and Tacoma radio broadcasts. Seventh day Adventist.

1631. Osterhus, C. S. *How Long to the End?: When Did Jesus Say He Would be Back to Earth Again?* N.d [ca 1930]. 8th ed. [Minneapolis: s.n.] 16 p.

From 1926 sermons. 2,520 Years of Gentile Age from A.D. 604 (Omar's mosque on Jerusalem Temple site) to 1917 (General Allenby's entrance into Jerusalem).

1632. Overly, E.R. *The Second Coming of Jesus.* [1950s]. Louisville, KY: Herald Press. 50 p.

1633. Pache, Rene. *The Return of Jesus Christ.* 1955. Chicago: Moody Press. 448 p. Abridged ed. 1975; 246 p. Transl. by William LaSor.

Also wrote *The Future Life* (1962, Chicago: Moody). Antichrist = Sea Beast.

1634. _____. *Notes Sur le Prophete Daniel.* 1970. Vennes sur Lausanne: Editions "Emmaus." 109 p. Also wrote *La Desitinee d'Israel* (1969).

1635. Panacea Society. *Who is Joanna Southcott? What is Her Ark or Box?* [1930s]. Bedford [England]: The Panacea Society. Tract.

1636. _____. *The "Whosoever" Religion.* [1930s]. Bedford [England]: Panacea Society at their Garden Press. [4] p.

Approaching "end of unhappy conditions in the world: last religion for the last times."

1637. Pankhurst, Christabel. "*The Lord Cometh": The World Crisis Explained.* New York: The Book Stall. 115 p. Rev. ed. 1934.

"The Battle of Armageddon is as literal a fact of the history of the immediate future as the Battle of Waterloo and the Marne are facts of past history."

1638. _____. *Pressing Problems of the Closing Age.* [1924]. London: Morgan & Scott. viii, 194 p.

Pankhurst: former suffragist activist; here says suffrage won't help — campaign was "political childhood," a Utopian dream. Should look instead to the Second Coming. Tribulation in effect since 1914. "At any moment there may be announced some new discovery that will give the nations an unimaginable power to destroy — that will seem to put the very heavens at their mercy." It will be used at Armageddon.

1639. _____. *The World's Unrest: Visions of the Dawn.* [1926?]. New York: Harper. vii, 232 p.

Now "eve of Lord's return." Human leadership inadequate; divine ruler needed to save us. Iron/clay mix = Bolshevism and Fascism. Antichrist to come from Roman Empire. Italy under Mussolini is a reconstituted Roman Empire. Italy probably to form union with France to oppose Germany; Italy trying to get England to join too. North Africa, Turkey, Near East also part of Antichrist's Roman Empire. Antichrist makes seven year pact with Jews. Science now breaking laws of nature; thus not immutable. Heaven may be in fourth dimension. New physics of Einstein, Rutherford proving creation true, evolution false. Natural disasters increasing. Civilizations all die. Cataclysmic end with explosive disasters prophesied. Also wrote *Seeing the Future* (anti-evolutionist).

1640. Panton, D[avid] M[orrison]. *The Apocalypse of the Lord (Revelation XIX).* 1922. London: C.J. Thynne. 53 p.

Addresses of the Prophecy Investigation Society.

Vol. also includes E.H. Horne's *Lord's Return*, Charles Askwith's *Kings of the East,* and E.L. Langston's *Present Events in the East.*

1641. _____. *Rapture.* 1988 [1922]. Miami Springs: Schoettle. 72 p.

"It is impossible to exaggerate the importance of the doctrine of the Parousia (Rapture)...." Rapture will be secret: the shout is "heard only by those to whom it is addressed." "Unfilled prophecy all lies *after* the Rapture," which can occur at any moment and will be without warning. Argues for a "plurality of rapture" in "separate and graded installments." Advocates partial or "selective rapture": some believers raptured prior to Tribulation, others later. Earlier (Sept. 1920), in *Moody Monthly,* Panton suggested the 1905 Russian edition of *Protocols of Zion* was the "mystery of iniquity": "The Latest Preparations for Antichrist."

1642. _____. *The Panton Papers: Current Events and Prophecy.* 1928. New York: T.M. Chalmers. 150 p.

Editorials from Panton's journal *The Dawn.* 1923 Tokyo earthquake was God's wrath upon that sinful nation. The biggest earthquake, famine (in Russia), pestilence (1918 flu), and war (WWI) all occurred since 1912. Jews are purest-blooded race. King of North = Bolshevist Russia; King of South = Egypt. Antichrist (Nero revived) = Mussolini (or else he is a "remarkable understudy"). The World War began the process of the revival of the Roman Empire. Rebuilding of Millennial Temple. Cites Malachy's 12th century predictions of end-time Popes. The Pope will flee destruction of Rome and be rescued by fleets of airplanes.

1643. _____, James McAllister, C.J. Waehlite. *Startling Signs of Great World Changes Soon to Take Place.* [1930?]. Toronto: A. Sims. 56 p.

"We are in the time of the end." Communism, Mussolini, racial hatred, airplanes as signs. Drying up of Euphrates: British success in Mideast during WWI.

1644. Parker, William. *The Judgment of Nations: or, The Ending of Temporal Power.* 1920. Pittsburgh: Mt. Lebanon Pub. 234 p. Diagrams.

Pre-mill. "Adamic race must end in a cataclysm of judgment and destruction." World War was "at least preliminary to the beginning of the end in a literal, or historical sense." False Prophet = Mohammedanism, historically; also Fascism and socialism now. Parker also wrote book against woman's suffrage.

1645. Patmont, Louis Richard. *Perils of the Latter Days; A Survey of Apocalyptic Events.* 1936. Findlay, OH: Fundamental Truth. 177 p. illus.

1646. Payne, James. *Messiah's Kingdom Coming on the Earth: A Reply to the Mystic Interpretation of Scripture.* 1965. London: Sovereign Grace Advent Testimony. 54 p.

1647. Payne, J[ohn] Barton. *The Imminent Appearing of Christ.* 1962. Grand Rapids, MI: William B. Eerdmans. 191 p. illus. bibl. SEE ALSO 1970+

1648. Peak, Luther C. *Today! In the Light of the Scripture.* 1942. Dallas: Baptist Beacon. 39 p.

"All serious students of the Word of prophecy, almost without exception, are firmly convinced that we are now living in the last days of this age."

1649. _____. *The Atomic Bomb and the Approaching Crisis.* 1946. Dallas: Evangelist Press. 88 p. illus.

Includes "Bible prophecy and the coming world government," "Atomic power, the Beast of prophecy and the Great Tribulation," "Satan and the mystery of the atom."

1650. Pearce, Victor. *Advent Or Atom.* 1980? [1940s?]. Eastbourne, England: Prophetic Witness Movement Intl. 33 p.

"These predictions were written during the war, of events which have since been fulfilled." In 1944 Pearce said Bible prophesied European Confederacy (England, France, Belgium, Holland, Western Germany, Austria, Switzerland, Balkans, Italy, Spain, North Africa, the Levant) opposed to Northern Confederacy (Russia and most of Germany). He says this was fulfilled in 1945. Also predicted Jewish Return. Rosh = Russia. "Heaven" (Greek *Ouranon*) = uranium. Believes that Bible describes nuclear fission: "elements melt with fervent heat" (2 Pet. 3:10) because the "power of 'uranium' [heaven] shall be shaken" (Luke 21:26). Antichrist leads apostate Church in Rome. Russia invades Israel; huge battle at Armageddon against a Western Confederacy formed from remnants of the Roman Empire, followed by the Second Coming. Pearce claims that all his 1940's prophecies were fulfilled, and that this booklet influenced Billy Graham and was also approved by Winston Churchill.

1651. Pearson, Alfred Chilton. *The Climax of the Ages; Introducing Earth's Coming Glorious King.* 1923. Ashfield, Australia: Merchant. 492 p.

"A presentation of the divine purpose with mankind, and an examination of the workings of this purpose in human history, including our own times. Together with a consideration of prophesied events of the most momentous character, eventuating in the establishment of the divine Kingdom on earth."

1652. _____. *Noah's Days and Christ's Coming.* 1935. Sydney: Worker Trustees. 263 p.

Also wrote *Behold the Bridegroom Cometh* and *Creation and Its Sequel.* Remarkable parallels between Noah and the Second Coming. Ark 42,000 tons burden, 457 x 91 x 54 ft. 1,260 years covers revival of Roman empire, Papal leadership, up to 19th Century. Decries "False theories of "Modern Science"" that deny the creation and "fixed level earth as the centre and scene of all operations of human history." Gap Theory creationism: Flood of 2 Peter 3 not Noah's but of the original (pre-Adamic) earth. God made "second earth for human history." Noah recognized coming Flood was "duplicate" of previous. End time war only after believers removed. In one regard — acceptance of evolution — things are far worse today even than in Noah's day. "Speaking Coming" (Rapture) parallel to Noah entering Ark seven days before Flood; "Personal Coming" (Second Coming) seven years later parallel to actual Flood.

1653. Peeter, James. *World Holocaust: Prophecies, Predictions— Your Future*

from Now to the Year 2000! [1969?] Denver: J. Peeter. 3 v. illus., maps.

Occult prophecies.

1654. Penn-Lewis, Jessie. *All Things New: The Message of Calvary for the Time of the End.* 1917. London: Morgan & Scott. 94 p.

1655. Pentecost, J. Dwight. *Things to Come: A Study in Biblical Eschatology.* 1964 [1958]. Grand Rapids, MI: Academie Books (Zondervan). x, 633 p. indexes, bibl. Orig. pub. Findlay, OH: Dunham. 1967 ed. Dunham (Grand Rapids).

Pentecost: Presbyterian; professor Dallas Theological Seminary. Pre-mill pre-trib; systematically presents and criticizes range of other views; many citations. Argues for literal over allegorical interpretation. Day of Lord = Tribulation and Millennium (not Rapture, etc). Purpose of Tribulation is to prepare Jews for conversion to Messiah. Woman with Child = Israel. Two Witnesses: literal, but not identifiable. Rosh = Russia; Gog = Prince of Rosh. King of East = Asian coalition. Beast: leads new Roman Empire, becomes world Dictator, 7-year pact, commands worship as God, gains control over Palestine, elevated by Harlot (corrupt religious system), but then destroys her. Second Beast = False Prophet; a Jew. Antichrist = generic (either Beast). Armageddon: whole 3½ year campaign. Gather at Armageddon, but battle spreads all over Israel. Locusts not literal; the armies. Reformers weren't chiliasts, but aided rebirth of Millennial belief by expectation of Advent. New Jerusalem descends during Millennium but suspended; lands on earth later.

1656. _____. *Prophecy for Today: The Middle East Crisis and the Future of the World.* 1961 Grand Rapids, MI: Zondervan. 191 p.

The Great War prophesied in Ezekiel will break out any time now. Accept Christ in order to avoid Tribulation and terrible judgment. 1989 edition. (Grand Rapids, MI: Discovery House; 211 p.); subtitled "God's Purpose and Plan for Our Future." SEE ALSO 1970+.

1657. Perret, Paul. *Prophecies I Have Seen Fulfilled.* [ca. 1940]. London: Marshall, Morgan & Scott (Zondervan in U.S.). xvi, 136 p.

Orig. French. Perret: Swiss Reformed Church pastor. "Certainly the end of our present era is near at hand." Importance of "miraculous" Jews, prophetic significance of Zionism, Allenby's liberation of Jerusalem. Distinguishes "end of [earthly historical] time" and "end of world." 1898 establishment of Zionism almost 40 years ago (a generation): "The dread selection is about to take place." But hour unknown. First Balkan War: "drying up" of Euphrates (Turkey). End of Time of Gentiles already. Ten-Horn Beast = ten Catholic nations. 6th trumpet (one nation falls)= 1938 Austrian *Anschluss*. Little Horn after the 10 = Hitler. Second Beast = Mussolini. But can't identify Antichrist: could be Jew, German, or Pope. Parousia (Rapture), then Tribulation.

1658. Peterson, W[illiam] A. *In the Days to Come.* 1966. Sydney, Australia: W.A. Peterson. 128 p. chart.

Dispensationalist.

1659. _____. *Watching for the Morning.* 1990. Baulkham Hill, Australia: W.A. Peterson. viii, 390 p. plates illus., maps, index.

1660. Pettingill, William. SEE ALSO 1800–1910. *Simple Studies in the Revelation.* 1929 (6th ed.). Philadelphia School of the Bible. 132 p.

Orig. 1906; some editions titled *The Unveiling of Jesus Christ: Simple Studies in the Revelation.*

1661. _____. *God's Prophecies for Plain People.* 1923. Wheaton, IL: Van Kampen; Findlay, OH: Fundamental Truth. 246 p.

Present collapse of civilization clearly prophesied in the Bible.

1662. _____. *How We Shall Be Caught Up, or, The Electric Crane's Resurrection Sermon.* [1930s]. Wilmington, DE: Just a Word. 12 p.

"It is a great thing to know that everything is going on according to God's schedule.... We are not surprised at the present collapse of civilization; the Word of God told us all about it."

1663. _____. *Nearing the End: Sim-*ple Studies Concerning the Second Coming of Christ, and Related Events.* 1948. Chicago: Van Kampen. 93 p.

Papacy — the Little Horn — may disappear any day; then the End of the Age. Calculations show Papacy and Turkish Empire expire in 1898. Millennium starts 1928 by several calculations.

1664. Philberth, Bernhard. *Christliche Prophetie und Nuklearenergie.* 1982 [1961]. Switzerland: Christiana Verlag. 256 p.

Also wrote *Revelation* (1994; BAC Australia).

1665. Pickering, Henry, comp. *100 World-Known Witnesses to the Second Coming of the Lord; Personal — Pre-Millennial; "Perhaps To- day."* n.d. London: Pickering & Inglis. 48 p.

Alphabetically arranged.

1666. _____. *God's Own Plan of the Ages.* [ca. 1930?] England: S.n. 14 p. illus.

Daniel II.

1667. Pickett, L[eander] L. SEE ALSO 1800–1910. *Armageddon, or, The Next Great War.* 1924. Louisville, KY: Pentecostal Pub. 164 p.

1668. Pinch, Ernest Buckhurst. *The Approaching Crisis.* 1961 [1953]. London: Advent Testimony and Preparation Movement. 60 p.

"An exposition of Biblical prophecy in the light of present-day world events."

1669. _____. *The Return of the Lord Jesus Christ: A Concise Scriptural Survey.* 4th ed. 1959 [1948]. London: Advent Testimony and Preparation Movement. 46 p.

Pinch: Gen. Sec'y Advent Testimony and Preparation Movement; ed. of *Prophetic Witness.* Pre-trib Rapture. At start of Tribulation, an imperial leader emerges promising to save world from upheaval and confusion. "Week of millenniums" since Creation, paralleling the Six Days of Creation. Millennium will be "benevolent dictatorship" under Christ.

1670. _____. *Darkness and Dawn.* 1969 [1956]. Eastbourne: Prophetic Witness. 46 p.

Second Advent.

1671. Pink, Arthur W[alkington] *The Redeemer's Return.* 1918. Ashland, KY: Calvary Baptist Church Book Store. 331 p.

1672. _____. *The Antichrist.* 1988 [1923]. Grand Rapids, MI: Kregel. 308 p. With new Foreword. orig. 1923, Bible Truth Depot: Swengel, PA. Also 1979, Minneapolis: Klock & Klock Christian Pub.

First presented at Bible conferences, then in *Studies in the Scriptures.* Dispensational pre-mill pre-trib. Aims at complete biography of Antichrist. Real Antichrist yet to appear; Antiochus, Nero, Papacy very evil but only forerunners. Attribution of Antichrist to Papacy in Reformation led to post-mill error. Antichrist = a Jew, will destroy the Papacy (Harlot). Antichrist = The Beast, Little Horn, Son of Satan, "Judas Iscariot reincarnated." Antichrist's 6,000 year run almost over. Revealed after Rapture; arises from Babylon, part of Ten Kingdoms. A political, military, economic and religious genius, Antichrist makes pact with returned Israel, which acclaims him as Messiah. Then he tries to exterminate the Jews. God soon to pour "unspeakably dreadful judgments" upon world under Antichrist.

1673. Pitt, F.W. *Coming Events Cast Their Shadows in the Air.* 1936. London: Marshall, Morgan, and Scott. 144 p.

Pitt: editor of *Advent Witness.* Revelation is concerned with events that occur "in the air," notably the Rapture; the invention of airplanes proves Revelation true. Jews now returning to Palestine; when they recover their nationhood Antichrist will become their king, but Antichrist controlled by The Beast in Rome. Rapture precedes Antichrist's Jerusalem rule. Russian-led Northern Federation will include Germany and African states; these will fight Ten Kingdom Federation led by Rome and the 200-million man army of the East at Armageddon. Israel is invaded first by the Assyrian King of the North (not the allied Russian federation). Refers to Einstein as "atheistic Communist." World will see resurrection of the Two Witnesses by "television." The False Prophet's Image of the Beast is a robot. Death ray weapons at Armageddon.

1674. Polhamus, William R. *The Unveiling of Jesus Christ: The Things Which Must Shortly Come to Pass.* 1936. New York: Fleming H. Revell. 184 p. maps, diagrams.

1675. Pollock, Algernon James. *"Things Which Must Shortly Come to Pass."* 1978 [1918]. Charlotte, NC: Books for Christians. 288 p. maps. Vol. 18 of The Serious Christian series. Orig. 1918; London: Central Bible Truth Depot; 2nd ed. 1936.

Rev., Dan., and Zech. Also wrote *Evolution — Unscientific and Unscriptural* (1923).

1676. _____. *The Amazing Jew.* 1939 [1930]. 2nd ed. New York: Loizeaux Bros. 156 p. 12 leaves plates.

Zionism as portent: "IT IS THE BEGINNING OF THE END." "Surely the coming of the Lord is very very nigh." Latter rain literally in Palestine: miraculous increase of rain. "Promised Land" far bigger than Palestine proper. Hitler now driving Jews out of Germany, to Palestine. Western Confederation: revived Roman Empire. Northern Confederation: Gog-Magog. Deadly wound: barbarian sackings of Rome; healing is future revival of Roman Empire. Mussolini: probably not himself the Beast, but he is preparing revival of Empire, and his successor will be the Beast. Palestine to come under Roman control, then seven-year covenant with Antichrist, ruler of Israel. Germany allies with Russia; invades Israel but destroyed by God. Literal Armageddon battle. "Words utterly fail to paint the horror of the Great Tribulation." Also wrote *May Christ Come At Any Moment?* (says denial of any-moment Rapture is "Satanic").

1677. _____. *Will the Church Go Through the Great Tribulation?* [1930s]. London: Central Bible Depot. 63 p.

Review of Reese's *Approaching Advent of Christ.*

1678. Pont, Charles E. *The World's Collision.* 1956. Boston: W.A. Wilde. bibl.

Introduction by E. Schuyler English. Arabs ally with U.S. and Britain when Russia invades.

1679. Powell, F. E. *God's Calendar, or, Where Are We in Prophetic Time?*

[1950s]. Minneapolis: Osterhus Publishing House. 6 p.

1680. Prenier, H.S. *End of Time*. 1948. Orlando, FL: priv. pub. 139 p. illus.

Seventh-day Adventist. Trumpet Woes: Ostrogoths, Vandals, Huns, Heruli, Moslems. Catholic supremacy A.D. 538 to 1798 (1,260 years of "Dark Ages"). Then Protestant domination, then Last Days. 3½ years = during French Revolution. Two Witnessess = Old and New Testaments. Two-Horn Beast = U.S. (will unite church and state). National Recovery Act = precursor to Mark of the Beast. "Look for a disunited Europe at the end of time." Millennium is a "quarantine" of Satan and his evil angels: no one else left on earth during the thousand years.

1681. Price, Charles S. *The Battle of Armageddon*. 1938. Pasadena, CA: author.

Gomer = Crimea. "There is nothing to hinder now the hordes of Russia sweeping down through both Turkey and Persia to the very gates of Jerusalem. There is the valley of Armageddon."

1682. Price, George McCready. *The Time of the End*. c1967. Nashville: Southern Publishing Association. 171 p.

Seventh-day Adventist; major creationist and Flood Geology theorist. Two-Horn Beast and False Prophet = democratic Protestantism of U.S. After "sealing" of 144,000 saints, nations turn on one another — global Armageddon.

1683. _____. *When and What Is Armageddon?* N.d.? 63 p. Typescript.

1684. *The Prophetic Word: A Source-Book*. 1924. St. Paul, MN: Clymer-Huelster Printing. xix, 1,142 p.

"Prophecies that focus on our times. From each Bible book. Including the world end is war, the first resurrection a series, the mystery of Messiah solved, Babylon, Symbolism of the Apocalypse in light of twentieth century inventions."

1685. Pruitt, Fred. *Past, Present and Future of the Church*. [1960s]. Guthrie, OK: Faith Pub. House. 72 p.

1686. Purnell, Benjamin Franklin. *The Rolling Ball of Fire*. 1915–25. 6 vols (4–6 titled *Flaming Ball of Fire*). Benton Harbor, MI: Israelite House of David.

1687. _____. *The Book of Wisdom: The Flying Roll: Addressed to the Twelve Tribes of Israel Scattered Abroad*. Benton Harbor, MI: Israelite House of David. 7 vols.

Purnell: leader of House of David, Adventist community with British-Israel roots in Benton Harbor, MI (later led by his wife Mary). Emphasized Endtime ingathering of the Elect 144,000. Rigid celibacy demanded for followers; Purnell took most of the young women for himself.

1688. R.L.R. *Unmasked! A Word of Warning for All Who Are Not Too Blind to See, Nor Too Deaf to Hear*. 1926. New York: Loizeaux Bros. 23 p.

Pre-mill.

1689. Rader, Luke. *Mystery Babylon, From Which Comes the Anti Christ*. [1932?]. Minneapolis: Book Stall. 55 p.

"An exposé, of the most fearful menace the world has ever faced" — Communism.

1690. Rall, Harris Franklin. *Modern Premillennialism and the Christian Hope*. 1920. New York / Cincinnati: Abingdon Press. 255 p. bibl.

Argues against pre-mill interpretation, claiming it is hyper-Calvinist.

1691. Raud, Elsa. *Introduction to Prophecy*. 1960. Findlay, OH: Dunham Publishing Co. 236 p.

Introduction by Herman Hoyt. Raud: editor of *Prophetic Word*.

1692. _____. *The Church and the Tribulation*. Lebanon, PA: Bible Christian Union. 76 p.

1693. Rawson, Frederick Lawrence. *End of the World, and Proofs of its Coming in December, 1917*. 1917. London: Crystal Press. 200 p.

Rawson: electrical/civil engineer; claims both scientific and metaphysical knowledge; also wrote *Life Understood* (1914, 1920, etc.). Christian Science plus psychic power, Pyramidology, etc. Predicts "dematerialisation" of entire world three weeks after publication of this book: Dec. 3 or 4, 1917. New Heaven and Earth. Armageddon was WWI. Said he predicted role of Germany beforehand. "Individual"

Second Coming occurred 1866; "general" Second Coming occurring now. Millennium: not literal. "All the authorities on the subject of the end of the world agree that we are right at the end." Dates range up to 1934; majority think 1923.

1694. Reed, B.E. *Signs of Earth's Sunrise.* 1950. Watertown, NY: Christian Book Service. 141 p.

Pre-mill, pre-trib. Last 3 verses of Daniel refer to Pyramid. 1953 = Rapture. 1954–60 = Tribulation. 1960 = Second Coming, Millennium. Rapture can be dated, but Second Coming cannot be dated precisely. Antichrist comes for 3½ years: Great Tribulation. King of North probably Russia. Jews flee to Petra during Tribulation. National conversion of Israel. Pyramid shows Time of End as 1909–1953. Seven Seals: White Horseman = false savior (communism); Red Horse = WWI; Black Horse = Depression; Pale Horse = WWII. 5th seal: martyrdom from Communism. Seven trumpets: wrath during Tribulation (literal interpretation). Great Earthquake (7th Bowl): will straighten earth axis for paradisical climate during Millennium. Three resurrections of dead.

1695. Reese, Alexander. *The Approaching Advent of Christ: An Examination of the Teaching of J.N. Darby and His Followers.* 1937. London: Marshall, Morgan & Scott. 328 p. indexes, bibl. refs. 1975 reprint ed. (Grand Rapids, [MI] International), with author's corrections.

Reese: Presbyterian minister in Brazil. Post-trib; "historical" pre-mill. Spirited refutation of pre-trib Rapture; many citations. Visible public glorious Second Coming; argues impossibility of its being secret and separate. End = Day of Lord = Rapture (Parousia) = Revelation (Advent); all part of same event, at start of Millennium and Judgment. Silly to assume separate resurrection of Tribulation saints after Rapture; naive to believe Christians all escape Tribulation. Antichrist must *precede* Rapture; illogical to suppose Christians all gone first. "Stupid obsession" to focus on illusory any-moment Rapture rather than final Coming and Millennium. Signs and events still to be fulfilled, but denies this downgrades expectation of Coming. "History is moving at a gallop": prophecies are being rapidly fulfilled, so End must be near. "Concert of Ten Kings in Roman Europe" and Return of Jews may occur any moment now. World evangelism being fulfilled now. Antichrist to come from Greek part of Roman Empire. Lord's Prayer is refutation of pre-trib belief. Satan, cast from heaven, turns fury against Israelitish Christian Church (not Jews) during Tribulation. Then persecutes all Christians in world. Satan arises, miraculously healed in fight against saints, aided by False Prophet. Reese wrote book 1914, but not published til 1937. Charles Rolls incorporated part of manuscript without acknowledgment in his *King's Own Honors Roll* (1933).

1696. Reid, James. *God, the Atom, and the Universe.* 1968. Grand Rapids, MI: Zondervan. 240 p. illus. bibl.

Reid: systems engineer; shows how Bible anticipates nuclear physics. "The words used by Joel and Peter centuries ago could well have been a description of an atomic explosion on a gigantic scale; the great rushing sound as the huge pillar of smoke ascends and breaks out into a tremendous mushroom formation, the blazing fire and blood-red cloud, the fission of atoms and disintegration of elements — the whole picture of nuclear horror was painted in vivid but restrained language by the Biblical writers centuries ago." The six creation "days" were really each long ages.

1697. Reimers, Karl. *Stehen Wir in den letzten Zeiten? Eine schlichte Beantwortung dieser Frage.* 1921. Hamburg: Agentur des Rauhen Hauses. 71 p.

1698. Repp, George Douglass. *A Comprehensive Outline of Prophecy.* 1935. St. Louis: Faithful Words. 62 p. Orig. pub. in Brooklyn by author.

1699. Rice, John R. *World-Wide War and the Bible.* 1940. Wheaton IL: Sword of the Lord. 122 p.

Rice: Baptist minister. Radio evangelist; founded Sword of the Lord. WWII = prophesied Last Days. Mussolini likely the Antichrist. 10 Horns = Italy, France, Spain, Portugal, Greece, Turkey, Syria, part of England. U.S. reduced to subject of European dictator.

1700. ____. *Bible Lessons on the Book of Revelation.* [1950?]. Murfreesboro, TN: Sword of the Lord. 60 p.

1701. ____. *The Coming Kingdom of Christ.* 1945 [1941]. Wheaton, IL: Sword of the Lord. 202p.

Also wrote *Jewish Persecution and Bible Prophecies and Last Judgment of the Unsaved Dead* (1940s). SEE ALSO 1970+.

1702. Rich, James Walter. *After the Storm, the Restoring Fire.* 1960. Boston: Christopher Pub. House. 254 p.

1703. Richards, H[arold] M[arshall] S[ylvester]. *Great Events Impending.* 1963. Los Angeles, CA : Voice of Prophecy. 35 p. illus.

1704. Richey, E. N. *Is the Messiah at Hand ? Ten Messages on the Signs of the Times and the Unfolding of Prophecy.* 1928. Houston: E.N. Richey. 100 p., plates.

Sermons at the tabernacle, Richey campground, Lakeland, Florida

1705. Rideout, Richard Forrest. *The Battle of Armageddon.* N.d. [1940s?] S.l. : s.n. [2], 16 p.

Bible Research Fellowship (Angwin, CA).

1706. Riggs, Ralph M. *The Path of Prophecy: The Revelation of Christ.* 1937. Springfield, MO: Gospel Pub. House. xiv, 227 p. index.

Gap Theory creationism: Prior to Adam, Earth was abode of Satan and his rebel angels, then destroyed and re-created during Six Day creation. Denounces evolution. 445 B.C. + 69 "weeks" (of years) = A.D. 30 (Jesus revealed as Messiah). 70th week only after long parenthesis: future seven-year alliance of Antichrist with Jews, after the Rapture. Roman Empire revived in Tribulation. Half of world population killed. Russo-Teutonic-Mongolian alliance marches on Antichrist's empire. As they fight each other around Jerusalem, and Antichrist is emerging triumphant, Christ descends at Second Coming. Jews return to Israel and achieve full independence only after Second Coming (prior to

this only partially independent segment of revived Roman Empire).

1707. Riley, William Bell. *The Evolution of the Kingdom.* 1912. New York / London: C.C. Cook / S. W. Partridge. 188 p. Orig. serialized in *Grace and Truth.*

Riley: Baptist minister; founded Northwest Schools (Minneapolis); prominent creationist advocate. Strongly pre-trib pre-mill.

1708. ____. *Daniel and the Doom of World Governments.* 1935. Minneapolis: L.W. Camp. 27 p.

1709. ____. *Daniel vs. Darwinism.* N.d.? Minneapolis: H. M. Hall. 98 p.

1710. Rimmer, Harry. *When East Meets West: The Eastern Question a World Question.* 1929. Los Angeles: Research Science Bureau. 36 p.

Rimmer: convert to Presbyterianism; influential creationist proselytizer.

1711. ____. *The Coming War and the Rise of Russia.* [1944] 1940. Grand Rapids, MI: William B. Eerdmans. 87 p. Shadow of Things to Come series: vol. 2.

Gomer = the Balkans. Armageddon: after Millennium. Coming war "the next-to-last war that shall ever trouble this planet"—will "dwarf the sadistic nature of this present war ... no matter how bad this present war may be, there will be another after it, more terrible in its consequences than any conflict in history has ever been or ever will be...." Boasts he predicted WWII for last ten years; notes Jewish emigration to Palestine. Predicts Russo-Soviet split, with Germany defeated and Russia emerging with greatly enhanced power, but doesn't expect U.S. in WWII. Next war will be Battle of Valley of Jehoshaphat, at start of Millennial reign. Battle of Armageddon is at end of Millennium. Coming war: Russia leads allied horde against reconstituted Israel. Allies include some African states, some Balkan ("Gomer"), Armenia ("Togarmah"). Beamed radio/electronic power will spell "ultimate doom of metal weapons" which enemy can make red-hot; thus the prophesied wooden weapons, to be burned for fuel for seven years after war. "Our task is not to make a warless world, and bring universal peace. Our great commission empowers us only to strive to save out of the wreck of this age such individuals as may be persuaded to turn to Christ and be saved.... The earth and all therein shall be consumed by fire."

1712. ____. *Palestine, the Coming Storm Center.* 1945 [1940]. 7th ed Grand Rapids, MI: Eerdmans 72 p. illus. Shadows of Things to Come: vol 1.

Nations invade Israel because Jews all there, thus wealth all there. Birds = Allenby's WWI planes.

1713. ____. *The Coming League and the Roman Dream.* 1943 [1941]. 2nd ed. Grand Rapids, MI: Eerdmans. 87 p. Shadows of Things to Come: vol 3.

Ten-Nation League will probably be led by Russia. Tarshish is not Britain, but Spain. Bible doesn't require revived Roman Empire; Italian failures in WWII prove it won't become powerful. Believes we're in last days, but may not be this generation. Daniel's 4th world empire is future League; then 11th nation will arise to dominate it, then great Tribulation and Second Coming.

1714. ____. *The Coming King.* 1941 Grand Rapids, MI: William B. Eerdmans. 90 p. Shadows of Things to Come: vol. 4.

1715. ____. *The Shadow of Coming Events.* 1946. Grand Rapids, MI: William B. Eerdmans. 294 p.

Dead Sea's "rich harvest of chemicals" provokes Russia's greed. Predicts rise of Russia as superpower. Influenced Dallas Theological Seminary interpretation and Hal Lindsey.

1716. Roberts, Oral. *The Drama of the End-Time.* 1963. Tulsa: Oral Roberts. 95 p.

Pre-trib. Roberts: Pentecostal minister, faith healer. Also wrote *The Book of Daniel and the Book of the Revelation of Jesus Christ* (1968, Tulsa: Oral Roberts).

1717. ____. *God's Timetable for the End of Time.* 1969. Tulsa: Heliotrope. 96 p.

1718. Roberts, Theodore, and Peter Rose; and C.F. Hogg and Thomas Stockdale. *The River, the Epilogue and the Post-*

script *(Rev. XXII)*; and *The Progress of Revelation Concerning the Second Coming.* 1923. London: C. J. Thynne & Jarvis. 84 p. Aids to Prophetic Study series.

The Prophecy Investigation Society. *The River*: Parallels between Rev. 22 and Genesis. *The Progress*: Two-stage Rapture.

1719. Robertson, H.C. *A Brief Interpretation of the Revelation of St. John: Sowing the Four Visions of Time, Each Extending to the End of This Age.* 1928. London: C.J. Thynne & Jarvis. 2nd ed 63 p. plates.

1720. Rodd, John E. *The Last Days: Text Book of the Second Coming of Christ.* [1930s]. Chicago: Evangelical Pub. 55 p.

1721. Roden, Ben. *The Man on the White Horse.* 1958. [Waco, TX?].

Roden: leader of Branch Davidians prior to Koresh. When F. Houteff predicted End for 1959, when her husband would be resurrected after 1,260 days, Roden claimed his arrival at Mt. Carmel, Waco, was fulfillment of this prophecy. He announced that secret name for true believers Houteff had prophesied was "Branch," and predicted End for 1960. When Roden died his wife Lois took over. She pronounced a Seven Year prophecy from 1977, with climactic years 1981 and '84 — later explained as Koresh's arrival, and his splitting of the cult in 1984, drawing off most members.

1722. Roerich, Nicholas. *Altai-Himalaya.* 1929. New York: F. A. Stokes.

Roerich: Russian-American artist, Central Asian explorer. Taught coming age of unprecedented war of nations, with oceans of blood; then teachers of Lord of Shambhala emerge and triumph. Already many teachers reincarnated; unusual people about; the New Age imminent. This book cited as evidence that Jesus spent his "lost years" in Tibet, and of reality of UFOs in ancient Hindu sources.

1723. Rogers, W[illiam] H. "*The End from the Beginning": A Panorama of Prophecy, or, History the Mold of Prediction.* 1938. New York: Arno C. Gaebelein. 302 p. 2nd ed. (preface dated 1941). New York: F.E. Fitch.

Baptist pastor, New York. Pre-trib.

pre-mill; any moment Rapture. "Armageddon Imminent." Seven dispensations: to Fall, to Flood, to Babel, to Exodus, to crucifixton, to present, and Millennium. Antichrist (the Beast) leads Ten-Nation Roman Confederacy in 70th Week, exploits and persecutes Palestine. Current conditions give "emphatic confirmation of the near coming of this seventieth week." Papal system = "mother of harlots" who rides the Beast (Antichrist). Iron/clay = fascism, communism. Stalin, Hitler, and especially Mussolini "forerunners" of Antichrist. Northern Confederation = Russia. Southern Confederacy = Egypt. Eastern Kingdoms = Far East. All converge at Armageddon, results in "utter prostration of the world's powers" and destruction of Antichrist. Satan's fall (war in heaven) was pre-Adamic. Prophecies not always in chronological order. The "descendants of Ham have been the slave nations of the earth; a people of inferiority and servility." "The coming will be in two distinct stages like a scheduled train coming in two sections." During Millennium, a seven-fold increase in light destroys all germs.

1724. _____. *In the Last Days, or, Why I Believe the Coming of Christ Is Near....* Findlay, OH: Fundamental Truth. 44 p.

1725. Romeo, Antonino. *Il Presente e il Futuro Nella Rivelazione Biblica.* 1964. Rome / New York: Desclée. xxxv, 287 p.

1726. Rood, Paul William. *Who Will Win the War?* 1942. Grand Rapids, MI: Printed by Zondervan for Back-to-the-Bible Book Room. 22 p.

Rood: led Bryan Bible League, other anti-evolution groups; progident of Bible Institute, Los Angeles (BIOLA).

1727. Rose, George L[eon]. *Tribulation Till Translation.* 1943. Glendale, CA: Rose Pub. Co. 286 p.

Tribulation began with early persecutions. Plans other works on "The Beast — His Image, His Mark, and His Number; The Antichrist, and the Man of Sin." Pre-mill; post-trib Rapture. Beast = Pagan, Papal, and Ten-Nation Rome. Lit-

tle Horn = Papacy. Great Tribulation was against Waldenses, Albigenses, Hussites, Huguenots, other Protestants and dissenters, and was continued by Communists and Nazis. Great Earthquake = WWI. Four world dictators gather forces at Armageddon. King of East = Japan; of North = the democracies. Red Dragon = red atheism (communism). False Prophet = apostate Christianity. Three unclean spirits = Nazism, Communism, false Christianity (Rome). Armageddon fought at Megiddo and elsewhere, gigantic final battle; Antichrist's armies vs. remainder of Christians. Christ comes with a shout, raptures the saints, God destroys the armies. 7th vial poured in air = aerial bombings. 70 Weeks were continuous. "We do know that we are living in the 'last days'" — but we can't set the date. Speculates great End Time event for Aug. 9, 1953.

1728. Roseman, L.H. *Eight Radio Addresses on the Return of Jesus and Things which Must Shortly Come to Pass.* [1930s]. Little Rock, AR: Bible Lover's Revival. 62 p.

1729. Ruckman, Peter S. *Mark of the Beast.* 1969. 2nd ed. Pensacola, FL: Pensacola Bible Press. 113 p. illus.

Antichrist in Revelation.

1730. Ruhling, Richard. *In den letzten Tagen.* 1949. Hamburg: Advent-Verlag. 48 p. illus. Also pub Vienna: Rudolf Uberbacher (106 p.) and Pacific Press.

1731. Rupert, G[reenberry] G. SEE ALSO 1800–1910. *Time, Tradition & Truth Concerning the End of the World.* 1914 [1911]. Britton, OK: Union. 127 p.

1732. _____. *Consecutive Events at the Time of and Following the Close of Probation.* 1920. Britton, OK: Union. 31 p.

1733. _____. *The Seven Thousand Years and the Seven Lamps on the Golden Candle Sticks.* N.d. Britton, OK: Union Pub. Co. [8] p. With: *The Story of the Real Jew.*

1734. _____. *Three Woe Trumpets and the Close of Probation.* N.d. Britton, OK: Union Pub. Co. 14 p. ; 19 cm. With: *The Story of the Real Jew.*

1735. Russell, D.S. [David Syme] *Apocalyptic, Ancient and Modern.* 1978 [c1968]. Philadelphia: Fortress Press. viii, 86 p. bibl. refs, indexes.

1736. Rutherford, Adam. *Anglo-Saxon Israel; an Explanation of the Origin, Function and Destiny of the Norse-Anglo-Celto-Saxon Race in the British Empire, U.S.A., Holland, Scandinavia and Iceland.* 1939. 4th ed. London: author; Maplewood, NJ: J.A. Graeves. xii, 825 p. illus., tables, diagrams, maps, foldout plan.

Includes Pyramidology. 1934 ed. titled *Israel-Britain, or, Anglo-Saxon Israel....*

1737. Rutherford, J[oseph] F[ranklin]. *Millions Now Living Will Never Die!* 1920. Brooklyn, NY: International Bible Students Assoc. 128 p. illus. 1977 ed. by James D. Bales, Searcey, AK.

Jehovah's Witnesses.

1738. _____. *Deliverance; A Vivid Description of the Divine Plan, Particularly Outlining God's Progressive Steps Against Evil and Showing the Final Overthrow of the Devil and All of His Wicked Institutions; the Deliverance of the People; and the Establishment of the Righteous Government on Earth.* 1926. Brooklyn: International Bible Students Assoc., Watch Tower Bible and Tract Soc., 379 p. illus.

1739. _____. *The Kingdom, the Hope of the World.* 1931. Brooklyn: Watch Tower Bible and Tract Soc. 62 p.

1740. _____. *Vindication; the Name and Word of the Eternal God Proven and Justified by Ezekiel's Prophecy, and Revealing what Must Speedily Come to Pass upon the Nations of the World.* 1931. Brooklyn: Intl. Bible Students Assoc., Watch Tower Bible and Tract Soc.

1741. _____. *Enemies; The Proof that Definitely Identifies All Enemies, Exposes their Methods of Operation, and Points Out the Way of Complete Protection for Those Who Love Righteousness.* [1937]. Brooklyn: Watchtower Bible and Tract Soc. 379 p. illus.

1742. Ryder, D. L., and J.E. Taylor. *Signs of the Present Times.* 1920. Nashville, MI: [s.n.]. [16] p.

1743. _____. *Day of the Lord's Vengeance At Hand.*

Tribulation = Popery.

1744. Ryrie, Charles T. *The Basis of the Premillennial Faith.* 1981 [1953]. Neptune, NJ: Loizeaux Bros. 160 p. bibl. refs index.

Same title as his 1949 Dallas Theological Seminary Th.D. thesis.

1745. _____. *Dispensationalism Today.* 1965. Chicago: Moody Press. 221 p. bibl.

1746. _____. *The Bible and Tomorrow's News: A New Look at Prophecy.* 1969. Wheaton, IL: Scripture Press. 190 p. illus. SEE ALSO 1970+.

1747. Saarnivaara, Uuras. *Armageddon: Before and After: Biblical End-Time Prophecies and Their Fulfillment in Our Time.* 1966. Minneapolis: Osterhus [1967; author]. 108 p. bibl. refs. index.

1748. St. John, Harold, Reginald T. Naish, and W[illam] E[dwy] Vine. *The Lights and Shadows of the Millennium (Revelation XX).* 1922. London: Charles J. Thynne. 72 p.

Addresses delivered to Prophecy Investigation Society.

1749. Sainton, M. *The Return of Our Lord.* 1921. Tract.

Generation living during the Great War (WWI) will be alive for the End.

1750. Sale-Harrison, L. *Palestine: God's Monument of Prophecy: The Wonders of a Remarkable Book in a Remarkable Land.* c1933. New York: Sale-Harrison Publications. 250 p. photos Scripture index.

Account of visit there. Includes photo of walls of Jericho showing that God removed foundations, causing collapse.

1751. _____. *The Coming Great Northern Confederacy: or The Future of Russia.* [1928]. 6th ed. Harrisburg PA: L. Sale-Harrison, care of The Evangelical Press. 29 p.

Some editions subtitled *The Future of Russia and Germany.* Earlier ed. *titled The League of Nations: The Future of Europe, and the Resurrection of the Old Roman Empire.* Dispensational. Rapture; then Armageddon seven years later. Meshech = Moscow; Tubal = Tobolsk. Gomer = Germany. Jews resettle in Israel, then Russia attacks — Armageddon. Soviets now buying up Canadian horses; also trying to establish autonomous Jewish republic near Manchuria: "another effort of Satan to defeat God's plan" (of re-established Israel). Armageddon will include Eastern Hordes too.

1752. _____. *The Anglo-Saxon Nation: or Is Great Britain Israel?* 1951 [1928]. New York. L. Sale-Harrison. 39 p.

1753. _____. *The Resurrection of the Old Roman Empire: The Future Confederation of the Ten Nation Empire.* c1934 [c1928]. 13th ed. rev. New York: Sale-Harrison Publications. 130 p. New ed. of 1928.

Mussolini is not the Antichrist: Antichrist must arise from confederacy of ten nations, so must be future. Hitler's failure to conquer southern Europe proof of God's plan for coming Ten Nation Confederacy (Roman Empire) in southern Europe. Radar, robots, radio and TV will be perfected and exploited by Antichrist. Antichrist defeated at Armageddon; later, Northern and Eastern Alliances also crushed.

1754. _____. *The Remarkable Jew: His Wonderful Future.* N.d. London: Pickering & Inglis. 12th ed. rev. 223 p.

Other editions also subtitled *God's Great Timepiece.*" Zionist movement, Balfour Declaration, preparation for establishment of Israel: the Return.

1755. _____. *The Wonders of the Great Unveiling: The Remarkable Book of the Revelation.*

Sale-Harrison: Australian evangelist, prophecy writer.

1756. Saloff-Astakhoff, Nikita Ignatievich. *Antichrist and the Last Days of the World.* 1941. Berne: priv pub. 88 p.

1757. Sampson, H[olden] E. *The Rise and Consummation of the Æon; a Book of Interpretation and Prophecy Relating to the Present "Last Times" of Antichrist.* 1920. London: William Rider. xvi, 349 p.

Occult: much on astral dimensions, redemptive evolution, divine mysteries, reincarnation, karma, predestination. Now in age of Antichrist. World to face worst persecutions, tortures, tribulations ever. Humanity divided into the Elect,

non-elect, and reprobate; Divine vs. Demoniacal Race-Types. Ever since the Fall, these have been mixed. Now "uncontrollable and undetectable numbers of *incarnate* Demons and Astrals at a period of human depravity so materialized and corrupted that the most material, carnal and barbaric manifestations of the Demonical force, tyranny and oppression will appear exceeding an hundredfold the worst times of the Dark Ages, the cruelest period of Papal persecution, and the red riot of the French Revolution."

1758. "Sanctilean." *The Impending Golden Age: A Critical Analysis of the World Sickness and Its Cure.* 1948. Santa Barbara, CA: J.F. Rowney Press. vii, 127 p.

Sanctilean Cosmic Actuality series. Forecast intense cold and snows of 1948–49. New Age continent now rising in Pacific: "The Plains of Asturia will stretch far northward to the giant volcano, Mount Pelius, whose emergence from beneath the ocean will shake the Earth. Mount Pelius will stand at a point approximately west of Portland, Oregon, and south of Unalaska Island, in the Aleutian Islands. Earthquakes at this time in the Pacific Ocean are centered around: (a) The rise of the old Asturian land Bridge in the South Pacific Ocean, (b) the rise of Mount Pelius, and (c) the submergence of Japan."

1759. _____. *"Flying Saucers": Portents of These "Last Days."* 1953 [1950]. Santa Barbara, CA: J.F. Rowny Press. 44 p.

Sanctilean Univ., Florence, AZ; Hra Maiac Inst. of Technology. Copyrighted so as to be available for study in Library of Congress. "We are in the 'last days' of the recurrent sixth solar age of a solar cycle of progress." New Jeru Salem descending from outer space. New Age race to arise in Australia, New Zealand, Canada and U.S. Evil forces trying to destroy them, but UFOs are neutralizing their atomic radiation and other poisons. When people die, they are transformed into 17-inch tall manifestations which go to "Paradise," located just outside Earth's atmosphere. However, rockets and atomic bombs are now disrupting Paradise and harming the departed beings, and rendering UFOs (which also emanate from there) increasingly visible.

1760. Sargent, H[arry] N[eptune]. *The Marvels of Bible Prophecy.* 1940 [1938]. London: Covenant. 429 p. index bibl.

Sargent: Major-General. Pre-mill. Armageddon will be gathering of nations against Palestine. Restoration of Israel required by prophecy. British-Israelism: Britain and U.S.: Stone Kingdom = "Israel-Britain" = Israel in "latter days." Little Horn = Papacy. 70 Weeks continuous. "World order of the Mark of the Dictator" fast approaching. King of North = Russian; of South = Britain. Four Horses: historical Rome. Trumpets = Goths, Vandals, Huns, Saracens, Turks. Beast = Papacy = 666 (*Lateinos*). Last few verses of Revelation in future; all rest are historical. "It is plain that the general trend of present-day events is heading steadily" in prophesied directions of "warfare of the end."

1761. Savitri Devi. *The Lightning and The Sun.* 1958. Buffalo, NY: Samisdat. 432 p. illus.

Author born Maximiani Portas; went to India to uncover lost knowledge of the Aryans; took name honoring Indo-Aryan Sun goddess; became ardent post-war supporter of Nazism. Genghis Khan: the Lightning; Akhnaton (Pharaoh): the Sun; Hitler: both Lightning and Sun. Coming leader, predicted by Hitler in 1928: "Contrarily to Adolf Hitler, He will spare not a single one of the enemies of the divine cause: not a single one of its outspoken opponents but also not a single one of the lukewarm, of the opportunists, of the ideological heretical, of the racially bastardized, of the unhealthy, of the hesitating, of the all-too-human; not a single one of those who, in body or character or mind, bear the stamp of the fallen ages." Nazism will rise from ashes of defeat to triumph. Book praised by William Pierce (author of *Turner Diaries*, about apocalyptic race war) and James Mason (author of *Siege*, which combines philosophy of Hitler and Charles Manson [Manson tried to precipitate apocalyptic race war]).

1762. Schable, Walter. *Die glau-*

bende Gemeinde in der Endzeit; Schlusselfragen biblischer Prophetie. 1963. Giessen, Germany: Brunnen. 277 p.

1763. Schaumburg, J[ohn] J[ay]. *Changing Prof. Smyth's Pyramid Figures.* [1912]. Oakland, CA: Messiah's Advocate. 4 p.

1764. _____. *God's Finger of Prophecy Pointing to the Landscape of Last-Day Conditions.* 1912 . Oakland, CA: Messiah's Advocate. 16 p. illus.

1,290 Years: from A.D. 580 to 1870, when Papacy lost temporal power. Suggests End will be in 1915, when 1,335 Years completed.

1765. _____. *The Signs of the Times: a Scriptural Discussion of the Events of Today in the Light of Prophecy.* 1915. 2nd ed. Oakland, CA: Advent Christian Publication Society. 31 p.

1766. _____. *The Soon-Coming Glory to be Revealed to All: Being a Treatise on the Events of Today in the Light of Prophecy.* 1916. Oakland, CA: Advent Christian Publication Society. 31 p.

Advent Christian. Social, moral, physical signs of imminent Second Coming. Mohammedanism, Christian Science, Mormonism as false beliefs. 1870 Franco-Prussian war as harbinger: "drying up" of Euphrates — Harlot Papacy no longer protected by France.

1767. _____. *Jesus Is Coming! Signs and Tokens.* 1932 [1922]. Oakland, CA: Messiah's Advocate. [4] p.

1768. Schebo, W.A. *Gog and Magog: A Study of the 38th and 39th Chapters of Ezekiel.* [1940s?]. St. Paul, MN: priv. pub. 39 p.

1769. Schick, Erich. *Der göttliche Sieg: Biblische Betrachtungen.* 1950. Stuttgart: Evang. Missionsverlag. 80 p.

1770. Schlink, Basilea. *Lo, He Comes.* 1965 [1961]. London: Faith. 146 p. Originally published as *Das Ende ist nah* (Darmstadt-Eberstadt, Oekumenische Marienschwesternschaft).

1771. _____. *To-Day, a Time Like None Before.* 1963. Darmstadt-Eberstadt: Evangelical Sisterhood of Mary, Faith Press. 15 p.

1772. Schor, Samuel. *The Everlast-*

ing Nation and Their Coming King. 1971 [1933]. Eastbourne, England: Prophetic Witness. 122 p.

1773. Schrader, Anna. *Prophecies of the End-Time: Given by the Spirit of Prophecy to Anna Schrader.* 1967. Dallas: Voice of Healing [Christ for the Nations].

1774. Schwarze, Carl Theodore. *The Marvel of Earth's Canopies.* 1957. Westchester, IL: Good News. 62 p.

Schwarze: NYU engineering prof.; Plymouth Brethren; proponent of creationist Canopy Theory. The Canopy, which created the Edenic conditions of the pre-Flood world (and caused the Flood by its collapse), will be restored at the Millennium. Also wrote 1938 *Bibliotheca Sacra* article "The Bible and Science on the Everlasting Fire." Lake of Fire = a white dwarf star.

1775. _____. *Program of Satan.* 1947. Chicago: Good News Publishers. 220 p.

1776. Scofield, Cyrus. SEE ALSO 1800–1910. *What Do the Prophets Say?* 1918. Philadelphia: Sunday School Times. 188 p. 3rd ed. London: Marshall. Also pub. 1918 Greenville, SC: Gospel Hour.

"[But] that which ... has sought expression in the Utopias, stands boldly forth in Scripture as a revealed purpose of God" — world will only improve with "Kingdom Age"; all human efforts to improve are futile, and end in failure.

1777. Scott, W. *The Coming Great War, the Greatest Ever Known in Human History.* 1932 [1920s?]. 3rd ed. Toronto: A. Sims. 46 p. (Orig. pub. anon.?)

1778. Scroggie, W. Graham. *The Lord's Return.* 1939. London: Pickering & Inglis. 171 p.

1779. Scruby, John James. *The Great Tribulation — the Church's Supreme Test.* Vol. 1. 1933. Dayton, OH: John J. Scruby. 233, 34 p., index.

1780. Sears, William B. *Thief in the Night; or, The Strange Case of the Missing Millennium.* [c1961]. London: George Ronald. xiv, 303 p. diagrams bibl. refs.

Bahai. All evidence points to prophetic significance of 1843–44 for return of Christ, the End. Baha Allah is He.

1781. Sellers, Otis Q. *The Last Days.* 1950. Los Angeles: Word of Truth Ministry. 15 p.

1782. Seventh Day Adventist Church of the Primitive Principles of the Advent Movement of 1844. *The Coming and Final Crisis.* [1950s?]. Trenton, NJ: Religious Liberty Association. 57 p.

1783. Sheeman, Willis G. *The Last Days and the New Age.* 1969. Miami. vi, 116 p. illus.

Preface and copyright by Elizabeth G. Bartosch. Written by Sheeman in 1940. "We are indeed living in the last days." Teachings of "Koresh" (Cyrus R. Teed); with quotes from Koresh's 1890s *Flaming Sword* magazine and extracts from his *Great Red Dragon.* Koreshan Cellular Cosmogony: "The earth is a concave sphere and ... we live inside." Concave earth with sun in center provides the "only promise of that harmonious social order where will be reproduced the harmony of the spheres." Newton's gravity theory is wrong. Koreshanity is the "true religion"; Koresh explained "every mystery of life" and is "the Messiah of this age." Koresh is the "greatest scientist in the world," and revealed the most important truths in all fields, especially astrology. Golden Age ended 16,000 B.C. Pyramidology (from Koreshanite J. Augustus Weimar). Creation 4000 B.C., Sept. 22–23. The Great Step of Pyramid passage = birth of Koresh (the reincarnated Elijah) in 1839. Euro-Americans descended from the Ten Lost Tribes, but British-Israelism is "wrong" — the "great hoax of the last days." Ten Tribes mixed racially and lost identity. Reincarnation. Jews: first of new race. "Biune race" of superior beings. Koresh, a descendant of Ephraim in U.S., leads remnant of God's people (now gathering in Koresh's New Jerusalem: his planned great city in Florida which is to become world hub). 2,300 years of Dan. 8:14 ends in 1839. U.S. is "blessed country of predicted glorious destiny" but must undergo Tribulation: "war and universal cataclysm, the most terrible and bloody war the world has ever known." Gog = economic capital; Magog = labor.

1784. Shoghi, Effendi. *The Promised Day is Come.* 1961 [1941]. Wilmette, IL: Bahá'í Publishing Trust. x, 136 p. index.

Effendi: great-grandson of Bahai founder Bahá'u'lláh; head of Bahai community. "The time for the destruction of the world and its people," Bahá'u'llah's prophetic pen has proclaimed, "hath arrived." "The hour is approaching," he specifically affirms, "when the most great convulsion will have appeared."

1785. Shotwell, Forrest L. *The World Tomorrow.* 1942. Flint, MI. 102 p. foldout map.

City auditor, Flint, MI; studies biblical ethnology. Armageddon = all Asia, Germany, East Europe, Scandinavia, E. Turkey, Ethiopia, Libya vs. rest of world. Dispensations, 70 Weeks, Rapture, Tribulation (Armageddon at end). Three unclean spirits from Satan = Communism, Fascism, Socialism (Nazism). Jews regathered by end of Tribulation, all convert by Second Coming. Beast = Antichrist revealed immediately after Rapture, super world dictator. Second Beast = False Prophet. Rules from Babylon, at Communist/Fascist border. Revival of Roman Empire. North = Russia. Russia will defeat Germany in WWII. Tarshish = England. Italy will be great power = Kingdom of South.

1786. Shuler, John Lewis. *The Great Judgment Day: In the Light of the Sanctuary Service.* 1974 [1923]. Washington, D.C.: Review and Herald. 128 p. illus

Daniel: Sanctuary cleansed after 2,300 days, following Abomination of Desolation. Tabernacle was earthly sanctuary; sanctuary now is heavenly. 457 B.C. + 2,300 = 1844. 69 Weeks = to A.D. 27; 70th to A.D. 34 (stoning of Stephen), with Crucifixion at midpoint. Then 1810 years, to 1844, for cleansing of sanctuary. Stresses necessity of blood for cleansing, redemption, atonement. Christ engaged in judgment, removal of sin, since 1844 in preparation for Second Coming. Prefigured by Jewish Day of Atonement, with scapegoat ritual. Great Tribunal already in session; investigative judgment of all. At Second Coming Jesus executes judgments. Scape-

goat = Satan, will be declared guilty of all sins; confined to empty desolate earth during Millennium. Seventh-day Advent preserved message of true Sabbath (contra Papal Sunday) and ongoing judgment.

1787. _____. *Is the End Near?* 1928. Nashville: Southern Publishing Assoc. 128 p. illus.

1788. _____. *The Coming Conflict.* 1929. Nashville: Southern Publishing Assoc. 128 p. illus.

1789. Shuttlewood, Arthur. *Warnings from Flying Friends.* 1968. Warminster, England: Portway. 266 p. plates illus. SEE ALSO 1970+.

1790. Sidersky, Philip. *Hitler, the Jews, and Palestine in Relation to the Second Coming of Our Lord.* 1938. 2nd ed. Grand Rapids, MI. [27] p.

1791. Silver, Jesse Forest. *The Lord's Return, Seen in History and in Scripture as Premillennial and Imminent.* c1914. 2nd ed. New York: F.H. Revell. 311 p. index.

Silver: from Pittsburgh. Resoundingly pre-Mill. First half on history of pre-mill doctrine, compendium of pre-mill advocates and supporters. Claims today's pre-mill belief "exactly what the early Christians beliefed and taught." Second half: proof from Bible. Whole tenor of Bible is pre-mill. Folly of Jews in not accepting literal fulfillment of Messiah prophecies. World increasingly wicked. Russellism ostensibly pre-mill but really more post-mill; heretical. Cites Barnabas and others on 6,000 Years from creation to End. Praises Montanists, Waldenses, Cathars, Huguenots, almost all other chiliasts, except some Anabaptists and Millerites. Blames Constantine for leading church into apostasy. Denounces Jerome, "sworn enemy of Chiliasm" (a-millennialist), who taught that world's 6,000 year span would end A.D. 500. Claims that "Crafty Rome [Church] taught that the earth would be destroyed in 1000 A.D." Resurrection of saints at start of Millennium; of others at end of Millennium. Jews to be converted and restored. Matthew's "End of the World" means end of present dispensation; "Day of the Lord" includes Millennium.

1792. Simpson, A. B. *The Coming One.* 1912. New York: Christian Alliance. 228 p.

Founder of Christian Missionary Alliance. 1,260 Days = from Moslem capture of Jerusalem in A.D. 637 (the Abomination of Desolation) to the founding of Zionism in 1897. Little Horn, Mystery Babylon, the Beast = the Papacy (gained power after fall of Rome). "Papal worship is therefore devil worship." Islam is a second Little Horn. Antichrist is Satan himself; rules during Tribulation. Church raptured, but most of world killed. Two-thirds of Jews die, but rest convert. New Jerusalem will be cubical city 376 miles each side, with vertical roads (no gravity). Three starting points for end times from 2,520 year calculation: from French Revolution to 1934.

1793. Simpson, David. *Marching Millions: A Brief Sketch of Man's Age-Long Warfare and God's Final Intervention.* [1950s?]. Kilmarnock, Scotland: John Ritchie. 99 p.

1794. Sims, A[lbert]. *The Coming Golden Age: When Lost Eden Will Have Been Restored, and God's Redeemed Family Shall Reign on Earth.* [1920s?]. Toronto: priv. pub. 50 p.

1795. _____. *The Days of Noah.* [1920s?]. Toronto: A. Sims. 23 p. illus.

1796. _____. *The Coming Great War: The Greatest Ever Known in Human History.* 1932 [1920s]. Toronto: A. Sims. 46 p.W. Scott, co-author?

Literal Armageddon.

1797. _____. *Daniel's Prophetic Image and the Stone Which Smote It.* 1932. 3rd ed. Toronto: author. 54 p.

1798. _____. *Beacon Lights of Prophecy: For Heaven-Bound Travellers Amid the Deepening Shadows.* N.d. Toronto: A. Sims. 56 p. Subtitle: "A brief outline of what the Bible teaches respecting the premillennial Second Coming of Christ and related events."

1799. Smith, Eugene S. *Armageddon and Millennium.* [1950s]. Dallas: Gospel Broadcast Service. 95 p.

1800. Smith, Joseph Fielding. *The Signs of the Times: A Series of Discussions.* 1942. Salt Lake City: Deseret News Press.

170 p. Also pub. Independence, MO: Press of Zion.

Mormon. Second Coming.

1801. Smith, L.A. *Is It Armageddon?* Nashville: Southern Pub. Assoc. n. d. 15 p.

Prophecies about World War I.

1802. _____. *A Great Day Coming.* N.d. Nashville: Southern Pub. Assoc. 24 p.

1803. Smith, Oswald J. *Is the Antichrist at Hand?* 1926. 5th ed. Toronto: Tabernacle Publishers. 122 p. 1927; Harrisburg, PA: Christian Alliance; 128 p. (subtitled "What of Mussolini?") Also 1983 Burlington, Canada: Welch.

Smith: Presbyterian, pastor of Toronto's Alliance Tabernacle; later, The People's Church. Favors pre-trib. God used Bolshevism to stamp out Greek Orthodox Church, but now communists want to stamp out all religion. Armageddon: final world war, in Israel. Of all diligent Bible students there is "not one who sets any date [for the End] beyond 1934." Earliest date by experts is 1928. "Convinced" that "we are already living in the closing days of the present dispensation." 604 B.C. + 2,520 = 1917 — prophetic year: Balfour Declaration. 588 B.C. + 2,520 = 1933. Mussolini: living up to Antichrist prophecies. Millennium will follow 10-Nation amalgamation. Occult and demonic predictions also of even greater World War by 1925–35. Rise of false prophets (increase in occult). New Roman Emperor will be assassinated, then revived and possessed by Antichrist. He then establishes 10-Nation League and initiates Tribulation. World's greatest earthquake (in Japan), famine (Armenia, Russia), and pestilence (1918 flu epidemic) have all just transpired. Mother Shipton foretold automobile, submarine, airplane. 70th Week in future: second half of Tribulation. Christ destroys Antichrist at Armageddon. Jews to reclaim Israel. Since 2,520 years of Gentiles ends in 1933, Tribulation, Antichrist's reign, and Armageddon must occur by then.

1804. _____. *When Antichrist Reigns.* New York: Christian Alliance. 1927. 148 p.

1805. _____. *The Clouds Are Lifting.* 1937. London: Marshall, Morgan & Scott. 96 p.

Present world like pre-Flood and Sodomite world. "End Time Signs" herald that end is near: apostasy, hypocrisy, scoffers, persecution, evangelism, increase in travel and knowledge, great wealth, famine, pestilence, earthquake, war, fear, unemployment, rise of dictators, revolutions. "Earth's darkest hour lies just ahead. Democracy has had its day, dictatorship is coming." Jews especially to be persecuted during Tribulation, but supernaturally preserved from total annihilation. Premill: visible Second Coming, millennial reign of Christ. Ten Toes/Horns yet to come: League of Europe, Second Coming within 7 years. Second half of book: exegesis of Daniel's visions. 45 B.C. to Christ's entry: the 69 Weeks. Long Gap — entire Church Age — til 70th Week of 7 years. "Dark, dark is the outlook. The vision ends in hopelessness and despair."

1806. _____. *Prophecy—What Lies Ahead?* 1959 [1943]. London: Marshall, Morgan & Scott. 120 p.

"Signs of the End Times — The Antichrist — The Great Tribulation — Christ's Return — The Kingdom of God on Earth — The Northern Confederacy — The Coming World Ruler — The Second Coming of Christ — Christ's Picture of the Last Days — The Jew in Prophecy — The Drama of the End-Time — etc." Armageddon after Russia and North Confederation attack. Post-trib pre-mill. "If we are to find out what will happen next, we must turn to the Bible. There is no other source of information...." Now nearing "End-Time Days," so things will get much worse. "Earth's darkest hour lies just ahead." Antichrist will present himself as only leader able to solve world's problems; deceives populace through miracles. Forms Ten-Nation league (revived Roman Empire), makes 7-year covenant with Israel (broken half-way through by Abomination of Desolation), Tribulation ("unparalleled suffering" for whole world — especially Jews). False Prophet makes miraculous talking statue of Antichrist. Great Northern Confederation — Russia, with Germany, Persia, Libya, Ethiopia — also attacks. Defeated at Armageddon by

Second Coming. Smith enthusiastically describes the rotting flesh at Armageddon.

1807. _____. *The Voice of Prophecy.* 1950. London: Marshall, Morgan & Scott. 111 p.

1808. _____. *When the King Comes Back.* 1954. Wheaton, IL: Sword of the Lord. 136 p. 1957 ed. London: Marshall, Morgan & Scott; 128 p.

Introduction by Wilbur Smith. Also wrote *World Problems in the Light of Prophecy.*

1809. Smith, Rebecca J. *The Time of the End: An Exposition of the Prophecies of Daniel and Revelation Relating to the Closing Events of the Present Age.* 1911. New Haven, CT: Herald of Life. 55 p.

"We are *now* in the 'time of the end.'" 1,260 "days": from A.D. 532 (Justinian's edict) to 1792. End Times began then. King of North: Turkey. King of South: Egypt (in Napoleonic wars).

1810. Smith, Robert W., and Elizabeth A. Smith (comp.). *Scriptural and Secular Prophecies Pertaining to the Last Days.* 1945 [1931]. Salt Lake City: Pyramid Press. Prophecy index.

Mormon. Quotes many Mormon prophecies (many from Mormon Scripture and from the *Millenial Star*), including 1843 "White Horse Prophecy" (Mormons to settle in Rockies; invasion of Pacific U.S. by Asians or Russians; cataclysmic earth changes), and prophecies by Joseph Smith, Brigham Young, Heber Kimball, Parley Pratt, Heber Bennion, Orson Pratt, Joseph Fielding Smith, Wilford Woodruff, Melvin Ballard. Non-Mormon prophecies include "Washington's Vision" (of Three Perils, including invasion by Asia and world war), Pyramid prophecies, Mother Shipton.

1811. Smith, Wilbur M. *This Atomic Age and the Word of God.* 1948. Boston: W.A. Wilde. 363 p. bibl.

Orig 1945 pamphlet, then 1946 *Reader's Digest* feature. Smith: Presbyterian; Moody Bible Institute faculty, then Fuller Theological Seminary; "American's best-known prophecy expounder." The Bomb forced non-believers to reconsider Prophecy, annihilation, and Second Coming.

1812. _____. *World Crises and the Prophetic Scriptures.* 1952 [1950]. Chicago: Moody Press. 384 p.

The 5th cent. Byzantine, Proclus, identified the Huns with Rosh; called northern lands "Rucia / Rosh = Russia. One-world government to come; world dictator. Two final conflicts, at beginning and end of Millennium. Federation of 10 Kings (Mediterranean-Roman), plus Gog and Magog (Russia). Russia now bent on world domination. Great burst of demon activity in Last Days, demon-worship (already a problem) will become rampant. Hobbes, Darwin, and Nietzsche exalted power, sought Antichrist. Nietzsche and Hitler were demon-possessed.

1813. _____. *Israeli Arab Conflict and the Bible.* 1967. Glendale, CA: Regal. 162 p. illus., maps, bibl. refs. SEE ALSO 1970+.

1814. Smith, William M. *Imminent Signs of the Times.* 1963. Westfield, IN: Union Bible Seminary. 38 p.

1815. Smith, Worth. *Miracle of the Ages; the Great Pyramid of Gizeh, Revealing the Message of the Great Pyramid in its Relation to the Present Crisis and the Near Future of the Race and Correlating Bible Prophecies and Ancient Historical References to the Great Pyramid.* [1934]. London: L.N. Fowler; Holyoke, MA: Elizabeth Towne. 160 p. plates, maps.

1816. Snider, William E. *The Indignation and Redemption.* [1945]. Santa Cruz, CA: The Mission of the Open Road. [4] p.

Advent Christian. "Mission of the Open Road" is Snider's trailer ministry.

1817. _____. *The Second Coming of Christ.* 16 p.

No secret Rapture before Second Coming, which will probably occur by end of WWII, or immediately after.

1818. Snowdon, James H. *The Coming of the Lord: Will It Be Premillennial?* 1922 [1919]. New York: Macmillan. xvi, 288 p.

Snowden: Western Theological Seminary, Pittsburgh. Post-mill (anti-premill). Worldwide triumph of Christianity and civilization after the War. Good bibl.

1819. Solovyov, Vladimir Sergeyevich. *War, Progress, and the End of History: Three Conversations, including a Short Story of the Anti- Christ.* 1990 [1915]. Hudson, NY: Lindisfarne Press. 206 p. 1915; London. Orig. Russian.

Novel. Antichrist section presented as manuscript found by protagonists and appended to narrative. During 20th century Japan unifies Far East, conquers Europe. 21st century: Europe unites to repel Asians, young superman becomes leader over new Roman Empire: Antichrist. Establishes new capital in Jerusalem. Assisted by Asian magician: the False Prophet. Catholic and Russian Orthodox leaders = Two Witnesses, killed when they declare emperor the Antichrist, but resurrected. False Prophet summons demons, uses occult magical powers. Jews revolt.

1820. Sparks, W.A. *A Treatise on Bible Prophecy: The Beginning of the End was Foretold to Begin with Daniel's Prophecy Which Started on July 28, 1914.* 1924. Charleston, WV: Tribune Printing. 64 p.

1821. "Sphinx." *The Times Bear Witness.* [1932]. London: Rider. 96 p.

Between now [1928?] and 1936. "Biblical & Pyramid Prophecy." Failure of disarmament. Armageddon: victory for U.S., "final overthrow of Russian & all evil." Astrological cycles: ends A.D. 2481 A.D. Six Days of Creation: 4,320 years each. Bible prophecies literally fulfilled. "We are nearing the end of the times, and the fulfilling of the Latter Day prophesies...." White Horse rider: Sagittarius. 1928 A.D. end of Daniel's 2,520 years. Ominous planetary conjunctions now. Great death, suffering, tremendous natural disasters to come in Tribulation and Armageddon. Israel to return to Palestine. Dispensation ends 1934, then 42 months of Two Witnesses and 3½ year Tribulation. Pyramid prophecy is "addressed specifically to the British race." Tribulation May 29, 1928 to Sept 15, 1936. British-Israel: "we, the British, are the inheritors of every promise made by God" to His Chosen People. Russian head of confederacy = Man of Sin, Gog; invades Israel, defeated at Armageddon by God's

British army. Makes reference to just-completed Dec. 14 Balfour Report — Germany refusing reparations payments.

1822. Spicer, William Ambrose. *Our Day in the Light of Prophecy.* 1947 [1917]. Oshawa, Canada: Signs of the Times. 380 p. illus. bibl. refs., index. Orig. pub. Nashville: Southern Publishing Assoc. Many Asian language editions.

Seventh-day Adventist. Signs of the End: 1755 Lisbon earthquake, 1780 Dark Day, 1833 meteor shower (stars falling). 538–533 B.C. + 1,260 = 1793–98 (period of Papal supremacy). 457 B.C. + 2,300 + 1844. 1844: the "investigative judgment"— cleansing of the heavenly sanctuary.

1823. _____. *Beacon Lights of Prophecy.* 1935. Takoma Park, DC: Review and Herald. 415 p. illus. maps, plates.

1824. _____. *What Next?* 1939. Nashville: Southern Pub. Assoc. 96 p. illus.

1825. Spink, James F. *Will Hitler Obtain World Domination?* 1942. New York: Loizeaux Bros. 64 p.

No; according to prophecy he is doomed to defeat because of persecution of Jews.

1826. Sproul, Stewart F. *The Last Remnant of Time: The Past, Present, and Future of This World's History in the Light of Bible Prophecy.* 1940. El Dorado, KS: S. F. Sproul. 66 p.

1827. Staege, A[lbert] J. *The Time of the End and the War Problem, and, Do You Want to Be Saved?* [ca. 1920]. Chicago: Advent Christian Press. 16 p.

6,000 years allotted for world.

1828. Stanton, Gerald B. *Kept from the Hour: A Systematic Study of the Rapture in Bible Prophecy.* 1956. Grand Rapids, MI: Zondervan. 320 p. 1991. 4th ed. sub-titled *Biblical Evidence for the Pretribulational Return of Christ* (also title of British ed.); Miami Springs, FL: Schoettle; 423 p.

Pre-trib.

1829. Stephenson, E[dward] M[orris]. *Are We Nearing the End of the World?* 1919. American Bible Publication Society. 12 p.

Armageddon.

1830. Stevens, Jesse Columbus. *The End Draws Near: or, The Certainty of*

Christ's Second Coming. [1938]. Takoma Park, Washington, DC: Review and Herald Pub. 96 p. : illus.

Seventh-day Adventist.

1831. Stevens, William Coit. *Revelation, the Crown-Jewel of Biblical Prophecy.* 1928. Harrisburg PA: Christian Alliance. 434 p. (2 vol. ed.) Also 1970 reprint ed.

Pre-mill. Series of partial raptures, to allow for martyrs during Tribulation: the "*Day of Doom.*" Literal interpretation but no dates, numbers, computations. The "time is at hand" — "proximate," "relatively imminent." Gives "full literal value" to Rapture. Anti-Christ, horrendous Tribulation. etc. Verse-by-verse exposition, with "intercalated" verses. 2,520 year theory "fallacious." Prophecy is simple, self-intelligible. Rejects 6,000 year theory; we're already probably in 8th millennium of world. Evolution is "completely refuted." Time period referred to is "entirely distinct and abruptly to succeed" present dispensation. Advocates "divisional and successional rapture." Literal locusts, other plagues, woes. But 200 million horde is not literal cavalry. Jews to return to Jerusalem, build new Temple. Antichrist makes 7-year pact. 70th week interrupted. Saints rule rest of world from Israel. Antichrist revealed after Rapture. Second Beast: counterfeit Christ = False Prophet; Jewish. First Beast = Roman Prince of 10-nation Europe confederacy. Gog = Russia. King of North = Syria, Arab confederacy. End of Tribulation: Beast loses grip; North, South, and East converge on Israel at Armageddon, will "leave the entire world in devastation." Survivors live into Millennium. World is so resistant to Christ that even after Christ's personal millennial reign humanity will still revert to Satan. World has just seen its worst war (WWI), worst earthquake (1920 China), famine (Russian), and pestilence (influenza pandemic). After Michael defeats Satan in War in Heaven, Satan expelled to Earth and then initiates Tribulation. Wounded head of beast is resurrected empire, probably Mussolini. Then absolute worldly authority given to Antichrist

(Beast from Sea). Beast from Earth is Antichrist's Prime Minister. Armageddon: where armies of world assemble, but destroyed outside Jerusalem at Jehoshaphat Valley (Jezreel) just prior to Millennium. Euphrates literally dries up. Clay-iron mix = popular as well as authoritarian acceptance of Antichrist. Mystery Babylon: corrupt apostate religion, false ecclesiasticism. Antichrist requires world to worship him. Hell located inside Earth. Pre-Adamic catastrophe of Gen 1:2 — "appalling disruption" of original creation, followed by re-creation. New Heaven and Earth: world will be similarly re-constituted after disruption of End. New Jerusalem = "divinely constructed space colony fifteen hundred miles square" hovers over earth at Millennium, then descends.

1832. Stewart, Basil. *Foretold & Fulfilled: The Church of Rome a Sign of the End: An Examination of Bible Prophecy Concerning Rome, and the Approaching End of This Age.* 1926. London: Covenant. 94 p. bibl. refs.

1833. _____. *The Witness of the Great Pyramid.* 1928. 2nd ed rev. London: Covenant. xvi, 271 p. illus. charts.

Armageddon: end of 1928–36 period.

1834. _____. *The Bible Chronology: Four Millenniums from Adam to Christ Proved by the Statements of Scripture, and Corroborated by the Scientifically-Recorded Chronology of the Great Pyramid.* 1930. London: G. Routledge. vii, 88 p. Plates. illus., bibl. refs., indexes.

1835. _____. *The Great Pyramid: Its Construction, Symbolism and Chronology.* 1931. 3rd ed, rev. London: Covenant. 58 p. illus., bibl. refs., index.

1836. _____. *"At Midnight a Cry!": The Present Crisis in Relation to the Second Advent, and Events Subsequent thereto Up to the Final Judgment; The True Nature and Sequence of these Events as Revealed in Prophecy and Corroborated in the Symbolism of the Great Pyramid.* 1932. London: Covenant Publishing Co. 185 p. illus., bibl. refs., indexes.

1837. _____. *Collected Addresses on Great Pyramid and Scripture Prophecy Respecting the Present World-Crisis and its Significance.* 1935. London: J. Bales Sons & Danielsson. vii, 139 p. diagr. Several addresses prev. pub. as pamphlets.

1838. Stranges, Frank E. *My Friend from Beyond Earth.* 1981? [1960]. Van Nuys, CA: I.E.C. new rev. enlarged ed. with added "chapter by Val Thor." 63 p. photos drawings.

1839. Strauss, Lehman. *Armageddon.* [c1959]. Findlay, OH: Dunham. 29 p.

1840. _____. *Christ's Literal Reign on Earth.* [ca. 1960]. Findlay, OH: Dunham. 36 p.

1841. _____. *The Man of Sin.* 1960. Findlay, OH: Dunham. 32 p.

1842. _____. *The Book of Revelation.* 1964. Neptune, NJ: Loizeaux Bros. 381 p. bibl.

1843. _____. *God's Plan for the Future.* 1965. Grand Rapids, MI: Zondervan. 198 p. index, bibl.

1844. _____. *The End of This Present World.* 1971 [1967]. Grand Rapids, MI: Zondervan. 131 p. bibl.

1845. _____. *The Prophecies of Daniel.* 1969. Neptune, NJ: Loizeaux Bros. 384 p. bibl.

Foreword by president of Moody Bible Institute. Strauss: Baptist minister. Dispensational pre-trib pre-mill. Insists on authenticity of Daniel, written ca. 600 B.C. Literal fulfillment in both past and future (double fulfillment). Daniel not in chronological order; some prophecies jump from past (already fulfilled) directly to End. Each chapter begins with some backtracking, overlapping. Clay mixed with iron = assimilation of peoples into Roman empire. 10 Toes/Horns = final (future) form of Empire. Democracy must crumble, fail; yield to theocracy. Contra claims of evolution, world is deteriorating. Lion's den = the Remnant during Tribulation. Little Horn= Antichrist during Tribulation. Abomination of Desolation = Antiochus, then (future) Antichrist. 70 "weeks" really 7 *heptads.* From 445 B.C. (Artaxerxes decree) to when Messiah "cut off" = 69 weeks. 70th Week in future, after parenthesis. Great Tribulation: second half of 70th. War in Heaven prior to

Tribulation: Good angels vs. bad (demons). Revelation 11: King of North, South = refers to past war (Antiochus, not Antichrist). But then Revelation jumps to End: Antichrist, Egypt (South) and Russia (North) vs. Israel. Literal Armageddon. "We are in that time period immediately preceding the seventieth week." SEE ALSO 1970+.

1846. Stroh, Grant. *When God Comes Down to Earth: or Epochal Crises, Past and Future.* 1914. Chicago: Bible Inst. Colportage Assoc. 220 p. Reissued as *The Next World-Crisis in the Light of Former World Crises.*

Introduction by James M. Gray. Pretrib.

1847. _____. *God's World-Program: God's Plans for Men and Their Consummation.* 1924. Chicago: Bible Inst. Colportage Assoc. xv, 204 p. New York: G.H. Doran.

Stroh: Moody Bible Institute professor. Jews to regather in Israel after their Tribulation. Spiritual authority removed from Jews, given to Church (temporarily). Ephesus: Apostolic church. Thyatira: Romish, harlot church. Sardis: Reformation church. Philadelphia: Modern missionary church. Laodicean: Apostate church. Rapture, then Satan's usurpation, then Christ-led army destroys him, then Millennium. Great Tribulation: 3½ years. "Year-Day" theory: Gentile age of 2,520 years from 604 – 588 B.C. (the destruction of Israel) to A.D. 1917 – 1933 (Time of the End). Disparages the "Hopelessness of Evolution."

1848. _____. *Panorama of the Ages.* 1940. Chicago: Moody Bible Inst. 106 p.

Bible-study correspondence course on dispensationalism.

1849. Strombeck, J[ohn] F[rederick]. *First the Rapture.* 1950. Moline, IL: Strombeck Agency. 197 p. 1992. Kregel reprint ed.

Foreword by DeHaan. 1982 ed.: Foreword by W. Wiersbe. Pre-trib. Imminent Rapture — Church will not go through the Tribulation (70th Week is future). Necessary to distinguish in the Bible between Israel and the Church. "Conditions in the world today indicate that the present age is rapidly drawing to a close." Holy Spirit is Restrainer of Satan during this Church Age, but Satan unrestrained during Tribulation.

1850. Stuernagel, A[lbert] E. *Christ's Coming Reign of Peace.* 1926. Sacramento, CA; World's Best Literature Depot. 122 p.

1851. Sunderwirth, Wilbert W. *What Time Is It, World? A Timetable of Prophecy.* 1953. New York: Vantage Press. xii, 231 p.

1852. Sweany, O. C. *Symbols of the Revelation Explained: A Historic View of Prophecy.* 1941. 29 p.

1,260 Days = era of the Papacy and barbarians.

1853. _____. *Is This That?* [1940s?]. Oakland, CA: Messiah's Advocate. [4] p.

1854. Talbot, Louis T. *God's Plan of the Ages.* 1946 [1936]. Grand Rapids, MI: William B. Eerdmans. 199 p.

Talbot: Presbyterian minister; Chancellor of Biola College and Talbot Theol. Sem. Dispensational pre-trib pre-mill. Fold-out chart. Gap Theory creationism.

1855. _____. *Russia, Her Invasion of Palestine in the Last Days.* [1940s?]. Glendale, CA: Church Press. 29 p. (radio address). Rev. ed.: *Russia Mobilizes for Armageddon.* 1955 [1946]. Glendale, CA: Church Press.

1856. Tanner, Jacob. *The Thousand Years Not Pre-Millennial.* 1934. Minneapolis: Augsburg. 57 p.

The Millennium is now. Contra premill; presents biblical objections. Not double Coming or double Resurrection: all are same event. The Millennium is symbolic, of powerlessness of Satan over believers. Revelation: literary parallelisms; not historical.

1857. Tatford, Frederick A. *Prophecy's Last Word: An Exposition of the Revelation.* 1974 [1947]. Eastbourne, England: Prophetic Witness. 270 p. Orig. pub. London: Pickering & Inglis.

Tatford: former director of United Kingdom Atomic Energy Authority; president of Institute of Governmental Purchasing (U.S.); editor of *The Harvester* and *Prophetic Witness*; also wrote *Is Evolution True?* (1970). "Futurist" interpretation:

present dispensation as parenthesis between 69th and 70th Week, before removal of Church at Second Coming.

1858. _____. *Daniel and His Prophecy.* 1980 [1953]. Klock & Klock reprint. Orig London: Oliphants. 256 p. bibl. indexes.

Long gap (Parenthesis) in account of last empire (ten-fold division [toes] refers to future period described in Revelation). Christ is the fourth figure who joins three friends in fiery furnace. Ten horns of last Beast are simultaneous (not consecutive) future rulers. Millennial Kingdom under Christ's personal rule. 70 Weeks began with 445 B.C. decree of Artaxerxes to rebuild Jerusalem. 69 weeks ended with Jesus entering Jerusalem. Great Parenthesis between 69th and 70th week: God ignores the in-between time when His people ignored him. Half of last "week" (7 years) is the Tribulation. (Many of the prophecies do refer to Roman times — not all are future.) Some refer to Roman destruction of Jerusalem, but Daniel 11:40–45 refers to End: battle of Valley of Jehoshaphat, Second Coming, and Millennium. Faithful (the Church) removed before Tribulation (1,260 days, or 3½ years); Second Coming allows for saving of godly remnant. Israel suffers the most during Tribulation.

1859. _____. *The Climax of the Ages: Studies in the Prophecy of Daniel.* 1964. Grand Rapids, MI: Zondervan. 256 p. indexes.

1860. _____. *God's Program of the Ages.* 1967. Grand Rapids, MI: Kregel. 160 p. bibl.

"The Old Testament prophets make it abundantly plain … that judgment will fall upon the Arab people …, the Arab will be swept out of the land and … Israel will be reestablished there."

1861. _____. *Will There Be a Millennium?.* 1969. Eastbourne, England: Prophetic Witness / Neptune, NJ: Loizeaux Bros. 124 p. bibl.

1862. _____. *Five Minutes to Midnight.* 1970. Fort Washington, PA: Christian Literature Crusade. 125 p.

1863. _____, and John McNicol.

Middle East Cauldron. 1971. Eastbourne, England: P.W. [Prophetic Witness]. 104 p. illus., map. SEE ALSO 1970+.

1864. Tatham, C. Ernest. *Daniel Speaks Today.* 1967 [1948]. Westchester IL: Good News. 93 p. Condensed ed.

1865. _____. *Revelation: The Climax of Prophecy: A Bible Correspondence Course.* 1960. Chicago, IL: Moody Bible. Inst. 172 p.

1866. _____. *Bible Prophecy.* 1972 [1960]. Dubuque, IA: Emmaus Correspondence School. Lessons separately paginated. diagrams.

Extension ministry of Emmaus Bible College. Pre-trib Rapture. Double reference, law of primary and secondary fulfilments. First Beast is political leader of Ten-Nation Roman Empire; Second Beast is religious leader — Jewish Antichrist.

1867. Taylor, George Floyd. *The Second Coming of Jesus.* 1950. Franklin Springs, GA: The Pub. House, Pentecostal Holiness Church. 225 p.

1868. Ten Boom, Corrie. *Marching Orders for the End Battle.* 1970 [1969]. Fort Washington, PA: Christian Literature Crusade. 91 p.

Author of *The Hiding Place* (anti-Nazi resistance) Don't rely on Rapture; Christians will suffer Tribulation.

1869. Tenney, C[larence] V. *God's Outline of Human History.* 1929. [New Hampshire] 24 p.

Armageddon will be a worldwide propaganda war. 7th Trumpet = WWI aerial war. Previous Trumpets were barbarian and Moslem invasions, French Revolution and Napoleonic Wars.

1870. _____. *Maranatha a Triple Witness of the Coming Kingdom.* [1930s]. Wolfeboro, NH. 60 p.

Also wrote *Is the Advent at Hand?* (1914); *Studies on Revelation* (1948); *A Fifth Universal Empire Now Due as Shown by the Harmony of Fulfilled Prophecy*; and *Matthew 24* (1950).

1871. Tenney, Merrill Chapin. *Interpreting Revelation.* 1957. Grand Rapids, MI : Eerdmans. 220 p. index bibl. charts.

Dean of Grad. Sch: Wheaton. Premill (but gives arguments for all positions); self-described "moderate futurist." Revelation is also message to its original audience (not only future). Seven churches refer to contemporary situation as well as Church Age in general. Argues for early date of composition. Series of seven: parallel not successive. Seals: general; Trumpets: specific. Bowls: specific and concluding judgments. Atomic bombs make literal interpretation of Trumpet judgments probable. Two Beasts: godless political/social/economic power in Last Days. The End "at hand" = fulfillment began with seven churches. Second Advent may be soon or not. May be long gap between Second Advent and Kingdom of God. Fulfillment may come very soon (but not necessarily); many accelerating trends today, however, suggest it is imminent. "Jerusalem" and "Babylon" are figurative. Two Beasts: real powers. Beast of Sea combines Daniel's Four Beasts; future dictator (one-world totalitarianism). Notes that greater literalism implies a more futurist interpretation.

1872. _____. *The Book of Revelation*. 1963. Grand Rapids, MI: Baker Book House. 116 p. bibl. refs.

1873. _____. *The War We Can't Lose: The Revelation*. 1968. new ed. Wheaton, IL: Scripture Press. 128 p. illus. Ed. by Henry Jacobsen?

1874. Tennyson, Elwell Thomas. *The Time of the End*. 1969 [1951]. Jefferson City, MO: Harvest Publishers. 195 p.

Also wrote *Deliverance in the Whirlwind*. (1959).

1875. Thiessen, Henry Clarence. *Will the Church Pass Through the Tribulation?* 1941 [1940]. NY: Loizeaux Bros. 63 p.

No, it won't; pre-mill Rapture.

1876. Thomas, James Henderson. *Tomorrow's World; Visualizing the Future Prophetically*. 1949. Kansas City, MO: Burton Pub. C. 127 p.

1877. Thompson, Fred P. *Bible Prophecies: Study Course for Youth and Adult*. 1964. Cincinnati: Standard. 127 p. bibl.

1878. Thurber, Robert Bruce. *Our Marvellous Times*. 1939. Poona [India?]: Oriental Watchman. 64 p.

1879. _____. *Toward a Better Day*. 1941. Poona: Oriental Watchman Pub. House. 272 p. : illus.

1880. Thurston, Herbert. *British-Israel and the Great Pyramid Scare*. 1928. London: Catholic Truth Soc. 28 p. bibl. refs.

From journal *The Month*; presumably a refutation.

1881. Titterton, C[harles] H. *Armageddon: or, The Last War*. 1916. London: Charles J. Thynne. xi, 108 p.

Titterton: professor of Hebrew and oriental languages, University of Edinburgh. World War is not Armageddon, but we're on the verge of it. Actual decisive combat at Jehoshophat, which is "represented" by term Armageddon. "Armageddon" is symbolic, as it was ancient place of decisive battle. Gog = northern anti-Christian and anti-Semitic world power. Gog of Revelation = all nations. Rosh = Russia. "Day of the Lord" = from the Parousia to the Millennium. Britain will be instrument of Jews' Return.

1882. Todd, Sam. *Flying Saucers, Atomic Bombs and the Second Coming of Christ*. 1955. Newnan, GA: 29 p.

Evangelistic Temple, Austin, TX

1883. Toms, Alan David. *"I Will Come Again": An Introduction to the Study of Prophecy*. 1963. London: Sovereign Grace Advent Testimony. 75 p.

1884. Torrance, Thomas Forsyth. *The Apocalypse Today*. 1959. Grand Rapids, MI: Eerdmans. 155 p.

Church of Scotland.

1885. Torrey, Reuben A. *The Return of the Lord Jesus*. 1966 [1913]. Grand Rapids, MI: Baker. 142 p. Orig. 1913; Los Angeles: Bible Institute of Los Angeles.

"The storm will be brief, and beyond the storm there is a golden day, such as philosophers and poets never dreamed of." Convinced of pre-mill truth by Danish theologian Martensen.

1886. Townsend, L.T. *End of the World: Biblical, Scientific and Other Points of View*. 1913. Boston: Advent Christian Pub. Soc. 62 p.

Presented 1884 in New Bedford as lecture. Natural and cosmic catastrophes, Zionism, militarism.

1887. Tracy, Edward. *The United States in Prophecy.* 1969. San Francisco: Convale. 77 p.

Babylon = New York; to be annihilated near End.

1888. Trumbull, Charles G. *Prophecy's Light on Today.* c1937. New York: Fleming H. Revell. 191 p.

Mostly from *Sunday School Times* articles. Strongly pre-mill. Astronomers seeing increasing signs in the skies of approaching End; also lawlessness, apostasy, spiritualism, decadent music; developments in Russia, rise of Hitler, and return of Jews to Palestine.

1889. _____, ed. *How I Came to Believe in Our Lord's Return and Why I Believe the Lord's Return Is Near.* 1934. Chicago: Bible Inst. Colportage Assoc.

1890. Tubby, C. S. *The Time of the End: Unmistakable Signs of Christ's Coming.* N.d. [1950s?]. 3 ed. rev. Stevensville, Canada. 117 p.

1891. Turnbow, A. *Watchman, What of the Night?* 1931. Chicago: Advent Christian. 11 p.

Advent Christian. The 6,000 years of world's history almost up.

1892. Turner, Gwin. *The Shape of Things to Come: Studies in the Revelation.* [ca 1970?]. Los Angeles: Leadership Development. 95 p.

Baptist.

1893. Tytler, William. *Plain Talks on Prophecy: Or, the Great Prophetic Cycles of Time.* N.d. Glasgow: Pickering & Inglis; Hulbert. 229 p. illus., charts.

Dispensationalist.

1894. *The Unsealed Book: An Exposition of the Book of Revelation.* 1968. Prophetic Light. 113 p.

1895. Vallance, G. F. *The Coming Universal Kingdom.* 1944. Easton, Suffolk, England: G. F. Vallance. 79 p.

1896. _____. *Proceeding According to Plan.* Woodbridge, England: G.F. Vallance.

Half-hour silence before 7th Seal: 21 years from Nov. 11, 1918 (Armistice) to Sept. 1939. "Last hour" is 42 years from 1918, thus Rapture will be 1960. 1918: 6,006 years after Adam.

1897. Vallowe, Ed. R. *Riches of Revelation.* 3 vols. Forest Park, GA: Ed. F. Vallowe Evangelistic Assoc.

Also wrote *Biblical Mathematics: Keys to Scripture Numerics* (1988 [1966]); *Budding of the Fig Tree* (Israel in prophecy; 1972); *Israel/Russia in the Last Days,* and *Revival Messages for the Last Days.*

1898. Valtorta, Maria. *The End Times as Revealed to Maria Valtorta.* 1994 [1985]. Sherbrooke, Quebec: Editions Paulines. xxii, 161 p. bibl. refs. Orig. Italian.

Posthumous pub. (Valtorta: d. 1961).

1899. Van Dyken, Peter L. *Premillennialism: An Absurd and Fantastic Illusion.* 1960. Ripon, CA: P.L. Van Dyken 14 p.

1900. Vennard, Iva May Durham. *The Revelation, a Student's Handbook.* 1914. Chicago: Chicago Evangelistic Institute Press. 112 p.

1901. Vine, W[illiam] E. *The Roman Empire in the Light of Prophecy: or, The Rise, Progress and End of the Fourth World-Empire.* 1916. London: Pickering & Inglis. 107 p. plates maps index.

1902. _____. *The Roman Empire: Its Coming Revival and End.* n.d. [preface dated 1936]. London: Pickering & Inglis. 96 p. index maps.

Daniel's Fourth Kingdom — Roman Empire — disappeared, to reappear, revived, as ten federated states. Clay = Jewish; iron = Roman militarism. Antichrist (Roman ruler) makes covenant with Jewish nation, shares power with the False Prophet (Jewish ruler). Treaty broken, Tribulation follows. Mystery Babylon = Catholic papal religion. King of South = a part of, or equal to, Roman confederacy (including Egypt), which is invaded by North. Armageddon: world's rebellion against God meets doom — Second Coming. Asserts that "present-day events indicate how rapidly we are approaching conditions destined to obtain at the close of the time of the Gentiles."

1903. Vos, Johannes Gerhardus. *The End of the Ages: A Study of Scripture Truth Concerning the Last Things.* 1960. S.l. : s.n. 43 p. First pub. booklet form in China in 1935, 2nd ed. 1936.

Reformed Presbyterian Church of North America.

1904. Walker, Allen. *Last Day Delusions.* 1957. Nashville: Southern Publishing Assoc. 128 p.

Seventh-day Adventist. Refutes secret pre-trib Rapture and denies the "second chance during the Millennium" theory (possibility of converting and being saved *after* the Second Coming). Also denies that Antichrist will only be revealed after the righteous join Christ in heaven.

1905. Walker, William H. *Will Russia Conquer the World?* 1978 [1960]. rev. ed. Dalton, GA: Span Pub. 109 p. 2nd ed. pub. Loizeaux Bros. 1962.

1906. Wallace, R. B. *A Three-Fold Cord: Creation, Revelation, Inspiration and the Purpose of the Ages.* 1963. 5th ed. Orange, CA: Ralph E. Welch Foundation. 195 p.

1907. Walvoord, John F. *The Return of the Lord.* 1955. Findlay, OH: Dunham.

Walvoord: Presbyterian; president of Dallas Theological Seminary; editor of *Bibliotheca Sacra.* Russian invasion of Israel midway through 7-year Tribulation; prepares way for Antichrist's takeover of world as head of revived Roman Empire.

1908. _____. *The Rapture Question.* 1975 [1957]. Grand Rapids, MI: Zondervan. 204 p. index.

Discusses various theories of the Rapture. Pre-trib; imminency of Rapture.

1909. _____. *The Millennial Kingdom.* 1988 [1959]. Grand Rapids, MI: Zondervan. xxiv, 373 p.

"A basic text in premillennial theology."

1910. _____. *The Nations, Israel, and the Church in Prophecy.* 1988 [1962]. Grand Rapids, MI: Academie (Zondervan). xiv, 176, 138, 183 p.

1911. _____. *The Revelation of Jesus Christ.* 1989 [1966]. Chicago: Moody. 350 p. bibl. SEE ALSO 1970+.

1912. Wangerin, Theodora Scharffenberg. *Our Lord's Great Prophecy: Evidences of the Rapidly Fulfilling Signs of Christ's Return as Given in Matthew Twenty-Four.* 1948. Seoul: Signs of the Times. 157 p. illus. In Korean.

1913. Ward, C[harles] M[orris]. *"... Waiting...."* 1959. Springfield, MO: Assemblies of God. 42 p.

Disasters; Revelation.

1914. _____. *The Bear and the Dragon.* 1966. Springfield, MO: Assemblies of God. 48 p.

1915. _____. *The H-Bomb and the Battle of Armageddon.* N.d.? Springfield, MO: Revivaltime. 23 p. SEE ALSO 1970+.

1916. Ware, Arthur E. *Some Last Hour Reflections; Recording the Solemn Condition of Affairs on Earth in the Year A.D. 1927, As Viewed from the Prophetic Sections of the Word of God.* 1927. 2nd ed. Edinburgh: Marshall Bros. 106 p. foldout chart.

Agrees with Anderson, Guinness. 19 years of crisis: 1915–34. 10-nation alliance, Armageddon. Evil Papacy, return of Jews. 1934: Second Coming; Armageddon, defeat of Antichrist armies. "Translation" of Church maybe 1927. 1917: Palestine mandate. Tribulation: 3½ years. Pre-trib Rapture: Christians *can't* be required to endure the "indescribable tortures" of the Tribulation.

1917. _____. *The World in Liquidation: The Coming of Christ at Hand.* 1953 [1930s]. Distr. by Simpkin Marshall (London). vi, 466 p. index chart.

Second Coming= "mystical first stage in 1933" — world economic conference. Christ pre-incarnated as Immanual before born as Jesus. 6,000 year lifespan of earth from 4075 B.C. creation to 1933. Then "unreckoned internal" before Millennium. Finally, Apocalyptic Era of 7 year Judgment which replaces "canceled" years A.D. 26–33.

1918. _____. *The Coming Exodus: A Chronological Demonstration from the Bible which, in the Belief of the Author, Affords Clear Evidence that Christ Will Return for His Church in the Year 1961 when the World Will Enter the Era of the Apocalypse.* 1961. Margate [Eng.]: Eyre and Spottiswoode. 100 p.

1919. Warn, Charles Lathrup. *Today, as in the Days of Noah: The Prophecies of Jesus, Peter, and the Apocalypse, Concerning* *the Events of Yesterday, Today, and Tomorrow.* 1948. Los Angeles. 58 p.

1920. *A Warning to All People of the Second Coming of Christ. Revelations of the Building of the Temple and Instruction to the Church of Christ. The Time Is at Hand....* 1971 [1938]. Independence, MO: Church of Christ, with the Elijah Message. 304 p.

(See also *Word of the Lord,* 1984.)

1921. Watchtower Bible and Tract Society. *The Truth Shall Make You Free.* 1943.

Replaced Russell's dates: invisible return of Christ was 1914, not 1874. Six periods of creation, each seven thousand years long; this is God's seventh period. Adam created 4028 B.C.; 1943 is Year 5971 of world. "We are therefore near the end of six thousand years of human history, with conditions upon us and tremendous events at hand foreshadowed by those of Noah's days." Implies 1972 as End. Time of End began 1914, when Satan's rule was broken — Satan and his wicked angels defeated in heaven and cast down to Earth. Abomination of Desolation = League of Nations. 7th Beast = Anglo-American world imperialism. Rome-controlled Kingdom of North; Anglo-American Kingdom of South. Armageddon: organized religion leads the war against God's people. (Written by Nathan H. Knorr?)

1922. ____. *"The Kingdom Is at Hand."* 1944. Brooklyn, NY: Watch Tower Bible and Tract Society. 380 p. illus. map, plates indexes.

1923. ____. *"New Heavens and a New Earth."* 1953. Brooklyn, NY: Watchtower Bible and Tract Soc. 380 p. illus.

1924. ____. *You May Survive Armageddon Into God's New World.* 1955 Brooklyn NY: Watch Tower Bible and Tract Soc. 379 p. illus.

1925. ____. *Life Everlasting in Freedom of the Sons of God.* 1966. Brooklyn, NY: Watchtower Bible and Tract. 410 p. illus., map.

1st ed.: 3 million copies. "A Worldwide Jubilee Approaching!" "Six Thousand Years of Human Existence Closing" — man nearing end of 6,000 years

existence and 7th thousand-year period about to begin. Man created 4026 B.C.; thus End is 1975, and Millennium begins fall 1975. Then will be what God intended: glorious freedom for mankind.

1926. ____. *"Then Is Finished the Mystery of God."* 1969. Brooklyn, NY: Watchtower Bible and Tract Soc. 380 p. drawings. SEE ALSO 1970+.

1927. ____. *In the Twinkling of an Eye.* 1961 [1910]. New York: Revell. 250 p. Pub. 1918, Los Angeles: Biola Book Room.

1928. Watson, Sydney. *The Mark of the Beast.* 1945 [1915]. New York: Loizeaux Bros. 245 p. Orig. pub. in England.

Fiction, sequel to above. In late 19th century a Jewess bore son "Lucien Apleon," the Antichrist, an incarnated demon, Judas reincarnated, skilled in all arts and sciences. Gains influence after Rapture (previous novel), as society sinks into appalling licentiousness and blasphemy. A revived Roman Empire of ten kingdoms makes Antichrist Emperor. Antichrist promises to protect Jews, who are militarily helpless, for seven years, and sets up base for world empire in Jerusalem. False Prophet assists Antichrist; they rebuild Temple, and unveil miraculous speaking statue. Populace branded with Mark of Beast: Greek letters "X S" with snake in middle (666). Babylon becomes world commercial center. Novel's heroes all suffer horrendous torture and beheading. Second half of Tribulation: all nations attack Israel, because financially indebted to Jews who are now concentrated in Israel.

1929. Webber, Edward Frederick. *A Study in the Revelation.* Fort Dodge, IA: Walterick. 220 p.

Father of David Webber; founder of Southwest Radio Church. Also wrote *United Nations Exposed* (1955; Southwest Radio Church). Hitler = Antichrist.

1930. Were, Louis F. *144,000 Sealed!: When? Why? Special Protection Promised for the Time of Trouble, God's Message of Love for His Remnant Church.* 1932. Victoria, Australia: author. 110 p.

Seventh-day Adventist.

1931. _____. *What Is Armageddon?* 1942. Adelaide Australia: author. 85 p.

Includes *Futurism and the Antichrist of Scripture.*

1932. _____. *Bible Principles of Interpretation: Establish Truth and Safeguard Against Last-Day Errors.* [1940s?]. [Melbourne, Victoria, Australia: Louis F. Were. 67 p.

1933. _____. *The Kings That Come From the Sunrising: A Survey, a Challenge, a Prophecy.* [1950s?]. Victoria, Australia: L. Were. 58 p.

1934. _____. *Power Unlimited: Righteousness by Faith and the Final Conflict.* [1960s?]. [Melbourne, Australia: Louis F. Were?]. 249 p.

1935. _____. *The Woman and the Beast in the Book of Revelation: Studies in Revelation 12–20.* 1983. Berrien Springs, MI: First Impressions. 237 p. "First Australian printing 1952" (priv. pub., titled *The Woman and the Resurrected Beast: Why is the Seventh Head Numbered 8? The Mysteries of Revelation 17 Solved*).

1936. Westwood, Tom. *Palestine: The World's Last Battleground: and, The Four Horsemen of the Apocalypse: Are They Riding in the Earth Today? and, The Antichrist: When Will He Appear?* 1968. Denver: Wilson Foundation. 91 p.

1937. White, Gordon. *Prophecies of the Bible: The Kaiser and the Turk, the Second Coming of Christ and the Millennium....* 1918. Tampa, FL. 64 p.

1938. Whitty, G. *The Coming Universal War: How Bible Prophecies Clearly Foretell Its Coming; How We May Escape This Great Catastrophe.* 1934. Wimbledon, England: priv. pub.

Believers raptured just as universal war begins.

1939. Wight, Francis Asa. *The Beast, Modernism, and the Evangelical Faith.* 1926. Boston: Stratford. 311 p.

Beast and False Prophet = last human ruler controlling earth. League of Nations = 7th Head of Beast. Beast from Sea is Bolshevism. Wight denounces evolution and modernism, and refutes Jehovah's Witnesses.

1940. _____. *Communism and Fascism Destroyed at Christ's Second Coming.* 1937. Harrisburg, PA; Evangelical Press. 72 p.

Things will get much worse (the Tribulation), but then the Second Coming and Millennium. "Christ offers no other alternative to this 'Atheistic Mass Man' when He appears, but entire destruction." America will be refuge nation during Tribulation, though it may become affiliated with the Ten-Nation confederacy. Pre-trib Rapture.

1941. _____. *The Catching Up of Christ's True Church ("The Rapture").* 1939. Grand Rapids, MI: Zondervan. 30 p.

Red Russia = Atheistic Beast Government. Ten-Nation confederacy arises from League of Nations. False Prophet = cultic, and ecumenical religious bureau.

1942. _____. *The Beast, the False Prophet, and Hitler.* 1941. Butler, IN: author. 48 p.

1943. Wilcox, Francis McClellan. *The Coming Crisis.* 3rd ed. 1933. Takoma Park; Washington DC: Review and Herald. 96 p.

Wilcox: editor of *Advent Review and Sabbath Herald.* Seventh-day Adventist; many quotes from E.G. White. "The prophetic word indicates that we have reached the closing days of earth's history." Papacy gaining power and permeating Protestantism; Catholics pushing for Sunday laws. First Beast = Roman Church. Two Horns = Republicanism and Protestantism (originally innocent but now corrupted). These last days characterized by "deceptive and mighty workings of Satan," who will impersonate Christ and perform miracles. Great persecutions ahead; believers will flee to mountains.

1944. Wilkinson, Ulysses Grant. *The Great Conflict: The Present World War and the Place It Occupies in Bible Prophecy and World History.* 1919. Comanche, OK: Wilkinson. 83 p.

1945. Williams, Charles. *The Coming End of the Age, Its Imminent Nearness and What It Means for Our Race.* 1916. London: Jarrold & Sons. 90 p. illus.

Williams: M.D. Declares that belief in imminent End is eminently sane.

1946. Williams, Henry Clay. *The Revelation of Jesus Christ: A Study of the Apocalypse.* 1917. Cincinnati: Standard. 370 p.

1914 prophesied as start of Stone Kingdom war (end of Gentile period) from verses about Nebuchadnezzar's madness. Millennium = 1972.

1947. Williams, Oliver E. *The Glorious Appearing of Our Lord.* [1916]. Warren, PA.

Preface by W.B. Riley. "*Present world events* declare He is coming." Pre-trib. Sudden, imminent Rapture. World War is sign of nearness of End.

1948. Williams, Samuel Jacob. *The Jew, God's Timepiece.* 1935. [Cincinnati:] God's Bible School. 64 p. illus. bibl.

1949. Williamson, George Hunt. *Other Tongues—Other Flesh.* 1954. Amherst, WI: Amherst Press. 448 p. illus. bibl.

Benevolent and malevolent interactions with extraterrestrials through history, some allied with sinister "International Bankers" who are hidden force behind governments. Right-wing, anti-Semitic undertones. Williamson was one of the first flying saucer contactees. Member of Brotherhood of the Seven Rays which also included Charles Laughead and Dorothy Martin. (Laughead and Martin were subjects of classic sociological study *When Prophecy Fails* [Festinger, Riecken, and Schachter, 1956]. They predicted apocalyptic flooding of most of Earth for Dec. 21, 1954, and expected to be transported to safety by flying saucers.) "Time is *very, very short!* ... Disaster will come before Dec. 1st, *this year!*"

1950. _____. *The Saucers Speak! A Documentary Report of Interstellar Communication by Radiotelegraphy.* 1954. Los Angeles: New Age. 127 p. illus.

Flying saucers arriving to warn and teach Earth. "The saucer people are the 'hosts' that were prophesied about as coming to earth preceding the Second Coming of Christ." Catastrophic earthquakes and judgments, then Golden Age.

1951. _____, and John F. McCoy. *UFOs Confidential.* 1958. Corpus Christi, TX: Essene Press. 100 p.

1952. Wilson, Art. *Am I Kidding Myself and Just Playing "Christian," Or Do I Really Believe That Christ's Return Is Very Near?* [1960s?]. Wichita, KS: A. Wilson. 30 p.

1953. _____. *According to the Bible ... How Near Is the End of the World?* N.d. Wichita, KS: A. Wilson. 24 p.

1954. Wilson, Lilly Dever. *The Apocalyptic Vision Revealed to John.* 1944. Des Moines, IA: Garner. 234 p.

1955. Wimbish, John Summerfield. *Three Prophetic Sermons.* 1951. New York: Calvary Radio Ministry. 20 p.

"The Red Russian menace prophesied; World War III; when the world's on fire." Baptist.

1956. Winrod, Gerald B. *The Prophetic Destiny of the United States.* 1943. Wichita, KS: Defender Publishers. 60 p.

1957. _____. *Antichrist and the Atomic Bomb.* 1945. Wichita, KS: Defender Publishers. 78 p. illus.

Also wrote *Mussolini's Place in Prophecy* (1933); *Hitler in Prophecy; United States and Russia in Prophecy and the Red Horse of the Apocalypse* (1937); *Communism in Prophecy* (1946). Winrod was pro-Nazi.

1958. Witty, Robert Gee. 1969. *Signs of the Second Coming.* Nashville: Broadman Press. 127 p. bibl.

1959. Wolff, Richard. *Israel Act III.* 1967 Wheaton IL: Tyndale. 94 p. bibl.

Wolff: his Jewish family fled Nazi Germany; Wolff then became a Christian. Exec. Secretary Intl. Christian Broadcasters; based in Wheaton. Act 1: God's call to Abraham. Act II: survival, dispersion, persecution. III: the Return; ends with Second Coming. Gentiles gain supremacy, but Gentile Age almost over. Nations will gang up on Israel, but God will destroy them. Temple rebuilding will be literal. King of South = Egypt. Cush = Sudan.

1960. Wood, A. Skevington. *Prophecy in the Space Age.* 1963. Grand Rapids, MI: Zondervan. Also pub. 1964, London. Marshall, Morgan & Scott.

1961. _____. *Signs of the Times: Biblical Prophecies and Current Events.* 1971 [1970] Grand Rapids, MI: Baker. 126 p. Orig. 1970, London.

Armageddon includes siege of Jerusalem; all nations invade; saved only by Second Coming, followed by Millennium. Reports rumors of 60,000 tons of pre-cut limestone from Bedford, IN, being warehoused for Temple rebuilding. Confederation probably of 10-nation former Roman Empire, vs. Northern alliance and Eastern bloc. All meet at Armageddon. Psalm 83 foretells 10-nation Arab confederacy. Signs of End: earthquakes, famine, war, disease, immorality, apostasy, cults, evangelism.

1962. Wood, Harold. *Where Are We in Prophecy?; Or the Second Advent of Christ, Is It Near at Hand, Or Distant?* 1929. Surrey, England: author. viii, 227 p.

Includes sections on global Flood of Noah (by D.M. Panton); Mussolini as Antichrist (by Ewart Kingston).

1963. Wood, Leon James. *Is the Rapture Next? An Answer to the Question: Will the Church Escape the Tribulation?* 1956. Grand Rapids, MI: Zondervan 120 p. SEE ALSO 1970+.

1964. Wood, Ross. *The Present in the Light of Prophecy: A Study of Some Outstanding Modern World Events and Conditions in the Light of Old and New Testament Prophecy.* 1933. Cincinnati: author. 208 p.

World War was "without precedent." Worst famines, earthquakes, pestilences also occured in 20th century. Jews now returning (Zionism).

1965. Woods, John Purvis. *The Final Invasion of God.* 1951. Boston: W.A. Wilde. 87 p.

"God is going to invade the planet!" Evidence that End is near: establishment of Israel in 1948, existence of weapons that can easily destroy all life. Woods doesn't discuss sequence of events, merely assurance of sudden, decisive Coming. Glorified bodies and heaven on earth afterwards.

1966. Woodson, Leslie H. *Antichrist and Armageddon.*[1950s]. Louisville KY: Pentecostal Pub Co. 37 p.

1967. Woodward, E[dward] P[ayson]. SEE ALSO 1800–1910. *The Threefold Witness (Daniel, Christ, John) Concerning the Final Consummation.* 1912. Westbrook, ME: Safeguard. 400, cxii p. illus.

1968. _____. *Mohammedanism in Prophecy and History and Its Approaching Downfall.* 3rd ed. 1957. Washington, KS: Vern Sizemore/Prophetic Literature. 104 p.

1969. Woodward, J. Elwin. *The Story of the Ages from Creation to Redemption; Key to Historic and Prophetic Diagram, and God's Plan of Salvation for Law Breakers* 1912. Chicago: Historic and Prophetic Publishing Co. 219 p. folded chart.

1970. Wuest, Kenneth S. *In These Last Days. II Peter, I, II, III, John and Jude in the Greek New Testament for the English Reader.* 1954. Grand Rapids, MI: W.B. Eardmans. 263 p. Wuest's Word Studies series no. 14.

1971. _____. *Prophetic Light in the Present Darkness.* 1955. Grand Rapids, MI: William B. Eerdmans. 135 p.

"At no time in past history has the universal situation of the human race been so desperate as it is today." Antichrist's armies will be obliterated at Armageddon when Christ returns with His saints and raptured believers. Christ then rules as "absolute dictator" during Millennium. Heaven is outside the universe, "at least 2,932,848,000,000,000,000,000 miles" away.

1972. Wyatt, Evelyn. *Holy Ghost or Holocaust?* 1965. Los Angeles: Wings of Healing. 32 p.

1973. Wyngaarden, Martin J. *The Future of the Kingdom in Prophecy and Fulfillment: A Study of the Scope of "Spiritualization" in Scripture.* 1955 [1934]. Grand Rapids, MI: Baker Book House. 211 p. indexes

Some prophecies literally fulfilled; others will be spiritually fulfilled. Disputes pre-mill, but expresses "fervent hope" for soon Second Coming.

1974. Yamagata, Toshio. *Highway to Truth.* 1952. Yokohama: Japan S.D.A. Publishing House. 254 p. illus. In Japanese.

Seventh-day Adventist.

1975. Young, E.J. *The Prophecy of Daniel.* 1949. Grand Rapids, MI: Eerdmans.

Young: Orthodox Presbyterian; Westminster Theological Seminary.

1976. Young, W[illiam] R[obert].

1924—What May We Expect in That Year?
[ca. 1920?]. San Diego: priv. pub. 24 p.

604 B.C. + 2,520 Years = 1924.

1977. _____. *How Long to the End?:
The Answer to the Above Question in Dan.
12:6 Given in Four Periods which All Cul-
minate in a Single Year.* 1923 [1922]. San
Diego: priv. pub. 116 p. illus.

"This long-sealed mystery of Dan.
12 now disclosed in the time of the end as
the finished mystery of Rev. 10:7 and the
measuring rod of Rev. 11:1."

1978. _____. *Time Fulfilled and the
Kingdom At Hand.* [1925?]. Priv pub. 30 p.

Predicted 1924 as End, but now realizes necessary to add eleven years (extending End to 1935).

1979. _____. *The Stone Kingdom:
Our Present Position in God's Prophetic Pro-
gram: End Events in Daniel 2.* 1928. San
Diego: s.n. 23 p.

Concerns Turkey.

1980. _____. *The Mystery of Revela-
tion 17 Now Unfolding; or, The Woman, the
Beast, and the Eighth Head.* N.d. [1929?].
San Diego: priv. pub. 36 p.

Mussolini and Papacy colluding in
1929. Mussolini as new Roman Emperor
(the Beast) and Church as the Harlot.

1981. _____. *Unsealed at Last: The
Prophetic and Chronologic Mystery of
Daniel 12 Now Entirely Disclosed....* 1931.
San Diego: s.n. 35 p. illus.

Prophecies of Daniel 12 fulfilled in
1924–25, as he predicted in 1922. A.D. 634
(Omar builds mosque on Temple site) +

1,290 Years = 1924. Caliphate abolished
that year; Papal power also doomed then.

1982. _____. *God's Prophetic Pro-
gram of End Events Now in Process of
Fulfillment, or Current History Exactly
Fulfilling Chronological Prophecy.* [1920s?].

1983. _____. *The Future Antichrist
Theory Versus the Fulfilled Premonitory
Signs.* [1930s]. San Diego. 62 p.

"The Last Generation Expiring."
Affiliated with *The World's Crisis* journal
(Advent Christian).

1984. _____. *"Nearly Arrived": 1934
the Closing Year of a Prophetic Decade
which Commenced in 1924.* [1930s]. Los
Angeles: Free Tract Society. 4 p.

Islamic Caliphate abolished in 1924.

1985. _____. *Where Are We Now?*
[ca. 1928]. San Diego. 28 p.

Significance of four grooves in Last
Tribulation passageway of Great Pyramid:
point to May 29, 1928 (after Davidson's
calculations). The "great Day of the Lord
must be close at hand."

1986. Zader, Willis H. *Gentile
Times When Fulfilled Examined in the Light
of Bible Prophecy and History.* [1918?].
Colton, CA: 103 p.

1987. Zahn, Theodor. *Offenbarung
des Johannes.* 1924. Leipzig: Deichert. 346
p.

Historic pre-mill.

1988. Zoller, John. *The Second
Coming of Christ and the Coming Ages.*
1968. New Era, MI: John Zoller. 255 p.

Works from 1970 On (Alphabetical)

1989. Aaseng, Rolf E. *When Jesus Comes Again: What the Bible Says.* 1984. Minneapolis: Augsburg. 96 p.

1990. _____. *Lift Up Your Heads: He Is Coming Again.* 1995. Lima, OH: CSS. 47 p.

1991. Abbott, John L. *The Time of the End.* 1982. Hornsby [Australia]: Stewart Printing. 73 p.

1992. Abent, John A. *Signs in the Heavens: Biblical Prophecy and Astronomy.* 1995. Shippensburg, PA; Destiny Image. 408 p. bibl. refs., index.

"The signs in the heavens are agreeing with the signs in the earth" regarding the "imminency of the Day of the Lord."

1993. Adams, Ken. *UFO, the Final Warning.* 1989. Video. Evansville, IN: Atlantic Video.

"Documentary" which links UFOs with Nazis, occult, and Antichrist.

1994. Adams, Laurice M. *Omega ... Now — the Test.* 1984 [1983]. Payson, AZ: Leaves-Of-Autumn Books. 25 p.

1991 reprint. Orig priv. pub. (Morristown, AZ).

1995. Adams, Matthew H. 1976. *UFO: Earth Invaded from Outer Space.* New York: Vantage Press. 67 p.

1996. Adams, Moody. *New Signs of the Second Coming.* N.d. [1980s?]. Baton Rouge: Moody Adams Evangelistic Association. 108 p.

1997. Agee, M[arilyn] J. *The End of the Age.* 1994 [1991]. New York: Avon. 320 p. charts. bibl. refs. index. Prev. pub. as *Exit 2007: The Secret of Secrets Revealed.*

"The 'time of the end' has come." Pre-trib. 1967 Six-Day War, with possession of Jerusalem: Sign of the End of the Age. Last generation born in 1967, will see Second Coming. Earth to undergo explosive holocaust Sept. 13, 2007: Day of the Lord, and expire in agony. At end of Tribulation Israel attacked by multi-nation army of North, which God destroys. Stresses we are nearing end of 6,000 year span. Adam created Sept. 18, 4043 B.C. Earth older though — pre-Adamic life. Approves Ussher, admires Anstey's chronology. 454 B.C. to A.D. 29 = 69 Weeks. Heavenly "hour" = 41⅓ days (= 1,000 hours); thus we're in last "hour" of 6,000 years. Pre-Adamic catastrophe ca. 11,000 B.C.: asteroid hit Pacific, blasted out moon, shifted earth axis. 7,000 years plus 49 (7 x 7). Great Week began 4003 B.C. (Adam in Eden for 40 years). Gentile Age 4003–2003 B.C.; Age of Jews 2003–3 B.C.; Age of Church began 3 B.C., also lasts 2,000 years, plus extra nine for rebellion. Rapture precisely dated to 1998 on Pentecost (but possibly 1992 or 1995). Tribulation begins 2001. Rapture II = translation of Tribulation saints at end of Tribulation. Second Coming, with tremendous cataclysms and death, Apr. 6, 2008. Final Judgment Apr. 21, 2008; Armageddon (world army vs. Christ's) lasts 40 days; then Millennium. False Prophet (an Israeli possessed by Satan) = Second Beast = Pale Horse rider = Antichrist. Common Market: Ten-Horn Beast; now 13 members but three to be incorporated into others. First Beast is world kingdoms; its tail is Satan. Babylon literally rebuilt. Satan hurled to earth mid-Tribulation after losing war in heaven with Michael. Two Witnesses = Elijah and Moses. Believers flee to Petra; literal fulfillment of plagues, woes, terrible catastrophes. Cosmic collision annihilates Babylon, capital of the Harlot (False Church), and forms the Lake of Fire by crashing through Earth. Satan lives on this asteroid; he rides it to Hell. New Jerusalem is sphere (not cube) slightly smaller than moon, and will orbit earth.

1998. Aguilera, Raymond. *Prophecies, Visions, Occurrences and Dreams.* 1990. El Sobrante, CA: priv. pub.

"These prophecies are all end time prophecies." "Day of the Beast" has arrived; Armageddon — will be in our lifetime.

1999. Ainsworth, Dick. *End Times Means Hard Times.* Video.

For those who miss the Rapture.

2000. Alder, Vicki Allred. *The Signs of the Last Days: A Scriptural Guide to the Future.* 1990. Sandy, UT: Wellspring. [14], 248 p. illus. index.

Mormon.

2001. Allen, Stuart. *World Conditions and the End of the Age.* 1977. London: Berean Pub. Trust. 16 p.

2002. Allnutt, Frank. *Kissinger: Man of Destiny?* 1976. Mission Viejo, CA: Allnutt Pub. 237 p. bibl. refs.

Kissinger as Antichrist.

2003. Alnor, William M. *Soothsayers of the Second Advent.* 1989. Old Tappan, NJ: Power Books. 222 p. bibl. refs.

Also wrote *UFOs in the New Age: Extraterrestrial Messages and the Truth of Scripture* (1992, Grand Rapids: MI: Baker, 293 p.) Suggests that UFOs are part of a "deliberate, other dimensional, otherworldly plan to deceive mankind in what could very well be the era when Jesus Christ returns to Planet Earth." After Rapture, Antichrist is acclaimed as Messiah.

2004. Alston, Lucille. *On Bible Prophecy.* 1992. New York: Vantage 55 p.

2005. *The Amazing World of the Apocalypse.* n.d. Candler, NC: Revelation Seminars. pamphlet.

2006. Ambassador College Department of Theology. *Is This the End Time?* 1973. Pasadena, CA: Ambassador Coll., 44 p. Illus.

2007. Amini, Ibrahim. *Al-Imam al-Mahdi: The Just Leader of Humanity.* 1996. Ontario, Canada: Islamic Education and Information Center. xvi, 350 p. bibl. refs. Orig. Farsi (Persian).

Amini: Iranian Ayatollah. Shiite Islam. The Twelfth Imam (successor to Muhammad) as the "Hidden Imam" who disappeared in the 800s A.D. (went into "occultation") and will reappear in the Last Days as the Mahdi (Savior).

2008. Ammi, Ben. *The Messiah & the End of this World.* 1991. Washington, DC: Communicators Press. xx, 164 p. illus. bibl. refs. Also pub. Nashville: Winston-Derek.

Also wrote *God, the Black Man and Truth.* Black nationalism: "African Hebrew Israelite"— ancient Hebrews were black; African Americans are Chosen People, Elect of God. Ben Ammi's group moved to Liberia, then to Israel in 1969, striving to establish Kingdom of God here on Earth. End of age of "Euro-gentiles." Science and technology "relegated to the status of guilty bystanders."

2009. Anderson, David. *The Omega Prophecy.* 1990 [1980]. <http://www.visi.com/~sonshine/background.html>

Anderson: Lutheran pastor. "The Omega Prophecy makes use of the classical form and imagery of Old Testament prophetic writings."

2010. Anderson, Loren E. *Prophecy and Antichrist, 666.* 1976. Fresno, CA: L.E. Anderson. 54 p. charts, diagrams

2011. _____. *Theo-History: The Parallel Covenants Theory.* c1983. Fresno, CA: Day Book. 120 p.

2,000 years of Jewish Covenant beginning with Abraham, then 2,000 years of Christian Covenant. Antichrist appears 2000 A.D., then 7 Years of Revelation, then Millennium. Cites Washburn and Lucas's *Theomatics.*

2012. Anderson, Roy Allan. *Abandon Earth: Last Call.* 1982. Mountain View, CA: Pacific Press. 78 p.

2013. Andrews, Valerie, Robert Bosnak, and Karen Walter Goodwin, eds. *Facing Apocalypse.* 1987. Dallas: Spring Publications. 195 p. bibl. refs.

2014. Ankerberg, John. *One World: Biblical Prophecy and the New World Order.* 1991. Chicago: Moody Press. 180 p. bibl. refs.

2015. _____, and John Weldon. *The Coming Darkness.* 1993. Harvest House. 342 p. bibl. refs., index. Occultism.

2016. Anstey, B. *Outline of Prophetic Events Chronologically Arranged from the Rapture to the Eternal State.* 1987. [Vancouver, B.C.?: B. Anstey?]. 176 p. illus.

2017. _____. *The Church Will Not Go Through the Tribulation.* [1980]. [Vancouver, B.C.?: B. Anstey?]. 32 p.

2018. *The Antichrist 666.* 1995. rev. ed. Brushton, NY: TEACH services. 262 p. illus.

W.J. Sutton and R.A. Anderson.

2019. Appleton, Helen. *The Second Coming of Christ at the End of This World.* 1992. Toowong, Australia: Jollen. 16 p.

2020. *Are We Living in the Last Days?* 1973. Pasadena: Ambassador College.

2021. *Are We Living in the Last Days?* <http://www.thebook.com/papax7/proph13.htm>

Babylon = U.S.— destroyed by Russia in nuclear war before Antichrist makes seven-year covenant with Israel. "Horrible sin" of abortion: "Hitler, heinous in his destruction of 6 million Jews, shrinks in comparison to America — swimming in the blood of 31,000,000 of her own babies." 1967 + 40 = 2007. "Apocalypse will start in or before 2007 A.D." Or before 2028 (1988 + 40). Any-moment Rapture. Every 3,600 years a Comet-Planet three times the size of Earth passes near Earth. Caused global catastrophe in 12,400 B.C.: Noah's Flood; lesser destruction on other passes (e.g. sun standing still for Joshua). Next pass (the big one): Aug. 11, 1999.

2022. *Are We Nearing the End Times?* <http://www.kansas.net/~duncan/olympics.html>

"Did you know all the signs Jesus said would signify His second coming are occurring in our time?" Pre-trib.

2023. Argüelles, José. *The Mayan Factor: Path Beyond Technology.* 1987. Santa Fe, NM: Bear & Co. 217 p. drawings bibl.

New Age: planetary conjunction and Mayan prophecies from extragalactic race. Harmonic Convergence: Aug, 16–17, 1987; Armageddon averted if 144,000 participate. End of Mayan Long Count (Calendar end date): A.D. 2012. Also wrote *Earth Ascending.*

2024. *Armageddon: The Return of the Messiah.* 1988. Video. Tel Aviv: Doko Video (for Chosen People Ministries).

2025. Armerding, Carl Edwin, and W. Ward Gasque, ed. *Handbook of Biblical Prophecy.* 1978 [1977]. Grand Rapids, MI: Baker Book House. 262 p. bibl. 1977 title *Dreams, Visions, and Oracles: The Layman's Guide to Biblical Prophecy.* 1989 expanded edition titled *Guide to Biblical Prophecy.*

Armerding: Plymouth Brethren.

2026. Arminjan, Charles-Marie-Antoine. 1986. *The End of the Present World and the Mysteries of the Future Life.* Britons Catholic Library. xvi, 196 p.

2027. Armstrong, Garner Ted. SEE ALSO 1910–1970 *Cosmos in Convulsion.* 1994. Tyler, TX: Church of God, International. 28 p.

2028. _____. *Europe and America in Prophecy.* 1994. Tyler, TX: Church of God, International. 148 p.

2029. Armstrong, Hart. SEE ALSO 1910–1970. *Christ's Twofold Prophecy—: The Olivet Discourse.* 1993. Wichita, KS: Christian Communications. 240 p.

2030. _____. *The Last Seven on Earth, and the First Seven in Heaven.* 1994. Wichita, KS: Christian Communications. 352 p.

Tribulation, Second Coming. Also writes on creationism and UFOs.

2031. Armstrong, Herbert W. SEE ALSO 1910–1970. *The Wonderful World Tomorrow: What It Will Be Like.* 1982. Pasadena: Worldwide Church of God. 99 p. indexes.

2032. _____. *Are We in the Last Days?* Pasadena, CA: Worldwide Church of God. 1985. 18 p. illus.

2033. Arnese, Pietro. *Apocalypse Soon.* c1997–1998. <http://apocalypsesoon.org/english.html>

"The appointed times of His patience are coming to an end. Soon, His holy and righteous judgment will be poured upon rebel mankind." There must be a purpose and final destination to human existence, otherwise we would be mere animals. Anti-evolution.

2034. [Arrabito, James]. *Adventists and World War III.* 1986. 4 videos. Angwin, CA: LLT Productions.

Seventh-Day Adventist.

2035. Arthur, Kay. *God's Blueprint for Bible Prophecy.* Eugene, OR: Harvest House. 132 p. illus. maps.

Arthur: runs Precept Ministries with husband Jack. Daniel's 70th Week to come, with Ten-Kingdom empire.

2036. Asahara, Shoko. *Supreme Initiation: An Empirical Spiritual Science for the Supreme Truth.* 1988. New York: AUM USA. 231 p. 4 p plates illus. Another transl. titled *The Teachings of the Truth.*

Asahara: Japanese leader of Aum Shinrikyo. Asahara attained enlightenment in Himalayas, founded AUM Shinrikyo (AUM = *om*, the Hindu mantra; Shinri-Kyo = "divine truth"). Yoga, Tantric Buddhism, Tao. If AUM gains enough practitioners, nuclear war in 1999–2003 can be averted. Also wrote *Declaring Myself the Christ.* Predicted 1997 World War in which U.S. attempts takeover of Japan. Increasing eclectic doctrine: later received vision from Shiva, incorporated Christian apocalyptism, Atlantis, Nostradamus, Tesla.

2037. _____. *Day of Annihilation.*

Japan destroyed 1996, sinks into ocean 1999, war with Mongols. Conspiratorial forces start nuclear war Nov. 2003; Disciples survive, gain superhuman powers.

2038. _____. *Disaster Approaches the Land of the Rising Sun.* 1995. Shizuoka, Japan: Aum. 312 p. Illus.

Asahara now decides Armageddon will start in 1996, with increasing disasters from 1995, and End in 1997, '99, or 2000. 1995 Kobe earthquake was triggered by electromagnetic devices of sinister conspiracy. Secret attacks by U.S. and Japanese aircraft using lasers and poison gas already underway. WWIII: U.S. vs. Japan. U.S. ruled by Freemasons (elsewhere says Jews). "There will only be a 21st century for those who read and practice the contents of this book." Describes Aum as "Buddhistic version of [Isaac] Asimov's Foundation [sci-fi series]." Aum members developed chemical, biological, and explosive weapons, and tried to ignite apocalyptic war in 1995 with nerve gas attacks.

2039. Ashmore, Ralph. *The Two Beasts.* 1971. Eastbourne, England: Prophetic Witness. 15 p.

2040. "Ashtar." *Survival is Only Ten Feet from Hell.* Carlsbad, CA: America West. 1989. iv, 123, 6 p.

Phoenix Journal series. Nuclear war, occult prophecy.

2041. _____. *From Here to Armageddon: I Am Ashtar.* 1990. Bozeman, MT: America West. 129 p. illus. *Phoenix* Journal series.

2042. Atat, Faysal. *Al-Harb, al-Alamiyah al-Thalithah wa-al-Akhirah min al-Manzur al-Qurani wa-al-Riwai.* 1992. Beirut, Lebanon: al-Irshad. 15 p.

2043. Aune, Kenneth E. *God, History, and the End of the World.* 1971. Savage, MN: Invictus. 290 p. illus.

Day of Lord: comet collides with Earth. Cometary cataclysm Oct. 1986: Halley's. Temple worship begins 1983; Antichrist declares himself God in Temple 1986. Dead resurrected; Church gathered. Living and resurrected believers raptured just before comet strikes, causing darkening of sky, biblical hail, earthquakes; kills over a billion. 1990 greatest war in all history, Tribulation 1983–90, Second Coming, Armageddon battle. Antichrist = King of South (Egypt). Millennium = May 1990. Harlot/Scarlet Woman = Catholic Church; Beast = UN. Harlot destroyed by UN Beast and Antichrist. "Final Age" starts 1945. Antichrist's armies invade Israel; other Arab armies invade southern Europe. All driven by "hatred of the white

race." Russia responds by attacking Antichrist's armies: Russo-European army
passes through Armageddon, assaults
Jerusalem; confronts massive Asia-Afro
armies there (final battle, with 18 million
gallons of blood). Then second comet
strike: comet nucleus falls in Atlantic,
great catastrophes. Many seals, trumpets,
vials are simultaneous (comet effects).

2044. Aust, Jerold. *Armageddon:
The End of the World.* 1997. United
Church of God.

2045. Austin, E.L.C. *Earth's Great-
est Day.* c1979. Glendale, CA: Heaven and
Home Hour. 65 p. Rev. ed. pub. 1980
Grand Rapids, MI: Baker (127 p.).

Appendix on Shroud of Turin.

2046. _____. *God and the Russians.*
1982. [Glendale, CA: Heaven & Home
Hour?]. 79 p maps.

Ezekiel.

2047. Austin-Sparks, T[heodore].
*The Work of God at the End Time: End-
Time Principles Set Forth in Simeon.* N.d.
London: Witness and Testimony. 58 p.

2048. _____. *The Ultimate Issue of
the Universe.* [1980s]. Washington, DC:
author. 59 p.

2049. Averehi, E. A. J. (Emmanuel
Afolabi James). 1993. *Rapture: Testimonies
of Jesus Second Coming.* Ilorin [Nigeria]:
Funkay Publishers, v, 34 p.

2050. Averkii, Archbishop of Jordanville. *The Apocalypse of St. John: An Orthodox Commentary.* 1985. Platina, CA:
Valaam Soc. of Amer. 240 p. illus index.

2051. Bacchiocchi, Samuele. *The
Prophetic Role of Pope John II.* tapes.

Seventh-day Adventist.

2052. _____. *The Advent Hope for
Human Hopelessness.* 1986. Berrien Springs,
MI: Biblical Perspectives. 384 p.

2053. _____. *Hal Lindsay's Prophetic
Jigsaw Puzzle: Five Prophecies That Have
Failed.* 1987 [1985]. Berrien Springs, MI:
Biblical Perspectives. 148 p.

2054. Baer, Randall N. *Inside the
New Age Nightmare.* 1989. Lafayette, LA:
Huntington House. v, 201 p.

Baer: expert on crystals; former New
Age promoter. Here says New Age is
Satan's deception — lies and fake miracles.

2055. Bailey, Keith M. *Christ's
Coming and His Kingdom: A Study in Bible
Prophecy.* 1981. Harrisburg, PA: Christian
Publications. 191 p. indexes bibl.

Bailey: Nazarene, minister with
Christian and Missionary Alliance; editor
of Christian Publications. Pre-trib pre-
mill. Imminent, now living in end-time
days. Church to escape awful acts, dark
hours of God's wrath (Tribulation). Apostasy and false religions abound. Rapture,
Tribulation, 144,000 Jewish Witnesses,
Second Coming, Millennium. False
Prophet will be Jewish leader. Beast will be
Roman prince, totalitarian ruler. Raptured
believers return with Christ to earth at
Millennium.

2056. Bainbridge, Bruce. *Why Do
Only 144,000 Go to Heaven?* 1988. Bend,
OR: Maverick. 165 p.

Jehovah's Witnesses.

2057. Baker, William W. *Theft of a
Nation.* 1982. West Monroe, LA: Jireh
Publications. xii, 192 p. bibl. index.

Palestine; Zionism.

2058. Bakker, Jim, and Ken Abraham. *Prosperity and the Coming Apocalypse:
Avoiding the Dangers of Materialistic Christianity in the End Times.* 1998. Nashville:
Thomas Nelson. 256 p.

Bakker: former televangelist convicted of fraud after sex scandal was exposed. Now rejects Prosperity Gospel he
formerly espoused, and the pre-trib Rapture. "The more I studied the Scriptures,
the more I became convinced that we are
living in the last days, and that we will
soon begin seeing the fulfillment of the
predictions in the prophetic books of the
Bible, including the cataclysmic conditions on earth, which will precipitate the
rise of the Antichrist." "By preaching 'another gospel,' with its emphasis on ease of
living, material wealth, and sensational
miracles, prosperity preachers and teachers have unwittingly set the Christian
community up for the arrival of the Antichrist." "For me, belief in the Rapture
played right into prosperity theology. It
made a perfect package: people could get
saved by saying a few words, they could
live in luxury and excess throughout this

lifetime, and then Jesus would return to take them out of the tough times that others were to experience during end-time tribulation. It was pure escapism."

2059. Baldwin, Robert F. *The End of the World: A Catholic View.* 1984. Huntington, IN: Our Sunday Visitor. 112 p.

Charismatic Catholic. A-mill. "Last Days" have been since Christ's resurrection until Second Coming, which may occur very soon, or much later.

2060. Baldwin, Stanley C. *1999: A Novel.* 1994. Downers Grove, IL: InterVarsity. 206 p.

Matt, a Christian radio talk show host in Oregon, interviews John Profett, author of book *1999* on Second Coming. Reveals to Matt he is really prophesied prophet Elijah, quoting Bible persuasively. Persuades Matt to work for him promoting his ministry. Matt's wife is suspicious, but Profett poisons Matt against her, railing against "Jezebels." Profett arranges kidnap and rape of Matt's wife, then "rescues" her. Radically anti-feminist, he eventually murders female theologian who criticizes him. Then murders former seminary roommate who identifies him despite name change (he had dropped out after becoming convinced he was Antichrist). Profett is foiled and shot at end; book contains no supernaturalism. Profett argues for 6,000 year creation-to-End span.

2061. Balizet, Carol. *The Seven Last Years.* 1979 [1978]. Lincoln, VA / Grand Rapids, MI: Chosen Books [distr. by Word Books]. 376 p.

Fiction. Balizet: Tampa hospital nurse who received "revelation" in form of this novel. Appendix gives Tribulation prophecies. Meteor hits Cyprus, triggers earthquakes (great signs and destructions); Rapture, even greater destruction, plagues. Millionaire media mogul and religious organization led by "Bishop" takes over power after disasters. Earthquake moves oil from Arabs to Israel. Christians replace Jews as Chosen, but after Rapture, Jews fill in again. Scramble to rationalize Rapture disappearances, as most "official" (non-true) Christians remain. Novel characters read Bible, discover all events were predicted (mostly literally). Bishop becomes Pope Sixtus VI (666). Nefarious astrologer helps religious and political leaders (Antichrist and False Prophet). Israeli leader complicit in plot. U.S. of Europe with capital in Rome led by secular leader: Antichrist. Antichrist signs treaty with Israel. Antichrist wounded, revives, possessed by Satan. Two Witnesses killed, return to life and are raptured on TV. Giant computer to control finance, personal information. 1992: all except faithful receive Mark of Beast. Subliminal messages to worship Pope. Underground convert communities in Judean hills: 144,000 (others in U.S.). Antichrist and Satan supernaturally prepare for Armageddon. 1995: Arab-African coalition attacks Israel; then Russian coalition does. Russians then turn on Arab-Africans. Then 200-million man Chinese army invades. U.S. of Europe and America support Israel, launch nuclear attack on Russia; a third of world's population killed. Chinese reach Armageddon, join other armies. Nuclear battle rages. Second Coming. Fire and brimstone on Russia, Europe, America; all civilization destroyed. Believers get glorified bodies for the Millennium.

2062. Bancroft, Sam. *The Mark of the Beast: A Study in the Book of Revelation Chapter Thirteen.* 1995. Peterlee (UK?): Petorlan. 19 p. illus.

2063. Barclay, Mark T. *Preachers of Righteousness: Critical to End Times Survival.* 1991. Midland, MI: M. Barclay. 151 p.

2064. Barela, John. *Antichrist Associates and Cosmic Christianity.* 1986. Broken Arrow, OK: Today, the Bible and You. 191 p.

Barela: runs Today, the Bible, and You Ministry (Tulsa area). The dangers of occultism.

2065. Barney, Kenneth. *Preparing for the Storm.* 1975. Springfield: Gospel. 96 p.

Pentecostal.

2066. Barsoum, F. *Coming Mideast Wars in Prophecy.* 1980. Dallas: International Bible Assoc. 284 p. illus.

2067. Bates, Leon. *Project for Sur-*

vival. 1977. Dallas: Bible Believer's Evangelistic Assoc.

After Gog's invasion of Israel, radioactive contamination necessitates seven month period to bury dead. Cruise missiles.

2068. Baxter, Irvin. *A Message for the President.* 1986. Richmond, IN: Endtime, Inc. 160 p. [2] leaves plates. bibl.

"For the first time, absolute proof that the United States is in the Bible!" "Unalterable" events of the next 10–15 years. Emphasizes Reagan's public references to Armageddon and includes newspaper clippings. Coming one-world government; world dictator (Antichrist, a Gentile) comes out of Common Market, heads revived Holy Roman Empire, a "Fourth Reich." False Prophet = a Pope (maybe present Pope John Paul II), enforces diabolical 666 money program. Whore of Babylon = papacy. Religious persecution "much worse than the Holocaust." Russia invades Israel. Nuclear war with China. The "deadly wound" divided Germany; to be reunited by Antichrist. Four Horses: Catholic Church, Communism, Capitalism, Southern Hemisphere Third World. Mandatory birth control. Antichrist forces way into forbidden Temple, declares himself world ruler. Russia = Gog Magog. U.S. may be base for religious revival during Tribulation. Rapture at end of Tribulation. All believers receive immortal bodies when raptured; given their own cities to rule over during Millennium. Armageddon = world armies try to destroy Israel. Literal bridle-high blood for 160 miles. Second Coming then, Millennium established. Russia vs. China nuclear war (one billion killed) leads to European unification and rise of Antichrist who promises peace. Also wrote *Will the Church Go Through the Tribulation?* (cassette).

2069. _____. *Mideast Treaty: Greatest Prophetic Fulfillment in 2000 Years.* 1994. Richmond, IN: Endtime Inc. 157 p.

2070. _____. *Understanding the Endtime.* 6 videos. Prophecy Home Bible study series. Richmond, IN: Endtime.

2071. Baxter, Mary K[athryn]. *A Divine Revelation of Hell.* c1993. Springdale, PA: Whitaker House. 216 p.

Copyright held by T.L. Lowery of National Church of God. Author member National Church of God, minister of Full Gospel Church of God. Cover: "Time is Running Out!" Revelations from Christ in 1976; taken to Hell for 40 days, chosen to tell world about Hell. Descends funnel into earth, spirits embedded in walls. Sees all manner of tormented sinners, unbelievers, apostates, satanist, occultists, etc., pleading for mercy but suffering for all eternity. Hell shaped like human body, crowded with demons and evil spirits waiting to emerge to earth. Shown visions of "time of the end": 666 Beast becomes world leader after promising peace, wealth; people deceived into getting 666 branded on forehead, "mind eraser" machines turn them into zombie slaves. Rapture, Antichrist and Tribulation, Millennium, then New Jerusalem descends from heaven.

2072. Beals, Ivan A. *The Great Expectation: the Promised Savior and Our Coming King.* 1976. Kansas City, MO: Beacon Hill Press. 381 p. bibl. refs.

2073. BeauSeigneur, James. *In His Image.* 1997. Rockville, MD: SelectiveHouse Publishers. 366 p.

Fiction; vol. 1 of Christ Clone Trilogy. Christ is cloned from DNA contained in the Shroud of Turin by atheist scientist attempting to prove that Earth was seeded by extraterrestrial life, raised as "Christopher Goodman."

2074. _____. *Birth of an Age.* 1997. Rockville, MD: SelectiveHouse Publishers. 241 p.

Vol. 2 of Christ Clone Trilogy. Nuclear wars in 2003 and 2019 devastate most of Asia. Two fanatical prophets summon asteroids to collision course with Earth.

2075. _____. *Acts of God.* 1998. Rockville, MD: SelectiveHouse Publishers. 433 p.

Vol. 3 of Christ Clone Trilogy.

2076. Beck, Harrell. *The End of Time.* 1985. Nashville: Graded Press. 64 p.

Official resource of United Methodist Church.

2077. Beckley, Timothy Green. *Psychic & UFO Revelations in the Last Days.* 1989. New Brunswick, NJ: Inner Light Publications. 184 p. photos, drawings.

Beckley: occultist, UFOlogist; also wrote *Prophecies of the Presidents: The Spiritual Destiny of America Revealed* (1992; Inner Light), and books on MJ-12 UFO conspiracy, Hangar 18, Planet Clarion, Inner Earth. Mass landings of flying saucers, elect of earth evacuated to another planet.

2078. _____. *Prophecies of the Presidents: The Spiritual Destiny of America Revealed.* 1992. New Brunswick, NJ: Inner Light. 128 p. illus.

2079. Beechick, Allen. *The Pre-Tribulation Rapture.* 1980. Denver: Accent Books. 288 p. illus. bibl., refs.

2080. Beholding Christ Ministries. *Daniel and Revelation.* 1992. Sparta, WI: Beholding Christ Ministries. 12 p.

Newspaper format. Seventh-day Adventist.

2081. Beirnes, Malcom E. SEE ALSO 1910–1970. *To Rule the World: The Conspiracy Influence on Modern History in the Light of Bible Prophecy.* 1975. Tequesta, FL: Midnight Cry. 82 p.

2082. _____. *After This the Judgment.* 1979? Tequesta, FL: Midnight Cry. 40 p.

2083. _____. *Millennial Reign of Christ.* 1979? Tequesta, FL: Midnight Cry. 112 p.

2084. _____. *Prophecies Fulfilled and Fulfilling.* 1979? Tequesta, FL: Midnight Cry. 38 p. chart.

2085. Benson, John L. *Truth About Tomorrow: A Study in Biblical Prophecy.* 1976. Denver: Baptist Publications. 96 p. bibl.

Adult teacher and adult student text eds.

2086. _____. *The Showdown That Will Rock the World.* 1977. Denver: Accent Books. 127 p.

Pre-trib Rapture. "Armageddon looms ahead as a dark and sinister reality." Antichrist, an apostate Jew, will negotiate Mid-East peace. Antichrist = the False Prophet. First Beast: political leader. Antichrist causes Roman Prince (European Dictator, Beast) to occupy Israel. Russian desolator = Gog-Magog. Satan cast out of heaven mid-Tribulation, provokes Russia to annihilate Israel. Israel consents to worship idol of Dictator to buy peace. "Palestine is the vortex which will draw all nations to destruction." Armageddon: whole campaign, most of second half Tribulation, all of Palestine. Arab North Africa invades, then Russians with satellites (to prevent Arab takeover), then Western nations to defend Israel, then Asia joins West = Armageddon. Russia pushes on to Egypt as Jews flee, then hears of Asian advance and/or Western landings in Israel. God destroys vast armies with earthquakes and storms. New Jerusalem probably orbiting Earth during Millennium. Most or all unsaved Gentiles killed at Second Coming. Glorified saints live in New Jerusalem but commune with unglorified folks on earth. Jerusalem becomes a seaport; other radical geological and meteorological changes.

2087. _____. *Who Is the Antichrist?* 1978. Schaumberg, IL: Regular Baptist Press. 127 p. bibl. refs.

Orig Dallas Theol. Sem. thesis. Antichrist = religious deceiver, heretic, apostate; a false Christ who claims divinity. Fraudulent miracles, magical delusions. First Beast = revived Roman Empire. Second Beast is Antichrist, leader of Ten-Nation coalition, makes 7 year pact with Israel. Israel trusts security to reorganized Roman Empire. Treaty negotiated by Antichrist, a Jew who collaborates with Empire, and is hailed as Messiah. Half way through 7 Years, Roman Prince emerges with absolute power in coalition. Demands Jews worship him as emperor, or will allow Arab attack. Antichrist cooperates, encouraging idolatry, then flees to Europe during Arab invasion, abandoning Israel to Holocaust that makes Hitler's "pale into insignificance." The North (Communist Russia) invades Israel also to prevent domination by South (Arabs). North conquers South, returns via Israel to face threats by east and north (probably mobilization of East Asian armies, and landings by armies of European Empire). Antichrist returns with armies of West after Russia's force destroyed supernaturally. Future will include many parallels with events of 1st-2nd century B.C. Daniel 11 refers to Ptolemies and Seleucids (Kings of South and North) as well as to future kings.

2088. _____. *What's This World Coming To?* 1979. Schaumberg, IL: Regular Baptist Press. 127 p. Adult Student series.

Urges "literal, normal, natural interpretation of prophecy." Pre-trib Rapture "imminent.... Get ready to blast off into space...." Temple rebuilt during Tribulation. Antichrist is Jewish miracle-working religious leader claiming to be Messiah. Second Beast = Roman prince who becomes ruler over Israel; forces Jews into idolatry in return for protection against Arabs. Satan is defeated in Heaven in mid-Tribulation; descends to earth and wreaks havoc on Israel. King of South = Islamic-Arab confederation which attacks Israel. Northern confederation attacks also and drives back Southern. Then Eastern armies invade. Christ destroys all these armies at Armageddon.

2089. _____. *Revelation: The Grand Finale of History.* 1982. Denver: Accent. 111 p.

2090. Bent, Wayne. *Shillum.* [1990s] Sandpoint, ID.

Much of book devoted to excerpts from *Protocols of the Learned Elders of Zion*, which Bent accepts as genuine document outlining Jewish conspiracy to control world politics and economy. Strongly anti-evolution. "The Battle of Armageddon is now to be fought." Book included in Bent's *The Winds* website (<http://thewinds.org>).

2091. Benton, Obie Folsom. *The Two Witnesses of Revelation.* 1988. Joelton, TN: Church of God, Philadelphian. 15 p.

2092. Benware, Paul N. *Understanding End Times Prophecy.* 1995. Chicago: Moody Press. 344 p. indexes, bibl. refs.

Foreword by Charles Ryrie. Ben-

ware: Moody Bible Inst. prof. Advocates literal interpretation, and pre-trib pre-mill view, but explains other approaches.

2093. Berg, David ["Moses David"]. *Teachings About the Endtime.* <http://www.thefamily.org/ourfounder/tribute/trib31.htm>

Berg: leader of the Children of God (a.k.a. Family of Love, gained notoriety for "flirty fishing"—sex as proselytizing tool). "We believe we're not only living in the Last Days, but the last of the Last Days, the end of the Last Days, the Endtime, the fulfillment of history! And if so, we're seeing the signs of the times! They include a lot of things, catastrophes, wars and all kinds of things that Jesus listed."

2094. _____. *The Book of the Future!* 1984. [Zurich?: World Services?]. xii, 500 p. illus.

2095. _____. *The Endtime News!* Tract. N.d?

Comet Kohoutek will destroy U.S.—the Whore of Babylon—in 1973. Tribulation = 1989; Second Coming = 1993.

End-time themes also featured in *The Basic Mo Letters* (1976; Geneva, Switzerland: Children of God).

2096. Bergin, Robert. *This Apocalyptic Age: A Commentary on Prophecies Relating to These Times ... And Their Portents.* 1973 [1970]. rev. and enl. 1st U.S. ed. Coconut Grove, FL: Fatima International. 159 p.

2097. Berlitz, Charles. *Doomsday 1999 A.D.* 1981. Garden City, NY: Doubleday. With "collaboration" of J[oseph] Manson Valentine. 226 p. [bibl.], index, drawings, maps.

Berlitz: grandson of language school founder; author of *The Bermuda Triangle*, etc. All evidence shows that Earth will undergo massive destruction A.D. 1999 or 2000. Planetary alignment, psychics and seers, Pyramidology, UFOs, Atlantis and Flood (previous destruction of world).

2098. Berry, M[arian] G. *A Warning.* 1990. Brushton, NY: TEACH Services. x, 197 p. illus.

Seventh-day Adventist.

2099. Bertrand, Neal, comp. *All the Scriptures You Need to Know About the Last*

Days: A Study Guide of End-Time Scriptures. 1981. [Lafayette, LA?]. priv. pub. 63 p. Available through Better Life Products (Lafayette, LA).

2100. Bettis, Joseph, and S[tanley] K. Johannesen, eds. *The Return of the Millennium*. 1984. Barrytown, NY: Int'l Religious Foundation. 233 p. bibl. refs.

2101. Betzer, Dan. *The Danger Zone.* 1980. Springfield, MO: Revivaltime. 31 p.

The Middle East. Betzer: Assemblies of God.

2102. _____. *And Greece Makes Ten.* 1981. Springfield, MO: General Conference of the Assemblies of God: Revivaltime. 31 p.

European Common Market as endtime Ten Nation revived Roman Empire. Greece is final member.

2103. _____. *The Beast: A Novel of the Future World Dictator.* 1985. Lafayette, LA: Prescott Press. 217 p.

2104. _____. *Revivaltime Prophecy Profile: Reports and Commentary on Today's Urgent Prophetic Events.* [1980s?]. Springfield, MO: Revivaltime Media Ministries. 13 p.

Includes "News Items"; "Hitler and the Antichrist"; interview with Freda Keet; Lebanon; "Kingdom Now" by David A. Lewis.

2105. _____. *The Handwriting on the Wall.* 1987. Springfield, MO: Revivaltime Media. 37 p.

Prophesied restoration of Israel.

2106. _____. *Tribulation the Seventieth Week.* 1987. Springfield, MO: General Council of the Assemblies of God. 40 p.

2107. _____. *A.D. 2000: Apocalypse? Or Golden Age?* 1990. Springfield, MO: Revivaltime Media Ministries. 29 p.

2108. _____. *The Last Generation.* 1992. Springfield, MO: Revivaltime Media Ministries. 34 p.

2109. _____. *The Seven Seals of Revelation.* 1993. Springfield, MO: Revivaltime Media Ministries. 33 p.

2110. Bhutta, A.R. *Propheziehungen über die Endzeit: Propheziehungen des heiligen Propheten Mohammed für das 14.Jahrhundert des Islam.* 1986. Frankfurt: Verlag "Der Islam." 92 p.

2111. *Bible Revelations.* <http://www.biblerevelations.org/toc.htm>

Seventh-day Adventist.

2112. [Biderman, Ken]. *Messianic End Times Prophecy.* <http://www.net-tally.coin/septuagint/messcvr.html> Tallahassee, FL.

Messianic Jew. Tribulation, Millenium; then Rapture and Second Coming.

2113. Billheimer, Paul. *Destined for the Throne.* 1975. Bethany House: Ft. Washington, PA: Christian Literature Crusade. 1991. Christian Literature Crusade ed. (London). 134 p. Also 1991 cassette ed. (Van Wyck, SC: Christians Listening).

"A Study in Biblical Cosmology setting forth the Ultimate Goal of the Universe which is the Church Reigning with Christ, with a New View of Prayer as 'On-the-Job' training in Preparation for the Throne." Foreword by Billy Graham. 650,000 copies (including 160,000 given away by TBN — Christian TV network). Billheimer: pres. emer. of Great Commission Foundation. Biblical cosmology, with church reigning with Christ at the End. Purpose of redeemed humanity is to join God on His throne.

2114. Birch, Desmond A. *Trial, Tribulation & Triumph: Before, During, and After Antichrist.* 1996. Santa Barbara, CA: Queenship Pub. lxxxiii, 635 p. map bibl. refs. indexes.

Catholic. Antichrist, Tribulation ("Chastisement"), Second Coming. Refutes Rapture and millennialism. Exhaustive search of Catholic texts, Church Fathers, hundreds of Catholic prophets and visionaries, teachings of Catholic Magisterium. The Parousia — Second Coming — shortly after death of Antichrist. Sometimes prophets and even saints don't understand all aspects of the prophecies revealed to them. E.g. 15th-cent. St. Vincent thought he was appointed "Angel of the Final Judgment." Before Second Coming occurs, new Roman Empire must arise, Antichrist must rule for 3½ years, all Jews must convert. May be "Minor Chastisement" first, but this can be averted if enough people convert. If not, then terrible heresy will prevail, civil wars, "natural" disasters, Russian invasion of Europe; Pope flees but is murdered by Moslem invaders, and Russians defeated at Bremen, Germany. Then Age of Peace. The "Major Chastisement" follows, after establishment of Ten Kingdom Roman Empire.

2115. Bisagno, John R. *Khomeini, Afghanistan and the Gold Crisis.* 1980. Houston: First Baptist Church Recordings. Cassette.

2116. Blaising, Craig A., and Darrell L. Bock, eds. *Dispensationalism, Israel and the Church: The Search for Definition.* c1992. Grand Rapids, MI: Zondervan. 402 p. indexes.

"Progressive dispensationalism": pretrib, but only vaguely, also claiming similarity to Ladd's historic pre-mill. This vol. includes Robert L. Saucy, the "father of progressive dispensationalism."

2117. Blank, Geraldine. *From the Beginning, But Emphasizing the Omega.* 1994. Snover, MI: Rainbow Press. 144 p.

2118. Blase, William. *End Times Truth About the "New Age"— the NWO— and the Last Days.* <http://www.zianet. com/wblase/endtimes/>

"UFOs, Aliens and Antichrist: The Angelic Conspiracy and End Times Deception."

2119. Blevins, Gary D. *666, the Final Warning: Beauty or the Beast—Ancient Mystery Code Revealed.* 1990. Kingsport, TN: Vision of the End Ministries. 494 p. illus.

Foreword by Texe Marrs. "The message of this book is one of *urgency!* The world is asleep concerning the *Last-Days* and the *fulfillment of prophecy!*" Illuminati, Freemasonry, Vatican, Communism, New World Order all part of End Time conspiracy; America now End-Time Babylon.

2120. Blodgett, Ralph H. *How Will It End?: Hope Beyond the Headlines.* c1984. Boise, ID: Pacific Press. 124 p. Also 1985; Warburton [Canada]: Signs Publishing.

Seventh-day Adventist. "If you've wondered what the Bible *really* does teach about Earth's final days...." Pre-mill but non-dispensational. Humans will be alive for Second Coming. But terrifying threat of nuclear weapons indicates that End is near: "powerful evidence that we have reached the end of time." Examines cases of Satanic possession. Second Coming: visible, not silent or secret. Prophecies to Israel were *conditional.* After Jews failed, God selected a New Israel: the Christian Church. Signs of End: Tribulation (especially A.D. 548 to 1798 under Roman Catholics); 1780 Dark Day; 1833 Falling Stars; increase in earthquakes and violence. "God's three final warnings": rejection of Creator God (i.e. evolution); "Babylon" (Catholicism) regains power; Mark of Beast (Sunday worship). Warns of coming enforced Sunday laws. During Millennium, living and resurrected righteous are transported to Heaven; Satan and evil angels will inhabit utterly desolate Earth. Wicked resurrected at end of Millennium; they and Satan battle Christ and righteous, who return to Earth only then. New Jerusalem descends.

2121. Bloomfield, Arthur E. SEE ALSO 1910–1970. *Before the Last Battle: Armageddon.* 1971. Minneapolis: Bethany House. 192 p. illus. maps. Orig. pub. as *A Survey of Bible Prophecy.*

Dispensational pre-trib. Satan reigns after Rapture, taking over control of world empire. 3½ year Tribulation (persecution of remaining Church) after Rapture, then seven years of 70th Week: Seven Last Plagues. Thus 10½ years from Rapture to Second Coming. Great White Throne Judgment may start during (not after) Millennium. Antichrist revealed as Satan himself only after Rapture, though he is active beforehand.

2122. _____. *A Survey of Bible Prophecy.* 1971. Minneapolis: Bethany Fellowship. 238 p. illus., index.

2123. _____. *How to Recognize the Antichrist.* 1975. Minneapolis: Bethany Fellowship. 153 p. illus.

Habakkuk describes radioactive fallout and Communist takeover. Antichrist [not God] will destroy Russia.

2124. Boatman, Russell. *What the Bible Says About the End Time.* 1980. Joplin, MO: College Press. viii, 422 p. bibl. indexes.

Describes different interpretations. Notes ambiguities and uncertainties of biblical text. Suggests non-literal interpretation. Rejects pre-trib Rapture doctrine.

2125. Bodunrin, J. *Subtle Deceit: (A Sign of the Last Days)*. [1970s?] [Nigeria?]: s.n. 51 p. bibl.

Holy Spirit glossolalia — speaking in tongues.

2126. Boersma, T. *Is the Bible a Jigsaw Puzzle: An Evaluation of Hal Lindsey's Writings*. 1978. St. Catharines, Canada: Paideia Press. 193 p.

Refutation of Lindsey.

2127. Boice, James Montgomery. *The Last and Future World*. 1974. Grand Rapids, MI: Zondervan xi, 148 p. indexes.

2128. Bonneau, Gilles A. *The Report Concerning Israel, the Nations and the Church: Past Present and Future: Foretold by Prophecy, Described in Scripture*. 1991. Willow Bunch, Canada: G.A. Bonneau. 221 p.

2129. Bowman, J.R. *God's 9 Major Events: Fruition of His Plan*. 1976. [Marion, NC?: priv. pub.] 150 p.

Pre-mill; imminence of Second Coming, "The enemies of Israel who will help the Anti-Christ will all be killed in the Battle of Armageddon. Not one of the persecutors of His 'brethren' will be left alive at the Second Coming of the King."

2130. Boyer, James L. *Prophecy — Things to Come: A Study Guide*. 1974 [1973]. Winona Lake, IN: BMH Books. 130 p.

2131. Boyer, Nicodemus E. *Adolf Hitler, the Black Horseman, and the Millennium in 2000*. 1985. Des Plaines, IL: Studeophile. illus. bibl. refs.

Vol. 1 of *Dr. Nostradamus: 1999, the Seventh Month*. Also wrote *A New Theory of Cosmology; Symmetrical Expansion of the Metagalaxy and of the Antimetagalaxy into the Opposite Directions of the Time Dimension and Changes of "Fundamental Constants" of Atomic Physics as a Function of Expanding Spacetime* (1983).

2132. Bradbury, Edward. *The Ships of Chittim*. 1994. [Shipley?]: E B Whitley. iv, 126 p.

Daniel prophecies.

2133. Bramlett, Jim. *Christ's Soon Return: The Overwhelming Evidence*. 1996. Orlando, FL: priv pub.

Second Coming A.D. 2000 (give or take a year). World Week; 6,000 Year scheme. Early Christians looked to A.D. 2000 as the End (Bramlett assumes they all considered 4000 B.C. the date of Creation). Also "Attack on U.S. imminent?" in Bramlett's *Prophecy Club* Web site: "Strange how a number of different sources are pointing to this same possibility in late 1998. In advance copy of his yet-to-be-distributed newsletter faxed to me two days ago, Pastor F.M. Riley says same thing, citing not a vision but unconfirmed Israeli Mossad intelligence tip to U.S. intelligence that Russia plans a preemptive strike against U.S. this fall so we will not interfere with their planned lightning blitzkrieg into Europe, essential to capture resources needed for their crippled economy and starving masses before Russian winter."

2134. Bransby, Lu Ann. *The Impending Hour*. [1981]. Oklahoma City: Impending Hour.

Foreword by Paul Crouch (Trinity Broadcasting Network). God said: "LuAnn, write a book on the last days before Christ returns!" "KEEP IT SIMPLE." God said there is no book which explains last days clearly and simply. Any-moment Rapture, then seven-year Tribulation. Section on "What to do if you miss the Rapture." Antichrist rules from Common Market nations. Russia (= Magog) invades Israel. "Gog" = Russia's military leader. WWIII: dead burned after 7 months: the "exact time" according to nuclear scientists for radiation to subside. "Hitler was a nice guy compared to Antichrist!" Armageddon = Antichrist (West), China and other Asian nations (East), North (Russia and allies), South (African nations); then the Second Coming. Blood bridle-deep for 200 miles. 120-pound hailstones: "scientific fact" that they are produced by mushroom cloud of nuclear bomb. Millennium under Christ's rule; then people will choose Satan or God. God promised that 5,000 people would be saved by reading this book.

2135. Bratt, John H. *The Final Curtain: Studies in Eschatology.* 1978. Grand Rapids, MI: Baker. 118 p.

2136. Bray, John L. *The Origin of the Pre-Tribulation Rapture Teaching.* 1992 [1982]. Lakeland, FL: John L. Bray Ministry. 36 p. illus.

2137. _____. *The Battle of Gog and Magog (in Revelation 20).* 1987. Lakeland, FL: priv. pub. 24 p.

2138. _____. *The Last Day of Resurrection, Rapture and Judgment.* 1991. Lakeland, FL: John L. Bray Ministry. 32 p. bibl.

2139. _____. *Are We Living in the Last Days?* 1994. Lakeland, FL: priv. pub.: 24 p. illus.

2140. _____. *"Coming in the Clouds of Heaven."* 1994. Lakeland, FL: John L. Bray Ministry. 36 p. bibl.

Matthew XXIV.

2141. _____. *Immediately After the Tribulation.* 1992. Lakeland, FL: author. 48 p.

2142. _____. *Then Shall Be Great Tribulation.* 1991. Lakeland, FL: author. 56 p.

2143. Bray, Raymond. *The Revelation Decoded.* c1995. <http://members. xoom.com/LordsWork/>

Bray: The Lord's Work, Incorporated, Austin, KY. Bray received the key to understanding Revelation from God in 1984. The Tribulation was in ancient Roman times; thus the Rapture is post-trib, but it precedes the Seven Last Plagues (the Seven Bowls of Rev. 16). Raptured faithful then return with Christ at Second Coming for Armageddon triumph. Beast from Earth with two horns like a lamb is Bilderbergers and Illuminati: secret societies which control the UN. Bray promotes Anglo-Saxon-Celtic people as God's Chosen Race, the Ten Lost Tribes of Israel, and reprints Henry Ford's *Dearborn Independent* anti-Jewish articles. Also promotes Gap Theory creationism and publishes *American Ephraimite* journal.

2144. Breese, Dave. *The Five Horsemen.* 1975. Lincoln, NE: Back to the Bible Broadcast. 48 p.

2145. _____. *These Last Days.* 1987.

Oklahoma City, OK: Southwest Radio Church. 25 p.

2146. _____. *Revelation Judgments.* 1994. Colton, CA: World Prophetic Ministry. 48 p.

2147. _____ et al. *Raging Into Apocalypse: Essays in Apocalypse IV.* 1996. Green Forest, AR: New Leaf. 312 p. bibl. refs.

Breese: Christian Destiny (Kansas). Contributors include J.R. Church, G. Jeffrey, David Lewis, C. Missler, Henry Morris, D.F. Webber, Gary Stearman, J. Walvoord.

2148. Briggs, Dennis Allen. *The End by God.* 1996. <http://www.theend-bygod.com/>

6,000 year theory.

2149. Brik, Hans Theodor. *Die Vision der letzten Tage: Weissagungen, Erscheinungen, Hellseher.* 1978. Stein-am-Rhein: Christiana. 1,215 p. bibl.

Occult prophecies; precognition, various seers and Christian prophets from medieval to modern times.

2150. Brim, Billye. *The Blood and the Glory.* 1995. Tulsa, OK: Harrison House. 158 p. bibl. refs.

Brin: worked with Kenneth Hagin. "We are at the end of the last days." How to call on the Blood of Jesus for protection, healing, and triumph. Gap Theory creationism: Six Day creation 6,000 years ago, but original creation was long before that. When Lucifer was expelled from heaven and cast to Earth, the resulting cosmic explosion killed the dinosaurs.

2151. Brogan, J.R. *20th Century Light on the End of the Age: An Assessment of the Protestant Continuing Historicist Interpretation of the Books of Daniel and the Apocalypse Brought Through to the Year 2000 A.D.* 1987. Southampton: J.R. Brogan. iv, 347 p. illus., maps, bibl., index.

2152. Brooke, Tal. *When the World Will Be as One: The Coming New World Order in the New Age.* 1989. Eugene, OR: Harvest House. 288 p. illus. bibl. refs.

Brooke: with Spiritual Counterfeits; former occult believer (disciple of Indian guru Sai Baba). Satanic delusions of the New Age, channeling, reincarnation, soul-travel. One-world government and religion, false Messiah. Demonic possession perhaps rediscovery of pre-Noahic secrets. Antichrist = Beast; False Prophet = Second Beast. Satan's Great Lie: Man can be as gods, and not die. Illuminati conspiracy. World ruled by secret cabal which manipulates the economy; international bankers (largely Jewish).

2153. Brooks, Keith. *Prophetic Questions.* 1954 [1951]. 3rd ed. viii, 165 p.

Actual questions and answers. Pre-trib. All believers raptured. Cars and planes foretold for Last Days. Rejects year-day theory. Rebuilt Temple will be proof of Jewish unbelief. First Beast = Antichrist; Second Beast = False Prophet. U.S. participates in Armageddon. Day of Christ = Rapture. Day of Lord = Second Coming. Armageddon at end of Tribulation. Armies assemble at Armageddon; blasted by Lord. Two Witnesses = Moses and Elijah. Babylon will be rebuilt. "Will animals be resurrected?"—No.

2154. Brooks, Pat. *Christian, Wake Up!* 1981. Fletcher, NC: New Puritan Library. 52 p.

2155. Brown, Arthur H. *Europe After Democracy.* 1993. South Plainfield, NJ: Bridge. 372 p. illus. bibl. refs.

"Examines Scriptural prophecy from Daniel and Revelation in the light of the rise of Europe, the foretold 'revived Roman Empire.'" Canadian evangelist. Common Market becomes New World Order: most ruthless dictatorship ever, led by a Jew. Church raptured pre-trib. Another, post-trib rapture, of Israel. Antichrist literally conceived by Satan (imitating Christ's virgin birth). Eastern millions invade when Euphrates miraculously dries up.

2156. Brown, Michael H. *The Final Hour.* 1993. Cassette. Lakewood, OH: Mary Foundation.

Catholic. Marian apparitions. Mary coming to warn "time of cataclysmic events threatens us all"— the "actual Anti-Christ himself, and to the hour of great tribulation that Christ spoke about." Medjugorje, Fatima, La Salette, Lourdes, Knock. Emphasizes that "wherever Our Lady appears the devil also turns up"; de-monic apparitions too, sometimes "camou-flaged as the Virgin." Lenin, Stalin, Hitler "forerunners" of Antichrist. Mary as "Virgin of Revelation." Some seers shown Tribulation, foresaw tremendous disasters. Third Secret of Fatima: akin to Revelation woes. Wrote book about Ukrainian visionary Josip Terelya. End of 1990s will be pivotal. Radical shift by 2040 (in lifetime of Medjugorje visionaries). Cosmic Warning visible to all world, and Chastisement. Now is "time of grace," chance to repent. Anti-Christ already in world. Accepts Walvoord's scenario. Tidal waves, earthquakes, fire from heaven, nuclear war.

2157. _____. *The Last Secret.* 1998. Ann Arbor, MI: Charis: 316 p. bibl. refs.

Mary's appearance at Fatima in 1917: Third Secret concerning coming One World Government, dire threat from Communist Russia, disasters.

2158. Brubaker, Ray. SEE ALSO 1910–1970. *Jerusalem in Prophecy.* [1970s]. St. Petersburg, FL: God's News Behind the News. Unpaged. illus.

Brubaker: does "God's News — Behind the News" telecast ("Detecting prophetic news, reflecting Bible views"). Formerly radio broadcast, with serial RaDar News (from *Ra*y and *Dar*lene Brubaker). Supported Korean-based Hyoo-go movement which believed End would be in 1994.

2159. Bryant, Page. *The Earth Changes Survival Handbook.* 1988 [1983]. Santa Fe: Sun Books. 440 p. illus., index, bibl.

2160. _____. *Earth Changes Now.* 1989 Santa Fe: Sun. 62 p illus

Occult prophecies. Foreword by Brad Steiger.

2161. Buechner, Howard A., and William Bernhart. *Hitler's Ashes — Seeds of a New Reich.* 1989. Metairie, LA: Thunderbird Press. 289 p. illus.

Sequel to *Adolf Hitler and the Secrets of the Holy Lance.* Real Third Reich hasn't started yet. Second Phase began 1985, lasts til May 1, 2015, when Thousand Year Reich starts, with purification of human race, or "Kingdom of the Rod of Iron." Armageddon after Millennium. Holy Knights recovered Holy Lance and ashes from Antarctica in 1979. Society of Saints of the Golden Circle worships Hitler as Prophet Elijah returned.

2162. Bullard, Rayford. *Glimpses Into the Revelation.* 1975. Franklin Springs, GA: Advocate Press. 275 p.

2163. Burkett, Larry. *The THOR Conspiracy: The Seventy-Hour Countdown to Disaster.* 1995. Nashville: T. Nelson. 324 p.

Fiction, sequel to *The Illuminati.* Burkett: founder-president of Christian Financial Concepts; was V.P. of electronics firm, manager at Cape Canaveral space project, wrote *The Coming Economic Earthquake,* has two radio programs. 1960s H-bomb rocket launch detonates in ozone layer, sets it afire, igniting chain reaction and expected End of the World, but it stops. Then cover-up; large ozone hole is blamed on industry and pollutants; used as excuse for environmentalists to establish dictatorial control. President becomes puppet of The Society (led by Chinese). Wisconsin challenges Feds, supports states rights, with religious opposition. Coverup exposed 50 years later.

2164. Burman, Michael (ed. by Leslie Chapman). *Unlocking End-Time Prophecy.* 1998. <http://www.geocities.com/Athens/Oracle/1525/unlock>

Follows and modifies H.W. Armstrong.

2165. Burnside, G[eorge]. *Daniel: Prophecy Unfolds the Future.* N.d. Reprinted 1993 by Leaves-of-Autumn Books. 250 p.

Australian evangelist

2166. _____. *Revelation's Wonders Unfolded.* 1985. Payson, AZ: Leaves-of-Autumn. 246 p. illus. Reprint ed.

2167. Burrill, Russell. *The New World Order: What's Behind the Headlines?* 1992. Keene, TX: Seminars Unlimited. x, 128 p. illus.

Seventh-day Adventist.

2168. Bush, Clifton H. *The Third Prophecy.* 1994. Indianapolis, IN: Fabco. xii, 240 p.

Fiction. Doctor McIver, retired Air Force colonel and archeologist, discovers truth of Third Prophecy of Fatima, hitherto unrevealed by the Vatican. World-

wide outbreaks of visions and psychic phenomena. Third Prophecy was ultimatum to humanity to reform by eve of A.D. 2000 or be destroyed as a failed experiment. Mankind was bioengineered by extraterrestrials; previous races were destroyed by Flood because of extensive interbreeding with animals.

2169. Buxton, Clyne W. *The Bible Says You Can Expect These Things.* 1973. Old Tappan, NJ: F.H. Revell. 160 p. bibl.

2170. _____. *End Times: A Biblical Study of Current and Future Events.* 1993. Cleveland, TN: Pathway. 153 p. bibl. refs.

Buxton: End Time Ministries, Cleveland, TN. Straight pre-mill, pre-trib; quotes, cites many other pre-mill expositors. "The thesis of this book is that we have abundant proof from the Bible showing that the end may be very near." Computer numbering system, UN, 200-million man Chinese army, all as prophesied. Turkey is now able to stop (by damming) flow of Euphrates. Mark on hand already in use in France (computerized electronic credit system). Any-moment Rapture, then Antichrist and Tribulation. But exact time unknown. "These times also offer tremendous opportunities to witness to the unconverted, using end-time events as a backdrop." 144,000 Jews to convert and evangelize during Tribulation. Partial and later complete fulfillment of prophecy: e.g. Abomination of Desolation partially fulfilled by Antiochus Epiphanes desecrating Temple, complete fulfillment at End. Major topics include Money control; Common Market; Israel; Rapture ("We will vanish into thin air — think of it!"). Rejects Pyramidology — God wouldn't use "tomb of a dead heathen King" to reveal the End. Author's "saintly mother" immobilized with paralytic stroke will arise "physically perfect." Tribulation will be worse than Auschwitz. "The world is headed for upheaval and destruction of catastrophic proportions. [More than half population will die].... If this sounds like the talk of a prophet of doom, it is not meant to, for that is exactly what awaits the world — doom." Literal interpretation of Trumpets (after all,

God did those things to Egypt before). At Second Coming, Christ destroys armies assembled at Armageddon. "Evidently, our Lord will employ atomic fission at this time...." Hordes of Christ's enemies die horrible deaths. During Millennium, some men will live almost a thousand years.

2171. Byers, Marvin. *The Final Victory: The Year 2000.* 1994 [1991]. Shippensburg, PA: Treasure House. 315 p. bibl. refs. [1991 Companion Press ed. 458 p].

Byers: missionary in Guatemala. Hebron Ministries. Post-trib Rapture. 1993 Israel peace treaty = 2,300 days from Jan. 1, 2000. Isaac Newton correctly predicted Daniel's prophecies (Byers discovered Newton's prophecy writings after first edition of this book; thrilled that Newton reached same conclusion concerning 70th week). God wants us to know about Last Days but most people are not listening. Stresses relationship with beginnings, origins, in Old Testament. 3½ not 7 year period. Revelation chronology is repeated: angel gives it, then John. 144,000 preach gospel during Tribulation. Rapture occurs 42 months after Antichrist revealed. 69 Weeks argument wrong. 62 Weeks = 434 years of independence for Israel til First Coming. 7 Weeks (49 years) = 1947–1996 (command to restore Israel to Second Coming). "Cut off" after 62 Weeks = Jesus circumcised. 1996 Second Coming is "spiritual," then Tribulation, Antichrist, then March, 2000 Rapture and Second Coming. Millennium starts 1996. Church Age lasts 2,000 years; Adam 4,000 years prior. 6,000 year theory — Ussher's 4004 B.C. creation date probably right.

2172. Cahill, Matthew E. *Recipe for Armageddon.* 1985. Cincinnati: Esmond Julie Pub. 156 p. maps.

2173. Campbell, Roger F., and David A. Campbell. *Prosperity in the End Time.* 1983. Fort Washington, PA: Christian Literature Crusade. 129 p. bibl.

Financial prophecy.

2174. Camping, Harold. 1979. *When Is the Rapture?* Oakland, CA: Family Stations. 46 p.

Camping: founder/owner of Family Radio Network, Oakland. Also wrote *Adam When?*

2175. _____. *The Seventy Weeks of Daniel.* 1979. Oakland, CA: Family Stations.

2176. _____. *1994?* 1992. New York: Vantage Press. xxi, 551 p. Scripture index.

Rapture and End in 1994. Lots of numerology. The 70 Weeks historically fulfilled 609–539 B.C. End-time information sealed until the Last Days (i.e. now). Final Tribulation = 2,300 days (six years plus). Creation 11,013 B.C. Flood = 6,000 + 23 years later. Creation to Messiah (born 7 B.C.) = 11,000 + 2,300 days. Flood to Messiah (Crucifixion) = 5,000 + 23 years. Satan was bound at the Cross (the Millennium). "Apparent" 12,000 years duration of world: 11,000 plus the Millennium (from the time of Christ). (Also, 120 years warning from Noah before Flood is multiple of 12,000). But really *13,000* years, just as the Twelve Tribes are really *thirteen.* 13,000 from Creation is 1988, plus 2,300 days is 1994. 7,000 years after Flood is A.D. 2011, with predicted 23 year Tribulation, but Tribulation is shortened for the sake of the Elect. The world lasts precisely long enough so all who are to be saved — the Elect — can be born. End will come between Sept. 15th and 27th, 1994. Antichrist is Satan himself. Believers undergo Tribulation. Rapture occurs "simultaneously with the end of the world." Birth control violates God's plan, and abortion is especially evil: "The murder of babies in the womb emphasizes that Romans 1 points to the end of the world." AIDS is endtime judgment on sin of homosexuality. Jews continue to reject Christ, so are rejected by God.

2177. _____. *Are You Ready?* 1993. New York: Vantage Press. xxiii, 403 p. illus. charts, Scripture index.

2178. Cantelon, Willard. *The Day the Dollar Dies.* c1973. Plainfield, NJ: Logos Intl. x, 149 p.

Pre-trib.

2179. Capps, Charles. *End-Time Events: Journey to the End of the Age.* 1997. Tulsa, OK: Harrison House. 252 p. illus. Bibl. refs.

2180. Caringola, Robert. *Seventy Weeks: The Historical Alternative.* 1991. Shippensburg, PA: Companion. 147 p. bibl. refs.

2181. Carman, Oneal. *Golden Age 2000: The Coming of the Prince.* 1993. Elizabethtown, KY: Gospel Gold. xii, 230 p. bibl. refs.

6,000 Years; literal Millennium. 1990s will be "the last decade of a two thousand year period since the birth of Jesus, and the last ten years of a 6,000 year period." 70th Jubilee begins Sept. 1996. Russia to lead Moslem Confederation against Israel. Antichrist arises from revived Roman Empire after Tabernacle (Temple) erected. Magog Battle near beginning of 7 Years; Armageddon (involving all nations) at end of 7 Years, then Second Coming (= Rapture). Israel reborn 1948, circumcised by first Arab war; bar mitzvahed with Eichman's capture. Ark of Covenant hidden under Temple Mount. Carman participated in various digs seeking Ark, ashes of Red Heifer, and other Temple treasures.

2182. Carr, Marc. *Last Sands in the Hour Glass: Revelation Explored.* 1988. Son-Rise. 294 p.

2183. [Carr, Tom]. *[Armageddon,] The Last Battle.* 1991. Torrance, CA: Silver Odyssey. Video.

Carr: director. Features Hal Lindsey.

2184. Carter, John. *A Prophetic Look at the Impending Financial Crisis.* 1993. Thousand Oaks, CA: The Carter Report. Video.

Sermon by Carter; Carter Report TV program; Community Adventist Fellowship.

2185. Carver, Everett I. *When Jesus Comes Again.* 1979. Phillipsburg, NJ: Presbyterian and Reformed. ix, 339 p. bibl. refs., index.

Carver: professor emeritus Gulf-Coast Bible College Refutes dispensational pre-mill scheme. Single judgment at Second Coming; single resurrection of dead. Kingdom of God inaugurated at First Coming, not future.

2186. *Catholic Prophecy on the Coming Great Chastisement and Personal Salva-*

tion. 1997 [1996]. <http://www.webcom. com/enddays/enddays.html>

The End Days website. Maitreya is Antichrist. WWIII; great comet called the Ball of Redemption. Then Millennium: 1,500 years; then Final Judgment. 8,000 years total.

2187. Caw, Frank. *The Ultimate Deception.* 1996–98. <http:/www.frank caw.com/>

Pre-trib. "Read about the most incredible, earth-shaking Bible prophecy predictions poised to be fulfilled at the dawning of the new millennium!!" Middle East peace agreement will fail, with Arab-Israeli war probably in 1999. All Arab states join forces; also Iran. Antichrist, from Lebanon, makes spectacular entrance, and defeats invading armies. Gives Jerusalem to the Palestinians, then conquers Syria, Iraq, Iran, and even resurgent Russia. Antichrist then enforces world peace and inspires world prosperity, not revealing his true nature until after the pre-trib Rapture. Also discusses Pre-Adamic rule of Satan on Earth (Gap Theory creationism).

2188. Cephas, David. *The Witness of the Times.* 1993. Scarborough: University of Western Australia Chaplaincy. 221 p. illus., maps ; bibl. refs., indexes. On title page: Christophorus.

2189. Cha, Dang-ho. *Rapture October 1992: The True Holy Spirit Comes from a Single Root.* [1992?]. San Diego: Taberah World Mission.

Korean-based Taberah World Mission: part of Hyoo-go (Rapture) movement. Follows boy prophet Bang-Ik Ha.

2190. Chaij, Fernando. SEE ALSO 1910–1970. *The Impending Drama.* 1979. Nashville: Southern Pub Assoc. 128 p.

Seventh-day Adventist. "Time is running out." Satan trying to distract us. Cites E.G. White frequently.

2191. _____. *The Key to Victory.* 1979. Nashville: Southern Publishing Assoc. 126 p.

2192. Chambers, Joseph R. *A Palace for the Antichrist.* 1996. Green Forest, AR: New Leaf Press. 294 p., plates, illus.

Saddam Hussein rebuilding Babylon.

2193. Chambers, Leon, and Mildred Chambers. *Interpreting End Time Events.* 1973. Fairfax, AL: Leon Chambers. 81 p.

2194. _____. *Interpreting Satan-Antichrist: His World Empire.* 1973. Fairfax, AL: Leon Chambers. 97 p.

2195. Chan, Kai Lok. *The Antichrist Beast Identified and Revealed.* 1979. Singapore: [K.L. Chan?]. xi, 181 p. illus., maps, bibl.

Post-trib pre-mill. Includes Epilogue against evolution. Indebted to Gordon Lindsay. Natural, social, and moral order falling apart. Prophecies have dual fulfillment: near and far. Russia = 4th Beast (red = communist). Not 10-toed revived Roman EEC. Dan. 11:40: King of North (Antichrist) and South (America) will battle in Israel. The "Assyrian" (rod and staff = hammer and sickle), Gog and Magog, Isaiah's Babylon: all are Russia, which is destroyed at Armageddon. Discusses various theories about Antichrist and Beast identities. Iron / clay mix = fascism / communism. Abomination of Desolation: nuclear destruction. Trumpets: nuclear, tactical, missiles, fallout radioactivity. "Beast" computer set up 1975 at Brussels EEC headquarters; will use three 6-digit numbers for each person for all buying, selling. Antichrist will take over EEC. Wounding of Antichrist: Hitler's attack on USSR. Papacy = 666, Mystery Babylon. Russia breaks treaty with Israel, invades mid-trib, with Persian, Ethiopia, Libya. An "absolute certainty" that Khomeini's Iran will turn communist and Soviet puppet. Armageddon at end of Tribulation. Tarshish = England. U.S. attacks Russian invaders via Egypt and Arabia. China then aids U.S., retreating into Egypt; EEC also aids U.S. vs. Russia. Armageddon: climax of war, Second Coming. Grand scale nuclear destruction. Russia destroyed at Armageddon — not before. Jupiter Effect confirms author predictions. Antichrist (successor of Brezhnev) emerges 1979, Tribulation. 1981–83: EEC surrenders to Russia. 1982–84: Russian invades Israel. 1984–88: U.S. attacks Russian armies; Armageddon. 1986–90: Second Coming.

2196. Chant, Barry, and Winkie Pratney. *The Return.* 1988. Chichester, England: Sovereign World. 256 p.

2197. Chase, Neal. *Ezekiel's Temple in Montana.* 1990. Missoula, MT: Baha'i Center. vi, 56 p.

"Over one hundred years ago the Mormon prophet George Williams prophesied the return of Jesus in this prison." Leland Jensen, founder of Baha'i offshoot BUPC, was imprisoned here starting on the prophesied day.

2198. Chatelain, Maurice. *La Fin du Monde.* 1982. Montreal: Presses de la Cite. 235 p. illus. bibl. refs. and index.

Natural disasters, prophecies.

2199. Chen, Hon-Ming. *God's Descending in Clouds (Flying Saucers) on Earth to Save People.* 1997. Garland, TX: priv. pub.

Chen Tao (Right Way) God's Salvation Church moved to Garland, Texas, with followers to prepare for God's Kingdom; prophesied God would appear on TV on March 25, 1998 on channel 18 nationwide; Second Coming March 31, 1998. Great Tribulation by devil spirits or King Satans, floods in Japan, China, conquest of Southeast Asia, ⅚ world's population die, refugees flee to America then escape holocaust on flying saucers, God's spaceships.

2200. Chiappalone, Joseph S. *Death of an Evil God: An Explanation of the Coming Destruction and an Exposé of the Evilness of Religions.* 1991. Malanda, Australia: Annwn Publications. 566 p. index.

Gnosticism.

2201. Chick, Jack T. SEE ALSO 1910-1970. *Chaos.* 1976. Crusaders comic series.

Aftermath of the Rapture.

2202. _____. *The Only Hope.* 1985. Chino, CA: Chick Publications. 24 p. illus. Comic book format.

2203. _____. *The Four Horsemen.* 1985. Crusaders Comic vol. 16. (Alberto series). 32 p. illus.

Chick advertisement: "clear description of how the papacy fulfills Bible prophecies of the antichrist." First horseman = Pope.

2204. _____. *The Last Generation.* 1992 [1972].

Hitlerian future; Christian believers savagely persecuted; World Court in Rome. Ends with Rapture.

2205. Chilton, David. *The Days of Vengeance: An Exposition of the Book of Revelation.* 1987. Ft. Worth, TX: Dominion Press. xxxiii, 721 p. bibl., index.

Preterist, post-mill. Christian Reconstructionism.

2206. _____. *Paradise Restored: A Biblical Theology of Dominion.* 1985. Ft. Worth, TX: Dominion Press. x, 342 p. index.

2207. _____. *The Great Tribulation.* 1987. Ft. Worth, TX: Dominion Press. xvi, 195 p.

2208. Chitwood, Arlen L. *Judgment Seat of Christ.* 1986. Norman, OK: The Lamp Broadcast. 181 p. Scripture index.

2209. _____. *Prophecy on Mount Olivet.* 1989. Norman, OK: The Lamp Broadcast. 329 p.

2210. _____. *Focus on the Middle East.* 1991. Norman, OK: The Lamp Broadcast. 79 p.

2211. Cho, David Yong-gi. *Daniel: Insight on the Life and Dreams of the Prophet from Babylon.* 1990. Lake Mary, FL: Creation House. 174 p.

Pastor of Full Gospel Church, Seoul; world's largest church.

2212. _____. *Revelation* 1991. Orlando, FL: Creation House. 172 p. bibl. refs.

2213. _____. *The Apocalyptic Prophecy.* 1998. Orlando, FL: Creation House. x, 227 p.

Also wrote *The Babylonian Prophecy* (1997).

2214. Christian Science Endtime Center. <http://www.endtime.org/> Denver.

Christian Science variant stressing founder Mary Baker Eddy's eschatological teachings, with End in 2000 or 2001 (6,000 years after Creation). Eddy was herself "representative of the Second Coming" and "Woman clothed with the sun." Denies literal physical Millennium. Eddy's "catastrophic prophecies" were later rejected by Mother Church.

2215. Chromey, Rick. *Revelation: a 4-Week Course to Help Senior Highers Un-* lock the Secrets of the End Times. 1992. Loveland, CO: Group. 40 p. illus.

2216. Chrysler, C. Donald. *The Handbook of Unfulfilled Bible Prophecy.* 1994. Marne, MI: Chrysler Books. x, 371 p.

2217. [Chumney, Eddie]. *Bible Prophecy and End Time Events.* 1998. <http://www.geocities.com/Heartland/2175/prophecy.html#EndTime>

Hebraic Heritage Ministries International (Strasburg, OH).

2218. Chung, M. Kirkpatrick. *Revealing Last Day Events from the Bible Books of Daniel & Revelation.* 1991. Siloam Springs, AR: Creation Enterprises International. 88 p. illus.

2219. Church, J.R. *Guardians of the Grail—and the Men Who Plan to Rule the World!.* 1991 [1989]. Rev ed. Oklahoma City, OK: Prophecy Publications. vi, 318 p. illus. Written with Ralph G. Griffin and G.G. Stearman.

Unified Europe under Karl von Habsburg (= 666), perhaps by 1992. Emerging dynasty to impose One World government and deceive humanity into worldwide slavery. Book prompted by *Last Temptation of Christ. Holy Blood, Holy Grail* thesis: Jesus married Mary Magdalene, had children; ancestors of Merovingian dynasty. Descendants also founded Priory of Sion in Jerusalem, inner Templar organization. Conspiracy to rule world related to Spear of Destiny. Antichrist, from tribe of Dan, to come from this group. U.S. = Mystery Babylon.

2220. _____. *Hidden Prophecies in the Psalms.* 1990 [1986]. Oklahoma City, OK: Prophecy Publications. 380 p. illus. bibl.

Research asst.: Patricia Berry; also lists ed. and res. by Jack Jewell, Ralph G. Griffin, and G.G. Stearman. Psalms are year-by-year prophecies of 20th century. Ps. 1–41: Israel recognized as nation. Ps. 42–72: Exodus psalms—persecution in Egypt (Germany). Ps. 73–89: Leviticus—establishment of Temple worship. Ps. 90–106: Numbers—ends with Armageddon and coming of Messiah. Ps. 107–150: Deuteronomy—the Millennium as God's Law or Word. Ps. 14 and 53: Fool says there is no God: refers to Stalin. Ps. 19: Heavens declare the glory of God: confirmation of Einstein. Ps. 23: green pastures, still waters: establishment of Jordan as boundary of Jewish territory, increased Aliyah (return). Ps. 48: Tarshish = Britain; 1948 start of last generation. In 1986 ed. suggested Rapture and Tribulation in 1988, Armageddon in 1994, but changed this prediction in 1990 ed.

2221. _____. *Hidden Prophecies in the Song of Moses.* 1991. Oklahoma City, OK: Prophecy Publications. 363 p. bibl. refs.

Sequel to Psalms book. Song of Moses in Deut. 32 plus Psalms 90–100 (the Mosaic psalms). Connections between symbols, numbers. 6,000 Year Theory. Song of Moses named in Rev. 15:3. Whole is coded prophetic mystery, fulfilled in 1990s. Simeon "bound" in the Law (story relegated to Deut.) because of Israel's spiritual deafness — can't "hear" secret message until Last Days (Joseph's "return," prefiguring Christ's, and release of Simeon). Song of Moses = predicts Israel exiled, rise of Christianity, Return of Jews, Antichrist and Armageddon, Second Coming. Antichrist from tribe of Dan: said to "judge" Israel during Last Days. Antichrist may already control international banking. 70th Week; Messiah cut off. Gog and Magog battle, start of Tribulation. Half world dies in Tribulation. "Noisome pestilence" = AIDS, or Iraqi chemical weapon. Ps. 96: Gog and Magog war (Russian invasion). End of Tribulation = Armageddon (East invades); Tribulation survivors doomed to be killed, saved only by Second Coming. Tabernacle dimensions prophetic [cf. Pyramidology]. Jewish festivals are symbolic of End events.

2222. _____, and Gary Stearman. *Prophecy in the News.* 1994. Oklahoma City, OK: Prophecy in the News. Tape.

Includes "Rise of the Mark; Biotechnology: Return of the Demon Seed; Omen: Profile of the Antichrist." 6,000 year scheme with A.D. 2000 start of Millennium.

2223. Civelli, Joseph R. *The Messiah's Return.* 50 p. Author.

Advertised in Whisenant's *88 Reasons.*

2224. Clark, Doug. SEE ALSO 1910–1970. *Earthquake—1982: When the Planets Align—(Syzgy).* 1976. Garden Grove, CA: Lyfe Production. 94 p. illus.

2225. _____. *Is Kissinger Giving the U.S. to Russia?* 1976. Orange, CA: Amazing Prophecy Center. 96 p. illus.

"Doug's Amazing Prophecy Facts on these Hot Issues: War, Detente, Soviet Agreements...."

2226. _____. *Seven Years of Hell on Earth.* 1976. Garden Grove, CA: Lyfe Production. 28 p. plates.

2227. _____. *They Saw the Second Coming.* 1979. Irvine, CA: Harvest House Publishers, 239 p.

Novel. Stanos Papilos (= 666), head of Common Market Ten Nations, revealed as Antichrist. Russian-Arabs attack Israel 1983. Overrun Israel, but God destroys invaders, and blasts their homelands too. Papilos takes over their nations, moves capital to Jerusalem, becomes world leader but is opposed by U.S. Jews are savagely persecuted by Antichrist; many flee to Petra. Mark of the Beast is a tattoo. Millions martyred. China marches against Antichrist across trans-Himalayan highway and dammed Euphrates. Americans join attack, destroy Europe. But Chinese turn against U.S. after taking Jerusalem. Armageddon = Chinese vs. Antichrist in Israel.

2228. _____. *The Coming Oil War: Predictions of Things to Come.* 1980. Irvine, CA: Harvest House. 178 p.

2229. _____. *Shockwaves of Armageddon.* 1982. Eugene, OR: Harvest House. 237 p.

Rumored Temple rebuilding in Israel. (Priv. pub ed. titled *Final Shockwaves of Armageddon.*)

Clark: formerly on Paul Crouch's Trinity Broadcasting Network; now wanted for mail fraud.

2230. _____. *Last World Government.*

2231. _____. *666: The Mark of the Beast.*

2232. _____. *Antichrist's Temple.*

2233. _____. *The Chinese Are Coming.*

2234. Clark, Gordon. *New Heavens, New Earth: First and Second Peter.* 1993 [1967]. Jefferson, MD: Trinity Foundation. viii, 271 p. bibl. refs., index.

2235. Clark, Pam. *Trumpet Wind Ministries.* <http://www.prophetic.net/toc.htm> Houston.

2236. Clendennen, Bert. *The End Time.* 6 cassettes.

Pentecostal (Assembly of God) evangelist; School of Christ International.

2237. Clouse, Robert G., ed. *The Meaning of the Millennium: Four Views.* 1977. Downers Grove, IL: InterVarsity Press. 223 p. select bibl.

Contributions by G. E. Ladd (historic pre-mill), H. A. Hoyt (dispensational pre-mill), Loraine Boettner (post-mill), and A. A. Hoekema (a-mill).

2238. Coder, S. Maxwell. *Israel's Destiny.* 1978. Moody 185 p. maps bibl. refs.

2239. _____. *The Final Chapter: Understanding What the Bible Says about the Last Pages of Human History.* 1984. Wheaton, IL: Tyndale House. 249 p.

Pre-mill pre-trib, any-moment Rapture. Part of book included in *Israel's Destiny.* Destinies of Jews, Gentiles, and church of God. Coder indefatigably devises literal interpretations for everything. Antichrist: ruler of world confederacy, to sign 7 year treaty with Israel. Jerusalem is literal center of earth. God gave Jews whole Arabian geological plate. Tribulation: Temple rebuilt, in second half Antichrist demands he be worshipped, ⅔ of Jews killed in horrible persecution, others convert. Rosh invades; destroyed by God. "All nations" invade Israel; Christ returns with armies of heaven: Armageddon. "Dry bones" not yet fulfilled — all Jews regathered only after Second Coming. Magog, Rosh = USSR, leader of Northern confederation. Gog = Prince of Rosh. Second Coming: Rift Valley opens, Jerusalem lifted up, with "Canopy of glory" over it. Other earth changes at Millennium include Dead Sea linked to Mediterranean Ocean, becoming world's greatest port.

Tribulation days literally shortened. "This generation" refers to the Tribulation generation. Rapture is next prophesied event. Then, "lawlessness and evil will exceed anything ever known in history" when Church and Holy Spirit removed. America comes under Antichrist rule with other nations; Antichrist controls world economy with Mark of Beast. U.S. troops invade Israel with other nations at end of Tribulation. Gog invasion early Tribulation; Antichrist with all the nations invades at end of Tribulation. "Weapons" of defeated invaders burned by Jews for 7 years = military fuel stores; or lignostone (treated pressurized wood). Antichrist, a Gentile, "indwelt by Satan and possessing supernatural powers." "Antichrist" can also refer to 2nd Beast (False Prophet). Literal death wound, miracle healing. Armageddon: gathering of all armies, focal point of battle. Those who hear and reject God before Tribulation will follow Antichrist. Those who didn't hear can be saved at Tribulation. Three Resurrections: of dead believers (at Rapture); of Old Testament and Tribulation saints (Second Coming), and the rest (end of Millennium). During Tribulation, supernatural will burst in upon the earth with horrible plagues, demons, evil beasts, worst ever earthquake, fire and brimstone, killing 2/3 of world. Mystery Babylon (Harlot) = "ecumenical monstrosity" during Tribulation. Literal Babylon becomes world center after Antichrist destroys Mystery Babylon. Coder unsure whether Raptured return physically during Millennium. New Jerusalem: probably pyramidal shape; literal descent to earth (but may remain suspended in orbit). When Christ rules, "Edom will be gone forever, along with other Arab nations which have sought to destroy the chosen people of God."

2240. Cohen, Gary G. SEE ALSO 1910–1970. *The Horsemen are Coming.* 1991 [1987]. Chattanooga, TN: AMG. 206 p. Orig. 1974 titled *Civilization's Last Hurrah.* [1974, Moody, 208 p].

Cohen: converted Jew, prof. Biblical School of Theology, Hatfield, PA. Fiction, set around A.D. 2000. Any-moment Rapture, though might be preceded by start of 7-year Tribulation. Rome capital of communist European United Republic. Rapture occurs, world baffled. EUR Premier, Turkish-born Baruk Mindor (i.e. Nimrod), makes 7-year treaty with Israel. Russo-Arab coalition attacks Israel with 100,000 air-cav paratroopers. Israel reduces USSR to radioactive wasteland with U.S.-supplied nuclear powered laser-firing superplanes. Communist China attacks rest of Far East, wars in Africa, famine, massive earthquakes, China exports food made from corpses. Two witnesses preach, would-be killer struck dead supernaturally, later killed but televised corpses rise to heaven. Literal Tribulation: waters turn red, giant lethal locusts. Mindor assassinated, revives. Adopts 666 as emblem, required as tattoo. Arabs attack. 144,000 Jews convert, flee to wilderness. The new Pope, Pius 666, becomes the False Prophet. People worship animated computerized statue of Mindor. New Babylon constructed. Siege of Jerusalem in Armageddon Valley, armies supernaturally destroyed, Second Coming.

2241. _____, and Salem Kirban. *Revelation Visualized: Never Before So Crystal Clear and Current an Explanation of the Last Book of the Bible!* 1971. Huntingdon Valley, PA: S. Kirban. 480 p. illus. maps.

2242. _____. *Salem Kirban Reference Bible: King James Version.* 1979 Chattanooga, TN: AMG. 1524, 479 p. illus.

Commentary by Cohen; background by Kirban. With: "Revelation Visualized."

2243. Cohen, Tim. *The Antichrist and a Cup of Tea.* 1998. Aurora, CO : Prophecy House, 444 p. illus. bibl. refs.

Reveals the British monarchy's "long endeavor to establish a 'new world order' and for the first time gives hard evidence to suggest the identity of the AntiChrist — Prince Charles of Wales." Prince Charles's name equals 666 in English and Hebrew; he has already taken a biochip implant; his heraldic symbols are those of the First Beast; and he has New World, Templar, Rosicrucian, Freemason and Illuminati connections. Cohen (a pseudonym) has forthcoming book *Messiah, History, and*

the Tribulation, which is dispensationalist post-trib, emphasizing Christology aspects.

2244. Collier, Gordon W. *God's Eternal Purpose in the Great Controversy Between Christ and Satan.* 1971. Jackson, TN: Author: 203 p. illus.

2245. Collier, John R. *From Rapture to Wrath: An Easy-to-Read, Simple-to-Understand, Yet Comprehensive and Up-to-Date Review of End-Time Prophecy.* 1996. Columbus, GA: Brentwood Christian Press. 382 p.

Pre-trib Rapture, between 1998 and 2001. Day of the Lord is the Tribulation, the 70th Week. The "Last Trumpet," when Rapture occurs, is Feast of Rosh Hashanah, not later 7th Trumpet of Revelation. During Tribulation, "literally *billions* will die"; rest all suffer horribly. Because Tribulation is so horrible, Church can't still be present. After Rapture, Antichrist takes over Ten Nation European Union. Russia and Moslem nations attack Israel in second half of Tribulation. Antichrist and U.S. then attack these invaders. God destroys most of the Russians; then Chinese attack the Western forces, and world is engulfed in nuclear exchange. World's armies attack at Armageddon. 6,000 Year theory: "The Scriptures show that Adam was created about 5000 years B.C. Therefore, at about 2000 A.D. the active part of earth's history would cease and a 1000 year period of rest would begin." Many converted during Tribulation, but all martyred.

2246. Collins, Della Sue. *The Prophets Identify the U.S.A. and Foretell Her Destiny.* n.d.

End-time Babylon, with Satanic base-6 number system and rampant homosexuality.

2247. Comfort, Ron. *The Five Horsemen in the Book of the Revelation.* 1976. Murfreesboro, TN: Bill Rice Ranch. 26 p.

2248. Conyers, A.J. *The End: What Jesus Really Said About the Last Things.* c1995. Downers Grove, IL: InterVarsity Press. 151 p. bibl. refs.

2249. Coombes, R.A. *America, the*

Babylon: America's Destiny Foretold in Biblical Prophecy. 1998. Liberty, MO: REAL Pub. 250 p.

2250. Cook, Terry L. *The Mark of the New World Order.* 1996. Indianapolis: Virtue Intl. xii, 720 p. illus. bibl. refs.

Cashless economy, implantable biochip technology, bar codes, etc. Cook — retired Los Angeles deputy sheriff, real estate broker, pilot, fundamentalist minister, Second Coming Ministries, Nevada; publishes *Pressing Toward the Mark* newsletter. Technology of Revelation's Beast. Biochips, bar codes, implants, computerized 666 economic system, global positioning system. Many news clippings.

2251. Coppi, Michael J. *Are the "End Times" Truly Upon Us?* 1998. <http: www.arch-angel.net/MJC/31.htm>

Writings by Coppi included in this Catholic "Marian Visions/End Times" website. "Many prophecies and apparitions, in addition to "signs of the times" indicate that they are...." Fatima visions; Great Jubilee Year of 2000.

2252. Cordner, Michael. *The Rapture of the Church.* 1995. <http://www.xmission.com/~gastown/revival/rapture.htm>

Only one rapture. Post-trib: Christians must go through the Tribulation.

2253. Cote, Armand J.N. *The End of Times.* 1973. New York: Carlton Press. 112 p.

2254. *Countdown to Armageddon.* 1998. <http://www.countdown.org/home. htm>

By "The Family." Comet Hale-Bopp is herald of Tribulation and Antichrist. Abomination of Desolation "some incredibly high-tech supercomputer, linked to the New World Order's telecommunications network."

2255. *Countdown to Armageddon: 1967 to 2007 A.D.* <http://www.prophecysite.com/ref.htm>

White Horse of Revelation = 1998 Middle East peace accord. Gog of Magog = Russia. Russia attacks Israel 1999, starting WWIII and Antichrist's Tribulation. Rapture at start of Tribulation. Creationist; 6,000 Year theory.

2256. The Covenant, the Sword, and the Arm of the Lord. *C.S.A. Survival Manual.* 1982. Pontiac, MO: C.S.A.

Covenant, Sword, and Arm of the Lord (C.S.A.): highly militarized Christian Identity group founded by James Ellison, who ran End time Overcomer Survival Training School. Imminent Tribulation: final battle between forces of God and "Satanic blood-line Jews..." After C.S.A. was raided by government, Ellison moved to Robert Millar's Elohim City Christian Identity group, where Oklahoma City bomber McVeigh had contacts.

2257. [Cox, Kenneth?]. 1994. *Last Day Events.* 6 videos. Riverside, CA: Family Enrichment Resources: Dimensions of Prophecy. Producer/director, Jeff Wood.

2258. _____. 1994. *End Time Prophecies.* 6 videos. Riverside, CA: Family Enrichment Resources: Dimensions of Prophecy.

2259. Crawford, Jarah B. *Last Battle Cry: Christianity's Final Conflict with Evil.* 1984. Knoxville, TN: Jann Publishing. xvii, 597 p. indexes. Distr. by CPA Books.

Crawford: Vermont minister; Christian Identity advocate.

2260. Crews, Joe. *The Last Night on Earth.* 1993. Frederick, MD: Amazing Facts. 32 p.

Seventh-day Adventist.

2261. Cribb, C.C. *From Now Till Eternity: The Sequence of Prophetic Events.* 1976. Raleigh, NC: Manhattan. [14], x, 422 p.

Founder and president of Evangelical Ministries, Raleigh, NC. We are now living in *"the very last days of the age!"* Rapture and Tribulation to occur "this generation." Ghastly, horrible violence during Tribulation under Antichrist's rule. Adam created 4005 B.C. 6,000 years for humanity to Armageddon and Millennium. Gap Theory Creationism "vast, indeterminate time lapse between Genesis 1:1 and the following verse 2." Tribulation preceded by forty years of increasing trouble, probably started 1948. Antichrist will be one of ten leaders; conquers three, then other seven submit to him. Antichrist is assassinated, then resurrected. Harlot of Revelation = Papacy. Bottomless Pit is inside earth. Rapture will be sudden and unexpected, but loud and public. Rapture mid-Tribulation (3½ years before End), thus believers endure much of Tribulation. False Prophet's image of Antichrist supernaturally endowed with satanic life. "Great Tribulation" final half of seven years: destruction and death beyond description, some 1½ billion killed by fire. Horrors of Tribulation persuade millions to turn to Christ. Armageddon: armies of whole world invade Israel to annihilate Jews, but themselves obliterated by God. Then Second Coming, Millennium. Gog and Magog battle at end of Millennium. Primitive weapons used because modern weapons destroyed after Armageddon. Our resurrected bodies won't have any blood, or freckles (but martyrs will retain their scars). Heavenly City 3,375,000,000 cubic miles.

2262. _____. *Man's Earth-Lease Is About to Expire.* 1977. Selections from *From Now Till Eternity*, vol. 1. Raleigh NC: Manhattan. 127 p.

2263. _____. *The Devil's Empire.* 1977. Selections from *From Now Till Eternity*, vol 2. Raleigh, NC: Manhattan.

2264. _____. *Armageddon, Dead Ahead.* 1977. Selections from *From Now Till Eternity*, vol. 3. Raleigh, NC: Manhattan. 160 p.

2265. _____. *The Coming Kingdom.* Selections from *From Now Until Eternity*, vol. 4. Raleigh, NC: Manhattan. 154 p.

2266. _____. *The Horrified and the Glorified.* 1977. Selections from *From Now Till Eternity*, vol. 5. Raleigh, NC: Manhattan. 139 p.

2267. Cristof, Boris. *La Gran Catastrofe de 1983.* 1979. Barcelona: Martinez Roca. 172 p. Also Montreal: Presse de la Cite; 1980, 208 p.

Occult and biblical. Author from Montevideo. Velikovsky, Hörbiger, Nostradamus, UFOs, ESP, Cayce, Atlantis, Antichrist. Prophecies of Ulrich de Mayenco (contemporary of Nostradamus): A.D. 2544 as End. "Una purificación personal desde ahora hasta 1983."

2268. Criswell, W[allie] A. *What to Do Until Jesus Comes Back.* c1975. Nashville: Broadman Press. 152 p.
Baptist minister.

2269. _____. *Welcome Back, Jesus!* 1976. Nashville: Broadman Press. 189 p.

2270. _____. *Eschatology. Great Doctrines of the Bible: Vol 8.* 1989. Grand Rapids, MI: Zondervan. 154 p.

2271. Crockett, Arthur. *Nostradamus' Unpublished Prophecies: Including Persian Gulf Update.* 1991. New special ed. New Brunswick NJ: Inner Light. 62 p. illus.

2272. Croff, John. *Why Worlds Are Made.* 1990. Las Vegas, NV: Light House Books. 182 p. indexes.

Human history as "Devil History": story of Satan's influence. Sizable community of descendants of Adam and Eve alive in Cain and Abel's time. Armageddon, universal earthquake, catastrophic astral disturbances. Then Millennium, world conversion to Christianity. Then iniquity spreads again, then Second Coming during Millennium. Earth destroyed, burned; church raptured, returns when Earth cools down enough. Christ shows himself at Armageddon, converting Jews. Earthquake re-unites continents; single land mass (as in pre-Flood period). Armageddon = Day of Lord. Earth changes orbit. At actual Second Coming, nothing left alive — all incinerated. During Millennium, Satan not bound; Jesus not on Earth ("extra terrestrial reign"); then nations rebel against God. Spirits of faithful procreate in space; new spirits, new worlds, new heavens. Worlds made for spirits to inhabit, then changed into heavens. Pre-Earth existence as spirits too. Final chapter: Evolution = Antichrist. 666 = Darwin's father Robert Waring Darwin. Beast from Sea = voyage of Darwin's *Beagle*. Seven heads: seven evolution-based science fields. 10 Horns: evolution theory "horns in" on other fields. Fatal Wound = Piltdown hoax. The 42 Months = 1827 to 1831 (start of *Beagle* voyage). "If we have understanding we will realize that all of Revelation 13 is about the theory of evolution."

2273. Crowther, Duane S. *Prophetic Warnings to Modern America.* 1977. Bountiful, UT: Horizon. xii, 415. illus. bibl. refs, index.

2274. _____*World War III, God's Judgments upon the Nations.* 1979. Bountiful, UT: Horizon.

Mormon. Warns of "the cursings God has placed on America, and the desolation and abomination" ahead.

2275. _____. *The Prophecies of Joseph Smith.* 1983. Rev. ed. Bountiful, UT: Horizon. 413 p., plates bibl. refs., index.

2276. _____. *Inspired Prophetic Warnings.* 1987. Bountiful, UT: Horizon. 315 p.

2277. Cruz, Nicky. *Armageddon by Morning.* 1992. Green Forest, AR: New Leaf Press. 272 p.

2278. _____. *David Wilkerson: A Final Warning.* 1991. Green Forest, AR: New Leaf Press. 207 p.

Witnessing to "a world in despair as disaster plunges humanity headlong toward the end of time."

2279. Cumbey, Constance [E.] *The Hidden Dangers of the Rainbow: The New Age Movement and Our Coming Age of Barbarism.* rev. ed. 1983. Shreveport, LA: Huntington House. 268 p. bibl.

Anti-Christian nature of New Age belief; New Age as a revival of Nazism.

2280. _____. *A Planned Deception: The Staging of a New Age "Messiah."* 1985. East Detroit: Pointe Publishers. 282 p. index.

Threat of New Age occultism. Satan will stage a fake Second Coming prior to the real one. Image of the Beast = hologram. Matthew Fox (Catholic New-Ager) = 666. Pat Robertson's goal of helping to usher in and establish the Kingdom of God is heretical.

2281. Cummings, L.O.N. *Our Health Message, the Cleansing of the Sanctuary and the Judgment of the Living 144,000 Melchizedek Priests.* [1980s]. Ringgold, GA: Inst. of Natural Health Science. 22 p.

Seventh-day Adventist.

2282. Curle, George. *God's Hidden Plan.* 1991. New Wine. xiv, 192 p.

Antichrist: 1999; Tribulation: 2002; Second Coming and Millennium: 2005.

2283. Curtis, C.R. *The Apostasy and Redemption of Latter-Day Israel: The Church of the Devil, the Strange Act, the Two Witnesses, the Davidic Servant, the Anti-Christ, Armageddon, the Divine Timeline....* c1992. S.l.: Author. 114 p. illus.

2284. Cutler, Gary L. *Rapture Reality: What Jesus Did and Did Not Say About His Second Coming.* 1997. Sheridan, IN: Holiness Renewal Press. 70 p. illus.

2285. Dahl, Mikkel. SEE ALSO 1910–1970. *The Book of Revelation Unveiled.* 1989. Fulton, MO: Shepherdsfield. 160 p.

Also wrote *The Lord's Day.* Rapture of the 144,000 "ever so near". Seven days later they return to witness to others. Second Rapture 1,260 days later. Two weeks after first Rapture, the Beast of Revelation emerges, with Moslem nations, and attacks Rome. Atomic holocaust near end of 3½ years (1,260 days).

2286. _____, and Jon R. Welker. *The Great Panic and the Coming Apocalypse.* 1993. 2nd ed. Fulton, MO: Shepherdsfield. 122 p.

2287. Dailey, Timothy J. *The Millennial Deception: Angels, Aliens, and the Antichrist.* 1995. Grand Rapids, MI: Chosen Books.

Dailey: with Chuck Colson's BreakPoint radio show. UFOs, etc., as demonic preparation for Antichrist. Started 1947 when UN gave up on Palestine problem, resulting in explosion of paranormal activity. Stage set for final end-time confrontation between God and the forces of evil: Armageddon. Antichrist probably on hand now preparing to enter world stage. UFOs maybe from other dimensions, psychic, quasi-physical. Dark angels engage in spiritual deception. Dailey began reading rightist publications such as *The Intelligence Digest* and believed Antichrist was leader of worldwide conspiracy, but then realized conspiracy theories were wrong. Antichrist can't be discovered until he reveals himself. Antichrist from Roman Empire, 7-year rule, invades Israel, conquers other countries, most powerful leader ever, greatest persecution ever. Nero, Napoleon, Mussolini, Creme's Maitreya all declared to be Antichrist. Appendix: critical review of Texe Marr's *Dark Majesty* (conspiracy theory).

2288. Dake, Finis Jennings. SEE ALSO 1910–1970 *The Rapture and the Second Coming of Christ.* 1977. Lawrenceville, GA: Dake Bible Sales. 119 p.

Over 7,000 scripture references confirming the truths expounded herein.

2289. Damien, Michel, and Charles Hirsch. *La Crainte de l'an 2000.* c1979. Paris: Seghers. 319 p. bibl. refs.

Occult prophecies.

2290. Daniel, John. *Scarlet and the Beast.* 3 vols. 1994. (vol 1). Tyler, TX: Jon Kregel. illus. bibl. refs.

Author: founder of business security company, writes about corporate fraud. Conspiracy. Vol. 1 (The Political Wars) subtitled "A History of the War Between English and French Freemasonry" (900 p.). Vol. 2 (The Religious Wars) subtitled "English Freemasonry, Mother of Modern Cults vis-a-vis Mystery Babylon, Mother of Harlots" (200 p.). Vol. 3 (The Financial Wars) subtitled "English Freemasonry, Banking, and the Illegal Drug Trade" (200 p.). Revelation 17–18. English Freemasonry is Scarlet (Mystery Babylon; aristocratic, capitalistic, rightist, pantheistic); French will produce the Beast (proletarian, communistic, leftist, atheistic).

2291. Daniel, Roger P. *An Outline of a Chart of the Course of Time from Eternity to Eternity.* [1980s?]. Sunbury, PA: Believers Bookshelf. 43 p.

"An Outline of A.E. Booth's *Chart of the Ages.*" See also A. Booth 1896.

2292. Dankenbring, William F. *The Last Days of Planet Earth: A Survival Guide to the End of the World.* [1977?] c1981. Altadena, CA: Triumph xiii, 490 p.

A.D. 539 + 2,520 = 1982. Thus 1982 may be Tribulation, End may be 1989, or 1997 (Ussher was very close). Coming economic crash will be worst ever. Cites Jupiter Effect and astrological predictions of catastrophe. Lost Tribe of Joseph = United States and England (white Anglo-Saxons). Northwest Europe = other Ten Tribes. Assyrians = Germany = King of North, God's instrument, leader of 10-Nation European confederacy; will make treaty with Middle East nations; all then attack Israel. Ethiopia and India (= Cush) ally with Soviet Union. King of South = Egypt. King of North establishes base for False Prophet (future Pope; the Second Beast) in Jerusalem. Then invades Russia, but army perishes in Russia. Russia then attacks with 200 million men; faithful flee to Petra and similar refuges around the world. 70th Week in future = 7 year Tribulation. Ten revivals of Roman Empire: Vandals, Heruli, Ostrogoths, Justinian, Charlemagne, Holy Roman Empire, Hapsburgs, Napoleon, Hitler-Mussolini axis, and future revival. Coming Ten Nations turn in wrath upon Vatican, destroy Rome. Mark of Beast in minds and labor (head and hand): computerized ID system — maybe based on German Deutschmark. First of Four Horsemen = false messiahs. Great Tribulation = no Rapture, believers subjected to persecution, martyrdom. Comet to hit Earth, maybe causing faster rotation (shorter days). Locusts = German helicopter gunships. Horsemen = motorized cavalry, tanks. Germany and 10 Nations attack "Israel" (i.e. United States and England). "Israel" returns after Second Coming. After Second Coming and Return, Soviet Russia , China, and African allies invade (Gog and Magog). United States can avoid prophesied destruction if it truly repents. Millennium = Dead Sea healed, huge population explosion, all earth fertile and cultivable. Saints not going to heaven: "heaven is coming to earth!" Men will travel in space faster than light, become "Creators," create life throughout universe. Offers dehydrated survivalist foods from his Triumph Foods for use in Tribulation. Mentions there is "an Elijah in our midst" now (referring to H. W. Armstrong?). Dankenbring now publishes *Prophecy Flash* magazine and runs Triumph Prophetic Ministries website.

2293. Daschbach, Edwin. *Is the End Near?: A Catholic Understanding.* 1989. Huntington, IN: Our Sunday Visitor. 29 p.

Inc: "Is fundamentalism's end-times scenario about to begin?—Commencement of subsequent end-times events—Tribulation—Better end-times scenario—When will all of this happen?"

2294. Davidson, Elishua. *Islam, Israel, and the Last Days.* 1991. Eugene, OR: Harvest House. 130 p. illus. map, bibl. refs. Transl. of *Wie is God.*

Author lives in Holland. We are now in "last phase of a battle" being waged between God and forces of evil. Islam is distortion of true religion of Christianity.

2295. Davies, Kirk. *Earth's Final Hours.* 1982. San Diego: Pacific Institute. ix, 330 p.

Seventh-day Adventist. World rapidly approaching final events. Millennium, the end of time, "not many more years away." But because Satan has caused many false predictions, people ridicule belief in imminent End. Righteous will be raptured, wicked all killed; Earth thus completely empty during Millennium. At end of Millennium, New Jerusalem descends like a giant space ship, 118,750 square miles (biblical dimensions of "side" are for entire perimeter). At end of Millennium wicked all resurrected; Satan gets them to rebel. Then Second Coming, Christ shows a "movie of the entire history of earth" from Creation to End. Wicked turn on each other in fury and despair after seeing it; literal blood up to bridles for 184 miles. Every Saturday righteous go to New Jerusalem to worship Christ. Fulfilled 6th Seal of Revelation: 1755 Lisbon earthquake, 1780 dark day, 1833 star fall (meteors). Ten Horns: successor barbarian kingdoms after Rome. Little Horn = Sea Beast = Catholic Church (1,260 year rule, then deadly wound 1798). 666 = Vicarius filii die. Chapter on Sabbath as required commandment; Satan spread the "Sunday lie." 2nd Beast = United States; which has surrendered to communists. Tragically, as world approaches final catastrophic events, most ignore God's warnings and instead believe scientists and false ministers. Christ waiting only for last of 144,000 perfect people. Armageddon = places of refuge (not battle) all over world where righteous escape Wrath of 7 last plagues. Cites right-wing conspiracy books. Denies eternal Hell for wicked. Pacific Institute also pub. *When the United States Passes the National Sunday Law* and *Proof that the Pope is the Antichrist.*

2296. Davis, John, and Naomi Rice. *Messiah and the Second Coming.* 1982. Wyoming, MI: Coptic Press. 222 p.

Davis: dir. of Coptic Fellowship International (founded in Egypt by Hamid Bey). Atlantean Doctrines and Christ Consciousness. Aquarian Messiah arrived 11 AM, Nov. 11, 1949, near Mt. Shasta.

2297. Davis, John Jefferson. *Christ's Victorious Kingdom: Postmillennialism Reconsidered.* c1986. Grand Rapids, MI: Baker Book House. 148 p. bibl., scripture index.

2298. Davis, Leo. *The Seventy Weeks Prophecy of Daniel; Ancient Prophecy Up-to-Date Fulfillment.* 1970. Bedford, IN: Leo C. Davis. 30 p.

2299. Deal, Colin Hoyle. *Christ Returns by 1988?—101 Reasons Why.* 1979. Rutherford College, NC: Colin H. Deal. xv, 175 p. illus.

Deal: New Life Assembly Church; publishes pre-mill *End-Time News.* Predicts "greatest wars of all time just prior to Christ's return." "Specific last-day fulfillments" include worsening moral conditions, natural disasters, discovery of Noah's Ark and Ark of Covenant, psychic revival, Communist Russian invasion of Palestine. After invasion, Jews to burn weapons for seven years: refers to Soviet weapons made of flammable "lingostone" [sic], atomic fuel (including nuclear dirigibles). Other signs: Temple being rebuilt, Soviets purchasing grain, Beast computer system installed in Belgium, European confederation being readied for Antichrist. UCLA helped Iraq rebuild the Tower of Babel. Petra ready for fleeing Jews. Earthquake from 1982 Jupiter Effect; Satanic UFOs; Karakorum Highway as Chinese invasion route to Israel; vultures already gathering at Armageddon. Enoch built Great Pyramid, with a "pre-recorded prophetic date" showing 6,000 years from Creation to Second Coming and Millennium. Great Tribulation by 1986; Rapture within 3-4 years.

2300. _____. *Armageddon & the 21st Century*. 1988. Rutherford College, NC: Colin H. Deal. 153 p.

2301. _____. *The Day and Hour Jesus Will Return*. 1988. Rutherford College, NC: Colin H. Deal. x, 153 p.

Intricate dispensational pre-mill interpretation. "God set a date for every major event to occur" including the End. "Armageddon, is on the horizon!" 2,520 years of Gentiles = 607 B.C. to 1914 (when Gentile powers begin to relinquish Palestine). 604 B.C. + 2,520 = 1917. 598 B.C. (Babylonian exile) + 2,520 = 1923 (Balfour Declaration confirmed). Many Raptures: the Church before the Tribulation, all new believers mid-Tribulation, then the 144,000 Jewish witnesses, then two more groups of Tribulation converts and martyrs at end of Tribulation. 6,000 year age of earth. Pyramid incorporates immense advanced knowledge, including precise chronological and prophetic measurements. It was covered with 144,000 limestone blocks, now scattered. Rapture will be in Sept. (day varies according to which year it occurs), then Armageddon and Second Coming follow according to strict schedule seven years later.

2302. _____. *Revelation of the Beast*. 1995. 118 p.

2303. *Decoding the Book of Revelation*. 1998. "Beastwatch" (www.BEAST WATCH.com). 158 p. maps.

Post-trib. Message of Revelation message is obscure because chronology is jumbled, but author discovered that Revelation 14:6–20 is key to interpretation, outlining events in proper order. Time of Warning (now), Years of the Beast, Ingathering of the overcomers, Day of God's Wrath. America is Mystery Babylon, cesspool of abominations, evil, decadence. Seven Kings of Rev. 17: five fallen empires, 6th is Rome (that still "is"), and Arab empire which was "not yet come" when Revelation was written. The Beast ridden by Mystery Babylon is the Eighth, and also "of" the Seventh: End Time Islamic Empire of almost same territory as Islam's

greatest extent in 8th century. "Hear this, by the Word of the Lord; the USA is going to be destroyed by a surprise attack from radical Muslims" with nuclear weapons. Moslems then rule US tyrannically for 3½ years. End-time "Restored Israel" not the current State of Israel, which is a heresy. Jews are to be persecuted terribly "beyond imaging," hunted down and killed by Moslems worldwide "in a manner that will make Hitler's time look like a dress rehearsal." Rapture is at end of Tribulation, just before day of God's wrath — same day as Two Witnesses raptured. Saudi Arabian terrorist Osama bin Laden especially is End Time threat; Moslems will take advantage of Y2k computer vulnerability to strike at end of 1999.

2304. DeMar, Gary. *Last Days Madness: Obsession of the Modern Church*. 1994 [1991]. Updated ed. Atlanta: American Vision. x, 395 p. bibl. refs., index. Orig. Brentwood, TN: Wolgemuth & Hyatt.

Christian Reconstructionism.

2305. Dennis, John. *Revelations About the Rapture*. 1977. Kansas City, MO: Any Moment Press. 53 p. bibl. refs.

2306. Denton, John. *Armageddon A.D. 2033: Facts on Bible Time Prophecies*. 1995. London: B.R.I.C. 284 p.

Denton: Los Angeles / London businessman. Based on Charles Taze Russell (Jehovah's Witnesses). 50,000 year cycle. Seven creation days 7,000 years each, ending with Millennium, and followed by 1,000 year Jubilee. Pre-Flood Canopy (later restored). A.D. 33 midway in 8,000 year period beginning 3968 B.C. with Adam (Eve 70 years later). 2,520 years ends 1996; Russia may be destroyed: head of Beast that is resurrected in 1996. Great Tribulation 2029–33; Millennium begins 2033.

2307. Derstine, Gerald. *The Kingdom of God Is At Hand*. 1973. Bradenton, FL: Harvest Time. 66 p. index.

Mennonite. Also wrote *God, Government, Guns: A Christian Perspective*.

2308. _____. *Fire Over Israel: Supernatural Happenings & Miracles*. 1993. Shippensburg, PA: Treasure House. viii, 130 p. illus.

2309. Deyo, Stan. *The Vindicator Scrolls.* 1989. Perth, Australia: West Australian Texas Trading. xiii, 254 p. index, photos, drawings, maps. Distr. by CPA (Christian Patriot Assoc.)

Deyo: says he's one of the men Isaac Newton predicted would rise up in the "time of the End" to decipher prophecy. Also wrote *The Cosmic Conspiracy*. Praises Vendyl Jones, Setterfield, Trevor Norman, Tatford. Antichrist's 7-year treaty, "Nimrud" 666 Computer identification numbers (Babylonian base-6), the European Confederacy. Nimrod Novik, Israeli advisor to Peres, may be the Antichrist. Russians and Arab allies invade Israel, then are destroyed. America (= Babylon) destroyed too. United Europe — revived Roman Empire — led by re-Nazified Germany, the Papacy (briefly), Chinese and Moslem forces all war against Israel. Creation ca. 6000 B.C.; Adam created 5690 B.C.; Garden of Eden = Gulf of Aden. Flood 3428 B.C. Shift of Earth's axis 2345 B.C. Continents split apart 2600 B.C. UFOs began as human conspiracy of Nazi origin, but taken over by real ETs. Flying saucers — Antichrist's chief Armageddon weapon.

2310. DeYoung, Donald B. *Jupiter Effect, a Proof of the End?* 1981. Winona Lake, IN: Grace Theological Seminary cassette

2311. Di Gangi, Mariano. *End of the World: The Prophecies in St. Mark's "Little Apocalypse" Demand Obedience to Our Lord's Great Commission.* 1980. Phillipsburg, NJ: Harmony Press: 23 p. bibl. refs.

2312. Dillard, Raymond B. *Gog and Magog: The Coming Conflict.* 1993. Philadelphia: Westminster Media. Cassette. Based on commencement seminar Westminster Theol. Sem. 1992, about Russian invasion of Israel.

2313. Ding, George D.D. *Prophecy and the World.* 1988. Monterey Park, CA: author. xii, 244 p. maps.

2314. Dobson, Ed. 1997. *50 Remarkable Events Pointing to the End: Why Jesus Could Return by A.D. 2000.* Grand Rapids, MI: Zondervan. 192 p. bibl. refs. Pre-trib. Rapture likely by 2000.

Dobson: pastor of Calvary Chapel, Grand Rapids, MI. Revived Roman Empire of Ten Kingdoms from Common Market nations; Antichrist and False Prophet establish one-world government. Antichrist's Ten-Kingdom armies (probably joined by or including U.S.) opposed at Armageddon by Arab-Islamic coalition joined by 200 million Chinese at Armageddon.

2315. Dodrill, Rufus McKinley. *Keep Your Eye on the Sky.* 1972. S.l.: Dodrill. xv, 160 p. illus., foldout plate.

2316. Dolan, David. *The End of the Age.* 1995. Grand Rapids, MI: F.H. Revell. 330 p.

Dolan: Israel-based CBS and CBN broadcast journalist; publishes *Israel News Digest.* Fiction. Syria attacks Israel (Israel P.M. named Nimrod). Two Israelis called up to fight are Messianic Jews ("Yeshua" believers) who realize End Time prophecy is being literally fulfilled. Damascus destroyed by nuclear attack. Russia provokes Islamic nations to avenge, sends own troops; this attack defeated. Prince Andre of European Union assassinated by Muslim on TV; revives, arranges world peace, hailed as Savior. Made Emperor; teams with Urbane Basillo — the False Prophet. Temple rebuilt on northern end of Mount. Andre declares himself divine leader of world religion. Antichrist statue speaks miraculously. Microchip implants; miracles abounding. John of Revelation is one of the Two Witnesses with fantastic supernatural powers; he befriends protagonists. 144,000 Jewish witnesses (the Man-Child) assemble. Believing Jews evacuate to United States. Antichrist army conquers Russia. Antichrist attacks China; China and United States resist Antichrist league with nuclear attacks, results poison oceans, air, trigger immense quakes. When Temple Abomination is complete, demons (including locusts) released from inside earth to ravage. Chinese, Muslims, and Russians send armies. Woes and judgments interpreted literally. At end of Millennium there will be another war: all nations against fully regathered and converted Israel. Second Coming; then Rapture.

2317. Dolphin, Lambert. *Jesus and*

His Church During the Tribulation: Supplemental Notes on End-Time Events and Israel's Exile in Edom. <http://www.ldolphin.org/bozrahsupp.html>

2318. Doughten, Russell S. *Thief in the Night.* 1988. Video. Des Moines, IA: Mark IV Pictures.

The Rapture. 4-part video series (see following); orig. film.

2319. ____. *Distant Thunder.* 1988. Video. Des Moines, IA: Mark IV Pictures.

The Great Tribulation.

2320. ____. *Image of the Beast.* 1988. Video. Des Moines, IA: Mark IV Pictures.

The Antichrist.

2321. ____. *The Prodigal Planet.* 1988. Video. Des Moines, IA: Mark IV Pictures.

Doughten: exec. prod. Prod. and dir.: Donald W. Thompson. Story: Thompson and Doughten. Screenplay: Jim Grant. Also "Study Guide" for film series *Finding God in the Final Days* (1978; Mark IV Pictures; 55 p., illus.).

2322. Douglass, Herbert E. 1979. *The End: Unique Voice of Adventists About the Return of Jesus.* Mountain View, CA: Pacific Press. 192 p.

2323. Doward, Jan S. *Footsteps of an Approaching God.* 1992. Frederick, MD: Amazing Facts. 116 p.

Seventh-day Adventist. The world is hopelessly corrupt, perverted, and violent.

2324. Downey, Mark. *Will the Real Armageddon Please Stand Up?* 1993. White Throne Pub.

Israel = Anglo-Saxons. Internet version posted by Northwest Kinsman.

2325. Draper, James T. *The Unveiling.* 1984. Nashville: Broadman Press. 285 p.

2326. Duck, Daymond R. *On the Brink.* 1995. Lancaster, PA: Starburst. 251 p. bibl. refs, indexes; illus.

"Easy-to-Understand End-Time Bible Prophecy." Duck: lay pastor (United Methodist). Dispensational pre-trib, premill. Any-moment Rapture. Tribulation begins not with Rapture, but with 7-year treaty with Israel (possibly years later).

Nation of Israel "exists so prophecies can be fulfilled." Two unsuccessful attempts to lay Temple cornerstone already (1989, 1990). Garments are now being made for the Temple priests, including crown and breastplate; also furniture, music instruments. Birds of prey now gathering in Israel for Armageddon. Rosh = Russia. "Do not be fooled" by break-up of Soviet Union; Yeltsin may still be Gog. God will force Russia to invade Israel with coalition. Germany (= Gomer) will join too. Daniel: feet of iron / clay = EEC; ruled by Antichrist. White Horse rider is Antichrist. Timothy: signs of evil, decay at End Times being fulfilled now. China now readying 200-million man army. Armageddon Battle rages whole second half of Tribulation. Two Russian invasions; invasion by King of North is *not* Armageddon. First *precedes* Tribulation. Second in 2nd half of Tribulation. Rapture probably precedes Tribulation. Endorses 7,000 Year theory (World Week). Four Beasts of Daniel: England-U.S.; Russia; Arab coalition; EEC (Revived Roman Empire). Billy Graham scheduled to preach to "entire world" on March 1995 by satellite.

2327. ____. *Revelation: God's World for the Biblically Inept.* 1998. 251 p. bibl., indexes.

2328. Duncan, Homer. SEE ALSO 1910-1970. *Prepare Now for the Second Coming of Christ.* [1970s?] Lubbock, TX: Missionary Crusader. vi, 230 p.

2329. Dunlap, Reg. *The Next Invasion from Outer Space.* 1978. Eliot, ME: Evangelism for Christ Assoc. 75 p.

Second Coming.

2330. Dunlop, Reginald. *Flee to the Mountains — God's Message for Survival — No Time to Spare — Imminent End-Time Destruction.* 1975. Ontario, Canada: priv. pub. 153 p. illus.

Great Pyramid is scientific proof of Bible truth and prophetic chronology. Important dates enshrined in Pyramid include A.D. 33 (Crucifixion), 1914 (end of 60 Weeks and of 2,520 Years). *Ouranos* = uranium: "heaven shaking" is nuclear bomb. Millennium = 1979–2,979, then 15 years when Satan is loosed, with final End

2994. No pre-trib Rapture. Truth of Bible-Pyramid chronology first revealed 1859 by Taylor's Pyramidology book; truth "finalized" 1957 when absolute proof of Pyramid-Bible chronology published by Adam Rutherford (thus 120 years of preaching paralleling Noah's warning to world before Flood). Adam created 5407 B.C.

2331. _____. *The Coming Russian Invasion of America: Why?—Where?—When?* 1978. Ontario, CA; Waynesville, NC: R.E. Dunlop; New Beginnings Kingdom. ix, 338 p.

"Considerable portions of this book were derived from discussions given on the radio broadcasts of … Bertrand L. Comparet" (Christian Identity advocate). War begins in Israel, but U.S. is primary target of Russian (and Chinese) attacks.

2332. Dunning, H. Ray, ed. *The Second Coming: A Wesleyan Approach to the Doctrine of Last Things.* 1995. Kansas City, MO: Beacon Hill Press. bibl. refs.

Including Frank G. Carver; Roger Hahn; Jirair Tashjian; George Lyons; William Greathouse; Harold Raser; Dunning; Harvey Finley; William Charles Miller; Rob L. Staples.

2333. Duty, Guy. *Escape from the Coming Tribulation.* 1975. Minneapolis: Bethany Fellowship. 157 p. bibl.

Pre-trib. Antichrist will "dazzle the eyes of an evil and adulterous generation with displays of the supernatural from heaven." The Church alone will recognize Antichrist at first, by his secret code, but Antichrist will be revealed to world when he enthrones himself in the rebuilt Temple. "The Arab world is an Antichrist world." Believers endure present pre-trib signs, but will escape the Great Tribulation by Rapture. Armageddon is place of mobilization for final battle; battle itself is at Jerusalem. Also wrote *Christ's Coming and the World Church* (1971; Minneapolis: Bethany Fellowship; 171 p.).

2334. Duvernoy, Claude. *L'Apocalypse a Deja Commence.* 1986 [1980] Paris: Atlantic. 267 p.

Collection "Action chretienne pour Israel."

2335. _____. *Controversy Over Zion: A Biblical View of the History and Meaning of Zion.* 1987. Green Forest, AR: New Leaf Press. 224 p. bibl. Orig. French.

Prophecies, restoration of Israel.

2336. Dyer, Charles H. *World News and Bible Prophecy.* 1993. Wheaton, IL: Tyndale House. 303 p. index.

Dyer: Extension Dean, Dallas Theological Seminary.

2337. _____, with Angela Elwell Hunt. *The Rise of Babylon: Sign of the End Times.* 1991. Tyndale House. 236 p. plates illus., bibl. refs., index.

Saddam Hussein is rebuilding Babylon, fulfilling biblical prophesies of Last Days just prior to Armageddon. "Could ours be the last generation?" This book was published just before the Gulf War.

2338. Earle, Ralph. *What the Bible Says About the Second Coming.* 1973 [1970]. Grand Rapids, MI: Baker Book House. 90 p. Orig. pub. titled *Behold, I Come.*

2339. Ebon, Martin, ed. *Doomsday! How the World Will End—and When.* 1977. New York: New American Library. [10] 241 p. bibl.

Ebon also wrote books about prophecy, the occult, parapsychology, ESP, ghosts, miracles, psychic warfare, reincarnation, Bermuda Triangle, Pyramid power, exorcism, Atlantis.

2340. Eden, Jerome. *Planet in Trouble: The UFO Assault on Earth.* 1973. New York: Exposition Press. 214 p.

Wilhelm Reich's orgone: Cosmic Life Energy. "Deadly" orgone accumulating in atmosphere from nuclear testing but mostly from evil flying saucers. Reich heroically intervened with Cloudbuster; mankind must unite to continue orgone defense to avoid "complete and total planetary annihilation." Concerns "*the most important critical event in the History of Earth*— the invasion of our globe by Space Men from other worlds!"

2341. Edgemon, Anna Marie. *The Bible Speaks to End Times.* 1993. Nashville: Convention Press. 76 p illus

"Teaching workbook."

2342. Efird, James M. *Daniel and Revelation: A Study of Two Extraordinary*

Visions. c1978. Valley Forge, PA: Judson Press. 144 p.

2343. _____. *End-Times: Rapture, Antichrist, Millennium.* c1986. Nashville: Abingdon.

Efird: Professor at Duke Divinity School. A-mill, preterist; no literal, earthly Millennium. Future known only to God. Strongly critical of "Darbyism" (pre-mill dispensationalism); calls it completely fictitious, "unbiblical and nonsensical." Well written; good presentation of Biblical writers' probable intent.

2344. Egbert, Elaine. *Till Morning Breaks: A Story of the Millerite Movement and the Great Disappointment.* 1993. Boise, ID: Pacific Press. 256 p. bibl. refs.

Fiction.

2345. Egner, David. *The Bear Goes South: When Russia Invades Israel.* 1979. Grand Rapids, MI: Radio Bible Class. 126 p.

Egner: editor of Radio Bible Class's *Discovery Digest.* "We could be standing on the threshold of the endtimes." "Even the most jaded skeptic will agree that the stage of international politics is set for the events Ezekiel described." Russia will invade Israel shortly. Rapture any time now, then Tribulation, with revival of Ten-Nation Roman Empire dominated by Antichrist. Russian invasion utterly destroyed; wreckage supplies Israel with fuel for seven years. Then, Antichrists's world armies are destroyed at Armageddon by the Second Coming.

2346. Eisenman, Robert H. *If I Forget You, O Jerusalem: A Handbook of Zionist Prophecy.* 1978. Fountain Valley, CA: Yahwist Press.

2347. Eller, Vernard. *The Most Revealing Book of the Bible: Making Sense Out of Revelation.* 1982 [1974]. Grand Rapids, MI: Eerdmans. 214 p. illus.

182-p. Study Guide pub. by La Verne College Press (CA), 1977.

Also wrote play *The Time So Urgent* about Church of the Brethren beginnings in Germany, 1708.

2348. Ellisen, Stanley A. *Biography of a Great Planet.* 1975. Wheaton, IL: Tyndale House. 272 p. illus. index.

2349. _____. *Three Worlds in Conflict.* 1998. Sister, OR: Multnomah. 280 p. illus.

"God, Satan, Man: the High Drama of Bible Prophecy." Ellisen: professor at Western Seminary. God's various covenants "show the beautiful symmetry of the Lord's program for His people." Covenants overlap, some for Israel, others for the Church. 70th Week put on hold because Jews rejected the Messiah. Meteoric rise of Antichrist after the Rapture, leader of Mediterranean nations. 70th Week begins when Antichrist makes covenant with Israel. The pre- mill pre-trib scheme shows "amazing symmetry and consistency of history and prophecy." Satan defeated in War in Heaven, vents wrath on Earth during Tribulation. Russian, Islamic, or combined confederacy attacks Israel; then Antichrist attacks them. God kills most of the Northern invaders. Antichrist killed mid-tribulation, then resurrected for new role: terrible persecution of Israel and devil worship. At end of Tribulation, armies of all nations converge at Armageddon. New Jerusalem orbits Earth during Millennium, descending at end.

2350. *The End of Time: The Messiah Comes: Elijah Two.* 1975. Dallas: C.M.I. 286 p.

(Picture of author on back cover but no name given.)

2351. *End Time Warnings.* <http://www.sirinet.net/~cloefke/warnings.htm>

From the End Time Information Center.

2352. *The End Times FAQ.* 1996. <http://www.catalog.com/endtimes/faq.html>

Created with the assistance of Father Andrew (The Trumpeter). Catholic.

2353. *The End Times Information Center.* 1998. <http://www.headingforhome.com/etic/index.html>

Also publishes *EndTimes Online.* Heading for Home ministries (Lawton, OK).

2354. *The Endtimer.* <http://www.geocities.com/Area51/Dimension/8443/index.html>

2355. Enfiedgian, Boghos. *The End*

of the Times of the Gentiles and the Coming of Christ. 1971. Khartoum, Sudan: Govt. Printing Press. 68 p.

2356. Engel, Marty. *End Times Dictionary.* 1982. Libertyville, IL: Charismatic Bookshelf. 144 p. illus., chart; scripture index.

Over 200 simple, paragraph-length entries. From "Abomination of Desolation" to "Wormwood" and "Young Lions." Also entries for prophetic numbers. Author believes in pre-trib Rapture. 70 Weeks as Church Age; date of start of 70th Week not known. New Jerusalem = cube or pyramid. Presents various proposed chronological sequences for seal-trumpet-vial events. Differentiates Armageddon from the "Last Battle" at end of Millennium. U.S. not in prophecy: either it becomes insignificant, or God remains silent about its role.

2357. Engleman, Dennis Eugene. *Ultimate Things: An Historical and Orthodox Perspective on the End Times.* 1995. Ben Lomond, CA: Conciliar Press. 296 p. bibl. refs. index.

Eastern Orthodox Church. "The world is doomed — its collision course with catastrophe cannot be diverted." Antichrist: man who appears Christlike. Millennium: period from First Coming to coming of Antichrist. Communism is millennialist, a "chiliastic heresy." Widespread nihilism in the End Times. Gog-Magog = ancient Russian tribes. Antichrist born with artificial insemination. Satan seeks population control, but God doesn't. Antichrist becomes world ruler, reigns 7 years. 70th Week separated from others by figurative Millennium. Two Witnesses: Enoch and Elias. End-time conversion of Jews. Pre-trib Rapture is wishful thinking; "satanic deception" to lull believers into complacency. Rapture really refers to Second Coming at end of Tribulation. Horrific persecution second half of Tribulation. Literal Armageddon; destruction of Satan's forces around Jerusalem.

2358. Epperson, A. Ralph. *The New World Order.* 1994 [1990]. Tucson, AZ: Publius. xxi, 357 p. index.

Freemasonry, occultism, New Age.

Author of *Hidden Hand*; conspiratologist, creationist.

2359. Erickson, Millard J. *Contemporary Options in Eschatology: A Study of the Millennium.* 1992 [1977]. Grand Rapids, MI: Baker Book House. 197 p. bibl., indexes.

2360. Eserhut, Charles L. *Careen: The Third Geologic Revolution.* c1986. Priv. pub. xi, 120. maps, bibl.

Eserhut: Christian Identity believer. "Our Time is Limited — the Next Careen is Overdue." Buildup of polar ice causes Earth to be imbalanced, so that every six thousand years or so it flops over, resulting in new axis with poles in completely different locations. Theory based largely on Hugh Auchincloss Brown's 1967 *Cataclysms of the Earth*, and on Allan Eckert's 1976 novel *The HAB Theory*. These "careens" have caused recurrent destruction of life in past ages, completely destroying many previous civilizations; the last caused Noah's Flood. Safest areas will be west of the Rockies. Eserhut approvingly cites creationists Henry Morris; also Donald Patten and various catastrophists.

2361. Esses, Michael. *The Next Visitor to Planet Earth.* 1975. Plainfield, NJ: Logos International. xi, 173 p.

Edited by Irene Burk Harrell. Author: a "completed Jew"; minister at Melodyland Christian Center. Also wrote *Jesus in Genesis*. Book is largely about Zechariah and other prophets (but not Daniel or Revelation). Pre-trib pre-mill; any-moment Rapture (Christ is the "next visitor"). "The end times *are* with us." All prophecies being fulfilled. Beast: Coming world dictator already alive but not revealed. Worldwide computerized credit system, number stamped on everyone (except resisters.) Already California steam buses, Israeli taxis and Italian (EEC) shoes with 666 serial and trademarks. Rabbis calculate the 1,290 and 1,335 years from 721 B.C. Assyrian conquest to A.D. 1904 (Azusa Pentecostal revival). But rabbis wrong about 1974. Jews flee from "north" (Russia) to Israel. U.S. to join other nations against Israel after Rapture — all true believers having been raptured. Literal Armageddon. "Every general who has looked at it [Armageddon] has agreed that it is an ideal place to have a battle. Russia has prepared the largest horse army in the world." No sun during Millennium: sunless light like before the 4th Day of Creation.

2362. Evans, Michael D. *JerUSAlem, D.C. (David's Capital).* 1984. Bedford, TX: Bedford Books. 162 p. illus., maps.

2363. _____. *The Return.* 1989 [1986]. New York: Charter Books. x, 293 p. bibl. Orig. 1986; Thomas Nelson.

2364. _____. *Seven Years of Shaking: A Vision.* 1995. Euless, TX: Bedford Books. 222 p. "In the next seven years, the world will wake up in a state of shock as ... flaming nuclear threats surge." Clinton's inauguration was the start of the End Time degeneration.

2365. _____. *Jerusalem Betrayed: Ancient Prophecy and Modern Conspiracy Collide in the Holy City.* 1997. Dallas: Word. xvii, 313 p.

2366. Ewert, David. *And Then Comes the End.* 1980. Scottsdale, PA: Herald Press. 192 p. bibl. refs., index.

Samuel Gerber's *Und dann kommt das Ende* (1981; Liestal: Worte des Lebens; 64 p.) is based on this work.

2367. Ezell, Douglas. *Revelations on Revelation: New Sounds from Old Symbols.* 1977. Waco, TX: Word Books. 124 p. diagrams bibl.

Decries "sinful, unchristian" desire to know the future. Must understand Old Testament references, which Revelation relies upon. Much symbolism applies to past. Everything after Christ's Resurrection could be the End.

2368. Faid, Robert W. *Gorbachev! Has the Real Antichrist Come?* 1991 [1988]. Tulsa: Victory House. 230 p. bibl. refs.

Faid: nuclear engineer. Post-trib. The End-Time 10-Nation Confederation prophesied in Bible is Soviet Union and Communist bloc (Latvia, Estonia, Lithuania, Poland, Czechoslovakia, Hungary, Romania, E. Germany, Bulgaria, and Afghanistan). Seven Heads of Beast are Warsaw Pact members. "Gorbachev" in Russian = 666 (according to Theomatics): Antichrist. "The End" within a generation

from 1967; Tribulation very soon. First Antichrist's, then God's wrath, poured upon world. Revelation woes describe effects of nuclear war. Antichrist will occupy Middle East. U.S. pulverized by nuclear war. All Christians killed except 144,000 sealed by God. 1st Vial: AIDS resulting from Mark of the Beast tattoos. Demonic locusts: mutated creatures. Armageddon: Russia and Eastern armies overrun Israel, slaughter most Jews. Then Second Coming. Surviving Jews realize Jesus is Messiah. 6,000-year lifespan of world since Adam. Faid also wrote *A Scientific Approach to Biblical Mysteries* (1993) and ... *More Biblical Mysteries* (1994) on Genesis as eye-witness account, pre-Flood conditions, Noah's Ark.

2369. Falwell, Jerry. *Dr. Jerry Falwell Teaches Bible Prophecy.* 1979. Lynchburg, VA: Old-Time Gospel Hour. viii, 81, [41] p. illus.

Falwell: Baptist minister; televangelist. "Last Days; the Rapture; the Two Judgments; the Tribulation; the Second Coming of Christ; the Millennium; Final Events." 41–p. final section includes charts (from Willmington's *The King Is Coming*, 1973) and questions and answers.

2370. _____. *Nuclear War and the Second Coming of Jesus Christ.* 1983. Lynchburg, VA: Old Time Gospel Hour. iv, 47 p. illus.

Soviet Union totally destroyed after attacking Israel, ⅚ of their army killed.

2371. Faris, Fayiz. *Harb al-Khalij wa-Nihayat al-'Alam.* 1991. Al-Qahirah: Dar al-Thaqafiyah. 55 p.

Iraq-Kuwait War.

2372. Feinberg, Charles Lee. *Israel at the Center of History & Revelation.* 1980. 3rd ed. Portland, OR: Multnomah Press. 240 p. bibl. refs indexes. Prev. eds. titled *Israel in the Spotlight.*

Feinberg: converted Orthodox Jew; PhD in archeology and Semitic languages (Johns Hopkins); Dean emeritus of Talbot Theological Seminary. Pre-mill.

2373. _____. *A Commentary on Revelation: The Grand Finale.* 1985. Winona Lake, IN: BMH Books. 178, [1] p. indexes.

2374. _____. *Millennialism, the Two Major Views: The Premillennial and Amillennial Systems of Biblical Interpretation Analyzed and Compared.* 1985. [3rd ed. 1980] BMH Books. First two eds. titled *Premillennialism or Amillennialism?* bibl.

2375. Feldick, Les. *Through the Bible with Les Feldick.* c1990–98. <http://www.lesfeldick.org/lesbk1.html> Kinta, OK.

Stage is being set for 70th Week. The 6,000 year span allotted to mankind is just about up.

2376. Fenley, Ward. *The Second Coming of Christ Already Happened!* Kingdom of Sovereign Grace: Sacramento.

Preterist.

2377. Ferrell, Vance, and Ellen G. White. *Mark of the Beast.* 1985. Altamont, TN: Pilgrims' Books. 204 p. index.

Pt 1: "The Truth About the Mark" (by Ferrell); Pt 2: "The Crisis of the Mark" (by White).

2378. Finley, Mark. *Coming Events: A Study of the Closing Scenes of This World's History.* [ca 1990]. Berrien Springs, MI. Cassettes.

Seventh-day Adventist.

2379. _____. *Prophecy Lectures: God's Last Day Message Revealed.* [ca 1990]. Berrien Springs, MI: New Life Discoveries. 2 cassettes.

2380. _____. *Studies in Daniel: The Time of the End Prophecy Seminar.* [Ca. 1990]. Berrien Springs, MI: New Life Discoveries. 10 cassettes.

2381. _____. *Living in the End Time: Prophecy Study Guides.* 1992. Fallbrook, CA: Hart Research Center. 64 p.

Pub. for *It Is Written* TV broadcast.

2382. _____. 1996. *Discoveries in Prophecy 2000 & Beyond.* 1996. 13 videos. S.l.: Seminars Unlimited. *It Is Written* telecast. Mark Finley, speaker.

2383. _____, and Steven Mosley. *God's Last Altar Call.* 1995. Boise, ID: Pacific Press. 48 p.

"An urgent message for these final days."

2384. Flewelling, Frederic. *Atomic Energy Revealed in the Bible.* 1982. Crouseville, ME: author. 6 p.

2385. Flurry, Gerald. *The Ezekiel Watchman.* 1992. [Edmond, OK]: Philadelphia Church of God. 71 p.

Worldwide Church of God televangelist. Follower of H.W. Armstrong.

2386. _____. *Jeremiah: Prophet of Doom — Or Hope?* 1993. [Edmond, OK]: Philadelphia Church of God. 45 p.

2387. _____. *Lamentations and the End-Time Laodiceans.* c1993. Edmond, OK: Philadelphia Church of God. 37 p.

2388. _____. *Isaiah's End-Time Vision.* c1994. Edmond, OK: Philadelphia Church of God. 87 p.

2389. _____. *The Prophecy of Habakkuk: "At the End It Shall Speak."* 1995. [Edmond, OK: Philadelphia Church of God]. 25 p.

2390. Flynn, Ted, and Maureen Flynn. *The Thunder of Justice: The Warning, the Miracle, the Chastisement, the Era of Peace: God's Ultimate Acts of Mercy.* 1993. [United States]: MaxKol Communications. 428 p. index. bibl. refs.

Catholic. Marian visions warn of worldwide destruction if God's messages are not heeded.

2391. Fogle, Lerry W. *Revelation Explained.* 1981. Plainfield, NJ: [distr. by] Logos International. xv, 270 p. bibl.

Fogle: past president Full Gospel Business Men's Chapter, of Frederick, MD; Church of the Brethren minister. Verse-by-verse commentary. Revelation is intended as a "blessing" and is "a revealing of Jesus"; symbolic because unable to express literally. The Kingdom came with Jesus; He is ruling already in heaven. Great Tribulation: not just End times, but tribulation throughout Christian history. Denies Rapture; Church always subject to Tribulation. Earthly, physical, national Israel "prefigures" Church, which is "spiritual Israel." Beasts really describe aspects of Jesus. Seven Seals: Redemption story, Christ as Priest. Seven Trumpets: Christ as King. Seven Vials: Christ as Judge. Two Beasts: not Antichrist (Antichrists are all those who oppose Christ, not any false Messiah). Head of Beast wounded and revived may be nation of Israel. Armageddon: spiritual; now as well as future.

Thousand Years is symbolic: now and forever. New Jerusalem is the "completed Church."

2392. Foglein, Stephen A. *The Age of "One Fold and One Shepherd" Is Coming: An Analysis of World Events Based on Biblical and Christian Prophecies.* 1981. Mountain View, CA: Atlas Books. 189 p. bibl., index.

Catholic. Hungarian mining engineer, escaped to U.S. Bible prophecy *plus* recent messages from God. Second Coming at End (not pre-mill). "The history of mankind is approaching its end." Now living in last days, but these may last centuries. "One fold and one shepherd" = Antichrist's reign. "This generation" refers to Jews as a people. Jews will acclaim Antichrist as Messiah. 3rd Secret of Fatima: WWIII (U.S.-Soviet nuclear conflagration): "the predicted chastisement approaches day by day, and it will strike us without warning"—(but not final End). Red Dragon of Apocalypse and Beast from the Sea = World Communism. Endorses Wurmbrand's 1979 *Was Karl Marx a Satanist?* The Millennium, when Satan was bound for thousand years, was A.D. 400 to 1400 (Dark and Middle Ages); Satan was loosed again in Renaissance. UFOs are Satanic manifestations. Satan sends messages via contactees. Prophecies are largely conditional (e.g. Fatima): repent or else. Only a million or so will survive Chastisement; the "whole earth will be in ruins." World renewed by Angelic Pope and Great Monarch (probably Otto Habsburg). John Paul II maybe penultimate Pope, prior to Angelic Pastor prophesied by Malachy. Several more Popes after Angelic Pastor, then Antichrist for seven years. Antichrist arises under Ten Kings, makes covenant with Israel, rebuilds Temple.

2393. Forbes, Gary A. *Last Days Worldwatch.* <http://www.ozemail.com/au/~adamgosp/lastdays.htm>

Australian: Adamstown Gospel Chapel (Newcastle).

2394. Ford, Desmond. *Daniel.* 1978. Nashville: Southern Pub. Assoc. 309 p. bibl.

2395. _____. *The Abomination of Desolation in Biblical Eschatology.* 1979. Washington, DC: Univ. Press America. xiv, 334 p. bibl. Orig 1972 PhD thesis.

Re: Mark 13; scholarly, technical.

2396. _____. *Daniel 8:14, the Day of Atonement and the Investigative Judgment.* 1980. Casselbury, FL: Euangelion Press. iii, 425, A-269 p.

Seventh-day Adventist. Also wrote *Physicians of the Soul: God's Prophets Through the Ages* (1980).

2397. Foster, T. *Amazing Book of Revelation Explained!* 1983.

Foster: co-founder Christian Revival Crusade. Seven Churches span entire Church Age, with Laodicean ending 1967. Millennium proper begins about 2000. Beast related to papal worship starting A.D. 533. 1,260 years = papal power from A.D. 606 to 1866. Armageddon: Soviets versus U.S. and England.

2398. Fraley, Robert ["A Fellow Servant"]. *God Reveals the Identity of the Beast.* 1975. Scottsdale, AZ: Crane. 180 p. bibl. refs.

"Avoid Being Marked by the Beast." Fraley: Watchman Nee follower. Satanic activity and deception. Computers and technology control society, economy, and education. First Beast and Antichrist: our U.S. Empire, which arose from sea, out of 10 European nations, and defeated 3 of them (England, Spain, France). The "mortal wound" it recovered from: Pearl Harbor attack. Second Beast (False Prophet) = U.S. society.

2399. _____. *The Beast of Revelation 13: A Comprehensive Bible Study About the Beast.* 1995. Scottsdale, AZ: Christian Life Services. 94 p. illus.

2400. Franz, Norman. *Bulls, Bears, and the Beast.* 1992. Video.

"Commercial Babylon Exposed"; when and how will the U.S. dollar will collapse; how to prepare for financial crisis in light of Bible prophecy.

2401. Franzmeier, Alvin H. *Countdown to Armageddon: An Amillennial Look at the End Times.* 1989. St. Louis, MO: Concordia.

Lutheran.

2402. Frazee, Willmonte Doniphan.

Coming Events and Crisis at the Close. 1978. Payson, AZ: Leaves-of-Autumn. xiii, 160 p.

Seventh-day Adventist.

2403. Freeborn, Leland F. *Prophecy Today: "The Coming War" When, Where, and Those Who Will Survive It.* 1980. Parowan, UT: Millenial Press of Zion.

Mormon.

2404. Friend, D. L. *A Summary of the Events of the Last Generation.* 1978. [S.l. s.n.]. 34 p.

Seventh-day Adventist.

2405. Friesen, Jake. *Time of the End.* 1974. Calgary: J. Friesen. 28 p. illus. "Time Is Running Out."

2406. Frisby, Neal. *The Revelation of the Written Scrolls and the Word of God.* N.d. [ca 1970?]. Phoenix: s.n. (20th Century Life). 127 p. illus.

Frisby: follower of William Branham. The Seven Seals and Thunders. Visions given personally by God: "startling revelations concerning the end of the world." Atomic war between U.S. (with Western Europe) and Russia. New Roman Empire joins the Soviets. Woman riding the Beast is Catholic Church. Parts of California float away; Florida inundated by tidal wave. Anti-gravity devices invented. Flying saucers involve "demons disguised as odd men." Musical rhythms as cause of sexual lust perversion. Appeals to Great Pyramid dates. Rapture, then Church and state fuse, resulting in Tribulation in the 1970s ("It has to take place by 1980...."). "1977 ought to terminate the world systems and usher in the millennium." Also available in scroll format.

2407. _____. *Prophet in Eclipse.* 1973. Phoenix: author; 20th Century Life. 35 p. illus.

Vol. 1 of Shadows of the End series.

2408. _____. *"The Sting of the Trumpets!"* 1973. Phoenix: author; 20th Century Life. 35 p. illus.

2409. _____. *The 7th Trumpet—the 3rd Woe!: The Unveiling of the Last Vials (Plagues).* 1974. Phoenix: author; 20th Century Life. 30 p. illus. Shadows of the End vol. 6.

2410. _____. *Atomic Holocaust!* 1974. Phoenix: author; 20th Century Life. 35 p. illus. Shadows of the End vol. 8.

2411. _____. *The Great Prophetic Image.* 1974. Phoenix: author. 20th Century Life. 26 p. illus. Shadows of the End vol. 15.

2412. Froese, Arno. *How Democracy Will Elect the Antichrist: the Ultimate Denial of Freedom, Liberty and Justice According to the Bible.* 1997. West Columbia, SC: Olive Press. 283 p.

2413. Froese, Arno, ed. *Toward the Seventh Millenium.* 1998. West Columbia, SC: Olive Press. 286 p. illus.

Contributors: Moody Adams, David Webber, Dave Hunt.

2414. Fruchtenbaum, Arnold G. 1983. *The Footsteps of the Messiah: A Study of the Sequence of Prophetic Events.* Tustin, CA: Ariel Press. xii, 471 p. illus index.

Fruchtenbaum: "Hebrew Christian," founder of Ariel Ministries. Foreword by Ryrie. Encyclopedic study of Tribulation and End Time events. Dispensational pretrib pre-mill. "Double reference" law: two referents separated by time (but denies "double fulfillment"). Law of Recurrence: same event described twice. Roman Empire split East and West (two-division stage of Empire); then East largely transferred to Russia, then Soviets. Seven churches = apostolic to A.D. 100, Roman persecution to 313, Constantinian to 600, Dark Ages to 1517, Reformation to 1648, missionary to 1900, apostate to present (end). Nine specific events to occur before Tribulation: Russian or "Ezekiel" invasion of Israel (Gog-Magog); entire army annihilated. Then one-world government, then 10-Kingdom stage, then Antichrist (of Roman origin). Seven-year covenant, not Rapture, starts Tribulation (Rapture could be some time prior—any moment). Seals = first quarter of Tribulation. Trumpets (third of all land, water, people destroyed) = second quarter of Tribulation. Bowls = second half of Tribulation. Purpose of Tribulation: to break the will of Jewish nation. 200 million horsemen = demons. Two Witnesses = unknown Jews (not revived ancients). Antichrist is literally resurrected from wound. Mid-Tribu-

lation war of Antichrist (based in Babylon) vs. Ten Kings. Ten Kings are of *entire* world, not just Europe. Literal mark
of beast. Armageddon campaign: Antichrist continues to Jerusalem after his
capital Babylon destroyed to annihilate
Jews. Second Coming at Bozrah (Petra)
south of Jerusalem. Christ vs. Antichrist —
armies continue all through Israel. Millennium starts 75 days after Armageddon
victory. Standard Millennium, final rebellion, Resurrection of wicked, Judgment.
World Wars I-II signs that "end of the age
has begun." Rapture date not knowable.
Second Coming exactly 7 years after
covenant, with Abomination of Desolation halfway.

2415. _____. *An Outline of the End
Times.* N.d. S.l. priv. pub.? Various pagings illus.

Also wrote *The Rise and Fall of the
Antichrist* (1970); *The Arab States in
Prophecy* (1970) etc. Also cassettes includ-
ing *The Basis of the Second Coming*; and
The Campaign of Armageddon.

2416. Fry, Richard W. *The King
Comes! A Study in the Book of Revelation.*
1982–96. San Diego: Promise of Life Ministries.

2417. *Future Events You Should
Know Today.* 1984. Zanesville, OH. 64 p.
illus.

"A modern day parable ... presenting
key last day Biblical truths done in a
fictional setting"

2418. Galley, Virginia. *Is Jesus Coming in This Generation?*

End = 1988.

2419. Gano, Raymond. *Apocalypse
Warning: What the Bible Says About the
End Times.*

Includes Terry L. Cook, Carl Lud-
wigson, Derek Mailhiot, Gordie Tong.
Gano: editor of online *Prophe-Zine*
(<http://www.prophezine.com/>).

2420. Gardner, Fran R., Jr. *The
Identification of Gog and Magog in Revelation 20:7–10.* 1972. Dallas Theol. Sem. 55
p. MA Thesis

2421. Garner, Guy. *The Key to Understanding Endtime Prophecy.* Porterdale,
GA: Voice of Liberty Ministries.

2422. Garrison, William. *Holocaust
II: The Truth About the New Age Plan.*
1985. Tulsa, OK: End-Time Ministries.
viii, 151 p., bibl.

(This ministry is not the same as
Charles Meade's End-Time Ministries of
Lake City, Florida.)

2423. Gaulke, Stephen. *He Shall
Come Again: A Study of the End Times.* 1991.
St. Louis: Concordia. Vol 1, Study guide:
31 p; vol 2, Leader's guide, 31 p. illus.

2424. Gaverluk, Emil. *Prophecy for
the Present; Planets of the Future; People for
Eternity.* [ca 1970?]. Nashville: Thomas
Nelson. 43 p.

Gaverluk: educational TV producer.

2425. _____. *Fiber Optics: The Eye
of Antichrist.* 1979. Oklahoma City:
Southwest Radio Church. 37 p. illus., map.

2426. _____. *The Rapture Before the
Russian Invasion of Israel: With 22 References to the Rapture in the Old Testament
and 32 References to the U.S.A.-Canada
Judgment as Prophetic Babylon in Jeremiah
and Revelation.* 1988. Woodburn, OR:
WPT. xiv, 321 p.

Two Russian invasions of Israel; Rapture precedes the first.

2427. _____, and Robert D. Lindsted. *Suddenly — No More Time!* 1981. Oklahoma City: Southwest Radio Church.
[iii], 67 p. illus.

Lindsted: mechanical engineer. Dispensational pre-trib. Exponentially-in-
creasing signs of the End. It is now "just
prior" to the Rapture: "The End is in
sight." Sun will be seven times hotter during the Millennium, and the Pre-Flood
Vapor Canopy will be re-established.
6,000 year existence of man, then the Millennium.

2428. Gentry, Kenneth L. *The Beast
of Revelation.* 1989. Tyler, TX: Institute
for Christian Economics. 209 p. bibl.
refs., indexes.

Preterist, post-mill.

2429. _____. *He Shall Have Dominion: A Postmillennial Eschatology.* 1992.
Tyler, TX: Institute for Christian Economics. xliii, 584 p. indexes, bibl.

Gentry: Presbyterian Church in
America minister near Greenville, SC.

Foreword by Gary North. Forthcoming: *The Abomination of Desolation: A Study in Eschatological Evil.*

2430. George, Barney. *God's Countdown to Doomsday: It's Much Later Than You Think.* [1970s]. [Melbourne, FL: GTS Book. 114 p. illus.

2431. Ghost Wolf, Robert. *Last Cry: Native American Prophecies: Tales of the End Times.* 1997. Spokane, WA: Mistyc House. 319 p. illus.

2432. Gibson, Ronald R. *Living in the Last Days.* 1983. Lancaster, PA: Lancaster Bible College. Cassette.

2433. Gibson, Thomas S. *The Prophetic Word.* <http:www.telusplanet.net/public/tsgibson/propheticword.html>

End-time prophecies received from God by Gibson and others.

2434. Gibson, Ty Forrest. *The Final Generation.* 1989. Malo, WA: Lightbearers. 12 cassettes.

Remnant theology.

2435. Giesbrecht, Kathy. *Unmasking the End Times.* 1997. Newton, KS; Winnipeg, Canada: Faith & Life Press. 44 p. Fast Lane Bible studies. bibl. refs.

"Bible studies for junior high."

2436. Gilbert, Adrian, and Maurice Cotterell. *The Mayan Prophecies: Unlocking the Secrets of a Lost Civilization.* 1995. Rockport, MA: Element. xiii, 337 p. illus bibl. refs, index.

2437. Gileadi, Avraham. *The Last Days: Types and Shadows from the Bible and Book of Mormon.* 1991. 2nd ed., rev. and enl. American Fork, UT: Covenant Communications. 323 p. bibl. refs, indexes. Orig. pub. Salt Lake City: Deseret.

Gileadi was excommunicated from Mormon Church after this book, but reinstated after following book (more moderate) was published.

2438. _____. *The End from the Beginning: The Apocalyptic Vision of Isaiah.* 1997. 2nd ed. Cave Junction, OR: Hebraeus Press. ix, 150 p.

2439. Glenn, Richard B. *The Mystery of Iniquity: An Indepth & Electrifying Message of End Time Prophecy.* 1994. Detroit: Richard Glenn Ministries. 171 p.

2440. Gloyd, Jim. *On Unto Perfec-*

tion: The Choice of the Last Generation. 1998. Ashville, OH: Glory! Publishing. 67 p.

Gloyd was miraculously healed by an angel (and?) at a Benny Hinn crusade in Cincinnati. AIDS as first of end-time pestilences.

2441. Goard, Dottie Mae. *These Last Days: Angelic Messengers Reveal the Future.* 1994. Pasadena, CA: Hope Pub. House. xi, 239 p.

Private revelations to author about the Second Coming.

2442. Goertzen, Harry C. *Prophecies of Daniel and Revelation.* 1981. National City, CA: Sidekick Enterprises. xiv, 197 p. illus.

Pre-trib pre-mill. Divided Roman Empire = Common Market. 6,000 year history for world ends 1982; 70th Week starts then.

2443. Goett, Robert. *How to Interpret the Apocalypse: As Naturalists? Or, as Supernaturalists?* 1985. Miami Springs, FL: Conley & Schoettle. 60 p.

"A Refutation of the Historic Interpretation, with Especial Reference to the Rev. G. Guinness' *Approaching End of the Age.*" Pre-mill. Insists on literal (supernatural) not symbolic or historic (naturalist) interpretation of Revelation (though some parts are symbolic). Revelation is an unveiled, not a veiled book. Mystic Babylon (Rev. 17) = Rome; in Rev. 18, the rebuilt literal Babylon is utterly destroyed.

2444. Goetz, William R. *Apocalypse Next.* 1991 [1980]. Camp Hill, PA: Horizon House. Updated and expanded ed. 386 p. bibl. refs.

Goetz: pastor of Sevenoaks Alliance Church, Abbotsford, B.C., editor at Christian Publications. Nearly 300,000 copies. Pre-trib pre-mill. Rapture; then invasion of Israel by Russia and allies supernaturally crushed. Antichrist becomes head of ten-nation confederacy, then moves to Israel after becoming world dictator. Dreadful persecution of Jews. Armageddon at end of seven year Tribulation: Antichrist, Arab confederation, Russia, and 200 million man Eastern army defeated at Second Coming. Liberalization of communist regimes just clever ploy. Russians will use lignostone weapons (superstrong wood which evades radar) fulfilling prophecy of Jews using their weapons for firewood. Karakorum Highway from China across Himalayas will be used as invasion route for Eastern hordes. Soviets stockpiling vast military supplies in Lebanon for use in their invasion, but will revert to horses because of oil shortage.

2445. _____. *The Economy to Come and Other Signs of Earth's Impending Climax.* 1983. Beaverlodge, Alberta: Horizon House. 391 p.

Coming cashless economy, Mark of the Beast, 666, Antichrist.

2446. Goldberg, Louis. *Turbulence over the Middle East.* 1982. Neptune, NJ: Loizeaux Bros. 292 p. illus. bibl.

In future war a missile from Syria or Jordan could accidentally destroy Dome of Rock (Mosque of Omar) to clear way for the Temple of the Last Days.

2447. Goldstein, Clifford. *1844 Made Simple.* 1988. Boise, ID: Pacific Press. 96 p. illus.

Seventh-day Adventist. 1844 was the cleansing of the Sanctuary in heaven.

2448. _____. *Day of the Dragon: How Current Events have Set the Stage for America's Prophetic Transformation.* 1993. Boise, ID; Pacific Press. 127 p.

Notes that E.G. White's anti-Catholicism sounds very bigoted now, but argues that it is all coming true. Soviet collapse has resulted in U.S. and Catholic Church as the leading world powers. Catholic Church is the First Beast of Revelation and America is the Second Beast.

2449. _____. *One Nation Under God?: Bible Prophecy—When the American Experiment Fails.* 1996. Boise, ID: Pacific Press. 160 p. bibl. refs.

2450. Good, Joseph. *Rosh Ha-Shanah and the Messianic Kingdom to Come: A Messianic Jewish Interpretation of the Feast of Trumpets.* 1989. Port Arthur, TX: Hatikva Ministries. 197 p.

Good; resident of Hatikva Ministries. Also wrote *Rosh-Hash-Ana, the Messiah's Return.* Predicts End for 1988, or Rapture for 2000.

2451. Goodman, Jeffrey. *We Are the Earthquake Generation: Where and When the Catastrophes Will Strike.* 1978. New York: Seaview Books. xv, 265 p. bibl, index drawings, maps

Psychics predict tremendous earthquakes, confirming biblical prophecy. Also wrote *Psychic Archeology.*

2452. Goodman, Phillip. *The Assyrian Connection: The Roots of the Antichrist and the Emerging Signs of Armageddon.* 1993. Lafayette, LA: Prescott Press. x, 306 p. illus. maps charts bibl index.

Goodman: founded Spiritual Armour Project. Dispensational pre-trib. Signs show imminent start of End. Antichrist to arise from revival of long-dead Assyrian Empire. As Israel was resurrected, so too Assyria. Holocaust, and following statehood for Israel, was fulfillment of Ezek. 37 ("dry bones"). Fourth Empire is Rome; clay / iron feet are fusion of barbarians with Romans. Antichrist comes from 11th "Roman" nation (i.e. from periphery of revived Empire). Rev. 13:3: Assyria "slain," then revived. Antichrist will convince world he is reincarnated God-King; really a Satanic spirit of demon-controlled man. Able to deceive world after shock of Rapture disappearances. Thirty end-time events: Rapture, followed by treaty with Israel, then Russian-Islamic coalition attacks Israel (War of Gog at start of Tribulation), God destroys army but Antichrist claims credit. Day of Lord = great signs in Heavens, final plagues; world reacts by sending army to Armageddon. Assyrian conquers or takes over U.S. after controlling Europe and Mid-East. All prophecies of devastation will be literally fulfilled at End. Saints not raptured during Tribulation will be "escorted" to safety near end of Tribulation, to escape destruction at Second Coming. Destruction of world of 2 Peter 3:10 = Day of Lord/Second Advent (which is not *post*-mill). New Heaven and New Earth *precedes* Millennium. "I sometimes wonder if the editors of our daily news are not plagiarizing their stories and clipping their headlines right out of the prophetic pages of Scripture." Breakup of Soviet Union "very significant" prophetically: "an even clearer sign of the latter days than was the former state of affairs"; it is the prophesied coalition of Gog.

2453. Goodman, Watson. *Look Out, Everybody!* 1985. Elkhart, IN: Enterprises for Emmanuel. xii, 339 p. illus. index.

The Rapture.

2454. Goseigen. *The Holy Words.* 1982. Tujunga, CA: Bishop of North American Region of Sekai Mahikari Bunmei Kyodan. 291 p.

Revealed by creator god to former Lieut. Col. Yoshikazu Okada, founder of Mahikari sect. Armageddon: Aug. 1999. "The crisis of perishing, ending and collapse of civilization is imminent." "Time is extremely near when I must change the surface of the earth into the sea of fire and mud again." Only cult members will survive this "intense cleansing of impure and contaminated mankind. It may become inevitable for god to put an end to the great mass of shabby and rotten mankind.... For this reason, as a transitory necessary step to cause a great change for the true civilization, chaos will appear in the world.... This is the End of the World." "Then, Ningen (Sub Humans) as well as religion, will not only become unnecessary on the Earth, but also cause foul disaster to god. Therefore, I must throw them into the foul fire of Gehenna." God created Japanese as the King race (Obito), above five inferior "branch" races (yellow [Chinese], red, white, blue, and black races).

2455. Graff, Ron. *The Registration.* 1997.

Fiction. Rapture, Tribulation, Mark of the Beast. Graff also runs *Prophecy Central* website (<http:www.bible- prophecy/com>) with "The Rapture Study Guide" ("How the world's rejection of the pre-trib rapture proves its validity").

2456. Graham, Billy. *Approaching Hoofbeats: The Four Horsemen of the Apocalypse.* 1983. Waco, TX: Word Books. 236,[3] p. bibl. SEE ALSO 1910–1970.

2457. Graham, Jimmy, and G. Lamar Wilkie. *Truth Or Myth: Deception*

of the Ages. 1993. Virginia Beach: Cornerstone. 139 p. bibl.

Graham: Georgia physician, pastor of independent Full Gospel Church, black. Wilkie: electronics instructor and Christian radio broadcaster. Intend to show "beyond doubt that we are the last generation." 1993 Waco incident, African famines, European Parliament all End signs. Catholic-headed World Church and world government under Antichrist just ahead. Pre-trib.

2458. Grant, Jean. *The Revelation: A Novel.* c1992. Nashville: T. Nelson. 249 p.

2459. Grant, Jim. *A Thief in the Night.* 1974. Chicago: Moody Press. 120 p. illus. Based on the Mark IV Pictures film. Original story by Donald W. Thompson and Russell S. Doughten; screenplay by Jim Grant.

2460. Greed, John A. *End of the World?: Or Is It a New Age?* 1977. Bristol: St. Trillo. 212 p. illus., maps, plans.

Northern forces allies attack Israel, Second Coming. Millennium, then all nations attack Israel, then world destroyed. First horseman may be Christ. 10 Nation treaty at start of seven-year Tribulation. Rapture at Last Trumpet (during last 3½ years). North = Gog = Russia (plus Germany and others). 10 Nation league as response to conventional war by Russia. U.S. may be knocked out in World War resulting from escalation of Russian attack. Roman leader rules world after World War; Antichrist destroys world church. Discusses ley lines, Uri Geller, UFOs (anti-Christian manifestations). Bahai = False Messiah of 1844. Armageddon just before Second Coming. Literal Armageddon with 450 million soldiers. New Jerusalem is pyramid, 1,500 miles each side; Glastonbury and Stonehenge also models for New Jerusalem.

2461. Greene, Richard. *The Rebuilding of Noah's Ark as a Last Day Witness to the World.* [1990s]. Frostburg, MD.: God's Ark of Safety Ministry. Unpaged. illus.

Life-size replica of Noah's Ark, begun 1976, as "tool to tell the world ... that Jesus is coming soon!"

2462. Greer, Lee. *When the Son of Man is Revealed!* 1993. Priv. pub. 101 p. bibl., refs.

Seventh-day Adventist. Universe is expanding from central point (Big Bang theory), which is God's Throne. Appeals to Robert Gentry's creationism and denial of relativity (claiming absolute frame of reference).

2463. Grenz, Stanley. *The Millennial Maze: Sorting Out Evangelical Options.* c1992. Downers Grove, IL: InterVarsity. 239 p. bibl. refs. 1979 ed. (320 p.) pub. as *The Next Twenty Years.*

Grenz: theology prof., Carey/Regent College (Vancouver). Started as dispensational pre-millennialist, then switched to "historic" pre-millennialism (post-trib), then moved to a sort of a-millennialism sympathetic to post-millennialism. Evaluates each position.

2464. Greene, Oliver B. See also 1910–1970. *The Second Coming of Jesus.* 1971. Greenville, SC: The Gospel Hour. 380 p.

2465. _____. *The End of the World.* [1970s?]. Greenville, SC: Oliver B. Greene. 31 p.

2466. Griffith, L.L. *When Earth Burns.* 1989. Levittown, PA: Dovetree Press. 215 p.

"Revelation's earthquakes, hails and fire, that signal God's wrath."

2467. Griswold, Millie H., ed. *God's Prophetic Calendar.* 1983. Charlotte, NC: Advent Christian General Conference of America. 137 p.

Advent Christian. Contributors include Oral Collins, Stephen C. Brown, David A. Dean, Freeman Barton, Carlyle Roberts.

2468. Gromacki, Robert Glenn. *Are These the Last Days?* c1970. Old Tappan, NJ: Fleming H. Revell. 190 p. Also pub. Worthing [England]: Henry E. Walter; Schaumburg, IL: Regular Baptist Press.

Pre-trib, dispensational. Belief in imminent any-moment return is essential. "If God ever wanted to introduce the great tribulation, He couldn't ask for a better time than this. The stage is set...." May be up to 50 years between Rapture and 7-year Tribulation. Rapture = spirits of dead saints descend with Christ, get resurrection bodies, and go up along with living saints. No families in heaven (thus avoiding problems such as remarriages). Harlot = apostate Christendom, rides Beast = Antichrist (political empire). Antichrist = gentile Roman Prince with huge appeal. Covenant between Antichrist and Israel. Satan cast by Michael to earth mid-Tribulation. During Tribulation, Hitler's persecution "*will* be surpassed." Israel driven out during Tribulation by Antichrist, Jews then convert. Also great revival during Tribulation = 144,000 Jews, many Gentiles saved. Antichrist breaks covenant mid-Tribulation, then invades. TV will show him rise from casket. Then he demands to be worshipped in Temple. North = Soviet Russia, South = Arab-African, East = Red China. Armageddon probably whole second half of Tribulation. Armies of West led by Antichrist invade after North destroyed. Then East attacks West, then both fight against Christ at Second Coming. God annihilates all armies, but it produces "many beneficial results." Flood proof of supernatural intervention. Water Canopy from Creation to Flood. Wicked and unbelievers will be provided with resurrected bodies able to survive eternal torment of Lake of Fire. Armageddon "climactic struggle between two diametrically opposed worlds of race, color, and creed": the white segment of the world's population" vs "the yellow, Oriental peoples of Red China and her neighbors."

2469. Grosboll, Marshall J. *The Whole Armour of God: Preparing to Be One of the 144,000.* [ca. 1990?]. Wichita, KS: Steps to Life. 20 p.

2470. Grossman, Randall A. *The Rapture: Is It Before Or After the Tribulation?* 1981. Hatfield, PA: Interdisciplinary Biblical Research Inst. 15 p. bibl.

Post-trib.

2471. Grotheer, William H. 1991. *The Hour and the End: An In-Depth Study of Luke 21:24.* [S.l.: s.n.] 50, [13] p. illus. Seventh-Day Adventist.

2472. _____. *The Sign of the End of Time.* 1995. Ozone, AR: Bible Prophecy Seminars.

2473. Gruss, Edmond C. *The Jehovah's Witnesses and Prophetic Speculation: An Examination and Refutation of the Witnesses' Position on the Second Coming of Christ, Armageddon and the "End of the World."* 1972. Nutley, NJ: Presbyterian and Reformed. 127 p. illus charts. bibl. refs.

2474. Gulley, Norman R. *Final Events on Planet Earth.* 1977. Nashville: Southern Pub. Assoc. 124 p. bibl. refs.

Gulley: prof. at Madison College, then at Southern Adventist Univ.; Seventh-day Adventist. Popularity of occultism as sign of Last Days. Satan performs wonder-working miracles in End Times to deceive the world prior to Second Coming.

2475. _____. *Christ Our Refuge: Making It Safely Through the Last Days.* 1996. Boise, ID: Pacific Press. 124 p.

2476. _____. *Christ Is Coming! A Christ-Centered Approach to Last-Day Events.* 1998. Hagerstown, MD: Review and Herald. 585 p. bibl. refs, indexes.

Textbook format. Thorough, heavily referenced, scholarly and well written. "It's the End-time. Final events are upon us." America is the Beast. Warns of end-time push for Sunday laws. Several chapters opposing evolution. Rejects 6,000 years scheme.

2477. Gundry, Robert Horton. *The Church and the Tribulation.* c1973. Grand Rapids, MI: Zondervan 224 p. bibl.

Post-trib. Church endures Tribulation, then raptured at Second Coming. Converted Jews also raptured, but non-converted survive into Millennium unraptured (converting at Second Coming). Temple restored in Tribulation, but worship led by Antichrist. Denies that 144,000 will evangelize; these may be orthodox Jews who resist Antichrist and remain during Millennium. Church persecuted in Tribulation but won't suffer *God's* wrath. Says post-trib view not necessarily less literal than pre-trib: may interpret woes *more* literally than some pre-tribs. Actual divine "Wrath" occurs only at close of 70th Week. Rapture = believers ascend in order to escort Christ back down again. No point for two sets of Endings (for Church,

and for others). The Early Church fathers were all post-trib.

2478. _____. *First the Antichrist.* 1997. Grand Rapids, MI: Baker Books. 200 p. bibl. refs., indexes.

"A book for lay Christians approaching the third millennium and inquiring whether Jesus will come to take the church out of the world before the tribulation."

2479. Hadley, E.C. *Prophetic Events: Soon to Come to Pass.* 1973. Sunbury, PA: Believers Bookshelf. 83 p.

2480. Hagee, John C. *Beginning of the End: The Assassination of Yitzhak Rabin and the Coming Antichrist.* 1996. Nashville: Thomas Nelson. xi, 196 p. illus., maps.

Hagee: founder/pastor Cornerstone Church, San Antonio, TX; president of Global Evangelism Television. Emphatically literal interpretation. Says Rabin's assassination was sign of imminent End, but rest of book is simply pre-trib pre-mill presentation. Any-moment Rapture; then, Tribulation, Antichrist revealed, "very soon" Second Coming. Israel given to Jews eternally by God. Iron-clay ten toes: mix of autocracies and democracies in 10-member modern European confederation. Extensive proof of fulfilled prophecy regarding the First Coming. World to End at Armageddon. Prophesied plagues to be like Ebola virus; AIDS, etc., also signs of imminent End. Excited descriptions of aftermath of Rapture, when many are discovered missing; UFOs will be blamed. Devil and demons have supernatural powers too (e.g. psychic); miraculous counterfeit deceptions. Antichrist from European union, maybe from merging of Serbia, Bosnia, Croatia. Computerized economy. Antichrist not revealed til after Rapture, but probably alive now. King of South: Islamic-African federation. Magog may not be Russia, but Soviet Empire will prob be revived, and take over Magog region. Russian-Islamic coalition attacks Israel halfway through Tribulation; but blasted by God. Jews then convert. Antichrist then steps in to impose world religion, economy, and government. He is assassinated, then reanimated by Satan in

Hell, returns to Earth, then worshipped. North and South then attack Israel (Russia-Islam again), with 200-million army from East: Armageddon. But instead join with Antichrist forces to battle Christ's forces. Literal blood up to horse bridles for 200 miles.

2481. _____. *Day of Deception: Separating Truth from Falsehood in These Last Days.* 1997. Nashville: T. Nelson. 245 p. bibl. refs.

2482. _____. *Final Dawn Over Jerusalem.* 1998. Nashville: T. Nelson. x, 211 p. bibl. refs.

Pro-Israel; Jews as God's people forever. All nations judged on their treatment of Jews. Pre-trib. Reborn Russia will lead pan-Islamic invasion of Israel. Antichrist will be great deceiver, perhaps Nobel Peace Prize winner, but "will make Hitler look like a choirboy" after making seven-year covenant with Israel. Argues against "replacement theology"—the assumption that was Israel replaced by the Church. Seven Festivals; Rapture at Rosh Hashanah, Second Coming at Yom Kippur, Millennium at Sukkot.

2483. _____. ed. 1997. *[NKJV] Prophecy Study Bible.* Nashville: Thomas Nelson. li, 1,792 p

2484. Halff, Charles. SEE ALSO 1910-1970. *Israel, Nation of Destiny.* 1974. San Antonio, TX: Christian Jew. 26 p.

Also wrote other books for Christian Jew on Israel (*Palestine, the Land of Fulfilled Prophecy*, 1955).

2485. _____. *Great End Time Prophecies.* 1975. San Antonio, TX: Christian Jew Foundation. [ii]. 48 p.

Now "fast approaching the midnight hour." Russia ("Gog") already preparing to invade Israel. Antichrist declares himself God in rebuilt Temple after Rapture, initiating Tribulation. Revived Roman Empire—United States of Europe—from Common Market. Two Witnesses = Enoch and Elijah: world sees them killed ("Well, naturally, it will have to be by television"). No rain for 3½ years during Tribulation. Roman Catholic Church: Great Whore, False Prophet.

2486. Hall, John G. *The Eternal*

Program of God of the Ages and Dispensations. 1972. [Newcastle, OK]: J.G. Hall. color chart.

2487. Hall, Marshall, and Sandra Hall. *The Connection Between Evolution Theory and the Doctrine of a Future Millennium.* 1976. Lakeland, FL: P/R Pub. 31 p. Monograph #11 from *The Connection Papers.*

"A demonstration that this "Jewish Fable" will not stand after the exposure of the Evolution Lie." Denies literal Millennium. *All* false teachings will be destroyed after the evolution myth is vanquished.

2488. Hall, R. Henry. *Ominous Portents of the Parousia of Christ.* 1984. Las Vegas: Hall Pub. Co. 356 p. illus. index. Spine: *Revelations of Brimstone.*

Hall: ex-professional gambler, writer on gambling, lives in Las Vegas. Sections written by Oral Roberts, Hargis, Swaggart, Gary Greenwald, Constance Cumbey, and journalist Lois Reed ("contributing writers"). Pre-trib Rapture. Rails against atheists, communists, liberals; U.S. sinking in corruption. Antichrist is 33 years old now. God sent Reagan as a "wise man" for the End Times. Psychic surgery is God's healing. Cites Greenwald on satanic rock music. Wants to "get rid of the Anti-Christs in the Senate!" Creation of Adam 4002 B.C. "God has given man 6,000 years from Adam," of which "5,986 have been already used up ... the remaining fourteen years are the LAST FOURTEEN, or the end of human time...." The "Final year in human history should be in the year 1998 (the end of the 6,000 year period of GOD's plan)." Antichrist revealed just prior to 1991; Rapture 1991. Man's number = 6; God's = 7: the Millennium. 666 + 666 + 666 = 1998.

2489. _____. *R. Henry Hall's A.D. 1991, the Genesis of Holocaust.* 1985. Las Vegas: Spirit of Prophecy Evangelical Ministries. xviii, 360 p. illus.

Moral conditions.

2490. _____. 1991. *The Secret of the Seven Thunders.* Las Vegas: Spirit of Prophesy Bus Ministries. viii, 120 p. illus., index.

"The true story of the endtime vision that was given to Rick Hall in 1991."

2491. Hallmann, Robert A.G. *Saddam Hussein, the Final Antichrist.* 1998. <http://www.magi.com/~rah/antichst.html>

Saddam Hussein, manipulated by evil extraterrestrials, will rule the world after being killed in U.S. attack and resurrected (probably 2001). Unimaginable horrors for those with Mark of the Beast. A Quantum Computer now orbiting Earth is the Beast. "Very Important Warning: Don't be deceived by the Aliens known as the 'Greys'.... For they are 'Fallen angels,' or 'Satan's Soldiers.'"

2492. Hammaren, Nils W. *The Seal of the End Times.* 1992. Somerville, NJ: End Times Press. xi, 307 p. illus. [12] p. prophecy charts

Hammaren: inventor, businessman. "The world is moving swiftly to the *Time of the End.*" Dedicated to survivors of coming Tribulation. Post-trib. Scofield Bible ("Do not be tempted to buy other books at this time," as they will mislead). One out of 62,000 is member of the Elect, but there are other believers, so non-Elect shouldn't be discouraged. Argues that "gravity is a Spirit-Force and has *no* physical cause...." Daniel sealed up his prophecies until Time of End. Holy Spirit can lift Seal for believers (i.e. author). 1914: Israel starts regathering; end of Gentile times (Russell was basically right). Two regatherings, Tribulations, and Second Comings. Ark of Covenant in Ethiopia. Spear of Longinus, forged by Tubal-Cain in 3061 B.C., pierced Christ on the Cross, owned by Hitler, spirited to South Pole for 34 years, then went to Antichrist (born 1961) in 1979. Spear's evil is now reactivated; Antichrist will use it for "aggression and control." First Tribulation = Hitler, Holocaust. New law now that government can confiscate any person's money if above a secret limit. Blavatsky's *Secret Doctrine* is "Anti-Bible ... Satan wrote this book." Agrees with Church's *Guardians of the Grail.* By 1992: a unified Europe under Karl von Habsburg. Russia and Arab consortium suddenly attacks Israel; then U.S. of Europe attacks Israel: Battle of Armageddon. Messiah predicted by Jeane Dixon is really Antichrist. Israeli believers flee to Petra after assassination of Beast, intensification of Tribulation. 70th Week — the Tribulation — starts in 1994 (after Russian invasion). Great (second half) Tribulation starts 1998, ends 2001 with Armageddon. Believers killed by U.S.-Russian atomic wars in Tribulation. Second Coming at Petra. Rapture only *after* Tribulation, then Millennium. Sun overheats, melts earth at End after Millennium. Buechner helped with Spear part of book (though he doesn't say Antichrist will inherit Spear). Advises believers to transfer funds to Israel to survive Tribulation. Author was buffeted by both Satanic and Godly forces and received revelatory visions.

2493. Hamon, Bill. *Apostles, Prophets and the Coming Moves of God: God's End-Time Plans for His Church and Planet Earth.* 1997. Santa Rosa, FL: Christian International.

2494. Hancock, Graham. *Fingerprints of the Gods.* 1995. New York: Crown Books. [iv], 578 p. illus., maps, charts, 32 p. plates. bibl., index.

Ancient advanced civilization based in Antarctica, then temperate. Earth's crust periodically slides; land position relative to poles shifts (Hapgood; explanation for so-called Ice Ages); Antarctica became polar. Scientific wisdom cult of survivors of this ancient civilization then established in Egypt 14th century B.C.; but destroyed by floods and Ice Age 11th century B.C. Immense building projects to preserve knowledge, history. Sphinx is equinoctial marker for Age of Leo by using processional movement; three pyramids precisely reflect Orion's Belt stars' positions 10,450 B.C. Also as warning of future Last Time catastrophe ca. 2000 A.D. "In short, through metaphors and allegories [myths, building alignments], I suspect the ancients may have tried to find many ways to tell us exactly when — and why — the hammer of global destruction is going to strike again."

2495. Harman, James T. *The Coming Spiritual Earthquake.* 1998. Maitland, FL: Prophecy Countdown.

Comet Hale-Bopp is "a sign that Jesus is Coming back again." Previously appeared just before Noah's Flood. 6,000 Year theory. 144,000 of Rev. 7 are Jewish, sealed during Tribulation; different from 144,000 of Rev. 14, who have mark or seal of Jesus. These latter are "first fruits"— only Christians to escape Tribulation, raptured to heaven prior to Tribulation. All other Christians must undergo horrible Tribulation. Thus both pre- and post-trib are partly right. Most who suffer Tribulation will be martyred. Martyrs (before and during trib) resurrected at beginning of Millennium to rule with Christ. Those who survive unmartyred through Tribulation not resurrected till end of Millennium.

2496. Harmston, James. *True and Living Church of Jesus Christ of Saints of the Last Days.* <http://www.tlcmanti.org/> Manti, UT.

Mormon variant. Armageddon imminent; Second Coming Apr. 6, 2000. Utah base is haven for Elect during Last Days. Website includes Harmston's *Book of Mormon Warning in the Last Days.*

2497. Harrison, James. 1995. *The Pattern and the Prophecy: God's Great Code.* Peterbrough, Ontario, Canada: Isaiah Productions. 399 p. illus. bibl. refs., indexes.

Intricate numerological calculations from the Bible. Dangers of Satanism. Napoleon and Hitler as prototypes of Antichrist. Newton's tragic rejection of the Trinity. Disbelief really started with Darwin. 6,000 year lifespan for world, from Creation ca. 4000 B.C. Daniel's 69 Weeks: 445 B.C. to A.D. 32. Age of Gentiles to 1992–3. Then 70th Week, ending 2000–1 with Armageddon and Millennium. Satan's post-millennial rebellion A.D. 3002–3. Gematria: "Name of the Lord" = 2001; "Name of Jesus" = 1999; "Power of God" = 2000. Satan, Antichrist, and False Prophet (Evil Trinity): 666 x 3 = 1998.

2498. Harrop, G. Gerald. *Armageddon.* 1985. Hantsport, NS, Canada: Lancelot Press. 65 p. bibl. refs.

2499. Hartman, Jack. *Strong Faith for the Last Days.* c1992. Dunedin, FL: Lamplight. 221 p.

Hartman: in insurance (wrote *Trust God for Your Finances*). Predicts economic collapse.

2500. Hartsaw, John W. *End Time — God's Glory.* 1982. Smithtown, NY: Exposition Press. x, 100 p.

2501. Harwell, Huey W. *Were We Once Angels.* 1994 [1986]. Flomaton, AL: Jubilee. 319 p. illus., maps., bibl. refs.

Armageddon may happen in this generation, before A.D. 2000. Stage set for WWIII and Armageddon. Pre-trib pre-mill. Russia and allies to invade Israel but suffer horrendous defeat. Gap Theory creationism. Seven Times Seven theory. Each "day" of creation = 7,000 years. Future Seventh Day also. Earth's 6,000 years almost up. War between U.S. and Russia. Then Antichrist, the reincarnation of Judas, becomes head of ten-nation Western Europe confederacy (the revived Roman Empire). Long discussion of Kissinger as probable Antichrist. Israel supernaturally helped in all recent wars. Great persecution during Tribulation, but some conversions. 144,000 Jewish witnesses. Gog, Magog = Gorbachev and Georgia. Babyon is New York.

2502. "Hatonn, Gyeorgos Ceres" [George Green?]. *Firestorm in Babylon: The Time Is Come.* 1990. Carlsbad, CA: America West. v, 197 p. *Phoenix* Journal series.

2503. _____. *R.R.P.P.* 1990. Carlsbad, CA: America West. *Phoenix* Journal series. Vol 1: "Rape, Ravage, Pillage and Plunder of the Phoenix"; Vol 2: "Rape of the Constitution, Death of Freedom."

Armageddon.

2504. _____. *Shrouds of the Seventh Seal: the Anti-Christ Whore of Babylon!* 1991. Carlsbad, CA: America West. *Phoenix* Journal series. iv, 210 p.

2505. _____. *As the Blossom Opens.* 1993. Las Vegas: *Phoenix* Journal series. 255 p.

2506. _____. *Tattered Pages.* 1993. Las Vegas: *Phoenix* Journal series. 228 p.

2507. Hauser, Robert W. *Give Glory to Him: The Sanctuary in the Book of Revelation.* 1983. Angwin, CA: R.W. Hauser. 249 p.

Seventh-day Adventist. "Secondary" futurist as well as (primary) historicist fulfillment of prophecies. When National Sunday Law passed, then exact date of all End Time events will be known.

2508. Hawkins, Yisrayl. *Unveiling Satan: Her Identity Revealed.* 1995. Abilene, TX: House of Yahweh. 493 p. illus.

Hawkins claims his brother and he were the Two Witnesses of the End Times. Changed his given name from Buffalo Bill to Yisrayl. Brother moved to Israel, changed name to Yaaqob; then founded House of Yahweh in Odessa, TX. Yisrayl founded House of Yahweh in Abilene, TX. Anglo-Israel teachings. Says all other churches are part of Satan's last days' deception. "This soon-coming Time Period will BEGIN the LAST Seven Years of Satan's rule upon the earth." Satan cast to earth mid-tribulation, kills 2nd Witness. By 1994 Hawkins was teaching we are already in "the midst" of Tribulation. Also publishes *Prophetic Word* magazine. (*Book of Yahweh* sacred to House of Yahweh.)

2509. Hawtin, George R. *Eschatology, the Doctrine of Last Things.* [1980?]. Battleford, Saskatchewan: George R. Hawtin. 152 p.

2510. _____. *Portrait of Things to Come.* [1980?]. Battleford, Saskatchewan: George R. Hawtin. 143 p.

2511. Hayden, Keavin. *What the World Doesn't Know: Uncovering Political and Religious Secrets that Affect Us All.* 1996. Daystar. 383 p. illus. bibl. refs.

2512. Hayes, Zachary. *What Are They Saying About the End of the World?* c1983. New York: Paulist Press. 73 p. bibl.

2513. Hayford, Jack W. *Until the End of Time: Revealing the Future of Humankind: A Study of Daniel and Revelation.* 1994. Nashville: Thomas Nelson. 158 p. bibl. refs.

2514. Haynes, William L. *A New World Order is Coming: Who Will Usher It In?* 1993. Oroville, CA: Golden Feather Books. 128 p. bibl. refs.

2515. Helffrich, Reginald Boone. *Revelation 14:1–5, the 144,000 Identified.* 1976. Live Oak, FL: author 26 p.

2516. Hendley, Jesse M. *The End is Near.* 1978. [Atlanta: Radio Evangelistic Publications].

2517. _____. *The Unfolding Drama of Bible Prophecy.* 1993. Atlanta: Radio Evangelistic Publications. 285 p.

2518. Henry, Carl F.H., ed. *Prophecy in the Making.* 1971. Carol Stream, IL: Creation House.

1971 Prophecy conference in Jerusalem, announced by Henry, editor of *Christianity Today*; featured Prime Minister Ben-Gurion, singer Anita Bryant, Wilbur Smith, Criswell, faculty from Dallas Theological Seminary, Talbot, and Gordon-Conwell; reported on by future Surgeon Gen. Koop. All agreed on "the soon return of the Lord."

2519. Heras, Antonio de las. *Explosion Extraterrestre.* c1977. Buenos Aires: Editorial Rodolfo Alonso. 121, [3] p. bibl.

UFOs, nuclear war.

2520. Hermann, L. William. *The Fire Storm.* 1993. Nashville: Winston-Derek Publishers. 89 p.

2521. Herrell. V.S. *Christian Epiphanological and Eschatological Teachings.* Kodak, TN: Christian Separatist Church. 80 p.

Preterist, anti-dispensational. White supremacist. Hitler was a good Christian. 6th Commandment (against adultery) really forbids race-mixing.

2522. Hickey, Marilyn. *Armageddon.* 1994. Denver: Marilyn Hickey Ministries. 86 p.

2523. Hicks, Roy H. *Another Look at the Rapture.* 1982. Tulsa: Harrison House. 120, [8] p. bibl.

2524. _____. *Final Days and Counting: Containing Instructions for Those Who Miss His Coming.* 1990. Priv. pub. (San Marcos, CA). 61 p.

Hicks: former Gen. Supervisor of Foursquare Gospel Churches. Any-moment Rapture. "We who live in the end time will have to be ready twenty-four hours a day!" Describes meeting Larry Goshorn, developer of Beast computer system installed in Brussels. All who refuse 666 Mark of Beast will be killed.

2525. "Hilarion" [Maurice B. Cooke]. *Threshold: A Letter for Michelle on the Meaning of Love, Karma, the New Age, Death, Rebirth & the Apocalypse.* 1980. Toronto: Marcus Books. 58 p.

2526. _____. *The Tribulation.* 1981. Toronto: Marcus Books. iv, 19 p.

Spirit communication channeled from Hilarion to Cooke. Another 1981 Hilarion book, *Dark Robes, Dark Brothers,* explains that humans not evolved from apes but descended from spiritual astral beings. Final decision "in a few years" when good separated from evil spirits of humanity, former to rise to astral state, latter obliterated.

2527. Hill, Brenda D. *Preparation for the Final Crisis: Study Work Book.* 1994. Douglassville, PA: Treasures of Heaven. 182 p.

Seventh-day Adventist. Based on Fernando Chaij's book.

2528. Hindson, Edward E. *End Times, the Middle East, and the New World Order.* 1991. Wheaton, IL: Victor Books. 204 p. illus., maps, bibl. refs. [Victor acquired by Scripture Press]

Vice President and professor at Missouri Baptist College (St. Louis). Cautions against undue speculation and reckless date-setting, rash identifications. "Babylon" is symbolic. EEC, computers may be of prophetic significance. Prophetic significance of Saddam Hussein's invasion of Kuwait and Desert Storm. Personal Antichrist, but not revealed until too late. Second Coming end of Tribulation at Armageddon, then Millennium. Portrays Islam as inherently anti-Christian. Magog may be Islamic (not Russian) confederation. Sea Beast = Antichrist. 2nd Beast = False Prophet. Pre-trib, but concedes elements of truth in rival views. "We are genuinely convinced that the march to Armageddon, the last great battle, has already begun."

2529. _____. *Final Signs: Amazing Prophecies of the End Times.* 1996. Eugene, OR: Harvest House. bibl. refs., illus. 224 p.

2530. _____. *Approaching Armageddon.* 1997. Eugene, OR: Harvest House. 334 p. illus., map, bibl. refs.

2531. _____. *Is the Antichrist Alive and Well? 10 Keys to His Identity.* 1998. Eugene, OR: Harvest House Publishers. 229 p. illus. bibl. refs.

2532. Hitchcock, Mark. *After the Empire: Bible Prophecy in Light of the Fall of the Soviet Union.* 1994 [1992]. Wheaton, IL: Tyndale House. xiii, 178 p. map, bibl. refs.

Confederation of Islamic states from southern part of former Soviet empire.

2533. Hobbs, Herschel H. *The Cosmic Drama; an Exposition of the Book of Revelation.* 1971. Waco, TX: Word Books. 212 p. bibl.

Chapter-by-chapter exposition. Not dogmatic, but most sympathetic to "historical background" interpretation: Revelation addressed to persecuted Christians of Roman Empire, but applicable to all believers in all times. Emphasizes symbolic meanings. Suggests First Horseman is a Parthian.

2534. Hocking, David. *The Final Holocaust: Will Anyone Survive?* 1987. La Mirada, CA: Biola Hour Ministries. 13 p.

Hocking: heads Biola Hour broadcast; minister at Calvary Church, Santa Ana. Pre-trib Rapture (possibly some years prior to Tribulation). Tribulation (70th Week) will be far worse than Nazi Holocaust. Armageddon: world's armies converge in Israel.

2535. _____. *The Coming World Leader: Understanding the Book of Revelation.* 1988. Portland, OR: Multnomah Press. 319 p. bibl.

Coming world leader: Jesus. Antichrist arises from Ten-Nation confederacy to become world dictator; defeated by Christ at Armageddon.

2536. _____. *What Does the Future Hold?* 1991. La Mirada, CA: Biola Univ. / Calvary Communications. 48 p.

Biola Hour Study Guide, based on radio broadcasts; also as cassettes. Pre-trib. Half the world killed during 7-year Tribulation. Israel accepts Antichrist's false promises of peace, only to suffer worse persecution than under Nazis.

2537. Hodges, Zane Clark. *Power to Make War: The Career of the Assyrian Who Will Rule the World.* 1995. Dallas: Redencion Viva. 135 p.

2538. Hoekema, Anthony A. *The*

Bible and the Future. 1982 [1979]. Grand Rapids, MI: William B. Eerdmans. rev. and updated ed. xi, 343 p. bibl. indexes. A-mill. Critical of dispensationalism.

2539. Hoeven, Jan Willem van der. 1994. *Babylon oder Jerusalem: Endzeitliche Verführung: Was kommt auf uns zu?* Neuhausen/Stuttgart: Hänssler. 223 p.

2540. Hoffman, John C. *What In Hell Is Going On? The Coming of the Lord!* 1972. Hollywood: author, and Universal Brotherhood Confederation. 163 p.

In 1952, ET craft carrying God's representatives were shot down when trying to communicate with U.S. government leaders about Second Coming.

2541. Hogue, John. *The Millennium Book of Prophecy.* 1997 [1994]. San Francisco: Harper San Francisco. xvi, 384 p.

"777 visions and predictions from Nostradamus, Edgar Cayce, Gurdjieff, Tamo-san, Madame Blavatsky, the Old and New Testament prophets and 89 others."

2542. _____. *The Last Pope: The Decline and Fall of the Church of Rome: The Prophecies of Saint Malachy for the New Millennium.* 1998. Boston,: Element Books. xx, 403 p., plates illus. bibl. refs., index.

Prophecies attributed to 12th-century St. Malachy: a roster of future Popes, each identified only by ambiguous verse epitaph, up to Judgment Day. Hogue suggests Pius XII (1940s) is Malachy's "Angelic Pastor." John Paul was poisoned for attempting reforms. (Dupont said he was backed by Satanic forces.) New Pope elected ca. 2000: "Glory of the Olive" (De Gloria Olivae), re: Olivet Discourse (End Times). Then Last Pope; Rome utterly destroyed, Judgment Day.

2543. Hollaway, Kevin. *The Final Countdown?* <http://www.ghgcorp.com/contdown.html>

Hollaway: "born-again Black conservative." Antichrist, Tribulation, etc. Second Coming within generation of 1948 Israel reestablishment. Creationism as necessary foundation for prophecy.

2544. Hook, Jack D. *Babylon the*

Great is Falling. 1984. Waterloo, IA: Blessed Hope. 191 p.

2545. Hooley, Robert. *Egypt: Trigger of Armageddon.* 1976. Denver: Liberty Pub. 79 p.

2546. _____. *Russia's Sudden Defeat.* 1978. Denver: Liberty. 136 p.

Hooley: pastor of Faith Bible Chapel (Denver). Russian-led invasion of Israel prophesied in Ezekiel: a "total diabolical plot from the Satanic councils of hell to utterly destroy the Jewish people." Russians allied with East Europeans, Turkey, Middle Eastern nations. Daniel's Four Beasts: lion is Great Britain; Bear is Russia. Invasion occurs "in the seven-year period of tribulation directly preceding the Second Coming." God destroys the invaders. Armageddon consists of seven major campaigns of which this is the second. Also wrote booklets *Armageddon*; *Flee Into the Mountains*; *Antichrist*.

2547. Horan, Neil. *What Will Happen in the Year 2000? Will It Be the End of History?* [London: Father Neil Horan]. Tract. illus.

Also wrote *Why I Believe the Prophecies Made in the Bible* (1998).

2548. Hornock, Gary L. *When in the World Will the World End?* 1997. Pittsburgh: Dorrance Publishing. vi, 34 p. bibl.

2549. [Horsley, Neal]. *Y2K Meltdown Preparation: Self-Defense in Action.* <http://www.christiangallery.com/yrk.htm>

If Y2k problem not stanched with massive government offensive, "it is no exaggeration to say Armageddon could well be on its way." At 2000, total chaos, all services and utilities shut down. Rulers possibly allowing Y2k meltdown in order to establish U.N.-controlled New World Order after total breakdown of society and national governments. No way to avoid this "unless your ticket to the Rapture gets collected before the chaos strikes." Recommends Gary North, Michael Bray. Horsley best known for ChristianGallery's and Creator's Rights party's strident anti-abortion websites calling for "Nuremburg Trials" for abortionists and all who aid them, accusing them of murder and genocide. Anti-evolution; rails against "Grand Conspiracy ... precisely designed to annihilate the idea of the Creator...." Calls for vigilante "army of God" to continue literal "war" against abortionists.

2550. Horta, Al. *Signs Which Point to Jesus' Soon Return.* Tape series. Irvington, NJ: End Time Ministries.

English-Spanish ministry. Also tape *Hastening the Coming of the Lord,* and *Last Call* newsletter. Tongues-speaking, faith-healing, and prosperity gospel ("Financial prosperity is part of God's redemptive plan").

2551. Horton, Stanley M. *Bible Prophecy: Understanding Future Events.* 1995. Springfield, MO: Gospel Publishing House. 110 p. Plus 124 p. leader's guide.

2552. Horvath, James. *He's Coming Soon!* 1995. Orlando, FL: Creation House. 190 p.

"Your complete guide to the End Times" (cover). "Includes the Teachings of: David Yonggi Cho, Kenneth Copeland, Creflo Dollar, Kenneth Hagin, Jack Hayford, Marilyn Hickey, Benny Hinn, T.D. Jakes, Fred Price, Oral Roberts, Lester Sumrall, Bod Yandian, [and] many others." Hinn said elsewhere that 1993 Israeli-PLO accord was predicted in Bible, indicating Second Coming to occur within our lifetime.

2553. Hoskins, Bob. *The Middle East and the Third World War: Ezekiel's Prophecy.* 1982. Miami, FL: Life Pub. 47 p.

2554. _____. *Babylon the Great is Fallen.* Cassette. N.d.? San Jose: Bob Hoskins Middle East Outreach.

2555. *How and When "Heaven's Gate" (the Door to the Physical Kingdom Level Above Human) May Be Entered: An Anthology of Our Materials.* 1998 [1996]. Mill Spring, NC: Wild Flower Press. Various pagings.

Cult led by Marshall Applewhite, former church music director and opera singer. Applewhite and Bonnie Lu Nettles (a nurse), calling themselves Do and Ti (first and last notes of musical scale) or The Two, attracted followers in the 1970s,

lecturing on UFOs. Applewhite resurfaced publicly in 1990s (Nettles d. 1985) warning of imminent collapse of civilization. This book includes Introduction by "Do," manifestoes, lecture transcripts, posters and ads, and articles by Heaven's Gate members (Lvvody, Wknody, Smmody, Jwnody, and other '-ody's'). The Two saw themselves as the Two Witnesses of Rev. 11 who would be assassinated after 1,260 days, then resurrected and transported to heaven 3½ days later. 2,000 years ago the Kingdom of God sent Jesus to Earth, but Luciferians (evil fallen angels, actually extraterrestrial aliens) perverted his message. Heavenly emissary is sent to Earth every other day; since a heavenly day is like a thousand years, two thousand Earth years between visits. Ti (Nettles) was incarnation of God the Father; Do (Applewhite) was Jesus incarnated. Do and Ti also referred to themselves as Admiral and Captain of extraterrestrial mission, with followers as Crew. Influenced by *Star Trek* and *X-Files* TV shows. Taught that Earth was dominated by Luciferian forces. "These 'Luciferian' space races are the humans' GREATEST ENEMY." Earth is "ruled by malevolent adversary races of space aliens" who have enslaved humans, extracting our DNA to produce human-alien hybrids to use for their own bodies, and who compete amongst themselves for Earth's spoils. But Do brings the message that "the Earth's present 'civilization' is about to be recycled—'spaded under.' Its inhabitants are refusing to evolve," instead following "Anti-Christ" by remaining faithful to "mammalian humanism" and Luciferian addiction to sex and procreation (Kingdom of God is sexless and genderless). "The Luciferians are about to be 'recycled' (annihilated) at the same time...." "Once we have disconnected from these bodies and gone back to the Next Level, we will receive new bodies ... issued like 'suits of clothes'.... The shedding of our borrowed human bodies may be required in order to take up our new bodies belonging to the Next World": the Evolutionary Level Far Above Human. The human body ("undercover costume") is like a cocoon or chrysalis from which to emerge with heavenly "glorified body." Only two ways to leave this level: either carried away by spaceship, or by meta-morphosing by "dropping out" of human shell (i.e. suicide). "If their Father does not require this 'disposition' of them, He will take them up into His 'cloud of light' (spacecraft) before such 'laying down of bodies' need occur." But in 1997 Heaven's Gate members decided Comet Hale-Bopp was followed by a UFO coming to trans-port them to heaven, so Do and many members committed suicide.

2556. *How to Prepare for Armaged-don.* 1980. Studio City, CA: World Liter-ature Crusade. 111 p. bibl. refs. Former title *Jesus Christ Solid Rock.*

2557. Howard, Donald R. *World Awakening.* 1988. Green Forest, AR: New Leaf Press. 240 p. illus.

2558. Howard, W. B. *Despatch Magazine.* 1998. <www.cth.com.au/corp/despatch/>

Endtime Ministries (Australia). UFOs, extraterrestrials and Last Days. Vatican masterminding New Age takeover of world. Rapture of believers.

2559. Howe, Ralph R. *End Times: An Exposition of Daniel and the Revelation for the Layman.* 1981 [1977]. Sayre, PA: Bible Lighthouse. 297 p. illus. bibl. Orig-inally Doctorate of Theology thesis.

2560. Howell, Leo. *Mid East Peace Treaty: God's Timetable, Will the Real Anti-Christ Please Stand Up?: Comparison of Daniel and Revelation.* [1990s]. New Al-bany, NY: cassette.

2561. Hoyt, Herman A. SEE ALSO 1910–1970. *Is the United States in Prophecy?* 1977. Winona Lake, IN: BMH Books. 16 p.

2562. Hubbard, David Allan. *The Second Coming.* 1984. Downers Grove, IL: InterVarsity Press. 121 p. Also titled *Jesus Is Coming Back!*

Tribulation, Second Coming, Mil-lennium. (No pre-trib Rapture).

2563. Huckaby, Scott. *End-Time Chronology.* <http://www.mastnet.net/~shucka/end_time.htm>

Huckaby: with Brazos Bend Baptist

Church. Also wrote *Jesus Christ Is Coming Soon,* etc. Computer technology, AIDS, Islam, Mormonism, Satanism, occultism, other spiritual deceptions.

2564. Hudson, Colin. 1994. *Europe and the Beast.* St. Austell: C.G. Publishing. 63 p. illus., maps.

The Common Market.

2565. Huebner, R.A. *The Truth of the Pre-Tribulation Rapture Recovered.* 1976 [1973]. Millington, NJ: Present Truth. 81 p. bibl.

Plymouth Brethren. Argues against D. MacPherson on origin of pre-trib Rap-ture doctrine; claims a Darbyite (Ply-mouth Brethren) origin.

2566. _____. *Future Events: Jacob's Trouble, the Hour of Trial, the Great Tribu-lation, the Day of the Lord, the War of that Great Day of God, the Almighty....* 1990. Morganville. NJ: Present Truth Publish-ers. v, 104 p. bibl. refs., indexes.

2567. Hughes, Dave. *The Secret of the End of the World.* 1998 [1998]. <http://www.newjerusalem.com/worldsend.htm>

"The 'Great Tribulation' *precedes* the Antichrist at the world's end! It will be a sudden astronomic cataclysm, followed by a surprise divine intervention! The reign of the Antichrist, and the end of the world will follow afterward." Comet strikes Earth, then U.S. is knocked out in nuclear war. Antichrist hailed as Jewish Messiah; sudden Second Coming after Pope John Paul's successor. Catholic prophecies.

2568. Hultgren, C. A. *God's Count-down in the 70's?* 1975. Los Angeles: C. A. Hultgren. liii, 116, 24 p.

2569. Humbard, Rex. "*... And Then Shall the End Come.*" N.d. Akron, OH: Rex Humbard World Outreach Ministry. 35 p.

Among "sure signs of the End Time" are increasing earthquakes, famines, pesti-lence. San Francisco devastated by 1906 quake because of its evil ways. Massive 1923 quake in Japan because it is the "most immoral of civilized nations." Rapture "at the close of the six thousand years."

2570. Hunt, Cyril. *Daniel's 70th Week: "According to His Word."* Kil-marnock, Scotland: John Ritchie. 23 p.

Plymouth Brethren.

2571. Hunt, Dave. *Peace, Prosperity, and the Coming Holocaust.* 1983. Eugene, OR: Harvest House. 282 p. bibl. refs.

2572. _____. *End Times Scenario.* [1980s]. Issaquah, WA: Saints Alive in Jesus. cassette.

Influence of occult and secular humanism on Mormons.

2573. _____. *The Mind Invaders.* 1998 [1989]. Eugene, OR: Harvest House. 378 p. Orig. pub. 1989 as *The Archon Conspiracy.*

Fiction. Satan attempts takeover exploiting US and Russian psychic research, UFOs, New Age religions. Parapsychologist invents Psitron device which results in demonic possession. Demons exorcised, but then Jesuit priest Del Sasso becomes channel for The Nine — the Archons — and Satan's agent Antichrist. He attempts to take over leadership at World Congress 666 by demonstrating miraculous powers. Takeover prevented by Russian and American parapsychologists who converted to Christianity, but Antichrist and Satan still at large at end of book.

2574. _____. *Global Peace and the Rise of Antichrist.* 1990. Eugene, OR: Harvest House. 321 p.

Man hailed as world's savior will prove to be the Antichrist.

2575. _____. *How Close Are We?* 1993. Eugene, OR: Harvest House. 323 p.

Pre-Trib. Imminent Secret Rapture; church must be removed, then Tribulation. Bible promises two Comings. Impossibility of evolution. "No Excuse for Unbelief." Revived Roman Empire. Soviet breakup strengthens prophetic scenario. Catholic interpretation of Rev. 12:1 — the woman as Mary — is heretical, a demonic apparition. Millennium, then final rebellion proof of evil in human heart. Exactly 42 months from Antichrist's image in Temple to Second Coming.

2576. _____. *A Woman Rides the Beast: The Roman Catholic Church and the Last Days.* 1994. Eugene, OR; Harvest House. 544 p.

Planned role as One World Church.

Catholicism is fundamentally anti-Jewish, a danger to Israel, God's Chosen.

2577. _____. *A Cup of Trembling.* 1995. Eugene, OR: Harvest House. 458 p. bibl. refs.

Title refers to Jerusalem in the Last Days. Pre-Trib. 69 Weeks: 445 B.C. to Apr. 6, A.D. 32. Mid-East "peace process" is satanic deception — will lead to destruction. Israel given eternally to believing Jews by God. Decries Israeli cozying up to Vatican, which is "Mystery, Babylon." "Vicar of Christ" (Pope) means anti-Christ, literally. Jewish "return" prophesies Last Days. Anti-Semitism satanically inspired; Islam is false religion, inherently anti-Jewish and terrorist. Moslems built Dome of the Rock on Temple site to prevent Jews from rebuilding Temple. Rapture of ca. 200 million believers to occur "very soon," then Antichrist revealed: with believers gone, he becomes world dictator, welcomed as a Messiah, rebuilds Temple, makes people worship his image. 7-year Tribulation. Two Witnesses arise halfway through. Antichrist's pseudo-peace to be exploded by Armageddon. Lutheran a-millennialism is false "Catholic" doctrine. Reconstructionists' "spiritualizing" (non-literal) interpretation is wrong.

2578. Hutchings, Noah W. *War in Heaven.* 1984 [1982]. Oklahoma City, OK: Southwest Radio Church. 43 p. illus.

"Signs in heaven" heralding the End include the space program and the Face on Mars. Extraterrestrials now battling each other in space. Also wrote *The Persian Gulf Crisis and the Final Fall of Babylon* (1991), and *Rapture and Resurrection* (1995), and *The Revived Roman Empire.*

2579. _____. *Europe Is Rising!* [1990]. Oklahoma City: Hearthstone. 116 p.

2580. _____. *Petra in History & Prophecy.* 1991. Oklahoma City, OK: Hearthstone. 160 p., illus.

2581. _____. *Y2k = 666?* 1998. Oklahoma City, OK : Hearthstone Pub. 208 p. illus.

The Y2k "millennial bug" computer problem causes massive shutdowns and disruption in year 2000.

2582. _____. *The Revived Roman*

Empire and the Beast of the Apocolypse. 1993. Oklahoma City, OK: Hearthstone Pub. 149 p. illus., maps.

2583. _____ et al. *Why I Believe These Are the Last Days*. 1990. rev. ed. Oklahoma City: Hearthstone. [ix], 184 p.

Authors: Hutchins, J.R. Church, Carl Baugh, Grant Jeffrey, Robert Lindsted, Emil Gaverluk, Don McAlvany, David Breese, William Sillings.

2584. Hymers, H.L. *Encounters of the Fourth Kind*. 1976. Van Nuys, CA: Bible Voice. 132 p.

Formerly titled *UFOs and Bible Prophecy*. Hymers: leader of Fundamentalist Army.

2585. Ice, Thomas, and Timothy J. Demy. *The Truth About the Last Days Temple*. 1996. Eugene, OR: Harvest House. 46 p. Charts, diagrams. Booklet in *Pocket Prophecy* series. Other titles in series include *The Truth About the Antichrist and His Kingdom*; *The Truth About the Rapture*; *The Truth About the Tribulation*; more titles to come.

Ice: executive director of Pre-Tribulation Research Center (Washington, DC). Rebuilding of Temple in Jerusalem being planned now. It will be desecrated by Antichrist's Abomination of Desolation halfway through Tribulation.

2586. _____. *Fast Facts on Bible Prophecy*. 1997. Eugene, OR: Harvest House. 237 p. illus. bibl. refs.

175 Bible prophecy definitions, chronological outlines of events, information on various interpretations.

2587. _____. *Prophecy Watch*. Eugene, OR: Harvest House. 279 p. illus. bibl. refs., index.

2588. _____, and Timothy J. Demy, eds. *When the Trumpet Sounds*. 1995. Eugene, OR: Harvest House. 471 p. illus bibl. refs.

21 chapters, each by different contributor. Dedicated to Walvoord; foreword by Ryrie. All pre-trib Rapture. Contributors: Ice, Mal Couch, J. Randall Price (Old Test terminology), Larry V. Crutchfield (views of Apostolic Fathers), Floyd Elmore, John S. Feinberg, Edward Hindson, J W Pentecost, Elliott E. Johnson,

Gerald B. Stanton, Walvoord (6,000 year scheme has "no scriptural support"), H. Wayne House, Stanley D. Toussaint, Paul D. Feinberg, John McLean, Gromacki, Jeffrey L. Townsend, Arnold G. Fruchtenbaum, Robert L. Thomas, LaHaye. 1992: LaHaye and Ice organized Pre-Tribulation conference; led to 1994 founding of Pre-Tribulation Research Center (Wash. DC). Ice says no signs for dating Rapture (that would be historicist), but status of Israel indicates now in Last Days: condition of Iraq, Russia, Israel, etc. is "stage-setting" for End.

2589. _____, and Randall Price. *Ready to Rebuild: The Imminent Plan to Rebuild the Last Days Temple*. 1992. Eugene, OR: Harvest House. 288 p. illus. bibl. refs.

Current efforts in Israel by small group of devotees to reinstitute ancient priesthood and sacrifices.

2590. Ingham, Stan. *Understanding Armageddon*. <www.pwmi.org/armagdon.htm>

Prophetic Witness Movement International (England): "proclaiming the pre-millennial Return of Christ."

2591. Inglesby, Eric. *UFOs and the Christian*. 1978. New York: Regency Press. 162 p. bibl.

Inglesby: became Anglican minister. Includes (excerpts?) his earlier *Sins and Saucers* (1955). "Without sound Christian advice, young people in their millions will be led astray by false gods." Inspired by friend's revelatory wartime vision of an atomic war with Satanic demons. Satan tricks humans astray prior to Second Coming so they won't be ready; deludes people into thinking End *isn't* near. "World destruction, in some form or another, is inevitable ..." due to sin. "Spiritual Armageddon." Hitler controlled by Satanic powers, like many UFOs (some are godly). Admires Walter Stein; Steiner. Fatima was a UFO illusion; demonic, as is Lourdes, Catholic church generally. *Close Encounters* film will deceive many. Adamski probably demon-possessed by saucerians. Moonies part of same deception. "Interplanetary body-snatching" (ET abductions). Satan got Book of Enoch excluded from Bible. It describes Watchers (fallen Angels) who corrupted and seduced humans. Praises von Braun's conversion to Christianity.

2592. Intrater, Keith. *From Iraq to Armageddon: Has the Final Showdown Begun?* 1991. Shippensburg, PA: Destiny Image Publishers. 178 p.

2593. _____. *Israel and the Last Days: Interpreting Current Events in the Middle East According to Bible Prophecy.* 1991. Gaithersburg, MD: Tikkun Ministries. video. [See Juster and Intrater].

2594. _____. *The Five Streams: A Prophetic Message on the Unity of the Church in the End Times.* 1995. Shippensburg, PA: Treasure House. vi, 147 p.

2595. Jackson, P. L. 1996. *Coming Up on Seven.* Ada, MI: Mainstream Christian Books. xi, 194 p.

Jackson: engineer. 6,000 Year theory; world is now approaching seventh thousand. Creation to Christ = 4,000 years. Evolution is false, but earth existed long before the Six Day creation of 6,000 years ago (Gap theory creationism). Rapture occurs simultaneously with or very soon after re-start of prophetic clock: 7-year 70th Week. Raptured believers in heaven during Millennium, other survivors on earth for Kingdom.

2596. Jakab, Desi. *"Watchman, What of the Night?" (World War 3).* 1984 [1982]. Nelson, Canada: D. Jakab. 40 p.

2597. James, Edgar C. *Arabs, Oil, & Armageddon.* 1991 [1977]. Chicago: Moody Press. 108 p. illus. maps. bibl. refs.

Arab involvement in Armageddon.

2598. _____. *God, Man, and Disaster.* 1981 Chicago: Moody Press. 127 p. bibl. refs.

James: Moody Bible Institute professor Natural disasters: volcanoes, earthquakes, fires, floods, hailstones and storms, famine, plagues, pestilence. "One day great devastating judgments will be poured out upon this earth." Russia, with Iran, Ethiopia, and Libya, attacks Israel; but is destroyed by hailstones.

2599. _____. *Armageddon and the New World Order.* 1991. Chicago: Moody 120 p. Rev. ed. of *Armageddon!* (1981).

Gulf War as forerunner to Armageddon. Rapture is the "Great Snatch." Russia, Libya, and Iran = Great Northern Confederacy. Antichrist comes from European confederacy, which develops from Common Market. China, Japan, and India = Eastern Confederacy. Armageddon (after Rapture) will result in literal bridle-deep river of blood.

2600. James, Timothy. *The Messiah's Return: Delayed? Fulfilled? Or Double-Fulfillment?* c1982. [Ashtabula, OH: Northeast Bible Inst.] 85 p. bibl.

2601. James, William, ed. *Storming Toward Armageddon: Essays in Apocalypse.* 1992. Green Forest, AR: New Leaf. 335 p.

2602. _____. *The Triumphant Return of Christ: Essays in Apocalypse II.* 1993. Green Forest, AR: New Leaf. 399 p. bibl. refs.

Contributors include Arms (Houston evangelist); Church; John Barela; David Lewis; Brubaker; Breese; J. White. Creationism required for true Christians. Liberal media bias; New Age mysticism, secret global ruling elite. Occult basis of Nazism, and connection with Christian Identity movement. Instability in former Soviet empire leads to Gog-Magog War. Damascus destroyed by Israel, then Russia invades, near start of Tribulation (= Gog Magog; Armageddon). Arms: Antichrist alive now. Babylon religion from Nimrod. U.S. drastically declines in influence, nuclear attack by Russia, then Antichrist, 10 King Europe, treaty with Israel. White: Millennium could start in 7 years. Lewis: Rapture unpredictable, but exactly 1,260 days from Abomination to Second Coming.

2603. _____. *Earth's Final Days: Essays in Apocalypse III.* 1995 [1994]. Green Forest AR: New Leaf. 367 p.

Contributors: Bob Anderson, Sumrall, Breese, Steve Butler, Phil Arms, John Barela, Webber, McAlvany, D.A. Miller, Missler, J.R. Church, J.W. White.

2604. _____. *Foreshocks of Antichrist.* 1997. Eugene, OR: Harvest House. 418 p. bibl., refs.

Nearing time when "earth's final and most terrible tyrant" gains control: Antichrist and Great Tribulation. Believers raptured before this, seven years prior to Armageddon and Second Coming. Overwhelming apostasy; the rise of China. Contributors: James (public relations director); Bob Anderson (sports broadcaster; Take Heed Ministries); David Benoit (Glory Ministries, writes about Satanic rock music); Breese (Christian Destiny); Church; Christopher Corbett (Intl. Christian Media); Feinberg; Froese (Midnight Call); Jeffrey; Berit Kjos (nurse, writes about occult [*Under the Spell of Mother Earth*]); Levitt; Missler; Walvoord; Webber.

2605. _____. *Forewarning: Approaching the Final Battle Between Heaven and Hell.* 1998. Eugene, OR: Harvest House. 385 p. illus. bibl. refs.

Includes Hunt (who criticizes Billy Graham and Paul Crouch of Trinity Broadcasting Network for cozying up to Pope and endorsing Marian apparitions; also Campus Crusade, Promise Keepers); Terry L. Cook of Second Coming Ministries (Mark of Beast technology, biochips); Levitt (Islamic Antichrist to make 7-year treaty with Israel); Hutching (Chinese preparing for overland invasion of Israel); Missler (Russian-Islamic coalition); Ice (denies that pre-trib doctrine is recent innovation); Bill Perkins; Duck; Randall Price; LaHaye; Christopher Corbett; Breese; Walvoord.

2606. _____. *Foreshadows of Wrath and Redemption.* 1999. Eugene, OR: Harvest House. Bibl. refs.

2607. Jean-Gregoire de la Trinite. *Peter Speaks to the World: Universal Encyclical for Christian Unity.* 1993 [1975]. 2nd ed. St. Jovite, Canada: Editions Magnificat, 287 p. Orig. French.

LaSalette apparitions. Infinite Love group. Brother John is the new mystical pope (Gregory XVIII) opposing the Antipope in Rome.

2608. Jeffrey, Grant R. *Armageddon: Appointment with Destiny.* 1990 [1988]. New York: Bantam. 249 p. bibl. illus.

Recovery of Ark of the Covenant, true site of Temple, timetable for invasion of Israel and Armageddon. Oct. 9, 2000: "probable termination date for the 'last days'"— 6,000 year scheme. 606 B.C. + 2,520 Years (Time of Gentiles) of 360–day years = 1878, plus 120 years (as before the Flood) = 1997.

2609. _____. *Messiah: War in the Middle East & the Road to Armageddon.* 1992. rev. ed. New York: Bantam. 347 p.

2610. _____. *Apocalypse: The Coming Judgment of the Nations.* 1994 [1992]. New York: Bantam [orig. Toronto: Frontier Res.] viii, 406 p.

2611. _____. *Prince of Darkness: Antichrist and the New World Order.* 1995 [1994]. New York: Bantam [Toronto: Frontier Research]. 355 p. plates.

2612. _____. *Final Warning.* 1996. Eugene, OR: Harvest House. 508 p. illus. maps, plates, bibl. refs.

"Economic collapse and the coming world government."

2613. _____. *The Mysterious Bible Codes.* 1997. Video. Toronto, Frontier Research.

2614. _____. *The Millennium Meltdown: The Year 2000 Computer Crisis.* 1998. Toronto, Ontario: Frontier Research Publications. 249 p. bibl. refs.

"At midnight, Dec. 31, 1999, millions of computers throughout the world will begin to crash.... Many experts suggest that the Year 2000 Crisis will be the most devastating and expensive problem in history. This crisis may set the stage for the creation of the coming world government that was prophesied to arise in the last days...."

2615. _____, and Angela Elwell Hunt. *Flee the Darkness.* 1998. Nashville: Word Pub. xiii, 363 p.

Novel. Software entrepreneur solves Y2k computer problem by developing a "millennial chip" with code which every person must use in order to buy or sell. Head of newly-formed European Consortium, Adrian Romulus, uses this technology to gain world control, setting the stage for Armageddon.

2616. Jenkins, Jerry B., and Tim F. LaHaye. *The Vanishings* . 1998. Wheaton, IL: Tyndale House. 148 p.

Vol. 1 of *Left Behind—The Kids* series (based on LaHaye and Jenkins' *Left Behind* series). "Four kids face Earth's last days together." The Rapture. Pastor: "Someday, Jesus will return to take his followers to heaven. Those who have received him will disappear in the time it takes to blink your eye. We will disappear right in front of disbelieving people. Won't that be a great day for us and a horrifying one for them?"

2617. _____. *Second Chance.* 1998. Wheaton, IL: Tyndale House. 144 p.

Vol. 2 of *Left Behind—the Kids.*

2618. _____. *Through the Flames.* Wheaton, IL: Tyndale House. 146 p.

Vol. 3 of *Left Behind—the Kids.*

2619. _____. *Facing the Future.* 1998. Wheaton, IL: Tyndale House. 150 p.

Vol. 4 of *Left Behind—the Kids.*

Other vols. in series planned: *Nicolae High,* and *The Underground Paper.*

2620. Jenkins, John Major. *Mayan Cosmogenesis 2012.* video lecture.

From Borderland Sciences. Also wrote *Tzolkin: Visionary Perspectives and Calendar Studies* (1994; Garberville CA: Borderland Sciences Research Foundation; 329 p. bibl. refs., index.)

2621. Jennings, J. Don. *Coming Events.* 1987. Chattanooga: Highland Park Baptist Church Tape Ministry. 12 cassettes.

2622. Jensen, Leland. *The Most Mighty Document.* 1979. Missoula, MT: Baha'i Center.

Jensen: former chiropractor, expelled from main Baha'i group. Founded BUPC (Baha'is Under the Provisions of the Covenant) in 1973 after imprisoned for molesting a patient. Armageddon followed by 20 years of disasters, then God's Millennial Kingdom for 144,000 survivors. Jensen predicted End for April 1980, then later for 1987 (Halley's Comet finally striking Earth after causing a year of catastrophes).

2623. *Great Pyramid of God: Chronological Book of Prophecy in Stone.* 1987. ("Fireside" transcript in <http:www.bahaullah.net/>website.)

6,000 Year Adamic cycle from 4000

B.C. Zoroaster 1000 B.C. Millennium A.D. 2000. Second Coming ministry began 1963: Jensen himself. Muhammad + 1,335 = 1963.

2624. Jeremiah, David. *The Handwriting on the Wall: Secrets from the Prophecies of Daniel.* c1992. Dallas: Word. 248 p. refs.

2625. _____, and C. C. Carlson. *Escape the Coming Night.* 1990. Dallas: Word. xiv, 240 p. bibl. refs.

Pastor at Scott Memorial Baptist Church, El Cajon, CA (affiliated with Institute for Creation Research). Carlson: Hal Lindsey's co-author. "Nothing in the world has experienced to date will equal the grand-scale calamities of earth's final seven years." Pre-mill, pre-trib. After Rapture, during Tribulation, many who are left will seek out Bibles. Two Witnesses = Moses and Elijah. Antichrist , leader of United States of Europe (Revived Roman Empire), indwelt by Satan, assassinated then resurrected. Armageddon = long campaign culminating in final battle. Israel invaded by South and North (Russia), then Russia overruns South. Then Antichrist mobilizes against North, as does East, which marches across dried-up Euphrates. At Second Coming, Christ obliterates all armies.

2626. Jeremiah, James T. *Converging Signs.* 1974. Cedarville, OH: Christian Educational Publications. 31 p. bibl.

Radio messages on Second Advent from Cedarville College (Regular Baptist). End Times catastrophes; apostasy, demon activity, world government. "Never in all church history have so many things said unitedly that the coming of Christ is at hand."

2627. *Jesus Is Coming Soon ... Are You Ready?* <http://www.sunlink.net/~bmurray/>

We're In the Last Days Ministry. America = Babylon. 6,000 Year theory. End within a generation — 40 years — of Israel's 1967 recapture of Jerusalem, thus by 2007. "Terrible Judgment from the Lord is coming upon the whole earth ... INCLUDING THE UNITED STATES.... Turn to Jesus NOW while there's still time...." "In

10 years or less, the Great Tribulation will be over ... at least 50%-70% of the population will be dead." First manifestation of revived Roman Empire is new Euro currency.

2628. *Jesus Is Finally Coming: Are You Ready for the Rapture? October 28, 1992.* 1992. [Downey, CA?] : Mission for the Coming Days. [106] p.

Korean-based Mission for the Coming Days is largest sect of Hyoo-go ("Rapture") or Jong Mal Ron ("end time theory") movement led by Jang Rim Lee. "God has set a day of judgment." Following Rapture, European Union Jan. 1993, Tribulation from 1993 to 1999, Second Coming 1999. "Dear Friends, DO NOT TAKE THE MARK #666 during the Great Tribulation if you miss the Rapture."

2629. *Jesus, the Only Hope for a Dying World.* 1992. Briar Hill, Vic.: Berean Bible Institute: 23 p. Berean series Bible studies. "Reprinted, abridged, from *The Dawn.*"

2630. Jewett, Robert. *Jesus Against the Rapture: Seven Unexpected Prophecies.* c1979. Philadelphia: Westminster. 147 p. bibl.

Critical of fundamentalists who welcome and seek to precipitate Armageddon and End, e.g. "Christians for Israel" campaign. Jesus didn't advocate apocalyptic war, rather he sought to avoid it: this is "unexpected" aspect because it is contrary to much evangelical teaching. Cites many books on the End. Also criticizes Rapture doctrine for its glib assumption that believers will avoid trouble but others will be horribly punished.

2631. Jezreel. *Prophecies of the Day of the Lord.* 1995. New York: Vantage. viii, 53 p.

2632. Jimenez del Oso, Fernando. *El Fin del Mundo.* 1979. Madrid: Ediciones Uve. 161 p.

Occult.

2633. Jina. *Revelation: The End of Time: A Selection of the End Time — Visions and Revelations.* 1978. London: Jina/White Horse Books. 48 p. illus. maps.

Jina also publishes *End Time Report.*

2634. Joab, Father, comp. *Predic-* *tions for the End: A Process Anthology.* 1972. [Toronto: The Process, Church of the Final Judgement.] 80 p. illus.

Process Church of the Final Judgment. Satan, Jehovah, Lucifer, Christ all equal deities. Jesus returns to judge mankind after it destroys itself; Satan (reconciled with Jesus) carries out his judgments. Johnian advocates "Holy Laughter" — though "Demonbuster" at End-Time Deliverance center opposes these signs as Satanic manifestations, Process founded by Robert de Grimston, wrote a sequel to Revelation ("the Time of the End is now"), and *And Now the Judgment* (1970).

2635. Jochmans, J[oey] R. *Rolling Thunder: The Coming Earth Changes.* 1980. Albuquerque: Sun Books. 240 p. illus. index.

Ghost-coauthored Noorbergen's *Secrets of the Lost Races.* Director of Forgotten Ages Research Society. Honorary doctorate from biblical research institute for "antediluvian" research. "Thunders": paraphrase of Revelation seals. Famines, earthquakes; abrupt pole shift in 1998. Highly eclectic: quotes, relies on Nostradamus, Cayce, Jeane Dixon, various psychics. California superquake; then even worse Atlantic seaboard quake submerges New York. Much of Japan also slides into sea. Russia and U.S. vs. China in 1980s nuclear and germ warfare. Antichrist revealed in 1980s, leads Catholic Church. Avatars, muntazars, pyramidology. Four Horsemen: first is imperialism starting 1881, second is 20th century wars, fourth is future war killing over billion people. The few survivors rebuild a better world. Can avert catastrophes by changing consciousness with New Age techniques.

2636. John, Samuel. *The Unholy Betrothal: The Abomination of Desolation.* 1990? Elanthur, Kerala, India: E.S. George. vi, 454 p. illus.

Author: Australian. Orthodox Eastern Church (Malankara, India). Armageddon = 1997 (or maybe 2004). Legal contract between God and Lucifer re: latter's authority over the world. Strong connection between Armageddon and ordination of women, which author denounces as evil abomination. Armageddon also equivalent to Kurukshetra of Mahabharata. Rule of Antichrist is Age of Kali; Hindus say Kali Yuga ends A.D. 2000 Antichrist born 1962, will rule for 3½ years from 1993 to '97. Fall caused by sex, which author is very worried about. Domination by women is End Time sign. Evolution is "perverted theory." "The end is not far away." Now at end of 3rd of Daniel's empires (belly and thigh of image means ruled by sex); 4th (10-Horn) empire will be Iron Age: had its birth with communism, will be either communist, Islamic, or from EEC. Jews are "arch enemies of Christ." Armageddon war is initially between Muslims and Jews, others join. "Man's life here on the earth is meant for six thousand years," then Millennium. 7,000 Year scheme related to 7 heavens and 7 hells. Cain mated with the Devil's "bionic" daughter. Indian Church descended from Lost Tribe of Dan.

2637. Johnian, Mona. *Life in the Millennium.* 1994 [c1992]. South Plainfield, NJ: Bridge Pub. iv, 195 p. 1994 printing "rev & expanded." "Logos book."

Foreword by Van Impe. Pentecostal. Johnian: Christian Teaching and Worship Center, Winchester, MA. We only use 10 percent of our brains, but will use 100 percent Millennium. Curse of Satan lifted first time in 6,000 years. Second Coming, then restoration with gradual perfection during Millennium. "In the last days, Satan-inspired men will have power to perform great miracles." Tribulation before Second Coming, includes rise of Antichrist, invasion of Israel. Antichrist tries to kill all Jews, will be worse than Holocaust. Armageddon will be site of major tourist attraction after Battle. People will talk with all animals like in Eden; horses may tell farmers when soil nitrogen is low, e.g.

2638. _____. *Countdown to the Millennium.* 1994. Bridge / Logos. 242 p.

2639. Johns, Varner Jay. *The Secret Rapture and the Antichrist.* n.d. Redlands, CA: The Quiet Hour. 125 p.

2640. Johnsen, Carsten. *Endtime Drama of the Western World: What Does Biblical Prophecy Say about Modern Communism?* [1970s?]. [Mentone, CA: Schmitke Pr. 93 p. Cover title: *World Communism in Endtime Prophecy.*

"Super-power atheism."

2641. Johnson, Alan F. *Revelation: Bible Study Commentary.* 1983. Grand Rapids, MI: Zondervan. 220 p.

2642. Johnson, Carl G. *Prophecy Made Plain for Times Like These.* 1972. Chicago: Moody. 272 p. bibl.

All members of the invading Northern Confederacy will be killed.

2643. Johnson, Kenneth Rayner. *Armageddon 2000: Countdown to Doomsday?* 1996 [1995].

Rev. ed. London: Creation Books. 248 p. bibl. refs. Pub. 1975 as *The Zarkon Principle* (Everest).

Occult end of world. "The book that goes further than *Chariots of the Gods.*"

2644. Johnson, Kevin. *Look Who's Toast Now!* 1997. Minneapolis: Bethany House. 144 p.

Explains "what the Bible has to say about Christ's return and the end times" for teens. "Ticking toward doomsday — Living on the edge of the end — The bopponauts missed their spaceboat — This means war — The grapes of wrath — All hail King Jesus — Liar, liar, pants on fire — Where are we through all of this? — Are we there yet? — Since the world is spinning down — The end is near, really."

2645. Johnson, Lance B. *The Two Witnesses.* 1994 [1991]. Davis, CA: priv. pub. (Come & See Ministries).

Sixth Seal is WWI; Fifth Trumpet is WWII.

2646. Johnson, Miles Beardsley. *The Setting of the Stage.* 1975. S.l.: Clarion. 160 p. bibl. refs.

I.e., for the Second Coming. Johnson: journalism, history and sociology teacher, California State University, San Luis Obispo. Mostly very long quotes from others, especially Walvoord, also Estep, DeHaan, etc. Pre-mill. Rise of Russia and Return of Jews. Gap (Parenthesis) before 70th Week. Magog = Russia. Revival of Roman Empire.

2647. Johnston, Jerry. *The Last Days of Planet Earth.* 1991. Eugene, OR: Harvest House. 227 p. bibl. refs.

Evangelist: Jerry Johnston Ministries (Overland Park, KS). Insists "the hour of His return is very soon." Pre-trib Rapture. Apocalyptic apostasy, rampant immorality, Satanism. Tribulation: Antichrist sets up Jerusalem-based empire. Half of world's population killed during his reign. Plagues include AIDS and radiation sickness. Israelites flee to Petra at end of Tribulation. America probably destroyed prior to Armageddon. Russia wars with Egyptian coalition, 200 million man Chinese army invades, then all fight against Christ at Second Coming.

2648. Jones, Brian. *Prophets of Fire: The Elijah Message for the End Time.* 1999. Boise: Pacific Press. bibl. refs.

2649. Jones, George Elliott. *The Millennial Issue.* 1996. Nappanee, IN: Baptist Bookshelf. 115 p. Also pub. in Texarkana.

A response to Albert J. Kempin's *Why the Millennial Doctrine Is Not Biblical.* Baptist minister. Pre-mill.

2650. _____. *The Truth Versus Non-Millennial Tradition.* Morrilton, AR: author. 154 p.

Refutes non-millennial allegorical interpretation (esp. of book *Gold Tried in the Fire*). Literal Millennium, with first resurrection before, second after.

2651. Jones, Herbert A. *Until the Day Dawn: or the Drama of the Ages: The Story of the Course of Christianity as it Wends its Way through History from the Time of its Beginnings, its Background in Jewish History, and its Trials and Triumphs Yet to Come, as Revealed by Biblical Prophecies.* 1974. Unpub. MS. 4 vols. Indexes.

2652. Jones, Jim. *The Last Supper/ The Jonestown Massacre.* 1993. Brighton, England: Temple Press. 28 p. [Prev. pub. TOPY].

Transcript of talk just before 1978 mass suicide in Peoples Temple in Guyana. "Final moments of Jonestown community as Jones demands collective suicide of his followers as the ultimate revolutionary act." Jones earlier said Brazil and Califor-

nia were the only safe places in the Last Days, and expected End in 1977.

2653. Jones, Robert Roy. *Covenant with the Beast.* 1997 [1996]. Oklahoma City: Hearthstone. [Orig. M.A. thesis, Univ. Central Okla.]

Novel. Pre-trib. News anchor goes to Israel to report catastrophic natural disasters and supernatural preaching of the Two Witnesses. World leader, the Antichrist, is assassinated, then revives. Arab and Russian armies destroy each other outside Jerusalem, followed by the Rapture.

2654. Jones, Russell Bradley. SEE ALSO 1910–1970. *What, Where, and When is the Millennium?* 1975. Grand Rapids, MI: Baker. 144 p. bibl.

2655. _____. *The Great Tribulation.* 1980. Grand Rapids, MI: Baker. 123 p. bibl. refs.

2656. Jonsson, Carl Olof, and Wolfgang Herbst. *The "Sign" of the Last Days—When?* 1987. Atlanta: Commentary Press. xv, 271 p. illus. bibl. refs.

Last days really started during Christ's lifetime. Date of Second Coming is unknown. Book mostly argues against Jehovah's Witnesses and other date-setters. Denies any increase in famines, earthquakes, pestilence, war.

2657. Jorgensen, Bob. *The Controversy Ended.* [1980s?]. Ashville, NC: Time for Truth. 8 p.

Also wrote *The Impending Conflict* (1980s?).

2658. Joyner, Rick. 1993 [1989]. *The Harvest.* New Kensington, PA: Whitaker House. Orig pub: Pineville, NC: Morning Star.

Joyner received divine visions and can foresee future. "Harvest" is End of the Age. Post-trib. AIDS is one of the judgments against evil; Islam is the greatest anti-Christian power. Rampant Satanic rituals with human sacrifice indicative of End Times evil.

2659. _____. 1997 [1995]. *Epic Battles of the Last Days.* New Kensington, PA: Whitaker House. 224 p., illus. Orig pub. Charlotte, NC: Morning Star.

Last Days strongholds of evil: racism, witchcraft, New Age beliefs, "religious spirit" (pride, heresies, misguided zeal), homosexuality, and abortion (Joyner had vision from God blaming church for abortion because church has aborted its "spiritual seed"). Special role of Cologne, Germany, as the city where Satan corrupted Christianity: birthplace of the misguided Crusades, Christian persecution of Jews, and of communism. Work halted on Cologne Cathedral 1560– 1842 due to pact with Satan, but resumed when Marx moved away. But Cologne also birthplace of Zionism. Uses America's Gulf War strategy as metaphor for dealing with End Times. Two follow-up vols. planned.

2660. ____. *Final Quest*. 1996. Charlotte, NC: Morning Star. 158 p. Illus.

The vision received by Joyner of the Last Battle between Good and Evil. Shorter version pub. in *Morning Star Journal* as *The Hordes of Hell are Marching*.

2661. Judson, Jeremiah. *The End Times Illustrated*. 1993. priv pub. (Glen Mills, PA: End Times Ministries). vii, 271 p. index, bibl., illus., drawings, charts.

Judson: religious training but also much knowledge through private Bible study and "listening to the voice of the Lord in the stillness of His presence." Naive amateurish exposition; drawings are very crude, seven churches as seven church ages up to present.

2662. Juster, Dan, and Keith Intrater. *Israel, the Church and the Last Days*. 1990. Shippensburg, PA: Destiny Image. 221 p. chart, bibl. refs.

Authors both Maryland pastors affiliated. with "Beth Messiah, Tikkun Ministries" (Gaithersburg, MD): restorationist organization committed to salvation of Israel. Non-dispensational, "historic" pre-mill (pre-1830, like Ladd), post-trib. Pentecostal; signs, miracles, healings, exorcisms. Companion vol.: *The Book of Revelation, the Passover Key*. Kingdom of God is here already, but only partially. Kingdom not postponed (as in dispensationalism); will increase gradually until climax. Saved remnant of Israel, who acknowledge "Yeshua" as Messiah. Postmills supporters include Ern Baxter, Dennis Peacock (Coalition for Traditional Val-

ues), Bob Weiner (but now wavering). "Critical mass" achieved in this age, judgment and salvation explode. "When Israel confesses the Messiah, *BOOM!*" Pre-mill, but victory of Body of Believers, who help usher in the Coming. World will get more evil, but Restored Church also grows, with messianic revival in Israel. Worldwide destruction, also outpouring of miracles. God will turn back assault from North, then great revival and Tribulation, then later Armageddon. Lord will "consume the wicked in a horrible annihilation" manifested as nuclear holocaust. As Jews about to be destroyed by invaders, Lord intervenes: "Yeshua will land like an Israeli paratrooper" with His saintly army. All flesh melts in Fire of God. Resurrection and glorification of the living. Millennium: resurrected saints rule over others. Probable scenario: after miraculous victory over Russia-Arab invasion, Orthodox Jews declare war hero the Messiah; he becomes world figure; many Gentiles convert to Judaism under relaxed Noachide ordinances. Jewish Yeshua believers persecuted intensely. Satanic regime emerges in Europe. Combined Euro-Russo-Arab forces attack; nuclear devastation. Tribulation Body of Believers immune to Revelation plagues, but many are martyred. Those born during Millennium will decide whether they are with or against God.

2663. Kah, Gary. *En Route to Global Occupation*. 1992. Lafayette, LA: Huntington House. 224 p.

New Age, Freemasonry, Omega point. Kah: former government operative invited to help one-world efforts.

2664. ____. *The Demonic Roots of Globalism*. 1995. Lafayette, LA: Huntington House. vi, 208 p. bibl. refs., index.

2665. Kaiser, Walter C. *Back Toward the Future: Hints for Interpreting Biblical Prophecy*. 1989. Grand Rapids, MI: Baker Book House. 152 p. bibl. index.

Prof. and dean: Trinity Evangelical Divinity School (Deerfield, IL). Pre-mill. Relies largely on Girdlestone 1901. Some prophecies conditional or sequentially fulfilled. Dependent on past: Creation, Eden, Flood (fulfillments refer to these past conditions). Importance of relating prophecies to rest of Bible. Kaiser describes tension between *now* and *not yet* referents of prophecies, but doesn't agree with "double sense" theory (hidden meaning to be decoded later).

2666. Kanzlemar, Joseph. *The End of the Age and Beyond: A Commentary on Revelation.* 1982. Marion, IN: Wesley Press. 190 p. illus.

2667. Karleen, Paul S. *The Pre-Wrath Rapture of the Church: Is it Biblical?* 1991. Langhorne, PA: BF Press. 102 p. bibl. refs indexes.

Consulting ed. for New Scofield Study Bible. Refutation of Rosenthal's "pre-wrath" theory. Says it's unbiblical, and wrong logically, theologically, and linguistically.

2668. Katterjohn, Arthur D., and Mark Fackler. *The Tribulation People.* 1975. Carol Stream, IL: Creation House. 137 p. bibl.

Post-trib. "First rapture, then wrath." Antichrist will appear deceptively saintly, not demonic.

2669. _____. *Lord, When?* 1976. Carol Stream, IL: Creation House. 87 p.

2670. Kay, Tom. *When the Comet Runs: Prophecies for the New Millennium.* 1977. Charlottesville, VA: Hampton Roads Pub. 239 p. bibl. refs. index.

Spectacular comet as harbinger of the End. Cites many Christian, occult and New Age prophets with similar predictions of cosmic signs and catastrophes.

2671. Kemp, Karl. *The Mid-Week Rapture: A Verse-by-Verse Study of Key Prophetic Passages.* 1991. Shippensburg PA: Companion Press. 360 p. illus. bibl. refs. fold-out chart.

Christians saved from Day of Wrath. 70th week = 7 years. Antichrist covenant with Israel. Abomination of Desolation near end 3½ years, then "super evil" reign of Antichrist next 3½ years. Rapture mid-week, Christ then begins rule over earth. Babylon destroyed, Bowls of wrath in 2nd half, Jewish remnant purified with travail. Christ destroys Antichrist's armies end of 70th week, Millennium begins. Two Witnesses killed, resurrected (raptured with others). 6th Trumpet initiates savage nuclear war, right after Abomination and before Mid-Week. 7th Trumpet: Mid-Week point. Second Coming "very soon, probably before the end of this century." But 70th Week probably hasn't started yet (3½ years prior to Second Coming).

2672. Kennedy, D. James. *Messiah: Prophecies Fulfilled.* n.d. Ft. Lauderdale, FL: Coral Ridge Ministries. 120 p.

Televangelist; Presbyterian. "God's Intricate Timetable": 70 Weeks prophecy. 69 Weeks from 458 B.C. to A.D. 26.

2673. Kennedy, Lawrence. *Foundations of Order: Understanding the Need for Biblical Church Government in the Last Days.* 1998. Carrollton, TX: North Church. vii, 68 p. illus.

2674. Kik, Jacob Marcellus. *The Eschatology of Victory.* 1978 [1971]. Phillipsburg, NJ: Presbyterian and Reformed. ix, 268 p. bibl. refs

Foreword by R. Rushdoony. Postmill. Tribulation was the destruction of Jerusalem in A.D. 70, and the 70 Weeks were continuous. Darkening of the sun and stars was extinguishing of the Jewish nation.

2675. Killian, Greg. *The Watchman.* <http://members.aol.com/gkilli/home/>

Refutes pre-trib Rapture. Unseen Planet X — the 12th Planet of the Sumerians (and of Zechariah Sitchin's books) — will trigger the Tribulation.

2676. Kimball, William R. *What the Bible Says about the Great Tribulation.* 1984. Phillipsburg, NJ: Presbyterian and Reformed. x, 291 p. illus. bibl. indexes. Orig. pub. 1983 Joplin, MO: College Press.

2677. _____. *The Rapture: A Question of Timing.* c1985. Joplin, MO: College Press. 193 p. bibl. index.

2678. Kincheloe, Raymond McFarland. *A Personal Adventure in Prophecy: Understanding Revelation.* 1974. Wheaton IL: Tyndale House. x, 214 p. bibl.

Pre-mill, "modified-futuristic" (generally dispensational). Now in sixth (Philadelphian) of seven church ages; seventh is apostate Tribulation church following Rapture. Overlapping chronology of Revelation. Extended Rapture, during first half of Tribulation. Woman clothed in sun = visible church; the Man-Child = invisible church. Russia and Egypt attack Israel, God destroys them at Armageddon, then Antichrist, leader of European Ten Kingdoms, becomes world ruler.

2679. King, Geoffrey R. *The End of the World*. 1971. Eastbourne, England: Prophetic Witness. 1971. 15 p. Prophetic Witness Manual No. 15.

Other pamphlets in series by Tatford, Lockyer, Maybin, Ashmore. Rapture, 7-year Tribulation, Millennium. Final revolt after Millennium: Christ reigns from Jerusalem, but population increases tremendously and many on world periphery only feign obedience.

2680. Kinman, Dwight L. *The World's Last Dictator*. 1995 [1993]. Woodburn, OR: Solid Rock Books. 322 p. illus. bibl., notes.

2nd ed. "updated with explosive new information."

2681. Kirban, Salem. SEE ALSO 1910–1970. *I Predict*. 1975 [1970]. Iowa Falls, IA: Riverside Book and Bible House. 144 p. illus.

Orig. priv pub., Huntingdon Valley PA. "THE BOOK THAT DARES TO REVEAL THE DISASTERS OF THE FUTURE!"

2682. _____. *1000*. 1973. Huntingdon Valley, PA / Iowa Falls, IA: Riverside Book and Bible House. 185 p. plates illus. maps, charts, music.

The sequel to *666*. Some eds. include both works.

2683. _____. *20 Reasons Why This Present Earth May Not Last Another 20 Years*. 1973. Huntingdon Valley, PA: [author]. 191 p. illus.

Stresses he "carefully culls" thousands of periodicals for items that can be interpreted as prophetic fulfillment. Any-moment Rapture. Antichrist = Beast from Sea = Little Horn — sudden sensational rise to power, hailed as Savior by Europe, U.S., Israel. Antichrist rules European Confederacy, possibly including the U.S. False Prophet = religious ruler, partner with Antichrist. Satanic miracle of statue makes statue talk, come to life. Kirban cites population pressure, pollution, famine, moral decay, other signs in news of impending crisis. Includes many news clippings (literally). Many predictions: including laws in U.S. limiting families to two children by 1980, 3-day work week by 1985, legalization of marijuana by 1977, nuclear bomb exploded by terrorists by 1982, no school by 2000 (children learn through TV receivers "built into their heads"), cloned human by 1989, churches taxed by 1979, Russia dominates Mid-East oil by 1978, tattoo number system for identification by 1984, UFOs solved by 1982. etc. Notes many of his past predictions fulfilled even quicker than he expected. Horses during Russia attack of Israel and Armageddon. At end of Tribulation, four blocs collide at Armageddon: Arab, Russian (North), United Europe, Far East. Arab Confederation moves against Antichrist's European Confederation, now based in Jerusalem. Russian confederacy joins against Antichrist. Then 200 million Chinese attack Israel to oppose European confederacy. Then Second Coming: all forces unite to oppose Christ.

2684. _____. *Kissinger: Man of Peace?* 1974. Huntingdon Valley, PA: Salem Kirban. 64 p., illus.

Kissinger as Antichrist.

2685. _____. *The Day Israel Dies!* 1975. Old Tappan, NJ: F. H. Revell. 233 p.

2686. _____. *Day of Judgment: A Cantata of the Second Coming, the Tribulation Period and the Battle of Armageddon*. 1975. audiocassette. Huntingdon Valley, PA: Salem Kirban.

The Second Coming Choir. Janet C. Hutchinson. Based on book *666*. Kirban also did "photo commentary" for Lowell Hart's *Satan's Music Exposed* (1980) on danger of rock and jungle-rhythm music.

2687. _____. *Countdown to Rapture*. 1977. Huntingdon Valley, PA: Salem Kirban, Inc. 189 p. illus.

Teheran, Iran, may be new Babylon of Revelation. Rapture in 1980, 1984, or 2000. Antichrist will be hailed as bringer of peace. Chinese-Japanese army of 200 million at Armageddon versus Antichrist's forces.

2688. _____. *The Rise of the Antichrist.* 1978. Huntingdon Valley, PA: Salem Kirban, Inc. 202 p, [16].

"We are already living in the Age of Antichrist!" Within next five years: mind programming, design your own child (genetic supermarket); within ten years: "your brain will be controlled by outside sources! Your memory will be transferred into a live embryo." Appendix "How to Identify Antichrist" Also wrote *Satan's Mark Exposed* (1978) and did photos for *Satan's Music Exposed* (1980).

2689. _____. *What in the World Will Happen Next? Answers to Life's Four Most Important Questions: What Is Life! Rapture! Hell! Heaven!* 1994. Huntingdon Valley, PA: Salem Kirban. 320 p. illus.

2690. Kirkpatrick, George. *What Time Is It?* 1995. Chesterville, OH: New Foundation.

"The Seventh Day rest is directly ahead of us." Kirkpatrick: runs New Foundations ministry with wife Jeannie.

2691. _____. *Mystery Babylon Revealed.* 1999. Chesterville, OH: New Foundations.

US = Babylon, Whore. U.S. government = Antichrist. 4 kingdoms of Statue (ancient empires) different from 4 beasts: lion=England, eagle=U.S., bear=Russia, Leopard = NATO, 10 horns + little + 3 (14 total). NATO to turn on and defeat US. Beast from Sea = U.N. U.S. to be utterly devastated by Russian-led NATO war, then by God. No Rapture: believers must flee and be "overcomers," surviving to rule with God during Millennium. Also wrote *God's Prophecy in Stone* (1996): the Great Pyramid as God's end-time sign. "We are coming to the end of the sixth-seventh of the Horizontal Passage, or to the end of the sixth one thousandth year day": Kingdom Age next.

2692. Kistler, Don, ed. *The Arithmetic of God.* Vol 1. 1976. 3rd ed. Kings Mountain, NC: Arithmetic of God. 187 p.

Mathematical structure of the Bible. "Words can be changed and given private interpretation, but numbers remain the same in all languages ..." the "infallible proof" of God. Kistler: a completed Jew.

Wrote "what the audible voice of God revealed to him." Kistler is "scribe of this revelation hid since the foundation of the world for this end-time generation."

2693. Kleier, Glenn. *The Last Day.* 1997. New York: Warner. 484 p.

Novel. Meteor destroys secret Israeli bioengineering facility Dec. 25, 1999. On Jan. 1, 2000, the sole survivor announces she is Jeza the Messiah. Imitating Christ, she performs miracles and demands end of all institutionalized religion. The Pope and others denounce her as Antichrist. World threatened by Armageddon: war between pro- and anti-Jeza millenarians (MeGoG and GoG).

2694. Klein, Kenneth. *The False Prophet.* 1992. Eugene, OR: Winterhaven. 224 p. bibl. refs., index.

Daniel saw last form of Beast; John saw whole historical panorama. Beast = one-world government under Satan, nearing completion now. Mystery Babylon — Harlot = world religion descended from Nimrod's Babylon. Ten Confederated Kings follow Antichrist, 1st Beast. Seven heads of Beast = Egypt, Assyria, Babylonia, Medo-Persia, Greece, Rome, and Britain. Since Napoleonic Wars, all wars orchestrated by International Bankers. False Prophet, agent of Antichrist, resurrects the 7th head (slain by WWII), as Common Market. False Prophet is 2nd Beast, the Two-Nation confederacy (U.K. and U.S.) Illuminati, Freemasonry, Communists: globalist conspirators who fomented American wars and Russian Revolution. Cites many conspiracy theorists, including Nesta Webster, J. Robinson (*Proofs of Conspiracy* 1978), and John Birch Society authors. Jerusalem will be world capital by A.D. 2000. Image of Beast = TV. Fire called down = bombs. 666 used by laser scanning systems.

2695. Knechtle, Emilio B., and Charles J. Sohlmann. *Christ's Message to the Last Generation.* 1997 [1971]. Brushton, NY: TEACH Services. 160 p.

Seventh-day Adventist. Two-Horn Beast (Rev. 13:11) = lamb or bison, representing America. First Beast = Papacy: 1,260 years to 1798.

2696. Knight, George. *Millennial Fever and the End of the World: A Study of Millerite Adventism.* 1993. Boise, ID: Pacific Press. 384 p.

2697. Kolberg, Bruno. *The Final Tribulation—Days of Vengeance.* 1998 [1993]. Carindale, Australia: B. Kolberg. xii, 291 p.

2698. Kolenda, E. J. *Armageddon Now!* 1979. Marked Tree, AZ; Ontario, Canada: E.J. Kolenda ; G. Erauw. 63 p.

"On the road of no return: Armageddon now! After 1980–1985, then what?"

2699. Kolosimo, Caterina. *Sopravviveremo al 1982?* 1979. Milan: A. Mondadori. 193 p. bibl. refs.

Occult. Kolosimo: wife of Peter Kolosimo (ancient astronaut promoter). 1982 "Jupiter effect" (planets all align to cause catastrophic disruption of Earth), Nostradamus, Catholic seers, Hörbiger, André Barbault.

2700. Koresh, David. *The Decoded Message of the Seven Seals of the Book of Revelation.* 1993. s.l.: s.n. various pagings.

Koresh: born Vernon Howell; leader of Branch Davidians. Text of Koresh's exegesis, produced by Phillip Arnold and James Tabor from Koresh's computer disks. Koresh believed the Tribulation had started, and that he was the Lamb of God of the Branch of David who would open the Seven Seals to bring in the Second Coming. After federal agents first attacked the Waco, TX, compound in 1993, Koresh began to believe the standoff could be the "little season" after the Fifth Seal, and was persuaded to write down his interpretation of the Seals. Before he finished the government attacked again, and most inside were killed in the resulting fire. Text also included in Tabor and Gallagher's *Why Waco?* (1995). See also *Seven Seals Revelation* (1998).

2701. Kortner, Ulrich H.J. *The End of the World: A Theological Interpretation.* 1995. Louisville, KY: John Knox Press. bibl. refs.

2702. Kosinski, D.S. *The Alexandria Letters: The Final Prophecies of the*

20th Century. c1985. Chicago: Devonshire. 135 p.

2703. Kraak, Willem. *El Fin del Mundo, Esta Muy Cerca?: Un Pensiamento Evangelico en Tiempo Oportuno Basado en las Profecias Biblicas.* 1973. Malaga: Biblioteca Biblica. 63 p.

2704. Kraut, Ogden ["compiler"]. *Visions of the Latter Days.* 1983. Salt Lake City: Pioneer. 148 p.

2705. ____. *Prophecies of the Latter Days.*

Mormon. Also wrote *Jesus was Married; Adam, Who Is He?; The White Horse Prophecy; Polygamy in the Bible; Mysteries of Creation.*

2706. Kremers, Marion Fleming. *God Intervenes in the Middle East: The God of Precision Timing in History.* 1992. Shippensburg PA: Companion Press. 353 p. index.

6,000 year chronology of earth history, importance of Jewish feasts for chronology, imminent Second Coming.

2707. Krupp, Nate. *The Omega Generation?* 1977. Harrison, AR: New Leaf. 213, [15] p. illus., bibl.

"We are living in that period of time that the bible calls 'the last days.'" Increasing communist infiltration will lead to coming totalitarian rule and one-world government. Doesn't take position on Rapture timing (pre-, mid-, or post-trib), but it must occur soon. Quotes 1973 vision of Roxanne Brant of Tribulation beginning within a few years. 1948 + 40 = 1988 for End, thus Tribulation may begin in 1981. Urges believers to become self-sufficient in food and shelter.

2708. ____. *The Church Triumphant at the End of the Age: Characterized by Revival, Restoration, Unity, World Evangelization, and Persecution.* 1988. Shippensburg, PA: Destiny Image. xviii, 368 p. illus., maps.

2709. "Kryon." *The End Times, New Information for Personal Peace: Channeled Teachings Given in Love.* 1994 (rev). Del Mar, CA: Kryon Writings. c, 172 p.

Channeled by Lee Carroll. Kryon: "magnetic master" who "created the magnetic grid system of your planet." Performed third "major global adjustment" in 1989, to bring about loving harmonious future.

2710. Kuhlman, Kathryn. *Distress of Nations.* [1970s]. Pittsburgh: Kathryn Kuhlman Foundation. Cassette, from radio broadcast.

2711. _____. *Famine.* [1970s]. 3 cassettes. Pittsburgh: Kathryn Kuhlman Foundation.

From radio broadcasts.

2712. Ladd, George. SEE ALSO 1910–1970 *Last Things.* Grand Rapids, MI: Eerdmans. 119 p.

Ladd: professor at Fuller Theological Seminary. Disagrees with standard dispensational pre-mill scenario; said returned Israel and rebuilt Temple are not to be taken literally. Prefers older (non-dispensational or "historic") pre-millennialism.

2713. LaHaye, Tim. *Beginning of the End.* 1972. Tyndale House. 173 p. illus., bibl. refs. Rev. ed 1991. xvii, 198 p.

LaHaye: Baptist minister; founded Christian Heritage College with creationist Henry Morris. "Discussion Guide" booklet 1973; 32 p. Pre-trib pre-mill. "Amazing fulfillment of prophecies tell earth's future" (1972, 1981 subtitle). Our generation is probably the last. "This generation" probably means those alive during World War One. "There is no question that we are living in the last days." "Almighty God is going to destroy Russia's massive armies by his supernatural power.... Russia will be almost entirely destroyed." Taking of Jerusalem during 1967 Six Day War proved everything is now ready for the Rapture.

2714. _____. *Revelation: Illustrated and Made Plain.* 1975 [1973]. Grand Rapids, MI: Lamplighter Books (Zondervan). 323, [3] p. illus.

2715. _____. *Coming Peace in the Middle East.* 1984. Grand Rapids, MI: Zondervan. 189 p. illus. maps.

Russia has to knock out Israel in order to take on U.S. in order to dominate world. "God's Original Land Grant to Israel" includes Lebanon, part of Arabia, most of Jordan, Syria, Iraq.

2716. _____. *How to Study Bible Prophecy for Yourself.* 1990. Eugene, OR: Harvest House. 203 p. illus.

2717. _____. *No Fear of the Storm.* 1992. Sisters, OR: Multnomah [Questar]. 252 p. illus. bibl.refs. 1998 ed. titled *Rapture: Under Attack.*

"Why Christians will escape *all* the Tribulation." Pre-trib Rapture: millions of Christians — all who have accepted Christ — suddenly disappear. Tribulation immediately afterwards: "The day is coming when the worst traumas in history will be eclipsed by a seven-year period that will be far more terrifying than anything man can imagine." Refutes criticisms of pre-trib view. Russia must attack soon because due to weakening caused by Soviet breakup it won't be able to do so in a few years.

2718. _____, and Jerry B. Jenkins. *Left Behind: A Novel of the Earth's Last Days.* 1995. Wheaton, IL: Tyndale House. 468 p.

The Rapture. In the year previous to Rapture, Russia mounted massive invasion of Israel with Libyan, Iranian and Ethiopian allies; invading forces obliterated by Israelis and God. Nicolae Carpathia, a Romanian politician of Italian descent, becomes U.N. leader. Seven Year Tribulation: 21 months of Seal judgments, 21 months of Trumpets, 42 months (3½ years) of Vials.

2719. _____, *Tribulation Force.* 1996. Wheaton IL: Tyndale. x, 450 p.

Second novel in *Left Behind* series. After the Rapture, several people join to form the "Tribulation Force" realizing that all remaining humans must come to Christ or be lost. Carpathia appears as a world Savior, but is really Antichrist, and uses hypnotic brainwashing and supernatural tricks to promote his rule. Establishes capital at (New) Babylon, disarms all nations, establishes one-world religion. New nonorthodox Pope was raptured, but successor (Bishop of Cincinnati) becomes head of world religion (Pontifex Maximus). Tribulation Force realizes Tribulation will start when Carpathia signs 7-year treaty with Israel: horrific seal judgments, ¾ world population killed. Elijah and Moses, the Two Witnesses, prophesy in Jerusalem.

2720-2733   *1970 On*   264   LaHaye

Rabbi friend reveals his lifelong study proves that Christ was indeed the Messiah (not Carpathia); cites Edersheim's 109 messianic prophecies. Egypt, Britain, and U.S. militias revolt against Antichrist government.

2720. _____. *Nicolae: The Rise of Antichrist.* 1997. Wheaton, IL: Tyndale House. xiii, 417 p.

Third novel in *Left Behind* series.

2721. _____. *Soul Harvest: The World Takes Sides.* 1998. Wheaton, IL: Tyndale House. x, 426 p.

Fourth novel in *Left Behind* series.

2722. _____. *Apollyon: The Destroyer is Unleashed.* 1999. Wheaton, IL: Tyndale House Publishers, ix, 403 p.

Fifth novel in *Left Behind* series. Believers, who use Internet to communicate, gather in Jerusalem, leading to showdown with Antichrist Apollyn is leader of demon locusts. Next two titles in series: *Assassin* and *The Glorious Appearing.* 12 planned.

2723. Lake, Eileen. *Arion's Utopia from Future.* 1997. Japan: Tarna.

In Japanese. Apocalypse and Aquarius too. Book of Revelation, but also UFOs, Atlantis, telepathy, and time travel. "Fire Baptism": 1945 atomic bombs on Japan. "Water Baptism" (huge Flood) in 1999 from pole shift, cosmic alignment. 144,000 survive, some live inside Earth. Kingdom of God follows, governed by "Eileenism."

2724. Lalonde, Peter. *One World Under Antichrist.* 1991. Eugene, OR: Harvest House. 182 p. 307 p. bibl. refs.

2725. _____, and Patti Lalonde. *Left Behind.* 1995. Eugene, OR: Harvest House. 182 p. bibl. refs.

Also title of 1994 video from "This Week in Bible Prophecy" TV program (hosted by Peter and Paul Lalonde).

2726. _____. *The Edge of Time.* 1997. Eugene, OR: Harvest House. 340, [12] p. bibl. refs.

2727. _____, and Paul Lalonde. *The Mark of the Beast.* 1994. Eugene, OR: Harvest House. 202 p. bibl. refs.

"Your Money, Computers, and the End of the World." Electronic identification and surveillance systems, coming cashless economy, computerized financial management. Armageddon soon. Also video (1992), and *Mark of the Beast II.*

2728. _____. *2000 A.D.: Are You Ready? How New Technologies and Lightning-Fast Changes are Opening the Door for Satan and His Plan for the End of the World.* 1997. Nashville: Thomas Nelson. ix, 192 p.

"Our Lord is going to return very, very soon": the Rapture. Satan will explain this disappearance of millions with his false gospel of extraterrestrial and paranormal phenomena, and is preparing for it by exposing us to *Star Trek*, the *X-Files*, and the like. Rapture date can't be known precisely because Creation date is not known precisely.

2729. _____. *Apocalypse: Caught in the Eye of the Storm.* 1998. Niagara Falls, NY: This Week in Bible Prophecy. 270 p.

Novelization of Jack van Impe's film of same title (screenplay by Lalonde). President of European Union, Franco Macalousso, is hailed as true Messiah when he appears to bring world peace. Christian believers then persecuted. Armies from sixty nations converge on Armageddon. Just as nuclear weapons launch worldwide, true believers are raptured to heaven. Reporter digs up his father's grave to see if he's been raptured.

2730. Lam, Joseph. *China: The Last Superpower.* 1996. Green Forest, AZ: New Leaf Press. 240 p.

2731. Lambert, Lance. *Battle for Israel.* 1975. Wheaton, IL: Tyndale House. Rev. Brit. ed. 1976 (Eastbourne, England: Kingsway). U.S. ed. titled *Israel, a Secret Documentary.*

2732. Lansdowne, Janet E. *The End of the Days.* 1972. s.l.: s.n., Association of the Covenant People. 70 p. bibl.

2733. LaRondelle, Hans K. *Chariots of Salvation: The Biblical Drama of Armageddon.* 1987. Washington, D.C.: Review and Herald. 192 p. illus. index.

Seventh-day Adventist. Elijah message of the Last Days to worship the Creator on Seventh-day Sabbath. Mt. Carmel, where Elijah defeated false prophets of

Baal, overlooks Megiddo. Modern Babylon = apostate religious-political totalitarianism.

2734. _____. *Good News about Armageddon*. 1990. Washington, D.C.: Review and Herald. bibl. refs.

Critical of dispensationalism.

2735. Larson, Anthony E. *And There Shall Be a New Heaven and a New Earth*. 1986. Orem, UT: Zedek. 154 p. illus.

2736. _____. *And the Earth Shall Reel To and Fro*. c1983. Orem, UT: Zedek Books. 179 p. bibl.refs.

Vol 2 of Prophecy Trilogy. Mormon

2737. Larson, Kenneth. *The Trumpet of Zion: Measures of the Earth, the Day of the Lord, and the Celestial New Jerusalem*. 1995. Los Angeles: author. xli, 494 p. illus. bibl. refs.

UFOs, Pyramidology.

2738. LaSelle, David P. *The Final Deception*. <http://www.angelfire.com/ak2/TheFinalDeception/

Novel. "Written in the hope that more people will seek the LORD and not be deceived in the end times." Before creation of Adam, Satan ruled from Mars; that world, with the dinosaurs, was destroyed. Flying saucers are Satan's deception. Post-trib.

2739. LaSor, William Sanford. *The Truth About Armageddon: What the Bible Says About the End Times*. 1982. Grand Rapids, MI: Baker. xiii, 226 p. indexes bibl. Also pub. 1982 (Harper and Row).

Emeritus professor at Fuller Theological Seminary; philologist. Thoughtful, scholarly. Pre-mill but doesn't accept whole dispensational scenario. Many biblical refs., "additional reading" lists. Stresses need to refer to whole Bible, not just selected proof texts. Concerned about proper understanding of eschatological terms. "End" as end of present age, not of existence; prior to "age to come." Confusion regarding interpretation of "People of God," "present age," and other terms. Believes Satan is superhuman individual who attacks full-scale during the Tribulation; wrath of God then poured out. But not certain about sequence of events. Ar-

mageddon = final conflict, centered around Jerusalem, ended by Second Coming and Millennium. Points out exegetical problems while accepting outline of pre-mill interpretation. Faithful resurrected for Millennium; others raised at end of Millennium for Judgment.

2740. *The Last Call: The Preparation of the Bride for the Rapture of the Church*. 1994. Lannon, WI: Clarion Call. 263 p.

Companion vol. to *Prophecies of the End-Times*.

2741. *Lastdays Ministry*. <http://www.clark.net/pub/apettey/lastday1.html>

Post-trib. Refutes "the false doctrine of the pre-tribulation rapture and [shows] how to be prepared to face the coming tribulation."

2742. Laurie, Greg. *Spiritual Survival in the Last Days*. 1982. Eugene, OR: Harvest House. 142 p. Formerly titled *Occupy Till I Come*.

Former Jesus People hippie, now pastor at Harvest Christ Fellowship (Riverside, CA). Tribulation to bring cataclysmic judgment to earth. Russia will invade Israel. Noah as last-days believer prior to destruction by Flood — we must act like him. 10-Nation European confederacy led by Antichrist will be world's strongest power. U.S. may be part of 10 Nations, or might lose nuclear war with Russia, or may be depleted by Rapture if revival is strong enough.

2743. "Lawrence, Troy" [Darick T. Evenson]. 1991. *New Age Messiah Identified: Who is Lord Maitreya? Tara Center's "Mystery Man" Alive and Living in London*. Lafayette, LA: Huntington House. v, 196 p.

Maitreya, the Hindu, Buddhist, Islamic, Jewish and Christian Messiah combined is London-based Pakistani Rahmat Ahmad.

2744. Laxton, William, David A. Dean, Oral Collins, and Barton Freeman. *Apocalyptic and Its Numbers*. 1980. Lenox MA: Berkshire Christian College. 144 p. bibl. refs.

Laxton: "Introduction"; Dean: "Argumentation for the 1843 Date"; Collins: "Is There a Mysterious Age Parenthesis in Biblical Prophecy?"; Barton: "The Mysterious Numbers of Biblical Literature."

2745. Leamen, Bob. *Armageddon: Doomsday in Our Lifetime?* 1986. Richmond VA: Greenhouse. 108 p. plates, illus. Photog. by Michael Coyne.

Survivalism.

2746. Lee, Francis Nigel. *Will Christ or Satan Win This World?: Or, the Increasing Christianization of the Great Straight Planet Earth.* 1981. Wavell Heights, Australia: Jesus Lives. [32 p.]

Post-mill. Also wrote *Communist Eschatology*; books on creation, communism.

2747. Lee, Jang Rim. *Getting Close to the End.* [1987?].

Korean Hyoo-go ("Rapture") movement. Groups include Lee's Mission for the Coming Days Church and Taberah World Mission (of 12-year old boy prophet Bang-Ik Ha). Christians to supernaturally depart Earth — the Rapture — on Oct 28, 1992. 1948 + 51 (one generation) = 1999, with Tribulation and Rapture 1992. Lee convicted of fraud after 1992 date. Lee also wrote *Rapture!* (1992) and *The Last Plan of God.*

2748. *Left Behind.* 1994. Niagara Falls, NY: This Week in Bible Prophecy. video.

Subtitled "Where'd Everybody Go?" Dramatization of Rapture, followed by teaching on End Times.

2749. Lelus, Charles-Andre. *La Fin du Monde Approche: Pourquoi il Faut Craindre les Prochaines Annees.* 1994. Montreal: Edimag. 111 p.

"Nostradamus, Edgar Cayce, and Jeane Dixon."

2750. Lemesurier, Peter. *The Great Pyramid Decoded.* 1977. New York: St. Martin's. 350 p. illus. index, bibl. Also 1996 rev. ed.

4000 B.C. start. Christ: 2 B.C. to A.D. 33. Final Age begins 1844. 1914 critical date. 1977–2004: collapse of materialist society. Feb. 21, 1999: Kingdom of Spirit founded. 2039: Second Coming. Humanity and Messiah shuttle to different planes of existence until 84th century.

2751. _____. *The Armageddon Script: Prophecy in Action.* 1983, c1981. New York: St. Martin's Press. 255 p. illus bibl.

Weight of prophetic belief makes it self-fulfilling or true, but usually in ways different than anticipated. Urges "co-operation" with prophecy. Similarity of many psychic revelations and ancient traditions to biblical prophecies; Great Pyramid as pre-biblical time-line. Jesus and Essenes deliberately sought to make Messianic prophecies come true, then re-interpreted them as heavenly Ascension and future Millennium when Jesus died. Recommends that aspiring Messiah enter Jerusalem by 1985 and follow script carefully.

2752. Levitt, Zola. *Israel in Agony: The Beginning of the End?.* c1975. Irvine, CA: Harvest House. 100 p.

Book is "virtually a timetable of those 'future events' which will lead to worldwide tribulation and the final war, the battle of Armageddon.... Through Israel, [God] will conclude His plan for the world." "The sad state of current world affairs is remarkably predicted in the Bible." "... the consummation is coming in the next twenty-five years...." To those now alive: "we're really going to see all this." About half of prophecies already fulfilled, the other half for the end time. Book largely about 1973 Yom Kippur War, as beginning of End: "pre-invasion" — preparation for Russian invasion. Russian invasion was stymied by the Arab defeat, but is still imminent — at beginning of seven year period. Antichrist will probably take credit for God's stunning defeat of Russia. Antichrist will be the "ultimate Communist." Good reasons to suppose that Kissinger is Antichrist, but says he personally doubts it. The 144,000 are Hebrew Christian evangelists; some will come to Christ during Tribulation. Pretrib Rapture. Can't "prevent" fulfillment of biblical prophecy (Armageddon, etc.). Book cites Arab and Soviet "Jew-hating."

2753. _____. *The Signs of the End.* c1978. Dallas: Zola Levitt. 31 p.

2754. _____. *"The Beginning of the End!"* 1987. [Dallas]: Zola Levitt Ministries. 59 p. maps.

2755. Lewis, Arthur H. *The Dark Side of the Millennium: The Problem of Evil in Revelation 20:1-10.* 1980. Grand Rapids, MI: Baker Book House. 65 p. charts, bibl. refs.

2756. Lewis, Daniel J. 1998. *Three Crucial Questions About the Last Days.* Grand Rapids, MI: Baker. bibl. refs., index.

"Are we living in the last days?" — yes. "Should Christians try to predict Christ's Return?" — no. "What must Christians believe about the last days?" — particular interpretation isn't important.

2757. Lewis, David Allen. *Things to Come.* 1975. Fairmont, WV: David A. Lewis Ministries. 5 cassettes.

"Things to Come," "Rapture, Judgment of Believers," "Tribulation," "AntiChrist, Russia," "Armageddon, Judgment of Nations."

2758. _____. *Magog 1982, Cancelled.* 1982. Harrison, AR: New Leaf Press. 143 p. illus.

Assemblies of God minister, president of National Christian Leadership Conference for Israel. Israeli invasion of Lebanon prevented Russian takeover and WWIII; canceled Magog invasion. Russia stockpiled arms in Lebanon for planned PLO-fronted invasion for Aug. 4, 1982, but thwarted when supplies captured by Israel. Lambert Dolphin supports theory. Huge underground base in Sidon, miles of air-conditioned tunnels, vast ammunition stores and sophisticated equipment. "Of course we know we are living in the 'end times' and the 'final era.'" Documents strident fundamentalist support for Israel.

2759. _____. *The Rapture of the Church; Essential Truth for End Time Victory.* 1986. Springfield, MO: Menorah Press. 19 p.

2760. _____. *Smashing the Gates of Hell: In the Last Days.* 1987. Green Forest, AR: New Leaf Press. 220 p.

2761. _____. *Prophecy 2000.* 1992 [1990]. Rev. 6th ed. Green Forest, AR: New Leaf Press. 428 p. illus.

2762. _____, and Robert Shreckhise. *UFO: End-Time Delusion.* 1992.

1991. 2nd ed. Green Forest, AR: New Leaf Press. 246 p. bibl. refs.

Lewis: researched UFOs since 1952. UFOs are occult, paranormal "manifestations of evil spirits that serve Satan" and figure in End Time and Antichrist prophecy. UFOs set people up for false hope of deliverance by ETs. They are "ancient evil foes of mankind and of God ... here for deception and the final destruction of the race of man once and for all." UFOs have a supernatural, spiritual dimension; but can also have physical reality and are definitely real. Includes case study of evangelical UFO victim. Chapters on "UFO Delusion vs. the Genesis Record" ("Evolution — Foundation for Deception"). UFOs and SETI belief as New Age evolutionism. Demonic Men in Black. Final chapters present End Times scenario. Appendix on creationism.

2763. Liardon, Roberts. *Spirit Life Tapes.* 1990. Minneapolis: Roberts Liardon Ministries. 12 cassettes.

Includes "The Militant Church," "How to Live in the End Times."

2764. _____. *Final Approach: The Opportunity and Adventure of End-Times Living.* 1993. Orlando, FL: Creation House. 191 p.

Pentecostal, founder of Spirit Life Bible College. "This generation" ushers in Second Coming. Says "Who cares!" about charts, chronological disputes, sequences. Instead offers "pan-trib" view: everything will "pan out" in the end. "Isn't it exciting to be alive in these last days?" Praises Aimee Semple McPherson, Kuhlman. Urges not to worry about End, but to "have fun," perform healings, and work for God. "God likes to have fun." But engaged in spiritual war with Satan and demons.

2765. Lightner, Robert Paul. *The Last Days Handbook: A Comprehensive Guide to Understanding the Different Views of Prophecy: Who Believes What and Why.* 1990. Nashville: Thomas Nelson. 223 p. illus. bibl. refs., indexes.

2766. Lightninghawk, William. *A Book of Prophecy. Vol 1: The Times of the End of the World.* 1988. Oakland, CA: Regent Press.

2767. Lindsay, Gordon. *God's Plan of the Ages: As Revealed in the Wonders of Bible Chronology.* 1982 [1971]. 4th ed. Dallas: Christ for the Nations. 254 p. charts.

Nebuchadnezzar of Babylonia conquered Israel 588 B.C.; then 60 years to empty it (make it desolate) = 528 B.C. + 70 years = 458 B.C. (end of Captivity; beginning of 70 Weeks). 69th Week A.D. 26 — "cut off" midway through by the Crucifixion.

2768. _____. *Red China in Prophecy.* 1972. Dallas: Christ for the Nations.

Nixon's China rapprochement was a "tragic miscalculation."

2769. _____. *Revelation Series.* 1970s. Dallas: Christ for the Nations. 16 vols. in 1 (513 p.).

1-2. *The Seven Churches of Prophecy.* 3: *The Judgment Throne and the Seven Seals.* 4: *The Great Day of the Lord and the Seven Trumpets.* 5: *The Tribulation Temple and the Three Woes.* 6: *The Two Witnesses.* 7: *The Sun-Clothed Woman and the Man Child.* 8: *The Rapture and the Second Coming of Christ.* 9: *The Rise of the Antichrist and the Mark of the Beast.* 10: *The Antichrist and the Beast from the Bottomless Pit.* 11: *The 144,000 on Mt. Zion and the First Fruits.* 12: *The Vial Judgments or the Seven Last Plagues.* 13: *The Two Babylons.* 14: *Armageddon and the Doom of the Beast.* 15: *The Millennium or the Coming World of Tomorrow.* 16: *The New Heavens and the New Earth.* Abomination of Desolation = nuclear ("A-BOMination")

2770. _____. *Prophecy Series.* 1973–74. Dallas: Christ for the Nations. 17 vols. in 1. illus.

1: *Those Amazing Prophecies that Prove the Bible.* 2: *The Antichrists have Come!* 3: *40 Signs of the Soon Coming of Christ.* 4: *It's Sooner than You Think!* 5: *My Visit to Red Russia, Land of the Godless.* 6: *Red China in Prophecy.* 7: *Prophecy Fulfilled in the Fateful 1960's.* 8: *The Prophetic Significance of the Life and Death of President John F. Kennedy.* 9: *The Second Coming of Christ.* 10: *The Signs of the Times in the Heavens.* 11: *The Rapture.* 12: *The World: 2000 A.D.* 13: *The 1970's in the Light of Prophecy.* 14: *The United States in*

Prophecy. 15: *Will the Christians Go Through the Great Tribulation?* 16: *Will the Antichrist Come out of Russia?* 17: *After Vietnam, What?*

2771. _____. *End of the Age Series.* 1973–75. Dallas: Christ for the Nations.: 9 vols. in 2. illus.

1: *Signs of the Coming of the Antichrist.* 2: *Antichrist and His Forerunner.* 3: *The Antichrist's Rise to Power.* 4: *The Great Tribulation.* 5: *Israel, the False Prophet and the Two Witnesses.* 6: *The Great Trumpets and the Vial Judgments.* 7: *The Judgment Seat of Christ.* 8: *A Thousand Years of Peace.* 9: *The Great White Throne.*

2772. _____. *Israel's 48 Signs of Christ's Return.* 1981. Dallas: Christ for the Nations. 78 p. photos.

2773. _____, and Jarry Autrey. *Israeli's Prophetic Signs.* 1982. Dallas: Christ for the Nations. 71 p.

2774. Lindsell, Harold. 1984, 1985. *The Armageddon Spectre.* Westchester, IL: Crossway Books. 135 p. illus. bibl.

Former editor of *Christianity Today.* God won't destroy all life, or allow us to. Millions must survive nuclear war for Christ to rule over at His Second Coming. World only destroyed afterwards. Need for deterrence against communist aggression. Belief in Jews' destiny ought not blind one to plight of Arabs, however.

2775. Lindsey, Hal (with C[arole] C. Carlson). 1990 [c1970]. *Late Great Planet Earth.* New York: Bantam Books. 1977 ed: Grand Rapids, MI: Zondervan. x, 180. bibl. refs.

Best selling "non-fiction" book of 1970s (28 million copies by 1990). Lindsey: former speaker for Campus Crusade for Christ; minister in Palos Verdes (Los Angeles). Return of the Jews to Palestine the most significant prophetic sign. Any-moment pre-trib Rapture, then 7-year Tribulation. Second Coming is within a generation of the blooming of the "fig tree" (establishment of modern state of Israel), so it must occur within "forty years or so of 1948." Temple will be rebuilt. Ten-nation confederacy led by Antichrist arises from Common Market as revived Roman Empire. Antichrist given supernatural powers by Satan; performs miracles and proclaims himself God after recovery from fatal wound. 144,000 Jews evangelize during the Tribulation. Harlot Church = ecumenical religion employing astrology, witchcraft, and occultism. Northern Confederacy, Gog = Russia, allied with Persia, Ethiopia (Black Africa), Libya (Arab Africa), and Gomer (Iron Curtain nations). Egypt with other Africans attack Israel first, then Russia by land (using horse cavalry) and sea. Russians continue into Egypt, but Antichrist's European Confederacy and Eastern Confederacy mobilize (200 million Chinese — "The Yellow Peril" — pour down Karakorum Highway through the Himalayas), so Russians return to Israel. Fire and brimstone rain down on Soviet army, utterly annihilating it. Then, at Armageddon, Antichrist battles the Easterners. All major cities of the world obliterated. Then, the Second Coming. Though the prophets themselves were unable to understand the meaning of their visions, Lindsey translates their biblical phrases into vocabulary of nuclear destruction, nerve gas, missiles, space combat, radiation, etc.

2776. _____. *The World's Final Hour.* 1976 [1971]. Grand Rapids, MI: Zondervan. 46 p.

Summary of *Late Great*, previously pub. as *Homo Sapiens: Extinction or Evacuation.*

2777. _____ (with C.C. Carlson) *Satan is Alive and Well on Planet Earth.* [1972]. Grand Rapids, MI: Zondervan Publishing House. 255 p. bibl. refs also Bantam ed.

2778. _____. *There's a New World Coming.* c1973. Santa Ana, CA: Vision House Publishers. 308 p. Also Bantam ed.

Two Antichrists.

2779. _____. *The 1980's: Countdown to Armageddon.* 1981 [c1980]. New York: Bantam. xii, 178 p. charts, bibl. refs.

Since Korean War, U.S. has been tricked into helping China "prepare for their role in the last awful war."

2780. _____. *The Rapture.* 1983. New York: Bantam Books. 211 p.

"Few people today doubt that history is moving toward some sort of climactic catastrophe." The countdown has started: "... all the predicted signs" necessary for seven-year Tribulation already evident. Seven-year treaty between Antichrist and Israeli pseudo-Messiah starts 2,250 day Tribulation which ends at Second Coming. First Seal: Antichrist emerges as leader from Common Market. Second Seal: Mid-Tribulation — Abomination of Desolation: Then Arabs, led by Egypt, attack Israel, followed by Soviets and their allies. But then Antichrist's Western forces threaten the Soviets, as do Eastern armies. Armageddon: Soviets return to Israel to meet this challenge. Sixth Seal: nuclear war. Trumpets: effects of nuclear war — firestorms, radioactive fallout, atmospheric debris blocks sunlight; also chemical and biological warfare. Only 50 million survive worldwide. Seven dispensations: to Fall, Flood, Babel, Abraham, Moses, Christ, Second Coming and End.

2781. _____. *The Road to Holocaust.* 1989. New York: Bantam Books. viii, 295 p. bibl.

Says post- and a-mill views lead to anti-Semitism, because they assume Israel replaced by the Church for rejecting the Messiah.

2782. _____. *Planet Earth — 2000 A.D.: Will Mankind Survive?.* 1994. Palos Verdes, CA: Western Front. 312 p. bibl. refs.

2783. _____. *The Final Battle.* 1995. Palos Verdes, CA: Western Front. xxi, 286 p.

Based on J. de Courcey's *Intelligence Digest.* Islam is the real "evil empire." Planned third temple will ignite Islamic attack. Suggests Northern attack of Ezek. 38 will be fulfilled by plan outlined in Zhirinovsky's 1993 *Last Dash to the South* (though in Fact Zhirinovsky fantasized attack *against* Moslem states.)

2784. _____. *The Messiah.* Formerly titled *The Promise.* 1996. Eugene, OR; Harvest House. 189 p. bibl. refs.

2785. _____. *Apocalypse Code.* 1997. Palos Verdes, CA: Western Front. 311 p.

2786. _____. *Planet Earth: The Final Chapter.* 1998. Beverly Hills, CA : Western Front, 295 p. bibl. refs.

Also wrote novel *Blood Moon.*

2787. Lindsted, Robert D. *The Next Move: Current Events in Bible Prophecy.* [1980s?]. Wichita, KS: Bible Truth. 187 p. illus. "Lindsted" misspelled on title page.

Lindsted: taught engineering; does *Bible Truth* radio program. Already fulfilled prophecies statistically impossible by chance. Stage set for End; any moment Rapture, then Tribulation, Second Coming at Armageddon. 224 promises of Second Coming in Bible. Rise and decline of Russia foretold. Gog = famous "Gogh" mountain in Russia. Ethiopian Jews = lost tribe of Dan. Israeli strike into Lebanon prevented Russian invasion then. U.S. = young lion of Tarshish. Because of world disarmament, future invaders will use bows, horses. Mideast petroleum foretold. Ten Nations = today's Common Market: the world's "last political power." Allied with New Age world religious movement = Harlot. Red heifer sacrifice: Vendyl Jones found location of ashes required to reinstitute; film *Raiders of the Lost Ark* based on him. Suggests 6,000 Year total: 4,000 to Christ, 2,000 more til end of Tribulation: begins 1980s? First Horseman = Antichrist. Nuclear destruction in Tribulation. 200 million Chinese army. Blood "literally" up to horses' bridles for 180 miles at Armageddon.

2788. _____. *Saddam Hussein, the Persian Gulf, and the End Times.* 1990. Wichita, KS: Bible Truth. video.

2789. Lloyd, James. *Beyond Babylon: The Last Week of the World.* Jacksonville, OR: Christian Media.

Also does *Apocalypse Chronicles* radio show and newsletter. Agent of Tribulation destruction is Z. Sitchin's 12th Planet.

2790. Lockyet, Herbert. SEE ALSO 1910–1970. *All about the Second Coming: the Drama of the Ages.* 1998 [1980]. Peabody MA: Hendrickson. xxvi, 241 p.

Also wrote *The Rapture of the Saints* (1979, Oklahoma City: Southwest Bible Church). Pre-trib Rapture.

2791. Logan, A.E. *Is This the Last Generation?* 1974. Athens, GA: Georgia Bible Institute. 26 p.

2792. _____. *"Things Which Shortly Must Come to Pass."* 1980. Athens, GA: Georgia Bible Fellowship. 34 p.

Second Coming.

2793. Logsdon, S. Franklin. SEE ALSO 1910–1970 *The Church Will Not Go Through the Tribulation.* 1980. Schaumburg, IL: Regular Baptist Press. 24 p.

2794. Logston, Robert. *The End-Times Blood Bath.* 1992. Nashville: Winston-Derek. 100 p.

Second Coming, but first "the most dreaded of all periods in human history"— the Tribulation. "This period must happen ... [it] cannot be stopped ... it will occur!" Christians must go through Tribulation. "I cannot overemphasize the need to understand that many of us today will be in the Great Tribulation." Two-thirds of world's population killed. Insists on Seventh-day Sabbath (Saturday). Two End Times leaders — political and religious Beasts. Democracy: "*In reality, it is the wishful system of Satan.*" AIDS: "punishment of misery from God." 666 economic mark, central computer in Brussels. "The Nazi's [sic] spent more money on occult research than the U.S. did on the atomic bomb project." Hitler was demon-guided. End Time leader will be even worse.

2795. Longley, Arthur. *God Will Destroy Communism; World War II to Armageddon in Bible Prophecies.* 1985. Hamilton, OH: Expositor Pub.

2796. Lorie, Peter. *Revelation: St. John the Divine: Prophecies for the Apocalypse and Beyond.* 1995. London: Boxtree. 224 p. illus. maps.

2797. Lovely, George. *"The Night Is Far Spent, the Day Is at Hand"; or, Lessons on Unfilled Prophecy.*

Also wrote *The Second Coming and the Fiery Trial.*

2798. Lovett, C.S. SEE ALSO 1910–1970 *Latest Word on the Last Days.* 1980. Baldwin Park, CA: Personal Christianity Chapel. 363 p. illus.

President of Personal Christianity ministry. Post-trib pre-mill. Russia to attack Israel soon. Start of 7-year Tribulation, ending with Armageddon, probably "within the next few years." Jews to embrace Antichrist as Messiah, and will suffer the most. Antichrist to come from revived Roman Empire, becomes emperor of world, allied with Pope. Satan "indwells" Antichrist. "Pre-wrath" Rapture: Tribulation different from "God's wrath": Christians raptured after Tribulation but before horrors of Seven Bowls. Armageddon = destruction of Antichrist's forces at Second Coming. Creation ca. 4000 B.C.; Second Coming and Millennium ca. A.D. 2000.

2799. Lowe, A[lister] J. *The Creative and Redemptive Weeks: The Foundation of Prophetic Truth.* 1981. Brisbane: End Time Publications. 129 p. illus. End Time Events: vol 1.

2800. _____. *The Tabernacle of Moses: The Divine Pattern.* 1981. Brisbane: End Time Publications. 155 p. illus. End Time Events: vol 2.

2801. _____. *Feasts of the Lord: The End Time Harvest of the Church.* 1982. Brisbane: End Time Publications. 107 p. illus. End Time Events: vol 3.

2802. _____. *A Guide to Things That Are to Be — Part 1.* 1982. Brisbane: End Time Publications. 345 p. illus. map. End Time Events: vol 4.

2803. Ludy, Claude E. *The Vile & the Holy: A Commentary on the Book of Daniel.* 1978. Saginaw, MI: Claude Edward Ludy. 100 p. illus.

"The angel, Gabriel, who gave Daniel the message, said it was to be kept secret 'till the time of the end'.... Cryptic expression & symbols masked true meanings in the Book of Daniel until the time was ripe for their revelation. Then, early in the twentieth century, truth began to emerge!" These include WWI, Hitler's rise and demise, Mussolini, the Holocaust (Time of Trouble). Vile Person and Little Horn of Daniel is Hitler. King of South refers to Allied armies attacking via Italy; King of North is Eisenhower invading Nazi Germany.

2804. _____. *The End of the Age: A Commentary on the Revelation.* 1989. Saginaw, MI: McKay Press. xviii, 125 p. bibl. refs index.

Hitler was the first (political) Beast of Revelation or Antichrist; the future (religious) Antichrist will rule much the same area: Europe, North Africa. "His power is expected to be great! A resurrection of Hitler (probably an occult simulation of one) is expected to take place, at which many will believe Hitler to be a true Messiah! That character, in partnership with the coming Antichrist, will rule much of the world!" Everybody marked on forehead or hand with Beast symbol 666. Ten-kingdom Empire composed of Albania, Algeria, Bulgaria, France, Hungary, Italy, Rumania, Tunisia, and Yugoslavia.

2805. Lundstrom, Lowell. *The Wind Whispers Warning: A Review of End Time Events.* c1979. Sisseton, SD: Lowell Lundstrom Ministries. 110 p.

2806. _____. *Prophecy Handbook: with Up-to-Date Mideast Prophetic Forecast.* 1980. Sisseton, SD: Message for America. 31 p.

2807. Lutheran Church — Missouri Synod. Commission on Theology and Church Relations. *The "End Times": A Study on Eschatology and Millennialism.* 1989 St. Louis: The Commission. 56 p. illus. bibl.

2808. Lutzer, Erwin W. *Coming to Grips with the Antichrist's New Age Roots.* 1990. Chicago: Moody Press. 41 p.

2809. _____. *Coming to Grips with the Role of Europe in Prophecy.* 1990. Chicago: Moody. 42 p.

2810. _____. *Hitler's Cross.* 1995 Chicago: Moody. 216 p. illus. bibl. refs.

Hitler as precursor of Last Days Antichrist. Uncritical acceptance of Nazi reliance on occult beliefs.

2811. Lynn, Betty. *Pathways to Armageddon ... and Beyond.* 1992. Eugene, OR: Harvest House. 263 p. bibl. refs.

Standing at doorstep of "last days": Christ "about to appear." Analysis of history and current events in light of Bible prophecy. Birth-pangs of End Times are closer and closer together. Jesus stressed importance of prophecy. Examines geopolitical trends: "pathways." Pathways of government (to one-worldism), power (from democracy to monarchy), Europe (mastery of world through economic power), Russia (one final strike at Israel despite Soviet breakup), Arab/Moslem (also attack Israel, Gulf War related to prophecies of Babylon), Israel (to host messianic kingdom). Evil prince — Antichrist — to rule over Europe and unite it with Israel. Usurper messiah; declares himself God in Jerusalem after Russian-Moslem invasion. 70 Weeks stopped with Crucifixion, last 7 years about to resume ticking. Church to be Raptured. Gomer = Ukraine, southern Russia, central Turkey (not Germany). Breakup of Soviet Union — hardliners now more apt to launch wild military adventure. Armageddon: world's armies assemble at Megiddo plain before the Messiah comes to attack Israel. New Jerusalem to descend from heaven, a cube 1,500 miles on each side, with city and streets of gold. God is now sending 15 million raptors commuting across Israel on various migratory pathways, as preparation for corpse feast at Armageddon.

2812. Lytle, C.D. *The Day and the Hour.* Hemet, CA: Prophetic Research Assoc.

The day and hour of Second Coming can be known.

2813. McAlvany, Don. *Toward a New World Order: The Countdown to Armageddon.* 1990. Oklahoma City: Hearthstone. 248 p. bibl.

Foreword by Tim LaHaye. McAlvany: undercover intelligence work, investment advisor; publishes *McAlvaney Intelligence Advisor.* America in disastrous moral, social, legal, and economic decline. Turning into government-controlled police state: e.g. disarming of citizens with gun laws, computer checks, cashless economy. Bush, the UN, environmentalists, and New Age advocates are pushing U.S. into this New World Order. Communists still seek world domination; warns of Russian treachery. 1991 overthrow of communist regime was really "pseudo-coup." "Could we soon see the rise of Antichrist? Is the stage being set for a one-world government, for Armageddon?"

2814. MacArthur, John. *The Second Coming of the Lord Christ.* 1981. Panorama City, CA: Word of Grace Communications. 218 p.

Study notes to 23-cassette collection of same title. Edited by David Sper. Includes: "Why Jesus Must Return; The Catching Away of the Church; Will the Church Go Through the Tribulation?; The Terrors of the Tribulation; Israel in the Tribulation; The Destruction of the Nations; the Earthly Kingdom of Jesus Christ; Is the Doom of the World Near?; How to Survive in the Last Days of Apostasy."

2815. McBirnie, William Steuart. SEE ALSO 1910–1970. *The Antichrist.* 1978. Dallas: Acclaimed Books. viii, 152 p. plates, illus.

McBirnie: "biblical consultant" for movie *Damien: Omen II*; pastor United Community Church (Glendale, CA). Ph.D. from and prof. at Calif. Graduate School of Theology. Antichrist must be alive now; may by revealed as Antichrist before Rapture; probably after defeat of Russian invasion of Israel. All nations referred to in Ezekiel are now identifiable. Magog and Rosh = Russia. Tarshish = Cadiz; Young Lions of Tarshish = Americans (cites Barry Fell on pre-Columbian Celts in America). Antichrist will persuade people to accept him as Messiah. Mark of Beast: invisible mark on body; Beast computer already in Brussels. Armageddon: East revolts against Antichrist, then Second Coming, then all armies battle Christ.

2816. McCall, Thomas S., and Zola Levitt. *The Coming Russian Invasion of Israel.* c1974. Chicago: Moody Press. 96 p. illus., bibl. refs.

Foreword by Hal Lindsey. 1987 update links coming famine to Chernobyl nuclear disaster. Organization of African Unity established in 1963 in Ethiopia foreshadowed Gog's alliance with King of South.

2817. _____. *Satan in the Sanctuary.* 1975 [1973]. New York: Bantam. 159 p. bibl. refs. Orig. pub. Moody.

Rumored rebuilding of Temple. Site actually slightly east of Dome of Rock, so it could be rebuilt without destroying mosque. Film *The Temple* based on this book (producer Malcolm Crouch).

2818. _____. *Raptured.* 1975. Dallas: Zola Levitt Ministries. Eugene, OR: Harvest House. 147 p.

Jewish feasts correlated with Christian history: Passover = Crucifixion; First Fruits = Resurrection; Rosh Hashana (Feast of Trumpets) = Rapture; Pentecost = Church Age; Yom Kippur (Atonement) = Tribulation and Second Coming; Feast of Tabernacles = Millennium. At Millennium, souls of dead "joined to eternal, victorious, sinless bodies." Russian invasion is blasted by Israel (helped by God), then Jews accept Leader, undergo Tribulation, Temple desecration. 144,000 witness, believers flee to Petra. Invaded by world armies. Two-thirds of Israel killed, but rest become "first Christian nation" at Second Coming.

2819. _____. *Coming: The End! Russia & Israel in Prophecy.* 1992. Chicago: Moody Press. 191 p.

Half the chapters revised versions of 1987 book. Tribulation and End Times "very soon." Russia (Gog, Magog) will attack Israel. Allies include Eastern Europe, Libya, Iran. Invaders annihilated, Israel burns their weapons for seven years (weapons may be made of wood, or the prophecy may refer to nuclear power, or fuel stores).

2820. McConnell, Lorne. *There Shall Be Signs: And You Shall Know.* 1998. Kemptville, Canada. bibl. refs., index.

Bible and astrology.

2821. McCune, James A. *America the True Church and the End of the Age.* 1980. Fairfield, OH: Yorkshire. ix, 227 p. illus.

2822. McDearmid, Andrew. *Eschatology: A Study Guide.* 1980. Brussels, Belgium: International Correspondence Inst. 206 p. illus. bibl.

Based on H. Hoyt's *End Times.*

2823. MacDonald, John. *The Great Tribulation.* 1971. Eastbourne, England: Prophetic Witness. 16 p.

2824. MacDonald, Sheri. *The End Times.* <http:/www.christianfaith.com/Christ/end/endtimes.html>

2825. MacDonald, William. *Armageddon Soon? What the Bible Says about the Future.* 1991. Kansas City, KS: Walter-

ick Publishing 42 p. illus. [also Canadian ed. in French, 1991].

Pre-trib Rapture (any-moment, imminent). Antichrist, 666, greatest persecution ever during Tribulation. Spread of Satanism and AIDS: signs that End is near.

2826. McDowell, Josh. *Daniel in the Critic's Den: Historical Evidence for the Authenticity of the Book of Daniel.* 1979. xiv, 148. bibl. refs, indexes.

2827. McElmurry, Tom. *The Tribulation Triad.* 1983. 235 p.

2828. _____. *The Key of the Bottomless Pit.* 1987. Texarkana, AR/TX: Bogard Press. 166 p. illus. bibl.

McElmurry: meteorologist, science teacher, Baptist preacher. Tribulation destruction and violence not caused by mere human activity: "God will do the destroying, and He does not need the puny weapons of science to fulfill His end-time prophecies." Earthquakes, volcanoes, tsunamis, tectonic plate shifting. Geological diagrams and maps of changes in Jerusalem topography at the Millennium. Comet causes poisoning of Earth by cyanogenic gases ("Wormwood" judgment). "Rolling up of heaven like a scroll" is cloud cover from volcanoes. Second Coming after Tribulation seen worldwide: Christ reflected throughout the stratosphere. Humans battle at Armageddon, but killing mostly from lava and earthquakes; "winepress of blood" is 185-mile long basaltic valley from which red liquid squirts up when crust is torn open, destroying the armies.

2829. McGee, J. Vernon. SEE ALSO 1910–1970. *3 Worlds in One.* [1990?] Los Angeles: J. McGee. 48 p.

2830. _____. *On Prophecy: Man's Fascination with the Future.* 1993. Nashville: T. Nelson. 248 p.

2831. McGhee-Siehoff, Estella M. *Hope in the End Time Prophecies.* <www.dial-a-prophecy.com/endhope.html> Orlando, FL.

"Hell has enlarged itself to accept this end-time generation."

2832. McGuire, Paul. *From Earthquakes to Global Unity: The End Times*

Have Begun. 1996. Lafayette, LA: Huntington House. iv, 223 p.

2833. McKee, Bill. *Orbit of Ashes; Jesus Is Coming!* 1972. Wheaton, IL: Tyndale House. 142 p. Also published under title *28 Things to Look for Before Jesus Comes*.

Pre-trib pre-mill. Following Rapture, Africans and Russians invade Israel, but then attacked by 200 million man army from East; all then battle Christ at Second Coming.

2834. McKeever, James M. *Christians Will Go Through the Tribulation: And How to Prepare for It*. 1978. Medford OR: Alpha Omega. 351 p. illus., graphs, tables, bibl. refs.

Consulting economist and Baptist evangelist; publishes *End Times News Digest* and investment newsletter. Post-trib: emphasizes that Rapture will occur at *end* of Tribulation. Believers meet Christ in air at Second Coming to join his army for Armageddon. Russia ("Gog") allies with China. Billions die horribly in Tribulation, including unprepared Christians. Explains in detail how to survive coming nuclear war, famine, earthquakes, Beast's One World economic system.

2835. _____. *Now You Can Understand the Book of Revelation*. 1980. Medford, OR: Omega. 351 p. illus.

Verse-by-verse exposition. Rapture occurs only after Tribulation well underway, at the Last Trumpet — the 7th Trumpet of Revelation. Purpose of Tribulation is to get rid of evil before the Millennium starts. Tribulation doesn't have clearly demarcated start — may have already begun. Events in Revelation not reported in chronological order. "I think Satan is probably using the UFOs very significantly." Demonic locusts could be killer bees or helicopters. Woman clothed in Sun is probably the Church; Man-Child is the "overcomers" who survive the Tribulation. Mystery Babylon may be literal rebuilt Babylon, or London or Jerusalem. Antichrist is probably Jewish.

2836. _____. *The Future Revealed*. 1988 [1982]. Medford, OR: Omega. 308 p. map. Orig. titled *The Coming Climax of History*.

2837. _____. *The Rapture Book: Victory in the End Times*. 1987. Medford, OR: Omega. 240 p.

2838. _____. *Preparing for Emergencies: Disaster Can Strike You Suddenly!*. c1993. Medford, OR: Omega Publications. 216 p.

2839. Mackler, Floyd. *Canaan Calling: A Challenge for the End Time*. 1994. New York: Carlton Press. 192 p.

"Spiritual life."

2840. McLeod, Merikay. *Now!* [Orlando, FL: World-Wide Bible Lectures]. 28 p.

Seventh-day Adventist. Allegory written by 17-year-old girl while at Grand Ledge Academy, MI (1963?). Events during Time of Trouble, up to Second Coming. UN troops in Iraq, US passes National Sunday Law.

2841. McMahon, T[homas] A., and Roger Oakland. *Understanding the Times: A Simplified Biblical Perspective*. 1990. Costa Mesa, CA: T.W.F.T. Publishers. [v], [172] p. illus. bibl. refs.

Science now agrees with the Bible that Earth will suffer cosmic collisions.

2842. McMillen, S.I. *Discern These Times*. 1971. Old Tappan, NJ: Revell. 192 p. bibl. 307 p. Study Guide available, bibl. refs, index.

Suggests Antichrist comes from Russia.

2843. MacPherson, Dave. *The Incredible Coverup*. 1975. Medford, OR: Omega Publications. xv, 171 p. plate. bibl. Combines *The Unbelievable Pre-Trib Origin* [c1973] and *The Late Great Pre-Trib Rapture* [c1974]; both revised and updated. Also pub. Logos Intl. 1975.

MacPherson: Dir: Heart of America Bible Soc., son of Norman MacPherson. Investigation into origin of pre-trib Rapture doctrine, which he opposes. Debunks Darby; reprints 1830 document by Margaret Macdonald, member of Irving's Glasgow church, whose trance revelations Darby appropriated. Macdonald's 1830 vision was of two-stage Coming, with believers raptured prior to Tribulation.

2844. _____. *The Great Rapture Hoax*. 1983. Fletcher, NC: New Puritan

Library. Condensed version pub. 1987 as *Rapture.*

2845. ____. *The Rapture Plot.* 1995 [1994]. Simpsonville, SC: Millennium III. xii, 290 p. bibl. refs.

Darbyites of the Plymouth Brethren tried to claim credit for formulating futurist pre-trib doctrine, but really introduced by Macdonald, a follower of Irving. Macdonald in turn influenced by John Tudor's 1829 *Morning Watch* articles. MacPherson claims coverup of true origin was largely perpetrated by William Kelly in *Bible Treasury.*

2846. ____. *Why I Believe the Church Will Pass Through the Tribulation.* Kansas City, MO.

2847. Macpherson, Ian. *News of the World to Come: Panorama of Biblical Prophecy.* 1973. Eastbourne, England: Prophetic Witness. 299 p.

Pre-trib Rapture will be visible and loud. Seven Years, with Antichrist, a "dazzling dictator," controlling United States of Europe, then the "Revelation" (Second Coming). Revived Roman Empire; 200-million Chinese army. Astrology is accurate but demonic. Discusses many books, especially British, not listed here, e.g. T.H. Salmon's *Christ Is Coming* (1910, London), T.L.B. Westerdale's *The Coming Miracle* (1918, London), J.A.T. Robinson's *In the End, God* (1950, London). When Allenby entered Jerusalem in 1917, Arabs shouted his name as "Allah Nebi!" (God's Prophet). 1934 = 587 B.C. + 2,520. 1934 + 33 years (for Christ's age) = 1967. Bible describes aerial warfare, paratroops, nuclear bombs.

2848. ____. *Dial the Future: A Book about the Second Coming of Christ.* 1975. Eastbourne, England: Prophetic Witness. 69 p.

2849. ____. *Bright Tomorrow: The Christian's Future.* 1980. Eastbourne, England: Prophetic Witness. 88 p.

2850. McQuaid, Elwood. *It Is No Dream! Bible Prophecy: Fact or Fanaticism.* 1978. West Collingwood, NJ: Spearhead Press. 260 p. illus. bibl.

Israel as prophetic fulfilment. McQuaid: dispensational "Evangelical Christian." Purpose: to explain Israel (in history and prophecy) to Christians, and explain true Christianity (as opposed to the kind which persecuted Jews) to Jews. The drama of Jews from through the Holocaust, 1948 founding of Israel and recent wars. Russia as prophesied foe, King of North, coveting Israel's vast resources. King of South is Egypt; of East: China; of West: revived Roman Empire. Antichrist, Tribulation, Armageddon; then Millennial rule of Christ from Jerusalem. Author's poems scattered throughout book.

2851. McRay, Ron. *The Last Days?* 1990. Bradford, PA: Kingdom Press. xii, 127 p. illus.

2852. MacWilliams, E. J. 1989. *The Last Days of God's Church.* Eau Gallie, FL: Harbour House, 192 p. bibl. refs.

2853. Maddoux, Marlin. *Seal of Gaia: a Novel of the Antichrist.* 1998. Nashville: Word Pub. 476 p.

Fiction. After Soviet collapse, secret sinister forces forecast ecological disasters as ploy to gain power, and seize control of world banking A.D. 2022 by computer manipulation and form New Earth Federation. 2031: NEF attacks Russia, China attacks India, NEF defeats China. The Antichrist, son of Helena Rousseau, taught by Ascended Masters in India, takes over as NEF leader in 2033, and imposes pagan and New Age religion of Gaia — pantheistic worship of Earth — by staging miraculous events with technological wizardry. Rapture occurs when Antichrist gains world control. Seal of Gaia — biochip implant — is Mark of the Beast. Antichrist hounds all Christians and implements genocidal programs to eliminate 7 billion people by 2040, but Omega computer runs amok and releases new virus which will destroy all humanity — saved only by Second Coming.

2854. Madray, George. *The End.* 1998. <http://www.theend.org/>

Rapure: A.D. 2020; Second Coming on Yom Kippur, 2020. Dispensational premill. 6,000 Year theory; opposes "Satanic lie" of evolution. Pre-Flood Water Canopy to be restored at Millennium. Antichrist: King of North from rebuilt Babylon; may defeat Russia at start of Tribulation.

2855. Mahan, Walter L. *The Unveiling of End-Time Events: A Prophetic Novel.* 1993. Nashville: Winston-Derek. vi, 453 p.

The Second Coming at Armageddon.

2856. Mails, Thomas E. *The Vultures Gather, the Fig Tree Blooms: A Study Concerning the Fulfillment of Prophecy in Our Time.* 1972. Hayfield, MN: Hayfield Pub Co. 100 p. illus., tables, charts, maps, bibl.

"Primarily a book for beginners" concerning End Times. Lutheran, but decries Lutheran shunning of End prophetic fulfillments. Many scholars say A.D. 2000–2100 as End. 7-year Tribulation begins when Antichrist leads 10-nation European confederacy. Then, Second Coming, Millennium, Judgment. Fulfilled prophecies: Israel restored, Gog (Russia) a power, 10-nation Europe, Russian-Arab-African alliance, world church. Rapture. Antichrist, Tribulation, Antichrist subdues 3 of 10 nations, allies with Jews, leader of Europe, the Mark, martyrs believers, desecrates Temple mid-Trib, then the Jews rebel, Russia and Arabs invade, Russia fights Egypt, God destroys Russians; China coalition invades, West resists, Armageddon. Third of world dies. Second Coming, Christ defeats both East and West armies. Millennium; Judgment. Rapture: anytime until 1988 (especially 1981), if generation= 40 years. Discusses pre-, mid, post-trib Rapture. Doesn't choose — could be any time until Second Coming. All Tribulation survivors will live in Millennium (they are not resurrected or destroyed); including those who join Gog at end of Millennium. But don't avoid marriage because of coming End. Ezek. 3-2: 2520 years after return from captivity (536 + 516 B.C.) = 1984 or 2004 as the End. A.D. 2000 or 2040 using Hosea 6:2 and 70 weeks.

2857. Mains, David R. *The Rise of the Religion of Antichristism.* 1985. Grand Rapids, MI: Zondervan. 133 p. bibl.

Later titled *The Truth About the Lie.*

2858. Malgo, Wim. *The Rapture: 1 Thessalonians 4:13-18.* 1969. Zurich, Switzerland: Midnight Call Mission. 27 p.

Malgo: Born and raised in Holland (uses German maps).

2859. _____. *1000 Years Peace.* 1984 [1974]. West Columbia, SC: Midnight Call. 90 p. illus.

2860. _____. *Shadows of Armageddon.* 1976. Hamilton, OH: Midnight Call. 182 p. illus.

2861. _____. *Begin with Sadat.* c1978. Hamilton, OH: Midnight Call.

2862. _____. *50 Questions Most Frequently Asked About the Second Coming.* 1980. Columbia SC: Midnight Call. 84 p. illus. maps.

2863. _____. *Russia's Last Invasion.* 1980. Columbia, SC: Midnight Call. 104 p. illus.

Invasion of Afghanistan is beginning of Ezekiel's End Time invasion of Gog.

2864. _____. *There Shall Be Signs in Heaven and On Earth 1948-1982.* c1980. Columbia, SC: Midnight Call. 90 p. illus.

The "entire universe … [is] subordinated by God to Israel's calling." Cosmic catastrophes fall upon Israel"s enemies. UFOs especially during Israel's wars. "Natural" catastrophes have increased with Return of Israel. Born-again men keep hair short, women realize that wearing slacks is an "abomination."

2865. _____. *Nuclear Catastrophe in the Mideast.* 1981. Columbia, SC: Midnight Call. 107 p. illus., maps.

All Lebanon given by God to Israel. Gomer = Germany. "In the end-battle of the nations, nuclear weapons will be used according to the Prophetic Word."

2866. _____. *In the Beginning Was the End: and After the End There Is a New Beginning.* 1983. West Columbia, SC: Midnight Call Publications. 140 p. illus.

"The Second Coming of Jesus is imminent … the end is, indeed, at hand!" Many prophecies fulfilled in past but will also be fulfilled again in the future (double fulfillment). Natural catastrophes rapidly increasing. Moral collapse. Rapture, then Antichrist. Approaching end of sixth millennium since creation of man. Antichrist's kingdom (Roman World Empire) already becoming apparent. Antichrist probably already active (but not revealed).

2867. Manker, Dayton A. SEE ALSO 1910–1970. *Invasion from Heaven.* 1979. Salem, OH: Schmul Publishers. 271 p.

2868. Mann, A.T. *Millennium Prophecies: Predictions for the Year 2000.* 1992. Rockport, MA: Element. xv, 143 p. illus. bibl. refs., index.

2869. Mansell, Donald Ernest. 1998. *The Shape of the Coming Crisis: A Sequence of Endtime Events Based on the Writings of Ellen G. White.* Nampa, ID: Pacific Press. 191 p. bibl. refs.

Mansell: former curator of E.G. White estate. Chronology of events with multiple citations for each from White. Forthcoming: *Adventists and Armageddon: Have We Misinterpreted Prophecy?* (Boise, ID: Pacific Press).

2870. Marcussen, A. Jan. *National Sunday Law.* 1998 [1983]. Thompsonville, IL: Amazing Truth. 95 p.

Seventh-day Adventist. Coming law requiring Sunday worship (forcing all to "worship the Papacy")is the End-time Mark of the Beast. Two-Horn Beast is U.S.

2871. Margoian, Mark. *God's True Prophet for the End of the World.* [1980s]. Waukegan, IL:

2872. Maria Devi Christos. *Uchenie Marii Devi Khristos.* 1993. [Moscow?]: Great White Brotherhood. 79 p. illus.

Formerly Marina Tsvigun, promoted as Christ's Second Coming and "living God" by fellow Ukrainian Yuri Krivonogov, her prophet, who formed Great White Brotherhood. Proclaimed End for Nov. 14, 1993; arrested just prior to this. Maria's *Teachings* = Third Gospel. She and her prophet would be killed, lie dead for 3½ days, then be resurrected just before the End.

2873. Marrs, Texe. *Dark Secrets of the New Age: Satan's Plan for a One World Religion.* c1987. Westchester, IL: Crossway Books. x, 288 p.

Also wrote *Ravaged by the New Age: Satan's Plan to Destroy Our Kids*; and *America Shattered: Unmasking the Plot to Destroy Our Families and Our Country* [by New Age occult conspiracy].

2874. ____. *Rush to Armageddon.* c1987. Wheaton, IL: Tyndale. 265 p. map, bibl.

2875. ____. *Mega Forces: Signs and Wonders of the Coming Chaos.* 1988. Austin, TX: Living Truth. 265 p. bibl.

End Time approaching. Computers, robotics, bioengineering, mind-controlling drugs, psychic warfare Satan's tools of deception for his New World Order, and will be used by Antichrist to attempt to create a super-race. New Age is a Satanic takeover plot: a "scientific religion for the end time." Bible foretells nuclear Armageddon, chemical-biological warfare, tanks, aircraft, rockets, lasers.

2876. ____. *Mystery Mark of the New Age: Satan's Design for World Domination.* c1988. Westchester, IL. Crossway Books. 287 p. illus., bibl. refs.

Satan's plan for world domination, via occultism.

2877. ____. *Millennium: Peace, Promises and the Day they Take Our Money Away.* 1990. Austin, TX: Living Truth. 270 p. bibl. refs.

2878. ____. *Circle of Intrigue: The Hidden Inner Circle of the Global Illuminati Conspiracy.* 1995. Austin, TX: Living Truth. xiii, 303 p. illus. bibl. refs.

Bible predicts Satanic conspiracy to rule world by A.D. 2000. "Ten Unseen Men Rule the World!" Capital in Jerusalem Temple. Ten Signs of the End of the World. Usual conspiracy suspects, and then some: CFR, Trilateral Commission, Bilderbergers, Priory of Sion, Skull & Bones, Freemasons, CIA, KGB. The wicked Clintons are occultists. U.N. plans to force State Religion of nature worship. Non-KJV Bibles are false deceptions.

2879. ____. *Project L.U.C.I.D.: The Beast 666 Universal Human Control System.* 1996. Austin, TX: Living Truth. xix, 244 p. illus. bibl. refs.

Hideous cyber-electronic mind control now in the works: "Lucifer's Identification System." Implantable biochips, world surveillance and slavery, Illuminati conspiracy. World is "about to enter a sinister period of blood, terror, and slavery unparalleled in human history."

Events must "rigorously and exactly fulfill the prophetic scenario for the last days" prophesied in the Bible.

2880. _____. *UFOs over Israel: Strong Delusion in the End-Times.* 1997.

Marrs also has videos and tapes including *The Cult of Diana* (Princess Diana's son is Antichrist).

2881. Martin, Donald L. *To the People: Prepare for War.* 1980. Great Neck, NY: Todd & Honeywell. 68 p. Revelation.

2882. Martin, Ernest L. *1998 in Prophecy.* <http://www.askelm.com/p971 209.htm> Portland, OR: Associates for Scriptural Knowledge.

Post-trib. Sept. 20, 1998 is exactly 2,000 years after birth of Christ. Revelation prophesies devastation of Earth by asteroid. 6,000 Years for world, but can't tell when 6,000 years is over exactly because creation date of Adam is not yet known precisely. Thus Millennium starts either 2028, 2030, or even 2068.

2883. Martin, Ralph. *The Return of the Lord.* 1983. Ann Arbor, MI: Servant Books. viii, 116 p. bibl. refs. Also wrote *What Time is It?* (1984).

2884. Mason, Roy. *Are We Facing the End of the World?: A Study of God's Plan's for the Ages and the Starting Signs of the Near End of the Present Age.* 1971. Orlando, FL: Christ for the World. 126 p.

2885. Massegee, J. Charles, Jr. *Five Minutes 'Till Midnight.* 1974. Ranger, TX: Charles Massegee Evangelistic Service. viii, 95 p.

2886. Matera, Dary. *Strike Midnight.* 1994. Ann Arbor, MI: Vine Books. 277 p.

Fiction: "Is this their final hour, the last desperate drama of human history?'" Biblical advisors from Baptist International Ministries, Chattanooga. Monster earthquakes, hurricanes. Rapture occurs, world baffled. American hero pilots Israeli superplane. Russia reverts to communism, attacks Israel. Israel then reduces Soviet Union to nuclear wasteland. Texas-born Palestinian becomes Israeli Prime Minister, then ruler of Europe, then elected president of U.S. as well and leader of United Earth. Established world religion, and "Chip of Life" wrist implant. New believers form and devise ways to beat computer system and resist Antichrist. Christian Underground

2887. Matheny, James F., and Marjorie B. Matheny. *Come Thou Reign Over Us.* 1981. Arlington, TX: Jay & Assoc. x, 167 p. bibl.

2888. _____. *Is There a Russian Connection?: An Exposition of Ezekiel 37-39.* 1987 Enid, OK: Jay & Assoc. 77 p. bibl. refs.

2889. _____. *The Four Beasts of Daniel 7: Prophecy for the End Time.* 1992. Brevard, NC: Jay & Associates 190 p. illus. bibl.

2890. _____. *Collision Course: The Ram and the Goat of Daniel 8.* 1993. Brevard, NC: Jay & Assoc. 178 p. map, bibl.

2891. _____. *A Kingdom Divided: The Rise of the Antichrist: An Exposition of Daniel 10-12.* 1994. Brevard, NC: Jay & Assoc. 195 p. bibl. refs.

2892. Matiasz, G.A. *End Time: Notes on the Apocalypse.* 1994. Edinburgh; San Francisco: AK Press. 299 p. maps.

Science ficion set in A.D. 2007. Civil war in former Soviet lands, U.S. trying to stamp out populist uprising in Mexico with sophisticated weapons; Oakland, CA revolts, establishes commune, revolutionaries plan to nuke establishment.

2893. Matrisciana, Caryl. *The Pagan Invasion.* 1994. Eugene, OR: Harvest House.

Also video version in series by Matrisciana and Chuck Smith of same title (1991, Jeremiah Films); series includes "Evolution: Hoax of the Century?" "Doorways to Satan," Antichrist, false messiahs.

2894. Maupin, Bill. 1981. *A Key to the Book of Daniel and 40 Year Generation.* Tucson: Lighthouse Gospel Tract Foundation. iii, 273 p. illus. maps, charts.

Maupin: with Lighthouse Gospel Tract Foundation (Tucson). Rapture = June 28, 1981; Second Coming = May 14, 1988. (Later re-calculated date for Aug 7.)

2895. Maxwell, C. Mervyn. *Magnificent Disappointment: What Really Happened in 1844 and It's Meaning for Today.*

1994. Boise, ID: Pacific Press. 175 p. illus. bibl. refs.

2896. Maybin, William James. *The Millennium.* 1971. Eastbourne, England: Prophetic Witness. 25 p.

2897. Mayers, Hector F. *The Strong Man is Coming.* 1979. Toronto: H.F. Mayers. 138 p.

2898. Mayhue, Richard L. *Snatched Before the Storm: A Case for Pretribulationism.* 1980. Winona Lake, IN: BMH Books. 16 p.

2899. Mayrhofer, Hermann. *Armageddon & Thousand Years is Past, "Little Season" Gog & Magog Battle in Progress.* 1984. Seattle: Mayhower Christian Foundation. xiv, 334 p.

2900. Mazakis, R. Winston. *Nations of Bible Prophecy: Current Events as Predicted in the Bible!.* 1994. Huntertown, MD: Institute of Biblical and International Studies. 314 p.

Mazakis grew up in Lebanon. His Institute of Biblical International. Studies is dept. of Middle East Mission. Pre-trib. Truth of prophecy and "inevitability of history": "No one can interrupt or undermine God's schedule." Lebanon civil war was prophesied. Gulf War ("east of Kedar") prophesied (especially by Jeremiah). Babylon vs. North (U.S.-led alliance). Disputes levitation model of Rapture; prefers Elijah's chariot of fire, followed by ferocious destructive worldwide tornadoes. Because U.S. has the most born-agains, it will suffer the most tornadoes. Will occur "definitely this generation." "Hooks in jaws" refers to return of Russian dictatorship. Rosh = Russia. Togarmah = Turkey. Gomer = Germany. Russia invades Israel for wealth of Jews. Attacks with international army, but most destroyed. Egypt will divert Nile to Red Sea when Israel bombs Aswan Dam, to prevent flooding of Nile Valley, fulfilling prophecy. "Ezekiel's war" is Russian attack on Israel, not Armageddon. Armageddon led by Antichrist, with world army, end of Tribulation. Ridicules belief of Russian attackers on horseback. Roman Empire comes from EEC. World seems safer now, thus the End near — when least expected.

Also wrote *Yesterday, Today, and Tomorrow in Bible Prophecy* (1974; Huntertown IN: Inst. Biblical Intl. Studies).

2901. Meier, Paul. *The Third Millennium: A Novel.* 1993. Nashville: T. Nelson. 311 p.

Over 150,000 copies. Author: Los Angeles psychiatrist; studied at Dallas Theological Seminary. A Jewish family in Newport Beach discovers events unfolding exactly as Bible predicted. Antichrist = U.S. President Damian Gianardo (part Jewish); survived explosion which killed previous president; engineered 1993 Mid East peace (7 year pact with Israel); creates New Roman Empire, with Britain, Italy, Japan, then seven other European nations. Jewish VP = False Prophet. Babylon capital of United Muslim States. Institutes 666 monetary system; renames presidential plane "White Horse"; ridicules and persecutes evangelicals. Rapture 1995. Russia, with Moslem and African allies, invades Israel on horseback: 1996. Attackers wiped out by nuclear weapons, supernatural earthquakes. Antichrist moves in to "protect" Israel, but disrupts restored Temple sacrifices, demands he be worshipped as God. Armageddon = Oct. 2000, then Second Coming and Millennium 45 days later. Two Witnesses = Moses and Elijah, descend from clouds, televised, supernaturally protected. Believers flee to Petra and Bozrah, supernaturally protected. Feinbergs part of the 144,000; some go to Israel, some witness at UCLA. Muslims, Asians, others revolt against Antichrist's New Roman Empire, tremendous nuclear destruction. Antichrist becomes world emperor, terrible persecution, martyrdom of believers. Science advisor "Terbor Esiw" (= Robert Wise, who advised author). Asteroids fulfill trumpet woes, literally interpreted. China vs. NRE nuclear exchanges, then Babylon destroyed. Antichrist invades at Armageddon: Moslems and 200 million Chinese confront him there. Meier: insists evolution impossible. Rapture not precisely dateable, but Second Coming exactly 1,260 days after Temple desecration (mid-Tribulation). Bible numerology; Equal Letter Sequence cited as proofs of supernatural origin, truth of End chronology.

2902. _____, and Robert L. Wise. *The Fourth Millennium: The Sequel.* 1996. Nashville: T. Nelson. 311 p.

2903. _____. *Beyond the Millennium.* Nashville: T. Nelson. 309 p.

Another sequel.

2904. Meredith, Roderick. *14 Signs Announcing Christ's Return.* [San Diego?] Global Church of God.

2905. Meresco, Donald. *New Light on the Rapture.* 1980. New York: Bible Light. 63 p. Scripture index.

Mid-Tribulation Rapture. Antichrist will be hailed as Israel's Messiah, but will desecrate the Temple midway through the Tribulation (the Abomination of Desolation) and turn on the Jews.

2906. Meyer, C.O. *At the Time of the End.* 1971. New York: Vantage Press. 300 p.

2907. Meyer, David J. *Last Trumpet Newsletter.* <http://www.biblerevelations/ org/articles>

Last Trumpet Ministries: Beaver Dam, WI. "As 1999 dawns we see the "Masterminds of the Great Illuminati Conspiracy scrambling like mad to finalize their hoped-for Luciferian New World Order objectives." Roman Catholicism is another component of this Satanic secret conspiracy: the Pope's signature "Dvx Cleri" = 666. Antichrist's Beast computer will take over after Y2k crash in 2000. "Voraciously blood-crazy" Chinese, eat aborted fetuses, are the Eastern hordes of Revelation. Meyer takes credit for praying Newt Gingrich out of power, calling him a Freemason and Illuminist who got the nefarious House Bill 666 passed. The government releases engineered diseases as an excuse to enforce debilitating vaccinations as a biological control mechanism.

2908. Meyer, Nathan M. *The Patmos Prediction.* 1989. Oklahoma City, OK: Prophecy Publications. 261 p. illus.

Meyer: ex-pastor and professor at Grace Brethren, Grace Theological Seminary. Nathan Meyer Bible Prophecy Assoc., Worthington, OH. Chatty exposition of book of Revelation. From sermons, chapter by chapter: "future history of the world." "Prepare for 'take-off'— soon!" Any-moment Rapture. Seven Churches: periods of church history: Ephesus to A.D. 100, Smyrna to 300, Pergamos to 500, Thyatira to 1500, Sardis to 1700, Philadelphia to 1900, Laodicean to present (age of apostasy). Rapture: probably a few hundred million beamed up. Antichrist = the coming world ruler = the Beast = First Horseman. Demands worship as God. 7-year Tribulation: over a billion killed. Plagues, woes literal. Image of Antichrist in the Temple comes alive. Literal mark of 666. Armies march across Euphrates to Armageddon. Giant hailstones, earthquakes. Antichrist may send UFOs after Rapture to deceive us into blaming ETs. Rome (Vatican) to be world capital. Invaders on literal horses — modern weapons rendered useless during Tribulation. Hell in earth's center. Literal Millennium, final rebellion end of Millennium. Final Judgment: the "end of time — the end of the world literally." New Jerusalem may be cube but probably pyramid shape. New Earth will be much bigger. God turns all atoms into energy, then reconstitutes matter. "We will eat in heaven." Eternal Hell for non-believers. Meyer also involved with search for Noah's Ark, Ark of Covenant, ashes of red heifer, Pharoah's chariots in Red Sea.

2909. Miceli, Vincent P. *The Antichrist.* c1981. Harrison, NY: Roman Catholic Books. 297 p. bibl. index.

Foreword by Malcolm Muggeridge. Collapse of Christianity and civilization; worldwide apostasy allows Antichrist, the false messiah, to appear. Mary: Prophetess of Last Days. Pope John Paul II realizes this is mankind's final struggle. Antichrist is leader of final revolt against God; last and worse oppressor of the Church; "culmination and recapitulation of all evils." Nero and Domitian were "types" of the Antichrist, but not Antichrist himself. Miceli refutes chiliasm (millenarianism — belief in literal Millennium on earth). Satan was bound during the present (6th) millennium. Two Witnesses = Enoch and Elias.

2910. Michael, Allen. *UFO-ETI World Master Plan.* 1977. Berkeley: One World Family Starmast Publications. 159 p.

"Channelings from the EVERLAST-ING GOSPEL" (of the Universal Mind cybernetic intelligence). Advocates bringing prophesied "New Order for the Ages." Life throughout universe. Space beings from Galactic Command here to channel peace messages. Evil "cyborg capitalism" = Beast of Revelation, Gog and Magog. Michael: "New World Comforter" prophesied in John 14:15-17,26 to bring forth "One World Nation of Israel." "Orthodox science" is leading mankind to Doomsday. Urges we get rid of money and punitive justice; advocates non-violent World Master Plan. Ominous Jewish bankers; Babylon money system run by Zionism. Fed Reserve and CIA is seat of "Gog" world bank "set up by the USSR tribe of Judah." U.S. = Tribe of Joseph. "Christ Communism" = heaven on earth. "Common sense tells everyone that there should be a sharing of all things...." 1,290 day period to rid world of nationalism. Last war will be in Mid East. 144,000 = telepathic ETI incarnates. Gog forced Russia and will force U.S. into communism. If ETIs don't bring peace now, then will after Tribulation. Cleansing process began 1914. Hitler and followers had psychic power from astral entities. Ridicules orthodox denominations' belief of Jesus. WWII= Armageddon; fulfilled Ezek. 38. Nazism was CIA plot to destroy USSR Israel, but ETIs prevented U.S. from joining Nazis. ETI may rig WWIII Armageddon in U.S. and Mid East to allow world communism to win. Messiah Michael sent to warn U.S. what to do to "offset a terrible Karmic cleansing revolution that is coming over this country resulting from a war that erupts in the Middle East."

2911. Michaelson, Sylvia J. *The New World Order: "The Mark (Dollar Sign) of the Beast."* 1991. Helena, MT: Ministering Angel Publications. 178 p. illus.

Also wrote *Lucifer the Beautiful* (1988).

2912. Michaelson, Victor. *Delayed Time-Setting Heresies Exposed.* 1989 [1985]. Payson, AZ: Leaves-of-Autumn Books. 86 p. charts.

Seventh-day Adventist. Refutation of Hauser 1983; condemns futurist heresy by Hauser and other Adventists, calling it "fortune-telling wizardry" and a "hydra-monstrosity" of "Babylonian-Mosaic-Adventist concepts" contaminated by "Jesuitical infiltration tactics." Insists on day-for-a-year principle ("day" means year) and historicist interpretation. Refers to other "time-setters" (""C.W." [Charles Wheeling], "W.W.," and "H.C.") who predict Second Coming for Aug. 3, 1987, for 1991, and for Aug. 27, 1996.

2913. Michell, John F. *City of Revelation: On the Proportion and Symbolic Numbers of the Cosmic Temple.* 1973 [1972]. London: Garnstone. 176 p. illus.

New Jerusalem will be a pyramid.

2914. Mickelsen, A. Berkeley. *Daniel and Revelation: Riddles or Realities?* 1984. Nashville: Thomas Nelson. xi, 266 p. bibl., indexes. ("Mickelson" misspelled on title page.)

Mickelson: prof. Bethel Theological Seminary (St Paul, MN). Dan. prophecies fulfilled in time of Antiochus. But argues for early date of composition of Dan. Disavows obsessive predictions, criticizes "crystal ball" approach and literalist interpretation of apocalyptic numbers. Prophecy is both foretelling and "forth-telling" (i.e. relationship of humans to God). Symbols have multiple referents, past and future.

2915. *The Midnight Cry: William Miller & the End of the World.* 1994. Lthika Intl. Film & Entertainment, in assoc. with Alpha Prod. and Pacific Press. video.

2916. Miladin, George C. *Is This Really the End?: A Reformed Analysis of The Late Great Planet Earth.* 1974 [1972]. Cherry Hill, NJ: Mack. v, 56 p. bibl. refs.

Post-mill. Refutes dispensationalist futurism (the "Thieme-Lindsey" scheme). Exact date of End can't be known for sure.

2917. *Millennium: Frightful Things to Come?* <http://home.sprynet.com/sprynet/astanton/> (Arnie Stanton's site.)

Antichrist's treaty with Israel A.D. 1999, Second Coming 2006. Most of the 144,000 Jewish Witnesses in End Times from Lost Tribes of Israel (now amongst Gentiles). Antichrist will try to fool us into believing that Armageddon and Tribulation are already past and that we are entering new Golden Age. Emphasis on UFOs.

2918. *Millennium Superworld.* 1981. Rochester, NY: Megiddo Mission Church. 142 p. index.

Meggido Mission Church founded by L.T. Nichols. "Social and moral conditions in the world today are precisely those predicted for the '*last days*'...." Imminent Second Coming, preceded by Elijah, who begins moral reformation. Rapture at Second Coming but people remain on earth; also Armageddon.

2919. Miller, Betty. *Mark of God, or, Mark of the Beast.* 1991. Dewey, AR: Christ Unlimited Ministries. iv, 104 p. End Time series.

2920. _____. *Personal Spiritual Warfare.* 1991. Dewey, AR: Christ Unlimited Ministries. iv, 83 p. End Time series.

2921. Miller, C. Leslie. *Goodbye World.* 1972. Glendale, CA: G/L Regal. [viii], 147 p. chart.

Foreword by Wilbur Smith. Miller: editor at Gospel Light. Pre-mill pre-trib: apostasy and occultism as signs of coming End, then Rapture, Antichrist appears, Tribulation, False Prophet proclaims Antichrist is God, Two Witnesses perform miracles, Antichrist's armies invade Jerusalem, Second Coming, Armageddon, Millennium. Very literal interpretation. False Prophet displays miraculous talking statue of Antichrist demanding he be worshipped. U.S. is place of refuge for Jews during Tribulation. Newspaper headlines will scream "MILLIONS MISSING" at Rapture, then "BE BRANDED OR DIE" (with the Mark of the Beast) during Tribulation. Literal river of blood at Armageddon.

2922. Miller, D.A. *Forbidden Knowledge: Or Is It? Unlocking Biblical Prophecies and New Insight Into the Last Days.* 1994 [c1991]. San Juan Capistrano, CA: Joy. 175 p. illus.

Foreword: Chuck Missler. Jewish Feasts as key to dates. Rapture to occur on Rosh HaShana, but year not certain. Second Coming may not be exactly seven years later, so can't be predicted precisely.

2923. _____. *Watch & Be Ready: 1992 Millions Disappear?* c1992. Stockton, CA: Prophetic Research Assoc. 90 p. charts.

Proposes "exact dates ... God is a date setter." 1992 = Rapture and beginning of 7-year Tribulation. Unified world religion and New World Order global leader (= Anti-Christ) emerges; those who cooperate with this are doomed. Anti-Christ signs 7 year treaty with Israel, literal False Prophet, Two Witnesses. Midpoint of Tribulation: abominable sacrifice in Temple, Antichrist worshipped as god. End of Tribulation: Second Coming, defeat of Anti-Christ and False Prophet, destruction of world empire. Creation ca. 6000 B.C.; geologists wrong. Added proof: occultist Jeane Dixon predicts savior before A.D. 2000 — Satan's counterfeit. Russian invasion of Israel probably at start of Tribulation (Sept. 28, Rosh HaShanah 1992). Millennium begins 75 days after Second Coming.

2924. Miller, David Arthur. *The Song of Moses and the Lamb: A Layman's Interpretation of the Judgment Hour Message.* 1985. Ringgold, GA: Inst. of Natural Health Science. [2] l, ii, 118 p.

Seventh-day Adventist.

2925. Miller, Ernest J. *The Final Battle.* 1987. New Wine. rev. ed. vi, 201 p.

2926. Miller, Harland W. *Make Yourself Ready: Preparing to Meet the King.* 1998. Lafayette, LA: Prescott Press. xi, 217 p. bibl. refs.

2927. Miller, [Monte] Kim. *The Fourth Dimension Mind Power and the Apostate Church.* Cassette. 1988. Denver, CO: Concerned Christians.

Miller: leader of Denver-based Concerned Christians, which began as cult-exposing group. Here Miller attacks Yonggi Cho of Korea, and he becomes increasingly critical of all "apostate" influences. He prophesied destruction of Denver for Oct. 10, 1998, then left for

Jerusalem with some of his followers. Miller claimed he was one of the Two Witnesses, and would be killed in Jerusalem in 1999 prior to the Second Coming. Israel deported members of his group fearing they would try to precipitate these events by violence. Whore of Babylon = America (the Little Horn, which arose from Ten Nations of Europe).

2928. Mills, Newt V. *This Is the Last Message: The End Time — the Lord's Return.* 1975 [Monroe, LA?]: Newt V. Mills Crusade. viii, 145 p.

Former U.S. Congressman from Louisiana (1937–43). Hour of End is "very eminent [sic]" — "Closer than you expect." God's miraculous interventions (author instantly healed of cancer on his nose); fulfilled prophecy. All international events prove remaining prophecies are being fulfilled now. Also satanic supernatural feats such as Uri Geller's; false prophets able to raise dead. 7-year Tribulation, including greatest ever earthquake. Perfect timetable from Creation, Flood, to End. Pre-trib Rapture. Coming 666 economic system of Beast: federally operated computer; 666 inscribed on Social Security card; those who accept this mark are eternally lost. Russia attacks at beginning of Tribulation (Gog Magog); Christ smashes Russian attack with earthquake. 10 Nation European (Roman) Empire becomes dominant after Russia is destroyed by Christ. Stresses difference between Russia attack and Armageddon. Two Witnesses = Enoch and Elijah. Beast from Sea = Antichrist. Second Beast = False Prophet. Righteous flee to Rock City (Sela) in Moab. WWIII (= Tribulation) starts one year, one month, one day, and one hour before the Second Coming. Wicked raised after Millennium for Judgment. Stresses eternal punishment and damnation.

2929. Milne, Bruce. *What the Bible Teaches About the End of the World.* 1979. Wheaton, IL: Tyndale. 159 p. bibl. index.

2930. Missler, Chuck. 1995. *The Magog Invasion.* Palos Verdes, CA: Western Front. 311 p. illus. maps, bibl. refs.

Ezek. 38–39. Hal Lindsey wrote *Magog Factor* (1992), reportedly plagiariz-ing from Edwin Yamauchi's 1982 *Foes from the Northern Frontier* (Yamauchi refuted claim that Rosh, Magog, etc., refer to Russia). Lindsey didn't publish this, but Missler's *Magog Invasion* has much of same text (including sections from Yamauchi).

2931. Mitchell, E., P. Jones, and J. Scharf. *The Mystery of Babylon Revealed.* 1980. Hesperia, CA: Truth Station. 211 p.

"Inspired by The Holy Spirit." Pentecostal; consists largely of Bible quotes. Now reaching climax of struggle between Satan's master plan and God's. Pagan worship continued via Catholic Church. "Catholicism is an unholy anti-Christ SPIRIT!" "CATHOLICISM IS THE NUCLEUS FOR THE SUPER-HAR-LOT CHURCH THAT IS FORMING IN THE END-TIME." America = Modern Babylon. Demonic spirits cause ESP, occult, psychic phenomena. Frantic writing style.

2932. Moatti, Pierre-Jean. *1984, l'Apocalypse?—.* Montreal: Presses de la Cité. 1982. 397 p. illus. maps, bibl.

Jews and Israel in prophecy. Also pub. Nice(?): A. Lefeuvre, 1980. Occult prophecy.

2933. Montague, George T. *The Apocalypse: Understanding the Book of Revelation and the End of the World.* 1992. Ann Arbor, MI: Servant. 246 p. illus.

2934. Montgomery, Ruth. *Threshold to Tomorrow.* c1982. New York: G.P. Putnam's Sons. 269 p. 1994 Ballantine ed.

Coming world war and natural catastrophes. Continues author's *Strangers Among Us* (extraterrestrials).

2935. Moore, Marvin. *The Crisis of the End Time: Keeping Your Relationship with Jesus in Earth's Darkest Hour.* 1992. Boise, ID: Pacific Press. 253 p.

Seventh-day Adventist pastor and editor at Pacific Press. Well written. Follows E.G. White. "Prior to the second coming of Christ, the entire planet will be engulfed in disasters more severe than anything the world has ever known." "Jesus is coming very soon." Satan will present himself as extraterrestrial Messiah — Christ. Close of "Probation," then Time of Trouble (Tribulation — Seven last plagues), then

Second Coming. Natural disasters, Sunday laws, rise of spiritualism. First Beast = Papacy; Second Beast = America. Believers to receive "latter rain"—spiritual outpouring of Holy Spirit—in End Times. Armageddon is final spiritual battle.

2936. _____. *The Antichrist and the New World Order.* 1993. Boise, ID: Pacific Press. 127 p. illus. bibl. refs.

A "'plain folks' explanation of the end times for non-Adventists."

2937. _____. *The Coming Great Calamity.* 1997 [1996]. Boise, ID: Pacific Press. 190 p. bibl. refs.

Follows E.G. White closely. "God is about to intervene again with His weapons of warfare." "A terrible crisis is coming upon the world"—probably within our lifetime. Second Coming preceded by horrible natural disasters, probably including asteroids or comets colliding with Earth. These disasters result in "paradigm shift"—world comes under religious control. Satan's end-time deceptions include belief in the Rapture, Marian visions (Catholic), and false miracles. Uses M. Barkun's analysis of millennialist belief.

2938. Moore, Philip N. *The End of History: Messiah Conspiracy.* 1996. Atlanta, GA: The Conspiracy, Inc. xiv, 1207 p. illus. bibl. refs.

Conspiracy by rabbis to hide and deny messianic beliefs of Jews, institutionalized A.D. 70-110 at Yavne yeshiva. Early Jews believed Messiah would die first, then come a second time to defeat Gog and Magog. Seven years prior to this Antichrist (= Armilus of Hebrew writings) would dominate and deceive Jews. Jeanne Dixon, Cayce, Nostradamus: all false demonic prophets. The "end" of the Cold War and breakup of the Soviet Union was just a clever ploy to disarm the West. Final Seven Years probably to start between 2020 and 2048, with Russian and Arab attack on Israel. Antichrist will then try to take credit for their defeat at beginning of Tribulation. The Rapture will be rationalized as UFO abductions. "The time key is that there is a biblical history of 7000 years marked off—the Kingdom lasts 1000 years and we are nearing the end of 6000

years...." After the Millennium, the whole world is molecularly transformed into imperishable elements—mostly precious gems—and the laws of decay and gravity are abolished. Evolution is false: Gap Theory creationism—pre-Adamic fall of Lucifer followed by Adamic creation 6,000 years ago. Praises Isaac Newton's prophetic writings. Author of Book of Revelation "was actually catapulted by God into a time-warp" in order to see future events. Hitler, demon-possessed, foresaw Satan's plan and predicted End for about 2045. Columbus was a Messianic Jew. Includes charts from Larkin; Jack Chick material.

2939. _____. *Nightmare of the Apocalypse: The Rabbi Conspiracy.* 1997. Atlanta: The Conspiracy xii, 370 p. illus. bibl. refs.

"Researcher for Hal Lindsey." Foreword by Sid Roth. Endorsed by Moishe Rosen (Jews for Jesus). Nephilim: half-breed demon monsters; from rape of women by Satan's fallen angels; tried to prevent Christ by destroying Jesus before birth; but destroyed by Flood. Endorses ELS gematria (prophetic messages encoded in Bible). Russia invades Israel ca. 2020. End any time up to 2055. "We believe Jesus' return is almost a certainty between 2017 and 2033!" U.S. may escape worst Tribulation if it develops SDI and other military defenses. Claims Golda Meir accepted Christ. Correlations and parallels between Genesis and Revelation. Petra for Jews during Tribulation. Abortionists eternally in Hell, aborted fetuses eternally with God. AIDS created by World Health Org. Early rabbis covered up Bible prophecies of Jesus as Messiah.

2940. Morris, Henry M. *The Flood Last Time and the Fire Next Time.* 1977. San Diego: Inst. for Creation Research. Tape.

2941. _____. *The Revelation Record: A Scientific and Devotional Commentary on the Book of Revelation.* 1983. Wheaton, IL: Tyndale House; San Diego, CA: Creation-Life. 521 p. illus. index.

Verse-by-verse commentary, using King James version. Revelation is a "sequel to Genesis"; together they are "foundation and capstone" of God's divine word. "Literalistic, futuristic, sequential, pre-mill, pre-trib interpretation." Suggests his is the "*most* literal" interpretation, viewing Revelation as "real, future history." World is ruled by Satanically-controlled Beast in second half of Tribulation, preceded by miraculous deeds and prophesying of Two Witnesses. Day of Lord, of Wrath = start of the Tribulation. Russia = Magog; Gog = probably Georgia. Tarshish = Carthage; probably Western nations generally. Russia and Islamic allies attack, using paratroops and modern weapons (made of lignostone, which Jews later burn for fuel). God sends cataclysmic catastrophes. Israel then razes Dome of Rock, rebuilds Temple. All Western allies then forge vast politico-commercial-religious alliance for world domination: nucleus is 10-nation empire. Rapture could be before or after Russian invasion. First of Four Horsemen is Christ. "Oil" of Third is probably petroleum. 144,000 "completed Jews" witness after series of plagues, convert multitude of Gentiles (Tribulation saints). Oceans literally turn red, a third of ships and of ocean life destroyed, by asteroid or meteorite strike. Angels reduce solar output. Shaft to Hell opened ("bottomless pit"), demonic spirits ("locusts") emerge to torment mankind. 200-million demonic "horsemen": maybe Centaurs, kill an average of six people each. Two Witnesses (Enoch and Elijah) bring about plagues, thwart the Beast. The Beast kills them, and the demonic horsemen, but Two Witnesses resurrected on TV. Satan is defeated, thrown out of heaven mid-Tribulation, vents wrath on Israel. Second Beast = False Prophet. Gog battle at beginning of Tribulation; Armageddon at end. Four Beasts of Daniel 7: not sequential but contemporaneous: West (Britain, U.S.), Bear (Soviets), Leopard (East), 4th (European confederacy) eventually dominates. First Beast of Sea = 4th of Daniel. Seven heads = historical kingdoms. Beast is both kingdom and leader. Leader assassinated, revives on TV. When Beast becomes global dictator, he turns against monstrous religious complex (Harlot). Babylon rebuilt as world capital. Beast conquers other nations of world first half of Tribulation. All religions amalgamated into one, led by the False Prophet. Satan speaks through "audio-animatronics" of the Beast's image. Three kinds of brands: Mark (logo), name, and number of Beast. 1st vial: loathsome sores = react with chemicals of Mark. Sun increases, oceans are poisoned. Euphrates blocked by tectonic upheavals; cripples Babylon. Hordes converge on Israel, many on horseback, to battle Christ and heavenly army assembled at Armageddon. Armageddon yields 180 miles of bridle-high blood. 200-million army from most nations, led by Beast, literally crushed by Christ. Tremendous earthquake levels all cities except Jerusalem. Angel in the sun calls for all birds to clean up Armageddon carnage. River from Dead Sea to Mediterranean. Earth's surface largely levelled, returns to antediluvian conditions, with Water Canopy and worldwide Edenic environment. Morris estimates there will be 4 billion resurrected saints. Only a small remnant population is alive at beginning of Millennium, but undergoes spectacular increase. By end of Millennium, a huge population is susceptible to Satan's final deception. During the Millennium, the New Jerusalem is suspended in the atmosphere, occupied by an estimated 20 billion saints (1/30 cubic mile for each). They travel over the universe in spiritual bodies. "Revelation is not difficult to understand. It is difficult to believe. If you believe it, you will understand it."

2942. _____. *Creation and the Second Coming.* 1991. El Cajon, CA: Master Books. xii, 194 p. bibl.

Evolution linked to New Age occultism, racism, Satanism — last days apostasy and deception. Evolutionists are the scoffers of the Last Days who doubt creation and the Second Coming (2 Pet. 3).

2943. Moss, Ralph. *Fire Bell in the Night.* 1993. Brushton, NY: TEACH Services. Iv, 105 p., bibl. refs.

Seventh-day Adventist. Coming Catholic domination. Great Whore = Catholic Church. Papacy allied with One World government. Devil will deceive world with spiritualistic miracles.

2944. Mostert, Orlando. *South Africa in the End Times.* 1980. 2nd ed. Braamfontein: Private Bag. 136 p. map.

Author heads Agápe ministry. In ten years South Africa will be world's greatest nation. God created South Africa for special purpose: specific end-time role as Ark of Safety, Second Israel, and World Liberator after Armageddon. "These are the 'end-times' which are prophesied...." Certain catastrophe by early 1980s. Russia will invade Middle East; Europe and Japan will collapse; China attacks with 200-million man army. America attacked by Russia and Warsaw Pact nations, both sides destroyed in world nuclear holocaust. South Africa will then lead survivors of world into New World Order. "Beyond the rivers of Ethiopia" (Isa. and Zeph.) = South Africa. New York = Babylon. UFOs are occultic apparitions used by Satan to deceive humanity.

2945. Mould, David. *The Pope, the Jesuits and the New World Order.* 1991. DeLand, FL: Laymen for Religious Liberty. 2 videos.

Service from Kingston, Jamaica, about fulfillment of prophecies in Daniel and Revelation. Adventist.

2946. _____. *A Call to Arms.* N.d. Jesus Behind Bars: Laymen for Religious Liberty.

2947. Mowll, Basil C. *The Approaching Day of Glory.* 1979 [1970]. Eastbourne, England: Prophetic Witness. [14], 38 p. plate, illus.

2948. Munilla, Luis. 1991. *The 7 Feasts of the Lord and the 1994 Jubilee.* Jemison, AL: priv. pub. 199 p. illus. maps. bibl. refs. "New updated ed."

Judaism.

2949. Murillo, Mario. *Fresh Fire (in the End Times).* 1991. Danville, CA: Anthony Douglas. 137 p.

"When you are finally serious about power in the end times." "Satan, sensing impending doom, has broken into a sprint. He is submerging America as fast as possible in despair, violence and filth."

2950. Musser, Joe. *Behold a Pale Horse.* 1970. Grand Rapids, MI: Zondervan 140 p.

Novel. Includes "Beast" computer in Brussels (which many fundamentalists subsequently accepted as non-fiction).

2951. Nagele, Kenneth. *The Elegan Files: A Guide to Understanding Life in the End-Times.* Orange, CA: Elegan Publishing.

Nagele: former Worldwide Church of God member (H.W. Armstrong). Posttrib. Antichrist may be a Balkan of Jewish descent. The final seven years will be time of extreme prosperity, allowing Antichrist to deceive the whole world into accepting him. After he kills the Two Witnesses, who he accuses of being the Beast and False Prophet, he claims he is the real Christ. Nagele recommends Ernest L. Martin, who describes spectacular astronomical display Sept. 21, 3 B.C. at Christ's birth, and predicts increasing knowledge of Christ in the seven years from 1997 to 2004.

2952. Nageley, Jack R. *The Dissolution of Society.* 1971. Miami: Review Printing. iii, 88. illus. maps.

2953. Nathan, K. Shanmuga. *Even So Come, Lord Jesus; The Second Coming of the Lord of the Sabbath: the Time and the Delay.* 1990. Madurai, India: author. 71, 102 p.

Seventh-day Adventist.

2954. Neighbour, Ralph Webster, and Gerald L. Stover. *Planet Earth: On the Brink of Eternity.* 1973. Elyria, OH: Morning Sunshine. 96 p.

2955. Neil, Richard L. *His Coming: God Has a Plan to End Suffering on Earth and Bring His People Into a New World.* 1988. Washington, DC: Review and Herald. 94 p.

Seventh-day Adventist.

2956. Nelson, Dwight K. *Countdown to the Showdown.* 1992. Fallbrook, CA: Hart Research Center. 128 p.

Seventh-day Adventist. Pastor of campus church at Andrews Univ. Literate presentation. 538 (A.D.) + 1,260 = 1798. U.S. prophesied to be the sole superpower near End. Beast = Papacy. Proposed laws requiring Sunday worship. Second Beast (False Prophet) = U.S. Satan will impersonate Christ and be acclaimed as Savior.

World plunges into all manner of disasters, then Second Coming.

2957. _____. *The Jesus Generation.* 1993. Fallbrook, CA: Hart Research Center. 142 p.

Sequel to *Countdown to the Showdown.*

2958. The New World Foundation Staff, eds. *The Bible II: How to Get to Heaven.* 1991. Midland, TX: New World Press. 630 p.

How to Get to Heaven abridgement of *The Bible II.* 600 B.C. God sent Israelites to America. Unbelieving survivors of great war (Indians) later succumbed to Gentiles. "Then, at the end of the age, the records would come forth to reveal more of God's mysteries. 'And when that day shall come they shall be visited of the Lord of Hosts, with thunder & with earthquake, & with great noise, & with storm, & with tempest, & with the flame of devouring fire.'"

2959. Newport, John P. *The Lion and the Lamb.* 1986. Nashville: Broadman Press. 381 p. bibl. indexes.

Newport: Ph.D. Univ. Edinburgh. Historic pre-mill. Stresses literary framework, dramatic and symbolic, of Revelation; dangers of both rigid dispensationalist approach and liberal (which denies any prophetic validity). Serious study of context, various views, very broad overview. Personal Antichrist. "Foreshortened future" concept: far events seen as close. Some "trans-historical" meanings. Includes verse-by-verse commentary with different interpretations. First Horseman = Gospel truth (if not Christ himself). Great Tribulation is final convulsive effort of Satan. Steers between literal and totally symbolic approach. 200 million = demonic hordes. Armageddon more judicial than military. Millennium: duration uncertain; perfect justice, but human rebelliousness manifested in final rebellion.

2960. *The Next Nuclear Wars: Bible Study Guide on End Time Prophecy.* 1986. New York: Vantage Press. xiii, 39 p.

2961. Nicholas, C.L. *The Bridegroom Is Coming.* 1994. Coloma, MI: Double A Pub. ii, 152 p. bibl. refs., index. rev ed. 1995 ed. has vii, 348 p.

2962. Nixon, Thomas C. *The Time of the End in the Book of Daniel.* 1990. Sandpoint, ID: Elmira Press. iii, 259 p.

2963. Nodrog [Orville T. Gordon]. *State of Time Station Earth.* Weslaco, TX: Armageddon Time Ark Base.

God to destroy U.S. by Flood. 6,000 years ends Sept. 3, 1996. Nodrog's 5th dimensional Time Ark will rescue believers from Armageddon; then transported by flying saucers.

2964. Noe, John R. *The Apocalypse Conspiracy: Why the World May Not End as Soon as You Think and What You Should Be Doing in the Meantime.* 1991. Brentwood TN: Wolgemuth & Hyatt. xii, 279 p. bibl. refs. indexes.

2965. Noebel, David A. *The Homosexual Revolution: End Time Abomination.* 1977. Tulsa, OK: Center for Christian Conservative Studies, Amer. Christian Coll. 100 p.

2966. Noone, Richard William. *Ice: The Ultimate Disaster.* 1982. Dunwoody, GA: Genesis Publishers. 380 p. photos, drawings bibl. refs. *5/5/2000* later prefaced to title. Also pub. Astraea (Atlanta) and Harmony Books (1986).

Great catastrophe on May 5, 2000. 6,000 years since last time planets were in straight line.

2967. Noorbergen, Rene. *Nostradamus Predicts the End of the World.* 1982 [1981]. New York: Pinnacle Books. 226 p. illus. bibl. 1981. ed titled *Invitation to a Holocaust* (NY: St. Martins; 200 p).

2968. _____. *A.D. 2000: A Book About the End of Time.* 1984. Indianapolis: Bobbs-Merrill. xiii, 166 p. bibl., index.

"Research by Joey Jochmans."

2969. Nori, Don. 1996. *The Angel and the Judgment.* [s.l.]: Don Nori. 179 p. illus.

2970. Norman, Bruce. *Preach the Word: Last-Day Events.* 1993. Silang [Philippines]: 1000 Missionary Movement Publications. 157 p.

Seventh-day Adventist.

2971. Norman, Ruth. *History of the Universe: And You— A Star Traveler.* 1983 [1981]. El Cajon, CA: Unarius Educational Foundation. 3 vols. illus. "Inspired by Uriel" (Norman's extraterrestrial manifestation) but actually written by Charles von Spaegel, Uriel's "sub-channel." UFOs, psychic channeling, reincarnation, energy forces, higher vibrational planes, different dimensions, Atlantis, etc. In 2001, flying saucers from 33 planets will stack up on Earth to usher in the age of Unarius (Christ's Second Coming) and welcome us into the Intergalactic Confederation. Satan is evil force seeking to prevent our psychic evolution who gained control over the demonic sub-astral planets of Orion. "Aryans" from Aries have achieved the highest consciousness.

2972. North, Gary. *Is the World Running Down?: Crisis in the Christian Worldview.* 1988. Tyler, TX: Inst. for Christian Economics. xxxiv, 345 p. indexes.

North: Christian Reconstructionist; post-mill. Claims that pre-mill interpretation breeds defeatism and apathy because of expectation that the world is decaying and getting worse. Urges post-mill conviction that Christians will take dominion over all aspects of society and establish the Millennium prior to the Second Coming. The Resurrection of Christ refutes entropy; the world is not running down, and Christians will take over the world and set up a strict Bible-based theonomy.

2973. _____. *Millennialism and Social Theory.* 1990. Tyler, TX: Inst. Christian Economics. xvi, 393 p. bibl. refs., index.

Argues that post-mill belief is evangelically more effective and results in stronger conversions. Historical *progress* is biblical idea. Claims Augustine really more post- than a-mill. Harshly critical of dispensational pre-millennialism. Advocates "neo-Puritanism." Allows that Millennium will probably come only after crises — economic failure, diseases — scare people into repentance. Vehemently denies that post-mill interpretation was invented by Whitby; but says much early post-millennialism (i.e. Jonathan Edwards) was pietistic rather than judicial.

2974. _____. *Rapture Fever: Why Dispensationalism is Paralyzed.* 1993. Tyler,

TX: Inst. Christian Economics. xxxv, 246 p.

Aims to "refute in print every aspect of dispensational theology." Savages dispensational pre-mill writers; says leading pre-mill theologians are afraid to confront post-mill arguments, leave field to sensationalizing writers. Pre-mill doomsday books sell millions, but are very unscholarly, and cannot effectively oppose humanism; "pietistic defeatists." Pre-mills don't trust Bible as guide and rulebook; resign themselves to eschatological ghetto. Pre-mill "any moment" doctrine means no prophecies left to be fulfilled before Rapture; clock has stopped ticking; Rapture may or may not be imminent. But sensationalists realize "ticking clock" books of prophecy being fulfilled now sell, so they betray official dispensational pre-mill doctrine. Hal Lindsey is an "intellectual fraud." Says Walvoord dropped "any-moment Rapture" doctrine in favor of Lindsey's ticking clock. Accuses pre-tribs of not wanting to convert Jews because ⅔ are required to be killed in Israel during Tribulation to fulfill scenario. "Biblical prophecy" vs. "eschatology": former may not be *our* future (i.e. already fulfilled). "Last Days" vs. "End Times": former applies to Old Covenant Israel, latter to *our* end. Suggests that "Constance Cumbey" may be pseudonym of Salem Kirban. Claims that many dispensationalists quietly abandoning or de-emphasizing doctrines. Chapter on "Dispensationalism vs. Six-Day Creationism." The Tribulation was A.D. 70; Nero was the Beast and Antichrist.

2975. North, Stafford. *Armageddon Again? A Reply to Hal Lindsey.* 1991 [1982]. 2nd ed. Oklahoma City: Oklahoma Christian Univ. 124 p. bibl. Orig priv pub.

1982 ed. titled *Armageddon When?*

2976. Oakes, Raymond F. *The Sealing & The 144,000.* N.d. 40 p. Reprinted 1992 by Leaves-Of-Autumn.

2977. _____. *The Mark of the Beast— The Badge of the Lost.* 1990. Payson, AZ: Leaves-of-Autumn Books. 53 p.

"A Special Study of this subject for Seventh-Day Adventists." Based on previous pamphlet *The Sealing and the 144,000.*

Argues that the 144,000 are "entire number" of the saved, including the dead (but notes this isn't official Seventh-day Adventist doctrine). The Mark is Sunday worship, which Seventh-day Adventists succumb to from desire to assimilate, thus mixing with false religions. Cites Loughborough. Condemns interracial marriages.

2978. Obu, O(lumba) O. 1994. *The Armageddon War.* Calabar, Nigeria: Everlasting Gospel Centre, Printers, Brotherhood Printing Press. iv, 35 p.; 23 cm.

Sermons delivered by His Holiness, Leader O. Brotherhood of the Cross and Star (Nigeria).

2979. Odendall, Dirk H. *The Eschatological Expectation of Isaiah 40-66 with Special Reference to Israel and the Nations.* 1970. Philadelphia: Presbyterian and Reformed. 202 p. bibl.

Odendall: Decoligny Theol. Coll. (South Africa). Book orig. Ph.D. thesis (Westminster Theological Seminary).

2980. Odle, Joe T. *Is Christ Coming Soon?* 1971. Nashville: Broadman Press. xvii, 127 p.

2981. Odom, Robert Leo. *Israel's Preexistent Messiah.* 1985. Bronx, NY: Israelite Heritage Inst. 75 p. bibl. refs.

Earth created 6,000 years ago. Messiah existed prior to Creation. World about to experience unprecedented time of trouble. Little Horn of ten confederated Roman states: Papal Rome (A.D. 538 to 1798 = 1,260 years; then from 1929 to End).

2982. _____. *Israel's Prophetic Puzzle.* c1987. Washington, DC: Israelite Heritage Inst. 109 p. bibl.

2983. O'Hara, Richard. *Leader's Guide for God's Prophetic Calendar.* 1983. Charlotte, NC: Advent Christian General Conference of America. 61 p. illus.

2984. O'Neill, Dan, and Don Wagner. *Peace or Armageddon? The Unfolding Drama of the Middle East Peace Accord.* 1993. Grand Rapids, MI: Zondervan. 112 p. maps.

Foreword: Richard Halverson, Chaplain of U.S. Senate. Both authors with Mercy Corps Intl. About the 1993 Israeli-PLO Peace Accord. Evangelical, but addresses Arab Christians and Moslems as well as Jews. Agrees that events are of prophetic significance, but critical of hardline dispensational pre-mill interpretation, noting it encourages hastening of Armageddon.

2985. Oropeza, B.J. *99 Reasons Why No One Knows When Christ Will Return.* c1994. Downers Grove, IL: InterVarsity Press. 225 p. bibl. refs., indexes.

Oropeza: with Christian Research Institute (Irvine, CA). Discourages date-setting and tying prophecy to current events. End *could* come at any moment—or not for thousands of years.

2986. Orsden, Donald B. *The Holy Bible—The Final Testament: What is the Significance of 666?* 1992 [1988]. Sunnyvale, CA: Orsden Press. 46 p. illus.

"The Rapture will take place in 1998. Only those who have completely devoted themselves to Jesus will be saved. The numbers prove it. For God has left us with the number 666 to forewarn us of the end of the world and Judgment Day in Revelations 13:18. Numbers do not lie!.... 'For God, with all his powers, laid down the laws of numbers at the beginning of creation.' Take your super computers, you scientists, and feed the number 666 into them. The output will be the proof God gives that 1998 is the year Jesus will take the faithful with him.... Jesus is now in Japan, preparing for the struggle against Satan and the Beast. You must repent of your sins before 1998. If you miss the Rapture, your only hope of being saved is to die a horrific death as a martyr in the Great Tribulation that will start on June 7, 1998. Repent sinners!"

2987. Osborn, LaVerle. *Prepare to Meet Thy God and Survive the Coming Holocaust.* 1981. Ringgold, GA: Lamplighter's International. 180 p. illus.

Seventh-day Adventist.

2988. Osborne, John. *Unveiling the Apocalypse.* 1991. [Grand Island, FL]: Prophecy Countdown. 91 p. illus.

Seventh-day Adventist group; promotes neurolinguistic programming.

2989. _____. *The Military Takeover*

of America. 1994. 4 videos. Mt. Dora, FL: Prophecy Countdown.

An interview with Bob Trefz by John Osborne on Last Day events in America.

2990. Otis, George. *The Last of the Giants: Lifting the Veil on Islam and the End Times*. c1991. Tarrytown, NY: Chosen Books (Revell). 272 p. map, bibl.

Foreword by David Aikman (of *Time* magazine). Otis: president of The Sentinel Group (missionary). Islam, not Russia, is the End Time enemy. Advocates "spiritual mapping"—a sort of geopolitical strategy—to oppose Satan's powerful but not impregnable army. Demonic deceptions: Hinduism, materialism, witchcraft. Ominous rebuilding of Babylon and reviving of its spiritual evil. Mesopotamia again the geopolitical capital of world. "Islamic Beast Theory": Revelation interpreted as Islamic-Magog 10-nation, and Tribulation oppressor. Magog=10-nation Islamic coalition, with many former Soviet members, from Turkic-speaking areas from Turkey proper to China, joined by Arabs and Persians. Antichrist: al-Mahdi, faith-healer and miracle-worker. End-time invasion of Israel by this northern-led confederation. Rebuilding of Temple may trigger this "Islamic jihad." Armageddon, the terrible battle in Mid-East, will destroy all human kingdoms. Urges concentrated missionary activity in Mid-East ("back to Eden") to save as many as possible; pro-Israel. Also wrote *Ghost of Hagar*. Hinted that Kissinger was Antichrist.

2991. Otto, Helen Tzima. *Our Revelationary Age: The Prophecies for WWIII and the Year 2000*. 1994. Houston, TX: Verenikia Press. xvi, 489 p. illus. bibl. refs., index.

2992. Ouellette, Raymond. *1998, the Year of Destiny: Dramatic Prophecies of the Bible, Great Pyramid, Astrology, Numerology, Nostradamus, Edgar Cayce*. c1978. Fall River, MA: Aero Press. 511 p. (2 vols). illus., diagrams, tables, charts.

Pre-mill. Bible is God's word ("We shrink in horror from an atheist..."). Revelation Vials have "literal as well as a moral significance" Obvious we're living in prophesied last times; Second Coming "near." Computer proof of Joshua's Missing Day (gives no attribution): "computer came to a standstill"; engineers discovered "day of elapsed time lost in space...," plus Ahaz's 40 min. Advocates "Divinity of man." Great cosmic catastrophes in ages past: Mu, Atlantis. Shift of poles April 19, 1998: 6,000 Years ends, Millennium begins. Uses base date of 2001, subtracts a few years as correction. Predicted in Pyramid; relies on Davidson. Bible also basis for accurate date-fixing. Book full of intricate calculations. Cayce: authority on pole-shifting. Vol 2: Biblical analysis; Atlantis, Mu. Whites advanced "highest" of all the races. Also wrote *Psychic Magic*.

2993. Overbey, Scot. *Vladimir Zhirinovsky: The Man Who Would Be Gog*. 1994. Oklahoma City, OK: Hearthstone. 150 p. illus.

Ezekiel foretold Gog-led invasion of regathered Israel.

2994. Oyedele, Ezekiel Ola. 1995. *The Church of the Latter Day and God's Plan for the End Time*. [Ikeja?: Lagos State Baptist Conference?] 72 p. bibl. refs.

2995. Ozanne, C.G. *The First Seven Thousand Years*. 1970. Exposition Press.

2,500 years: 539 B.C. to A.D. 1982. Tribulation: 1989–96. 6,000 years from 4004 B.C. 1999. Sanctuary cleansed, Antichrist thrown out.

2996. Pacheco, Nelson S., and Tommy R. Blann. *Unmasking the Enemy: Visions Around the World and Global Deception in the End Times*. 1994 [c1993]. Arlington, VA: distr. by Bendan Press. 436 p. Rev ed. illus. bibl. refs.

Pacheco: U.S. Air Force Lt. Col. (ret.). Blann: chemical technician; UFO investigator. UFOs, the paranormal, Holy Shroud of Turin, Marian apparitions, New Age; also cattle mutilations, Satanic cults (including human sacrifices), crop circles, black helicopters. Flying saucers are evil manifestations: psycho-physical intrusions of "metaphysical intelligent entities" from "parallel universes" into our world, luring many into harm or false beliefs. Good manifestations also evident, such as apparitions of Virgin Mary (including faces in the clouds). Biblical Nephilim of fallen angels interbreeding with humans: Hitler may have been involved with demons trying to create physical bodies to inhabit.

2997. Pack, Charles L. *Dry Bones, Two Sticks & Falling Dominoes.* 1979. Oklahoma City, OK: Southwest Radio Church. 79 p. illus., maps.

Ezekiel's prophecy.

2998. Packer, Maurice Edwin John. *Christ's Second Coming Explained.* 1972. Eastbourne, England: Prophetic Witness. 15 p.

2999. Paisley, J. Kyle. *Reasons Why the Great Tribulation Must Precede the Church's Translation.* 1987. London: Sovereign Grace Advent Testimony. 8 p.

3000. [Palmer, Bobby]. *Prophecy Links!* 1998. <http:/www.tribulation.com/>

Atlantis Station website. Pre-trib.

3001. Panteleimon, Archimandrite, and Michael Hilko. *A Ray of Light: Instructions in Piety and the State of the World at the End of Time.* 1996 [1991]. Jordanville, NY: Holy Trinity Monastery. 96 p. illus.

Eastern Orthodox.

3002. Paquette, Jacques. *Apocalypse: Propheties de la Fin des Temps.* [Quebec, Can.]: priv. pub. 237 p.

Bible prophecies.

3003. Paredes Vielma, Cesar. *Preludio del Fin.* 1984. Merida, Venezuela: ULA. 120 p.

Biblical prophecy.

3004. Parsley, Rod. *An Approaching Apocalypse.* 1988. Columbus, OH: World Harvest Church. 3 cassettes.

3005. _____. *The Final Awakening: A Vision for the Endtime.* 1988. 4 cassettes. Columbus, OH: World Harvest Church.

3006. Pasedag, Willy Jack. *Letztes Geschehen nach der Bibel.* 1975. Bieselsberg: Morgenland-Verlag. 256 p. illus.

3007. Pate, C. Marvin. *The End of the Age Has Come: The Theology of Paul.* 1995. Grand Rapids, MI: Zondervan. 256 p. bibl. refs., indexes.

3008. _____, and Calvin B. Haines. *Doomsday Delusions: What's Wrong with Predictions about the End of the World.* 1995. Downers Grove IL: InterVarsity. 180 p. bibl. refs.

Any-moment, pre-trib, and "deeply committed to God's prophetic words" but extremely critical of date-setters, those who force prophecy to fit current events. Wrong to read current events into historical aspects. First Coming had eschatological significance. Stresses "already/not yet eschatological tension": parts fulfilled historically, parts future, parts both; multiple fulfillments; combination of futurized / realized eschatology; living in overlap age between age that was and age to come. Signs of the times began in Jesus's generation. Authors believe in Rapture, Tribulation; Antichrist to lead 10-Nation confederacy against Israel, but will be opposed by vast Chinese army, resulting in Armageddon, then Second Coming, Millennium. 4th Empire of Daniel really Greek (Macedonian), not historical and endtime Roman. Nero: precursor of Antichrist. Harlot = unfaithful Israel (destroyed by Empire).

3009. Patrick, F. Chris. *The Zodiac Conspiracy.* Orangevale, CA: Christian Research Ministries.

"God's Hidden Message in the Stars Revealed." Hale-Bopp and Hyakutake Comets among the endtime signs of Christ's soon Second Coming.

3010. Paulien, Jon. *As Speculation Builds, Let's Keep Our Eyes Focused on What the Bible Says About the End Time.* 1994. Hagerstown, MD: Review and Herald. 159 p. charts. bibl. refs.

Seventh-day Adventist. Studied under Hans LaRondelle. Seals and Trumpets are partly historical, some yet to come. Mentions being taught that End would come in 1964 (120 years after 1844), because Noah preached for 120 years before the Flood judgment.

3011. Paulus, Stefan. *Nostradamus 1999: Who Will Survive?* 1996. St. Paul, MN: Llewellyn. xvii, 282 p. maps. bibl. refs., index.

3012. Payne, J. Barton. SEE ALSO 1910–1970. *Encyclopedia of Biblical Prophecy; The Complete Guide to Scriptural Predictions and Their Fulfillment.* 1980

[1973]. Grand Rapids, MI: Baker. xxv, 754 p. indexes tables Reprint ed. of 1973 Harper & Row orig.

7th seal, 5-7th trumpets, 5-7th bowls all *after* Second Coming. "Classical" post-trib: 70th Week (Tribulation) is historical.

3013. Peace, Richard, and Dietrich Gruen. *Revelation: Looking at the End of Time.* 1989. Littleton, CO: Serendipity House. 111 p. illus. map. bibl.

3014. Peisker, Armor D., and Richard Shelly Taylor. *End Times: A Doctrinal Study on the Shape of Things to Come.* [1970s]. s.l.: s.n. 128 p. Teacher ed. Aldersgate doctrinal studies.

3015. Pekarek, Art Leon. *The End-Time Holocaust.* 1994. 161 p. bibl.

Antichrist, Rapture, WWIII. Also wrote *The Naked Truth About Gays* (1993, Oakland, CA: Lamb).

3016. Pemberton, Owen Richard. *The Truth About the Rapture of the Church.* Roswell, 1993. GA: Old Rugged Cross Press. 106 p.

3017. Penn, P. *The Remnant Seeds of Creation: A Strategy for Survival: King James and Charles Darwin Revisited.* 1990. Kansas City, MO: AAHAA Books. ix, 247 p. illus.

"The preservation of non-favoured races in the struggle for life." Orig. title: *The Origin of the Race, Society by Means of Good and Evil; or, Spirit and Creation — Flesh and Evolution.* Black creationism.

3018. Pentecost, J. Dwight. SEE ALSO 1910–1970. *Will Man Survive? Prophecy You Can Understand.* 1990 [1971]. Chicago: Moody Press. 208 p.

Pre-trib pre-mill. Pentecost: emeritus professor Dallas Theological Seminary.

3019. Perfect, Dick. *The Coming Invasion of Israel: A Brief and Easy to Read Exposition of Ezekiel 38.* 1992. Cardigan: Good Stewards. 27 p.

3020. Perkins, Bill, ed. *Steeling the Mind of America.* 1995. Green Forest, AR: New Leaf. 304 p. bibl. refs.

Contributors: John Ankerberg, Missler (Islam as Satanic occultism, collapse of U.S. and emergence of endtime European super-state, Yeltsin and Zhiri-novsky in prophecy, Russia [Magog] to invade Israel), McAlvany (emerging police state in America, black helicopters, surveillance and disarmament of populace, occult explosion), Hal Lindsey, Henry Morris (importance of creationism).

3021. Perkins, Donald. *According to Prophecy.* <http://www.according2prophecy.org/>

Perkins: black evangelist, formerly with Jimmy Swaggart, now with Immanuel Bible College, CA. Pre-trib pre-mill.

3022. Peters, Ted. *Fear, Faith, and the Future: Affirming Christian Hope in the Face of Doomsday Prophecies.* 1980. Minneapolis: Augsburg. 124 p. bibl. refs.

3023. Peters, Wes. *In Light of Biblical Prophecy.* <http://www.ionet/~wes/>

Mid-trib pre-mill. Final Seven Years ends with Second Coming, but Rapture occurs after the Sixth Seal, thus Christians undergo Antichrist's Tribulation, and many are martyred. Following Rapture, the Seventh Seal, then the Seven Trumpets and Bowls (the "wrath of God," here distinguished from the "Tribulation"). Russia, with Iraq, Iran, Turkey and others to invade Israel. Also does *The End Times* journal (Bakersfield, CA).

3024. Petersen, Bill. *The Last Days of Man.* 1977. Old Tappan, NJ: Spire Books. 190 p. Also pub. by Warner.

"Is Today the Day before Doomsday?... A serious look at our future as events the Bible says are Omens of the End come to pass." Accuracy of Bible prophecies. Not a coincidence that nuclear weapons, establishment of State of Israel, and UFOs all started around the same time.

3025. Petersen, Gordon E. *Daniel's Four Faces of Antichrist.* c1991. Colton, CA: World Prophetic Ministry. [iii], 66 p.

Pre-trib Rapture. The "world is ripe" for Antichrist to begin his reign. Revived Roman Empire now forming; to be ruled by Antichrist, who will kill at least 9 million Jews during 70th Week Tribulation.

3026. Peth, Howard. *Vanishing Saints: Is the Rapture Real?* 1988. Frederick, MD: Amazing Facts. 128 p. illus. bibl. refs.

3027. Petrisko, Thomas W. *Call of the Ages.* 1995. Santa Barbara, CA: Queenship Pub. 509 p. bibl. refs.

"Apparitions and revelations of the Virgin Mary foretell the coming fall of evil and an era of peace." Also wrote *The Sorrow, the Sacrifice, and the Triumph* (1994) about Irish prophetess Christina Gallagher.

3028. Pfandl, Gerhard. *The Time of the End in the Book of Daniel.* 1992. Berrien Springs, MI: Adventist Theol. Soc. Publications. 360 p. bibl., indexes.

Based on 1990 Ph.D thesis Andrews University.

3029. Phillips, Bob. *The Great Future Escape.* c1973. Santa Ana, CA: Vision House. [ii], 108 p.

Foreword by Tim LaHaye. Former title *When the Earth Quakes.* Phillips: dir. youth ministries at Hume, CA, Christian camp. Pre-trib; Rapture very soon. Tribulation: "wars, famines, pestilences, earthquakes, and other disasters of the past will be mild in comparison to this time of worldwide devastation." At Armageddon, revived Roman Empire, Russia (King of North), Egypt (King of South), and China (King of East, with 200-million man army), will all converge on Jerusalem. Battle results in literal 200-mile long bridle-deep river of blood. All enemies of God will be dead by the Millennium.

3030. Phillips, John. *Only God Can Prophesy!* 1975. Wheaton, IL: Harold Shaw. 147 p.

Pre-trib. "The time cannot be far distant when the trumpet will sound, the Church be swept upwards to glory, and the closing events of the age take place." Gog — Russia — will invade Israel, with Persia, Libya, Ethiopia, Egypt, and Gomer (Germany or the Balkans), but invaders will be annihilated. Nazi occultism; increase of demonic activity. Miraculous healing of Antichrist as Satanic imitation of Christ. Thermonuclear attack: "The entire East Coast, from Portland, Maine to Norfolk, Virginia and up to 150 miles inland would become a lake of fire."

3031. _____. *Exploring the Future.* c1983. Nashville: Thomas Nelson. 342 p.

Phillips: Moody Extension staff and Moody Monthly writer. Also wrote *Exploring Revelation.*

3032. Phillips, Michael R. *A Survival Guide for Tough Times.* 1979. Minneapolis: Bethany Fellowship. 176 p. bibl. refs.

Phillips: Christian bookstore owner. Doesn't take position on timing of Rapture (pre-, mid-, or post-trib). But Second Coming in this generation. 6,000 Year theory: epochal events every 2,000 years: Adam, Abraham, Jesus, and imminent Second Coming. Financial, physical, and medical preparation for Tribulation.

3033. Phillips, O.E. *When the Messiah Should Have Appeared.*

Daniel's 70 Weeks.

3034. Pierson, Robert H. *Good-Bye, Planet Earth.* c1976. Mountain View, CA: Pacific Press. 175 p.

"The end is near." Social, economic, moral, political chaos now; natural disasters. End likely ca. 2000 A.D. World dictator to emerge. Mark of the Beast = Sunday laws in U.S. Also wrote *The Final Countdown* (1966).

3035. _____. *What's Just Ahead.* 1978. Nashville: Southern Pub Assoc. 32 p.

Second Coming and the End.

3036. Pippenger, Jeff. *The Rise and Fall of the King of the North.* 1997. Hope Intl. 140 p.

3037. Pittman, Howard O. *The Fourth Beast.* Video. Christian Broadcasting. 98 p. illus.

Pittman died for fifteen minutes. God allowed him to see a person in the process of being possessed by demons. Also showed him the three great conspiracies and the five point plan that Lucifer will use to take over the world.

3038. Plueger, Aaron Luther. *Things to Come for Planet Earth: What the Bible Says About the Last Times.* 1977. St. Louis: Concordia. charts bibl. refs.

Plueger: Chino, CA, Lutheran pastor. Argues that dispensationalist interpretation is misleading many Christians, and that they may forsake faith because of its false teachings. Defines pre-, post-, a-mill positions. Argues for "historic" pre-mill position: non-dispensational. The Second Coming is followed immediately by the End of the World. Plueger denounces "second chance" doctrine of accepting Christ during Tribulation, after Rapture / Second Coming: if we miss salvation before Second Coming, there will not be time later. Bible speaks of "the end of the world, never of a secret rapture." End will come when least expected. May be any day, but can't predict it. Earth will physically disintegrate in explosive fire. "Near" and "far" fulfillment of prophecy — some things already partly fulfilled but more fulfillment later. 70th Week is whole Christian era. Great Tribulation is earthly life in this era. Armageddon may involve WWIII or Mid East conflict, but it is also current spiritual battle between Good and Evil. Desolations of Revelation are mostly "recapitulations" of First Advent or inter-advent conditions. The time just prior to the End may be both better *and* worse: great increase in belief, believers (reign of Christ — Millennium) and of Satan's increased activity (apostasy will increase). Many confessions and creeds affirm "traditional" pre-mill position on Millennium. Rev. 20: "summary of church history." Millennium: "Christ's inter-advent period of restraint on Satan until a final, brief release." Not literally 1,000 years. Antichrist probably will be real person. Includes chapter devoted to critique of Lindsey's *Late Great Planet Earth.*

3039. _____. *Things to Come and Not to Come: Bible Prophecy and Modern Myths.* 1990 2nd ed. Yucaipa, CA: TRUTH versus Truth and Error. 110 p. illus., bibl. refs. indexes.

3040. Podaras, William. *Signs in the Now of the Coming of the Lord (to a Dying Earth).* [1980s]. Gastonia, NC: Tabernacle of God. 69 p. illus.

3041. Pohle, Joseph. *Eschatology; or, The Catholic Doctrine of the Last Things.* 1971. Westport, CT: Greenwood Press. 164 p. Reprint of 1917 ed., transl. from German.

3042. Poland, Larry W. *The Coming Persecution.* 1990. San Bernardino, CA: Here's Life. 225 p. bibl. refs.

Rampant fear. Book largely lurid anecdotes illustrating sorry state of world today: declining morals, porn, occultism, Satan-worship, phony Messiahs, increasingly anti-Christian; fulfilling 2 Tim. signs of Last Days. Glib style; rails against blatant anti-Christianity. False Messiahs will perform *real* miracles. Includes fictional stories: 1947 Demonic Council plans how to corrupt post-war society; Christian living in Millennium future recalls days of increasing terror and evil prior to Rapture with society flagrantly anti-Christian, and bliss of joining Christ at Rapture. First of 4 horsemen: Antichrist. Discussion Guide for Group Study at end, with questions for each chapter.

3043. _____. *2084: A Novel.* 1991. San Bernardino, CA: Here's Life. 263 p. biblical refs.

We are "now moving toward a climax, an end to life as we know it." Fictional account of three unsaved (non-believing) Americans exposed to life in A.D. 2084, during the Millennium, by being transported through time. Satan's agents try to tempt them into rejecting God's Kingdom.

3044. _____. *The Great War.* 1993 Nashville: T. Nelson.

3045. Poole, Willie L. *The Rapture and the End of Time.* 1991. New York: Vantage Press. vi, 71 p.

3046. Poole-Connor, Edward J. *Christ's Millennial Kingdom.* 1987. Chelmsford, England: Sovereign Grace Advent Testimony. 11 p.

3047. Pope, Joe ["Elijah III"]. *Welcome to the New Earth.* Vancouver: Urantian. tract.

7-year Tribulation starts in 1990; nuclear holocaust; 2 billion saved by angelic transport to planet Graceland (includes 144,000 Elect — religious martyrs). Judgment Day Resurrection A.D. 2021 (will be televised). Later, saved are transported back to new earth.

3048. Popoff, Peter. *Calamities, Catastrophies, and Chaos.* c1980. Upland, CA: Faith Messenger.

Popoff: faith-healer, televangelist. Chronicle of recent natural disasters, societal ills, UFOs, occult manifestations. Jesus to return any moment. God gave Popoff visions of humanity's history from beginning to End, which all signs show is very near. Predicts earthquake will destroy Dome of Rock; much of west coast to fall into sea; new virus kills much of population but Christians "supernaturally protected"; terrorists explode nuclear bomb in U.S. city; revolution will "paralyze" the Soviet Union; etc. Great spiritual revival too. Also wrote *Tribulation Money Is Here!*

3049. Posey, A.R. *Gamlhkon the Man 666.* 1981. Seminole, TX: A.R. Posey. 53 p.

"A chronological narrative with a merging of prophetical scriptures, by using an acrostic term for Gog and Magog, Little Horn, King of the North, in which the rising of the seventh and final Beast, and the Second Coming of Jesus is foretold."

3050. Powell, Ivor. *What in the World Will Happen Next?* 1985. Grand Rapids, MI: Kregel. 176 p. Rev. ed. of *The Rising of the Son* (1973).

Mysterious increase of vultures now in Israel — to eat Armageddon corpses. Ships from Chittim (Ezek. 39)=U.S. and British forces based in Cyprus.

3051. Preston, Don K. *II Peter 3: The Late Great Kingdom.* Shawnee, OK: 1990. 126 p.

Preterist. Refers to end of Jewish state in A.D. 70. Restoration Movement.

3052. ____. *Seal Up Vision & Prophecy: A Study of the 70 Weeks of Daniel 9.* 1991. Shawnee, OK. 47 p. bibl.

3053. Price, Randall. *In Search of Temple Treasures: The Lost Ark and the Last Days.* 1994. Eugene, OR: Harvest House. 378 p., plates illus., map, bibl. refs.

3054. ____. *Jerusalem in Prophecy.* 1998. Eugene, OR: Harvest House. 434 p. illus. maps, bibl. refs. indexes.

3055. Price, Susan. *Judgment and Holocaust: Israel and the Church, Are We Ready? Scriptural Analysis of Creation, Covenant, and Coming Judgment, a Messianic Perspective.* 1994 [c1993]. Ann Arbor, MI: Revelation. 576 p. illus. charts diagrams, bibl. refs.

Price: book designer. Coming Holocaust parallel to Nazi's; reaction to American economic collapse, then reaction to reinstituted Temple sacrifice. "This book is an understudy, a preparation for other pieces to be written before the curtain falls on this decadent world." Apocalypse prepared when Carter helped surrender Israel. Accelerated by Gulf War (new Babylon parallel to old). "Soon the sun will sink and a quarter of the world will turn black and America will burn. For most, Hell will follow." Urges blacks to return to Africa, American Indians to a separate Canadian homeland, Jews to Israel.

3056. Price, Walter K. *The Coming Antichrist.* 1985 [1974]. Neptune, NJ: Loizeaux Bros. 240 p. bibl. indexes. Orig. 1974 (Moody).

Price: Baptist pastor, Lexington, KY. Good discussion of history of beliefs. Pretrib Rapture. Antiochus Epiphanes as "type" for Antichrist. Real Antichrist only revealed following Rapture; then forms ten-nation confederation, based in Israel; defeats Russian invasion mid-Tribulation. Armageddon = Antichrist's forces vs. 200 million man Oriental army. "Western Europe and America have always dreaded invasion by vast hordes of Asiatics. Like the plague of locusts described in Joel, these hordes, if we did not have the deterrent of nuclear weapons, could swarm over the western world and deluge it with the sheer weight of their numbers. This seems to happen at the close of the tribulation."

3057. ____. *Next Year in Jerusalem.* 1975. Chicago: Moody. 199 p. bibl. index.

3058. ____. *In the Final Days.* 1977. Chicago: Moody Press. 192 p. bibl.

3059. Prince, Derek. *The Last Word on the Middle East.* 1982. Grand Rapids, MI: Zondervan. 157 p. bibl. Also pub. Lincoln, VA: Chosen Books; orig. priv. pub.

3060. ____. 1992. *The Destiny of Israel and the Church: Restoration and Redemption at the End of the Age.* 1992. Milton Keynes, England: Word. 148 p.

3061. ____. 1992. *Prophetic Destinies: Who is Israel? Who is the Church?* Lake Mary, FL: Creation House. 123 p.

Prince: lives in Jerusalem; heads Derek Prince Ministries. Satan knows his falsehood will be revealed to all when Israel's redemption is completed, so trying to thwart this. Holocaust caused Jews to return to Israel. Increase of Messianic Jews. Both Jews and Gentiles purified by Tribulation; only a remnant will survive from each. Jews will convert. End-time Tribulation, like Holocaust, is caused by ignoring God's warnings.

3062. *Prophecies from the Fourth Book of Esdras (aka Ezra).* 1998. <http://members.aol.com/Chosen72/ezra.html>

(Fourth Book of Ezra in Catholic Bible = 2 Esdras in Protestant versions.) According to 2 Esdras, 9½ of 12 parts of world's history was already past in Ezra's time. According to "Christopher" (Catholic website author: main site *Jesus Christ Will Return Soon*), first six parts were the Six Days of creation. Second six parts are a thousand years each. Thus we are now (1998) in last four years of the 12th part. Other sites by Christopher include *"Behold, the calamities draw near, and are not delayed," The "End Time" Event List,* Marian apparitions, and effect of Y2k computer bug on nuclear weapons.

3063. *The Prophecy Club.* <http://prophecyclub.com/pc.order.htm>

Prophecy Club, Topeka, KS. Includes many videos on creationism, Oklahoma City bombing, the Y2k computer "Millennial bug," UFOs, the New World Order, etc.

3064. Prophet, Elizabeth Claire. *Forbidden Mysteries of Enoch.* 1992 [1983]. Livingston, MT: Summit Univ. Press. viii, 492 p.

Book of Enoch. The Watchers: fallen angels who co-habited with human females, contaminating human race with evil. Enoch warns of Tribulation and signs of coming End. Prophet: leader of Church Universal and Triumphant (CUT), moved from Malibu, CA, to Livingston, Montana.

3065. _____. *Archangel Michael's Rosary for Armageddon.* 1985. [Livingston, MT?] : The Church Universal and Triumphant. 32 p.

Prophet predicted U.S.-Russian war for 1989, then indicated (though not explicitly) that nuclear Armageddon would begin April 23, 1990.

3066. Prophetic Research Assoc. *Tribulation Comic Book.* Vol 1. Hemet, CA.

Seventh-day Adventist?

3067. *Prophets and Prophecies for the 20th Century.* c1983. Oklahoma City: Southwest Radio Church. 70 p. illus.

3068. Pruitt, Robert J.—*And Then Shall the End Come.* [1970s]. Cleveland, TN: White Wing. 67 p.

Church of God.

3069. Rabanne, Paco. *Has the Countdown Begun?: Through Darkness to Enlightenment.* 1994. London: Souvenir. 213 p.

Rabanne: Spanish-born fashion designer. During 1930s astral voyage he attained 7th vibratory plane, and foresaw WWII. Coming cataclysmic destruction is prophesied by all religions and seers. Galactic civilization billions of years old presides over Earth; extraterrestrial Elohim started life here, producing monstrous hybrids which were later eradicated. 666 was telephone number Nixon used to dial Armstrong on the Moon. Science has lost its ancient moral foundation, and is now new Tower of Babel. John Paul II is 110th pope of Malachy's 112. Quotes 10th century *Tuba Seculorum* prophesying 20th century World Wars. Invokes Atlantis, Marian apparitions, Nostradamus. Moslems to overrun Europe. Tremendous Earth cataclysms, then three days of total darkness. Then Antichrist takes over to "save" world. Millennium is new age of sacred knowledge. The Parousia: all mankind achieves 7th vibratory plane.

3070. Rafferty, James M. *Prophetic Insights into the New World Order.* 1992. Malo, WA: Light Bearers Ministry. 147 p. illus. bibl. refs.

3071. _____. *Prophetic Insights Into Current Events.* 1994. Malo, WA: Light Bearers Ministry. 126 p. illus. bibl. refs.

3072. Ramsey, Willard A. *Zion's Glad Morning.* 1990. Simpsonville, SC: Millennium III. xii, 308 p. illus. bibl. refs., indexes.

Post-mill.

3073. Ramtha, the Enlightened One. *Last Waltz of the Tyrants.* 1989. Hillsboro, OR: Beyond Words. 157 p.

Ramtha: 35,000 year-old spirit from Atlantis channeled by J.Z. Knight. Ramtha's teaching about the End: massive catastrophes by 2042. Judi Pope Koteen, ed.

3074. Ransom, Elaine, and Darryl Skytta. *Understanding the Book of Daniel.* 1997. Appleton, WI: priv. pub. illus.

Fiction in which Daniel is explained to children.

3075. Rasmussen, Roland. *The Post-Trib, Pre-Wrath Rapture.* 1996. Canoga Park, CA: The Post-Trib Research Center. 404 p. illus.

3076. Ravenscroft, Trevor, and Tim Wallace-Murphy. *The Mark of the Beast: The Continuing Story of the Spear of Destiny.* 1997 [1990]. York Beach, ME: S. Weiser. 245 p. illus.: Orig. pub.: London: Sphere Books. bibl. refs., index.

The Holy Lance which pierced Christ on the Cross has supernatural powers, and is "symbol of the Apocalypse." Hitler, a vessel of the Beast, realized its power and tried to use it for black magic. The Antichrist Beast will ensoul the coming World Dictator and conquer the world. Joshua Ben Jesu set up demonically-inspired Academy in Persia in A.D. 666; A.D. 1332 (666 + 666) saw destruction of Knights Templar in France. Another 666 years — 1998 — will see "tremendous sequence of apocalyptic events," with Antichrist establishing world rule in 2020s.

3077. [Ray, Mike]. *The Last Days.* n.d. Napa, CA: Hopewell Baptist Church [10 p].

3078. Ray, Pearl J. *Beyond Today.* 1986. Kannapolis, NC: Harvest Age Ministries. 288 p.

3079. Reagan, David R. *The Master Plan: Making Sense of the Controversies Surrounding Bible Prophecy Today.* c1993. Eugene, OR: Harvest House. 243 p. index. diagrams.

Radio host of "Christ in Prophecy"; Lamb and Lion Ministries near Dallas, former professor of international law and politics. Also wrote *Jesus is Coming Again!*

(1992; Harvest House), a children's book on End Times prophecies. Pre-trib. Satan inspired abuse of prophecy to discredit it. Many prophecies "telescoped": refer both to events near and far in time. Purpose of Tribulation: to "soften the hearts of the remnant so that they will accept Jesus as their Messiah." After Millennium, God superheats Earth, "reshapes it like a hot ball of wax." New Jerusalem is a cube 1,500 miles square with vertical streets. Argues for *conditional* immortality: wicked punished in hell for duration proportional to their sins, then permanently destroyed.

3080. Reckart, Cohen G. *Endtime Tribulation Survival.* <http://members.aol.com/acts0412/>

Apostolic Mission Fellowship, Tampa, FL. Vehemently post-trib. Israel = Whore of Babylon. Talmudic Pharisees (Jews) are Antichrist. "Cohen" = Reverend.

3081. Reese, Ron. *The Midnight Hour Approaches! Your Time is Almost Over.* N.d. Brooklyn, MI.

6,000 years ends in 1992–93. In 1991 tract *Is Jesus Coming in '98?* figured Second Coming for 1998. In Oct. 1998 in his newsletter, Reese announced he had "overwhelming evidence" that the Tribulation would start Nov., 1998, based on 6,000 years for mankind and 2,000 between the First and Second Comings.

3082. Reid, G. Edward. *Even at the Door.* 1994. Hagerstown, MD : Review and Herald Graphics, 250 p.

Second Coming ca. 2000.

3083. _____. *Sunday's Coming.* 1996. Fulton, MD: Omega. 251 p.

3084. Reinhold, Roy A. *Prophecy Truths.* <http://members.aol.com/prophecy04/> [may switch to http://A.D.2004.com.]

Pre-wrath Rapture. Last Days Temple dedicated Sept. 2003. Hidden Bible codes.

3085. Reiter, Richard R., Paul D. Feinberg, Gleason L. Archer, and Douglas J. Moo. *The Rapture: Pre-, Mid-, or Post-Tribulational?* c1984. Grand Rapids, MI: Academie Books (Zondervan). 268 p. bibl. refs. indexes.

3086. Relfe, Mary Stewart. *When Your Money Fails: The "666" System Is*

Here. 1981. Montgomery, AL: Ministries Inc.

Israelis already conditioned for The Beast's 666 system by acceptance of 666 phone and car numbers. Mid-trib rapture.

3087. Renfro, James. *The Sure Word of Prophecy's Final Message as Given by Jesus.* 1992. Louisville, KY: priv. pub. 92 p.

3088. Repairers of the Breach. *The Antichrist 666.* 1980. Brownsville: Repairers of the Breach. 262 p. illus. Orig. priv. pub.: Brooklyn.

3089. *The Revelation of Jesus Christ.* 1985. Orangeburg, NY: Revelation Research Foundation. 181, 139 p. illus.

3090. Rice, John R. SEE ALSO 1910–1970 *"Behold, He Cometh!": A Verse-by-Verse Commentary on the Book of Revelation.* 1977. Murfreesboro, TN: Sword of the Lord. 348 p.

Imminent Coming, no further signs necessary, but wrong to predict time or date. Pre-trib Rapture. Seven churches *not* "foreviews" of historical epoch or views. Ten Kingdoms out of Roman Empire. Antichrist revealed after Rapture, makes treaty with Jews. Antichrist = First Beast = 10-Nation confederation. Whore = false Christianity = Catholic Church. Mid-Tribulation: Antichrist becomes worldwide dictator, Abomination of Desolation. Folly to try to identify Antichrist now. 144,000 sealed Jews, many Gentiles saved during Tribulation. "Locusts": Demons arise to torture wicked. Two Witnesses = Moses and Elijah. Satan works miracles via Antichrist and False Prophet (Antichrist's priest). First Horseman = Antichrist. Gog/Magog = probably Russia. Later post-Mill Magog is Russia too. 200 million literal horsemen: all the wicked. All armies of world vs. Israel, then vs. Christ's hosts. Second phase of Coming: with 10,000 saints to Armageddon battle. Cosmic collisions, as in Flood (Velikovksy, Canopy). Hell center of earth. Eternal Hell for unbelievers. Evolution "foolish, wicked" idea. Gigantic cataclysm, end of Millennium, new heaven and earth. New Jerusalem cubic in shape: "A new system of coherence and gravity will hold this redeemed planet and the Heavenly Jerusalem together," and will provide oxygen for all its 1,500 mile height.

3091. _____. *The Second Coming of Christ in Daniel.* n.d.? Wheaton, IL: Sword of the Lord. 43 p. chart.

"No speculation nor theories, but what the Word plainly teaches."

3092. Richards, H[arold] M[arshall]. *Startling Evidence that Christ Is Coming Soon.* 1991. Newbury Park, CA: Voice of Prophecy. 24 p.

Seventh-day Adventist.

3093. _____. *Daniel and Revelation Series.* 9 cassettes. Toledo, OH: Toledo First SDA Church Tape Ministry.

3094. Richman, Chaim. *The Holy Temple of Jerusalem.* 1997. Temple Institute/Carta. 96 p. illus., maps.

3095. *The Mystery of the Red Heifer: Divine Promise of Purity.* 1997. 79 p.

Ashes of red cow needed to purify Temple. Rabbi Richman of Temple Institute collaborating with Mississippi farmer Clyde Lott to breed pure red cow.

3096. Rietkerk, Wim. *The Future Great Planet Earth.* 1989. Mussoorie, India: Good Books. vi, 69 p.

3097. _____. *Do We Live in the End Time?* [1990s] Michigan City, IN: L'Abri Cassettes. Tape.

3098. Riley, R.M. *The Year of Destiny.* 1994. [Missouri: Last Call Ministry?]

3099. Ripp, Bobby. *End-Time Deceptions.* 1996. Mandeville, LA: True Light Ministries.

Pentecostal. Post-trib — most of world will be deceived by Satanic delusions. Marian apparitions, New Age, and UFOs Satan's three greatest tools for deception. 6,000 Year theory.

3100. Robbins, John W. *Pat Robertson: A Warning to America.* c1988. Jefferson, MD: Trinity Foundation. xii, 158 p.

Robertson is a false prophet: his claim that God speaks directly to him violates truths of Protestant Reformation. Also wrote *The Pursuit of Power: Dominion Theology and the Reconstruction Movement* (1988).

3101. Robertson, Pat, with Bob Slosser. *The Secret Kingdom.* 1982. Nashville: Nelson. 223 p. bibl., refs.

Robertson: charismatic Southern Baptist; televangelist. Annihilation of Russia (Ezek.) either from nuclear bombs or direct act of God.

3102. _____. *The New World Order.* c1991. Dallas: Word. xiii, 319 p. bibl., index.

3103. _____. *The End of the Age.* 1995. Dallas, TX: Word. 374 p.

Novel. Post-trib. Giant meteor hits near Los Angeles triggering global catastrophes. Charismatic Mark Beaulieu (demon-possessed since Peace Corps stint in India) becomes Vice President, then President after advisor Tauriq Haddad assassinates President. Beaulieu — the Antichrist — releases Satanic forces; demonic locusts of Revelation torment all non-believers. After restoring Babylon, Beaulieu is killed; then Haddad — the False Prophet — brings him back to life and world hails him as Messiah. Meanwhile, Bible-believers flee to "El Refugio" in New Mexico mountains and establish Christian Resistance movement. Taught by Pastor Jon Edwards, they realize all is happening precisely according to Revelation. Antichrist attacks El Refugio, but his forces blasted by Christ. Then he invades Israel, joined by Eastern armies. All forces destroyed at Armageddon, then believers get glorified bodies and are raptured to join Christ. New Jerusalem descends to orbit Earth. Chernobyl = Wormwood. AIDS: biblical pestilence. Suggests Tribulation starts ca. 2000 and End 2007: 1967 + 40 (biblical generation), also 400 years since first dedicatory prayer in America. (Earlier, Robertson predicted 1982 for Soviet invasion of Israel.)

3104. Robertson, Robin. *After the End of Time: Revelation and the Growth of Consciousness.* 1990. Virginia Beach, VA: Inner Vision. 254 p. illus. bibl. refs.

Beginner's Guide to Revelation: A Jungian Interpretation (1994) is revised ed. of above.

3105. Robinson, Freddy. *The Book of Daniel Unsealed: There is Another Antichrist After 666.* 1995. s.l.: Transfiguration Prod. 126 p.

Christ chose author to "reveal the se-

crets" in Daniel: "The future will be unveiled before your eyes." Author makes all mysteries "perfectly clear"; baffling questions finally answered with "amazing simplicity"; Christ showed him he was correct. Two Antichrists: the first, "666," already came and fulfilled role. First Antichrist = Reagan (author very explicit but doesn't actually use name): shot by John, healed, born 2-6-1911, had 666 address. 70 Weeks = 490 years from Cyrus's decree to Peter baptizing Cornelius. The second Antichrist (Beast) about to emerge; rules 3½ years; Two Witnesses (Elijah and Moses) oppose Antichrist; Antichrist kills them, desolates Israel. Antichrist in Israel 1,260 days, then returns 30 days later, following which he is destroyed.

3106. Rogers, Adrian Pierce. *Living in the Last Days.* 1987. Memphis: Bellevue Baptist Church. cassette.

Other tapes: *In the Second Coming and the Apostacy of the Last Days; Lebanon, Libya and the Last Days; Signs of the End of the Age* (1988).

3107. Rohr, Richard. *The End Time: The Book of Revelation.* 1988. Kansas City, MO: National Catholic Reporter. 4 cassettes.

3108. Rose, Seraphim. *The Future of Russia and the End of the World.* 1985. Liberty, TN: St. John of Krondstadt. 12 p.

3109. Rosen, Moishe, with Bob Massie. *Overture to Armageddon: Beyond the Gulf War.* 1991. San Bernardino, CA: Here's Life. 204 p. bibl. refs.

3110. Rosenthal, Marvin J. *The Pre-Wrath Rapture of the Church.* 1990. Nashville: Thomas Nelson. 319 p. illus. bibl. refs. index. Study guide also published (1992, Orlando, FL: Zion's Hope).

Jewish-born. Former executive director of Friends of Israel Gospel Ministry; now executive director of Zion's Hope. Devises new interpretation: neither pre-, mid-, or post-trib. Combines aspects of each: Rapture just prior to "Day of Lord," which is middle of second half of 70th Week, announced by opening of 7th Seal.) Thus Church preserved from "wrath." Second Coming is "ultimate absolute of history." 144,000 Jews sealed just before

Rapture, take over witnessing duties. Revived Roman Empire, led by Antichrist (Western European confederacy). Tribulation is wrath of *man,* not God; God's is Day of Lord. Great Tribulation is shortened; believers raptured, Day of Lord begins. Millennium not part of Day of Lord. Earth renovated *before* Millennium. Rapture signaled by cosmic disturbances. Seal judgments up to Rapture, then trumpets and bowls. Two Witnesses = Elijah and Moses. Antichrist revealed mid-Tribulation, revived from fatal wound, erects miraculous statue in Temple. 2/3 of Jews killed, rest convert. Six Seals of Revelation = Matt. 24:5-9: man-made disasters.

3111. *Roses from Heaven.* 1982. Orange, TX: 384 p. illus.

Catholic. Prophecies of Veronica Leuken (Bayside, NY). Marian apparitions, UFOs, comets, vampires, imposter Pope now in Vatican (real Pope was kidnapped). True believers raptured on the eve of the Apocalypse.

3112. Rosio, Bob. *Hitler and the New Age.* 1993. Lafayette, LA: Huntington House. ix, 198 p. bibl. refs.

"The Coming Holocaust — The Extermination of Christendom." Rosio: head of Cheswick Christian Academy and Fellowship (PA). "We are now living in the age which leads to the fulfillment of all prophecy." Hitler, like Nero, was type of Antichrist. New Age is based on Nazi occultism. "It is reported that Germany spent more money on psychic exploration than the United States did in developing the atomic bomb." New United Europe will be German-led Fourth Reich. "History will be repeated, but on a deeper, wider, and deadlier scale." After Rapture, Satan will try to exterminate Jews.

3113. Ross, Randal. *The Next 7 Great Events of the Future: And What They Mean to You.* 1997. Orlando, FL: Creation House. xxxii, 162 p.

Ross: pastor, Lubbock TX. Pre-trib. Says he used to be a prophecy fanatic; scared as kid when couldn't find his parents, thought Rapture had occurred without him. Describes local preacher who predicted July 28, 1978 for End. The seven

events are the standard dispensational upheavals, disasters, 7-year Tribulation, Jerusalem-based reign of Antichrist (the "consummate smooth-talking dude"), Russian-Arab attack on Israel.

3114. Roth, Sid. *Time Is Running Short.* c1990. Shippensburg, PA: Destiny Image. [xvi], 220 p.

Foreword by Derek Prince. Roth: "messianic Jew"; president of Messianic Vision (Jewish evangelism). Jews return from North (Soviet Union). Old Testament prophecies of Messiah definitely fulfilled by Jesus. Soviets want to destroy all Jews. 2nd Holocaust brewing in Russia. Jews returning from Russia = End Time sign. Book of Esther is "God's master end-time strategy." Satan makes Jews and Christians enemies. Roth exhorts Christians to imitate Esther; stand up for Jews. Satan targeting Jews: that's why so many are involved in occult. Will be 144,000 Jewish end-time evangelists. Some chapters by Michael Brown, Louis Goldberg, John Fischer, Keith Parker.

3115. Rowe, Everette. *Christ Reigns with 144,000.* [1980s?] S.l.: s.n. 15 p.

3116. Roy, Allen. *Daniel Prophecy Study.* <http://www.tagnet.org/another viewpoint/Daniel/>

Interactive website. Also leads "creationary geology tours" of Grand Canyon.

3117. Rudge, Bill. *The Last Days: What's Ahead for the Body of Christ, the Apostate Church, and the World.* 1998. Hermitage, PA: Living Truth.

3118. Rumble, Dale. *The Diakonate: A Fresh Look at the Church that is Being Built for the End Times.* 1982. Newton Abbey, England: Torbay Publishing. 195 p.

"How home churches and servant leaders are being raised up...."

3119. _____. *Crucible of the Future: A Prophetic Look into the Nineties.* 1989. Shippensburg, PA: Destiny Image.

3120. _____. *And Then Shall the End Come.* 1991. 135 p. bibl.

3121. Rushdoony, Rousas John. *Thy Kingdom Come: Studies in Daniel and Revelation.* 1978. Fairfax, VA: Thoburn Press. iv, 256 p. index.

Post-mill. Kingdom was taken from Jews, given to God. Bible declares Israel will fall (to the Romans), but that the world will continue, contrary to Jewish messianic expectations. Rushdoony: leading Christian Reconstructionist theoretician.

3122. Rusk, Roger. *The Other End of the World: An Alternate Theory Linking Prophecy and History.* 1988. Knoxville, TN: Plantation House. x, 268 p.

Rusk: Tenn. science professor; brother of former Secretary of State. Historicist interpretation, following Reformation leaders (Luther, Calvin, Newton). End Times from First Coming to Second. Agrees with earlier historicist advocates in denouncing Papacy as Little Horn, 2nd Beast, Whore of Babylon. Prophetic "day" = year. Astronomical significance of "days," especially 2,550 and 2,300. "70 Weeks" = 490 years. 70th week continuous (no parenthesis), from Christ's baptism to Sanhedrin's rejection of Gospel seven years later. Rejects secret Rapture. Makes distinction between Jews and Israel; House of Joseph = 10 Tribes = Israel. Also distinction between scepter, birthright, promises. Kazar Jews not of biblical descent. Gentiles grafted onto Israel. America and related northern Europeans now Israel and heir to promises. Stresses greatness, destiny of America. Endorses conspiracy ideas of Zionist aims at domination. Gog and Armageddon refer to invasion of America (not Palestine) by Russia.

3123. Russ, Mike. *The Battle for Planet Earth from Abraham to Armageddon.* 1983 [c1981]. New York: Ballantine Books. 176 p. bibl. notes. 1981 ed. Santa Ana, CA: Vision House.

3124. Russell, D.S. *Prophecy and the Apocalyptic Dream: Protest and Promise.* 1994. Peabody, MA: Hendrickson. viii, 136 p. bibl. indexes.

Russell: principal of Baptist colleges in England. Critical of fundamentalist approach (though believer himself); "utterly rejects" precise date-setting, identifying symbols with current figures and events, Rapture doctrine, and pre-mill approach.

3125. Rusten, E. Michael. *The End*

Times: Discovering What the Bible Says. 1997. Wheaton, IL: Harold Shaw. 92 p.

3126. Ruth, Merle R. *The Seventy Weeks Prophecy and Its Amazingly Remarkable Fulfillment.* ? [1980s?] Annville, PA: M. Ruth. 19 p.

3127. Ruzo, Daniel. *Los "Ultimos Dias" del Apocalipsis: Gurdjieff, Bo-Yin-Ra, Pak Subuh y Los Tres Caminos.* 1970. Mexico: M. Schultz. 287 p. illus.

3128. Ryalls, Charles. *The Paradigm Shift.* 1997. Belleville, Canada: Essence. 221 p.

Novel. The Rapture and Tribulation.

3129. _____. *Yeshua the King.* <ttp://www.yeshuatheking.org>

"I truly believe that we are quickly approaching the most important events in history, the Tribulation and the return of Yeshua, Jesus, to establish His 1000 year earthly Kingdom." Based in Bellinghame, WA.

3130. Rydel, Margaret. *The Blessed Hope and Glorious Appearing.* [Tampa?]

Predicts End for 1988.

3131. Ryrie, Charles T. SEE ALSO 1910–1970. *The Living End.* 1976. Chicago: Moody. 144 p. Later ed. (c1981) titled *The Best is Yet to Come.*

Jesus' forecasts regarding modern nations. Bible gives true answers to tomorrow's news. The situation will deteriorate for believers: hatred, torture, death. Antichrist will demand worship, intense persecution of resisters. Armageddon: carnage of unbelievable proportions. Second Coming accompanied by enormous catastrophes of earth and heavens. 10-nation revived Roman Empire just prior to Coming, led by Antichrist. Treaty with Israel; half way through, Antichrist seeks to conquer world, betrays Israel. Literal interpretation of Revelation. 7th Seal brings 7 Trumpets; 7th Trumpet brings 7 Bowls. Each brings catastrophic punishment. First seal is Cold War; Antichrist. Demon-locusts from Hell possibly "coming invasion of warlike UFOs." Gog and Magog = Russia; King of North. Meshech and Tubal probably in Turkey. Gomer probably in Turkey or Ukraine. Russians probably ride literal horses for invasion, as

Tribulation disrupts industry. 7 years fuel from arms, and for burying Russian dead. Turkey to ally with Russia. Kings of South = Ptolemies of Egypt. North and South invade Israel; Antichrist intervenes with European armies, defends Israel. Goes on to conquer Egypt, returns to fight North. Armies of North battle Antichrist's forces in Israel. God intervenes, destroys Russian armies. Armies of East (China) then cross dry Euphrates to battle Antichrist's forces, but they unite to battle Christ when he appears at Second Coming: Armageddon (end of Tribulation). U.S. either has no role in events, or is destroyed by nuclear war or Tribulation; maybe under European control. After Rapture, world church: Harlot. Millennium: completely righteous government, peace, prosperity; yet many still revolt at end, demonstrating that sin and rebellion always punished. New Jerusalem suspended 1,500 miles over Earth.

3132. _____. *What You Should Know About the Rapture.* c1981. Chicago: Moody 118 p. illus.

Come Quickly, Lord Jesus! 1996. Eugene, OR: Harvest House. 139 p. Retitled ed. of *What You Should Know About the Rapture.*

3133. _____. *The Final Countdown.* 1982. Wheaton, IL: Victor Books (Scripture Press). 120 p. diagrams. Rev. ed. of *The Bible and Tomorrow's News* (1969).

Pre-trib, any moment Rapture. Symbols of Revelation convey literal truth. Antichrist = Little Horn = Western leader from 10-Nation confederacy, establishes new Roman Empire. Two Witnesses commence spectacular, miraculous ministry. Antichrist kills them mid-Tribulation, but publicly resurrected. Satan fights Michael, but loses. Throws full power behind Antichrist, who demands worship in Temple. False Prophet = Second Beast, promotes First, requires Mark. Literal plagues, judgments, woes, including demonic locusts. Only Jewish survivors of Tribulation will be those who convert. Armageddon campaign: all nations vs. Israel. Mystery Babylon = Harlot = apostate Church, with political power, dominates 10-Nation federation. Egypt conquered by European Federation mid-Tribulation. Gog = Russia: invades with vast army; supernaturally destroyed by God; then armies of Orient invade Israel–Armageddon. Not all born during Millennium become saved, though Christ rules. Tribulation survivors in worldly bodies ruled over by resurrected saints. Unsaved join Satan's final rebellion. Ryrie stresses eternal torture of all unsaved.

3134. Safan, Kamil. *Al-Saah al-Khamisah wa-al-Ishrun: Al-Masikh al-Dajjal, Yajuj wa-Majuj, al-Mahdi al-Muntazar.* 1995. Cairo, Egypt: Dar al-Amin. 247 p.

Islamic. "False Messiah" (Antichrist), God and Magog.

3135. Sale, C. M. *7 Years to Go.* 1995. London: C.M. Sale. 52 p.

Earth's rotation; geomagnetism.

3136. Salim, Fahd. *Asrar al-Saah wa-Hujum alGharb (Qabla 1999): Indhar Khatir wa-Akhir lil-Alam al-Islami.* 1998. Cairo, Egypt: Madbuli al-Saghir. 159 p. bibl. refs.

Islamic millennialism; Arab-Israeli conflict.

3137. Salty Doc. *God's Great Eagle and Timetable: Satan's Deep Secrets Exposed.* 1984. Pasadena, TX: Revelation 2:24. viii, 135 p.

Author: from Houston area. Also wrote *Blessed Hope, 1996.*

3138. Samael, Aun Weor. *Nous Sommes Proches d'Une Grande Catastrophe.* 1980. Montreal: Ganesha. 22 p.

Neo-gnostic. Atlantis; Planet Hercolubus approaching Earth; radiation from Alcyone in the Pleiades.

3139. _____. *La Grand Catastrophe et "l'Experience du Soleil."* 1998. Montreal: Ganeshan. 132 p. Illus.

3140. Sanders, Paul L. *From Chaos to Glory.* 1990. [Fresno, CA: Prophetic Research]. 317 p. bibl. refs.

3141. Sarkett, John A. *After Armageddon.* 1996 [1983]. <http://homepage.interaccess.com/~jas/after_armageddon.shtml/>

3142. Sauer, Val J. *The Eschatology Handbook: The Bible Speaks to Us Today About Endtimes.* c1981. Atlanta: J. Knox Press. xiii, 144 p.

Advocates "inaugurated eschatology," combining elements of "realized eschatology" and dispensational belief that many End-time events are still in future.

3143. Savage, John Ashton. *The Scroll of Time: or, Epochs and Dispensations of Scripture, a Key to the Chart: With Special References to the Book of Revelation and Other Prophesies.* 1971 [1893]. Sudbury, PA: Believers Bookshelf. xv, 202 p. illus.

3144. Scallion, Gordon-Michael. *The Future Map of the United States: 1998–2001.*

3145. _____. *Tribulation: The Coming Earth Changes.* video. 1993. Westmoreland, NH: Matrix Video.

Occult prophecies, importance of self-sufficiency, spiritual empowerment.

3146. Schaffter, R.C. *The Last Call: The Preparation of the Bride for the Rapture of the Church.* 1994. Lannon, WI: Clarion Call. 263 p.

Companion volume to *Prophecies of the End-Times.*

3147. Schellhorn, G. Cope. *Extraterrestrials in Biblical Prophecy.* 1990. Madison WI: Horus House (distr. Inner Light). xii, 427 p. 6 p plates illus. bibl. refs., index.

ETs as messiahs from space. Wormwood of Revelation is Planet Marduk of the Babylonians, which will return to devastate Earth again, but some favored humans are rescued by flying saucers. These ETs gave us end-time Bible prophecies as warning. Two falls of angels: Lucifer (with Nephilim), then the Watchers (under Azazel). Flood ca. 4600 B.C. WWIII: Gog-Magog (Soviet bloc) and Southern Confederacy (Arabs) attack; then European confederation of the Beast attacks and defeats Soviets in Israel. European and Eastern armies then annihilate each other.

3148. _____. *2011: The Evacuation of Planet Earth.* 1998. Madison, WI: Horus House. 224 p.

Fiction.

3149. Schmidt, Kenneth. *What Next? The Glory of Anticipation.* 1974. Stow, OH: New Hope. 141 p.

3150. Schmitt, John W., and J. Carl Laney. *Messiah's Coming Temple: Ezekiel's Prophetic Vision of the Future Temple.* 1997. Grand Rapids, MI: Kregel. 191 p. illus., maps, bibl. refs., index.

The rebuilt Temple of Jerusalem which will be Christ's headquarters during the Millennium.

3151. Schmugge, Frederick K. *When These Things Begin: A Scripture Study on the End Times.* 1986. St. Paul, MN: Phylax Press. iv, 83 p.

3152. Schrock, J.B. *Daniel— Revelation and Prophecy of the End Times.* [1990s]. Congerville, IL: J.B. Schrock. 216 p.

3153. Schrupp, Ernst. *Israel und das Reich des Islam: Zeitgeschehen im Licht biblischer Heilsgeschichte: Endzeitliche Perspektiven.* 1992. Wuppertal [Germany]: R. Brockhaus. 263 p. illus., map., bibl. refs.

Also wrote *Israel in der Endzeit.* Antichrist will be like Hitler, Stalin, or Saddam Hussein.

3154. Schuldt, Lynn Louise. *a.d. 79: A Prophecy Paradox.* 1996. Concord, CA: Son Mountain Press. 338 p. illus., maps, bibl. refs., index.

Preterist: All prophecies fulfilled A.D. 79.

3155. Searcy, Jim. *Great Joy in Great Tribulation: Simplified Prophecy for the Last Days.* 1995. Shippensburg, PA: Companion Press. 364 p.

We are now in middle of final seven years: the Tribulation.

3156. Segraves, Kelly L. *The Great Flying Saucer Myth.* 1977 [1975]. San Diego: BetaBooks. 126 p.

Segraves: with Creation-Science Research Center. Flying Saucers as Satan's attempt to deceive mankind into accepting false messiahs.

3157. _____. *Sons of God Return.* 1975 New York: Pyramid Books. 191 p. bibl.

3158. Sena, Patrick J. *The Apocalypse: Biblical Revelation Explained.* 1983. New York: Alba House. viii, 116 p. bibl. refs.

Catholic. Good presentation of a-mill position; also describes others.

3159. Seng, Tan Khian. *The Winds of God.* 1995. Singapore : Hidden Manna Press, 64 p.

"A prophetic perspective on the move of God in this decade."

3160. *Seven Seals Revelation.* 1998. Jesup, GA: Hidden Manna. 2 vols. illus.

Written by Branch Davidians after the death of their leader David Koresh, who was working on new interpretation of the Seven Seals when the Waco, TX, compound was destroyed. Pre-Adamic creation with Michael and Lucifer (female) as original inhabitants. This earlier creation destroyed and covered with sea of glass (diamond) prior to Six Day re-creation. Earth now traveling backwards in time until 6th Seal when it returns to original creation. God's surname is Koresh. David Koresh is the Elijah messenger, the Lamb and the Man-Child of Revelation, and the Rider of the White Horse (also the Destroying Angel and rider of the 4th Horse — Death). Koresh, "anointed with the oil of his wives" during sexual intercourse, prophesies for 1,260 days, killed 69½ weeks after anointing (Apr. 19th, 1993) — the 5th Seal. Black Horse rider reveals that Koresh "can fulfill the prophecies even to the point of alluring his people deceitfully." Koresh wounded one head of the Babylonian Beast; Oklahoma City bombing was beginning of healing of the Beast. Elisha, the "Chosen Vessel," to preach for 42 months after death of Elijah (Koresh), with the Remaining Bride (survivors of Waco fire). 2,300 days from death of Koresh to 6th Seal (Cleansing of the Sanctuary), during which 144,000 are sealed ("Koresh" written on their foreheads) and five months torment of unsaved begins. At 6th Seal, the Lamb (Koresh) and 200 million godly (the locusts) are resurrected and taken to New Jerusalem, a spaceship. Earth destroyed by fire, then the Millennium, then wicked resurrected for 100 years ("short season"), then New Jerusalem returns to Earth.

3161. Sewell, Nancy. <http://members.aol.com/reinbeaux/prophecy>

"I believe that Jesus' coming for His church is very near. His coming for the church will be before the Seven Year Tribulation...." UFOs a delusion. Van Impe a Satanist because he accepts Catholics as Christians and endorses ecumenicalism.

3162. Shackcloth, H. Hazell. *Israel: The Family and Nation of Destiny: A Prophetic Study of Israel, the Church and Christendom.* 1988. Glasgow Scotland: Gospel Tract. 224 p. map, charts.

Plymouth Brethren. Jacob and his family as *types*: prophetic pictures of all mankind up to End. Rejects ecumenical movement as apostate and unbiblical. Papal system is distortion of Christianity. 69 weeks 454 B.C. to A.D. 29; then Church Age; then Rapture, then soon after the 70th Week = Tribulation; then Armageddon, Millennium. Book includes chart by Edward Denny. When church raptured, God focuses again on Israel, now regathered. Revived religious and political Roman Empire of Western Europe (Harlot and Beast). Sealed Jews live in peaceful Israel during Millennium. Then final rebellion of man.

3163. Shallieu, Frank. *The Keys of Revelation: Jesus' Testimony.* 1993. Orangeburg, NY: Revelation Research Foundation. ix, 723 p. illus. bibl. refs., index.

3164. Shank, Robert. *Until: The Coming of the Messiah and His Kingdom.* 1982 Springfield, MO: Westcott. 517 p. bibl. refs.

3165. Shanks, William H. *The Coming Savior and the World's Crisis (Signs of the Times and End of this Dispensation).* 1975. Arbroath, Scotland: Herald Press. 60 p.

3166. Sharfi, M[uhammad] Zaki-uddin. *Did the Prophet Muhammad (PBUH) Predict the Second Coming of Jesus and World War III?* 1983. Brooklyn, NY: Saut-ul-Islam. [24] p. Map, bibl. refs.

Qur'an and hadith (traditional sayings and acts of Muhammad) explain what is obscure or distorted in Bible. Jews accept Dajjal (Antichrist) as Messiah during WWIII, Gog and Magog (Russia and China) invade Israel. Jesus kills Dajjal at gate of Lydaa (Lod). Jesus declares he is not son of God, didn't die on the cross, and cannot atone for sins of others.

3167. [Sharrit, John T.] *Soon-Coming World-Shaking Events: As Foretold by — God Almighty.* 1980 [1978]. Phoenix, AZ: Christian Missionary Soc. 331 p. illus.

Sharrit: pres. Christian Missionary Soc. "THE END IS NOW NEAR!" 6,000 Year scheme. Announces reconciliation of pre-, mid-, and post-mill interpretations. "Soon Destruction of Russia and Probably America!" Magog = Russia. Tarshish and her "lions" = England, U.S., etc. Gomer = East Germany and other Communist satellites. Togarmah = Turkey. Common Market computer for laser tattoos (Mark of Beast). Antichrist from Ten-Nation European confederacy. Russia, with North and East Africa, attacks Israel. God destroys Russian armies: Russia launches nuclear strike at U.S. U.S. retaliates. Russian weapons used as fuel for years made of "Lingo-Stone," a "stronger than steel wood." Russia is now buying horses worldwide; new breed of vultures in Israel breeding furiously to accommodate corpses. Antichrist "must be a Roman"— Caesar Nero (666) resurrected. Makes covenant with Israel, rules 3½ years: the Tribulation (first half of 70th Week). Christians raptured end of Tribulation. "Wrath of God" different: second half of 70th Week. Christians suffer Tribulation; punished in Wrath of God. No salvation possible after Rapture. Wrath ends with Armageddon, probably before A.D. 2000, as Satanic world armies, including 200 million from East, attack Christ in Israel. Then Millennium, with greater Israel as world leader. New Jerusalem = 792,000 stories high. Offers $10,000 for disproof of scheme. Claims over 4½ million copies.

3168. Shaw, Gwen R. *God's End-Time Battle-Plan.* 1984. Jasper, AR: End-Time Handmaidens. 182 p.

"A Bible study on spiritual warfare."

3169. Shelley, Bruce. *What the Bible Says about the End of the World: A Historical Look at How End-time Beliefs Developed.* 1978. Wheaton IL: Victor.

3170. Shelton, Kenny. *Mystery Boom Revealed! A Study in Revelation.* <http://www.intowww.org/rev/revc.htm>

Adventist. King of South = Russia. King of North = Catholicism and apostate Protestantism. Little Horn = Rome.

3171. Shepherd, Brodrick D. *Beast, Horns and the Antichrist: Daniel: A Blue-print of the Last Days?.* 1994. Grassy Creek, NC: Cliffside Publishing. xiv, 135 p. illus. bibl. refs., index.

Convincing scholarly argument against futurist interpretation. Daniel refers not to future events, but events up to 2nd century B.C. Sheperd: runs Armageddon Books (West Jefferson, NC), online bookstore.

3172. Sheppa, Milton. *Is the "Tribulation Period" Real?* 1993 [1989]. Longview WA: Milton A. Sheppa. 61 p.

3173. Shifflett, Alvin. *The Beast of the East.* 1992. Lancaster, PA: Starburst. 111 p. illus. bibl. refs.

3174. Shorrosh, Anis A. *Jesus, Prophecy, and the Middle East.* 1981 [1979]. Nashville: Thomas Nelson. x, 145 p. plates illus bibl. Orig pub Daphne, AL: author. 1988 audio ed. (tapes).

Israel prophesied to grow 20 times its 1948 geographical size. "Incredible insights into the unique subject of the Second Coming by a native of the hometown of Jesus." Rapture, Antichrist, 70th Week of Daniel, "3 Armageddons," "The Mystifying Millennium."

3175. Shubert, Eugene, *The Ends of Time: Notes on the Evolution and Dynamics of Biblical Eschatology.* 1986 [1984] Richardson, TX; Priv. pub. 205 p.

3176. Shuttlewood, Arthur. SEE ALSO 1910–1970. *UFO Prophecy.* 1978. New York: Global Communications. 266 p. illus.

3177. _____. *UFO's, Visions of a New Age.* 1981. New York: Global Communications. 66 p. illus.

3178. *Signs of the Last Days.* <http://www.jeremiahproject.com/prophecy/signs.html> [Run by Vic Bilson.]

From the Jeremiah Project (Wichita, KS). "We are now living in the last days!"

3179. Silk, Ely, and Joan Silk. *Heaven Bound: A Practical Approach to Preparing for the Rapture.* 1997. Tamarac, FL: Silos. 108 p. illus.

"Getting ready for the most important trip of your life."

3180. Silva, Charles. *Date with the Gods.* 1986 [1977]. Pontiac, MI: Living Waters.

Cosmic disruption every 6,666 years. Planet "Hercolubus" = Wormwood of Revelation.

3181. Simmons, Larry. *42 Months to Glory: Unlocking the Mysteries of End Time Prophecy.* 1994. Oklahoma City: Ephriam House. iii, 231 p. Charts. bibl. rcfs.

Simmons: insurance agent; Baptist. Israel suffered because Jews didn't accept Christ. Day of Lord = End of the Age; including colossal earthquakes, sun blotted out. Then, sign of Christ in sky followed almost immediately by Rapture. WWI fulfilled earlier signs of wars, etc., so final signs must occur one generation from WWI. Lost Ten Tribes now in all nations = Ephriam: prophecies apply to them. At Rapture all descendants snatched up, then deposited in Israel, returning with Christ on horseback from sky. Tribulation catastrophes entirely manmade (though Satan controlled); different from God's Wrath. Tribulation not 7 years, only 3½. Denies Gap (parenthesis) before 70th Week. 42 months begin when Satan cast out by Michael from heaven. Believers won't suffer Wrath. Armageddon = all nations vs. Israel. Antichrist, probably from states of former Yugoslavia, forms a confederation and revives the Roman Empire. U.S. = End Time Babylon; its destruction by Antichrist will be "sudden" and "utterly complete." U.S. betrayed Israel by insisting on land for peace program. Rapture is shortly before Armageddon, then Second Coming within a few days (return as 144,000 with Christ). Temple site not directly under Dome of Rock. Ark of Covenant may have been returned from Ethiopia with airlifted Jews. Two Witnesses protect Israel from attackers, God protects whole country. Millennium: Mediterranean turns fresh. Pre-Flood Canopy restored. Urges we memorize Bible, as it will be confiscated.

3182. Singer, Jim Z. *"Use My Gifts": The Message of Our Lord.* 1993. Toronto: Ave Maria Centre of Peace. 64 p. illus.

3183. *666: The True Identity of the Antichrist.* 1991. Grants Pass, OR: White Lion. 62 p. illus.

3184. *666—The Uprise of Antichrist and the Battle of Armageddon.* 1977. Pasadena, CA: Christadelphian Bible Campaign. 16 p. map.

From *Herald of the Coming Age.*

3185. Skinner, Charles. *Strong Delusion—God's Plan to Damn.* Walterboro, SC: Overcomer Radio Ministry. 70 p.

Rejects the Rapture theory as "strong delusion."

3186. Skolfield, Ellis H. *Hidden Beast.* 1991 [1989] 2nd ed. rev. Fort Myers, FL: Fish House. 286 p. illus. bibl. refs.

3187. _____. *Hidden Beast, 2.* 1990. Fort Myers, FL: Fish House. 282 p. illus.

3188. _____. *SOZO: Survival Guide for a Remnant Church.* 1995. Fort Myers, FL: Fish House.

Describes "the cataclysmic events that will precede the soon return of the Lord." Also wrote *Daniel is Out of Chronological Order* (1983).

3189. Slater, George E. *The Last Night on Earth.* [1980s?] Unpub. 8 p.

Seventh-day Adventist.

3190. Smith, Chuck. *The Soon to Be Revealed Antichrist.* 1976. Costa Mesa, CA: Word for Today. 46 p.

3191. _____. *What the World Is Coming To.* 1977. Costa Mesa, CA: Maranatha Evangelical Assoc. of Calvary Chapel. xi, 211 p. bibl. refs.

Smith: Foursquare Gospel minister, pastor of Calvary Chapel, Costa Mesa (associated with the Jesus People). Maranatha is network of churches affiliated with Calvary Chapel. Smith also heads Maranantha! Records (Christian pop music). Verse-by-verse exposition of Revelation. Second Coming "very soon." Pretrib Rapture. Antichrist heads ten-nation confederacy based on Common Market. Christ destroys Antichrist, the world dictator, at Armageddon

3192. _____. *End Times: A Report on Future Survival.* 1980 [1978]. Costa Mesa, CA: Word for Today. 93 p. bibl. refs.

Excitedly says if Russia invades Israel as expected, "very soon we could be rejoicing around the throne of God in glory!"

3193. _____. *Snatched Away!* 1980. Costa Mesa, CA: The Word for Today. 82 p.

3194. _____. *The Tribulation & the Church.* 1980. Costa Mesa, CA: Word for Today. 47 p.

3195. _____. *The Final Curtain.* 1991. Eugene, OR: Harvest House; 96 p. 1984; Costa Mesa, CA: Word for Today; 73 p.

3196. _____, and David Wimbish. *Dateline Earth: Countdown to Eternity.* 1989. Old Tappan, NJ: Chosen Books. 192 p.

3197. _____. *The Last Days, the Middle East, and the Book of Revelation .* 1991. Tarrytown, NY: Chosen Books. 220 p. Rev. ed. of: *Dateline Earth* (1989).

3198. Smith, Elwyn A., ed. *The Religion of the Republic.* 1971. Philadelphia: Fortress Press. viii, 296 p. bibl. refs.

3199. Smith, Wilbur M. SEE ALSO 1910–1970. *You Can Know the Future.* 1971. Glendale, CA: G/L Regal. 118 p.

Also: *The End Times: You Can Know the Future.* 1971. Glendale: Regal Cassette. 6 cassettes.

3200. Snobelen, Clyde. *The Revelation.* <http://carver.pinc.com/~revpublishing/revpubnews.html>

Revelation Publishing. Snobelen advocates pre-Flood Water Canopy Theory.

3201. Sosebee, A.J. *End of Our Time.* 1994 New York: Vantage Press. xiv, 157 p.

Dispensational pre-trib pre-mill. Second Coming prophecies fulfilled slowly between Industrial Revolution and 1948, more rapidly since. Sosebee was chosen to write book to save people from Tribulation. Also wrote *Creation, Life and Time.* AIDS is End Time sign. Christians who miss Rapture must endure Tribulation, martyrdom, and refuse Mark of Beast. Confusion caused by Rapture exploited by Antichrist. Computer disk inserted in men's hand and women's forehead (like Hindu dot). Describes types of demons (fallen angels). Demons will possess all non-believers during Tribulation. Mussolini was probably Antichrist, and will be reinstated. First half of Tribulation: Antichrist and False Prophet establish control, bring peace to Middle East. Israel invaded by Moslems and northerners; Antichrist sets up headquarters in Temple. War in heaven (Rev. 12) occurs during Tribulation. Two Witnesses = Enoch and Elijah, televised. Antichrist is First Horseman of Four. Locusts = missiles with chemical warheads. Rev. 9: nuclear missiles. Battle of Armageddon at end of Tribulation, vs. army from East. Sun and Moon stand still over Palestine during Millennium. No childbirth during Millennium. New Jerusalem will descend to earthly Jerusalem. World Week: 6,000 Years plus seventh Millennium. Then, the "little season" lasting 6,000 years (or maybe some other unit), and a thousand year Great White Throne Judgment. These three 6s are Antichrist's 666. The New Jerusalem is a cube 375 miles on each side.

3202. Spillman, James Russell. *Omega Cometh.* c1979. Old Tappan, NJ: Revell. 154 p.

Doesn't take position regarding timing of Rapture (pre- or post-trib).

3203. Springer, Ernest. *1994? Argument for a Fair Hearing.* 1994. Audubon, NJ: Old Paths Publications 67 p.

About Harold Camping's 1994?

3204. Sproul, R[obert] C. *The Last Days.* 1985. Altamonte Springs, FL: Ligonier Ministries. 2 videos. Also 1979 audiotape ed.

3205. Sproule, John A. *In Defense of Pretribulationalism.* 1980. Winona Lake, IN: BMH Books. Rev. ed. 64 p. Prev. pub. as *A Revised Review of "The Church and the Tribulation" by Robert H. Gundry.*

3206. _____. *An Exegetical Defense of Pretribulationalism.* 1981. 224 p. Grace Theological Seminary. Th.D. thesis.

3207. Stackhouse, Reginald. *The End of the World?: A New Look at an Old Belief.* 1997. New York: Paulist Press. vii, 136 p. bibl. refs.

Stackhouse: professor emeritus Wycliffe College at University. Toronto. A-mill.

3208. Stair, R.G. *The Last Day Prophet.* Cassette. Walterboro, SC: Overcomer Radio Ministry.

Post-trib. 6,000 Year theory. Television is Satanic influence. Tells listeners not to go to doctors and to leave the cities. Rapture is "strong delusion"—a lie promoted by the Catholic Church, a religious monstrosity. Other tapes include *The Last Day Prophet, It Is Finished — Coming Judgment, The Day of the Lord is Near, Last Days in America, Tribulation Next, The Day and the Hour of Christ's Coming, Profile of the End, End Time Revelation, The Last Generation.*

3209. Standish, Colin D., and Russell R. Standish. *The Perils of Time-Setting.* 1992. Rapidan, VA: Hartland Publications. 83 p.

3210. _____. *The Antichrist is Here.* [1990s]. Rapidan, VA: Hartland Publications. 250 p.

Authors: Seventh-day Adventist ministers. Deadly wound of Beast which heals: Papal power destroyed when Pope captured by Napoleon in 1798, but later re-established. Fall of communism was orchestrated by Pope, who will lead world religion at End, persecuting true Christians fearfully. "We are living in the last days…. We are near the end of this world's history." U.S. becomes Second Beast of Daniel.

3211. Stanley, Charles F. *The Coming of Christ.* 1988. 4 cassettes. Atlanta, GA: In Touch Ministries.

3212. _____. *When They Cry Peace and Safety.* 1991. Atlanta, GA: In Touch Ministries. cassette.

Southern Baptist Convention sermon.

3213. Stanton, Don. *Mystery 666.* 1978. Secunderabad, India: Maranatha Revival Crusade.

3214. Stap, Mulraine, and Fred Stap. *Jesus of Galilee Will Walk the Earth Again.* 1997 [1993]. [Michigan:] Stap Ministries. 27 p.

Post-trib. Especially intended for woman. Russia, with Iran, Germany, others, invades Israel prior to Seven Years, which starts with treaty. First half of Seven Years at least Four Seals, then Satan is cast to Earth. Antichrist — Satan himself— declares himself God. Seven Heads: Egypt,

Assyria, Babylonia, Medo-Persia, Greece; Rome is Sixth (the head that "is"), United Europe or Germany is 7th ("yet to come"). No Rapture. After Seven Years and 75 days, the Second Coming, then 7 Bowls. Millennial reign, then literal New Jerusalem. M. Stap writes *Mulraine's End Times and Christ's Return* website (<www. geocities.com/heartland/Ranch/6240/>).

3215. Stedman, Ray C. *What On Earth's Going to Happen?* 1970. Glendale, CA: G/L Regal Books. 203 p.

Pastor Peninsula Bible Church, Palo Alto. Pre-trib. 144,000 Jews witness during Tribulation. Russian invasion is destroyed. Great natural disasters, "unprecedented human evil … terrible slaughter and human suffering." Then Second Coming. Rapture will be soon but date is not knowable.

3216. _____. *What's This World Coming To?: An Expository Study of Matthew 24-25, the Olivet Discourse.* 1986 [1970]. Ventura, CA: Regal Books. 2nd ed. 167 p.

3217. Steele, Ron J. *The Mark Is Ready—Are You?* 1978. Project Research. 112 p. illus.

Antichrist is black. Discovered government plan to change currency, tied to Universal Product Code, 666 Mark of the Beast, the secret Belgian computer. Entertainer Michael Jackson promoted as Messiah, but is really False Messiah. Plans book on "False Black Messiah Phenomenon."

3218. Steinbach, Tom. *God's Game Plan.* 1997. White Pine, MI: Times Ten Pub. 192 p. Illus.

3219. Stephens, William H. *The Bible Speaks to End Times.* 1993. Nashville: Convention Press. 157 p. bibl. refs.

Ed. of *Biblical Illustrator.* Text for course in Baptist Doctrine. Historic premill. Sometimes more than one fulfillment. Kingdom Age began with the First Coming; will be fully realized at Second. Prophecies refer to Church, not Israel. 1st Beast of Sea = Antichrist. 2nd Beast = false religion, state-controlled. Antichrist based in Babylon (= Harlot). Mortal wound is Antichrist's defeat at Armageddon, with renewed attack at end of Millennium. Armageddon not specific site. Second Coming combines Rapture and defeat of Satan, as same event. All the saved are resurrected at start of Millennium, all unsaved at end. Gog-Magog battle is at end of Millennium.

3220. Stephenson, John M. *Watchman Warning: The Endtimes Are Unfolding.* 1994. Sunnyvale, CA: Living-Faith Outreach. xiv, 470 p. Charts, bibl. refs., indexes.

God's Endtime judgment is coming. "The presented Pattern View of prophecy, founded on more than 30 doctrines, helps to resolve the issues between holders of different prophetic views.... Revelation's events, which end history, have started. The fourth-seal war will soon thrust people into divine discipline for their sin.... [This book shows that] the endtimes unfold in the sequence of apostasy, calamity [Tribulation], discipline, deliverance [Rapture], & retribution [Judgment]." "God is Bringing Judgment and Ending History." 70th Week is historical: no parenthesis. 2,000 years from Adam to Abraham, 2,000 years to Christ, thus 2,000 Christ to End, making it ca. A.D. 2030. "Human history may last a fixed period of 6,000 years." God bet Satan he wouldn't convert a single one of God's Elect in this 6,000-year span. Satan goes to Lake of Fire if loses. Seals 1-4 already broken (great apostasy). 4th Seal: major war which will initiate Judgment. Then great disasters of Tribulation: much of world killed. Mark of Beast, 10 kings reign with Beast. 5th Seal: Babylon the Great one-world system. Tribulation: people forced to decide between God and Satan. Apostasy including Satan worship, tongues speaking. U.S. becomes puppet of Beast Empire (Babylon) after 4th Seal War. Post-trib Rapture; occurs at Second Coming after Tribulation; then Millennium: the Last Day of Church Age. "Millennium" = one day only (reverses 2 Peter 3:8; the thousand years equals a literal day). "A [literal] Millennium will not occur." Antichrist = Beast. The Wrath bowls during the Last Day (Millennium), then Armageddon.

3221. _____. *Watchman, How Far Gone is the Night?* 1995. Sunnyvale, CA: Living-Faith Outreach, x, 246 p. illus. bibl. refs.

3222. Stevens, Neville V. *Zion Ministries: Bible Prophecy for the Endtime.* <http://www.omen.net.au/~zionmin/articles.html>

"The Bible is full of prophecy. It details horrific events that will occur in the endtime, and ultimately when the final battle between good and evil is fought. But before all this, many things will occur that will effect your life. You need to know what to expect! You may be shocked by the graphic detail revealed in the pages of your Bible. But you need to know!" Post-trib: horrible persecution before Second Coming. Ten Kings are Islamic superstate. Ten Lost Tribes now Anglo-Americans. Australian offshoot of H.W. Armstrong's Worldwide Church of God.

3223. Stevens, R. Paul. *End Times: Practical Heavenly Mindedness.* 1994. Downers Grove, IL: InterVarsity Press. 80 p. bibl. refs.

LifeGuide Bible Studies series for church or college study sessions. Also wrote *Revelation* for same series. Questions referring to different books of Bible. "Last Days" began with the Ascension of Christ (First Coming). Final End will be according to God's timing which is impossible to predict, but the Second Coming is the only prophecy not yet fulfilled, so could be soon. Evil to be incarnated in "anti-kingdom" of Antichrist.

3224. Stewart, Don, and Chuck Missler. *The Coming Temple: Center Stage for the Final Countdown.* 1991. Orange, CA: Dart. 238 p. illus., maps, bibl. refs.

Rebuilding the Temple in Jerusalem, triggering the End Time Tribulation.

3225. Stewart, Ed. *Millennium's Eve.* 1993. Wheaton IL: Victor Books. 475 p.

Novel. Journalist and police officer discover plot to blow up televangelists gathered for huge rally in Los Angeles on Dec. 31, 1999 just as millennium begins. Plotter, who refers constantly to Four Horsemen of Revelation, turns out to be rival televangelist who faked his own assassination after organizing the rally.

3226. Stewart, Tom. *1998: Year of the Apocalypse.* <http://whatsaiththescripture.com/Timeline/98.Yr.of.Apocalypse.1.Text.html>

Pre-trib Rapture of Church (the Apocalypse) May 31, 1998. Tribulation = Nov. 19, 1998 to Oct. 12, 2005. Russian attack Apr. 1, 2002. Pre-Wrath Rapture (second Rapture) Oct. 4, 2005. Second Coming = Oct. 13, 2005. Millennium = Oct. 18, 2005. In 1878 Amish minister Noah Troyer prophesied coming destruction of America if nation did not repent in 120 years (same time given in Noah's day: 1878 + 120 =1998). Also, in 1989, Dimitru Duduman, a Romanian Christian, was sent by God to warn Americans of God's coming judgment on the U.S. In 1993 Duduman shown book with 1¾ pages left blank. In 1996 shown same book with only single page left. By mathematical calculation can determine that destruction (no blanks left) will come by Jan. 24, 1999.

3227. Stokes, Roger. *The Jews, Rome and Armageddon.* 1995 [1987]. Strathalbyn, Australia: Strathalbyn Christadelphian Ecclesia. xii, 472 p. illus., maps, bibl. refs., index.

Christadelphian.

3228. Stone, Perry F. *The Perfect Day: a Novel on the Millennium.* 1985. [Cleveland, TN?]: Voice of Evangelism Outreach Ministries. 130 p.

Stone: on *God's News Behind the News* telecast.

3229. Stott, John R. *The Gospel and the End of Time: The Message of Thessalonians.* 1994 [1991]. Downers Grove, IL: Inter-Varsity. 218 p.

Rector emeritus: All Souls Church, London. Pre-trib Rapture.

3230. Strandberg, Todd. *Rapture Ready.* <http://www.novia.net/~todd/>

Pre-trib, any-moment Rapture. Includes *Rapture Indicator.* Also wrote "How the World's Rejection of the Pre-Trib Rapture Proves its Validity."

3231. Straughan, Alfred D. *God's Coming Wrath: A Study of the Creational Phenomena of the Tribulation in the Book of Revelation.* 1971. New York: Carlton Press. 79 p. illus

3232. Strauss, Lehman. SEE ALSO 1910–1970 *The Importance of Bible Prophecy.* 1977. La Mirada, CA: Biola College. 21 p.

From Biola Hour radio program.

3233. _____. *The Signs of the Times: A Prophetic Study in Matthew 24.* 1978. La Mirada, CA: Biola College. 22 p.

From Biola Hour radio program.

3234. _____. *Prophetic Mysteries Revealed.* 1980. Neptune, NJ: Loizeaux Bros. 255 p. index, bibl.

Dispensational pre-mill. Parallels between Matthew and Revelation; exegesis of parables. "Mystery" of Mat. 13:11 = the Church Age: long period of time in which Israel is set aside and God deals with Gentiles. Parable of mustard seed: Strauss denies post-mill interpretation of earthly progress of Church. Leaven = not the Gospel, but rather corrupting influences (deceit, hypocrisy, materialism). Seven Churches: personal, local, historical as well as prophetic interpretation of each. Ephesus: represents Church A.D. 30-160. Smyrna: to A.D. 312 (martyred, persecutions). Pergamos: to A.D. 600 (worldly). Thyatira: Medieval Church. Sardis: Reformation. Philadelphia: 18-19th century (small but faithful). Laodicaea: wealthy but complacent current church.

3235. _____. *God's Prophetic Calendar.* 1987. Neptune, NJ: Loizeaux Bros. 133 p. bibl.

"Collapse of civilization," racial conflict, huge advance of communism: "doom is certain."

3236. Stringfellow, Bill. *All in the Name of the Lord.* c1980. Clermont, FL: Concerned Publications. 172 p. bibl.

Stringfellow: attorney; Harvard Law. Satan's origins as Lucifer — God's favored angel in heaven. Satan's counterfeit teachings, especially about Armageddon. Nimrod and Semiramis in Babylon perverted true worship into paganism. Creation about six thousand years ago in six literal days. Seventh day — true Sabbath — is Saturday; Sunday worship is Mark of the Beast. Old Roman Empire was divided in ten successor states. A.D. 538 + 1,260 = 1798. Little Horn and the Beast = Catholic Church, Papal hierarchy.

3237. Strong, John. *The Doomsday Globe.* 1977 [1973]. Kensington, Australia: Clarendon Press. 275 p. illus., diagrams, graphs, maps, bibl.

"Doomsday is coming"—global and astral catastrophes. "Biblical prophecy is true" and supports his theory. Follows Melvin Cook and Gentry (young-earth creationists), Patten (catastrophes), and Rutherford (pyramidology). Communists want nuclear war to reduce population and competition from West. War is inevitable; radiation won't kill survivors. Earth: lubricated crust slides over mantle. Antarctica slides to equator when jolted by nuclear explosions, causing unprecedneted quakes, volcanoes, tidal waves. 1978 probably Doomsday. A.D. 643 (first mosque at Temple site) + 1,335 = 1978. A.D. 688 (Dome of Rock) + 1,290 = 1978. Pyramid is "chronograph" showing dates: Adam created 5407 B.C., Millennium 1979. "Faith is required because God's purpose is the testing of the individual."

3238. Sullivan, George. *The King Is Coming.* 1973. Garland, TX: The King Is Coming. Unpag. illus.

Sullivan: evangelist; publishes journal *The King Is Coming.* Last Days: this generation. Pre-trib. Antichrist will deceive world with Satanic miracles. Warns that Antichrist will kill all the unsaved, so urges evangelization.

3239. Sumburèru, Dale. *The Greatest Deception: An Impending Alien Invasion.* 1997. Mukilteo, WA: WinePress. 301 p. illus., maps, bibl. refs.

"Apocalyptic prophecy." Sumburèru: Seventh-day Adventist. March 22, 1997: "the date when all the dramatic events leading through the tribulation to the return of Christ should begin," with Second Coming somewhere between July 2000 and March 2001 (Tribulation "cut short" so date uncertain). 2,300 days: March 1994 to July 2000. 70 jubilees: 1437 B.C. to A.D. 1994.

3240. Sumrall, Lester Frank. *Iran, Russia and the End of the World.* 1980.

South Bend, IN: LeSea Tapes. audiocassette.

3241. _____. *I Predict 1984: Is Big Brother Watching You?* South Bend, IN: LeSEA publication. 63 p.

3242. _____. *I Predict 1985: Who will Survive in 85?* 1984. South Bend, IN: LeSEA Publication. 65 p.

3243. _____. *I Predict 1986: a Year of World Destiny.* 1985. South Bend, IN: LeSEA Publication. 65 p.

3244. _____. *I Predict 2000 a.d.* 1987. South Bend, IN: LeSEA. 114 p.

2000 as the Millennium.

3245. _____. *Time Bomb in the Middle East: Countdown to Armageddon.* 1991. Tulsa, OK: Harrison House. 118 p. map.

3246. Sungenis, Robert A., Scott Temple, and David A. Lewis. *Shockwave 2000! Harold Camping's 1994 Debacle.* 1994. Green Forest, AR: New Leaf Press. 176 p. bibl. refs.

Temple and Lewis: pre-mill. Sungenis (who formerly worked for Camping) is uncommitted. Appendix: manifesto declaring "we are living in the last days and nothing must be allowed to detract from the nobility and power of the message of end-time Bible prophecy." Camping's calculations, say authors, do detract, and violate literal interpretation.

3247. Sutton, Hilton. *The Beast System: Europe in Prophecy: A Study of Revelation Chapters 13 and 17.* 1981. Tulsa, OK: Harrison House. 109 p.

3248. _____. *World War III: God's Conquest of Russia.* 1982. 4th ed. Tulsa, OK: Harrison House. 93 p.

Russia launches missiles at U.S. during attack on Mideast, but prophesied earthquakes/hailstorms cause them to fall on Russia; meanwhile U.S. launches retaliatory strike "Russia totally wiped out." Sutton presented *Ezekiel File* (Gog = Russia) to Begin's advisors regarding planned invasion of Israel.

3249. _____. *He's Coming!* Tulsa, OK: Harrison House. 149 p.

3250. _____. *Revelation: God's Grand Finale.* 1984. Tulsa, OK: Harrison House. 251, [7] p. bibl. index.

3251. _____. *Death of an Empire: The Prophetic Destiny of the Soviet Union.* 1991. Tulsa, OK: Harrison House. 71 p. bibl.

"We are living in a time when Bible prophecies are being fulfilled daily." All evidence shows Day of the Lord is fast approaching. Pre-trib. Gog = "presently" Gorbachev. Russia still belligerent; will control Turkey and "Gomer" (part of Germany and eastern Europe), and will invade Israel. Soviet Union will be destroyed after Rapture: entire population killed. "Signs" in the sun, moon, stars are prophesied effects of our space program.

3252. _____. *Rapture: Get Right Or Get Left.* 1993 [1991]. Tulsa, OK: Harrison House. 90 p. Prev. titled *He's Coming.*

"Warning! This Book May Determine Your Destiny...."

3253. _____. *Abcs of Bible Prophecy.* 1994. Tulsa, OK: Harrison House. 130 p.

Relates prophecy to today's news. Hilton Sutton Ministries: Humble, TX. President of Christian Evangelist Zionist Congress of America. "Satan Hates Prophecy"—hates Revelation the most of all tells humans it is a horror story, but it's really a book of blessings. 'The Time of the End Is Here!" Pre-trib Rapture.

3254. Sutton, William Josiah. *The Illuminati 666 (Book 2).* 1995. Brushton, NY: TEACH Services. 294 p. illus., bibl. refs., index.

3255. _____, and Roy Allen Anderson. *The Illuminati 6666.* 1995. Brushton, NY: TEACH Services. 294 p. illus., bibl. refs., index.

3256. Swaggart, Jimmy. *The Great White Throne Judgment.* 1979. Baton Rouge: Jimmy Swaggart Evangelistic Assoc. 202 p.

Swaggart: Assemblies of God minister (before sex scandal); televangelist.

3257. _____. *A Study in Bible Prophecy: A Scriptural Approach to Eschatology.* c1986. Baton Rouge: Jimmy Swaggart School of the Bible. iv, 248 loose-leaf "Bible Study Course."

3258. _____. *Armageddon: The Future of Planet Earth.* c1987. Baton Rouge: Jimmy Swaggart Ministries. vi, 201.

Any-moment Rapture. Antichrist revealed; Tribulation (worst ever suffering); Second Coming and Armageddon; Millennium; final revolt of Satan. This "timetable clearly detailed in the Bible." America today: "We see sin, iniquity, and blasphemy erupting like a cesspool of evil, spewing forth from the very pits of hell" worse than Sodom and Gomorrah. Communists literally Satanic, "subhumans." Ten-Horn nations of "revised" Roman Empire: implies Russia will be defeated by Antichrist because Roman Empire includes parts of USSR. Gog = Antichrist (not Russia). Antichrist not resurrected or reincarnated man. "The rapture will be the most earth-shaking event in the history of the world." 144,000 Jews (= Man-child of Rev.) raptured during Tribulation; also other Tribulation saints. Not all saved Christians will be raptured: those "sleeping" (unaware), not vigilant, not sober, will miss it. Jews' purpose was to produce Christ; they have suffered because they "utterly rejected God." But only race to know God's plan, and Swaggart is stoutly pro-Israel. Antichrist: probably a Syrian Jew, who will subdue Greece, Turkey, Egypt. Israel welcomes Antichrist as Messiah; Antichrist conquers Israel, rules from Babylon half of Tribulation, then from Jerusalem. Abomination of Desolation, desecrates Temple, Jews flee. Then Antichrist moves to meet threat from Germany, Russia, and China. Returns to Israel; Battle of Armageddon = Christ arrives: Satan, demons, and Antichrists armies vs. Christ with heavenly armies and Israel. Armageddon and Second Coming will be televised: "Suddenly the camera will pan upward" as Christ arrives with army in the sky. Blood literally to horse bridles in whole valley. At the Millennium, the Dead Sea is raised, joined to ocean. New Jerusalem descends from heaven.

3259. _____. *Coming World Events.* [1980s]. 6 cassettes. Baton Rouge: Jimmy Swaggart Ministries.

3260. Swihart, Stephen D. *Armageddon 198?* 1980. Plainfield, NJ: Haven Books (Logos). xii, 269 p. illus. charts, maps, diagrams, bibl. refs.

Swihart: pastor Church of the Living Word, Elkhart, IN. Pre-mill, post-trib (but doesn't insist on latter). This generation will probably see the Second Coming. 70th Week divided: first half consecutive with 69 weeks, up to Christ's baptism; then long gap — the New Testament church; then second half of 70th Week prior to Second Coming (3½ year Great Tribulation). Rapture/Second Coming, then three battles (including Armageddon). Appendix of "Last Day" terminology in Bible (various synonyms, epithets, terms referring to). Rapture after Armageddon (Russia, China vs. Antichrist's Europe). Seal, trumpets, bowls: chronological within each set, but all three series run concurrently, in parallel. 6th and 7th follow Armageddon. Antichrist from Syrian region. Details deterioration of present: war, immorality, famine earthquakes crime, "mockers." Prophetic importance of Israel, America, Russia, China. Beasts of Revelation: Egypt, Assyria, Babylonia, Medo-Persia, Greece; Rome, and Revived Rome; 8th (in future) is Revived Greece. Antichrist gets control over Ten Nations to dominate Israel during Tribulation, unleash demons from Abyss, great persecutions. Satan then possesses him and he orders he be worshipped in rebuilt Temple. Russia will invade Israel — Armageddon (two parallel accounts). Gog = Russia; allied with Germany, Persia, Africans; then China joins invasion.

3261. Syme, Bob. *50 Evidences for the Pre-Trib Rapture.* <http://members.aol.comRSy2717/pretrib.htm>

3262. Talbott, David N. *Remembering the End of the World.* 1996. Video. Kronia Communications.

"Based on the book *The Saturn Myth* by Talbott [1979; Doubleday]." Talbott examines the possibility that the mythological symbols of our ancient ancestors told of great catastrophe caused by celestial bodies. He suggests that our solar system was configured differently at one time than it is now." Velikovskian catastrophism; Saturn theory; periodic cosmic collisions and destructions in myths.

3263. Tamura, Teresa. *Semarikuru*

Shumatsu: Sheisho No Yogen. 1993. San Jose, CA: Bay Garden-sha. 118 p. illus. bibl. refs.

"Coming Last Days: Bible Prophecy."

3264. Tan, Paul Lee. 1991. *A Pictorial Guide to Bible Prophecy.* Garland, TX: Bible Communications. 413 p. illus., charts, diagrams. Index.

"Perfect for overhead presentations and seminars." Dispensationalist.

3265. Tarkowski, Ed. *The Second Coming of Our Lord and Savior Jesus Christ.* <www.ncinter.net/~ejt/>

Post-trib. 6,000 Year theory. Refutes pre-Wrath trib. Catholics promote apostate Marian worship for Year 2000 Jubilee.

3266. Tasseos, Socrates G. *Bible Book Ezekiel Interpreted World War III Is Prophecised: End of the World As We Know It with the Battle of Armegeddon.* 1991. Sun City, AZ: SOC Pub. 48 p. illus.

3267. Tatford, Frederick A. SEE ALSO 1910–1970. *The Clock Strikes.* 1971. Fort Washington, PA: Christian Literature Crusade. 126 p.

Fiction. Antichrist.

3268. _____. *God's Plan for the Future: An Outline of Prophecy.* 1971. Eastbourne, England: Prophetic Witness. 16 p.

3269. _____. *Prophet of Judgment Day: An Exposition of the Prophecy of Joel.* 1974. Eastbourne, England: Prophetic Witness. 88 p.

3270. _____. *How Much Longer???* 1975. Eastbourne, England: Prophetic Witness. 86 p. bibl.

Fictional account of family during Antichrist's reign. Second Coming "imminent" (perhaps before 2000); preceded by Rapture and ten-nation confederacy.

3271. _____. *Dead Bones Live: An Exposition of the Prophecy of Ezekiel.* 1977, Eastbourne, England: Prophetic Witness. 275 p. illus. maps, plans

3272. _____. *Ten Nations, What Now?* 1980. Eastbourne, England: Upperton Press. 30 p. illus. map.

"The European Common Community and its future."

3273. _____. *The Final Encounter: An Exposition of the Book of Revelation.*

1983. Newtown, Australia: Christian Outreach Book Service. 660 p. bibl.

3274. _____. *The Revelation.* 1985 [1983]. Minneapolis: Klock & Klock. 647 p.

3275. Taylor, Charles R. *The Destiny of America.* 1972. Van Nuys, CA: Time-Light. 254 p.

Huntington Beach televangelist— "Today in Bible Prophecy." Russia bought bows and arrows from English companies; also using lignostone (specially treated wood) for weapons; huge numbers of cavalry ready — thus will literally fulfill biblical prophecies about weaponry at End (including Israel burning attackers' weapons for seven years).

3276. _____. *Get All Excited—Jesus Is Coming Soon.* 1975 [1974]. Redondo Beach, CA: Today in Bible Prophecy. 108 p. illus. maps.

3277. _____. *World War III and the Destiny of America.* c1979 [1971]. Nashville: Sceptre Books (Thomas Nelson). 390 p. illus. index. Orig. pub. Redondo Beach, CA: Today in Bible Prophecy.

Used book *Prepare for Armageddon* by Claude L. and Lydia R. Strother for "scientific data."

3278. _____. *Those Who Remain.* c1980 [1976]. Huntington Beach, CA: Today in Bible Prophecy. 99 p. bibl. refs illus.

Sequel to *Get All Excited—Jesus Is Coming Soon.* Pre-trib. Antichrist = King Juan Carlos of Spain. "Stones crying out" = videotape (made in part from stones).

3279. _____. *Watch 1988—The Year of Climax.*

Predicts End for 1988. Previously had predicted Rapture for several previous years, and later predicted Rapture for several subsequent years; e.g. Sept. 6, 1994, with Millennium for 2000.

3280. _____. *World War III: When the Arabs Attack Jerusalem.* 1991. Today in Bible Prophecy. 88 p. illus. 2nd ed. Orig. titled *When the Arabs Attack Jerusalem.*

Arab nations attack with full support of Soviet Union and Eastern Europe. To stop U.S. and Western Europe from defending Israel, Soviets launch all-out one day nuclear attack — this "according to

specific Bible prophecies. America will burn." Russian Middle East invasion "synchronized with an all-out CBW [chemical-biological warfare] and thermonuclear bombardment" of America.

3281. _____. *Those Who Remain, 1980 Edition.* Orange, CA: Today in Bible Prophecy. Ezek. 39: U.S. suffers hideously from Russia but responds in kind.

3282. _____. *The Antichrist—Juan Carlos.* 1994. Huntington Beach, CA: Bible Prophecy for Today. 134 p. illus.

3283. Ted. *The Climax.* 1982. St. Petersburg, FL: The Gospel Truth. 334 p.

"This book contains nearly every Scripture in the Bible dealing with the End Times and events from the past that have a bearing on the End Times." Author: no surname given.

3284. Telford, Shirley. *The Prince of Peace.* 1984. San Francisco: William & Richards. 56 p.

Telford (Telford Weston): earlier wrote book on economics and world peace; claimed it influenced Chinese leaders. A drama: Christ appears to heroine (who also wrote book on world peace), shows her future Millennium (apparently post-mill). Armageddon seems to be destruction of old economic regime ("Babylon"), beginning with abolition of slavery. When heroine is martyred, the Millennium begins.

3285. Temple, George. *Is Anyone in Charge?* [1980?]. El Reno, OK: Temple Press. 171 p. illus.

3286. Terrell, Steve. *The 90's, Decade of the Apocalypse: The European Common Market—the End has Begun.* 1994 [1992]. rev. ed. South Plainfield, NJ: Bridge Pub. 217 p. bibl. refs.

Terrell: taught at Biola, now actor, Lord's Player's founder (San Diego). Pre-trib pre-mill. 1992 EEC agreement to dissolve trade barriers, federate, unite currency, is prelude to Armageddon. C.F. Noble's theory that Three Beasts of Daniel are contemporaneous, not ancient empires (cites Morris of ICR); Israel is Fourth. Lion = England; bear = Communist Russia; Leopard = Indian Empire. Antichrist probably British; he rides all Four Horses of Revelation. "*Estimated time of impact: 1993.*" "The end time drama has already begun." Won't be one-world government before Second Coming; but Antichrist will rule EEC by Jan. 1993. England and another nation will withdraw from Common Market to reduce it to 10. Armageddon won't involve whole world. Seven year Tribulation: Pope crowns Common Market leader Holy Roman Emperor; Satan possesses him mid-Tribulation. Spain and Portugal rebel, are crushed. Empire then conquers Mediterranean and Israel. Mid-Tribulation: Emperor declares Temple worship of him as God. 144,000 believing Jews flee, preach, protected by God. Egypt, Ethiopia, Libya attack; Emperor defeats them (beginning of Armageddon). Russian confederacy attacks, overruns Israel; Christ Comes, destroys occupying army. Millennium. New Jerusalem descends at beginning of Millennium. Not 1,500 miles tall, but suspended 1,500 miles above Earth: a "glorified space station." Believers live in New Jerusalem, others remain on earth. End of Millennium: God destroys last Satanic army. Ezekiel's "Beloved City" (not same as New Jerusalem) is 9 sq. miles, for pilgrims going to Temple worship. Will feature highways, airport, motels. God wouldn't keep Rapture a secret; he must tell us approximately when it will occur. Tribulation 1993, then Millennium A.D. 2000.

3287. Tetsola, John. *Understanding the Time Zones of God*. 1993. East Orange, NJ: End Time Wave Publications. x, 160.

Religious aspects of time.

3288. *These Things Shall Be...: The Coming of Elijah, the Second Advent of Christ, the First Judgment, Armageddon, the Millennial Reign of Christ, the Second Judgment, Eternity*. 1983. Rochester, NY: The Megiddo Church. 57 p.

"We believe that the coming of Christ is now imminent": "there are not many of the allotted six thousand years remaining." Two-thirds of humanity will die. Armageddon, then Second Coming.

3289. Thibault, Roger. *Letters from the End Times*. <http://www.yellowstone-info.com/endtimes>

Catholic. Yellowstone Information Services. Y2k computer bug as proof of the coming Chastisements. Rejects pretrib Rapture: "we're all going to have to duke it out with the Antichrist and his minions." Clinton is tool of Satanic New World Order ("we have an antichrist for president"); UN is New World Order plot; abortion is horrible sin ("Ending abortion is at the heart of everything we do")— murdered abortionists were really killed by government agents to discredit anti-abortion movement; the Pope is surrounded by traitors in the Vatican. Anti-gun-control and pro-militia-movement. U.N. and other foreign troops now assembling in America preparing for subversion and takeover; biochips as Mark of the Beast (now being tested on humans). Marian apparitions: Agnes Sasagawa in Akita, Japan; Medjugorge, Fatima, Garanbandal.

3290. Thieme, Robert B. *Armageddon*. 1976. Houston: Berachah Church. 48 p.

Thieme: ex-Air Force; Seminary thesis on Armageddon; minister of Berachah Church. Apocalyptic. (Followers included Marilyn Quayle.)

3291. Thomas, I.D.E. *The Omega Conspiracy: Satan's Last Assault On God's Kingdom*. c1986. Oklahoma City: Hearthstone Publishing (div. of Southwest Radio Church of the Air). 254 p.

UFOs: humanoid ETs among us. Fallen angels sired super-race — the biblical Nephilim. Fallen angels are beings from another dimension: "spirit beings from outer space" who mated with humans — and are doing so again. They tried to thwart Christ by polluting race to prevent his Incarnation in pure human line. Endorses Book of Enoch. Pyramid dimensions encoded advanced astronomical knowledge. Omega Conspiracy is final gigantic attempt to corrupt humanity before Return of Christ — worse than pre-Flood assault. Paluxy "manprints" in Cretaceous strata are evidence of Nephilim. ETs suck energy from earthlings. Thomas: former pastor in Wales, now Baptist minister, Maywood, CA.

3292. Thomas, Lee. *Passage to a*

New World. 1991. West Covina, CA; Shiloh Ministries. xvi, 93 p.

3293. Thompson, George N., ed. *Augustine on the End of the World*. [date?] Tishomingo, OK: Mayflower Pilgrim Press. 55 p. reprint.

3294. Thompson, Linda. *America Under Siege*. 1994. Indianapolis: American Justice Federation (distr. by The Prophecy Club, Topeka KS). video.

Militia movement. Uncovers government plans for instituting New World Order by systematic brutality, harassment, and surveillance; international police and UN, and civilian prison camps run by Federal Emergency Mgt. Agency (FEMA).

3295. *The Time Is At Hand ...* <http:members.aol.com/timeathand/index.thml>

Pre-trib. Includes "What to Do If You Miss the Rapture": a "huge number" will be saved during the 7-year Tribulation. Antichrist will "easily put the likes of Hitler and Stalin to shame" during the Tribulation. Resist the Mark of the Beast, even though martyrdom is likely result.

3296. Timm, B.A. *Seven Giant Steps to World Peace*. 1989. New York: Vantage Press. 49 p. illus.

3297. Timmons, Tim. *Creation, the End of the World, Bethlehem*. 3 cassettes. South Coast Community Church sermons.

3298. *To Hope Again*. 1994. Thousand Oaks, CA: It Is Written; Adventist Media Center. 2 videos.

Includes "The Night the Stars Fell" and "The Right Stuff for the End Time."

3299. Tout, Charles A. *The Apocalypse and Last Day Prophecies*. 1992. Ilfracombe: Stockwell. 134 p.

3300. *Transit Letters*. Order of the Solar Temple.

Order of the Solar Temple: cult led by French homeopathic physician Luc Jouret and Jo DiMambro (author?) who believed they were reincarnated Knights Templars. Members murdered member family whose baby they claimed was Antichrist, then committed suicide in fires in Canada and Switzerland in 1994. Believed world will end in apocalyptic fire which will purify the Order, whose members will then be transported to the star Sirius.

3301. Traylor, Ellen Gunderson. *The Priest*. 1998. Nashville: Word. 370 p.

Novel. One of the Dead Sea scrolls, kept hidden, contains clues which can identity living descendant of Zadokite Priesthood (a Cohen living in England), thus allowing reinstitution of Temple worship in Jerusalem and ushering in Last Days. Investigators hampered by white supremacist and Islamic opponents.

3302. Treacy, Maura. *Focus on End Times: Today's Events and the Soon Return of Jesus Christ*. 1983. Burlington, Canada: Crown. 139 p.

3303. Tucker, Bill. *End of the World Final Events*. [1990s]. Video. Redlands, CA: The Quiet Hour. The Quiet Hour home video ministry Dir. by Bill Colwell.

3304. Tucker, J.L. *The Beast and His Mark*. Redlands, CA: The Quiet Hour. 55 p.

Same family as LaVerne Tucker. Beast = Roman Catholic Church; "Vicarius Filii Dei" = 666. Fatal wound recovered from was Napoleon's 1798 capture of Pope. Mark of Beast is coming compulsory Sunday worship laws. Also wrote *The Last Night on Earth*.

3305. Tucker, LaVerne [E.] *The Coming Battle of Armageddon*. [1980s]. Redlands, CA: The Quiet Hour. 26 p. illus.

3306. _____. *Coming World Events...*. [1980s]. Redlands, CA; The Quiet Hour. 27 p.

3307. _____. *End of the World: Coming Final Events*. 1981. Redlands, CA: The Quiet Hour. 132 p. illus.

"Your world is going to end!" A.D. 538 + 1,260 day/years = 1798 (Papal supremacy). 10-Kingdoms start 476 A.D. Beast = Little Horn = Papacy. Uproots 3 horns: Heruli, Ostrogoths, Vandals. Rome changed Sabbath. 69 weeks = 457 B.C. to 27 A.D.; the 70th ends A.D. 34 (stoning of Stephen). 457 B.C. + 2,300 day/years = 1844. "Pre-advent judgment" began 1844, when "truth restored." Second Coming any time now. Refutes Rapture and Gap (Parenthesis) theories. Quotes E. G. White.

Ribera's 1590 work written to refute charge that Pope was Antichrist. Second Coming = resurrection of righteous, saints go to heaven, wicked slain. Millennium = earth totally desolate, lifeless. End of Millennium = resurrection of the wicked, New Jerusalem descends. False Prophet = apostate Protestantism, persecuting dissenters especially Sabbath keepers, with civil penalties. False Prophet makes Sunday mark of authority. 666 = vicarius filii dei; 666 also "Latin church" in Greek, "Roman kingdom" in Hebrew. False spiritualistic revival in U.S. then church-state system resembling Catholic, with death penalty for Sabbath keepers. Tremendous judgment from Heavens: sea, skies, mountains, cites crumble. New Jerusalem: 375 miles each side.

3308. ____. *End of the World: How to Prepare for It*. 1983 [1980?]. Redlands, CA: The Quiet Hour. 20 p.

3309. ____. *End of the World: Final Events*. 1992. Redlands, CA: The Quiet Hour. 140 p. illus.

3310. Tuella. *A New Book of Revelations*. New Brunswick, NJ: Inner Light Publications. 160 p.

"Channeled thru Tuella." Global war in Middle East. Fallen angels try to enslave humanity. God's rebellious son Jehovah distorted the Bible to deceive humanity; Tuella corrects it here. Also wrote *Project World Evacuation: UFOs to Assist in the "Great Exodus" of Human Souls Off This Planet* (1993).

3311. Tunji, Abd al-Salam. *Al-Iman bi-al-Yawm al-Akhir*. 1986. Tripoli, Libya: al-Jamahiriyah al-Arabaiyah al-Libiyah: Jamiyat al-Dawah al-Islamiyah al-Alamiyah. 469 p.

The Islamic Imam of the Last Days.

3312. *12 Tribes of Israel*. <http://www.hodc.com/index.htm>

Disciples of YaHaWaShi (Jesus Christ). The true Biblical Israelites are Blacks; also Indians and Latin Americans. Jews are the Synagogue of Satan. "Time, times, and a half" = A.D. 1620 to 1970. White America = Babylon and Egypt. God is going to destroy America soon with terrorist attacks and nuclear bombs. Russia,

returned to Communism, will attack Israel, and WWIII. Angels will appear in UFOs to deliver the elect of the nation of Israel. "Jesus Christ will return to destroy the nations that are ruling and establish his Kingdom on Earth, under the Israelites."

3313. *UFOs, Aliens & Antichrist: The Angelic Conspiracy & End Times Deception*. <http://www.mt.net/~watcher/>

Watcher Ministries, Missoula, MT. "Satan has been preparing the earth for the event that the Bible has foretold — Satan and his angels shall be cast down to earth" to try to prevent the Millennium. Since pre-Adamic ages Satan has ruled over Mars and other planets, and now controls UFOs. Tribulation probably starts 1998; Satan presents himself as extraterrestrial Messiah at end of Gog-Magog War, counterfeiting the Second Coming.

3314. *UFOs and the Occult*. 1976. Oklahoma City, OK: Southwest Radio Church. 31 p. illus.

3315. Unger, Merrill. *Beyond the Crystal Ball*. 1973. Chicago: Moody Press. 189 p. bibl.

"Billions will perish in the coming cataclysm." Probably by H-bombs — but maybe a direct act of God's wrath on earth rather than human war. Some must survive for Christ to rule over in Millennium. A "huge Oriental army, equipped with nuclear weapons ... a scourge in God's hands" to punish wicked. Unger: Dallas Theological Seminary.

3316. *The United States in Prophecy*. 1970. Independence, MO: Gospel Tract Soc. 31 p. illus.

"The Future of America — The Age of the Apocalypse — Are We Facing Atomic Holocaust? — Is Destruction Our Destiny?" [etc.]

3317. *... Unto 2300 Days*. 1979. Mesa, AZ: Prophetic Research Assn. 85 p. Daniel 8.

3318. Van Auken, John. 1996 [1994]. *The End Times: Prophecies of Coming Changes*. Virginia Beach: A.R.E. viii, 168 p. illus. bibl. refs. Orig. pub.: Inner Vision.

"Includes Prophecies and Predictions

from the Bible, Nostradamus, Holy Mother [Mary], Edgar Cayce." Asserts there is "prophetic agreement that the coming of the Messiah may occur somewhere between 1996 and 1999." Great pole shift A.D. 2000. Cayce's Pyramid-derived dates show that new sub-race of humanity arises A.D. 2033-38. Nostradamus predicts Antichrist and Armageddon in 1999.

3319. Vandeman, George E. *Look! No Doomsday!: A Planet Struck by Lightning, Alarm Lights Blazing, and Rescue from the Skies.* 1970. Mountain View, CA: Pacific Press. 96 p.

3320. _____. *Showdown in the Middle East.* 1980. Mountain View, CA: Pacific Press.

3321. _____. *The Telltale Connection.* Boise, ID: Pacific Press. 80 p.

3322. _____. *The Rise and Fall of Anti-Christ in the Prophecies of Revelation* 1986. Boise, ID: Pacific Press Publishing Assn. 79 p.

3323. _____. *Showdown at Armageddon: Planet Earth's Final Crisis and the Events Preceding It.* 1987. Boise, ID: Pacific Press. 94 p.

Also as 2 videos (seven telecasts): Thousand Oaks, CA: It Is Written. Ten Kings: Germanic tribes which took over Roman Empire: three later absorbed into Papacy by A.D. 538. A.D. 330: Pope controls Rome after Constantine moves capital to East. Pope declared head of all churches. Rapture won't be pre-trib, thus no second chance if you miss it! At Millennium, Satan will be alone on Earth: "one day soon, within the space of a few short hours, this earth will depopulated — not one human being left alive anywhere in the world." At end of Millennium, Satan is loosed to lead resurrected wicked against New Jerusalem, and is destroyed by Christ at Second Coming.

3324. Van der Hoeven, Jan Willem. 1994 [1993]. *Babylon or Jerusalem?* Shippensburg, PA: Destiny Image. 187 p. bibl. refs.

3325. Vander Lugt, Herbert. *There's A New Day Coming! A Survey of Endtime Events.* c1983. Grand Rapids, MI: Radio

Bible Class. 160 p. Scripture index. Also pub. Eugene, OR: Harvest House.

Vander Lugt: research director of "Radio Bible Hour" (DeHaan). Pre-mill; any-moment Rapture. Antichrist — probably a homosexual and secret occultist — will head Western European confederation arising out of Common Market. Russia and allies (Iran, Ethiopia, Libya) attack Israel, but are destroyed mid-Tribulation by "supernatural judgments from heaven." Armageddon at end of Tribulation: Antichrist's Western armies vs. Southern Confederation, then the East. Seals, Trumpets, Bowls start in that order but all end together at Second Coming. Army of 200 million are really demons. The Tribulation will be the "worst time of suffering, devastation, and death in all human history"— but many will convert and their souls will be saved.

3326. Van Impe, Jack. *Signs of the Times.* 1979. Royal Oak, MI: Jack Van Impe Ministries.

3327. _____. *Bible Headlines.* 1980. Royal Oak, MI: Jack Van Impe Ministries. 125 p. illus.

"A compendium of current news releases examined in the light of Bible prophecy." Van Impe: Baptist; televangelist; publishes *Perhaps Today* magazine. Pre-trib pre-mill. Believers return with Christ to participate in Armageddon and Millennium warning about "that which is about to befall our planet and race" in these End Times. "Cavalcade of signs" proving End is imminent. Terrorism, inflation, space exploration, plague, famine, earthquakes, moral decay, drugs, occultism, Soviet threat, coming world government, Antichrist and his 666 computer in Belgium (next to EEC building). Communist Russia, with Moslem and African allies, will invade Israel (Van Impe sells map of this coming war). All nations attack Israel later at Armageddon. Persia will also ally with Russia — Khomeini is an imposter. China now building superhighway across Himalayas as invasion route.

3328. _____. *11:59 ... And Counting!* c1983. Royal Oak, MI: Jack Van Impe Ministries. 324 p.

Nuclear war (WWIII: Tribulation), then Millennium, then nuclear annihilation by God. Not just Russia, but U.S. destroyed too. Van Impe's 1975 TV special "The Middle East, World War III, and Christ's Return" won religious broadcasters' Angel award.

3329. _____. *A.D. 2000— The End.* 1990. Video (60 min.) Troy, MI: Jack Van Impe Ministries.

"Van Impe discusses the end of the world and the return of Christ from a biblical perspective." A.D. 2000 cited as momentous by everybody — including New Age, Naisbitt, etc. Thus End is 9-11 years hence. We can't know day or hour, but do know year (approximately). Pre-trib Rapture, so Christians should look forward to the End. 6,000 Year Theory from Epistle of Barnabas and other early Christian and Jewish authorities. 2 Pet. 3:3; Ps. 90:4. Russian Jews: last Tribe to return. Appeals to past advocates of 6,000 Year theory.

3330. _____. *The Great Escape.* 1990. Troy, MI: Jack Van Impe Ministries. Video.

"Dr. Jack Van Impe explains the Great Tribulation — a seven-year period of trouble, sorrow, and suffering such as the world has never known and which millions escape bodily … if prepared."

3331. _____. *Prophecy Portfolio: In-Depth Scriptural Studies of World Events and End-Time Bible Prophecies.* 1990s cassettes. Troy, MI: Jack Van Impe.

3332. _____. *The 90's, Startling End-Time Signs, & Your Future.* 1990. Video. Troy, MI: Jack Van Impe Ministries

"Factual reports and prophetic interpretations about: End-time terminology, numerology and chronology, Israel, Europe, leaders, organizations, space spectaculars."

3333. _____. *The Beginning of the End: The Prophetic and Historic Developments Leading to the End of the Age.* 1992. Troy, MI: Jack Van Impe Ministries. 3 videos.

Jack and Rexsella Van Impe. 1: Russia, World War III and Armageddon; 2: America in Prophecy: The Decline and Fall of the American Empire; 3: The Great Escape.

3334. _____. *The E.C. Antichrist: The New World Order and the Countdown to Armageddon.* 1992. Troy, MI: Jack Van Impe Ministries. video.

3335. _____. *Daniel Final End Time Mysteries Unsealed.* 1993 Troy, MI: Jack Van Impe Ministries. 4 videos.

Van Impe "believes the Holy Spirit guided him to a clear and comprehensive understanding of every verse in Daniel's 12-Chapter masterpiece. These utterances reveal everything Christians and Jews need to know to understand their future. Dr. Van Impe has poured more than 300 hours of research into this project, studying every book possible on the subject." Presented by him and Rexella in 7 hours.

3336. _____. *Everything You Always Wanted to Know About Prophecy: But Didn't Know Who to Ask!* 1993. Troy, MI: Jack Van Impe Ministries. 138 p. orig 1980; 61 p., illus. fold-out chart.

3337. _____. *Last Days: Hype or Hope?* 1997. Video. Troy, MI: Jack Van Impe Ministries.

3338. _____. *God's Promises of Prophecy.* 1998. Nashville: J. Countryman. vi, 137 p. illus.

Also wrote *2001: On the Edge of Eternity* (1996, Dallas: Word).

3339. _____, with Roger F. Campbell. *Israel's Final Holocaust.* c1979. Nashville: Thomas Nelson. 172 p. index.

"All prophetic truth revolves around the Jews."

3340. Van Kampen, Robert. *The Sign.* 1993 [c1992]. Wheaton, IL: Crossway Books. 2nd expanded ed 544 p. illus. map, bibl. refs., indexes, foldout chart.

"Bible Prophecy Concerning the End Times." Pre-wrath Rapture: believers undergo Antichrist's and Satan's wrath during better part of Tribulation but are raptured just prior to God's wrath at end of Tribulation. Magog = Goths, Germans; Antichrist will be Hitler healed of his deadly wound.

3341. _____. *The Fourth Reich.* Grand Rapids, MI: Fleming H. Revell. 445 p.

Novel. Two Jews return to Russia after working for Israeli intelligence. One supports Bulgakov, a Russian leader who gains world power and signs 7-year treaty with Israel; the other opposes him. 3½ years later he is revealed as Antichrist.

3342. _____. *The Rapture Question Answered: Plain and Simple.* Grand Rapids, MI: F.H. Revell. 211 p. illus. bibl. refs., indexes.

3343. Varner, Kelley. *The Time of the Messiah: A Prophetic Picture of the End-Time Church.* 1996. Shippensburg, PA; Destiny. 151 p. bibl. refs.

3344. Vasek, Everett. *Why Jesus Might Return Around 1998 or 1999.* <http://www.angelfire.com/tx/eternalhome101/>

3345. Veliankode, Sidheeque M.A. *Doomsday: Portents and Prophecies.* 1998. Riyadh, Saudi Arabia: Dar Ibn Khuzaima. 498 p.

3346. Venden, Morris L. *The Return of Elijah.* 1982. Mountain View, CA: Pacific Press. 110 p.

Seventh-day Adventist. Worship of the Beast is belief in human autonomy.

3347. _____. *Here I Come, Ready or Not.* 1987. Boise, ID: Pacific Press. 90 p. illus.

The Second Coming. Also 1977 cassette *Introduction to Last Day Events* and a forthcoming book *Nothing to Fear: Devotions for the End Time.*

3348. Verbeek, Aad, Jan Westein, and Piet Westein. *Time for His Coming.* 1995. Noordgouwe, The Netherlands: Westein. 223 p. illus.

150 year End Time period is 1844–1994. Second Coming 1994.

3349. Vigeveno, H.S. *In the Eye of the Apocalypse: Understanding the Revelation, God's Message of Hope for the End Times.* 1990. Ventura, CA: Regal Books. 215 p. bibl. refs.

3350. Vissarion. *A Little Grain of the Word of Vissarion Presenting the Last Testament of the Heavenly Father Who Sent Him.* 1995. Rev. ed. Moscow: s.n. 30 p.

3351. _____. *Last Testament.* <http://vissarion.com/jesus/gene/e2050.html>

Vissarion: former Russian policeman, Sergei Torop. During 1991 Communist putsch discovered the Truth: that he was the Second Coming of Christ and was to deliver the *Last Testament* and lead the Church of the Final Testament. "And here the time of Doomsday Judgment has come, when the harvesting begins, and the seeds will be separated from the weeds at last" (description by Irina Kuzmina). In 1994 Vissarion proclaimed the Holy Land for future humanity (his followers) in Krasnoyarsk region of central Siberia. *Last Testament* consists largely of "Narration" by disciple "Vadim."

3352. Voice of Light Mission. *Behold I am Coming Quickly and My Reward Is With Me.* N.d. Flushing, NY. Tract.

Pre-trib.

3353. Wadsworth, Robert, and Daniel Stockemer. *A Voice Crying in the Heavens.* 1997 [1996]. Oregon City, OR.

Biblical astronomy. Comets Hyakutake and Hale-Bopp portrayed the coming invasion of Israel, Antichrist, the Tribulation, and the soon return of Christ. Four eclipses that occur on Holy days also verify the coming invasion of Israel, pestilences and plagues. September 12, 1997, is Christ's 2,000th birthday.

3354. Wagner, Donald E. *Anxious for Armageddon: A Call for Partnership for Middle Eastern and Western Christians.* 1995. Scottdale, PA: Herald Press. 253 p. maps. bibl. refs, index.

3355. Walker, Celeste Perrino, and Eric D. Stoffle. 1998. *Eleventh Hour.* Nampa, ID: Pacific Press. 303 p.

Novel. "An End-Time Story. Sinister forces plot to take over the U.S. government in the name of God." Forthcoming: *Midnight Hour* (Nampa, ID: Pacific Press): "As America faces its final crisis, the choices become intensely personal."

3356. Walker, Frank. *The Beast His Image and the Two Horned Beast.*

3357. Walker, Ken, and Val Walker. *Escape from Armageddon.* 1997. Glen Waverly, Australia: Good News Australia. 218 p.

Novel. Three university students and their families deal with angels and demons during the Rapture, Antichrist's New World Order, Israel's war with Russia, the escape of the righteous Jews to Petra and Christ's Second Coming in Jerusalem.

3358. Walker, Tom. *An Invasion from Another World.* <http://www.icu2.net /preachers/invasion-from-another.htm>.

UFOs as Satan's ploy to get people to reject salvation. Pre-trib. 6,000 years of world's lifespan just about up.

3359. Walker, William H. SEE ALSO 1910–1970. *Progressive Revelation.* 1971. Cherokee, NC: Span Publications. 175 p.

Also wrote *God's Trademark: The Number Seven* (1980).

3360. Wallin, Robert E. *Last Days Study.* 1982. Phoenix, AZ: Brace. 153 p.

3361. Walsh, Daniel R. *Prophecy and the Comet: Biblical Impact of Shoemaker-Levy 9.* 1996. Orange Park, FL: Celtica. 96 p. illus., bibl. refs.

The 1994 comet as a Bible omen prophesied in Revelation (deliberate pattern of Black Eyes).

3362. Walthers, Harry. *Prophecy of the Church of Philadelphia and Two Raptures.* 1998. Condensed version of *The Answer (Two Raptures)*; 1986. Summarized at <http://www.escape666 .com/>

First Internet Church of Philadelphia. All prophecy "seems to converge round 2000 A.D.— the Millennium"; before that, "the world will soon be faced with an Apocalypse; some sort of cataclysmic destruction from both deep space and from the hands of man!" Comet will pass very close to Earth, Aug 11-14, 1999. Two Raptures: first for those "accounted worthy": "one day soon, the 'worthy' Church of Philadelphia will be 'caught-away' into Heaven (in the First of Two Raptures) which triggers the start of the Apocalypse!" Second Rapture is the Resurrection: two-fold, occurs midway through the Great Tribulation after Antichrist declares himself God in the Temple. Website includes Doomsday chat section.

3363. Walton, Lewis R. *Advent! World Events at the End of Time.* 1986. Washington D.C.: Review and Herald. 95 p. bibl.

Revival in 1850s almost led to Second Coming: "Jesus was trying to return." Similarly in 1890s. Economic crisis. All conditions necessary for Return can be accomplished in under 3 years. Adventists need to prepare. Urges we make things ready to coax Second Coming. Throne of God in Orion. Quotes E.G. White; she predicted nuclear bombs in 1909.

3364. Walvoord, John F. SEE ALSO 1910–1970. *Daniel, the Key to Prophetic Revelation.* 1971. Chicago: Moody. 320 p. bibl. index.

3365. _____. *Armageddon, Oil and the Middle East Crisis: What the Bible Says About the Future of the Middle East and the End of Western Civilization.* Grand Rapids, MI: Zondervan (HarperCollins). 1990 [1974]. 234 p. Rev. ed., also special Billy Graham Evangelistic Assoc. ed.

Son John E. Walvoord collaborated. Over 1½ million copies. "Many signs point to imminent, worldwide catastrophes." Technological advances, moral decline. Rapture is next event, probably very soon. 10-Nation revival of Roman Empire: Mediterranean confederacy, including North Africa and West Asia, with control of Arab oil. Led by Antichrist = Beast. U.S. and Russia fade as powers. World church movement is sign of last days; occultism = end-time false prophets; demon activity. 7-year covenant with Israel. Dictator desecrates Temple mid-Tribulation; destroys Harlot church. Russia invades (probably on horseback) mid-Tribulation, but crushed. Mediterranean Confederacy then tries to destroy Israel. World wide persecution will surpass Hitler's. Tribulation disasters may be nuclear as well as supernatural. Tremendous catastrophic divine judgments poured out second half of Tribulation. Huge physical upheavals level cities, mountains. Most of world killed. Then Armageddon: world revolt against world dictator; Satan connives to have all armies assemble around Armageddon in order to fight Christ: final suicidal world war centered in Mideast, attacked by armies of South (Africa), North (Russia), East (China and others). Antichrist repels African attack, then Russia attacks again.

Then China with 200 million. Interrupted by Second Coming; all armies destroyed. All unbelievers killed at Second Coming, but entire world would have been killed if not for intervention of Second Coming. Survivors live in Millennium, have kids who may or may not be saved.

3366. _____. *The Prophecy Knowledge Handbook.* 1990. Wheaton, IL: Victor Books. 809 p. indexes.

3367. _____. *Major Bible Prophecies: 37 Crucial Prophecies that Affect You Today.* c1991. Grand Rapids, MI: Zondervan. 450 p. indexes.

[Dwight Wilson says publication was delayed due to Russia coup, and says Walvoord probably changed falsified prophecies.]

3368. _____. *The Final Drama: Fourteen Keys to Understanding the Prophetic Scriptures.* 1998 [1993]. Nashville: Thomas Nelson. 185 p. indexes. orig. title *Prophecy.*

3369. _____. *End Times: Understanding Today's World Events in Biblical Prophecy.* 1998. Nashville: Word. xi, 243 p.

3370. _____. *Every Prophecy of the Bible.* 1999. Colorado Springs, CO: Chariot Victor: 685 p. illus., index.

3371. Ward, C.M. *World Without Children!* 1970. Springfield, MO: Assemblies of God. 48 p.

3372. _____. *Writing on the Wall: New Prophetic Sermons and Up-To-Data.* 1993. Columbus, OH: Quill. 179 p.

3373. Warden, Michael D., and Rick Chromey. *Revelation: Unlocking Its Secrets.* 1993. Loveland, CO: Group. 45 p. illus.

4-week adult course on "understanding the signs of the end times"

3374. Warner, Tim. *The Last Trumpet: Bible Prophecy & the Rapture.* 1998. <http://www.geocities.com/~lasttrumpet>

Post-trib. Christians must go through the Tribulation.

3375. Warren, Lee E. *Revelation & End Time Prophecies.* <http://plim.org/revelation.html>

Warren: headed Chicago branch of Inst. Divine Metaphysical Research, then founded offshoot PLIM (The Power La-

tent in Man). Discusses 6,000 Year theory with Creation 4000 B.C. but denies literal End or Second Coming in A.D. 2000. Armageddon and Second Coming are symbolic, not physical; non-literal Millennium (spiritually fulfilled since Christ). Vatican = Whore of Babylon.

3376. Warshofsky, Fred. *Doomsday: The Science of Catastrophe.* 1977. New York: Pocket Books. x, 260 p. bibl., index. Also Reader's Digest Press: NY

"In Search of Ancient Mysteries" TV writer.

3377. *Watch and Be Ready: Preparing for the Second Coming of the Lord.* 1994. Salt Lake City: Deseret Book Co. iii, 236 p. index.

Mormon. Contributors: Kent Jackson, M. Catherine Thomas, Joseph Fielding McConkie, R.J. Matthews, R.N. Holzapfel, Larry Dahl, R. L. Millet, Gerald Lund, Stephen B. Robinson. Joseph Smith taught Last Days began 1820 (First Vision). This dispensation (the last) includes greatest extremes (including greatest evil) of any age. Book of Mormon Christ's "instrument of preparation for the Second Coming." "Israel" = all descendants of Lost Tribes; thus most Gentiles have Israelite blood. Most Mormons literal descendants of Ephraim (and Manasseh). New Jerusalem in Independence, MO. Also in Missouri: Adam-ondi-Ahman, where Adam once met, and will meet in future. Mormons will undergo Judgments (Tribulation), but some will be divinely protected. 7,000 year earthly existence (including Millennium). Now nearing end of 6,000 years; End thus ca. 2000 A.D. 7 Seals symbolize the seven thousand years. Second Coming, then Millennium. Millennium: everything corruptible burns away (including people), earth returns to Eden conditions. Both mortals and immortals exist during Millennium. But mortals all "translated." Not all convert to Mormonism, though all will by end of Millennium. Final battle end of Millennium: Gog Magog; only mortals join Satan.

3378. Watchtower Bible and Tract Society. SEE ALSO 1910–1970. *God's Kingdom of a Thousand Years Has Ap-*

proached. c1973. Brooklyn: Watchtower Bible and Tract Society. 412 p.

"An examination of much evidence in the Holy Bible and Twentieth-Century World History on whether God's Millennial Kingdom will begin its blessing within our own generation."

3379. _____. *Revelation: Its Grand Climax At Hand!* 1988. Brooklyn: Watchtower Bible and Tract Soc. Intl. Bible Students Assoc. 319 p. illus. bibl. refs.

Published in 33 languages, 12,250,000 copies. Watchtower also published *Will the World Survive?* (1992).

3380. Watkins, Terry. *Warning! 666 Is Coming.* 1995. <http://www.av1611.org/666.html> Dial-the-Truth Ministries.

3381. Watts, Clay. *Lessons Learned from End Times Bible Prophecy.* 1996. <http://members.aol.com/ClayWatts/enddecep.htm>

3382. Waugh, Raymond A. *Why All Church-Age Endtime Prophets are False: A Scriptural Thesis that Endures.* 1994. Kearney, NE: Morris. 136 p.

3383. Weagle, Charles R. *Judgment Warning 2002 A.D.* <http://warning2002ad.com>

3384. Webber, David. *The Image of the Ages: Bible Prophecy: Iraq/Babylon, Armageddon.* 1991. Lafayette, IN: Huntington House. 158 p.

Largely long quotes from popular science, news, and religious magazines, searching news for prophetic confirmations. Saddam Hussein's rebuilding of Babylon: "foul source of Babylonish mysteries of the occult." Napoleon and Hitler tried to refashion Roman Empire. Common Market basis of new Empire. Single European Act = Beast from the Sea. Antichrist "will change times and laws that will result in worldwide catastrophe and upset the balance of nature in this solar system." War in heavens during Tribulation: SDI and other Star Wars weapons, electromagnetic weapons. Terrible judgments both man-made and divine. Antichrist will have large robot army. Computers, robots, mind-control, artificial intelligence, bioengineering: "end-time scenario for the Antichrist system" — a

metallic man-image of Nebuchadnezzar (Daniel's image): robot with 5th generation computer, a bionic man, will "utterly dominate" all people. AIDS = judgment from God.

3385. _____, and Noah Hutchings. *Prophecy in Stone.* 1974. Fort Worth, TX: Harvest Press. 82 p.

Tribulation begins 1981–85, ends 1988–92. Later wrote rev. ed. titled *New Light on the Great Pyramid*, with Tribulation 1988 to 1996.

3386. _____. *Signs of the Second Coming.* 1977. Oklahoma City: Southwest Radio Church. 88 p. illus

3387. _____. *Is This the Last Century?* 1979. Nashville: Thomas Nelson.

Rapture, Antichrist, 7-year Tribulation, Armageddon, and Second Coming (soon). "We are quickly approaching the six thousandth year after Adam was created." 6th day likely to end at close of century. Hosea 6: Israel raised and revived after "two days" (= 2,000 years). 1917 (Balfour Declaration) + 30 (age of maturity): lots of Jews in Palestine. 1917 + 50 (age of restoration) — Jerusalem regained. 1917 + 70 (end of generation) — 1987. 1948 + 40 years of testing = 1988. Tribulation probably 1981–1988. Russian invasion of Israel mid-tribulation. Allied with East Germany, Iran, Ethiopia, Libya, Turkey. Babylon being rebuilt now. Jupiter Effect (calamitous 1982 planetary alignment). Great Synagogue (Tribulation Temple) scheduled for 1981 completion. Russia so militarily superior that Brezhnev or successor may attack Israel any day now.

3388. _____. *Olivet to Armageddon: An Exposition on the 24th and 25th Chapters of Matthew.* 1979. Oklahoma City: Southwest Radio Church. 63, vii p.

3389. _____. *The Computers Are Coming.* 1980 [1978]. Oklahoma City: Southwest Radio Church. 80 p. illus.

3390. _____. *New Light on the Great Pyramid.* 1985. Oklahoma City: Southwest Radio Church. 117 p.

3391. _____. *Computers and the Beast of Revelation.* 1986. Shreveport, LA: Huntington House.

3392. _____. *666: The Mark Is*

Ready! 1997. [Columbia, SC]: Olive Press. 93 p. illus.

3393. Weber, Timothy P. and Bruce L. Shelley? *The Future Explored.* 1978 Wheaton, IL: Victor Books. 132 p.

3394. Wehr, Jeffrey Drew. *The New World Order in Bible Prophecy.* 1992. Sparta, WI: Beholding Christ Ministries. 90 p.

3395. Weldon, John, with Zola Levitt. *UFOs: What On Earth Is Happening.* c1975. Irvine, CA: Harvest House. xii, 167 p. bibl. refs. Also Bantam ed. 1976.

UFOs demonic manifestations of Last Days.

3396. Wells, Gary B. *Armageddon.* 1996. <http://www.gbwattorney.com/ARMAGEDD.htm>

Mormon. Cites LDS sources, especially Bruce McConkie's *Millenial Messiah.* (1982, Salt Lake City: Deseret).

3397. Wheeler, John L. 1996. *Earth's Two-Minute Warning: Today's Bible-Predicted Signs of the End Times.* North Canton, OH: Leader Co. xiv, 216 p. bibl. refs.

3398. Wheeler, Penny Estes. *The Appearing: An Inspiring Story of the End-Time.* 1996 [1979]. Hagerstown, MD: Review and Herald. 224 p.

Novel. Seventh-day Adventist. Awaiting the Second Coming, four believers undergo persecution and witness end-time destruction.

3399. Wheeling, Charles. *Armageddon Now.* 1992. Jemison, AL: Focus on Jesus: Countdown Ministries. 2 videos.

Seventh-day Adventist. Originally saw Iran-Iraq War (1980s) as start of Armageddon; then, the Persian Gulf War.

3400. _____. *The King of the North, the Time of the End Another Look at Daniel 7.* 1994. 2 videos. 1989. *The Time Is Now.* 2 videos. Jemison, AL: Countdown Ministries.

3401. _____. 1995. *The Time Has Come.* 2 videos. Jemison, AL: IBE.

3402. Whipple, Gary F. *Shock and Surprise Beyond the Rapture: The Mysteries of the Ages Revealed.* 1992. Hayesville, NC: Schoettle. 270 p. illus. bibl. refs.

3403. Whisenant, Edgar C. *88 Reasons Why the Rapture Will Be in 1988.* 1988.

Nashville: World Bible Society. Two-in-one ed. combined with *On Borrowed Time: The Bible Dates of the 70th Week of Daniel, Armageddon, the Millennium.* 69 and 55 p.

Two million copies. "GOD IS A DATE-SETTER." Rapture will occur between Sept. 11 and 13, 1988. WWIII will be Oct. 3 and will last one hour. (Biblical "three-score and ten" refers to lifetime of Communism). Rosh Hashanah (Feast of Trumpets) is symbol — type — of the Rapture.

3404. _____. *And Now the Earth's Destruction by Fire, Nuclear Bomb Fire in World War III, World War IV and World War V at Armageddon.* 1994. Little Rock, AR: Author. (various pagings).

"America! America! God shed his wrath on thee! United States prepare to meet thy God as shown in Bible prophecy."

3405. _____. *Resurrected, 88 Reasons Revisited in 1995.* 1995. Little Rock, AR: Author. (various pagings) illus. Incorporates materials copyrighted 1993 and 1994.

3406. _____. *75% of the Bible is Future as of 21 November 1995: These 5600 Original Pages in 21 Books as of About 300 Pages Each Prove It....* 1995. Little Rock, AR: author. (various pagings) map.

"But in this 20th book about 520 mysteries and questions are herein answered according to Daniel 12:4. At the time of the end the knowledge (of God) shall be increased."

3407. _____, and Greg Brewer. *The Final Shout: Rapture Report 1989....* 1989. Nashville: World Bible Society. 86 p. charts.

Realized he was off on 1988 prediction by one year because there was never actually a Year 0.

3408. Whitcomb, John Clement. *The Five Worlds of History, Science and Prophecy.* 1981. Winona Lake, IN: BMH Books. Large chart. BMH/Whitcomb — Brethren (fired from Grace Theological Seminary 1990)

3409. White, Frank H. *The Saints' Rest and Rapture: When and For Whom?*

1983 6th ed. Chelmsford, England: Sovereign Grace Advent Testimony. 32 p. Post-trib.

3410. White, John [Warren]. *Pole Shift.* 1980. Virgina Beach, VA: A.R.E. Press. xxvi, 413 p. drawings, photos index. Also 1982 Berkley ed.

Edgar Cayce Foundation. White: dir. educ. for astronaut Edgar Mitchell's Inst. Noetic Sciences. Cataclysmic inversion of Earth's axis is causing catastrophic slippage of continents around molten core. Evidence from ancient history, psychic prophecies, and science. Discusses Stelle community, Velikovsky, Jeffrey Goodman's 1978 *We are the Earthquake Generation*, Hugh Auchincloss Brown's 1967 *Cataclysms*, Adam D. Barb's 1955 *The Coming Disaster Worse than the H-Bomb*, Thomas Chan's 1965 *Adam and Eve Story*, Charles Hapgood's 1958 *Earth's Shifting Crust*, Emil Sepic's 1960 *The Imminent Shift of the Earth's Axis*.

3411. White, John Wesley. *Re-Entry: Striking Parallels Between Today's News Events and Christ's Second Coming.* c1970. Grand Rapids, MI: Zondervan. 164 p., indexes.

Foreword by Billy Graham. White: Oxford Ph.D.; chancellor of Richmond Coll., Toronto; now evangelist with Billy Graham's organization. Astronaut metaphors: re-entry of Christ at Second Coming. News items indicate we are near End. Militant apostasy, nuclear armaments, space program, rampant immorality, Return of Israel, menacing aggression of Russia. Cites accuracy of Jeane Dixon predictions, including birth of coming world leader (Antichrist). Magog = Russia. The Beast = Antichrist — rules new Roman empire. Rapture, then Armageddon seven or so years later: Southern bloc led by Egypt, North led by Russia, and East led by China with 200 million men converge near Jerusalem to confront Antichrist and his Western bloc.

3412. _____. *WWIII: Signs of the Impending Battle of Armageddon.* c1977. Grand Rapids, MI: Zondervan. 203 p.

Foreword by Billy Graham. Apocalyptic signs in the news, from popular magazines, newspapers, TV. Conflict and impending war all over world. Likelihood of worldwide nuclear war. Instantaneous global coverage made possible by TV = sign of imminent End. UFO cults as false messiah. Chemical and bacteriological warfare, increasing natural disasters, pollution. Satan increasingly active and visible. Antichrist on his way; the film *The Omen* was an accurate portrayal. 1908 Siberian explosion was a "Jugmon bomb" from space: God's judgment, precursor of widespread devastation God will hurl at Russia after it invades Israel.

3413. _____. *The Coming World Dictator.* 1981. Minneapolis: Bethany. 119 p. illus.

Soviet satellite-borne lasers. Shah's overthrow prelude to Russo-Muslim alliance. Rumored Temple rebulding in Jerusalem. New Temple is an "absolute necessity for the completion of the prophetic picture."

3414. _____. *Arming for Armageddon.* c1983. Milford, MO: Mott Media. [vii], 218 p.

Foreword by Billy Graham. Creationist. The Holocaust enabled Jews to return to Israel to fulfill destiny. Pre-trib pre-mill. Rapture, then Antichrist becomes head of European confederacy and establishes capital in Israel. Massive Soviet attack on Israel defeated (probably with neutron bombs). U.S. and Russia in nuclear conflict.

3415. _____. *Thinking the Unthinkable.* 1992. Lake Mary, FL: Creation House. 210 p.

Cover: "Are All the Pieces in Place?" Foreword by Billy Graham. Culling current events for signs of prophetic fulfillment. Mankind headed toward annihilation, but Christ will return to evacuate believers. Soviet breakup means greater danger of nuclear war. Terminal war to fulfill Armageddon prophecy. Rapture of half billion believers leaves U.S. greatly weakened. Russia and EuroAsia and Islamic allies then attack Israel, but 85% destroyed. Antichrist (Beast) emerges as Western European leader, signs 7 year pact with Israel. Relative peace for first half, then war killing ⅔ of mankind, then Armageddon involving all armies of world. "History cannot escape Armageddon." Desert Storm, with poison gas, burning oil wells, etc., was "precursor" to prophesied fall of Babylon. Neutron bomb will cause prophesied "flesh melting away." "Signs on moon" maybe mirrors installed by humans. Antichrist and Two Witnesses publicized via TV; preach to all world. 144,000 Jewish evangelists during Tribulation. Russia = Northern power, Gog. Gomer = Germany. Seven years to bury Russian dead. Russia is now making weapons of material harder than steel but flammable (the prophesied burning of weapons for fuel for seven years). Invasion probably beginning of Tribulation (same 7 years). Antichrist will seem like "nice guy." Great Synagogue may serve as Tribulation Temple (but Millennial Temple will be actual rebuilt Temple). 200-million army probably non-Arabic Moslems; possibly Chinese. End of Millennium: Satan, Gog and Magog again attack.

3416. *Why We Believe We Are Living in the Last Days.* Dearborn, MI: Omega-Letter / Christian World Report. 36 p.

Mark of Beast technology is already here; psychic powers rampant; populace is yearning for a world leader; false Messiahs abound; ozone hole was prophesied in Revelation; Soviets ("Gog") preparing to invade Israel.

3417. Wieland, Robert J. *Daniel and Our Times.* 1980. Kenilworth, South Africa: Africa Herald Pub. House. 216 p. illus.

3418. Wiers, Walter. *Last Battle for Earth.* 1978. Los Angeles: Walter Wiers. 429 p.

End Times according to *Oasphe,* Newbrough's 1881 "Cosmic Bible." UFOs, psychic powers, telepathy.

3419. Wiggins, Elizabeth. *The Final Countdown.* Pamphlet series. Hollaway's *Final Countdown* (Internet) inspired by it.

3420. Wiles, Herb. *It's About Time: The Solution of Time Enigmas from Adam to Armageddon.* 1993. Riverside, CA: IAT Pub. xxii, 666 p; 2: xiv, 468 p. (2 vols.: *History* and *Prophecy*). illus. bibl. refs.

Edited by Joan E. Hiatt. Wiles: ex–pool hustler. Acknowledges irreverent televangelist Gene Scott as his "spiritual father"; praises his wisdom and teachings. Also cites Z. Sitchin, Velikovsky, R. Capt (Pyramidology). ETs = Enoch's Watchers. Re-creation (Gap) Theory. Chapter on Canopy Theory. "4-2-1 Theory" (6,000 years). Adam created 4002 B.C.; Christ born 2 B.C.; Millennium starts A.D. 1999. Biblical genealogies (with ten-year correction) show 4,000 years Adam to Christ. British-Israelism: Britain is Ephriam; U.S. is Manasseh. Original Israelites were Celtic: "Together we are known in the Bible as 'Israel'" Vol. 2: Daniel's image (statue): legs are Roman Empire, but ankles are Islam. (Follows Gene Scott in interpretation of Daniel) Antichrist's kingdom from iron-clay Muslim confederation: the 10 Kings. Antichrist comes from Seleucid region, will conquer Israel, force Islamic worship in Temple; 7 year Tribulation. Opposed by Western alliance led by False Prophet. Antichrist secretly allies with Russia, then destroys Israel, attacks Egypt and destroys Babylon. Then Russia, the West, and Antichrist converge at Armageddon. "Unwalled villages" = U.S. Gomer = Germany. Gog-Magog = Russia. 1½ billion die in Tribulation; literal, demonic woes; most of mankind killed in nuclear war, God's Wrath unleashed, with celestial upheavals. 7 churches = church ages: Ephesus to A.D. 100, Smyrna to 310, Pergamos to 529, Thyatira (Catholic, i.e. pagan; Mystery Babylon) to 1529, Sardis to 1789, Philadelphia (the true church) to 1920. Apostasy since then. Two Witnesses: Moses and Elijah. 666 = Universal Product Code. Russian and Far East armies led by Satan himself. Rapture of Philadelphia church first, then False Prophet and Antichrist revealed, then Tribulation (to start within a few years). Detailed chronology of events, explanation of identities.

3421. Wiles, Richard D. *Judgment Day 2000: How the Coming Worldwide Computer Crash Will Radically Change Your Life.* 1998. Shippensburg, PA: Treasure House. 323, [8], p. bibl. refs.

Wiles: formerly with Christian Broadcasting Network. Y2k computer glitch will result in massive worldwide depression. Utilities will shut down, and drinking water and food will be scarce. Muslim and Russian "terrorities" with nuclear bombs will launch coordinated attach on America's 100 biggest cities.

3422. Wilkerson, David R. *The Coming Persecution.* 1973. Dallas: David Wilkerson Publications. Audiocassette.

Pentecostal. Wilkerson "details a prophetic vision he received from God concerning five tragic calamities."

3423. _____. *The Vision.* 1974. New York: Pyramid Books.

Vision received in 1973. Economic collapse, drastic weather changes, many disasters in next few years. Moral landslide with no restraints; super world church, Antichrist as superstar. Armageddon: literal bridle-deep blood 200 miles long. The Tribulation will be "thousands of times" worse than WWII and Stalinist terrors. "Israel is invincible, because it is flowing in the tide of divine prophecy." Man's landing on moon violated God's dignity.

3424. _____. *David Wilkerson Presents The End Times New Testament.* 1975. Chappaqua, NY: Chosen Books. 300 p.

New Testament paraphrased.

3425. _____. *Racing Toward Judgment.* 1982 [1976]. New York: Jove. 160 p. Orig. pub. Lindale, TX: David Wilkerson Youth Crusades; Tappan, NJ: Revell.

3426. _____. *Set the Trumpet to Thy Mouth.* 1985. Springdale, PA: Whitaker House. 240 p. Also pub. Lindale, TX: World Challenge.

Over million copies sold. "America is going to be destroyed by fire!" very soon because of sin and depravity: violence, abortion, lust, homosexuality, polluted and idolatrous TV ("Satan has taken full possession of secular television"), demon-possessed rock music (Wilkerson also wrote *Rock and Roll, the Devil's Heartbeat*). Wilkerson was called by God to be a Last-Days watchman in "Babylon" (America). When Russia invades the Holy Land, God blasts Russia "with supernatural destruc-

tion beyond all description." True believers transported into celestial bodies during the holocaust.

3427. _____. *America's Last Call.* 1998. Lindale, TX: Wilkerson Trust Publications. 141p.

Economic forecasting.

3428. *Will Humanity End This Way?* 1982. Yucaipa, CA: Universal Pub. Assn. 36 p.

3429. Williams, Dave. *End Times Bible Prophecy: My Personal Sermon Notes.* 1991. Lansing, MI: Mount Hope. 37 p. bibl.

Author: Mt. Hope Church pastor, televangelist, Lansing, MI. Also wrote *The Grand Finale: A Study on the Coming End-Time Revival.* In outline form. End of Age = Rapture. Second Coming is at end of Tribulation. False religion occultism increases during Last Days. Tribulation saints taken up at Armageddon. Antichrist revealed after Rapture. Unsuccessful Russian invasion of Israel. Gog = Russia. Antichrist = Beast: heads 10-nation federation of Western Europe (revived Roman Empire), then becomes world leader, forces use of the Mark 666. U.S. loses influence, suffers nuclear destruction. "Christian liquidation camps" in Tribulation; most of world population killed. "Diplomatic demons": Three Spirits convince nations to help Antichrist annihilate Israel.

3430. Williams, Julian E. *Henry Kissinger — Mystery Man of Power.* 1972. Tulsa, OK: Christian Crusade Pub. 32 p. illus.

3431. Williams, Sid. *Gog & Magog — The Last Prophecy: Operation of the Holy Spirit.* 1993. Granite City, IL: Save the Bible Ministry. 104 p.

3432. Williams, Steven D. 1998. *The Revelation Mysteries: A Complete Study on End-Time Prophecy.* West Hempstead, NY: Hosanna Pub. House. X, 365 p, illus., maps; bibl. refs., index.

Favors post-trib view. Revelation describes nuclear and chemical warfare. 4.5 billion killed. U.S. is 7th Head of Beast, "continental homeland of Antichrist." 1929 was the "fatal wound" which healed. Antichrist becomes world emperor, sets up headquarters in Jerusalem; defiles Temple with Abomination of Desolation middle of 70th Week. King of South = South America, allied with Antichrist. Antichrist attacked by ships stationed in Chittim (= Cyprus) from Western Alliance. Then armies from North (Russia, with Africa) attack, followed by 200-million man army from East. End-time clues in dollar bill design: satanic devices and symbols.

3433. Willis, C. Paul. *Christ of the Apocalypse.* 1993. Shippensburg, PA: Destiny Images Publishers. viii, 196 p.

3434. Willis, Charles DuBois. *End of Days, 1971–2001: An Eschatological Study.* 1972. New York: Exposition Press. 121 p. illus. bibl.

Second Coming "climactic end of human history." United world empire of Antichrist linked by computers. "UFOs represent the space force of the Lord Jesus Christ preparing for the Second Coming." War by late 1970s, WWIII in early '80s (China and African nations vs. Russia and West), worldwide famine mid-'80s. Apostate End-Time Church ("Whore of Babylon") by 1990s. Armageddon: Antichrist's armies converge on Israel, then (ca. 1992) the Rapture: believers whisked away by flying saucers, followed by Second Coming. Perhaps second Rapture at end of Tribulation, of Trib converts. Antichrist born in 1962 (cites Jeane Dixon), perhaps active in pan-Arab confederation. Peace symbol is sign of Antichrist.

3435. Willis, Wesley R., and Elaine Willis. *Unwrapping the Mysteries of Things to Come: a Study of Revelation.* 1996. Colorado Springs, CA: Accent. 111 p.

3436. Willmington, H.L. *The King is Coming: An Outline Study of the Last Days.* 1991 [1973]. rev. expanded ed. Wheaton, IL: Tyndale House. 345 p. Foreword by Jerry Falwell.

Author: Bible chairman of Lynchburg Baptist College (now Liberty Univ.), Dean of Falwell's Thomas Road Bible Inst. Pre-trib pre-mill. Much of book matches chronological account of scenario with citations of supporting biblical verses useful

for proof texts. Intended as concise text on Last Days. Day of Lord = Tribulation = End of This world = Time of End = Day of God's Wrath or Judgment = 70th Week. Also, Day of Christ = Millennium. Antichrist controls Western powers, seven year treaty with Israel, gains control over Mid-East after Russian invasion, tries to destroy Israel, sets himself up as God, becomes world ruler, crushed by Christ at Armageddon. Gomer = Eastern Europe; Togarmah = Cossacks and South Russia. Mystery Babylon = false apostate church; may arise from World Council of Churches. Additionally, a second, political, Babylon will be rebuilt. Common Market = originally Ten Nations, revived Roman Empire. White Horse rider of four = Antichrist. Magog = USSR. Two Witnesses — their corpses broadcast on TV. Egypt and Russia attack; Russia then continues to Egypt, returns to Israel, defeated there by God. Bows and arrows are used, maybe due to disarmament treaty. Antichrist assassinated, revives, worshipped as God. The faithful Israelites flee, probably to Petra. At the end of the Tribulation, Antichrist leads armies at Armageddon. Jerusalem destroyed, then Second Coming. Enthusiastically describes carnage of battle: literal 200 mile horse-bridle high lake of blood. Says post-mill view is now almost extinct. Final revolt at end of Millennium led by Satan proves man is "desperately wicked." Gap Theory creationism: world was re-created following pre-Adamic ages. It will similarly be re-created after the Millennium.

3437. _____. *Signs of the Times.* c1981. Wheaton, IL: Tyndale. 167 p.

3438. Wilmore, Gayraud S. *Last Things First.* 1982. Philadelphia: Westminster Press. 118 p. bibl.

3439. Wilson, B[ruce] McIntosh. *Death of the Church and the Long March of the Saints.* 1987 —. Warialda, Australia: Longmarch Christian Books. Vol. 1 about Babylon and God's People; vol. 2 about Zechariah and Ezekiel.

3440. Wilson, Clifford. *UFOs and Their Mission Impossible.* 1975 [1974]. New York: New American Library. x, 225 p.

bibl. Orig. pub. Word of Truth. 1988 expanded ed. titled *The Alien Agenda*.

3441. _____. *Gods in Chariots and Other Fantasies*. 1975. San Diego: Creation-Life Pub. 144 p. bibl.

3442. _____. *Close Encounters: A Better Explanation*. 1978. San Diego: Master Books. xiv, 354 p. bibl.

3443. _____, and John Weldon. *1980s: Decade of Shock*. 1978. San Diego: Master Books.

3444. Wilson, Dwight. *Armageddon Now! The Premillenarian Response to Russia and Israel since 1917*. 1991 [1977]. Tyler, TX: Inst. Christian Economics. xlii, 264 p. bibl. refs., index. Orig. 1975 UC Santa Cruz thesis

Claims he's pre-mill himself, but highly critical study of pre-mill works and doctrines, pub. and with foreword by leading post-mill (North). Useful criticisms.

3445. Wilson, H. Speed. *Rapture, Prophecy or Heresy: Will Biblical Christians be Removed from the Earth?* 1989. Canton, OH: Daring. 160 p. Scripture index.

Wilson: Col. USMC (ret.); former director Full Gospel Business Men's Fellowship. Denies Rapture — offers $10,000 reward if Rapture can be proved. Believers to be "overcomers" during Tribulation. Daniel's fiery furnace perhaps prediction of nuclear holocaust which end-time believers survive. "Restrainer" is Rome; Antichrist is Papal church. Mentions 1981 (1948 plus 40, minus 7-year Tribulation) and 1980 as predicted dates.

3446. Wilson, J.O. *The Way Out is Up!* c1982. Mountain View, CA: Pacific Press. 60 p.

"Earth Faces Doom, But a 'Remnant' To Be Rescued." "Little Flock": believers who realize, following 1844 disappointment, that the Sanctuary of Daniel 8:14 is in heaven, not on earth. Summary of Seventh-day Adventist history. Second Coming is not a secret Rapture. At Second Coming, faithful go to God's throne in Great Nebula of Orion.

3447. Wilson, James Larkin. *No More Babies: End of Human Race*. 1991. Houston: author. 102 p. illus.

3448. Wilson, Larry W. *18 End-Time Bible Prophecies*. 1992. Brushton, NY: TEACH Services. vi, 282 p. illus. "Wake Up America Seminars."

3449. _____. *Warning! Revelation Is About to Be Fulfilled*. 1994 [1988]. 6th ed. Brushton, NY: TEACH Services. 202 p. charts.

Copyright held by Wake Up America Seminars of Bellbrook, OH, whose "single mission is to herald the imminent return of our Lord Jesus Christ through whatever means possible." End Time events 1994–98. Rev. 8:5 earthquake in 1994. Then meteor/asteroid devastation. Denies Rapture; Christians must undergo Tribulation. Antichrist who becomes the world leader will be Satan himself—will awe humanity with miraculous powers. 1.3 billion killed in Tribulation. Literal interpretation of "trumpet" destructions. Sabbath is Saturday. Suggests Creation in 4105 B.C., Adam and Eve in Eden 100 years before Fall. Sin began 4002 B.C., thus 6,000 year span of existence up in 1998. (Previously Wilson had announced End for 1995.)

3450. Witcher, Charles K. *The Mystery of the Four Horsemen Revealed*. 1994. Vantage Press. 260 p. bibl. refs.

A study of biblical prophecy.

3451. Witherington, Ben, III. *Jesus, Paul & the End of the World: A Comparative Study in New Testament Eschatology*. 1992. Downers Grove, IL: InterVarsity Press. 306 p. illus.

3452. Witty, Robert G. 1969. *Signs of the Second Coming*. Nashville: Broadman Press. 127 p.

3453. Wlodyga, Ronald R. *The Restoration of the Kingdom to Israel*. 1992. Buffalo, NY: Sword & Shield. 436 p. illus.

3454. Womack, David Steven. *Developing a Concept of Life in the End Times in a Local Congregation*. 1987. D.Min. thesis: Southwest Baptist Theol. Sem.

3455. Wong, Kenneth. *The Return of Jupiter: End of the World in Light of the Bible*. 1996. Pittsburgh: Dorrance. viii, 44 p. illus., bibl. refs.

Subtitle: "End of the World in the

Light of the Bible." "A terrible earthquake is going to break the oceanic crust under the Pacific Ocean by the year 1996 A.D."

3456. Wood, Leon J. SEE ALSO 1910–1970. *The Bible & Future Events: An Introductory Survey of Last-Day Events.* 1973. Grand Rapids, MI: Zondervan. 208 p. bibl.

Any-time Rapture, then seven-year Tribulation, Second Coming, Millennium — all follow predictably. Antichrist, with False Prophet, based in Jerusalem; he invades Northern (Russian) and Southern (Arab) confederations. 200 million horsemen not an Eastern army, but are probably symbolic of Jewish revolt.

3457. Woodrow, Ralph. *Great Prophecies of the Bible.* c1971. Riverside, CA; Ralph Woodrow Evangelistic Assoc. 202 p. bibl. illus.

Post-trib. Rejects dispensationalism. Rapture occurs at Second Coming. Prophecy is "fulfilled" not "futurist." Tribulation was destruction of Jerusalem in A.D. 70. Papacy is the Antichrist. Rome was the "restraining power." Also wrote *Which Year Will Christ Return*; *The Abomination of Desolation*; *Daniel's 70th Week*.

3458. Woods, Dennis J. *Unlocking the Door: A Key to Biblical Prophecy.* 1994. Lafayette, LA: Huntington House. 224 p.

3459. *The Word of the Lord Brought to Mankind by an Angel.* c1985. Independence, MO: Church of Christ with the Elijah Message. 195, 36 p. illus.

3460. "The WordWeaver." *Endtime Events! Are You Ready for These Things?* <http://www.netpci.com/~tttbbs/grup_end.html#anchor4146969>

In WordWeaver's Endtime Discussion Group Exchange (E.D.G.E.). Post-trib. Jews were only God's people conditionally. The Ten Nations = an Islamic confederation. Islam is "doctrine of devils." Advocates Holocaust revisionism.

3461. Worley, Win. *Hosts of Hell* series. 1976–83. Lansing, IL: H.B.C.

Series includes *Battling the Hosts of Hell*; *Conquering the Hosts of Hell*; *Demolishing the Hosts of Hell*; *Annihilating the Hosts of Hell*; *Eradicating the Hosts of Hell.* Southern Baptist pastor: Highland, IN.

"Oh, that God in would in these last days raise up a mighty army to storm the enemy citadels and loose the captives in Jesus' mighty Name!" Demon exorcism. Worley names, describes, and classifies thousands of demons he has battled.

3462. _____. *End Time Mind Control.* Lansing, IL: H.B.C.

"Hosts of Hell" books and booklet series.

3463. Yacovsky, F. Jacob. *The Missing 200 Years: God's Timetable.* 1978. Fern Park, FL: Sar Sholem of Jerusalem. 106 p. illus. index.

"We are now approaching the dispensation of the 'end of the days'" about which the prophets spoke so much." Messiah coming soon. Creation date off by 190 years — really 5,924 years ago; thus 72 years till world's 6,000th (and final) year. Two-Horned Beast = Islam (Arab and Turkish branches). Four Beasts / Kingdoms = America, England, Russia, France. King of North, Gog-Magog = Russia. During Gog invasion of Israel, much of Jerusalem sinks in great earthquake which swallows all defiling Christian and Moslem graves. Then, the Messiah's Coming.

3464. *YAHWEH the Unknown God: The Mystery of HIS Secret Purpose Revealed.* 1988. McKee, NJ: Restored Israel of YAHWEH. xiii, 313 p.

Tribulation and Judgment Day.

3465. Yahya, Harun. *Mehdi ve altin cag: (Islam'in dunya hakimiyeti).* 1989. Cagaloglu [Istanbul, Turkey]: Nasajans. 296 p. illus.

Islamic.

3466. Yerbury, Ray W. *The Ultimate Event: A Bible Study in Prophecy.* 1988. McDowall, Australia: Cross. xiv, 186 p. illus. maps. index. bibl.

3467. _____. *Vital Signs of Christ's Return: the 77 Most-Asked Questions on Christ's Return!* 1995. Green Forest, AR: New Leaf. 192 p. charts, maps, tables, bibl.

1990 first ed subtitled "70 questions and answers"; published in Australia.

3468. Yerby, Robert B. *Up, Up, and Away: The Glorious Kingdom and Coming of Jesus Christ.* 1976. Wengel, PA: Reiner. 118 p.

Refutes futurist dispensationalism. "As believers we are seated *now* with Christ in heavenly places...."

3469. Yoder, J. Otis. *God, Daniel and the End!* 1975. Breezewood, PA: Heralds of Hope. 84 p.

Voice of Hope Radio Sermon.

3470. Yohn, Rick. *What Every Christian Should Know about Bible Prophecy.* 1982. Eugene, OR: Harvest House. 81 p. illus.

3471. Yonge, John. *Pre-Tribulation Planning for a Post-Tribulation Rapture.* c1997. <http://www.neptune.on.ca/~jyonge/>

Post-trib. Refutes pre-trib Rapture; advises survivalist methods to cope with Tribulation. False Prophet is probably an American (Pres. Clinton?); deceives world into accepting Antichrist. Antichrist is Russian (Zhirinovsky?) who will ally with Iraqi ruler. Antichrist invades Israel. "I for one, am eager for the tribulation to begin ... because it compares to crossing one last desert before reaching the Heavenly Oasis." But believers must endure purifying trials. Jews will suffer the most because they rejected the Messiah. Armageddon follows Second Coming.

3472. Young, Kim. *The Last Hour.* 1997. Phoenix: ACW Press. 247 p.

Young: student at Dallas Theological Seminary, Precept Upon Precept leader. Novel. Talk show host Josh Cohen investigates world plots, including sinister First Lady. Increasing anti-Jewish and anti-Christian persecution, then Antichrist arises as leader.

3473. Young, Woody, and Chuck Missler. *Countdown to Eternity; Prologue to Destiny.* 1992. San Juan Capistrano, CA: Joy Pub. 208 p. Maps, tables.

Missler: engineer in computer industry. Bible is "integrated message system." Importance of Creation and Flood accounts as setup for prophecy. "This is the time for Christian's [sic] to prepare for the end-time events." Rapture; then 7-day/year Wedding in heaven of Christ and raptured Church simultaneously with seven-year Tribulation on Earth. Working on Vol. 2: *The Vehicle of Destiny.*

3474. Youngberg, John, and Millie Youngberg. 1997. *Unbroken Circle: How to Take Your Family Through the End Time.* Nampa, ID:Pacific Press. 223 p. illus.

Seventh-day Adventist.

3475. Youssef, Michael. *Earth King.* 1988. Westchester, IL: Crossway Books. 381 p. 1992 ed. titled *Man of Peace: A Novel of the Anti-Christ.*

Fiction. Youssef: Egyptian-born social arthropology Ph.D.; Also writes on Islam and Christianity; evangelical Anglican, runs Leading the Way Ministries.

3476. Yusko, Alan. *Abominations in the Last Days.* <http://www.serve.com/rapture/>

Yusko: editor of *Rapture Report*, and Bible Prophecy and Rapture Report Home Page. Pre-trib. Computer proof that God wrote the Bible. Coming Russian invasion. Creationism; anti-abortionism.

3477. Zachary, John. *Mysterious Numbers of the Sealed Revelation.* 1994. Golden, CA: Harvard House.

Astrological signs of the Second Coming of Christ. "Biblical research aligns with occult phenomenon!" History is "designed and controlled by a Supreme Being." Tribulation: Aug. 28, 1998 to Oct. 4, 2005; 1,260 + 1,335 days (7 years).

3478. Zahner, Dee. *The Secret Side of History: Mystery Babylon and the New World Order.* 1994 Hesperia, CA: LTAA Communications. 216 p. bibl. refs.

3479. Zambrano, William. *The Seven Year Tribulation Has Begun!* <http://home.att.net/~eyedoctor/>

Tribulation began July 16, 1994, when Comet Shoemaker-Levy hit Jupiter. Zambrano: ophthalmologist.

3480. Ziegler, Gordon L. *The Mystery of the Second Advent.* 1991. Auburn, WA: Prophetic Literature Assoc. 144 p.

3481. Zinn, Jay. *The Unveiling.* 1997. Mukilteo, WA: WinePress. 402 p.

Novel. Post-trib. "The end of the world is right on schedule." Antichrist and False Prophet work with World Church and Ten Kingdom confederacy.

3482. Zollinger, W. Thor. *Our Future Prophesied.* 1995. <http://www.srv.net/~thor/thor/CR/TITLEPG.htm>

Author: robotics engineer for Lockheed in Idaho Falls. 6,000 Years for earth. Iraq, led by Antichrist, conquers Jordan, Syria, Iran (Saddam Hussein, or successor), becoming leader of Ten Nations. Arab states then invade Israel with 200-million man army (they are presently acquiring Apache helicopters). Invasion may be 2009, with Second Coming 2013; or 2030–34.

Index

References are to entry numbers

Parsing index